The Catholics of Ulster

Also by Marianne Elliott

The People's Armies: The Armies Revolutionaries:
Instrument of the Terror in the Departments
April 1793 to Floreal Year II

Wolfe Tone: Prophet of Irish Independence

Partners in Revolution: The United Irishmen and France

Watchmen in Sion: The Protestant Idea of Liberty

MARIANNE ELLIOTT

The Catholics of Ulster

A HISTORY

BASIC
BOOKS

A Member of the Perseus Books Group

For Marc
a book in a life

Contents

List of Plates ix
Maps xiii
Acknowledgements xxix
Prologue xxxiii

1 FROM CÚ CHULAINN TO CHRISTIANITY: 1
   RELIGION AND SOCIETY IN EARLY ULSTER

2 GAELIC ULSTER: LAND, LORDSHIP AND PEOPLE 23

3 RELIGION IN ULSTER BEFORE THE REFORMATION 57

4 THE LOSS OF THE LAND: PLANTATION AND 81
   CONFISCATION IN SEVENTEENTH-CENTURY
   ULSTER

5 THE MERGER OF 'IRISHNESS' AND CATHOLICISM 123
   IN EARLY MODERN ULSTER

6 LIFE UNDER THE PENAL LAWS 161

7 REFORM TO REBELLION: THE EMERGENCE OF 211
   REPUBLICAN POLITICS

8 THE REVIVAL OF 'POLITICAL' CATHOLICISM 267

9 THE FAMINE AND AFTER: CATHOLIC SOCIAL 303
   CLASSES IN NINETEENTH-CENTURY ULSTER

10 ACROSS THE DIVIDE: COMMUNITY RELATIONS 333
    AND SECTARIAN CONFLICT BEFORE PARTITION

11 CATHOLICS IN NORTHERN IRELAND 1920–2000 371

CONTENTS

12 A RESENTFUL BELONGING: CATHOLIC IDENTITY   429
IN THE TWENTIETH CENTURY

Notes   483
Select Bibliography   562
Index   601

Plates

1a) *Belfast from the River Lagan. Cave Hill in the Distance.* Engraving by Marcus Ward & Co., 1863, in the collection of the Ulster Museum, Belfast (Photograph reproduced with the kind permission of the Trustees of the National Museums and Galleries of Northern Ireland)

1b) *West Belfast Peace Wall separating the Loyalist Shankhill Road and Nationalist Falls Road*, 1994 (Photograph: © Pacemaker)

2a) Aerial photograph of Emain Macha (Navan Fort) (Photograph: Environment and Heritage Service, Belfast © British Crown Copyright 2000. Published by permission of the Controller of Her Britannic Majesty's Stationery Office)

2b) Statue of Cú Chulainn, republican plot, City Cemetery, Brandywell, Derry (Photograph: © Allan Leonard)

3a) *The Dartmouth College Map of the North East of Ireland*, Map 25, *c.* 1586. Detail showing Tullahoge, County Tyrone (Photograph: © National Maritime Museum, London)

3b) Aerial photograph of Tullahoge Fort (Photograph: Environment and Heritage Service, Belfast © British Crown Copyright 2000. Published by permission of the Controller of Her Britannic Majesty's Stationery Office)

4 *The Chief of the MacSweeneys seated at Dinner*, Plate III in *The Image of Irelande* by John Derrick, 1581, republished by Adam and Charles Black, Edinburgh, 1883

5a) Hedge Row School Mural, Ardoyne Avenue, Belfast (Photograph: © Allan Leonard)

5b) Orange banner, Loyal Orange Lodge 273, Portadown No. 1 District (Photograph: Carleton Orange Hall, Portadown)

6a) Mural of a Mass Rock, Ardoyne Avenue, Belfast (Photograph: © Allan Leonard)

6b) Mural of the Virgin Mary, Berwick Road, Ardoyne, Belfast (Photograph: © Allan Leonard)

7a) 'The Station' taken from *Traits & Stories of the Irish Peasantry, Vol. 1*, by William Carleton, William Curry, Jun., and Co., Dublin, 1844

7b) *Cabins, Mourne Mountains, Co. Down* by R. J. Welsh, *c.* 1900. In the collection of the Ulster Museum, Belfast (Photograph reproduced with the kind permission of the Trustees of the National Museums and Galleries of Northern Ireland)

8 *Battle of Ballynahinch, 13th June 1798*, (detail) by Thomas Robinson, *c.* 1798/99 (Photograph reproduced by permission of the Office of Public Works, Ireland)

9a) *Cardinal Paul Cullen*, artist unknown, nineteenth century (Photograph reproduced with permission from St Patrick's College, Drumcondra, Dublin)

9b) *At Doon Holy Well, Kilmacrenan* by R. J. Welsh, 1912. In the collection of the Ulster Museum, Belfast (Photograph reproduced with the kind permission of the Trustees of the National Museums and Galleries of Northern Ireland)

10a) *An Gorta Mór: 'Britain's Genocide by Starvation'*. Mural of the Great Famine, Whiterock Road, Ballymurphy, Belfast (Photograph: © Allan Leonard)

10b) *An Gorta Mór: 'They buried us without shroud nor coffin'*. Mural of the Great Famine, Ardoyne Avenue, Belfast (Photograph: © Allan Leonard)

11a) *Rioting in Sandy Row Belfast*, 1864, artist unknown. In the collection of the Ulster Museum, Belfast (Photograph reproduced with the kind permission of the Trustees of the National Museums and Galleries of Northern Ireland)

11b) *Riots in York Street, Belfast, 1922* (Photograph: © *Belfast Telegraph* Newspapers Ltd)

12a) *Walker's Pillar, Walls of Londonderry* drawing by W. H. Bartlett, engraved by R. Wallis, *The Scenery and Antiquities of Ireland – illustrated in One Hundred and Twenty Engravings, from the Drawings by W. H. Bartlett with historical and descriptive text by J. Sterling Coyne, N. P. Willis etc. – Vol. II*, James S. Virtue, London, *c.* 1825/1840 (Photograph: National Museums and Galleries of Northern Ireland, Ulster Folk & Transport Museum)

12b) Parliament Building, Stormont, Belfast (Photograph: © Pacemaker)

13a) Terence O'Neill with Councillor Robert Hart after opening O'Neill Road (Photograph: © *Belfast Telegraph* Newspapers Ltd)

13b) *"Biased!! How dare you, you long haired Fenian agitator."* – illustration by Martyn Turner from *Pack Up Your Troubles – 25 Years of Northern*

Ireland Cartoons, by Martyn Turner, The Blackstaff Press Ltd, Belfast, 1995 (Picture: © Martyn Turner/*Fortnight* Magazine)

14a) *Questionnaire* illustration by Martyn Turner from *Pack Up Your Troubles – 25 Years of Northern Ireland Cartoons*, by Martyn Turner, The Blackstaff Press Ltd, Belfast, 1995 (Picture: © Martyn Turner/*Irish Times*)

14b) August 1969 (Photograph: © *Belfast Telegraph* Newspapers Ltd)

15a) '*Free Ireland*' 1916 commemoration mural, Beechmount Avenue, Belfast (Photograph: © Allan Leonard)

15b) Bobby Sands Funeral, 1981 (Photograph: © *Belfast Telegraph* Newspapers Ltd)

16 Last rites by Father Alex Reid said over the body of one of the two British Army corporals killed at Andersonstown, March 1988 (Photograph: © *Mirror* Syndication International)

Maps

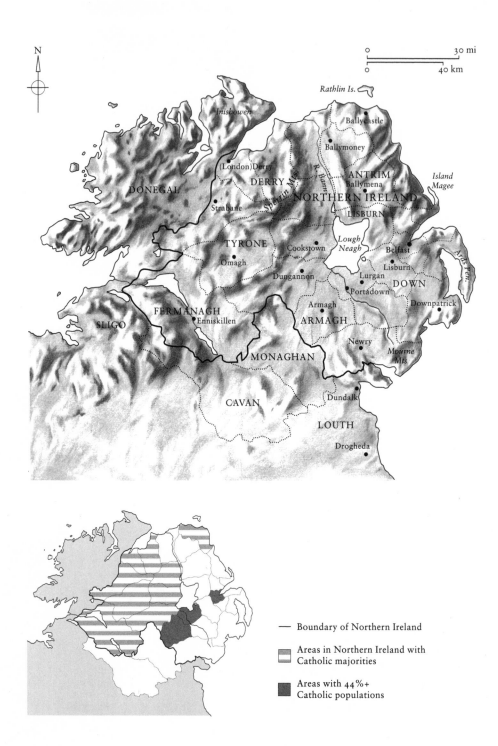

N

30 mi

40 km

Rathlin Is.

Inishowen

Ballycastle

Ballymoney

(London)Derry

DERRY

ANTRIM

Island Magee

Ballymena

NORTHERN IRELAND

Strabane

DONEGAL

LISBURN

TYRONE

Cookstown

Lough Neagh

Belfast

Omagh

Lisburn

Dungannon

Lurgan

Portadown

DOWN

FERMANAGH

Armagh

Downpatrick

SLIGO

Enniskillen

ARMAGH

Newry

Mourne Mts

MONAGHAN

CAVAN

Dundalk

LOUTH

Drogheda

—— Boundary of Northern Ireland

Areas in Northern Ireland with Catholic majorities

Areas with 44%+ Catholic populations

Map 1. Modern Ulster

N

○   30 mi

○   40 km

Inishowen

Ailech

R. Bann

Lough Neagh

Navan Fort
(Emain Macha)

Clogher

Strangford Lough

R. Bann

Downpatrick

Black
Pig's Dyke

Slieve Gullion

Black
Pig's Dyke

Dundalk

⩗ Linear earthworks

Map 2. Prehistoric Ulster

N

0 ——— 40 mi
0 ——— 50 km

L. Foyle

DÁL
RIATA

CENÉL   Ailech   CENÉL   ULAID
nEÓGAIN
NORTHERN   DÁL
UÍ NÉILL   nARAIDE
CONAILL   Uí
Thuirtri   DÁL
Airthir   FIATACH

Armagh   UÍ ECHACH
AIRGIALLA   COBO

Newry

Leth
Cuinn

CONNACHTA   SOUTHERN
UÍ NÉILL   •Tara

MIDE

Leth
Moga

EÓGANACHT

AIRGIALLA   Overkingdoms

DÁL   Subkingdoms
RIATA

Airthir   Other dynasties
and subject peoples

··············   Boundaries between
overkingdoms

————   Boundary between Leth
Cuinn and Leth Moga

Map 3. Political divisions to *c.* 800

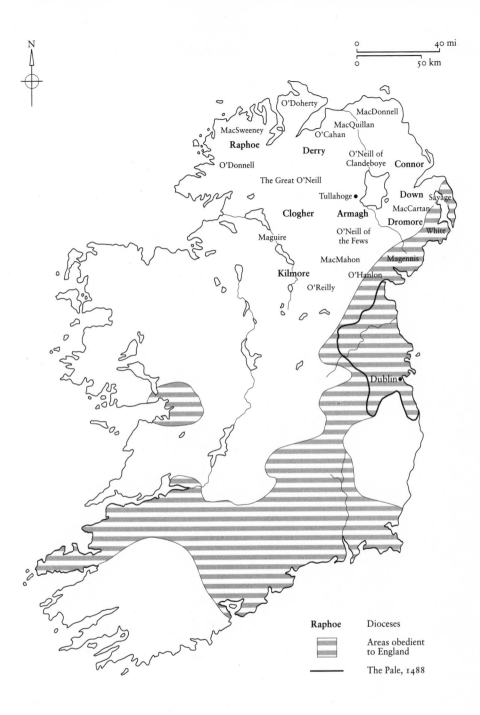

N

o_____40 mi
o_____50 km

O'Doherty

MacDonnell

MacSweeney

MacQuillan

O'Cahan

Raphoe

Derry

O'Neill of
Clandeboye

Connor

O'Donnell

The Great O'Neill

Tullahoge ●

Down Savage

MacCartan

Clogher

Armagh

Dromore

White

Maguire

O'Neill of
the Fews

Magennis

MacMahon

Kilmore

O'Hanlon

O'Reilly

Dublin ●

Raphoe Dioceses

Areas obedient
to England

The Pale, 1488

Map 4. Gaelic and Anglo-Irish lordships by the fifteenth century

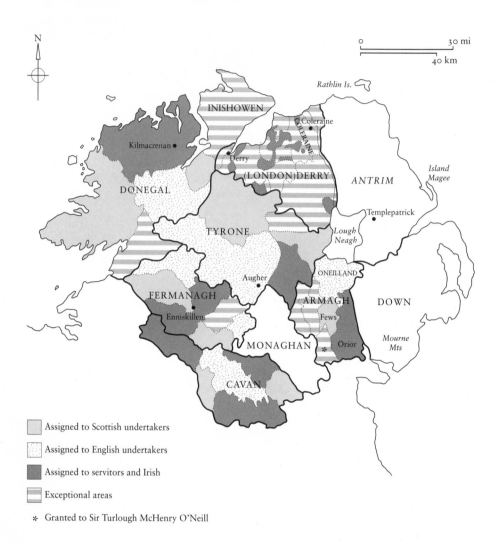

Map 5. The Ulster plantation
(after T. W. Moody, ed., *New History of Ireland*)

N

30 mi

40 km

Ballymoney

19%

ANTRIM

Ballymena

Randalstown Antrim

Strangford Lough

43%

(London)Derry

DERRY

24%

Maghera ◇

DONEGAL

Strabane

Templepatrick

Belfast

TYRONE

Barons Court
(Abercorn Estate)

Stewartstown

Lisburn

Killinchy ◇

Lough Derg

52%

Dungannon

Lurgan

Saintfield

Ards

Ballynahinch ◇*

Armagh

DOWN

Downpatrick

FERMANAGH

Monaghan

42%

ARMAGH

27%

MONAGHAN

Ballybay

35%

Newry

64%

Carlingford ◇

CAVAN

76%

* Charter Schools

● Main brown linen markets
  by size

% Percentage of Catholics
  in 1732

◇ Places referred to in account
  of 1798 rebellion

Map 6. Eighteenth-century Ulster

The Catholic population increased rapidly in the latter half of the century, particulary in south Ulster, where it reached 50% in Armagh by 1766 and 60% in south Down. By 1834 Catholics outnumbered Protestants in the province

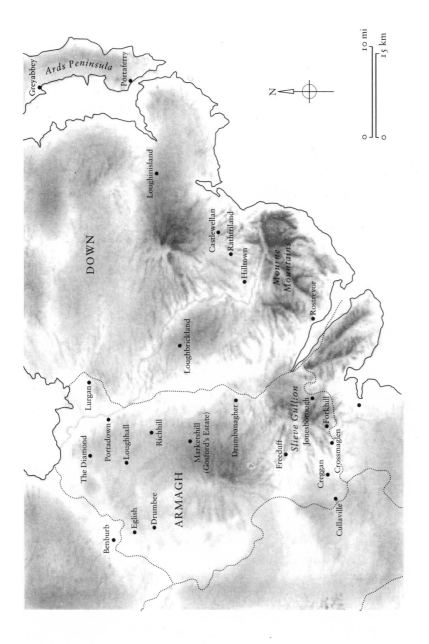

Map 7. Sectarian conflict in Armagh and Down, late eighteenth century

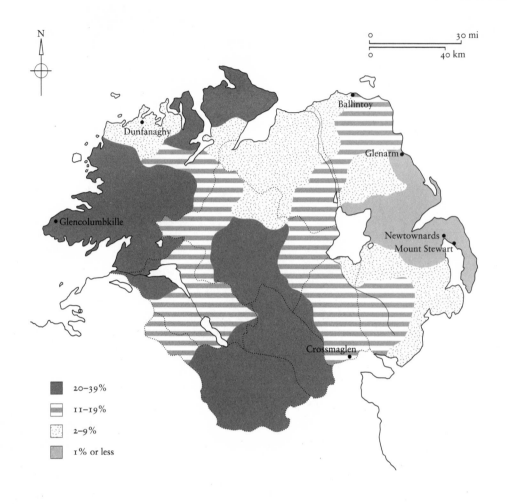

N

0   30 mi
0   40 km

Ballintoy

Dunfanaghy

Glenarm

Glencolumbkille

Newtownards
Mount Stewart

Crossmaglen

■ 20–39%

▤ 11–19%

▦ 2–9%

▨ 1% or less

Map 8i. Ulster in the famine era: dependence on soup kitchens after 1847
(after Frank Wright, *Two Lands in One Soil*)

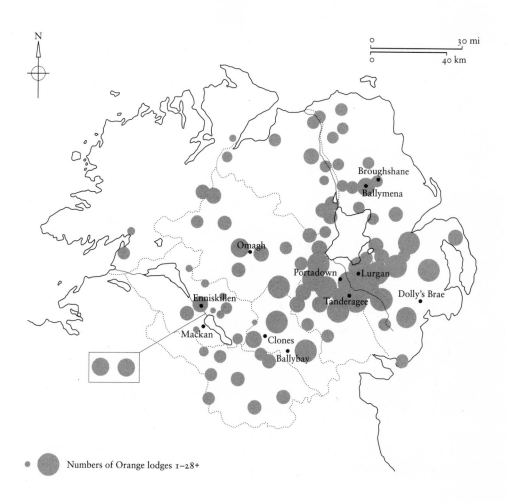

N

30 mi
40 km

Broughshane
Ballymena

Omagh

Portadown • Lurgan
Tanderagee   Dolly's Brae

Enniskillen
Mackan   • Clones
                   Ballybay

Numbers of Orange lodges 1–28+

Map 8ii. Ulster in the famine era: number of Orange lodges
(after Frank Wright, *Two Lands in One Soil*)

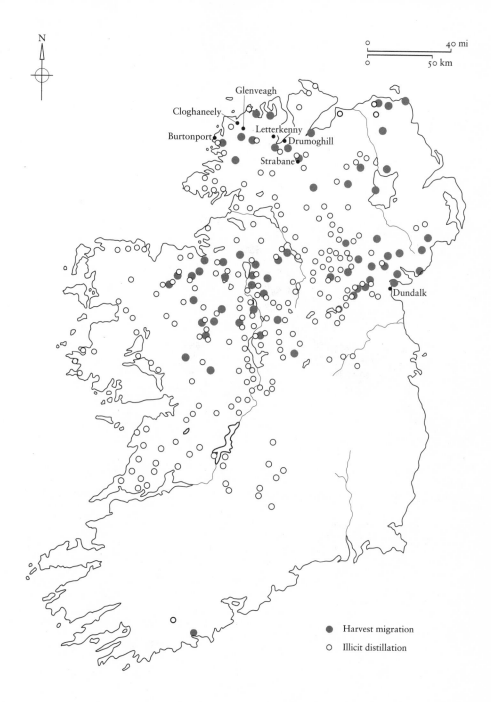

Map 9. Harvest migration and illicit distillation,
early nineteeth century

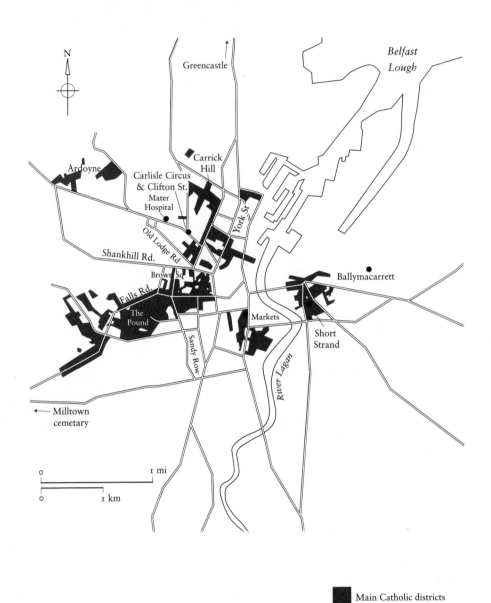

N

Belfast
Lough

Greencastle

Carrick
Hill

Ardoyne

Carlisle Circus
& Clifton St.

Mater
Hospital

York St.

Old Lodge Rd

Shankhill Rd.

Brown Sq

Ballymacarrett

Falls Rd.

The
Pound

Sandy Row

Markets

Short
Strand

River Lagan

← Milltown
cemetery

0   1 mi

0   1 km

Main Catholic districts

Map 10. Belfast in 1911
(from Sybil Baker, 'Orange and Green')

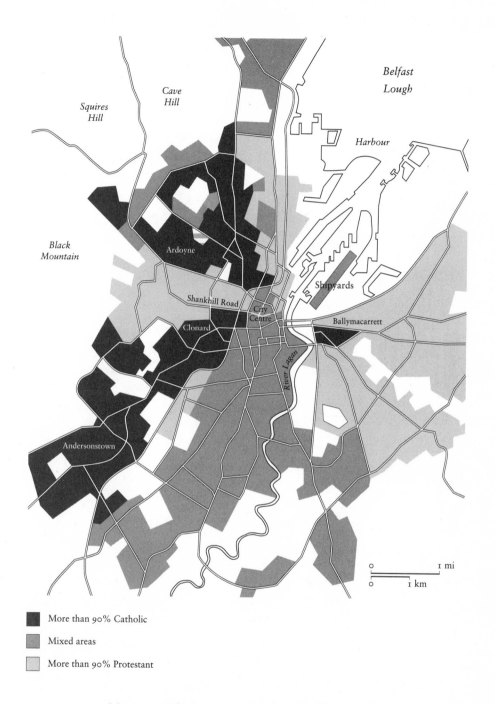

Belfast
Lough

Squires
Hill

Cave
Hill

Harbour

Black
Mountain

Ardoyne

Shipyards

Shankhill Road

City
Centre

Clonard

Ballymacarrett

River Lagan

Andersonstown

1 mi

1 km

More than 90% Catholic

Mixed areas

More than 90% Protestant

Map 11. Religious segregation in Belfast, 1990s

Acknowledgements

This book started out in conversations with Brian Friel and Anne Tannahill, after I had written a Field Day pamphlet about Ulster Protestantism. It has taken many turns and twists since then and ended up a much bigger project than first envisaged. It has been researched and written while I have been a full-time academic in the British University system, in the last three years as a Head of Department. In view of the current audit culture – a virus-like infection spreading through every aspect of British higher education, a culture which actively penalises long-term research projects such as this book – I am somewhat in despair about my ability to embark on such a major project again. It is unlikely that this one would have been brought to fruition without periodic research grants awarded by Birkbeck College, the University of Liverpool, the Leverhulme Foundation and most notably the Nuffield Foundation, which gave me time to write when it was becoming increasingly difficult to find. I acknowledge their generosity with deep gratitude. Like any writer, I have paid a price in neglected friends and family. I would like to pay particular tribute to my mother, Sheila Burns, my sisters Geraldine Walsh and Eleanor Dent, to friends like Susan Paton, Joanna Bourke, Anne Laurence, Moya Paul, Margaret and David Rankin, Angie and David Stovell, and Annie and Robin Gwyn, who have repaid such negligence with constant loyalty and support.

I have been blessed in my colleagues, notably Richard Evans, Hilary Sapire and Joanna Bourke at Birkbeck College, University of London; Linda Christianson, Elizabeth Malcolm, Dorothy Lynch, Ulli Kockel, Máiréad nic Craith, Conor mac Carthy and Harvey Cox at the Institute of Irish Studies, University of Liverpool, and Angela MacEwan in the School of History.

The staff at numerous libraries and archives have been consistently helpful, and I am deeply grateful to those at the libraries of Liverpool University, Birkbeck College, Boston College, the National Library of Ireland, the National Archives of Ireland, the Royal Irish Academy (notably Síobhain O'Rafferty), the Department of Irish Folklore (UCD), Queen's University Library, the Ulster Museum, the Ulster Folk and Transport Museum (especially Linda Ballard, Bill Crawford and Roger Dixon), Belfast Central Library (particularly Darren Topping and Suzanne Drake), the Public Record Office of Northern Ireland (notably Marian Gallagher and, formerly, Allan Blackstock), the Scottish Record Office, the Public Record Office, the British Library and the Institute of Historical Research. But I must single out the staff at the Linenhall Library in Belfast, most notably John Gray, John Killen, Mary Delargey, Yvonne Murphy, Bern Kane, Cíaran Crossey and Allan Leonard (particularly for his assistance with the illustrations), for making my innumerable visits there so rewarding and enjoyable.

I am humbled by the remarkable generosity of so many fellow scholars. Séamus Ó Catháin helped on many occasions with the riches and pitfalls of the folklore material; Aídan Mac Poílin, Bréandain Ó Buachalla and Art Hughes with the early stages of locating the Irish-language sources; Anthony Buckley shared his expertise on ethnicity, Trevor Parkhill his on local history and the riches of the Ulster Museum. Brian Walker was unstintingly generous with his time and expertise. Roy Foster was always there with helpful tips, support and friendship. Donnacha Ó Corráin, Katharine Simms, Cathy Swift, Bernadette Cunningham, Nicholas Canny, Roy Foster, Paul Arthur, Michael Parker and Maurice Hayes read and commented upon individual sections. Tracey Holsgrove and Phil Jimmieson of Liverpool University have helped defuse numerous crises. Tim Walsh helped with last-minute checking. Ian McBride, Don Akenson and Christopher Woods read the entire manuscript against a tight deadline, which, in retrospect, I had no right to ask. My debt to them is incalculable. Vincent Morley has provided research assistance (and critical commentary) throughout the research and writing of the book, most notably with the Irish-language sources. He brought a particular expertise to the translation of the poems. The book – and indeed my own experience in researching and writing it – would have been considerably impoverished without him.

My agent, Peter Robinson, and publisher, Simon Winder, have been patient beyond belief and the team at Penguin (particularly Jennifer Munka, Sophie Wright, Claire Pollak, Jennie Todd and Cormac Kinsella) have been a pleasure to work with. My thanks also to Oula Jones for the index.

But I owe more than I can ever repay to my immediate family: to my son Marc, for all those missed childhood experiences, and most of all to my husband Trevor, for all the times that he did the chores to let me write, or had to forgo holidays because I had no time, and most of all for his love and sense of humour and for making me laugh even on the dark days.

Prologue

'Whatever you say, say nothing'

(Ulster saying)

I still consider myself an Ulster Catholic, for that was the tradition into which I was born and in which I was raised and educated until the age of eighteen. I have always felt different from Catholics elsewhere in Ireland and this is a common feeling among Ulster Catholics. Yet I have found them consistently neglected in the histories of Ireland and of Irish Catholicism in particular, as if Irishness and Catholicism so dominated their sense of themselves that they could be safely included with all other Irish Catholics. The assumption is that Ulster is primarily Protestant. Had this been so, we would not have been left with that overwhelming insecurity which is such a feature of the Ulster personality, or such daily agonising over culture and identity. By the second half of the nineteenth century Catholics were in a small majority in Ulster. On the eve of partition they remained at 43.7 per cent and today (from the most recent 1991 census) account for 38 per cent. To a considerable degree their modern identity has been shaped by the Ulster Protestants and not always in a simple oppositional way. They needed a separate history which located them firmly in Ulster.

I have chosen to define them as 'Ulster' Catholics because it accurately describes that cultural and religious grouping for most of the period covered in this book. In addition, four-fifths of the book deals with the centuries before the state of Northern Ireland came into existence. However, I recognise that few Catholics today would admit to an 'Ulster' identity. Indeed, some go even farther in rejecting the very term 'Northern Ireland', dismissively calling the state the 'Six

xxxiii

Counties', with all its connotations of incompleteness and illegitimacy. In the recent past they disliked the way in which Unionists flaunted the term 'Ulster', when the new northern state contained only six of the so-called 'historic' nine counties (Cavan, Monaghan and Donegal having been included with the southern state). So they chose to reject it, except, pointedly, for all-Ireland occasions such as Gaelic Athletic Association sports fixtures. It is one of the many terms by which one can still identify the cultural and religious identity of the speaker in Northern Ireland. It is surely high time for Ulster Catholics to re-assert their regional identity and challenge the view that 'Ulster' necessarily means Protestant.

Conversely, I have opted on most occasions to use the name 'Derry' for both the city and county rather than the more politically correct 'Derry/Londonderry', except when the context dictates otherwise. I do so in the knowledge that County 'Londonderry' is technically more correct, since the county only came into existence after the seventeenth-century Ulster Plantation and was called after the London companies to whom it had been transferred. More than any place name, this one traditionally singles out Catholic from Protestant, for Catholics consider the ancient monastic site of Derry (Doire) as peculiarly theirs and seldom use the 'London' prefix. But since I am writing about the Catholics, it makes sense to adopt their terminology. Besides, I am beginning to tire of those mental contortions required before saying anything about Northern Ireland. We would like to believe that it is because we do not wish to offend. But there are equally valid and less complimentary explanations, including an effort to disguise our own background or to fathom that of others.

I have found this book very painful to write, not because the experience of Ulster's Catholics has been the doom-laden one of nationalist tradition, though there was enough of that to dispel any idea of this image as pure mythology, but because I have discovered in myself lingering prejudices and sensitivities which I either believed I had left far behind or never recognised in the first place, and I know that I am not alone. I do not subscribe to the belief voiced by many public figures associated with Northern Ireland that we must leave the past behind. The mistrust, prejudices and fears which lay behind the recent Troubles and many earlier periods of conflict have existed for a very long time and are unlikely to disappear overnight. I now know why I viewed the Bible College behind my school bus-stop as sinister, why I tagged certain areas and towns as Protestant or Catholic and felt uncomfortable in the former, why I, like my community, was instinctively anti-Scottish and anti-English, when I had no direct experience of either. I have since learnt that few people conform to stereotypes.

Although I was born in County Down, near Strangford, my family moved shortly afterwards to Belfast, my father's home city. We had moved to a new housing estate on the edge of North Belfast. Surrounded by fields rolling down from the Cave Hill and overlooking the sea, the White City never quite felt like urban living. The beauty of Belfast's setting has often figured in writings by its authors, a poignant contrast to the living conditions and sectarianism in the streets below, a form of escapism allowing that deep love of the place which I noted in my father and which I have retained, even through the Troubles. It is a love often heightened by a sense of embattlement, and I have noted similar feelings in the people of Liverpool, where I work.

The White City in the late 1940s was something of a new beginning in Northern Ireland, and so indeed it was remembered by my parents. The Northern Ireland government had a poor record in the provision of housing for its people and the Belfast blitz of 1941 highlighted the serious over-crowding and inadequate housing of the city. The White City was one of the model estates of the post-war Housing Trust, a body which has won general acclaim for its record in supplying affordable housing and allocating it on a non-sectarian basis. In our corner of the estate there were three Catholic families and five Protestant, just about reflecting the religious make-up of the population then. Large tracts of North Belfast and adjacent areas in those days were genuinely mixed religion. The jaggedness of sectarianism impinged rarely enough to be truly memorable. But in general one knew the codes of behaviour and said nothing to upset in mixed company. That perhaps was the problem. The undercurrents were always there, but suppressed in the interests of good neighbourliness. I recall, as a teenager, my first experience of what I now recognise as a particular characteristic of Ulster humour: using Ulster Catholics' and Protestants' stereotyped views of each other to induce laughter and a more relaxed atmosphere.

But it was a very long time indeed before I could do this myself and even now it does not come naturally. I am angered that I still have a habit of treading carefully in conversation with people in and from Northern Ireland, instinctively seeking out the tell-tale clues to their background before I can totally relax. And yet, when that point comes, it is so refreshing, so much we have in common. I am glad to say that younger generations – many who have grown up entirely in the Troubles – are much less reticent on such matters. On the downside, there are many other areas of Northern Ireland life which are very much worse. Today the White City is a loyalist stronghold, one of the many mixed neighbourhoods which fell victim to the polarisation of the Troubles, one of the latest (1999) to acquire a peace 'wall' (for which read 'barricade'), dividing it off from Catholics on the Whitewell Road. Those streets, where I used to play and walk safely, have become another sectarian frontier zone.

There was genuine friendship and total mixing of the children at play then. But we went to different churches (often several times a week), different schools (the uniforms publicly proclaiming our religion from an early age) and attended different social functions, more often than not associated with our church. By the time we had become teenagers, the childhood friendships had given way to ones with class-mates of our own religion. My family read the *Irish News* (the Catholic daily newspaper), bought southern papers outside Sunday mass, had a Catholic GP (even though there were others much closer), never voted in elections, and, like thousands of other Catholic families, took our summer holidays south of the border. For the mandatory 12 July shut-down, then as now, was the Orangemen's marching season, and as the estate became festooned with Union Jacks, it took on a new character. Admittedly we had more reason to go south than most, for my mother came from County Kerry. It meant that I was more familiar with every other province in Ireland than my own. Long summer days spent in Counties Antrim and Down (straddled by the city of Belfast) created a great affinity with the people and landscape of these areas, while the largely rural territory west of Lough Neagh and the River Bann seemed like a foreign country.

I was cured of much of my early prejudice by my first experience of working with Ulster Protestants and English and Scottish people. With many of my schoolfriends, I applied for holiday work to the newly opened British Home Stores in Belfast. The 'Religion?' portion of the application form and the very term 'British' interacted with my prejudices to convince me that no Catholic would be hired. In fact, we were all offered jobs. I learnt that the Protestant stereotype of the untrustworthy and lazy Catholic, about which our parents' generation had heard so much, was here turned on its head, for we found that our new 'British' employers thought quite the contrary.

After attending Catholic primary and grammar schools in north Belfast, I went up to Queen's University in Belfast in 1967 to study History and (in the first and second years of a four-year degree) I also took French and Scholastic Philosophy. Of course, the choice of the latter instantly marked me out as Catholic, for the Department had been created in response to a successful campaign to create separate Catholic teaching programmes in controversial subjects. But there was no obviously Catholic bias in the programme and, throughout my years at Queen's, I never experienced any sectarianism whatsoever. It is unlikely that I, the other members of my family or indeed very large numbers of Ulster Catholics would have gone through higher education without Queen's University and the grants provided by the Northern Ireland Ministry of Education. We were in a much more privileged position than the bulk of University students today. It was the time of Terence O'Neill's premiership and the civil rights marches and I remember a new optimism in the air. I think O'Neill was a courageous man, ahead of his time. I also remember one of his major critics, Bernadette Devlin, as an inspiring student leader and was saddened that her talents, alike with those of so many other Catholics, were lost in Ulster's sectarian undercurrents.

Although in this book I am critical of the Catholic Church when I believe it has deserved criticism, I do not remember an occasion when the clergy were not there for their flock at times of need. The authoritarianism of the Catholic Church in Ireland generally (and in Ulster in particular, because of the prevailing lower social status of Ulster Catholics after the seventeenth century) was a late development. It has not always worked in the interests of either the Church itself or its people and it played into the hands of those who never wanted to see Catholics in power in any event. The Church's dislike of internal criticism through the ages, its ethos of endurance, submissiveness and guilt has tended to crush initiative and individuality. There *is* something in the Ulster Protestant tendency to assume a herd-like mentality in Catholics. But the Church has never been able to take its people where they did not want to go and it gave much-needed leadership in the absence of a secular one in past centuries. For better or worse, it has played a major role in fashioning Catholic identity.

However, that other perception of Catholicism as some kind of dangerous conspiracy, with Rome at its head, is entirely misconceived. This most conformist of religions has sought rather to belong to the system and I have highlighted a number of occasions in past centuries where failure to so involve leading Catholics in the state structure (a resistance often insultingly expressed) not only transferred that leadership to the clergy and turned the Catholic community into a state within a state, but also created that sense of alienation and victimhood which deterred criticism of the Church and upon which militant nationalism was to feed. The post-1999 power-sharing executive is what most Catholics would have settled for in the past. But reasonable demands have a tendency to increase when resisted and only time will tell whether this is what they will settle for in the future.

But this is not a book about the Catholic Church. It is about the people who have called themselves Catholics, about their culture and sense of identity, about their relationship with people in the rest of the island and, above all, with their immediate neighbours: the Protestants and Presbyterians of Ulster. It is important to recognise that Ulster Catholics have been on the losing side for most of the past four centuries, and that the almost complete loss of the top tier of Catholic leadership, and progressive loss of land to Protestants from the time of the Ulster Plantation, placed them on a lower social and economic level than most of their co-religionists elsewhere on the island. From this it was perhaps predictable that the images of the downtrodden and dispossessed Gael or feckless 'taig' (depending on one's religion) established themselves several centuries ago. But the common assumption that Ulster Catholics are pure Gaels is wrong, as I have argued in the main body of the book, even though the association of Gaelic culture and Catholic religion from the time of the Reformation is accurate enough.

This is why I have felt it so necessary to go back to the very earliest of times when Catholics, strictly speaking, did not exist. I am very aware of how controversial this will be and of the centuries-old 'slanging match' (it can scarcely be dignified by the term 'debate') between Protestantism and Catholicism as to which was the true heir of Christ. However, it made no sense to commence this study at the end of the Gaelic order (1603–7), for Ulster was then the most Gaelic province in Ireland and Gaelic traditions were subsumed into Catholic culture. A return to the earliest history (even the pre-history) of Ulster people is, I believe, also essential because of the nationalists' claim to racial purity. The related issue of my treatment of the Irish language requires some clarification. I have taken advice from a number of early Irish historians and on the whole used Old Irish spellings in the early chapters. Thereafter I have adopted Irish or anglicised versions of names according to which had most currency at the time and have used English translations of Irish-language sources throughout. Although the counties of Ulster were only created between 1570 and 1613, I have chosen to use their names also in preceding centuries to facilitate understanding of the location of the events discussed. I have taken a largely chronological approach in structuring the book, chapters broadly outlining political developments prefacing those dealing with the social, religious, cultural and economic issues of a given period.

Ulster's physical environment has played a significant part in the development and reinforcement of cultural identities. Its proximity to Scotland – visible from the north-east coast on most clear days – is immediately apparent. Even before the Ulster Plantation and subsequent population movements made Scottish Presbyterianism such a dominant influence in the province, Scots had been arriving and settling for many centuries. Antrim and Down have remained the most Protestant in the province (with Presbyterianism the largest Protestant denomination).

The eastern counties, along with Armagh, also contain the main concentration of urban dwellers and industry in the province. Pivotal to this has been the spectacular growth of Belfast over the past two centuries, from a small market-town of some 8,000 inhabitants in the eighteenth century, to around 400,000 (a quarter of the province's entire population) in the twentieth. Ulster Catholics in the past have had an ambivalent relationship with the city. Incorporated in 1613, it was then a Protestant settler town, and has remained an essentially Protestant city both in reality and in the perception of Catholics elsewhere in Ireland. In the eighteenth century Catholics accounted for only 8 per cent of its population, largely clustered on its western fringes (from where the Catholic west-Belfast enclave would later develop). By mid-nineteenth century they were 33 per cent of its population, the rapid influx of often poor rural Catholics in preceding decades forming the backdrop to the ugly sectarian riots for which Belfast has become notorious. Because of the recent Troubles, there are more areas in Belfast today which Catholics (notably working-class males) would find inhospitable, even dangerous. On the other hand, members of the fast-growing Catholic middle class are moving in large numbers into those areas which I would have considered posh and Protestant as a child.

Even east Ulster, however, like the rest of the province, is largely rural. The volcanic plateau, which covers most of County Antrim, drops sharply to the coast and is dissected by deep gulleys. The result is one of Europe's most scenic coastlines. But much of it is bleak and inaccessible, today's coastal road – the product of a public works scheme of the Great Famine – only opening it to the outside world in the middle of the nineteenth century. Its remoteness locked in older traditions and, like other hillier and remote areas, the Glens of Antrim were and have remained a traditionally Catholic and nationalist area – though the county as a whole is largely Protestant.

In contrast County Down, south and east of Belfast, has a landscape of rolling, fertile countryside, home in past centuries to some of Ireland's most influential landed gentry. But the south and south-west of the county is more varied topographically, with the Mountains of Mourne rising to 852 metres and a belt of lower mountains stretching into south Armagh. This – alike with much of south Ulster – is largely Catholic territory and was in the seventeenth and eighteenth centuries the haunt of bandits and escapees from the defeated Jacobite forces. South Ulster also has a distinctive drumlin topography – a wide belt of hummocky hills, small lakes and boggy hollows – stretching from County Down to the Atlantic coast of Sligo and Donegal, causing particular distortion on the borders of Cavan, Monaghan and Fermanagh, where it opens into larger lakes and gives this county the appearance of a water wonderland. It makes for difficult access and has been a cultural and defensive barrier since prehistoric times. These drumlins defined such 'border' areas for many centuries before political units emerged.

Another such barrier between east and west was the River Bann, connecting with the outsized Lough Neagh (some 24km in width, 48km in length). It was one of the reasons why the Anglo-Norman settlement of the eleventh and twelfth centuries was largely confined to Antrim and Down, and all but collapsed a century later. Ulster was to remain much less culturally diverse than most of the rest of the island, the strongest Gaelic area in Ireland until the defeat of the Ulster chieftains in 1603 and subsequent Ulster Plantation. This resulted in large tracts of six counties (Armagh, Tyrone, Cavan, Fermanagh, Derry and Donegal) being confiscated and settled with imported English and Scottish Protestants. The religious demography has altered very little since then. The religious map of Armagh would remain particularly significant: the low-lying fertile north assigned to Protestants, the rising and higher ground from mid to south to Irish Catholics. Armagh was left with a number of internal religious frontiers and potential flashpoint areas. It was the only Ulster county with near-numerical parity of Protestants and Catholics, leaving neither feeling secure. In general, as in Armagh, low-lying areas were occupied by Protestants, with notable corridors along the Bann, Foyle and Lagan river valleys, while political and economic factors over the centuries tended to concentrate Catholics in poorer upland areas. It is important to add, however, that not all Catholics were poor and not all Protestants rich. Indeed, the poor Protestant has tended to be forgotten in all the propaganda about the downtrodden Catholic and superior Protestant.

Because of a very general absence of natural woodland and an inhospitable weather pattern – with two-thirds of the province experiencing 225–250 raindays per year, the north-west in particular, battered by Atlantic gales – much of Ulster is covered by blanket bog, most notably Donegal, but also much of Derry, Tyrone, Fermanagh and Antrim. The broad mountainous band of the Sperrins, spanning north Tyrone and south Derry, does not relieve this sense of barrenness, for even its highest point, Sawel Mount (683 metres), is flattish and bog-covered, and the Glenshane Pass, through which travellers from the east must access Derry City, is notoriously the first road to be closed in adverse weather. Although Tyrone has long been something of a religious patchwork quilt (with Protestant majorities in the south, east and west) the Sperrins area has remained largely Catholic, its inaccessibility, as with the Glens of Antrim, locking in old traditions. With Fermanagh, Tyrone has had a marginal Catholic majority, making for very close electoral contests between Nationalists and Unionists. County Derry has had a small Protestant majority. Derry City was, like Belfast, very much a Protestant town at the outset, incorporated in 1613 as part of the Ulster Plantation. Because it was a defensively walled town and because of its lengthy and successful resistance to Jacobite (Catholic) attack at the close of the seventeenth century, it has been considered as something of a siege city. As working-class Catholics began to arrive in large numbers from Donegal in the early nineteenth century (giving Derry a Catholic majority by 1851) that siege mentality intensified. Catholics clustered on the Donegal side of the city, in the Bogside and outside the city walls. The city has long had a dual personality, the Donegal side exercising a powerful emotional pull for many of its Catholic populace.

Donegal, like Monaghan and Cavan, has long had a Catholic majority, and on this crude numerical basis all three counties were joined with the south in 1920. But they all retained significant Protestant populations (as much as a quarter in Donegal) on the eve of partition. The magical mountainscape and Atlantic coastline of Donegal has made it a favourite holiday destination for many Ulster people. But its barren and boggy soil also made it the poorest county in Ulster, its people figuring prominently in the seasonal search for work in Scotland and travelling to the hiring fairs in Tyrone well into the twentieth century. The western parts of Donegal have remained Irish-speaking, even though the language had all but died out elsewhere in the province by the middle of the nineteenth century.

The boundary of Ulster has been something of a moveable feast in the two thousand years or so covered in this book. I have accordingly followed the political definition of the province current at a given period, so that Cavan, Monaghan and Donegal are included in my

discussion until partition, alike with some areas of north Leinster and
north Connacht which have had common experiences. After 1920,
however, my analysis is largely confined to the six counties of Northern
Ireland.

In 1992–3 I was invited to serve on the independent Opsahl Commission in Northern Ireland, headed by the international human rights
lawyer, Torkel Opsahl. It was the brainchild of the then editor of
the current affairs magazine *Fortnight,* Robin Wilson, and Queen's
University law professor, Simon Lee, and was one of the early land-
marks in the current peace process. There were particular years in the
Troubles when raw sectarianism overflowed into random assassina-
tions, and this was one of them. Inter-party talks had just broken
down, and with every initiative seemingly exhausted there was a very
widespread sense of helplessness. The Commission sought to give
everyone involved in and with Ulster the chance to talk, even if it
produced no infallible blueprint for peace, and talk they did: a huge
range of people, pacifists and paramilitaries, unemployed and execu-
tives, schoolchildren and teachers, clergy and voluntary workers, and
a lot of what is often termed 'ordinary' people. There was not much
of the naked hatred that outsiders have come to associate with the
province, but a lot of mutual fear, suspicion and misunderstanding.
We concluded that Ulster's problems were very largely internal to the
communities themselves, that the desire for peace was overwhelming,
but that securing it required an examination of the roots of their
mistrust and a more honest acceptance of responsibility. I hope that
this book will be a small contribution to that process.

I

FROM CÚ CHULAINN TO CHRISTIANITY: RELIGION AND SOCIETY IN EARLY ULSTER

'In the days when this took place there was in those parts a great king, a fierce pagan . . . by name Loíguire son of Níall . . . He had around him sages and druids, fortune-tellers and sorcerers . . . [who] prophesied frequently that a foreign way of life was about to come to them, a kingdom, as it were, with an unheard of and burdensome teaching, brought from afar, over the seas, enjoined by few, received by many; it would . . . seduce the crowds, destroy all their gods, banish all the works of their craft, and reign for ever . . . And so it happened afterwards: when Patrick came the worship of idols was abolished and the catholic Christian faith spread over our whole country.'

Muirchú, *Life of St Patrick*, seventh century AD
(Deane, ed., *Field Day Anthology*, i, 78–9)

1. Pre-Christian Ulster

Prehistoric man arrived in Ulster around 7000 BC and settled along the sea and lake shores, in the valley of the Bann, around Lough Neagh and the Antrim coast, later extending to Strangford Lough and the Inishowen peninsula. Defended by a band of hummocky drumlins,[1] interspersed with boggy marshes and lakes, human settlements in prehistoric Ulster were lost amidst primeval Atlantic forests and a carpet of prickly vegetation. Man made no catastrophic alteration to the landscape, its very inhospitality becoming part of outsiders' perception of its people: romantic and mysterious to primitivists, barbaric and threatening to those seeking to subdue it. Its multitude of tiny kingdoms defied easy conquest and its final subjugation in the seventeenth century was ironically facilitated by the novel, if unstable, political unity achieved under Hugh O'Neill.

The Mesolithic hunter-gatherers who first inhabited the province have left their mark in archaeological finds around the coast, lakes and river valleys. But our knowledge of this uncharted period is poor and uncertain. It was thought until recently that these northern arrivals were the first inhabitants of Ireland and that they had travelled over land-bars from Scandinavia and Scotland. This is no longer accepted by archaeologists as certain, despite the land-bar theory being well represented in Irish mythology, and the heaviest distribution of Mesolithic sites and megalithic tombs from the Neolithic period (c.4000 BC onwards) being in the northern part of Ireland.[2] To argue any cultural distinctiveness from these times before written records, however, would be impossible. Early Ulster man was well travelled and receptive to outside influences. As he entered history, he was already a mongrel.

By around 4000 BC Ulster had acquired its pastoral economy. But evidence of domestic and communal life is elusive. Survivals come rather in the form of sophisticated burial tombs and suggest well-developed religious cults long before Christianity. When Celtic-speaking peoples emerged as a distinctive entity in Europe or when they arrived in Ireland is a matter of some controversy.[3] However, despite some speculation that Ireland may have received large numbers of Celtic Gauls fleeing before the Roman invasions, the introduction of the more famous La Tène Celtic culture in the first century BC is thought to have come from Britain and Scotland.

In the 1940s, T. F. O'Rahilly put forward an elaborate schema for the arrival of successive waves of Celtic peoples in Ireland.[4] The first he identified as the Cruithin. Since they were also found in Scotland, they have been used by some Ulster Protestants to create an origin legend, separate and apparently older than the equally spurious claim that the Catholics are the pure descendants of the Gaels.[5] However, we simply do not know the origins of any people during Ireland's Iron Age.[6] Although the predominance of court tombs in Ulster suggests some element of cultural and regional distinctiveness, they are intermixed with other varieties which show substantial links with other parts of Ireland, notably the south-east. There is little agreement on whether the Ulster peoples of this age arrived from continental Europe via the Atlantic and western route, or through northern England and Scotland. But scholars now dismiss the idea of waves of invasion displacing one people by another, preferring to explain cultural change by contact with other countries. The names Cruithin, Ulaid and Érainn represented ruling dynasties, their territorial and military power based on confederations. Prehistoric Ireland was a considerable racial mix. Other parts of Ireland besides Ulster shared populations with Britain. In truth, little is certain about this period before written records. The fact remains, however, that, whatever the origins of the inhabitants of Ireland, Ulster, with the rest of the island, became thoroughly Celticised in language and social institutions half a millennium before Christ and remained so until early modern times.

But it is the Ulaid who dominate the sagas transmitted by the medieval writers to the future and who gave their name to the province. In the *Ulidian Tales* or *Ulster Cycle*, with their legendary hero Cú Chulainn, and their royal centre at Emain Macha (Navan Fort in County Armagh) the Ulaid have left one of the most striking records of

Celtic society. Though largely mythological and bearing the hyperbolic mark of generations of storytelling before it was committed to writing in the seventh century, the *Ulster Cycle* has come to epitomise Ireland's heroic age. It tells of the Ulaid king Conchobar (Conor) mac Nessa and his champions, the youthful hero, Cú Chulainn, Fergus mac Róich, his foster-father, and Conall Cernach, his foster-brother. Each is inexorably pulled along by his heroic destiny, doomed by irrational codes of honour to kill those whom they love most. It is also a tale of strong and passionate women: the vampish and ruthless Medb (Maeve) of the enemy Connachta, the faithful Émer, who was to die for love of Cú Chulainn, and the heroine who was to exercise most influence on modern Irish writing, the tragic Deirdriu (Deirdre).

She is a woman of startling beauty whose fate as destructress – 'a woman over whom there will be great slaughter' – was foretold at birth. Destined to wed Conchobar, she leaves him for love of Noíse, son of Uisliu, and goes into exile with him and his brothers. Enticed back by an offer of immunity from Conchobar, Deirdriu commits suicide after Conchobar has the sons of Uisliu murdered. Fergus takes 3,000 warriors into exile with the Connachta, in protest at such treachery. Thus is set the scene for the centrepiece of the *Ulster Cycle* and perhaps the most important tale in Irish literature, the *Táin Bó Cuailnge* (Cattle Raid of Cooley). The *Táin* recounts an episode in the long wars waged by the Connachta against the northern province. The conflict centres on the Boyne valley in County Meath.

It is an aristocratic warrior society, in which the traditional Irish preoccupation with lineage is already present – boastful, heroic, hospitable, much given to feasting and drunkenness, fine music and long stories. But it was only in raids and warfare that their aristocratic values could be measured and demonstrated. The theme of the *Táin* concerns a cattle raid, and the main festivals of the ritual year – Beltaine and Samain – mark the beginning and the end of the grazing season. There may have been some thirty-five *tuatha* or petty kingdoms in Ulster, each with its king – chosen from the kin-group of his predecessor – its nobles, its free commoners and its unfree population. Larger units were brought into being by more powerful kings exchanging military protection for hostages and tributes. But the kin-group (those sharing a common great-grandfather, the *derbfine*) was the important unit of social control. Usually no one had any legal rights outside one's own *tuath*. There were no urban centres, no state institutions as such. Assemblies were held by the king at festival times, and kings proclaimed law and regulations to meet emergencies. But the law was for the most part customary, accurately committed to memory in the law schools, and applied and transmitted by learned lawyers, whose status was equal to that of the nobles and who held positions of great respect in this pre-literate society. With the poets and other learned men, they alone in Celtic society had free right of movement between *tuatha,* and were fundamental to the extraordinary unity of language and tradition in early Ireland. They remained an important and revered element in that society into modern times and the customs and laws they transmitted were central to its stability.

The people of pre-Christian Ulster generally lived in circular structures known as raths. Like the identical ring-forts elsewhere in Ireland, they are distinctive to the island. Some fifty to sixty thousand have survived throughout Ireland, and County Armagh alone contains three to four hundred.[7] Excavations show that they – like the similar crannog lake-dwellings – tended to be built over existing settlements, sometimes of great antiquity. Such continuity belies the image of constant conflict portrayed by the sagas, and excavations of these domestic structures, for example, show no sign of warlike activity.[8] Certainly these predominantly single-family farms appear to have had no military purpose, their circular earthworks designed to keep animals in or out. They are generally located just below the tops of low-lying hills and their very wide distribution throughout the province suggests a close relationship between dwelling and pasture, short-range transhumance determined by the geography. Ancient field patterns suggest small, perhaps less wealthy, even unfree, communities involved in arable farming and pooling resources.[9]

It is the more spectacular ringed enclosures or hill-forts, however, which have left their mark on Irish mythology, even if archaeological excavations limp a long way behind. Four prominent hill-forts have been identified in Ulster. Grianán of Ailech in County Donegal, Clogher in County Tyrone, Downpatrick in County Down, and most important of all, Emain Macha (Navan Fort) in County Armagh. With the exception of the first, however, even these have no obvious defensive purpose. Rather, the presence of Megalithic burial mounds within the enclosures suggests a ritual importance and ceremonial function. Certainly excavations of Emain Macha suggest as much. The tradition of Armagh as the religious capital of Ireland does not start with St Patrick. There is a high density of pagan artefacts in the north, with the heaviest concentration around Armagh – lending credence to the Patrician legend that he chose the site because it had been a pagan cult centre.

It was the recognised centre of Ulaid power, said to have been named after the horse-goddess, Macha, a site which even today is staggering in its grandeur. A massive circular edifice, built in timber over the site of earlier structures, Emain figures prominently in the Ulidian tales. It was the scene of the Ulaid's great celebrations, and artefacts found nearby – including a splendid ceremonial bronze trumpet, some 186cm in length – amply bear this out. Indeed, Celtic feasting was a topic of much fascination with the classical authors. An entire pig was said to be the reward for the most fêted warrior (the so-called 'champion's portion'), voracious appetites incongruously linked with strict etiquette and codes of hospitality. It is not without reason that some of the greatest acts of treachery noted in Irish mythology and folklore should have been associated with betrayals of traditional hospitality. The highlight of such festivities was provided by the musicians and the bards and the tradition of courtly eulogies survived as long as the Gaelic order itself.[10]

The imaginary world of the *Táin* depicts a high-spirited, excitable and recklessly brave warrior society, one that was almost childishly fond of adornment. In the *Táin Bó Cuailnge*, the three companies of Ulster exiles gather with the Connachta armies to march against the Ulaid. One company was distinguished by speckled cloaks, clipped hair, knee-length tunics and full-length shields; the second, by dark-grey, wrap-around cloaks and calf-length, red-embroidered tunics, swept-back hair and bright shields; the third, purple cloaks, red-embroidered, full-length tunics, shoulder-length hair and curved, scallop-edged shields. The longer the cloak, the greater the wealth and status of the wearer. Physical beauty is central to their idea of perfection, and parading it part of the ritual of war.[11]

This warrior aristocracy also believed the afterlife to be very much like the present and was buried with enough earthly chattels to tide them over. The location of the otherworld is very often associated with water, which may explain why so many artefacts have been found in the Shannon and Bann valleys, and the longstanding fascination with the outsized Lough Neagh (the largest freshwater lake in the British Isles). In the twelfth century Giraldus Cambrensis found Lough Neagh fishermen claiming to have seen the submerged towers of the horse-god Eochu, from whom the lake derived its name (Loch nEchach).[12] Early Irish religion, however, was very much of this life. The gods were polymorphic and prominent actors in Irish mythology. The entire emphasis was on ensuring the well-being of the *tuath*. The gods were highly localised and the importance and strict observance of ritual was deemed to tame them and ensure prosperity. The king was ritually married to the earth-goddess and the well-being of the territory taken as a sign of her endorsement of his reign. All the great festivals were likewise designed to enlist the supernatural on the side of earthly prosperity and their importance was such that all were assumed into the Christian calendar. One of the effects of such close linkage between this and the otherworld was a sense of the beauty and enjoyment of this life.[13] These gods and goddesses, however, are rarely benign – the male gods, giant, club-wielding figures, presiding over magical cauldrons; the goddesses treacherously alternating from beautiful maiden to frightful hag, predicting catastrophe. Irish paganism appears to have been as localised as its politics. Every district had its *síd* (hill or mound) another possible location of the otherworld.[14] But the pervasiveness of the deities, both for good and evil, is a token of the intermingling of the real and the divine, the natural and the supernatural which has always characterised Irish folk religion. It is no accident that the Irish word for fairies is *síde* (from *aés síde*, or people of the hill) for they were believed to reside in such hills.[15]

The historic division of Ireland into four provinces was already in place. A fifth, Mide – defining an area roughly coterminous with modern Meath and Westmeath – was an artificial creation by the Kings of Tara. During the ascendancy of the Ulaid (450 BC to AD 324), according to the pseudo-historical dating of the medieval chronicles,[16] the boundary of Ulster seems to have fluctuated between a line from the modern counties of Donegal, Fermanagh, Monaghan, Armagh and

Down, to one taking in Leitrim, Cavan, Louth, Longford and parts of Meath and Westmeath. The events of the *Táin* show 'the border country' well defined by natural phenomena and in people's minds by the time it came to be written down. The 'province boundary' – traditionally extending from the River Drowes in the west, to the Boyne in the east – was guarded from Slíabh Fuait (the Fews mountain, between Dundalk and Armagh), protecting the route to Emain. 'Each of Ulster's heroic warriors had his day on Slíab[h] Fuait, to take care of every man who came that way with poetry, and to fight any others.'[17] It may have been reinforced by earthworks, thought to have predated Hadrian's Wall and popularly known as the Black Pig's Dyke. Surviving folk traditions tell of a monstrous black pig tearing up the earth and disappearing into the sea. Sometimes the story is associated with the defence of Ulster. But usually it has assumed portents of war to come, and in modern times has even been linked to predicted sectarian attacks.[18] Known to have been erected at the same time as Emain Macha around 100 BC, it runs across south Ulster, from Armagh to Donegal. Historically such earthworks appear to have been linked to a series of attacks on Ulster, the similar Dorsey and Dane's Cast of County Armagh acting as secondary lines of defence of the route to Emain Macha.[19]

Although the jewel of the Ulster Cycle, the *Táin Bó Cuailnge* portrays the Ulaid already in decline. The *Táin* recounts an episode in the long wars waged against the northern province by the Connachta, centred on Meath and the Boyne valley, the location of the conflict of the *Táin*, and the Black Pig earthworks. It is for the Uí Néill, sprung from the Connachta, that the most elaborate and entirely fictitious origin legend was created by the Christian compilers of the *Lebor Gabála* or *Book of Invasions*. They were said to have been a Goidelic (Gaelic) people. In fact, we have no real evidence of the ethnic origins of these dynasties. The term Goidelic more accurately describes the Irish form of the Celtic language, although it was in usage as an ethnic term by the eighth century.[20] However, the ascendancy of the Ulaid, and with it their capital at Emain, was destroyed around the time of the introduction of Christianity in the fifth century AD. The Ulaid were henceforth largely confined to the small kingdom of Dál Fiatach (most of eastern County Down), their kinsmen to Dál Riata (north Antrim).

The Cruithin were organised into the two sub-kingdoms of Dál nAraide (around Belfast Lough), and Uí Echach Cobo (central and west Down). This area east of the Bann acquired the general denomination of Ulidia. According to later historical speculation, the three sons of Niall of the Nine Hostages, King of Tara – Eóghan, Conall and Enda – set up kingdoms approximately covering Donegal, Derry and Tyrone. Two, Cenél Conaill and Cenél nEógain, later rose to prominence. Thus came into being the northern Uí Néill. In central and south Ulster were a number of vassal states, collectively known as the Airgialla (Oriel) – the group of ruling families now governing much of Armagh, Tyrone, Monaghan and later Fermanagh and including many from the mid-lands who had fought with Niall. As written history commences with the arrival of Christianity in the fifth century AD, Ireland is almost completely Gaelic in speech. So commenced the golden age of Gaelic Ireland, which would endure until the Norse invasions.

2. The historiography of pre-Christian Ireland[21]

In the realm of prehistory nothing is certain. Oral traditions were probably not written down till the seventh century AD, and the earliest written version of the *Táin* to survive dates from the eleventh century. Taming the past to suit the present is a process not unique to Ireland. Even so, the humanising of pagan gods to create fictitious dynastic ancestors or the portrayal of a golden Celtic age has had a particularly long history in Ireland. In this process the *Ulster Cycle* holds a special place. It was the most highly developed of all the mythological tales – possibly, as Robin Flower suggests, because they were first written down in Ulidian territory at the great monastic house of Bangor – and enjoyed considerable prestige into the Middle Ages. Although some scholars now think that the tales of the *Ulster Cycle* may have contained some genuine oral traditions and may well have initially been compiled by Ulaid literati, they can no longer be accepted as the reliable 'window on the Iron Age' that they once were.[22] However, their idealised picture of early Irish society as wedded to its land and its traditions was to exercise a powerful influence over future generations.[23]

Although that other great epic of Finn and the Fianna has enjoyed more popular appeal because of its lyrical romanticism, the *Ulster Cycle* became the perfect symbol of Ireland's glorious past. Its portrait of a heroic and aristocratic society was particularly adapted to rebut accusations of savagery and barbarism, which characterised English accounts from Giraldus Cambrensis onwards. By the early sixteenth century the Ulidian tales had long been out of fashion. In seventeenth-century poetry – after the destruction of the Gaelic order – they reappear in the bardic lament for a golden age when the poets moved in royal circles. 'They [the English] will be in our places', writes the late seventeenth-century poet Ó Bruadair, 'thick-hipped, mocking, after beating us from the flower of our towns . . . English-speaking, cosy, tasteful . . . [They are now] where Deirdre . . . Emer and the Liath Macha (Cú Chulainn's grey steed) used to be'.[24]

On the whole, however, the *Ulster Cycle* was 'a rediscovery of the romantic period', as Patrick Rafroidi has put it, a period when Catholic emancipation was the main issue of the day and when liberals generally saw the Celtic past as a period capable of reconciling all sides. In presenting the past to an English audience, its sophistication and aristocratic nature had much to recommend it. The intensity and violence of the *Ulster Cycle* did not lend itself easily to romantic primitivism. Yeats and Lady Gregory hoped to harness its energy to a new heroic present and, with Standish O'Grady, were largely responsible for the revival and survival of the Cú Chulainn myth. But it was perhaps predictable that its intensity would make the perfect vehicle for Patrick Pearse's fusion of heroic action and Christ-like sacrifice and that Cú Chulainn should have become the back-stage actor in the 1916 rising. It was used by O'Grady to argue that the qualities which advanced the North far beyond that of the rest of the island lay in its Gaelic past rather than its importation of Scottish and English settlers in the seventeenth century.[25]

O'Grady and other writers of Ireland's late-nineteenth-century literary revival were particularly interested in promoting the image of an organic link between an ancient Irish civilisation and a haunted landscape, such that it is sometimes difficult to disentangle later nationalism's tendency to associate mysterious landscape with ancient culture from genuine folk survivals. Indeed, Sinn Féin early last century made south Armagh's Slieve Gullion – overlooking the route to Emain Macha – a special place of pilgrimage. Suffice it to say that there is a wealth of Ulster folk material linking key figures from the *Ulster Cycle* with features of the landscape, features to which modern Catholic traditions often lay particular claim in the widespread (though largely unproven) belief that theirs is a culture rooted in a more ancient tradition than that of Protestantism.[26]

3. *The arrival of Christianity*

As Ireland emerges into history in AD 431, much of the world reflected in the heroic tales had already passed. A new order of things was emerging which would survive until the Normans. Fundamental to this was the arrival of Christianity. It is the only example in western history of Christianity establishing itself in a culture untouched by Roman conquest. As elsewhere, it did so by adapting to that culture, thereby preserving many of its features. It introduced a notional unity just when the political concept of High Kingship was itself developing and the two became mutually supportive. As early as the seventh century AD, St Patrick had been accepted as the country's saint and Armagh was promoting its claim to be its religious capital.

Patrick was the son of a minor Roman noble living somewhere in north-west Britain. At sixteen he was captured by a raiding party from Ireland and spent the next six years in slavery. Why Patrick's name became associated with the religious centre at Armagh is as mysterious as almost everything else about his life. There are suggestions that it occurred before the destruction of Emain Macha and it was common for early Christian bishops to seek the patronage of local rulers. This would explain the need of early Christian hagiography to invoke Cú Chulainn, the Ulaid's legendary hero, and Patrick's associations with Downpatrick, new capital of the Ulaid after they were defeated and forced east of the Bann.[27] Despite the seventh-century hagiographic lives of Patrick, depicting him moving about the country, converting huge numbers, anointing bishops, performing miracles and everywhere conquering paganism, the earlier establishment of Christianity in the south of Ireland seems to have come mainly from non-Patrician sources. It was another two centuries before Christianity became firmly established in Ireland and Patrick himself tells of early resistance. Indeed, the traditions of the bullish saint who could do no wrong are less than the man. In the two authentic documents left by Patrick – his *Confession* and *Letter to Coroticus* – he reveals himself as more than willing to accommodate native ways, provided they did not openly conflict with Christ's teachings.[28] It was to be the key to Christianity's remarkable success in Ireland. There are no martyrs in the history of early Irish Christianity. Giraldus in the twelfth century considered this a weakness, symptomatic of his notion of the general laxity of the Irish church, though he appreciated the barbed witticism of one Irish bishop's response that his own people, the Anglo-Normans, would soon change that. The Irish 'have always paid great honour and reverence to churchmen, and they have never put out their hands against the saints of God. But now a people has come to the kingdom which knows how, and is accustomed, to make martyrs. From now on Ireland will have its martyrs, just as other countries.'[29]

In later centuries both Protestants and Catholics claimed the early Irish church as their own. The former argued that the early Irish church was free from Roman control until imposed by Henry II in the twelfth century, that it was therefore never really 'Roman' Catholic in any significant sense and that the Reformation church was simply attempting to return it to its primitive purity.[30] Certainly Patrick's mission seems to have been unofficial and entirely British in origin and support. Indeed, he was frowned upon by other ecclesiastics as some kind of vulgar itinerant. Charges of unworthiness he readily admitted and he was desperately anxious to explain his conduct in Ireland to his fellow clerics in Britain. Claims for loose ties with Rome are accurate enough for the very early church. However, the collapse of the Roman Empire elsewhere caused Irish Christianity to be isolated for several centuries. But if native peculiarities were the result, historians have identified a strong emotional attachment between the early Irish church and Rome and a sense of belonging to one church with Rome as its head.[31] In the seventh century, Armagh successfully used native and Roman law to establish its primacy, interlinking its claims with those of the Uí Néill to the High Kingship, on the one hand, and to Rome's claims to be the final appeal court in Christendom on the other. Central to its case was the active promotion of the cult of Patrick (despite the embarrassing tradition of his burial at Downpatrick). It was then that the popular image emerged of Patrick the all-conquering hero, outwitting the druids and securing submission from Lóegaire, king of Tara (though given his patronage by the Ulaid, this could never have been the case).

It is unlikely that a Roman-type episcopacy, based on Roman administrative centres, would have succeeded in Ireland and, although bishops played an important role in the early Irish church, it was to develop largely as a monastic and rural organisation until the reforms of the twelfth century.[32] There was little in the way of parochial development until the time of the Normans, and later in Ulster, where Norman settlement was weak. The monasteries became important social centres, fulfilling many of the social functions normally associated with towns and attracting major settlements, lay and clerical alike, within their precincts. Monasticism accommodated Irish society's familial structure, and as Christianity gained ground, it became fashionable for the Irish aristocracy to help found monasteries on their family's land. But under Irish law, land could not be alienated from the family grouping without its consent, and so the tradition developed of monastic leadership and property being passed on naturally to the heirs of the founder. Abbots became the equivalent of territorial overlords, they were succeeded by their kin and family succession to land was guaranteed. The abbot was often elected from the family of the founder and the family retained that right of presentment for centuries.[33] Christianity did not fundamentally alter the existing social system. The communities settled in raths, crannogs and cashels (e.g. Nendrum in modern County Down) and the Irish monastic tradition of living in small huts rather than monastic houses was such that the introduction of great monasteries with the Cistercians in the twelfth and thirteenth centuries was frowned upon as un-Irish.[34] They followed Irish rather than continental rules that mirrored the diverse local traditions in which they operated. Far from opposing pagan survivals, they often simply Christianised them. They Christianised the native practice of fasting to enforce unmet claims.[35] Pagan festivals became feastdays, pagan deities Christian saints. The saints took over the druidical weapon of malediction, assumed responsibility for bestowing hospitality and holding public assemblies. The early saints' lives written in the seventh and eighth centuries reflected many barely Christianised beliefs. Qualities hailed by heroic societies are uppermost; miracles replace magic, litanies druidical incantations. Christianity had gone native. The saints, bishop-abbots and monks were members of royal houses. It is they who were responsible for collating and writing the country's history, traditions and laws.[36]

For, most of all, the saints took over the mantle of the learned classes and in Irish law the clerics enjoyed the same respect as the *file* (poets) and equal social status with the kings of *tuaths*. They were not only tolerant of Irish secular learning, they took most of it over. They created a new Irish identity by constructing the genealogies, sagas and tales of early medieval Irish literature. By the seventh century the early Irish church had become a deeply integrated one. In the new writings the heroes of the past are summoned from the dead to bear witness. Christianity has become the heir to native traditions.[37] By the eighth century, poet, cleric and king are represented as co-operating in the compilation of that great body of Irish law, the *Senchas Már*. The sixth to ninth centuries are recognised as Ireland's 'Golden Age'. As early as the sixth century, the monastic schools acquired a reputation for learning and Bede tells of many students being attracted from Britain by their reputation. Over the next two centuries many had developed highly professional scriptoria and the golden age of monasticism arrived the following century with the epitome of the successful combination of native and Christian: the illuminated manuscripts.

It is no accident that the earliest written chronicles, annals and vernacular poetry should have originated in south-east Ulster, or that some of the earliest recorded sagas are dominated by the Ulaid, by now a declining dynasty. For it was on Ulidian territory that the great monasteries of St Comgall at Bangor and St Finnian at Movilla actively cultivated vernacular literature and educated or influenced many of the leading scholars and saints of the period. In the *Book of Invasions* or *Book of the Taking of Ireland* (the *Lebor Gabála*) – the most influential of the narrative pseudo-histories, compiled between the eighth and twelfth centuries – a holy man is said to have come to Finnian. He claimed to be of the royal house of Ulaid and to have lived through many lives and shapes, witnessing the entire history of Ireland, which he then related. Thus was born that tradition of genealogical and historical lore, which became standard teaching in the schools for centuries to come and which produced the mythology of the Milesian (Spanish) origin-myth of the Irish race, a myth of such durability that a special blood relationship with Spain was still being claimed as late as the eighteenth century.[38]

In Ulster Catholic tradition, however, it is Colum Cille (Columba, AD 521–97) rather than the national Patrick who emerges as symbolising their particular identity.[39] A member of the Uí Néill royal house and particularly associated with Donegal and Derry, Colum Cille represents the merger of the early church with Irish society. A bard in his own right, he is particularly remembered for having saved the bards from expulsion at the famous Convention of Druim Cett near Limavady in AD 575. He came to symbolise that attachment to nature and the land so characteristic of Gaelic poetry, and the sense of physical wrenching from that land through exile which was to form such a part of Irish nationalist tradition. For Colum Cille is said to have gone to war with Finnian in a dispute over possession of a copy of St Jerome's gospel and to have accepted permanent exile as penance. It is not surprising to find that it is Colum Cille, as a saint with human failings, rather than Patrick, who is invoked as the Catholics' vengeful ally in prophesying the destruction of the Protestant heretics during periods of sectarian conflict in Ulster.[40] Folk traditions of the native saint ready to avenge his people probably have good groundings in reality.[41]

Ulster's domination of early Irish learning had faded by the beginning of the eleventh century. Central to its passing was the eclipse of Bangor, almost certainly through the continued decline of its political patrons in Dál nAraide. But the process was hastened by the destructive Viking attacks from the eighth century onwards. Christianity was confidently established and monastic art and learning was at its height when the Vikings struck in AD 795. They raided the defenceless coastal monasteries, destroying the manuscripts and plundering the precious objects. Iona, Bangor, Downpatrick and Armagh were raided repeatedly. They sailed up the Bann, Foyle, and Boyne, raiding from Lough Neagh, Strangford and Carlingford Loughs. The northern kings fought back with considerable success. The Ulaid attacked victoriously in 811 and again in 825, and Viking encampments were finally destroyed in the north by the Uí Néill in 866.[42] Thereafter there were no Viking settlements north of Dublin, though the Dublin Norsemen continued to raid the northern coasts and lakelands well into the tenth century. But the monasteries never recovered their earlier character. Many more monks fled to the Continent. Scholars are still guessing at the many manuscripts destroyed and the art of illuminating manuscripts never revived. Although the campaign against the Vikings may have achieved a fragile political unity, ultimately it simply aggravated dynastic quarrels and prepared the way for the Normans.

4. Dynastic changes: eighth–twelfth centuries

From the time of St Patrick to the establishment of Brian Boru's claim to High Kingship in the early eleventh century, the political history of Ireland is dominated by the Uí Néill and their claims to dynastic overlordship were encouraged and legitimised by the church. From around the eighth century the terms *Leth Cuinn* and *Leth Moga* began to be used to describe Uí Néill and Eóganacht hegemony in the northern and southern halves of the country respectively. Later monastic writings gave prominence to dominant lines and the Irish practice of kingship and succession was already modified in a feudal direction before the Anglo-Norman invasion. The twelfth-century church reforms which introduced a diocesan organisation mirrored closely the territorial and political changes that had occurred. The monastic familia of the early Irish church reflected a society based on the small units of *tuatha* and family groupings. By the twelfth century provinces had replaced peoples as the essential political unit and the development of strong provincial kingships provides the backdrop to the diocesan reorganisation.[43]

The period witnesses constant pressure by ascending dynasties on older or declining ones. It was this pressure which was behind the expansion of Dál Riata into Scotland in the fifth century and they were overrun entirely by Dál nAraide in the eighth century. The Ulaid (now confined to east Down) had shared the kingship of Ulidia with the Cruithin of Dál nAraide (roughly occupying the southern two-thirds of Antrim, half of Down and north Louth) until 972 when they killed the last Cruithin king, Áed mac Loingsich. They had been helped by the attacks on Dál nAraide by Uí Thuirtri of the Airgialla, who by the twelfth century had replaced them as the dominant element in Antrim. By then, however, the Ulaid themselves no longer held any authority in Ulidia, much of which had been subsumed into the expanding overlordship of the Cenél nEógain.

In the eighth and ninth centuries, the Cenél nEógain branch of the northern Uí Néill emerged from a long struggle with their rival branch Cenél Conaill and expanded from their Donegal–Derry centre to take control of the mid-Ulster territories of the Airgialla and become High Kings of Ireland.[44] During the centuries of the Norse attacks, the annals also record a bewildering series of dynastic feuds in Ulster. As the tenth century opened, the climate deteriorated, food was scarce and comets appeared in the sky.

Great snow and cold and unprecedented frost, in this year, so that the chief lakes and rivers of Ireland were passable, which brought great havoc upon cattle, birds and fishes. Horrid signs besides. The heavens seemed to glow with comets.[45]

Internal feuding in the Uí Néill facilitated the rise of Brian Boru to the High Kingship and destroyed their centuries-old monopoly. Thereafter Ulster became increasingly isolated from the affairs of the rest of the country.

But the continued aggrandisement of the Cenél nEógain and their allies was bringing about significant changes in Gaelic society. There was a considerable narrowing of power at the top, and there are hints in the annals of a growing distance and hostility between upper and lower orders.[46] The idea of the *tuath* and its king as the essential unit was being eroded by the surge towards dynastic aggrandisement. Familial land is no longer sacrosanct; there is a growing territorialisation of the idea of kingship, power over property as well as peoples, and the Cenél nEógain's subjugation of the Ulaid included the alienation of large tracts of territory in a way which would have been unacceptable at an earlier period. The early Middle Ages thus witnessed the oft-repeated process in Irish history of subject-peoples being pushed down the social scale and on to less fertile land.[47] Notable too in this period was the tendency both of conquered and conquerer to simply assume the pedigrees of the more ancient peoples.[48] Falsification and confusion of genealogies became a matter for complaint by the poets, one complaining in 1150:

Bad brotherhood within the *túath*, iniquitous law and great arrogance in kings, the needy transitory king will subdue the miserable husbandman, . . . many judges without justice, sovranty destroyed by base kindreds.[49]

By the time of the Norman invasion in the twelfth century, it had become impossible to trace lineages with certainty to an ancient past.

One sign of this narrowing of power was the trend towards surnames from the eleventh century onwards, further separating dominant from inferior family groupings. Most notable is the emergence of the Ó Néill from Cenél nEógain and, over the next two centuries, their defeat and reduction of their once-dominant kinsmen, the Mac Lochlainns, to the status of minor lords in Inishowen. The Ó Catháin (O'Cahan) likewise emerged from the proliferation of Cenél nEógain families in this period and established themselves in north Derry. At the end of the twelfth century the Ó Dochartaigh (O'Doherty) rose to dominance from the internal feuding of Cenél Conaill, only to be replaced themselves as overlords by the Ó Domhnaill (O'Donnell) at the beginning of the following century. The pressure of the Uí Néill dynasties had greatly reduced Airgialla territory by the twelfth century to that roughly co-existent with Fermanagh, Monaghan, Armagh and part of Louth. The Ó Cerbaill (O'Carroll) dynasty were replaced as kings of Airgialla in the twelfth century by the Mac Mathgamna (MacMahon), who remained effective rulers of Monaghan to the end of the old order at the beginning of the seventeenth century. Their lineage could be traced back to AD 700. More dubious was the Airgialla descent claimed by the Fermanagh Mag Uidir (Maguires), who only emerged into history at the end of the thirteenth century. The Airthir of Armagh had been chief rivals to the O'Carrolls, but their power was eventually eclipsed by Uí Néill encroachments and the only branch to retain prominence into modern times were the O'Hanlons. Further east, only the Cruithin, Mag Aonghusa (Magennises), and their kinsmen the Mac Artáin (MacCartans) of Down survived the dynastic aggression of the pre-Norman age and the Anglo-Norman invasion of Ulster.

Such developments, however, were largely confined to the upper echelons of society and did not alter the lives of most people in these centuries. Apart from a general increase in tillage, Ulsterman lived much as he had done in the past. He was still largely engaged in raising livestock; his home was still a circular wooden structure, heated by central fires and as ill ventilated and smoke-filled as those still remarked on by the Williamite forces in the seventeenth century. In this, little differentiated the upper from the lower social levels, despite the enormous noble contempt for the lower orders. Slavery persisted into the twelfth century, and, as elsewhere, pagan survivals continued to be complained about by the church into modern times.

5. The Irish church on the eve of the Norman invasion

What was the nature of the Christianity bequeathed by Gaelic society? Giraldus complained of the absence of a pastoral mission in the Irish church of the twelfth century. It is one of the few areas in which his criticism is well founded. There is little evidence that the monasteries gave much priority to preaching or to the care of souls, whatever the genuine ascetism of some, particularly during the period of the Céili Dé (Culdee) movement of the eighth century (which practised strict self-sacrifice and also included reclusive anchorites).[50] But the twelfth-century reformers exaggerated the worldliness of the early Irish church. They underestimated the elements of genuine piety and, more importantly, the deep impact it had made on Irish society.[51] The simple fact is that the Irish church on the eve of the Norman conquest was a 'popular' one. It had accommodated pagan survivals and existing secular society and succeeded in turn in permeating the culture of that society on common ground.[52] The authors of the early saints' lives had consulted popular tradition, so that the images transmitted to future generations were very often those developed by Irish society in the eighth century. The saints are endowed with virtues esteemed by that society, not least of which is their role in providing hospitality and entertainment and in later times they were deemed to have blessed the merriment and festivities of the patrons' days (or patterns) celebrated at local holy wells. The veneration of local saints almost as familial figures was a particular facet of Irish rural society.[53] 'Saint Patrick . . . didn't discourage the sport or myth that used to be at these places', a Fermanagh storyteller claimed in the 1970s, 'but he made these places holy places' – places still known to be good for 'a day's outin'.'[54] The relics of the saints became important tools of power for the leading dynasties, their bells in particular being vested with supernatural powers, their hereditary custodians becoming venerated figures. The holy wells and other pagan sanctuaries are still places of pilgrimage to the present day, damned as 'mere remnants of heathen superstitions, practised by our forefathers before the Christian era, and afterwards appended to the rites and ceremonies enjoined by the Church of Rome in the darker ages of Christianity', as one of the many critics put it in the nineteenth century.[55] Whatever the controversy about which church was the natural successor to Patrick's, Irish Protestantism generally – alike with the Catholic hierarchy of later centuries – would remain dismissive of the pagan survivals which were as much part of that church as its biblical teachings, and the rural nature which had transformed it at the outset remained to conserve those elements into later times.

2

GAELIC ULSTER: LAND, LORDSHIP AND PEOPLE

'It may be easily perceaved by this slender and brief description of Ulster, what hath ben and ar the reasons why this Province hath ben . . . more chargeable to Her Maj[ie] than any other Province, an namlie, the want of good townes and Fortified places . . . the sufferance of the Oneils to usurp the government of the Severall Captens and freeholders . . . [enabling them] to wage and mainteine the greater number of Scottes . . . and lastlie, the want of due exercises of religion and justice . . . the occasion of much impietie and barboresnes.'

Hore, ed., 'Marshal Bagenal's Description of Ulster,
anno 1586', 157–8

The beginnings of English rule in Ireland, or what became English rule in later centuries, came when Henry II, with papal support (granted by the letter *Laudabiliter* in 1155), arrived in 1171. This twelfth-century Anglo-Norman[1] 'invasion' was to alter fundamentally the cultural landscape of Ireland, though not by replacing one people or one culture by another. That never happened. Indeed, the Anglo-Norman colony contracted, virtually collapsed entirely in Ulster, and had been reduced to the eastern seaboard of the Pale around Dublin by the fifteenth century. The changes which occurred came about rather through the process of acculturation. Gaelic chieftains, initially defeated by superior Anglo-Norman military talent, soon copied their methods. These centuries witnessed a remarkable escalation in the militarisation of Irish society, the establishment of mercenary armies and a growing exploitation of Gaelic society to support them. Gone were the checks and balances, the strong personal bonds inherent in the old Irish law codes. Gaelic polity had not remained static, but on the eve of its destruction at the end of the sixteenth century it had deteriorated so far that many welcomed the Tudor changes. That said, Gaelic mores and culture remained as vital as ever, defying attempts at church reform, continuing to shape the landscape and people's lives. Ulster was to remain the most Gaelic part of Ireland till the opening of the seventeenth century and the lives of the people were not fundamentally affected by the changes at the top. This is why the events of the seventeenth century were to come as such a shock.

1. Anglo-Norman Ulster

The population increases of the twelfth and thirteenth centuries produced new migratory movements throughout western Europe. The move of the Anglo-Norman lords from south Wales was part of this process.[2] They moved into the fertile valleys of Leinster and Munster and held Connacht as a tributary kingdom. That they never settled throughout Ulster was as much a result of its natural defences as the defiance of the Gaelic lords. In Ulster, only the coastal territory of Antrim and Down was partially brought into the new system by the daring of John de Courcy (1177). It was not an 'invasion' in the strict sense of the word, but the kind of individual and localised exploit already so common in Ireland, and de Courcy was quickly accepted as just another element in traditional dynastic feuding.[3] By sponsoring local traditions and saintly cults, he was even seen as a leader who might revive the fortunes of ancient Ulidia. He was responsible for the heavy concentration of religious establishments and promotion of the Patrick cult in what became modern County Down. In the thirteenth century, de Courcy's successors built a strong power-base, laying claim also to the old 'Ulster' title (the earldom of Ulster was created in 1205). The Anglo-Normans had entered a region where the River Bann was already a cultural divide and had established themselves with the support of many of the lesser chieftains as a buttress against Cenél nEógain aggression. Thus did the O'Flynns of Uí Thuirtri (mid-Antrim), the MacCartans and Magennises of the Ulaid (Iveagh and Kinelarty, mid and south Down), that branch of the O'Neills later to become the Clandeboye O'Neills of Antrim and Down, the borderland Maguires of Fermanagh, the O'Hanlons of Armagh, the O'Reillys of Breifne (Cavan) and the O'Cahans of Derry survive and strengthen as allies of the Anglo-Normans.[4] Such pragmatism – allying with whatever side offered the most – was to characterise the Gaelic chiefs until the seventeenth century.

Likewise, the Anglo-Normans survived by adapting. They fitted easily into the complex network of Gaelic alliances. There was considerable intermarriage, so that most of the great families at the end of the period would have been of mixed descent. By the fourteenth century the Anglo-Irish in Ireland were in retreat and the Ulster colony effectively collapsed. Always insecure, occupying little more than an eastern coastal strip some 25km wide from Fair Head to Carlingford Lough, and excluding much of mid-Antrim and west and central Down, the colony's survival had depended on exploiting the perennial Irish dynastic divisions and on adaptability. The Anglo-Normans had imported settlers at every level, English peasants, merchants and crafts-men being brought into Ulster, largely from the north-west of England. There was displacement of native lords, notably in the Ards peninsula and Lecale, where the descendants of Anglo-Norman families such as the Russells, Whites and Savages retained a precarious and diminishing foothold throughout the period.[5] They did not, however, displace Irish tenants. Indeed, the sharp demographic decline of the fourteenth century made tenants a scarce commodity.[6] They adopted the native land system and very often native ways and outside observers came to make little distinction between them and the native Irish chiefs. There was some hostility between settlers and natives, notably with the O'Neills, but on the whole the relationship seems to have been one of compromise.[7] Flashes of nationalistic fervour occurred at the top, notably at the time of the invasion of Ulster by Edward Bruce of Scotland (1315). But the only sustained record of nationalistic or, more accurately, ethnic conflict is to be found in the church.[8]

We have little information about settlement on the ground. Broadly speaking, in Ulster east of the River Bann the hills, woodland and bogs remained the preserve of the native Irish and the lowland coastal areas that of the Anglo-Irish. Certainly in Ireland as a whole the uplands came to be associated in the minds of the authorities with a peculiarly Irish way of life.[9] It was a tendency accentuated by the colony's retreat from the fourteenth century onwards. North Antrim was lost around 1400 through marriage to the MacDonnells of the Isles. The Clandeboy O'Neills, driven from Tyrone, occupied south Antrim and north Down and the Anglo-Irish Savages and Whites became confined to the Ards peninsula and south Down.[10] By the time of Marshal Bagenal's famous description of Ulster in 1586, the descendants of the original colonists had contracted to the area around Strangford Lough (Ards, Lecale and Dufferin), 'somewhat degenerate [i.e. Gaelicised] and in poore estate', yet still having freehold rights to their lands and never totally assimilated into native society.[11] This area around Strangford Lough was to continue a special, if at times purely nominal, allegiance to England throughout this period. The result was to be a particularly striking cultural diversity, to which was added 'New English' such as Bagenal in the late sixteenth century (i.e. a new cohort of Protestant English arriving during the Tudor conquest, in turn giving rise to the terms 'Old English' and 'Old Irish' to describe the Catholic descendants of the Anglo-Irish and Gaelic Irish respectively). It was considered culturally different from the rest of Ulster and by the late sixteenth century naughty children would be threatened with removal east of the Bann 'where you never hear a word of Irish'.[12]

Neither the MacLochlainns nor the O'Neills were successful in subjecting eastern Ulster to their overlordship, despite successive attempts. It is one of the best examples of topography shaping the history of the province. Cut off by the Bann, the woods of Glenconkeine and the Mountains of Mourne, the area was accessible in only four eminently defensible places: over the Bann at Coleraine, the ford at Toomebridge, Glenn Righe (Vale of the Newry River) and the Moiry Pass (parish and townland of Moira, north-east of Magherlin).[13] Inland topography, therefore, and coastal location prevented the remnants of the Anglo-Irish colony from being totally overrun.

2. The Scottish influence

The cultural landscape was also altered by the importation of large numbers of Scottish mercenaries after the thirteenth century – Gaelic Ireland's response to the more sophisticated warfare of the Anglo-Normans. Gaelic in speech and tradition, and, unlike the seventeenth-century Scottish planters, largely from the Gaelic/Scandinavian Western Isles, they intermarried, settled (mostly along the coast from the Foyle to the Glens of Antrim), and assumed Gaelic Irish genealogies.[14] Marriages were contracted by the Gaelic lords for the purpose of recruiting more mercenaries, thereby producing a succession of formidable wives to the O'Neills and O'Donnells in particular. By the sixteenth century the greatest of the overlords – O'Neill of Tyrone and O'Donnell of Tyrconnell – were of mixed blood, the former contracting

Anglo-Irish, the latter Scottish marriages. Although the Anglo-Irish in the north-east looked south to the Pale, Gaelic Ulster's cultural and economic frontier had long operated on an east–west, rather than a north–south, axis. It already formed part of a cultural and linguistic community with the Isles and western Scotland, the poets in particular enjoying an easy interchange. Scots were settled by King John around Coleraine and in the Glens of Antrim at the beginning of the thirteenth century. The MacDonnells of the Isles established an hereditary claim in Antrim through marriage with the Bissets c.1400. They and other mercenaries, like the MacQuillans of the Route (north Antrim, probably Welsh in origin), were amongst the major beneficiaries of the decline of the Anglo-Irish colony in the fourteenth and fifteenth centuries.[15] By the latter half of the sixteenth century the collapse of the Lordship of the Isles had added successive waves of MacDonnells to the Ulster settlement and destabilised neighbouring territories. They eventually pushed out the MacQuillans from the Route and the Whites from Dufferin. They were to remain a law unto themselves, supporting whichever side furthered their interests, miraculously emerging at the beginning of the seventeenth century (despite the hostility of successive English governments) as untainted by treason and with a commanding hold over most of Antrim.

The greatest of these hereditary mercenary or gallowglass families, the MacSweeneys, were territorial lords in Donegal by the fourteenth century, while another branch of the MacDonnells, serving O'Neill in Tyrone, came to own the area around Ballygawley. Others came in the wake of the Bruce wars (1315–18) and stayed. By the fifteenth century we find the gallowglass families of MacSheehy, MacDowall (MacDougal), MacCabe (who became the Maguires' and Mac-Mahons' hereditary gallowglass), MacGill, MacRory and MacConnell, most, alike with the east Ulster hereditary poets, the Ó Gnímhs (Agnews), coming from the same Hebridean stock as the MacDonnells. Although these families spread into the other parts of Ireland, they did not do so until the sixteenth century and on the whole remained peculiar to the northern part of the country. They were treated like the hereditary professional families and were settled on gifts of free land. They became thoroughly absorbed into Ulster Gaelic society, establishing territorial lordships in their own right and becoming major patrons of the poets.[16] The high costs of their maintenance gradually altered the character of Gaelic lordship, replacing the personal service and periodic hospitality of the old law tracts with increasing exactions and billeting (or 'coyne and livery'). The numbers of Scots mercenaries increased dramatically in the wars of the sixteenth century, reaching an estimated 25,000 between the 1560s and 1590s, and placing an intolerable burden on the host population.[17] They were quartered throughout the province, most notably in convenient locations like the Inishowen peninsula and O'Cahan's country around Coleraine, while Rathlin Island became the MacDonnells' military way station between the Isles and the Antrim coast. There were Irish mercenaries too (kerne), likewise quartered by 'coyne and livery'. But the Scots gallowglass and mercenaries became a particular feature of warfare in the north, causing heightened English anxiety at the prospect of the Scottish enemy using Ireland as a base and producing that novel preoccupation with Ulster which would characterise Elizabethan policy.[18]

3. Daily life and social relations in Gaelic Ulster

Such localism was to intensify after the Anglo-Normans halted the eleventh- and twelfth-century moves towards unity and high kingship, and a European-wide decline in population impacted on Ireland from the fourteenth century onwards. Ireland, even by contemporary standards, was grossly underpopulated. This fostered assimilation in colonised areas. Labour and tenants were scarce. But it also made labour-intensive arable farming difficult. In Gaelic areas pastoralism increased. Once-cultivated land reverted to forest, intensifying outsiders' perception of Ulster in particular as another world, primitive and threatening. They were struck by the comfortless and impermanent housing of even the lordly classes. A people who seemed to move and live with their cattle, their largely outdoor life reflected in their distinctive clothing.[19] Although towards the end of the period there are signs of Gaelic lords periodically adopting the externals of European nobility in more comfortable housing and formal attire, many aspects of Gaelic life had remained unchanged since the dawn of history and power was still reckoned in terms of people and livestock rather than property and land.

Certainly the Irish were contemptuous of Anglo-Irish attachment to stone buildings. Even in church life the showiness of the new continental-inspired monasteries was ridiculed. 'He was not engaged to keep stone walls', MacMahon at the end of the twelfth century is reputed to have replied to the accusation of having abandoned his alliance with John de Courcy and destroyed his forts, 'he scorned to confine himself within such cold and dreary enclosures while the native woods were open for his reception and security'.[20] His words neatly capture the difference between Anglo-Irish and native Irish perception of man's relationship with the land: to the former native Irish areas seemed wild and wooded, hilly and hostile, full of 'narrow corners and glennes under the mountaines foote, in which they lurked',[21] a landscape requiring taming, clearing and civilising through building and enclosure. House-building was made compulsory in later plantation leases. The extension of English law depended on the existence of administrative centres. In 1606 Sir John Davies found it impossible to conduct court because of the absence of buildings in which to site sessions and gaols, 'for the habitations of this people are so wild and transitory as there is not one fixed village in all this county', Fermanagh.[22] Even the apparel of the Irish was adapted to the boggy terrain – most going bare-legged, breechless and shoeless. 'The bogs are so great on this island', wrote a fourteenth-century Spanish pilgrim after passing through Ulster en route for Donegal, 'that scarcely upon the highest mountains can one pass through the waters, and even if one goes knee-deep, so that on foot there is great difficulty, and on horseback even greater.'[23] The wildness – still a feature of the immediate northern side of the border today – was a threatening cordon for the medieval Pale, deterring settlement well into the eighteenth century. And just as such wild terrain protected the east from absorption by O'Neill, so the mountain ranges of Tyrconnell (Donegal) made the latter virtually unconquerable. The province was thus effectively divided politically and geographically into three blocks.

In the absence of towns and modern communications, physical relief dominated everyday life and local identity. Even O'Neill's country – though the largest and most powerful territorial lordship in Ireland, extending from Inishowen(Donegal) to south of the river Blackwater (Tyrone/Monaghan/Armagh border) – did not have a natural locus of power. The annals record a very real mental division created by the Sperrins, one part looking north-west to Derry and its hinterland from Omagh to Lough Foyle, the other south-east towards Armagh and beyond. It was a physical and mental divide reflected in the semi-independent status of O'Cahan's country and eventually in the creation of the separate county of Londonderry in the seventeenth century.

The insubstantial housing of the Ulster Gaels may have contributed to the remarkable mobility noted by all commentators. But to government officials they betokened the rootless man, and such mobile abodes were outlawed in 1608. The beehive wattle-and-daub, windowless and chimneyless huts – such a feature of early seventeenth-century maps – are very much a survival of ancient vernacular housing, more common in early modern Ulster than in areas influenced by the Anglo-Irish. They are depicted as clustered round the few towns, abbeys and royal residences. By the sixteenth century they would have been the housing of the poorer elements in society, regardless of race, and in the plantation surveys they were reported from every part of Ulster. The great lords were already living in tower houses, and middling septs like the O'Hagans of Tyrone in two-storey houses. But for most of this period the living styles of the lords did not differ greatly from the people at large. Cattle were the only valuable property and the quickly erected, temporary wood-framed house was the norm and a standard of great antiquity. In its most basic form, it permitted considerable mobility to the Irish during the Nine Years War, 1593–1603 (or Tyrone's – after Hugh O'Neill, earl of Tyrone – Rebellion). It came to represent for Elizabethans all that was worst in the Irish character and was heavily legislated against. The change to stone as a building material was one of the more visible revolutions in the cultural landscape of seventeenth-century Ulster. But like almost everything else in the medieval rural lifestyle, the nature of its housing was dictated by circumstances. Local building stone was in short supply, whereas wood was plentiful. The destruction of the forests in the seventeenth century soon changed that.[24]

The general disregard for domestic comfort by all classes was another cause of complaint. In this respect even the lifestyle of the lords seems not to have changed much over the centuries, and was lived out in great halls adjoining their fortresses, surrounded by crowds of people, including the mandatory poets, harpists and storytellers. It was even claimed of the early fourteenth-century Aedh Reamhar O'Neill that he maintained sixty houses other than his chief residence, twenty for entertaining the poets, forty for performers of the lesser arts.[25] The carelessness and lack of privacy in sleeping arrangements was thought to encourage promiscuity, the constant presence of animals squalor, the lack of etiquette and social distinction at table (or lack of one, as Fynes Moryson proclaimed) irreverence and want of social deference. Meat was cooked in skins, meals taken out-of-doors, tables and beds notable by their absence. 'They care not for pot, pan, kettil, nor for mattrys, fether bed, nor such implements of household', remarked one Tudor visitor.[26] Judging by similar comments from later centuries, the reality was probably not far removed from such statements, even if the idea of depravity requiring rescue was. Pastoral habits do not inspire order and cleanliness, and the promotion of tillage was as much a part of the Tudors' and Stuarts' mission to 'civilise' the Irish, as enclosures, towns, villages and stone houses.[27]

In contrast the typical native warrior lord disdained the apparent tameness of settler farming and housing, and Conn O'Neill in Henry VIII's reign cursed those who sought to 'learn English, sow wheat, or make any building in Ulster'.[28] It was, after all, not through good husbandry that one became *The* O'Neill or *The* O'Donnell, but rather through the skilled horsemanship, for which Gaelic lords were noted, the daring cattle-raid and generous gifts of the spoils.[29]

> Conn vow'd his race
> For ever to the fight and chase,
> and curs'd him of his lineage born,
> Should sheathe the sword to reap the corn,
> Or leave the mountain and the wold
> To shroud himself in castled hold.[30]

'Every prince eligible for high Kingship is taught love of plunder and hatred of peace', ran one fourteenth-century praise poem of the O'Donnells. In contrast those who slept in feather beds, cropped their hair and wore ruffs, hose and jewelled spurs, were satirised by the poets as effeminate and unmanly.[31] They seemed to be forever on the move, their very dress denoting lives generally pursued out of doors. The famous Irish mantle – a huge shag, a brightly trimmed and russet-coloured rug or cloak, worn over saffron tunics – was in general use, by male and female alike, in the sixteenth century. Acting both as bedding and clothing, and enabling woodkerne, cattle-herders and, Spenser thought, rebels and outlaws, to sleep rough and move rapidly, it was 'their house, their bed, and their garment . . . a fit house for an out-law, a meet bed for a rebel, and an apt cloke for a thiefe'. Spenser also thought it encouraged promiscuousness, providing the 'bad hus-wife' and 'wandring woe men . . . a coverlet for her lewde exercise'.[32] In dress and lifestyle little would have differentiated the lowly from the lordly, although, with the general trend towards greater distancing between lord and subject by the sixteenth century, this too was chang-ing. In common with their peers elsewhere in Europe, there was a move towards what English officials applauded as 'civility' among sixteenth-century Irish lords, both in dress and housing. Indeed, Mac-Mahon levied protection rents on the Pale in fine cloth, and Magennis of Iveagh (deemed the 'most cyviliest of all the Irishrie'[33] in Ulster), Manus O'Donnell and Turlough Luineach O'Neill wore satin and velvet on ceremonial occasions. In fact, Irish dress, like Irish housing, had been adapted to suit the terrain and way of life, and the Anglo-Irish settlers in Ulster adopted both, the Savages becoming wholly 'degener-ate' in Tudor terminology. And while the poor like the poor everywhere can have had little but rags below their mantles (which might explain the aforementioned Spanish pilgrim's belief that they were naked beneath their shag cloaks), all the evidence, visual and otherwise, from the heavily bejewelled women, with their elaborate linen head-dresses, to the long-flowing sleeves of the standard tunic and the long, fringed, curled (almost dreadlocked) hair of the men, betrays as much stylis-ation as that of the ancient Celts – primitive certainly, in the sense of being locked in an earlier age, but scarcely the symbol of barbarity as perceived by Spenser and others.

4. *The land and its 'ownership'*

To the Irish, the hills and forests were places of refuge – as much from the predatory Gaelic lord as the English. It was complained of O'Neill during an invasion of his lands in 1541 that he 'never made show of no power, but kept him and his and their cattell in grete woodes and fastnes, where we could not attayn them, nor yet have perfect knowledge where they were'.[34] They were also essential elements in the agrarian economy. The hills provided summer pasturage for the large herds which dominated that economy and in many cases were considered communal land for neighbouring communities. The forest clearings permitted arable farming in the unenclosed lowland ground, which would otherwise have been difficult to protect against livestock. Most estates were arranged to include a hilly area.[35] Often whole septs would move with their cattle to adjacent hill areas for summer pasturage. This was that seasonal movement of livestock termed trans-humance, at the time called booleying (from the Irish word *buaile* for enclosure or byre) or creaghting (after the Irish word *caoraigheacht*, Hiberno-English 'creaght', signifying 'a herd of miscellaneous livestock with its attendants, grazing or passing through other people's lands').[36] It gave rise to the misconception that the native Irish were a nomadic people. Although there are early signs of a cash economy (particularly in areas bordering Anglo-Irish settlements), cattle still formed the basic unit of value till the end of the Gaelic period. Most people would have been involved in herding livestock – the cattle being moved to summer pastures on 1 May and returned at the end of October. The economic basis for booleying was little understood by English observers. Its association with those maligned hills and fastnesses damned it as a rebelly way of life; its temporary nature conjured up the image of the rootless man, even though it was very often conducted by milkmaids. Rather it was a long-established response to local terrain; it was a particular feature in boggy and hilly areas and as such it continued in these areas, in various forms, down to the twentieth century.[37] But it would be wrong to romanticise this image of the Gael living in poorer, upland regions. In medieval society considerable power attached to the command of mountain passes, and throughout this period the

Magennis castles controlled the accesses to the Anglo-Irish of Lecale, whilst in the largely pastoral economy of Gaelic Ireland extensive woodland was no deterrent to settlement and pasturage. Creaghting was first described in the annals in the fourteenth century as a particularly northern phenomenon practised by Irish and Anglo-Irish alike. At times it was used aggressively, particularly by the Fews branch of the O'Neills – the cattle being deployed as a weapon to devastate enemy lands and was a particular feature of Ulster conflict in the seventeenth century.[38]

This association in the minds of the authorities between landscape and Gaelic and rebelly ways is particularly noticeable in the case of inauguration ceremonies for Gaelic chiefs. Here the symbolism of nature was allied with that of an ancient pagan past. Such ceremonies always took place on hills, which were usually ancient burial mounds or in some other way associated with the ancient history of the people or place, and the poet played a key role in linking the candidate to that past. Frequently the inauguration stone was encircled by trees, like some ancient druidical grove. Such ancient survivals seem to have died out or were suppressed after the Anglo-Norman invasion. But, in a clear anti-English political gesture, they were revived with particular emphasis on the Gaelic past in the fourteenth century and were adopted even by hibernicised Anglo-Irish families. There was considerable local variation in the ceremony, Donegal in particular originally retaining many more ancient, even pagan, rituals, though later O'Donnell inaugurations took place in the church at Kilmacrenan. By the sixteenth century the most powerful chief in Ireland was O'Neill of Tyrone, and his inauguration site at Tullahoge, just east of Lough Neagh, attracted particular attention from Tudor cartographers. Before the twelfth century, the church had played a major role in such ceremonies. But although the role of native monks seems to have continued undiminished, and that of the poets as perceived heirs to ancient druids was magnified, there was a marked turning away from the institutional church which had associated itself with Henry II and English ways.

By the sixteenth century, the narrowing of power in Gaelic Ireland was also reflected in changes in the inauguration ceremonies. The main overlords, for example, were now claiming the right of naming and inaugurating the sub-chiefs. The MacSweeneys claimed to have been inaugurated by Colum Cille's successors at Iona before they came to Ireland. It may well have been this tradition which explains their inauguration in 'Colum Cille's precinct', Kilmacrenan, 'and if any were inaugurated elsewhere, he could not be long in power'. But this seems to have been on the suffrage of O'Donnell, who exacted a hereditary tribute for the honour and inflicted bitter retribution when such approval was not sought.[39] Most notable, however, was the significance being attached to the surnames of the leading families and the public declaiming of 'the name' – *The* O'Neill, *The* O'Donnell – at the inauguration. To be called 'The O'Neill' signified lordship of the whole of Ulster, a counter-sovereignty to that of the Crown. Thus was Conn O'Neill obliged to forsake 'the name of O'Neill' prior to becoming earl of Tyrone in 1542 and his son Shane's use of it was part of his attainder in 1569:

Forasmuch as the name of O'Neill, in the judgements of the uncivil people of this realm, doth carry in itself so great a sovereignty as they suppose that all the lords and people of Ulster should rather live in servitude to that name than in subjection to the crown of England: be it therefore enacted that the same name of O'Neill ... shall from henceforth cease ... and be utterly abolished and extinct forever.[40]

To English governors Gaelic inauguration ceremonies held such potential for rebelliousness that they had symbolic sites such as the O'Neill inauguration stone at Tullahoge destroyed in 1601. Indeed, the revival of lapsed inauguration rites became a symbol of rebellion by many chiefs during the Nine Years War. Assisted by the cultivated anti-quarianism of the learned men, the retention of such ancient customs became part of a chief's armoury and the old idea of the marriage between chief and land continued to be voiced by the bards well into the seventeenth century. Although the sacral element had by then long been replaced by a more secular definition of the lord as head of a dominant family, the practice itself symbolised an alternative definition of power to that being assumed under English law (often readily so) towards the end of the period. In this respect it was also a reminder of the ancient status of declining families, the O' Cahans and O'Hagans for instance retaining the ceremonial role of conferring authority on

The O'Neill. For later nationalists, such sites were to retain their symbolic significance, as remnants of a Gaelic landscape which was considered peculiarly theirs.[41]

This traditional association of land with Gaelic tradition, however, owed little to secure ownership, and we must look to later centuries for the development of what Ulster folklorist Michael J. Murphy terms 'the peasant complex – which puts prestige, house, lands, cattle and everything else above people'.[42] But as the land surveyors set about assessing 'ownership' on the eve of the Ulster Plantation, they aroused an acute consciousness of who had rights to what. Gaelic landholding differed from region to region and even from kin-group to kin-group within the same area, and custom was often stronger than right. At the top of the landholding system the overlord controlled his 'country' (equivalent to the old *tuath*[43] or the modern barony). Each 'country' consisted of the lord's private family lands (technically the property of the sept rather than the individual); the mensal lands, which supplied him with food, probably farmed by freeholding septs; the demesne lands which went with his office, and which were farmed by rent-paying tenants; the freeholders' lands, owing him dues and services; and church lands, traditionally free from such exactions. But for most of this period, the lord's power was defined not in terms of landownership, but in a complex series of rights and clientship. Thus, although there might have been certain hereditary lands attached to his office (desmesne lands), more often than not such lands belonged rather to his particular sept. Indeed, he actually owned only about one-fifth of the land held. More important were the lands from which he could demand certain rights, and when these were not fulfilled he would simply take such land into his hands as forfeit, and time and custom established ownership. The process was mirrored on church lands, the bishop or abbot having assumed many of the lord's secular trappings and powers.[44]

Within each lordship actual ownership of land was confined largely to the lord and his relatives, officials, soldiers, poets, brehon (a lawyer or judge) and ecclesiastics. But there would also have been a number of formerly important landowning families reduced in status through the expansion of ruling lineages, and thereby several layers of presumed ownership, with groups theoretically reduced to tenants-at-will still claiming title. This downward social process was a particular feature of the period and was aggravated by the nature of Irish succession. Every male with a common great-grandfather in the chiefly line had a right to be considered for succession to the sept title. But very often force spoke louder than right, and the history of Gaelic Ulster is riven by bloody succession disputes, which, even when temporarily resolved, could leave behind aggrieved family factions ready to join forces with the new lord's traditional enemies. Even depressed septs and the lowliest farmer would have retained a keen sense of status – a point noted in 1607 by Sir John Davies (James I's attorney-general in Ireland). In Fermanagh he had interviewed the inhabitants of every barony, particularly the scholars, 'who know all the septs and families and all their branches, and the dignities of one sept above another, and what families or persons were chief of every sept, and who were next, and who were of a third rank, and so forth, till they descended to the most inferior man in all the baronies'.[45]

The patent rolls of 1615 list a multitude of small grants to persons described as 'gentlemen', revealing the existence of something approaching a peasant gentry.[46] 'All the Irish almost boast themselves to be gentlemen, no lesse than the Welsh', noted Spenser, 'for if he can derive himselfe from the head of any sept, (as most of them can, they are so expert by their Bardes), then hee holdeth himselfe a gentleman, and thereupon scorneth to worke, or use any hard labour, which hee saith, is the life of a peasant or churle.'[47] Lineage notions of status were to persist through and beyond the plantations. Stronger amongst those who had lost out than among those who had gained by the changes, it was to fuel a sense of grievance into modern times.

This downward social process was intensified by the much-criticised system of gavelkind or partible inheritance, whereby the sept's land was subject to periodic redistribution, as co-heirs died or families increased in size. Gavelkind also operated in Gaelicised areas of the Anglo-Irish colony. There was a wide regional variation in this practice; where it did occur regularly it was a disincentive to improvement. In some areas, however (e.g. Fermanagh), it happened so infrequently that by 1600 most farmers would have held their farms much as they do today. More powerful families could compensate for proliferation by extending control over other lands, further adding to the depression of status of those overrun. Given the right of illegitimate children to inherit, the sexual permissiveness of Gaelic society, and the enormous number of male heirs produced, by the end of this period the leading families had acquired possession of vast tracts of their respective counties, as much as three-quarters of Fermanagh, for example, being in the hands of the Maguires.[48] Consolidation by the dominant lord at the expense of freeholders, and their decline in status to that of tenants, was a prominent feature of late medieval Ireland, even the inauguration ceremonies changing in content to reflect the progressive transformation from king to landlord.[49] The tendency in the fifteenth and sixteenth centuries was for overlords such as O'Neill or O'Donnell to reduce free subjects to the status of tenants and transform their territories from lordships to estates. Such was their success that, in 1603, Hugh O'Neill was recognised as owning virtually the whole of Tyrone. The expansion of the junior branches of the O'Neills had caused the once-prominent Mac Cathmhaoil (McCawll, McCall) sept to disperse eastwards through Armagh and Down, and likewise encroached upon the territories of minor lords such as Magennis, O'Hanlon, MacMahon and O'Reilly (occupying the heavily wooded borderlands between Ulster and the Pale and Gaelicised midlands).[50] It was this class of minor lord which unsurprisingly responded most positively to the Tudor policy of 'surrender and regrant'.

Such depression in status would have been a recurrent feature of Gaelic Ireland, though we do not know enough about medieval landholding to assess how it was absorbed. In a society where linear succession did not operate, the sons of former chieftains also risked losing their father's lands to the sons of succeeding rulers. One way of avoiding this was to break away and form a new sub-chieftainship, as did the O'Neills of Clandeboy, those of the Fews in south Armagh and the Maguires of west Fermanagh, in the fourteenth and fifteenth centuries. Such an unsatisfactory system of landholding was one of the main factors in the violence of medieval Irish society. When power attached to overlordship rather than ownership, it required constant assertion through enforced tributes and services. Yet ancient customs die hard. Despite the proclamation of 1605 against Gaelic land tenure, older inheritance customs survived and were even recognised by the Dublin authorities until 1641.[51] Studies of land usage and settlement in County Derry show that such subdivision within a defined kin-group persisted, the same families occupying the lands of their ancestors and continuing to live in kin-groups into the twentieth century. At the most basic level, subdivision may not have been as destructive or anarchic as studies of the upper reaches of Gaelic society would suggest, and where rough land, bog or mountain adjoined restricted arable land, an element of communal farming was not incompatible with independent holdings within the family land.[52]

This picture of kin-groups possessing a long-standing stake in identifiable pieces of land would seem to conflict with the total absence of written proof. However, in a society without written land titles, no tradition of mapmaking or surveying, and where outright ownership was the exception rather than the rule, customary right and an acute awareness of who had what rights over what territory were vital. In the plantation scheme it could mean the difference between retention and dispossession to know whether one's land was demesne or freehold, as many in Fermanagh argued successfully, and in Cavan less so. It would appear that the humblest farmer knew every inch of the territory to which he was entitled.[53]

A particularly notable association of land and people was that of the O'Hagans of Tyrone, whose prominent role in the inauguration of the O'Neills seems to have come from their lengthy occupation of the Tullahoge site itself and the surrounding territory, an occupation which continued from at least the eleventh to the early seventeenth centuries.[54] The modern association of local people with certain townlands would appear to go back far beyond the keeping of records, and divisions became more precise where partition occurred, as under gavelkind. Indeed, Davies says as much of Fermanagh in 1607, where he found 'an exceeding great' number of freeholders, even occupiers of 'petty fractions and divisions' under gavelkind claiming such.[55] In Anglo-Irish areas, where occupation was more continuous, measurement was more rigorously defined. But in Gaelic areas units would have been seen as little more than 'a bundle of spade ridges',[56] boundaries loosely defined and periodically re-defined by the medieval practice of 'perambulation', symbolic location of burial grounds and crosses, and handed-down custom. When asked in 1543 to adjudicate in a territorial dispute between O'Donnell and O'Neill, Lord Deputy

St Leger complained that they produced no legal proof besides 'certain old parchments or bills, confirmed by no seal, signature or other testimony but such as are composed by vain poets ... blinded by affection for their lords'.[57] The extreme localism of Gaelic society and the apparent confusion of land title was to bewilder the Elizabethans. But it was a medieval concept of landholding defined by tradition which was to persist into modern times and to provide the emotional groundwork for the land campaign of the late nineteenth century. Moreover, although the trend by the early seventeenth century was towards individual ownership and primogeniture, the old identification of family groups with certain areas continued, and in the absence of other records was frequently accepted by seventeenth-century crown officials in the parcellation of land to new owners.[58] It would be wrong, therefore, to assume blanket instability of title. Historical geographers have identified an underlying stability in medieval Irish society which conflicts with the picture of mayhem in contemporary English accounts. Indeed, in areas of Ulster not torn by warfare at the end of the sixteenth century, crown officials were surprised to find a relatively well-ordered landscape.[59] In this mapless society, there was nevertheless a network of small territories whose boundaries were well-known to the resident population, and a well-established association between particular communities and certain parcels of land. Even the unfree gained a right of inheritance after thirty years' occupation.[60]

The lowest level of land unit was called different things in different areas – the 'poll' of Cavan, the 'tate' of Fermanagh and Monaghan, the 'ballybo' of Tyrone, Derry, Donegal and Down. But at the end of this period they were standardised as the modern townland, their local names and boundaries retained, thereby fossilising Gaelic settlement patterns. Averaging some sixty acres, these base units represented not so much a fixed geographic area as the measurement of agricultural potential, or land considered capable of grazing a certain number of cattle. It was a notional and fluctuating form of land assessment which survived the Ulster plantation and was still remarked upon in the eighteenth century.[61] The larger land units of ballybetaghs (averaging sixty ballyboes) were controlled by middle-level sept leaders, the inferior septs of the dominant lord. These were the free septs, the future freeholders of Tudor settlements, those most at risk from the system of periodic redistribution to the benefit of the senior lord, and those who increasingly resorted to English law for protection.

At the lower level of the 'churls' or under-tenants who actually worked the land (and we know that substantial areas of Ulster were under tillage, whatever the dominance of pastoral farming), their scarcity should have ensured some security. Certainly the appeals of Hugh O'Neill and the other Ulster lords for the return of those who had exercised the customary right to change lords and had fled to the Pale during the ravages of Shane O'Neill's rebellion and the Nine Years War, show them to have been a scarce and valued commodity. But this involved a further deterioration in their condition, removing traditional freedom of movement and reducing them to total subservience. There can be no doubt that this is exactly what the Ulster lords were attempting to do and it was specifically forbidden by royal proclamation in 1605.[62] The idea of a personal bond between lord and subject had long disappeared. The position of the Irish peasant generally was one of the worst in Europe, and, after the ravages of the Nine Years War, that of the Ulster peasants was the worst in Ireland. The poor and weak would have had little redress under what was left of the brehon laws, a fact noted by Spenser.[63] Little wonder that many saw England's common law as frequently providing more protection and the Anglo-Irish and English as the lesser taskmasters. Although we know very little about the people of Ulster during the Middle Ages, it is clear that ownership of land and memory of past ownership were more important in Gaelic Ulster than once thought and enmity between dominant and declining septs persisted through many generations.[64] Low densities of population would have cushioned the impact of dispossession. But by the end of the sixteenth century insecurity of tenure, erratic and increasing military exactions and absence of fixed payments were emerging as major grievances. The middling rank of chieftains might have welcomed the greater security offered by the introduction of English Common Law. But the confiscations and influx of settlers after the Ulster Plantation was quite another matter, exacerbating tensions which had been brewing for some time.[65]

An even more tortuous layering of landholding occurred in the case of church lands. These so-called termon lands dated from the very generous grants of land to the early monasteries, and to all intent and purposes had become the hereditary possessions of certain families. By the late medieval period the term encompassed coarb (technically heir or successor to the founding saint) and erenach (monk-steward) lands. The holders were not necessarily in orders, though many were. Even then hereditary transmission was still possible, given the continuance of clerical marriage, regardless of the statute of the Synod of Cashel (1101) forbidding it. Such families traditionally provided the members of the clergy.[66] They symbolised the economic basis of the medieval church, paying tithes, in addition to rents, fines, and tributes to the bishop or archbishop – as they would have done to the secular lord – providing supplies, upkeep of church buildings and hospitality. They were technically free from lay exactions, but suffered encroachment by Gaelic lords, notably the O'Neills.[67] Whatever their different status, however, these lands came to be treated by their erenach families in the normal Gaelic manner. There was as much precise local knowledge of their extent and their attendant duties and rights, as there was of neighbouring secular lands. The Inquisition of Dungannon in 1609 found 'that these septs or erenachs have, tyme out of mind, inherited the said lands according to the Irish custome of tanistrie' (whereby the successor was appointed by the existing holder within his own lifetime), and that neither abbot nor bishop had any right to remove them.[68]

Such lands were extensive in Ulster, particularly in those areas of early Patrician and Columban foundations. They may have accounted for as much as a third of the land in the Irish part of the diocese of Armagh (i.e. County Armagh, east Tyrone and south-east Derry). When the English archbishop of Armagh, John Colton, made a visitation to the see of Derry in 1397, hospitality and security was arranged through termon lands along the entire route from Termonagurk in east Tyrone. The contemporary account of Colton's visitation reveals the ubiquity of erenachs in Gaelic Ulster, suggests a large degree of co-operation between different areas and, most importantly, shows that the lands and positions had remained in the hereditary possession of the families of the founders. Even though they had fallen down the scale of power, they nevertheless still retained considerable local prestige through their erenachies. Notable examples were the O'Boyles in Donegal, the O'Loughrans of south Tyrone and the MacCawells of Clogher.[69]

Such lands were not considered part of native territory under the territorial arrangements of the late sixteenth and early seventeenth centuries, in which much land was regranted to native freeholders. In fact, they became the earliest effective plantations, most going to 'servitors' who were largely Palesmen.[70] Given the noted attachment of the people to holy places associated with the early saints, former church lands retained a special attraction for local Catholics even though no longer in their hands. 'The country around Downpatrick is now mostly Protestant', wrote Walter Harris in 1744, 'yet some remains of popery still continue, and will probably always do so as long as St Patrick's Wells . . . are held in such high veneration by the credulous vulgar.'[71] Special significance seems to have attached to the termon land of Colum Cille's successors, and MacSweeney family tradition claimed that the branch which despoiled it without restitution perished, while that branch which made restitution prospered.[72]

5. The poets and the preservation of tradition

Gaelic society on the eve of its extinction was a contradictory mix of remarkable survival, adaptation to the new circumstances and internal decline. The role of the learned men was unchanged for most of this period, bound by the continuing hereditary principle and centuries-old convention. If anything, their importance in proclaiming the lord's noble lineage and praising his prowess was greater than ever in the aggravated localism and instability of the fifteenth and sixteenth centuries. The brehon was still an important figure at the end of the sixteenth century, undergoing the same lengthy training, enjoying the same hereditary status as his forebears, presiding over the open-air arbitrations, and repeating passages from the law codes drawn up in the seventh and eighth centuries. But little remained of the ancient laws in practice. Their repetition by the brehons was little more than 'antiquarian window-dressing',[73] and the protection for the church and free landowning families, in-built in the early law codes, was long gone. The brehon was not seen as particularly dangerous by English officials, and Davies was clearly touched by the sight of Maguire's aged brehon, who had been summoned to give information on the lands and dues to which Maguire was entitled. No such sympathy, however, was reserved for the 'chroniclers, gallowglasses, and rhymers . . . persons that merit no respect . . . for they are enemies to the English government'.[74]

The poet and the musician were still mandatory figures in the Gaelic lords' retinue. Indeed, bardic poetry remains the most important surviving Gaelic source for the thirteenth to seventeenth centuries, even though its true significance continues to be hotly debated by historians.[75] There is little sign of immediate nationalistic response to the Anglo-Norman incursions. But it is a frequent element in bardic poetry – of its very nature a glorification of past traditions – which called up a pagan past and nature itself to produce a native messiah who would expel the 'foreigner'. In the conventional bardic format the 'foreigner' (*Gall*) always implied non-Gaelic, though it often referred to local enemies, and as time went on the distinction was made between 'fair foreigners' (*Fionnghallaith*) or Old English, and the *Saxain* or *Sax-Ghaill*, the New English. Traditional bardic calls to their hosts to rise against the intruder have sometimes been misinterpreted as reactions to English conquest, whereas many Ulster poets, whilst lamenting the passage of the old order, were, by the early seventeenth century adapting and accepting changed conditions.[76] Bardic poems mislead if interpreted as some early nationalistic expression, though no one has yet come up with a satisfactory concept to encapsulate the pride in culture and place clearly there in medieval Ulster. Moreover, although the content of the sixteenth- and seventeenth-century poems differs little from those of the thirteenth and fourteenth centuries, the poets excelled in their antiquarianism and sense of historical connectedness. The Gaelic revival of the fourteenth century in particular produced a new interest in Gaelic history and genealogy which continued to the seventeenth century.[77] But unless the context and identity of the patron are also taken into account, these praise poems can be unreliable source material and on that point Spenser made one of his more acute observations: 'Through desire of pleasing perhaps too much [the Bards] . . . have clouded the truth.'[78]

Bardic conventions were intensely conservative. Their training remained unchanged throughout the centuries, and they were critical of those few poets who broke free from the straitjacket of convention.

The turn of phrase, the cultivated irony and ambiguity of these poems are admirable. But one cannot expect to find much sense of vision or spirit or any fresh commentary on current events. We would learn more of popular opinion from songs – if any survived.[79] But these were disdained by the poets as the preserve of the unlettered, and Thomas Moore's nineteenth-century romantic image of the bard as minstrel has no basis in reality. The poets represented a highly elitist profession, which disdained the lowly-born of every race and whose lament for the demise of the Gaelic order often rose no higher than a criticism of the *arriviste*, the 'churl' and 'serf' who knew not their place in society. Indeed, there is in these poems a sense of respect for breeding, nobility and royalty regardless of nationality. The poets were typical of Gaelic society in their professed loyalty to the English monarch, whilst sometimes making the unreal distinction between the person of the monarch and the monarch's representatives in Dublin. Their main role was to praise their host chieftain and for this they were – and expected to be – richly rewarded in land and the spoil of battle.

But historians are often too dismissive of bardic poetry. The poets did reflect the interests of the elite, otherwise they would have been – indeed, some were – rejected by their patrons. Their real importance – with that of the other professional families – was their linkage between past and future, their task, 'to spin the threads of lore' and to 'follow up the branches of kinship'.[80] They were valued by their employers as genealogists, historians and preservers (sometimes creators) of princely lineages, and their poems were preserved by generations of the recipient family as proof of status. Their authority was equivalent to that of the clerics and lawyers as guarantors of legal agreements, as attested by the 1543 dispute between O'Donnell and O'Neill, mentioned above. In their claims to overlordship of all Ulster, the Great O'Neill and his son Niall Óg chose the symbolic site of Emain Macha to entertain a great gathering of the learned men of Ireland, the O'Neill poets tracing a fictitious connection with the ancient Ulaid dynasty.[81] The poets liked to be considered as heirs to the druids, their verses endowed with magical powers, their satire and criticism so influential in destroying reputation, that the famous west Ulster poet Tadhg Dall Ó Huiginn was said to have been murdered in 1591 by those who had been the subjects of his satire. 'Vain and Childish', wrote English Jesuit scholar

Edmund Campion in 1571 of the Irish, 'greedy of prayse they bee, and fearful of dishonour. And to this end they esteeme their Poets who write Irish learnedly, and penne their sonnets heroicall, for the which they are bountifully rewarded. But if they send out libells in disprayse, thereof the Gentlemen . . . stand in great awe.'[82]

The exact role of the poets in Gaelic society is elusive, but it was such a part of the fabric of authority that even such New English as Sir John Perrot felt compelled to employ them.[83] They tended to admire power in any quarter and had no difficulty serving those English who patronised the poets, or in adapting to the new anglicised order after the initial shock at the collapse of the society which had supported them. Indeed Maguire's chief poet, Ó hEódhasa, was among the 'deserving Irish' allotted land in the Ulster Plantation.[84] Their real importance to the later development of Catholic identity lies in their role as antiquarians and pseudo-historians. Although as custodians of historical tradition they could and did accommodate change, the history they perpetuated was that of the *Lebor Gabála* or *Book of Invasions* – the pseudo-history of Ireland which had created the myth of the Gaelic race. The *Lebor Gabála* was one of the central texts of the bardic schools. It was particularly popular in the first part of the seventeenth century, and through the learned classes became central to the writings of the Counter-Reformation, a distiller of the elements on which later nationalism was to draw. Ironically, it was the progressive decay of the bardic order which projected such historical readings to a wider audience; for, deprived of lordly patronage after the destruction of the Gaelic order in the early seventeenth century, the poets were obliged to abandon their former exclusiveness and write for a more popular audience. It was only then that they became purveyors of nationalist sentiment.

6. Gaelic lordships in late medieval Ulster

If we turn from the poems to reality, the idea of national consciousness is even less credible. Gaelic polity remained that of dynastic aggrandisement right up to the sixteenth century and in the giddy swings of alliances the Anglo-Normans and Anglo-Irish were just another factor.

Thus we find the Dunleavys (Mac Duinn Sléibhe), the Clandeboye O'Neills, the Magennises and the O'Hanlons successively in alliance with the Anglo-Irish against MacLoughlin, then O'Neill aggression; or the O'Neills and Whites in alliance against the Savages and Magennises; or the Anglo-Irish themselves as often as not in revolt against the crown and capitalising on the collapse of royal authority in Ulster. But there is a sense of provincial pride, and a constant effort to link into the lineage of ancient Ulster. The Mac Duinn Sléibhe kings of Dál Fiatach were profoundly conscious of their illustrious Ulidian past and, after the disappearance of the family from politics at the end of the thirteenth century, that claim was taken up by the Magennises of Uí Echach Cobo (Iveagh), a powerful if minor sept in south-west Down, who successfully resisted Anglo-Norman and O'Neill aggression alike and who taunted the O'Neills on their groundless claims to dynastic succession from Conchobar mac Nessa and the Ulaid. Their patronage of the poets outstripped their importance in numbers and power and they were rewarded by poems tracing the antiquity of their lineage back through the ancestors of the Ultonian heroes. Likewise, the O'Hanlons, though frequently vassals of the O'Neills, were conscious of their descent from the ancient Airthir and their association with Emain Macha, and there are signs that they too considered the O'Neills upstarts. Expelled by the O'Neills from north Armagh, where they had been kings of Loughgall, they were able to use the Anglo-Normans and the Dublin government to halt the O'Neill advance. They remained deadly enemies to the O'Neills of the Fews and the related McCanns, who had displaced them. Such identity with Ulster's past was therefore no premise for provincial unity, but another dynastic tool in the power struggle. It is significant here because it shows how doggedly the minor septs clung on to traditional definitions of status and lineage, preserving the elements from which a future Catholic and Gaelic identity would be forged.[85]

At the beginning of the sixteenth century the political situation in Ulster was much as it had been for centuries. The Gaelic lords had never challenged the validity of the papal grant of Irish lordship to England. They simply ignored it.[86] Throughout the period Gaelic Ulster contained a host of semi-independent lordships, paying nominal fealty to the English crown, each following their own interests and lacking any sense of common purpose. Indeed, it has been suggested that Gaelic Ulster before the Tudor 'conquest' was moving towards a Polish situation, an enserfed peasantry controlled by a host of territorial magnates.[87] Crown officials found agreements made with dominant lines would founder on the vagaries of the Irish succession system, new leaders simply ignoring those made by their predecessors. There was a long history of the crown supporting strong chiefs who could bring stability to Ulster and Tudor support for Hugh O'Neill was very much in this tradition. In the new thinking that followed Henry VIII's act of 1541 transforming the medieval Irish lordship into a kingdom, the Gaelic system of succession and landholding was identified as the main cause of instability. Tudor policy did not envisage the destruction of Gaelic Ireland, rather its accommodation in an extension of English law throughout the country. Central to this policy was the system of 'surrender and regrant', whereby the lord surrendered his traditional rights and lands, and received them back from the crown in outright ownership, normally to be held according to English inheritance custom. The Irish title of the O'Neill or the O'Donnell would likewise be converted into English-style earldoms, O'Neill becoming earl of Tyrone. It was a voluntary policy, to be worked out by slow accommodation over a lengthy time-span, and it was applied with much sensitivity to local custom. The aim was to create freeholders, holding directly from the crown and this, followed up by 'composition' – whereby fixed dues would replace the arbitrariness of 'coyne and livery' – would inject a stability so noticeably lacking in Gaelic areas. The policy, started in the 1540s, was continued into the seventeenth century by James I, progressing from the principal lords to much smaller landholders.[88]

Given the constant downward pressure exerted in Gaelic society by expanding dominant lineages, the process held obvious advantages for the lesser lords. It was espoused with particular eagerness by those borderland septs caught between O'Neill and the Pale: the O'Reillys of Breifne (Cavan), the Magennises of Iveagh (south Down), the Mac-Mahons of Monaghan, and there are signs of support for the administrative structures – including the shiring of Ulster in 1585 and the introduction of sheriffs and courts – which accompanied the process. It is wrong to think of some kind of independent Ireland pitted against an expanding colonial power in this period. The refusal of the English crown to extend the protection of the law to the Irish, was, claimed Sir John Davies, one of the key reasons why English rule had never been made effective in the country.[89] Such inequality of treatment before the law had indeed been a frequent complaint by the Irish throughout the Middle Ages, and even the greater lords welcomed the certainty of hereditary title. The O'Neills had been trying to introduce lineal succession since at least the fourteenth century,[90] and Conn O'Neill was among the first to accept the new policy, taking the title earl of Tyrone in 1542. But under Irish law such title was not in the possession of an individual lord to surrender, and customary law continued to be practised by all but the immediate kin of the parties to the original agreement.[91] In a system where so many had legitimate claims to the lordship, 'surrender and regrant' consolidated individuals at the expense of the family group and the collateral septs, and a series of major succession disputes destabilised Ulster in the latter half of the century. The most notable led to the rebellion of Shane O'Neill (d.1567), and dynastic instability continued in Tyrone for the rest of the period. Dynastic disputes in all the lordships weakened and ultimately destroyed 'surrender and regrant'. They were most destructive in those very counties – Monaghan, Fermanagh and Cavan – where the new policy had found most support. But it was the coincidence of similar dynastic challenges in the two strongest lordships of Tyrconnell and Tyrone which created the climate for rebellion in the 1590s.

With so many threats no lord could afford to be seen as entirely abandoning the Gaelic system of succession. No one had walked the tightrope between the English and Gaelic systems as successfully as Hugh O'Neill, seen by contemporary crown officials and modern historians alike as the key mediator between the two traditions and the one native leader capable of modernising Ulster and adapting to the new circumstances. But even he found himself compelled to join the rebellion against government policies in 1595, recognising that if he failed to do so, he would provoke rebellion from his rivals within the lordship. His taking of the title of the 'O'Neill' at Tullahoge was an open act of rebellion against the crown, and may have been his way of placating those septs who adhered to Gaelic ways.[92]

The policy also collapsed through lack of adequate crown support for those who had entered into such agreements. All the Tudors had preferred accommodation to confrontation. Dispossession was not official policy. But the introduction of English adventurers and settlers on to confiscated church lands after the Reformation (particularly in view of the kind of occupation system outlined above), the inefficient and sometimes brutal attempts at colonisation, and the activities of freebooting officials who exploited the weaknesses of the Gaelic system to acquire land for themselves, alienated even friendly Gaelic lords and contributed to the unusual, if transient, sense of unity in the end-of-century revolt.[93] The appearance of sheriffs and officials and perhaps, most of all, of mapmakers and surveyors was all very unsettling, and the best cartographer of the period – Barthelet – was beheaded by the Irish in Donegal. Government officials seemed to be everywhere. 'The greatest advantage that the Irish had of us in all their rebellions', commented Davies, 'was our ignorance of their countries, their persons, and their actions; since the law and her ministers have had a passage among them, all their places of fastness have been discovered and laid open ... how they live and what they do ... insomuch as Tyrone [Hugh O'Neill] hath been heard to complain that he had so many eyes watching over him as he could not drink a full carouse of sack but the State was advertised thereof within few hours after.'[94]

There was little consciousness that the Gaelic order was under threat. The lords entered into 'surrender and regrant' agreements and abandoned them with similar unconcern, when they wished to continue the traditional occupation of attacking their weaker neighbours. But to a situation already unsettled by the aggrandisement of Hugh O'Neill, the application of new crown policies and the build-up of mercenary forces, was added a remarkable concurrence of succession disputes. That in Monaghan resulted in the summary execution of Hugh Roe MacMahon by the Lord Deputy Fitzwilliam and the subsequent partition of the county. The denunciation of Hugh Maguire as a traitor in neighbouring Fermanagh, for claiming succession under Gaelic practice in defiance of an existing 'surrender and regrant' agreement, set in motion the train of events which by 1595 had brought almost the whole province into rebellion, finally bringing to a close the Tudor experiment and the collapse of Gaelic Ulster.[95] It was a collapse which was as sudden as it was unforeseen.

Internally it was collapsing anyway.[96] The downward pressure which had been part of the Gaelic land system was accelerated by 'surrender and regrant'. At the end of the sixteenth century there was a growing recognition of land as a commodity and this, accompanied by the painful introduction of a money economy, started the process of indebtedness through which the land system was progressively eroded. This was a much more corrosive process than the more dramatic Ulster Plantation and it affected plantation and non-plantation counties alike.[97] Ironically where government policy of 'surrender and regrant' was made effective lower down the scale, native landholders were cushioned from the new economic realities for longer (as in Monaghan), for the result was a host of independent landowners technically protected from the dispossession which followed the flight of their previous overlords in 1607. It was because 'surrender and regrant' had not proceeded beyond the top in the major lordships of Tyrone and Tyrconnell that the entire territory lay open to confiscation when O'Neill, O'Donnell and the other lords went into exile in 1607. But even before this it was becoming clear that the favourable terms granted in 1603 would not be allowed to stand.

By the Treaty of Mellifont in 1603, which ended the Nine Years War, O'Neill had been effectively granted the freehold of his entire earldom (modern Tyrone, most of Armagh and Derry), with the clear implication that all living within its confines – including some like O'Cahan who had fought on the English side – were dependent on him.[98] He had also successfully resisted the establishment of an Ulster presidency along lines of those already existing in Connacht and Leinster and restricted the interference of crown officials to periodic visits by justices, thereby effectively establishing his claim to be considered chief lord west of the Bann. But all this conflicted both with official policy to break the power of the overlords by creating freeholders and with the latter's ambitions to so be liberated, and created dissatisfaction on all sides. As O'Neill continued lineage expansion at the expense of collateral septs, their complaints were taken up by dissatisfied officials. Measures such as the 1605 proclamation compelling all principal landowners to introduce English landholding practices, followed by the 1606 commission for defective titles, bode ill for the lords who had survived the war so successfully. Both, in fact, were aimed against the power of the chief lords and were yet another attempt to weaken it by granting secure title to the inferior septs. A test case was brought against O'Neill by O'Cahan, with government backing. The recognition of O'Neill's ownership of O'Cahan's country (Coleraine) was contrary to both Gaelic law and assurances received by the latter from government. O'Neill was preparing to travel to London to answer the challenge when an invitation by O'Donnell and Maguire to join them in flight to the Continent dramatically altered the situation, baffling contemporaries and historians alike as to his motives for accepting. Through a skilful use of diplomacy and knowledge of English ways on the one hand, and a ruthless exploitation of Gaelic custom on the other, O'Neill appeared to have survived the end-of-century crisis rather well and there seemed little reason for his sudden abandonment of a position still apparently powerful. The activities of his younger and more volatile allies Maguire and O'Donnell threatened to involve him in new charges of conspiracy and when they announced that they were about to take ship for Spain in September and invited him to accompany them, he agreed. This event, closely followed by renewed rebellion in Inishowen and Derry, produced an abrupt change in government policy: from accommodation and gradual anglicisation (in the belief that the people were reformable) to outright confiscation and plantation.

Traditionally the Flight of the Earls in 1607 is taken as the end of the Gaelic order in Ireland and there can be no doubt that the events of the seventeenth century marked a sharp break with the past. The poets were the first to register the shock at this sudden destruction of the world which had sustained them. But it was to be many generations before Ulster generally did so and Gaelic practices continued far into the seventeenth century. The Nine Years War was in no way a popular rebellion. It was fought largely by mercenaries, and the experience of Fermanagh, where only two freeholders could be found to have actually participated in the rebellion, may not have been unusual. The Ulster chiefs were independent of their people and when they were removed, government officials experienced extraordinarily little resistance. In 1606 when Lord Deputy Mountjoy visited Monaghan he needed only 120 to 140 soldiers. In previous years he would have required between 800 and 1,000.[99] At first it seemed that those free septs and minor lords who had been seeking independence from over-lords like O'Neill would benefit from the attainder of their former overlords – and indeed many were confirmed in their land titles. But the Gaelic system, whatever its flaws, had allowed them considerable local autonomy – that famous 'liberty' which English observers thought made them such bad subjects. The operation of the new system pushed some into revolt, others into penury. Even Donal O'Cahan ended his days in the Tower of London, his case against O'Neill never resolved.[100]

Few at the end of the Gaelic period wished to perpetuate the old system of landholding. What seems to have been unrecognised, how-ever, was that with the introduction of the English system went a change in the notion of status, definable in future by ownership of land. In the seventeenth century there was a steady decline of native freeholders to the status of tenants. There were now many Palesmen and New English settled in Ulster, conversant with the new legal system and exploiting the very obvious weakness of Gaelic title to acquire more land. The support for measures which promised to give freehold-ers and tenants more security gave way to confusion at the operation of the new system. Inability to cope with an economy which required payment of money rents soon led to indebtedness. English officials eventually excluded the Irish entirely from operating the new legal system, because ties of kin stopped jurors convicting locals to whom, by the very nature of Gaelic society, they were invariably related.[101] Although the annals record frequent atrocities among the elite, medi-eval Irish society was not generally a violent one. People were much too valuable a commodity – lordship, after all, was defined by control of people rather than possession of land – and warfare generally took the form of 'harrying' (systematic destruction of property) and cattle raids, rather than the killing of people.[102] There was, moreover, no criminal code in Irish law, only collective fines and distraint, and the rural Irish never did quite come to terms with English laws which put people to death for attacks on property.[103]

Ironically the Flight of the Earls had removed the chief modernising element from Gaelic society in Ulster, an element prepared to operate within the new anglicising process.[104] But that process, coming so suddenly into the one part of Gaelic Ireland which had been left relatively untouched by English ways, did not allow for gradualism or accommodation, and the myth of the golden Gaelic past was already in the making among the first casualties of the process – the poets, the clerics, and the continental exiles.

3

RELIGION IN ULSTER BEFORE THE REFORMATION

Twisted their consciences, perverse their minds,
they desire no bishop or cleric;
they say no pater or creed –
I refuse to be one of their sort.

Fasts or feasts of the saints –
bad is the whim – they keep them not;
Mary is no more to them than a wisp,
a rude breed unblessed by God.

They hate baptism, cross and church,
a treacherous stock; a pity, O God,
is the decline of Patrick's faith
and a faith without direction being promoted.

> 1640 poem *Truagh mo Thurus ó mo Thír* ('Regretted
> is my Journey from my Country') of uncertain
> authorship, though attributed to Patrick Dunkin
> (Ó Muirgheasa, *Dhá Chéad*, 13–14)

At the end of the Nine Years War a general fear of religious persecution was preventing remaining rebels from surrendering.[1] O'Neill had identified religion as a common unifying force which would attach the Old English and the Spanish to his cause and win the support of the papacy. Certainly the new breed of English-born official in Ireland in the latter part of the sixteenth century was making Protestantism rather than obedience to the crown the test of loyalty, and increasingly identifying 'civility' with the new religion.[2] But even the Pope doubted O'Neill's sincerity and Jesuit and Spanish travellers to Ulster considered its inhabitants more pagan than Christian. Such tension between the 'universal' and 'national' church was quite common and in Ireland generally a central standard was not successfully imposed until the nineteenth century. But in Ulster in particular the old religion was too embedded in traditional ways to be easily supplanted and by the mid seventeenth century its future was reasonably secure. More dramatic was the speed and success with which the clerics and literati moved to create the image of the Gaelic past and Catholicism as an organic entity, providing the documentation for that exclusive nationalism which was to emerge two centuries later.

1. Decay and revival in the medieval church

The long isolation of the Irish church ended in the twelfth and thirteenth centuries with a series of church councils which introduced a system of dioceses and sought to end the many 'abuses' into which the Irish church had fallen. Bishops now replaced abbots as leaders of the church. More important in the decline of Gaelic monasticism, however, was the introduction of new continental orders: the Augustinians, Franciscans and, most of all, the Cistercians. With their strict rules, community life, grandiose buildings and distinctive dress, they remained apart from the laity. Although patronised by a few Ulster kings in the twelfth century, they were concentrated in Anglo-Norman areas and remained weak in Irish areas. Certainly, apart from the coastal strip of the earldom of Ulster, the province was relatively unaffected by the changes. The Columban tradition remained extra-ordinarily dynamic. Irish monks continued to prefer separate huts outside churches to the communal dormitories of the new orders, and many of the other 'abuses' associated with the Gaelic church continued.[3]

That the reforms of the twelfth and thirteenth centuries had such limited impact in Ulster owed not a little to the divisions that developed in the church between Irish and Anglo-Irish areas after the Anglo-Norman invasion. By the fourteenth century the see of Armagh was in the control of English or Anglo-Irish clerics and was to remain so till the sixteenth century. Ulster remained split between *ecclesia inter Hibernos* and *ecclesia inter Anglicos*. Whilst the Archbishop of Armagh chose to reside permanently in County Louth rather than in the cathedral city, the dioceses of Raphoe, Derry, Clogher and Kilmore remained relatively free from Anglo-Irish interference in church affairs, and although Down, Connor and Meath were *inter Anglicos*, a separate diocese of Dromore was created to take account of the increasing power of the Magennises. Even then it proved difficult to fill the see because it was considered 'as beynge . . . amonges wilde Irysh men'.[4] The ethnic conflict within the formal structure of the medieval church is undeniable, creating numerous incidents. The church leaders had welcomed Henry II as an ally in their programme for ecclesiastical reform. In consequence the Gaelic chiefs came to see the church as something foreign, and there was a significant revival of pagan practices in the early thirteenth century.[5] Indeed, Alan Bruford's study of medieval Irish romance and folk-tales shows that, unlike continental romances, Christian themes scarcely figure in the Irish ones. The traditional heroes were pagan, as was the landscape: 'They still lived for the most part in the world of Cú Chulainn.' Clerics when they do appear seem rather sinister, enchanters or abductors of women, whereas the druids are the poets.[6] It is important, however, not to exaggerate the internal conflict; the Ulster clerics and erenachs were perfectly happy to welcome the English primate of Armagh on his 1397 visitation.[7]

Although successive popes urged the Irish clergy and people to be loyal to the king of England under the terms of the initial 'grant' of *Laudabiliter*, they also intervened frequently to moderate the persistent tendency of English clerics to treat their Irish counterparts as inferior. The Irish clergy became great 'Rome-runners' in this period, and, as in later centuries, the papacy was widely recognised as a supranational arbiter in perennial local disputes. As elsewhere in late medieval Europe, there appears to have been genuine popular devotion to the Pope. 'In this place I could not walk in the street', wrote Bishop Chiericati, papal nuncio to the court of Henry VIII, of Downpatrick in 1515, 'because everyone ran to kiss my dress, understanding that I was nuncio from the Pope, so that I was almost compelled by force to stay in the house, so strong was their importunity, which arose from strong religious feeling.'[8]

As administrator-bishops continued to be appointed, however, and many English appointees to abbacies became absentees, formal religion declined. Monasteries attracted fewer vocations and fell into disrepair and as the Anglo-Irish colony retreated in the fourteenth century, so too did the monastic foundations which had spread with it. Border areas between the crown colony and the independent lordships – once seen as buttresses against encroaching rebelliousness – were particularly affected. Such was the decline in the Downpatrick area, that only the Franciscans survived the absorption of all the other foundations (five in all) into the cathedral in 1513.[9] Certainly the formal structure of the medieval Irish church was in poor shape on the eve of the Reformation. The first stages of the dissolution of the monasteries in the sixteenth century did not affect predominantly Irish areas in the west and north, where there were few large monasteries to dissolve. But to look for a formal, church-based religion in Ulster in this period would be unproductive. A preference for older monastic forms not only thwarted the medieval reforms but gave rise to a remarkable revival on the eve of the Reformation.

The rural, familial structure of Gaelic society provided an alien environment for the great continental orders. More congenial were the mendicant (or Observant) orders of friars, notably the Franciscans, with their emphasis on poverty and preaching, and travellers in sixteenth-century Ulster were impressed at the flourishing state of their friaries.[10] The revival had developed in the fifteenth century from an existing trend within the Franciscans for laity to follow a version of the rule while continuing to live in the community. This was the Third Order Secular, and, even though adopting a regular rule, it continued in closer communion with the locality than the older and now declining orders. Medieval Irish Christianity had retained the strong ascetic urge so notable in early centuries. Communities of Culdees survived in Ulster into the seventeenth century and holy men and places continued to be venerated.[11] Even Campion, often so critical of native Irish ways, found the people 'such mirrours of holiness and austeritie, that other nations retaine but a shewe or shadow of devotion in comparison of them'.[12]

These existing tendencies help explain the phenomenal popularity of the mendicant orders. They were noted for strict observance of their vows and preference for simple dwellings, often sited in remote and barren areas. It was almost a reversal to early church organisation. Unlike the Cistercians, their buildings and dress were simple and their mission was to minister to the religious and social needs of the local people. They did not have extensive lands, and they lived, not by tithes or compulsory dues, but by charitable alms usually given in kind. As they were credited with leading exemplary lives and sponsoring a spiritual literature in simple Irish, their criticism of fellow clerics who became Protestant as having 'sold Mary for meat and a wench', carried a particular relevance.[13] Their development seems to have had no parallel outside Ireland, and their existence must surely explain the failure of anti-clericalism to take root there. In contrast to English and Scottish preference for colleges of secular priests, the popularity of the friars testifies to Ireland's continuing attachment to monasticism and to the general conservative nature of Irish society. At the time of the dissolution of the monasteries, it proved particularly difficult to suppress the orders of friars. When ejected, they simply continued in the neighbourhood, sustained, as before, by the goodwill of the locals. Those of Armagh, when expelled at the beginning of the seventeenth century, split into two communities, one to Brantry, County Tyrone, the other to Creggan, south Armagh, and remained in the area into the eighteenth century.[14]

Their friaries in Ulster were founded by leading local families – the O'Donnells, the MacSweeneys and the O'Neills being particularly notable patrons in Gaelic areas, where they were most widespread. But we also find foundations by the MacQuillans, the MacDonnells and the Savages in Antrim and Down. The spiritual rewards of burial in the cemeteries and habit of the friars helped cement the links between Gaelic lord and the mendicant order. Indeed, this centuries-old attachment to monastic burial had made the monastic burial grounds ancestral mausoleums. It was very often the neglect into which these had fallen which motivated a local chieftain (or his wife) to introduce the mendicant orders.[15] The holy dead retained their powers in late medieval religion: penances were typically performed in cemeteries, the unworthy dead were thought to be repulsed by their worthier neighbours and families took great care to ensure the continued protection of their ancestral dead. There was much discontent among the descendants of the Armagh O'Neills in 1715 when a tree over the family vault was felled. It had been planted in the sixteenth century on the south side of the church just opposite the altar, so that the branches would grow over the O'Neill vault.[16]

To the Elizabethan mind the friars were particularly associated with native Irish culture and rebelliousness. John Derricke's woodcuts and commentary of 1581, claiming to depict the lifestyle of the Donegal MacSweeneys, is perhaps the most famous expression of this. Here the friar is constantly involved in the chieftain's everyday life and exploits, and while Derricke is hostile, and hardly a reliable source, he captures the respect for the friars among the Irish lords.[17] Nearly all were native Irish; many were members of hereditary learned families, closely linked with ruling dynasties, and almost all the Third Order friaries in Ulster owed their origins to local chiefs. Kinship with the exiled Gaelic lords made them spearheads of the continental Counter-Reformation and introduced a highly politicised tone into its literature.

The Franciscan Observant friars were particularly popular in Ulster.[18] Their spread was often a reaction against the exclusivity of the older orders (which were declining at the same time), and given their largely pastoral role, their expansion reflects a surviving popular piety independent of the fluctuations in church history. The debate over the failure of the Reformation in Ireland has singularly neglected the nature of popular piety.[19] It is wrong to think of medieval Christianity as rotten and ripe for reform. The problems lay rather in the higher church structure and its inflated bureaucracy. At local level it was flexible and accommodating of popular beliefs and practices. Few actually wanted a Reformation.[20]

2. Official and unofficial religion

In his study of devotional literature in the centuries before the Reformation, a Franciscan priest, Canice Mooney, found a ready availability of literature in Irish, much of it perpetuating pagan leftovers or peculiarly Gaelic interpretations of scripture. Significant is the continuing devotion to local saints, the familiar association of saints (and Mary in particular) with kin, and a sense of the vengefulness of the saints reminiscent of the heroic tales.[21] 'St Patrick is of better credit than Jesus Christ', it was observed in the 1580s, and Colum Cille was considered 'a god of great veneration with . . . all Ulster.'[22] Relic and image-worship was common throughout pre-Reformation Europe. But in Ireland both were symbols of power, part of the hereditary element so common throughout the history of the Irish church, and as such they were jealously guarded by secular rulers and families. Medieval churches seem to have been very ornate, their ornaments and relics prized by the local people and protected during the perennial warfare. Despite the ruthlessness of one of the Maguire chiefs in the fifteenth century, he was hailed by the Annals as one who had 'frequently set up oratories and churches and monasteries and holy crosses and images of Mary'.[23] While the complaint in 1530 of Nelan O'Neill against 'certain ecclesiastics' (including a McGurk and an O'Mellan) for 'fasting' and 'ringin bells' against him (including the bells of St Colum Cille and St Patrick, of which these families were respective hereditary keepers) represents the remarkable unbroken link of certain families with the early saints and their relics.[24]

Because of the failure of the medieval reform movement in Gaelic areas, the religion which continued to flourish in Gaelic Ulster retained traits left over from earlier times. Clerical marriage continued into the seventeenth century, as did hereditary clerical succession, lay claims to patronage and presentation (the right to nominate clergy), and a stronger attachment to kin than to church – resulting in persistent participation by clerics in inter-clan warfare. There was little social stigma attached to illegitimacy, concubinage and marriage to near relatives, and little inducement among the native clergy to enforce church decrees in such matters when clergy were as culpable as laity. As late as 1613 one Counter-Reformation missionary to Ulster still found it necessary to compel priests 'to put away their wives'.[25] Indeed most of the Rome-running of the period was in pursuit of dispensations for clerical illegitimacy, which Rome was more than happy to grant.[26] 'The clergy have more dispensations here than anywhere', commented Campion, 'and like to return a wife after only a year, if even a small quarrel.'[27] Indeed, clerical marriage was an essential part of the hereditary succession of professional clerical families like the O'Loughrans of Armagh and Tyrone. Benefiting from frequent papal dispensation for illegitimacy and marriage, members of the family dominated nearly all the important positions in the fifteenth-century *ecclesia inter Hibernicos* in the Armagh diocese. They were hereditary erenachs of Donaghmore near Dungannon, held various offices also under the O'Neills, and remained prominent in both church and politics throughout the seventeenth century. By then they were leading figures in the Counter-Reformation.[28] Cases of local clerical dynasties can be replicated from all over Ulster: the O'Corrys of County Armagh, whose descendants were still prominent in the twentieth-century parish of Lissane; the O'Boyles of Clondehorky parish, Donegal;[29] the Mac-Cawells of Clogher in Tyrone. A number of the leading clerical families were also members of ruling local dynasties, the names of the Maguires, the O'Donnells, the O'Gallaghers, the O'Reillys recurring regularly in episcopal succession lists.[30] The Protestant church's legitimisation of clerical wives and children both improved the legal status of women and had much to offer the hereditary Irish churchman. For such a cleric to support the Counter-Reformation, required, as Katharine Simms has forcibly argued, 'a transformation of outlook and ideals hardly less revolutionary than that involved in embracing Protestantism'.[31]

By the end of the sixteenth century little formal religion remained in Ulster. 'The people without discipline [and] utterly devoid of religion', complained Lord Deputy Sussex in 1562, 'come to divine service as to a May game.'[32] Nor was there much sense of belonging to the Roman church. The bishop was a distant figure, requiring the local lord's protection to enter an area, and seemingly unable to administer the one sacrament designed to bring bishop and laity together – confirmation. We have no positive information that sermons supposed to be delivered from the basic doctrinal handbook, the *Ignorantia sacerdotum*, were so delivered, and a good deal of evidence to the contrary – Elizabethan observers finding the Ulster Irish totally ignorant of doctrine and commandments. 'They are very religious', wrote Bishop Chiericati in 1515, 'but do not regard theft as a crime, and do not punish it.'[33] Nor was the taking of life considered wrong. Campion recounts an old tale of an Ulsterman attending confession for the first time with a travelling monk, who, when asked if he had committed murder, replied that he never knew before that it was a sin and confessed to five.[34] The novelty of Tuathal Balbh O'Gallagher capturing rather than killing prisoners in the early sixteenth century was attributed to a sermon in which he had heard a friar condemning homicide.[35] There are many such examples of the popularity and efficacy of these sermons (though the absurdity of some of the moral stories should guard against excessive romanticisation of the friars' integrity).[36]

Popular religious culture was largely one of localised folk practices and, with most of rural Europe at the time, the Ulster people would have been ignorant of the most basic elements of formal religion. Religion was rather a functional spirituality directed towards the needs of the community, honouring local saints like local chieftains, as much for their powers of protection and vengeance as for their spiritual example. A sense of sin scarcely existed, and confession – that most potent channel through which the Counter-Reformation sought to refashion the moral perception of the people – was largely unknown. But there was an age-old reverence for local devotional rituals and for learned and holy men which had transferred itself to the friars. Clerical training in Gaelic areas – though still a largely uncharted field – appears to have operated on a system of fosterage to clerical teachers operating in their own homes. Everything testifies to the complete integration of religion into Gaelic society, even the churches, as often as not, serving local secular needs.[37] So integrated, then, was religion with Irish society, particularly traditional kinship structures, but so lacking in formal structure, that the Reformation would have had to reform from the bottom up.

This must not, however, be confused with irreligion and Campion's dismissal of the religion of the 'uplandish' Irish as composed of 'idle miracles and revelations vaine and childish' was typical of that ageless disdain of the urban intellectual for the rural mind.[38] As in Europe generally, popular religiosity in Ulster was a mixture of the sacred and the superstitious, a profound identification of the mystical with local places and objects, a kind of pantheism which was a direct continuation of pre-Christian traditions.[39] In this mix, the friars supplied a devotional need. Surviving evidence – notably in the devotional literature translated from Latin into simple Irish, religious poems, many reflecting strong social preoccupations, and rhymed sermons testifies to the strength of their pastoral mission and to a genuine popular spirituality creating the demand. There exists in manuscript a considerable collection of compendia of moral tales used by Franciscan preachers in the late middle ages. Commentators note a lightness of touch, an absence of high moral theology, and a naturalness which helps explain why many of the tales survived into modern folklore.[40] Most are meditations on the life of Christ from the *New Testament*. But there is nothing sterile or inaccessible about them and they make moving reading. A notable example – and perhaps the most popular of all – is *Smaointe beatha Chríost*, a fifteenth-century translation by a Franciscan friar at Killala of a fourteenth-century Latin text. At least thirty-eight manuscript copies have survived, when less than half a dozen would be the norm, and some twenty survive for the nearest rival in popularity, a thirteenth-century life of Mary. *Smaointe* is shot through with typical Franciscan ideals of poverty, but even more significant is its sheer humanity. Christ is a loving son, close to his Mother, solicitous for her suffering. Mary is not the plaster-cast image of serenity and virtue as promoted by the modern Catholic Church, but a real person, suffering normal maternal anguish at loss, separation and death. This is Mary as the representative of humanity rather than the icon of the church, a theme common also in secular literature of the period.[41]

There is, moreover, some evidence that amongst the literate and aristocratic elite, particularly among those actively involved in the sixteenth-century revival, religion may not have been quite so divorced from the church's ideal as imagined. Maire MacSweeney was one of several aristocratic Irish women who commissioned pious and religious works in the sixteenth and seventeenth centuries. In 1513–14 she commissioned a 'Book of Piety' from a local scribe, which includes stories about the 'Finding of the True Cross', 'Christ's Descent into Hell', the infancy and passion of Christ, Adam and Eve's banishment from Heaven, lives of saints Margaret, Catherine, Colum Cille and Patrick, the vision of St Paul, some passages of St Patrick's Purgatory, various papal indulgences, a treatise on the Eucharist, the benefits of hearing mass, advice on how to make confession, a description of venal and mortal sins, a passage on the twelve golden Fridays (a precursor of the first Fridays practice), various homilies on drunkenness, hypocrisy and true piety, and advice for holy living. There is also evidence of the celebration of Easter as special. Maire, we are told, heard daily mass (sometimes more than once), fasted three days a week and during the fasts of Lent and winter, and observed the golden Fridays. She founded many churches in Ulster and Connacht, and was buried in the friars' habit and in the monastery which she founded.[42] Support for the Counter-Reformation by the Gaelic aristocracy may not have been so entirely cynical as once imagined.

3. The impact of the Reformation and Counter-Reformation

Lacking a working parochial structure and regular religious practice, however, Gaelic Ulster presented a problem to Reformation and Counter-Reformation alike and both proceeded on the premise that the populace required 'civilising' before they could be formally instructed in religion. Both were equally unsuccessful in the short term. Although Counter-Reformation Catholicism had a working church structure in Ireland by the 1630s, it was concentrated in Anglo-Irish areas and it would be some time before it penetrated Gaelic Ireland. But equally, the Reformation failed entirely to make any impact on Gaelic areas. Until quite recently even leading Irish historians wrote of a Catholic people predestined to triumph, ignoring the fact that other European states had been just as renowned for their popular piety, yet still adopted Protestantism.[43] It was not a case of positive choice between one or the other. In the seventeenth century people just continued as they had done before. The long-term difference lay in Protestantism's cultural rejection of Gaelic ways and Catholicism's compromise with them.

Until the seventeenth century, the progress of the Reformation was minimal in Ireland and non-existent in Ulster, outside Carrickfergus.[44] At the time there was certainly no great popular outburst against it, no immediate association between rebelliousness and religion. After the dissolution of the monasteries, there was some spectacular destruction and iconoclasticism[45] – a wanton destructiveness which left the Protestant church impoverished and dependent on the hated tithe. But such attacks on church property had been a common feature of Gaelic society,[46] and it was the earlier foundations in the urban areas which suffered most. Recusancy fines could only be implemented in the few areas where local government was in the control of the Protestant gentry, and overall there was a lack of will and consistency in the implementation of the religious reforms. Personal greed rather than religious zeal was often the motivating force. 'The ministers for disability, and greediness', remarked Lord Deputy Sussex in 1562, 'he had in contempt, and the wise fear more the impiety of the licentious professors, than the superstition of the erroneous papists.'[47] The New English, who had most to benefit, would have preferred a more repressive policy and the few spectacular executions of clergy which occurred (that of Bishop O'Devany of Down and Connor in 1612 being the most notable) were gratuitous acts by those in power in Ireland rather than policy developed in London. James I's government preferred accommodation.[48]

There is still considerable debate on the reasons for the success or failure of the Reformation in different localities. But much seems to have depended on the accessibility of the reformers, their residence in the area, their assiduous application to preaching and involvement of the laity in the new religion.[49] They were preconditions for success which proved unattainable in Ireland. James I believed that the native Irish areas would be more amenable to instruction, and successive English monarchs and their advisers were against forced conversion.[50] It was a policy of persuasion, however, which foundered on the absence of sufficiently trained preachers to bring the gospel to the Irish, and most of all on the developing exclusivity of the Church of Ireland.

Staffed predominantly with English and Scottish clerics – the existence of some genuinely Protestant native clergy not surviving into a second generation – the Church of Ireland pursued a policy of winning the Irish from their 'stubborn traditionalism and ignorant superstition' through compulsion and Anglicisation and simply succeeded in setting itself apart as elitist and foreign. Failure fed its existing assumption that the Irish were perhaps irredeemable in any event. More Calvinist than its English parent, its belief in predestination and justification by faith alone and its early identification of the Pope with Antichrist caused it to see the Irish generally as already damned. It fixed in Protestant imagination the fiercely anti-Catholic, apocalyptic and embattled identity which would afflict its relationship with Catholicism into modern times. Above all it was hostile to Gaelic ways and the pull of kin ultimately eroded the loose conformity of native Irish clergy.[51] Calvinism's hostility to the temporals of Catholicism alienated it from a native culture in which local saints were so revered. They 'neither fast nor keep the feasts of the saints and they don't care a rush for Mary', complained one poet of the Puritan ministers brought to County Down by the Scots planters.[52]

At first Counter-Reformation Catholicism too seemed at war with Gaelic mores. In particular it condemned those very elements in popular religious practice which had developed from existing kin and community structures: contractual, private and clandestine marriages, polygamy, excessive feastings and communal gatherings at wakes and funerals, money fines and compensation as part of penance; burials in monastic rather than church grounds. Tridentine Catholicism (as set out by the Council of Trent, 1545–63, in response to the Protestant Reformation) sought a priestly, church-centred religion, directly communing with the individual rather than the family or community. Most of all it sought instruction through catechism and education. Until the continental seminaries produced enough priests to serve such needs, which they did not before 1641, such aims remained unfulfilled. Before then the need for an Irish-speaking clergy required the frequent vesting of episcopal authority in the friars, and they mediated the strictness of Tridentine decrees. There was also only limited circulation of the vernacular catechisms and religious tracts issuing from the sole existing Irish-language printing press, which was in Louvain.[53] The Catholicism which survived the Reformation in Ulster was more the medieval than the Tridentine kind, and owed more to simple survival on the one hand, and the exclusiveness of Protestantism on the other, than to the Counter-Reformation.

Calvinism represented a move from religion based on locality and a sacralised view of the world, to an inward-looking one based on the individual and one's co-religionists.[54] As such it was in sharp opposition to the intertwining of religion, place and kin prevalent in rural Ulster (and in rural Europe generally). Tridentine Catholicism, strictly interpreted, was also hostile to popular religion. The Old English tended to be more strictly Tridentine and elitist, and in this there was some continuation of the medieval divisions between *ecclesia inter Anglicos* and *ecclesia inter Hibernicos*. There was no meeting of minds between Old English and native Irish prior to 1641. The Jesuits – the advanced guard of the Counter-Reformation – were concentrated in and around the Pale and had little contact with the Ulster chieftains. They persistently objected to the influence of Hugh O'Neill (even in exile) over episcopal appointments to Ulster, and to the continuing dominance of the friars, when Tridentine reforms envisaged authority flowing from the bishops.[55]

And yet, in the circumstances, it made sense to utilise the only clergy left in place – which in most cases meant the Franciscan friars. In 1561 papal permission had been given to hold masses in places other than churches, and half a century later the friars were fulfilling many of the duties of the absent secular clergy. Some religious communities simply set up again near their destroyed buildings, and by 1615 many were returning to re-occupy their old houses. Two years later the Franciscan provincial and guardian of their college at Louvain, Donatus Mooney, reported 18 houses of Franciscan tertiaries in Ulster, against 9 in Connacht, 2 in Meath and one in Leinster.[56] Because these were more dependent on the support of the laity than previously, traditional lay influence continued. The result was that by the 1620s, though there was an episcopal structure in place (something which failed to materialise in England till 1685), the kind of change envisaged by Counter-Reformation reformers had not materialised. For most of the sixteenth century the friars were still trained in the traditional manner in the localities (one of the factors, it was thought, rendering them hostile to Counter-Reformation changes). There were still married clergy and friar-bishops still closely connected with local Gaelic dynasties. Peter Lombard, the absentee Old English Archbishop of Armagh, attributed the otherwise inexplicable execution of O'Devany (when government policy was one of general leniency towards the clergy) to his association with O'Neill.[57] As the leading Irish cleric at the papal court he contributed to papal reconciliation with the Stuart monarchs and to the acceptance of the idea that Irish Catholics could be loyal to a Protestant monarch.[58]

But in Ulster, where organised religion had been so closely identified with aristocratic society, old traditions died hard and aristocratic lineage remained a major recommendation to church preferment long after the dismantling of the Gaelic superstructure. The Franciscan Bonaventure Magennis, appointed Bishop of Down and Connor in 1630, was recommended to the Pope as of true noble blood, kindred to the O'Donnells, the MacDonnells of Antrim, the O'Neills of Tyrone and of course, the Magennises.[59] The Ulster clergy as a result remained the most pro-Spanish, the most suspected of political subversion. They did not receive a welcome at the new continental seminaries set up by the Old English – a major factor in the institution of one of their own at Louvain, in the Spanish Netherlands.

In turn the Ulster clergy resented the appointment of outsiders to benefices, much as they had done throughout the Middle Ages. They considered the clergy outside Ulster soft on the Protestants, and prone to resist Ulster appointees as 'those who could give offence to the English'. In a lengthy memorial on the subject in 1626, Bonaventure Magennis explained that 'ecclesiastics have frequently to hide in woods and mountains and there assemble the people for the reception of the sacraments and for instruction, and the people have to carry to those places food and requisites for their ecclesiastics'. How then, he asked, would an outsider survive, unknown to the area, even if he did reside, which recent experience had shown to be unlikely? This was a thinly veiled attack on Lombard, who never took up residence in his archdiocese of Armagh. Magennis continued by pointing to the Ulster princes as preservers of the faith there. It is their influence, wrote another Ulster cleric the same year, through whom 'the faith is preserved whole and inviolate in the province of Ulster, more than in all the other provinces of Ireland'.[60]

Such provincialism was entirely typical of Gaelic society.[61] All the colleges on the Continent were subject to such rivalry. Provincial pride aside, the continuing strength of the Gaelic lords had preserved much of Ulster from the full force of the Reformation until James I's reign. When steps were taken to establish a Protestant episcopate after 1603, the first bishop, George Montgomery, found the medieval church infrastructure still intact.[62] Signs are that those remaining after the Flight of the Earls – even so-called 'deserving natives' who received land under the plantation scheme – continued to provide the focus of Catholic religious practice and sustenance to the friars. In May 1613 Shane McPhelimy O'Donnelly attended a Sunday mass in a glen in Brian Maguire's country between Fermanagh and Tyrone. Several of the Maguires, an O'Quin and an O'Neill were there, O'Neill 'enthusiastically saying they'd rather go into rebellion than lose religion'. The friar, the thirty-year-old Turlough McCrudden, a native of Tyrone 'lately come from beyond the seas', preached for most of the day, stating 'that he was come from the Pope to persuade them not to change their religion, but rather to go into rebellion'.[63]

The scene may have been repeated many times, for another deposition some months later told of McCrudden having preached while staying with the O'Hagans and again in the woods of Lisselby Roodan in the barony of Loghenesolyn, Londonderry. The informant estimated attendance at 1,000, including 'all the priests of those parts . . . to the number of 14'. Again he preached against the English 'damnable doctrine', inferring that greed alone induced their countrymen to turn. 'He told the people that the Pope had sent him unto them to comfort them . . . and that every year the Pope would send unto them holy men, lest they should be seduced and reasoned by the English, and that they should not despair or be dismayed; though for a time God punished them by suffering their lands to be given to strangers and heretics, it was a punishment for their sins; and he bade them fast and pray . . . for it should not be long before they were restored to their former prosperities.'

Information on this Franciscan mission reveals an already established system of local funding for the Louvain seminary through gifts to preachers such as McCrudden and more regular collections by the priests. 'There is nobody in the country of the Irishry, but has given somewhat according to their abilities', reported Teag McGlone, the informant, 'the poorer sort' giving twelve pence on the above occasion. His sermons also highlight the moral strictness of the Counter-Reformation, even if the Ulster clergy hardly measured up to its standards. 'He prayed long, exhorting them to reform their wicked lives, telling them of drunkenness, whoredom, and lack of devotion and zeal.' He deprived a number of priests of their livings 'some for keeping women, others for presuming to exercise the function of priest, who had not been properly called, and for having more benefices than one'. McCrudden is an example of the new continental-trained Franciscans, who were more politicised and pro-Spanish than their predecessors. It was these the authorities most wanted to exclude, and in a year when fears ran high of a Spanish-backed return by the exiled chiefs, McCrudden told his audience that Tyrconnell was returning with 18,000 men sent by the King of Spain 'and that, according to a prophecy in a book at Rome, England had only two years more to rule in Ireland'.[64]

In the long term continental-trained clergy were to play a vital role in bringing a certain uniformity to Irish Catholicism. But they remained a minority in Ulster. In the 1670s and 1680s Archbishop Oliver Plunkett was still complaining at the weakness of episcopal control and parish structure in Ulster, the poor quality (in his view) of the clergy, and, above all, the continuing dominance of the Franciscans over the spiritual life of the people. The influence of the local lords over Catholicism in their localities was still greater than that of the bishop. Various synods, such as that at Drogheda in 1614, may have promulgated the decrees of the Council of Trent, but half a century later there was little sign of change on the ground.[65] In this Ireland was not unique. The Tridentine reforms were rarely implemented in all their purity and the general picture throughout Europe was one of harnessing rather than repudiating popular practices.

4. The friars and the beginnings of 'patriotic antiquarianism'

Given this continuing position of the friars as part of the Gaelic elite, it is hardly surprising that it was the Franciscans who led the way in anchoring the Gaelic past to Catholicism. Such a development was not unusual to Ireland: the Counter-Reformation generally produced a kind of 'patriotic antiquarianism', prompted initially by humanist contempt for barbaric pasts.[66] The ancient traditions of monasteries as repositories of learning had continued with the friars, who recruited heavily from the families of hereditary poets and genealogists. And just as the crises of the Viking and Anglo-Norman invasions had sparked off major Gaelic revivals, so also did the Tudor conquest. From Ulster the leading figures were all Franciscans associated with the new Franciscan seminary in Louvain. It had been founded in 1606 by Florence Conry (Flaithrí Ó Maoil Chonaire), chaplain to Hugh O'Neill, confessor to Red Hugh O'Donnell, and member of a Connacht family of hereditary historians. He was the epitome of the politicised native Irish priest, conducting missions on behalf of Tyrone and Tyrconnell to Spain.[67] In similar mould was Hugh Mac Caghwell (Mac Aingil). Born in County Down, but descended from the hereditary erenachs, the Clogher Mac Cathmhaoils, he trained at one of the bardic schools still operating in Ulster in the late sixteenth century and became tutor to Hugh O'Neill's sons. On the Continent he became a noted theologian, and, like Conry, was appointed to an Irish see at O'Neill's request. He too had carried out political missions to Spain and, it seems, a papal mission to Ulster in 1613.[68] Over the next three decades Louvain produced a remarkable outpouring of Gaelic scholarship and devotional texts in Irish.

In 1626 Michael O'Clery was sent to Ireland by Aodh Mac an Bhaird (Hugh Ward), professor of theology at Louvain and member of the family of hereditary poets to the O'Donnells, to collect all the available manuscript material for an ecclesiastical history of Ireland. O'Clery had been a lay brother of the Franciscan Abbey in Donegal and, like Ward, a member of a family of ollamhs (poets/historians) to the O'Donnells. O'Clery was a trained historian, and he and his associates are credited with saving many of the Irish manuscripts now extant. Working mainly out of the remnants of the Donegal friary, they scoured the north and midlands of Ireland, and were given ready access to the manuscript collection of the Protestant Archbishop Ussher (himself a noted antiquarian, who shared the Franciscans' ambitions of defending Ireland's reputation as the island of saints and scholars from its detractors). Only in the western parts of Ulster and in Connacht did O'Clery find the chroniclers following the old ways. The outcome of the Louvain Franciscans' efforts was a number of saints' lives, in simple Irish, which set the standard of hagiographical religious writing thereafter, a new edition of the *Lebor Gabála*, a new martyrology, and, most famously, the *Annals of the Four Masters*.[69]

It has frequently been argued that the activities of O'Clery and his like represent the coming together of Catholicism, Gaelic heritage and anti-English nationalism, and that the works emanating from the continental seminaries played a major role in the process. If so the process was lengthy in its gestation for the Louvain works are not noticeably anti-English and were aimed at an Irish and continental elite rather than at the Irish people.[70] The portrayal of an unbroken link between the Irish people, Catholicism and learning, is however, unmistakable, as is the replacement of the multitude of local saints with the national trio of Patrick, Brigid and Colum Cille, and the denunciation of Protestantism as heretical – a word entering the Irish language for the first time. Certainly the purpose behind the 1625 Louvain life of Patrick, Brigid and Colum Cille, the compiler told his reader, was that 'you may learn the sympathy between us moderne Catholikes and St Patricke and the Primitive Christians, and on the contrary discover the discrepancy of the Protestants, not only with S. Patrike whome I am sure they will discarde for a very superstitious papist, but from all the current of the ancient Catholiks'.[71] Likewise the devotional work of someone like Florence Conry also incorporated contemporary religious issues, the repression of the clerics, the recusancy fines, an attack on Protestant bishops, interference of the state in religious matters, and an early claim that government derived its authority from the governed.[72]

Much of this continental-inspired revival falls into the established pattern of antiquarianism, the retrieval and copying of older Gaelic manuscripts, and scholars differ on the extent to which one can detect early glimmerings of nationalism in it. Certainly much of the Gaelic poetry of the early seventeenth century – like bardic poetry through the centuries – shows a pragmatism which attempts to accommodate the new political situation, hostility to Luther's and Calvin's 'breed' and praise for James I existing in equal measure. The coronation of James I was welcomed by many of the Ulster poets as ushering in a new age of tolerance. The king's Scottish and Catholic background, his past friendship with Hugh O'Neill, and most of all their belief that he was in fact descended from the third-century Irish king Feargal, all combined to reconcile clerics and poets to the new order. O'Neill's call for a religious crusade now found less favour with Rome and a pious formula on the theme of rendering unto Caesar what is Caesar's was put forward to allow Irish and English Catholics to reconcile their religion with loyalty to a Protestant monarch. As Breandán Ó Buachalla has detailed in a seminal article on the subject, the traditional occupation of the learned classes in supplying impeccable genealogies to victorious lords played a major role in the acceptance of the Stuarts as Ireland's rightful kings.[73]

This did not stop them, however, from lamenting their lost status and proclaiming a holy war against the new breed of upstarts, *Gael* and *Gall* alike; thus Eochaidh Ó hEódhasa (O'Hussey), Maguire's *ollamh*,

> Where have the Gaels gone?
> What is the fate of the mirthful throngs? . . .
> They have been given billeting far and wide,
> Away from bright, smooth Ireland; . . .
> They find no sweetness in devotion to poetry
> The sound of harps or the music of an organ
> Nor the tale of the Kings of Bregia of the turreted walls
> Nor the numbering of the ancient generations of their
> forefathers . . .[74]

And yet the same poet welcomed the accession of James as the end of mourning, a new dawn. Ó Gnímh (*ollamh* to the O'Neills) could write the haunting

> My heart is in woe,
> And my soul is in trouble,
> For the mighty are low,
> And the abased are the noble.[75]

> (A more literal translation would be:
> My woe at the condition of the Gaels!
> seldom a joyful mind
> has any of them at this time –
> all their nobles are annihilated!)

But he could also sing the praises of those who were profiting from the new system. Fearghal Óg Mac an Bhaird's 1608 lament on the death of O'Donnell spoke of the threat to Ireland from 'the sect of Luther, the legions of Calvin . . . the stewards of heretic bishops'. Yet he too accepted James as rightful king:

> Three crowns the right of James . . .
> For the King of the hosts of the Gael and the Gall . . .
> To you is the place of Ireland as well
> You are her husband and equal.[76]

Given such apparently mixed sentiments, scholars have questioned nationalistic readings of these poems.[77] Despite the remarkable outpouring of Gaelic literature which occurred at the beginning of the seventeenth century, it would be unrealistic to expect a major break by the poets and learned men with the strict, centuries-old conventions in which they were trained. Their preoccupations were still the elitist ones of the Irish bards, praising their traditional patrons by tracing kinship with the Irish saints. Moreover, in a continuing oral culture where few (even among the elite) could actually read, the direct influence of the printed works emanating from Louvain can have been minimal. The key link here would have been the clergy and particularly friars like McCrudden who would have used such works as manuals, and clearly had the power to draw large crowds. For over a century, even in times of practical tolerance, successive governments sought to curtail the influence of the continental-trained clergy: 'for they spare not to come out of Spaine, from Rome, and from Remes, by long toyle and dangerous traveyling hither, where . . . no reward or richesse is to be found, onely to draw the people into the Church of Rome . . . lurking secretly in their houses, and in corners of the country'.[78]

The Catholic Church, dominated as it was by members of the Gaelic elite, had moved quickly to define Catholicism as the 'ancestral religion', that 'received by their forefathers'.[79] In so doing it created the texts which fed into later nationalism. These texts were not generally printed until the nineteenth century. But to claim lack of impact because not in print till then would be to misunderstand the process of the transmission of ideas in the two preceding centuries. Gaelic manuscripts were highly prized by their owners. They were frequently copied, widely circulated, and often memorised for recitation in public. As the scribal tradition gradually disappeared with the cessation of the schools which had operated in the Gaelic system, clerics and schoolmasters increasingly became the main practitioners. Often older Gaelic manuscripts survive only in their seventeenth-century form, some corrupted by contemporary readings of the past. Ten surviving manuscripts would suggest that such a work had entered popular oral tradition. By this yardstick, the most celebrated work by Catholic priest, poet and historian of Anglo-Norman ancestry, Geoffrey Keating (*Foras Feasa ar Éirinn*, c.1634) must rank as the most influential Irish-language manuscript of all time. Though not printed in full until the twentieth century, hundreds of manuscript copies have been located from all over Ireland.[80] A popular history of Ireland written in Irish by a French-trained Munster cleric, it updated the pseudo-history of the *Lebor Gabála* to include the Old English and conveyed the notion of Catholicism and Ireland as an organic unit. The Louvain-produced devotional works in Irish would have been used as religious manuals, the sources of homilies and sermons by the clergy in Ireland. In time their message would have entered popular consciousness. Certainly the trend by the eighteenth century was for Irish scribes to write in a more popular idiom. The material from which 'the origin legend of the emergent Irish nation'[81] later developed was being created by these exiled clerics. The clergy were replacing the learned classes and frequently acting as patrons in this new order of things. The old elitism is still there and it is the Irish upstarts and churls who are objects of scorn in the poetry.[82] But the association between the Irish and Catholicism is unmistakable and the two would merge in the second half of the seventeenth century.

4

THE LOSS OF THE LAND: PLANTATION AND CONFISCATION IN SEVENTEENTH-CENTURY ULSTER

'Before the war the nobility of Ulster enjoyed their possessions . . . But now, only three Catholic gentlemen in all Ulster have recovered their estates and property . . . All the others have difficulty obtaining a lease of a part of their property . . . The peasantry – those who cultivate the land – are all right . . . But the gentlemen are completely ruined.'

Archbishop Plunkett, 1671 (Hanly, ed., *Plunkett Letters*, 247)

It would require over two centuries of erratic development for the kind of Catholic nationalism previewed in the continental writings of the early seventeenth century to emerge. However, the association between religion and dispossession – so central to modern nationalism – was well established by the close of the seventeenth century. The plantation of Ulster with British settlers was not initially intended as a religious campaign against Catholics. But it took on its own dynamic and effectively became such by the turn of the century. For Protestant settlers too the century established the perception of Catholics poised to take revenge and dispossess them at the first opportunity. The Ulster Irish had risen in 1641 and 'massacred' large numbers of the settler population. That the Ulster Plantation was never as total, nor the 1641 uprising as brutal, as tradition allows matters little. Both have continued to be axioms of respective communal identities for over three centuries, the one played up, the other played down according to one's religious affiliation. 'I was watching a programme on TV about the conquest of Northern Ireland and the setting up of the Plantation,' Paddy Doherty, prominent Catholic civic leader in Derry, told the 1993 Opsahl Commission.

'It featured the building of houses in order to protect the inhabitants. The seizing of the land and all of the activities and atrocities to maintain the ownership of that land is the root problem of the present troubles. They [the Unionists] are still building walls and it looks as if there has been no movement from those days when they saw everybody outside as being uncouth, violent and prepared to take their lives.'[1]

This 'seizing of the land' – the land confiscations of the seventeenth century – was to remain a symbol of communal injustice in the minds of Ulster Catholics long after it had ceased to be an issue in the rest of Ireland. It pervaded popular tradition and much otherwise scholarly local history. The post-1969 Troubles were to dispel much of that bitterness as a majority of Catholics became increasingly aware of the monster to which it had given rise. But it informed rural republicanism possibly more than is recognised. The sinister campaign against Protestant border farmers during the Troubles, the justification of hard-line attitudes by references to the sufferings of Catholics at the plantation, the implication that the settlers and their descendants are un-Irish, all fuelled the equally persistent Protestant fears of another 1641.[2]

The problem about the chaos which engulfed seventeenth-century Ireland (as indeed it did contemporary Britain and the rest of Europe) is that we know very little about the ordinary people, the 'churls' so valued by Hugh O'Neill and equally by the new settler landlords. The 'churls' may well have fared a good deal better under the new dispensation than under the Gaelic land system.[3] But the elite did not, and it is their voice we hear. Moreover, because of the nature of Gaelic society – with its extended kinship networks, multiple layers of declined and declining families, and regular division of lands – there were many more people claiming status as gentry than had land to support such claims, and this at a time when social status was increasingly measured in land-ownership rather than lineage. It was this, the sharp decline in status, the resentment at being lorded over by upstarts and *parvenus*, which most determined the reaction of that 'elite' to the plantation, rather than actual dispossession.

1. *The Ulster Plantation*

The Irish chiefs were scattered and King James was well content. He declared that all Ulster was forfeit to him . . . The bad land, bog and mountain and forest was divided among the Irish. The good land was given to the King's favourites or sold to Englishmen . . . This was called the Plantation of Ulster; for the king planted there men whom he could count on to be loyal to him, since they would always be at enmity with the Irish they had driven out; many of whom were living miserably on the bleak hillsides, in sight of their old homes.[4]

So ran a popular early twentieth-century school textbook. Like all popular history it contains both truths and distortions. From the government's point of view, the Ulster Plantation, like earlier plantations in Leix, Offaly and Munster, was driven largely by security and fiscal considerations. The Flight of the Earls, the subsequent rebellion of Sir Cahir O'Doherty and the vast tracts of church land (some 20 per cent of the province, technically confiscate, but relatively untouched till James I's reign) placed an unprecedented amount of territory at the disposal of the crown – virtually the whole of modern Armagh, Cavan, Tyrone, Fermanagh, Derry and Donegal. The sudden availability of so much territory presented the new monarch with the opportunity of creating a defensible colony and infusing Ulster Irish culture with habits of 'civility' and industry. Like all colonial ventures it was shot through with the cultural elitism of the colonising power. But it was not a blueprint for a general dispossession of the existing inhabitants. Sir John Davies, the attorney general, credited with master-minding the plantation, thought earlier plantations had failed because all the land was given to adventurers, forcing the local people into the hills and woods where they became outlaws.[5] He and the Lord Deputy, Chichester, considered the creation of a secure Ulster Irish population alongside the new planter element as vital to the scheme's success. Having cut off the 'heads of that hydra of the North', he predicted a rosy future.

'All the possessions shall descend and be conveyed according to the course of the Common Law. Every man shall have a certain home and know the extent of his estate, whereby the people will be encouraged to manure their land with better industry than heretofore hath been used, to bring up their children more civilly, to provide for their posterity more carefully. These will cause them to build better houses for their safety and to love neighbourhood. Thense will arise villages and towns, which will draw tradesmen and artificers. So as we conceive a hope that these countries in a short time will not only be quiet neighbours to the Pale, but be made as rich and civil as the Pale itself.'[6]

In other words, he thought the Irish could be made 'civil'. Time would reveal this cosy image of a settled peasantry to be inappropriate for a pastoral people, accustomed to transhumance and the mobile lifestyle dictated by it. But it held a certain attractiveness for those continuing to seek security of land title.

Such had been the insecurity (and resentment) created in Gaelic Ulster by the aggrandisement of overlords like Hugh O'Neill that a number of rival chieftains had not only fought in the war against him, but fully participated in and initially welcomed the Ulster Plantation as giving them greater security of title under English law. It was the Gaelic system of overlordship and all its trappings which England sought to destroy. Bringing the Irish into the benefits of the common law, granting rent relationships and leases in place of the customs tying man to lord in the Gaelic system was as important as planting British settlers in early schemes, and widespread dispossession of the Ulster Irish was not envisaged.

Ulster was to remain severely under-populated for most of the seventeenth century.[7] Loss of life in the Nine Years War, followed by famine and harvest failure, had taken a heavy toll. In contrast England and Scotland were over-populated and severe land-hunger was fuelled by a flood of pamphlets extolling the attractiveness of Irish land. At a time when voyages of discovery and colonisation were in vogue in Europe, a natural migration of peoples from Scotland and England to Ulster was already underway before the official plantation was conceived. We know of new settlements of Catholic Scots (almost certainly gallowglass families) at Strabane (in Tyrone), Inishowen (in Donegal), and there were almost certainly others.[8] But Counties Antrim and Down are the best documented and here we have a foretaste of how the indigenous population (or at least their lords) responded to settlement by newcomers. In these two counties that chronic instability of land rights, so noticeable in the closing decades of the sixteenth century, made many Gaelic lords eager participants in the new schemes. Partial surrender of family territory in return for secure title over the remainder seemed a good bargain. The hibernicised Catholic descendants of the old Anglo-Norman colony in County Down, around Downpatrick and Lower Ards (the Savages, Whites, Russells, Echlins, Audleys, Mandevilles, Smiths, Bensons, Jordans and

Fitzsimmonses) had participated in abortive attempts at new British settlements in the late sixteenth century, largely as part of their continued resistance to O'Neill's expansion.[9] The three leading Gaelic lordships in Down (those of Magennis, the MacCartans and the Clandeboye O'Neills) had all voluntarily accepted a reduction of their landed power in return for such title. However, there was more than a hint of shady dealing by Scottish speculators like Sir Hugh Montgomery and Sir James Hamilton in their agreement with Conn O'Neill in 1605, whereby they used their influence at the Stuart court, and O'Neill's parlous political situation (in prison for rebellion) to acquire one-half and then two-thirds of his land. Even still it granted O'Neill secure title to the remainder of his existing estate, recognised status as a figure of consequence in the new system, and guaranteed succession to his sons.[10] All of this reflected a recognition that the best chance of secure title now lay with the crown, and there was a rush to gain it from a new Scottish monarch who was expected to be more sympathetic. In fact, Conn's inheritance was whittled away in little over a decade by indebtedness and the need for ready cash, which he raised by selling off most of the remnants of his estate to Hamilton, Montgomery and Moses Hill. Few Gaelic lords would handle the new rent and money economy well and indebtedness was to cause more loss of land than confiscation.

But one east Ulster Catholic family was to profit spectacularly under the new regime of crown grants. When James became king of England in 1603, the MacDonnells of Antrim held a precarious, though legally unrecognised, hold over the whole of Antrim (including the Route, where they had displaced the MacQuillan lords). Good timing ensured that they had survived the Nine Years War, untainted by treason and favoured by James (whom they had helped against internal enemies in Scotland). The upshot was a royal grant of the entire territory of the Glens and the Route. The MacDonnells (soon to become earls of Antrim) were survivors. Despite a number of major setbacks, they succeeded in retaining both their estates and their Catholicism throughout the seventeenth century. The result was a Scottish-Irish hybrid population, speaking a 'Highland Irish'. Antrim became a haven for Catholicism, to which streams of Scottish Catholics resorted periodically, and one of the final remnants of Gaelic overlordship. It survived as such because of the earl's strong position within the Anglicised power structure. A leading courtier who married the widow of the duke of Buckingham and periodically raised troops for the Stuarts, he effectively straddled both worlds. His power and position at court also allowed him to retain all the trappings of a Gaelic chief which elsewhere the authorities were trying to stamp out. Like all Gaelic lords, his kinship network was wide, with the result that a call for help in 1639 to recover his family lands in the Western Isles elicited offers from nearly all the Gaelic families in Ulster – 'as many Oe's and Mac's as would startle a whole council board', according to Lord Deputy Wentworth.[11]

The unofficial settlement of the eastern counties set a pattern for the plantation. Even the earl of Antrim encouraged some three hundred families of Lowland Scots Protestants to settle on his land. There is no sign that they displaced sitting Catholic tenants, many of whom sub-let to incoming Protestants.[12] In contrast the Clandeboye estates were de-populated and waste, and the acquisitions by Montgomery and Hamilton produced the most concentrated settlement of Scots in Ulster in the first half of the seventeenth century, extending from the south shore of Belfast Lough to the Ards peninsula. Conn O'Neill had given away more territory than he was strictly entitled to, and, since the area was flooded with new settlers, it is likely that existing Irish were displaced.[13] By 1609 a vigorous building programme was already underway to accommodate the new settlers. The ruins of local monasteries disappeared in the search for building materials, much to the disgust of the Franciscan priest Edmund MacCana who toured the area in the 1640s. 'Of these monasteries not even the ruins remain, for a colony of Scots, who settled there, employed the stones of them for building houses for themselves – so great is the passion of heretics for demolishing sacred objects' – a statement seized upon two centuries later by Revd James O'Laverty, in his scholarly, though passionately partisan, history of the diocese of Down and Connor.[14]

However, Chichester (Lord Deputy, 1604–14), though he profited handsomely from the land deals of the period, disapproved of major clearances of the Irish. His was a continuation of the Tudor policy of breaking the powers of the overlords by making the lesser lords freeholders of the land they occupied. This is what happened in County

Monaghan in 1591, and the reason that Monaghan, like Antrim and Down, was excluded from the plantation settlement. But the new policy – first hinted at in Clandeboye – was directed from London and represents the missionary zeal which the new king was to bring to the policy of 'civilising' Ulster through plantation. In the nineteenth and twentieth centuries a series of legal contests of the Lough Foyle fisheries was to challenge what rights the crown possessed over such territory.[15] It has to be said that such rights were not challenged at the time. The Ulster Plantation was implemented with considerable co-operation from the Ulster Irish. The Irish elite responded as it had always done: as individuals, using England when it suited them against their enemies. The learned men too, after initial panic at the Flight of the Earls, accommodated themselves to the new situation.

A roll-call of the main Irish beneficiaries under the plantation settlement would read like a list of the rivals of the O'Neill, O'Donnell and Maguire lords who had fled in 1607. The O'Hanlons who had fought against O'Neill were rewarded with a total of 1,340 acres.[16] Maolmhuire MacSweeney, who had testified against Hugh O'Neill and attacked the crews of the ships taking the chieftains to the Continent, received 2,000 acres, as did Turlough O'Boyle and two other Mac-Sweeneys.[17] The various O'Neill branches in Tyrone and Armagh who had suffered in Hugh O'Neill's lineage expansion received grants. Notable among these were the O'Neills of the Fews in south Armagh, frequent allies of the Dublin administration in the sixteenth century. Turlough MacHenry O'Neill had been pardoned in 1603 and received a grant of 9,900 acres (the largest grant to any Gaelic lord), on which he was to settle considerable numbers of British tenants.[18]

In Fermanagh the senior Maguire, Conor Rua, had expected to be rewarded for his loyalty and surrendered his three baronies in Fermanagh. But it was not government policy to replace one overlord with another.[19] Usually the great were lowered and the middle-ranking consolidated. Conor Rua received less than a third of his territory back and lost the ancestral seat at Lisnaskea to a Scottish undertaker. The decline of the once great had been a running sore in Gaelic society. With the dismantling of that society in the seventeenth century such traditional restiveness found a new focus. Conor Rua's grandson was to be one of the initiators of the Ulster rebellion in

1641.[20] Paradoxically it was the junior Enniskillen branch, which had fought on O'Neill's side in the Nine Years War and participated in the Flight of the Earls, which became most reconciled to the new situation. Brian Maguire received 2,000 acres in the plantation scheme, and by pragmatically avoiding future involvement in rebellion, transmitted them to his descendants. For this he was posthumously damned by later nationalist tradition, a fate awaiting all the Irish landowners who survived the plantation. Other Maguires received smaller grants, a practice repeated in all the plantation counties to reconcile a handful of key 'deserving Irish' to the scheme.[21]

The descendants of Shane O'Neill, thwarted in their succession to the O'Neill title by successive earls of Tyrone, likewise received recognition in the new scheme, with land grants in Armagh and Fermanagh. But their position was a pale shadow of their former glory, and resentment at continuing decline (even if started long before the plantation) was undoubtedly a factor in Sir Phelim O'Neill's drift to rebellion in 1641.[22] Cavan was already settled by many Englishmen and the county's position had accustomed its chiefs to Pale ways. They were accordingly the first to use the English common law to argue their rights to the land, engaging a Pale lawyer and travelling to London to push their claims. Grants of land totalling 13,950 acres raised the O'Reillys to a position second in importance to the O'Neills in the new order.[23]

Despite Sir John Davies' dislike for Ireland's 'chroniclers . . . and rhymers', the government recognised that it was ignorance of the Gaelic land system which had prejudiced previous plantations and that it was the learned men who were the repositories of local knowledge. The multitude of surveys and commissions which accompanied the plantation – many conducted personally by Chichester and Davies – consciously sought out such 'clerks or scholars of the country who know all the septs and families and all their branches, and the dignity of one sept above another . . . till they descended to the most inferior men of all the baronies . . . [and] what quantity of land every man ought to have by the custom of their country'.[24]

No doubt there was an element of compulsion in this for Davies and Chichester in their 1609 inquisition were accompanied by a strong military force. But the very many cases of the learned men receiving grants under the plantation system, of the Gaelic gentry serving as sheriffs, jurors, justices, or electors, and using the new legal system to settle disputes, show that a substantial number were prepared to work within the new system. The Ulster Plantation was not imposed on a universally reluctant population. It was nonetheless a major revolution in land ownership. In all, two hundred and eighty Irish became land-owners of some 94,013 acres. But seen against an estimated 365,097 acres acquired by various English and Scottish grantees in the six plantation counties alone, the scale of the revolution in land ownership can be appreciated. These figures also disguise cases such as that of Hugh O'Neill's half-brother Art McBaron O'Neill. He had fought against O'Neill in the recent war. But his reward of 2,000 acres was to revert to the crown after the deaths of himself, his wife and their survivor. It also included an agreement to move from his O'Neilland (north Armagh) territory centred on Loughgall – then given to English undertakers – to the less fertile area of Orior in the south of the county. His son was Owen Roe O'Neill, military leader of the Irish Catholic Confederacy after the 1641 rising.[25] Always remembering the novelty and limited appeal of the modern concept of 'ownership' in Gaelic society, how did those not included among these two hundred and eighty fare in the new order?

The plantation scheme involved the division of six counties (Don-egal, Londonderry, Tyrone, Fermanagh, Armagh and Cavan) into three categories: first, land to be granted to English and Scottish undertakers; second, land to be granted to servitors (usually English government officials) and 'deserving' Irish; third, land belonging to or to be granted to the established church and Trinity College. The undertakers were required within three to five years to settle English or Scots on their lands at a rate of 24 per 1,000 acres, and to pro-vide defences and build stone houses and bawns, or risk hefty fines. No one who did not conform to Protestantism and no Irish could rent these lands. The other two categories were granted with no condition to plant or conform, and here the Irish inhabitants could remain. In fact, although some displacement did occur, the Irish re-mained even on undertaker land, for tenants were scarce. The Irish remained likewise on the lands given to the London companies: the new county of Londonderry, encompassing Derry and its immediate

Inishowen hinterland, part of north Tyrone, and O'Cahan's lands around Coleraine.

On the whole the Irish remained in occupation of the land. Only the remaining swordsmen of the Irish lords or 'kerne' were totally expelled, some transported to continental service, others taking refuge as outlaws in the woods. But 'occupation' and 'ownership' are quite different things. Those Gaelic lords who had participated in various 'surrender and regrant' schemes recognised as much, and so increasingly did the minor septs. The abundance of Irish families claiming freehold over the land they occupied, even though most such claims would have been untenable, testifies to this. Only a small number were to be satisfied. This and the loss of the top tier of Gaelic lordship (through the Flight of the Earls and death in battle) pushed the gentry of Catholic Ulster down a tier. A new tier of chief lords had been substituted for the old and generally the main undertaker in each barony ended up occupying the residence and demesne land of the former Irish chief.[26]

We simply do not know how the bulk of the Ulster Irish reacted to the plantation. The continuation of year-to-year leases on the estates of some Irish grantees (e.g. MacSweeney) suggests that they may have enjoyed greater security in new leases from the undertakers and servitors. Generally the Irish were supposed to receive shorter leases. But the 1619 and 1622 surveys suggest that many British settlers fared little better. In fact, such was the general insecurity of title under the plantation, with British grantees constantly under threat of confiscation for non-compliance with the original terms of their grant, and frequent prying commissions to check on them, that few were in any hurry to give tenants legal title.[27] The plantation had caused a frisson of anxiety about land title, and the investigations into defective titles during the lord deputyship of Thomas Wentworth, future earl of Strafford, continued such uncertainty into its third decade. Certainly the original concept of a strong, segregated British (and Protestant) colony had to be abandoned. The Irish remained in the majority on all estates. Many of the settlers showed a preference for Irish ways and did not always comply with the terms of the original grants. Indeed, the requirements for conformity to the established religion and the abandonment of Irish dress and agricultural methods were quietly set aside.

What then of popular tradition, of the dispossession of the Ulster Irish and their forced transfer to less fertile ground? In the 1940s a farmer in Killeavy parish, County Armagh, told the Irish Folklore Commission of a family tradition about their people having been driven from the good land in the north of the county to the boggy land of the south. Similar traditions were reported from Cavan, north Louth and Tyrone.[28] Such population movement certainly did occur in Armagh. As one of the most fertile areas of Ulster, it had already been more densely populated in Hugh O'Neill's time than elsewhere in his lordship, and was to prove particularly popular with British settlers.[29] In other areas the trend would have been more gradual, part of the progressive erosion of Catholic landholding over the century. It is not always clear why this movement took place. But judging from reports of Irish tenants, unable to pay rents or fines, and simply leaving with their stock in time-honoured fashion, compulsion may not have been the only factor. In the original plantation proposals there is no requirement to locate the Irish on less fertile land, even though the bulk of better land went to the English undertakers.[30] By the 1660s, however, although Irish and settler still occupied the most fertile land in about equal numbers, the tendency for marginal land to be occupied almost exclusively by Irish was already far advanced. These were to be the areas of Irish cultural survival and to a remarkable degree the figures show that the plantation and subsequent Cromwellian settlement had already set the pattern for the province's future political divisions: with the Ulster Irish heavily concentrated in Donegal, mid-Ulster, the Glens of Antrim, and the southern part of Armagh and Down.[31] 'The natives for the most part remained on their former lands, but degraded from the status of proprietors to that of tenants-at-will', commented T. W. Moody in a seminal article in 1938. 'The process by which they were driven out of the more fertile land and their places taken by British colonists was a gradual one, and was the product of economic forces rather than of any deliberate act on the part of the state.'[32]

However, it is difficult to find contemporary evidence of sustained Irish resentment against the settlers. Most complaints came from the other direction, as settlers told the various commissions of their inability to get secure leases because of landlord preference for Irish tenants, who were always willing to pay higher rents.[33] There were many stories of grumbling and restiveness in the early years of the plantation and, until his death in Rome in 1616, persistent expectations of a return of Hugh O'Neill with continental help. Another period of high tension occurred during the war between England and Spain (1625–30) and family connections with the continental exiles fanned lingering discontent. There was no open rebellion, yet a wide enough range of reported conspiracy among minor players to show rumbling discontents among the disappointed or declining. Anything like 'popular' support is impossible to gauge – though it was vaguely reported in a Fermanagh conspiracy to repossess the confiscated lands in 1625.[34] But however much the impositions of the overlords were disliked and burdensome in the closing days of the Gaelic political system, it is quite clear that the Ulster Irish continued to look for social leadership to the former Gaelic lords, however fallen in fortune, and would continue to do so well into the following century. What lay behind these rumblings was not so much loss of land (though that was a feature) as loss of status and failure to cope with the new landed and money economy.

Rents in the Gaelic system were largely nominal. Evidence suggests that many Ulster Irish grantees continued to exercise traditional lordships, when the various impositions of the new system required ready cash and good estate management. The remaining lands of Conn O'Neill, the O'Cahans, the O'Donnells, the Magennises, the Mac-Mahons and many more were progressively mortgaged or sold off for this very reason.[35] The reported poverty of the conspirators of 1615 and rebels of 1641 was clearly a major contributory factor in their actions. 'It may seem strange that those men who were accounted so great ... should have no better revenues', wrote Chichester of O'Cahan's and O'Donnell's poverty on the eve of the plantation, 'but it may be answered that their maintenance is not from the money they receive but from their provisions of meat, butter, cuttings and coshierings which [since the two men were then in prison, and remained so till their deaths in the 1620s] none of the people will afford to them ... whilst they are in prison or absent from their countries.'[36] Another aspect of Gaelic lordship which continued was the lavish hospitality. Maolmhuire MacSweeny was not the only beneficiary of the plantation to die in poverty, having, according to local tradition 'drank out his estate and mortgaged it'.[37]

Most of all, the plantation played havoc with this intensely status-conscious society. Suddenly people deemed their social inferiors (Irish and British alike) were rising in the social ladder while those who would normally have been in the elite were rapidly declining. This elitism and social snobbery of Gaelic society is frequently overlooked. But more than any loss of land it explains the sense of lost glory which later infused developing nationalist tradition. 'The people in general are great admirers of their pedigree,' commented an English traveller in 1674, 'and have got their genealogy so exactly by heart that though it be two hours work for them to repeat the names only from whence they are descended lineally, yet, will they not omit one word in half a dozen several repetitions; from whence I gather they say them instead of their Pater noster.'[38] This older lineage definition of status was to continue in Ulster Catholic society alongside the newer landed one, quite independently of wealth and property, and was undoubtedly responsible for the long memory of customary land rights.[39]

Randal MacDonnell (created earl of Antrim in 1620) and Brian Maguire were not alone in their attainment of a social position which would not have been theirs without the new dispensation. Even more obscure would have been the lot of the O'Haras of Crebilly in Antrim, who, through marriage alliances (in particular with the MacDonnells) and astute land deals, had pulled themselves from minor lords in the sixteenth century to become one of the most important lords in east Ulster in the seventeenth.[40] Brian Crossagh O'Neill, an illegitimate nephew of the earl of Tyrone, could have expected little under the old system. But he was granted 1,000 acres in the Ulster Plantation, as another of those potentially restless middle-ranking lords considered worth 'buying off' by government administrators. The plantation settlement gave rise to a new social category: the middleman, people like Patrick Groome O'Dufferne in north Tyrone, who managed to acquire a lease to Sir Claud Hamilton's entire estate at Gortin and then sub-let it to Irish and settler alike.[41] Certainly by the 1630s there was a sudden upsurge of Gaelic families applying to the Ulster Office (the Irish chief herald's office) signifying, if not a total acceptance of the new system, at least a recognition that new symbols of noble status were required.[42] Status, its retention or acquisition, appears to have been the crucial determinant of the Gaelic lord's response to plantation. The experiences of those creators of tradition, the learned men, may well be the key to much of the future bitterness and will be discussed more fully in a later chapter.

One class of learned men fared particularly badly: the septs holding the termon and erenach lands. These formed the lion's share of land deemed to belong to the established church (some 48,158 acres of a total 74,852 acres of church land). Parcelled throughout the counties involved in the Ulster Plantation, they amounted to 24 per cent of the confiscated territory in Tyrone, and from 21 per cent to 18 per cent in Londonderry, Donegal and Armagh. Technically the holders did not own the land. But their families had held them for many centuries and could be expected to be particularly sensitive to the changing interpretation of land title. Some may have done as well as the O'Loughrans of Donaghmore (County Tyrone), who survived as chief tenants to 1666. But the McCaseys of Tynan in County Armagh – granted a 21-year lease in 1615 of much diminished land and losing even this by mid-century – may have been more typical.[43] Such families seem to have remained on church lands where they were traditionally concentrated. But there are many cases of leases being questioned by former coarbs and erenachs and by 1641 most Irish on church lands had been depressed to the category of sub-tenants.[44]

Although the poets who remained quickly adapted, seeking patrons, as they had always done, among English and Irish alike, they were the traditional guardians of Gaelic ancestry and were the first to register their distaste for the pretensions of those not born to gentry status.

> Man after man, day after day,
> Her noblest princes pass away
> And leave to all the rabble rest
> A land dispeopled of her best.[45]

Already a highly politicised class, they were prepared to accommodate the new situation provided their own elite position continued to be recognised. The most accommodating were those who continued to be patronised by surviving Gaelic lords. Fear Flatha Ó Gnímh, the east

Ulster poet, at first fiercely critical of the new system, but latterly more accommodatory, is perhaps the best known of such pragmatists. Such accommodation by lord and poet, however, led to the traditional charge of 'selling out' by other poets who preferred a return to a heroic warlord past. And even Ó Gnímh had to admit that the craft of the poet was lost on 'men of low crafts' and 'serfs'.[46] The most comprehensive attack on this new breed of upstarts was the satirical *Pairlement Chloinne Tomáis*. Though Munster in origin, it epitomises the professional classes' reaction to the turmoil in the social hierarchy introduced by plantation policies. It recounts the history of Clan Tomáis, a low-born brutish breed, suddenly raised by the collapse of the old nobility. Then Clan Thomas began to accumulate land, create bogus genealogies, seek marriage alliances and educate their children to rhetoric and the priesthood – a 'race of churls', aping noble ways, but lacking the breeding to carry it off.[47]

2. The 1641 rebellion

By the 1630s evidence suggests that the plantation was settling down. Some 40,000 settlers had arrived. But this out of a likely population of between 200,000 and 300,000 left the Irish in the majority everywhere.[48] There was tacit religious tolerance, and in every county Old Irish were serving as royal officials and members of the Irish Parliament, inherent in which was the conferment of new status within the post-plantation settlement. Indeed, local government effectively collapsed in 1641 because so many such officials were among the rebels.[49] But all was not well with the Irish grantees. Most Gaelic lords were heavily in debt and the amount of land in their hands was being steadily eroded.[50] Declining branches of the Maguires or the O'Neills would have been a volatile element at any time in Gaelic society, but they would have been kept in check by their Gaelic overlord. With the overlords gone, their restlessness fed on every slight by English officials, many of whom would have been their social inferiors. The economic troubles of the 1630s had introduced a lesser breed of landowner than the original undertakers. The resentments of at least one future rebel (Hugh MacMahon) were aggravated by the lack of respect of one such newcomer. Old English cleric John Lynch would later describe the leaders of the Ulster rising of 1641 as 'a rabble of men of ruined fortunes and profligate character'.[51] There may too have been a restlessness for old ways and the earl of Antrim's call in 1638–9 for military recruits savoured of former 'hostings' by Gaelic chiefs.[52]

It would be wrong, however, to seek the causes of the 1641 rebellion in the restlessness of individuals among the old Gaelic elite or to see it as a delayed reaction to the Ulster Plantation. Many of the main surviving Gaelic families such as the Maguires of Tempo, the O'Neills of the Fews, the Antrim MacDonnells, the O'Neills of Killeleagh, the Magennises of Iveagh, did not take part – though their wider kin groups were heavily involved. There is every likelihood that the new system would have settled down had it not been for the heightened tensions and fears caused by the developing conflict between king and parliament in England, an economic crisis, the presence of thousands of unemployed soldiers and a general breakdown of order at every level. It was a classic revolutionary situation, and like all revolutionary situations, it did not start as such.

The lord deputyship of Viscount Wentworth, from 1633 to 1640, when he was made earl of Strafford, had succeeded in making a crisis out of existing insecurities over land title and religion. In principle his actions should have pushed settler and Ulster Irish closer together, for every sector of Irish society was affected by his 'thoroughness'. His renewal of a confiscation and plantation policy – this time in Connacht – sent a frisson through the remaining Catholic landowning class. But they were not alone. His failure to confirm earlier concessions on land titles – notably those modifying the articles of plantation in Ulster – was accompanied by new, unfavourable leases, higher rents and in some cases extortionate fines. The activities of his commission on defective titles meant that no landholder could rest easy. The high rents consequent on Wentworth's policies affected every level of Ulster society at a time when it was already deep in recession. By spring 1641, harvest failure, high food prices and a general deterioration of material well-being were already producing disorders in the east of the province, where an unusual concentration of military quartering was intensifying the religious and economic fears of the local population.[53]

The soldiers thus being quartered in Ulster were no ordinary soldiers. They constituted the largely Catholic 'New Irish Army', which had been raised for Charles I by Wentworth in 1639 for use against the Scottish Covenanters. It was to figure prominently in the anti-popery mania of the English parliament which was to provoke the Ulster Irish into the protective pre-emptive strike with which the 1641 rebellion began. Thereafter it was to supply the rebellion with its trained troops. More immediately it contributed to the unusually heightened religious tensions of 1640–41. Prior to Wentworth's deputyship there had been an easy-going tolerance in religion. The Catholic Church was able to re-establish some of its structures and to develop a *modus vivendi* over the increasing numbers of inter-faith marriages in Ulster.[54] All this was put in jeopardy by Wentworth's religious policies. The established Church of Ireland was to be brought into strict conformity with that in England, raising the spectre of revived recusancy fines for those who did not attend Anglican services and repossession of church lands. The covenanting war in Scotland brought Wentworth's religious policies to bear most heavily on the Ulster Presbyterians – till now accommodated within the Church of Ireland. In 1639–40 Wentworth sent agents into Ulster to force them to swear the so-called Black Oath against the Covenant, forcing some to flee back to Scotland, others to take to the hills and many more to riot. It is a token of the chaos and confused identities of the period that many English settlers thought the early stages of the 1641 rising was a Scots–Irish conspiracy against themselves.[55] The tensions of the period were causing people to look at their neighbours in a new light, for Ireland was about to be pulled into the vortex of impending civil war in England.

The calling of the Long Parliament in England at the end of 1640 unleashed a flood of puritan propaganda to implicate Charles I in a popish conspiracy, of which Wentworth's 'New Irish Army' was deemed the centrepiece. The net effect was to provoke in reality what was feared in theory, for the Ulster Irish rebelled in October 1641 in the firm conviction that they were themselves about to be attacked. It was a County Antrim English planter of puritan sympathies (Sir John Clotworthy, later Lord Massarene, and a member of the Long Parliament), who first alerted parliament to the threat posed by Wentworth's 'popish army' in Ulster. His accusations were seized upon and used first against Wentworth himself, then against the king. In language which thereafter became the stock-in-trade of anti-popery, John Pym denounced this international papist conspiracy to destroy Protestants' 'law and religion'. A host of pamphlets denied that papists could be loyal and Catholics in Ulster feared that Scottish puritans were poised to attack them. The propaganda further fuelled the developing crisis in Ulster and was claimed by the rebellion's leaders as one of the main reasons for their action.[56] The tragedy of the situation was that negotiations between London and the Catholic Old English that summer had started to remedy their grievances, notably over land title. But the Ulster Irish had not been included in the negotiations and they viewed the prorogation of the Irish parliament as another ploy by their enemies to silence their protests.[57]

On 22 October 1641 a number of Ulster Irish, headed by Sir Phelim O'Neill, attacked the principal fortified positions in Ulster. By the following day most of the province from Newry to Donegal was in their hands. It had been a comparatively bloodless rising which had taken most people completely by surprise. Thus opened eleven years of extraordinary confusion and complexity, which even now historians cannot completely unravel. It was to see the Ulster Irish successively in uneasy alliance with the Old English Catholics, the Protestant royalists and ultimately even Cromwell (against their former Catholic allies). Owen Roe O'Neill had returned from nearly four decades of service with the Irish regiment in Spanish Flanders to lead the Irish 'Confederate' army. But his Counter-Reformation zeal – and even more so that of the papal nuncio Rinuccini, who arrived in 1645 with the aim of fully restoring Catholicism – alienated the Old English and put paid to any chance of a negotiated settlement. It was very far from being the great Catholic nationalist uprising of later tradition. But its significance for the future of Ulster's Catholics, and for their relationship with their Protestant neighbours, cannot be overestimated.

Early proclamations from the leaders assured the English and Scots settlers that no harm would come to them and that the Irish were acting under a commission from the king. The latter was in fact a forgery, but most of the Ulster Irish were genuine enough in their belief that they were supporting the king. Certainly there was some disposition – particularly among the Scots – to believe them, and, at the very least, to remain neutral.[58] It was a disposition encouraged by many personal links between the Irish and the settlers, with whom many were now related by marriage. Certainly the early stages of the rising were marked more by plunder than bloodshed, suggesting envy among the lower Irish of new, more materialistic conditions among the settlers. 'He never saw such base covetousness as did show itself in these Irish robbers, such bitter envyings and emulations,' commented George Creichton, a Presbyterian minister who spent many months a prisoner among the rebels.[59] Lack of investment in chattels and material comforts had always been a feature of Gaelic society much commented upon by visitors. Aspiration to such comforts as symbols of civility had already been noted among the gentry and would have started to set apart the 'haves' and 'have-nots'.

The Catholic leaders, however, very quickly lost control in what fast became a total breakdown of order in Ulster. Miles O'Reilly was simply rejected by his men when he intervened to prevent the killing of Protestants at Kilmacrenan in Donegal.[60] Phelim O'Neill's notes of protection were ignored, and Philip O'Reilly, after numerous attempts to protect prisoners in Cavan, had to admit his loss of authority over his men and advised prisoners to flee to Dublin.[61] However moderate the aims of the initial rising, that breakdown of order generated vigilantism. Popular indiscipline gave rise to localised vendettas. Scotland's troubles finally spilled over into the province early in 1642 and the presence of thousands of unoccupied soldiers from Wentworth's now disbanded army added to the powder-keg.

Even today historians lavish thousands of words denying any general massacre of Protestants in 1641. Such denials are undoubtedly necessary, given the wild exaggerations of genocide and dreadful barbarities which were to exercise anti-Catholic opinion for centuries after the events and form the basis of dispossession and penalisation of religion until the nineteenth century. Pamphlet literature in England laid claim to anything up to 150,000 Protestants massacred, when the number of Protestants in Ulster may not have been much above 30,000. None the less, as many as 12,000 may have perished, the majority from cold and exposure after being stripped of clothes and possessions during an unusually cold winter. In this state thousands made their way to Dublin in a seventeenth-century preplay of famine-induced population movements in the Third World. Their sufferings were extensively documented in the commissions of 1641–2 and 1652 and in the trials of 1652–4. However unreliable they have been proved, one cannot read the statements of people such as Elizabeth Price of County Armagh, who had lost her husband and five children in circumstances of considerable brutality, without coming to understand the terror and suffering which occasioned the rumours and wild exaggerations of the period. Even Catholic folk memory is critical of the extreme brutality of the Irish leaders in 1641.[62]

We know less about losses among the Ulster Catholics. But retaliatory massacres of Ulster Irish at Templepatrick and Island Magee in County Antrim were not isolated incidents. Some 500, mostly women and children, were reportedly killed in a revenge attack in the Mourne Mountains in County Down, another 295 in Fermanagh. In the Mourne incident Sir James Montgomery could not contain his men, for they 'had seen . . . their houses burned, their wives and children murdered. So they were like robbed bears and tygers, and could not be sattisfied with all the revenge they took', and instead of open battle as Montgomery wished, they attacked the Irish from the rear 'being full of revenge . . . most partys killing many, and giving no quarter'.[63] Certainly the period decimated many Ulster Catholic families: an analysis of those of the Fews in Armagh shows a numerical decline of between a third and four-fifths.[64] The failure of the Irish Catholics – above all the Old English – to mount any effective defence until long after the event is surprising, particularly since it was their political enemies in Ireland who were effectively manipulating the evidence. It can surely only be adequately explained by their own anger at the Ulster Catholics' lack of moderation, which had given their parliamentary enemies the excuse to associate them too in the Ulster's guilt.[65] The fact remains, however, that even if the slaughter was spontaneous and not planned, even if there were barbarities on all sides, even if every Catholic was not involved, 1641 destroyed the Ulster Plantation as a mixed settlement and made religion for the first time the main justification for dispossession.

The first indiscriminate killings appear to have been those of a small force of Scots (some 300 to 400) at Augher, County Tyrone, in the first days of November, after they had already surrendered. The exact train of events has been impossible to trace. The main Irish leaders were horrified and, still anxious to keep the Scots neutral, they issued a number of statements, blaming the massacre on 'lewd people' or the 'common sort'. But bloodshed begot bloodshed. It was largely carried out by inferior leaders over whom the key figures quickly lost control. There was widespread plunder of property and livestock and cases of Irish and settler alike either fleeing from their homes for fear of neighbourly enmities escalating, or pre-empting such by killing the neighbour concerned.[66] There was a concentration of atrocities in that swathe of territory covering north Armagh and south Tyrone which had been most densely settled by English. All were the result of freebooting by local captains as groups of prisoners were transferred. There is no sign of a general assassination policy, and alcohol was frequently a factor. But local captains tended to be residents of the area, local sept leaders. The most notorious incident – which lives on in the commemorative banner of the local Orange lodge – was that at Portadown in County Armagh. Sometime in November 1641 a group of prisoners being moved from Loughgall were drowned in the River Bann in circumstances of extreme cruelty. No one, then or since, has discovered the precise reason or who gave the order, but ultimate responsibility would have fallen to the local captain, Toole McCann. Some 80 to 100 men, women and children perished and rumours quickly spread of portents and visions, ghosts of the victims rising from the water to call for vengeance. Other killings, such as that at Shewie in County Armagh, were carried out by Irish soldiers fleeing from defeat, helped by locals pursuing personal vendettas. At Kinnard (Caledon) in Tyrone, some Protestant tenants and servants of Sir Phelim O'Neill himself were murdered, an event which so angered him that he had a number of the attackers hanged.[67]

The first such killings in County Antrim were representative of this lack of any overall pattern, for the attackers were led by a Catholic Scot, recently arrived from Scotland. Alisdair MacDonald (Alexander MacDonnell), a kinsman of the earl of Antrim, was part of a mixed religion force of the earl's tenants, assembled to protect his estates against the rebels. On 2 January 1642 they were crossing the Bann at Portnaw to protect a Protestant settler, when MacDonnell turned his men on the Protestants within his own force and killed sixty of them. Thereafter all the earl of Antrim's Catholic tenants joined the rebels, largely in self-protection as the Portnaw incident set off a train of reprisals. Some days later settlers, reacting to news of such killings of Protestants, massacred the Irish in Islandmagee and Templepatrick, which in turn triggered killings of Protestants at a number of besieged locations in the north-east of the province. By now local leaders were unable to contain their followers, and it had become something of a rebellion without a cause, as fear turned low-level resentments at English fashions and language into murderous attacks.[68] But it was never general and there are innumerable incidents of clemency on all sides – the terrible events at Portadown being criticised by local Irish for their 'inhumanity and unchristianlike murder'.[69]

The action of Alisdair MacDonnell was symptomatic of the lack of common aim in the Ulster rising. He had joined as part of his own ambitions to use the Irish against his family's traditional enemies in Scotland, the Campbells. It was, in part, the same reason which kept his uncle, the earl of Antrim, neutral. Notwithstanding his neutrality, his Scottish Campbell enemy, in the form of the earl of Argyll, was permitted by the English parliament to occupy the earl of Antrim's estates and base his army on Rathlin Island, the population of which was systematically massacred.[70] Argyll was part of a Scottish force under General Robert Monro which arrived in Ulster in April 1642 and swept through Antrim and Down by May, wasting much of the land and destroying the Irish strongholds.

By the summer the Ulster Irish had all but acknowledged defeat. That the war continued for another ten years owed more to the eruption of England's civil war into Ireland than any coherent sense of purpose. In effect, the future of Catholic Ulster had already been sealed in those first few months of the Ulster rising. The Old English had been sucked into it by the spreading disorder at the end of 1641. But the next ten years witnessed persistent friction between them and the Ulster Irish, the former dismissing the other as 'a rabble of men of ruined fortunes and profligate character'; the Old Irish responding with taunts of 'sons of heretics and remonstrators'.[71] This was not the great Catholic uprising of tradition.

Early reports of the rising filled the press in England with histrionic and often fictional accounts. Thus began England's lurid fascination with 1641 which was to outlast anything similar in Ireland. More popular literature was generated in England by 1641 than by any other single event in Irish history, all alike depicting the rising as a popish conspiracy to exterminate Protestants. A particularly influential tract was the *Remonstrance* of Henry Jones. In March 1642, Jones, Dean of Kilmore and future Bishop of Clogher, delivered his own account to the English House of Commons. He portrayed the rebellion as 'a long-laid conspiracie' by the Church of Rome to extirpate Protestantism and undermine allegiance to the king. Popery was thus a political as well as a religious threat. The events of 1641 firmly implanted this notion of Catholicism as a dangerous political system and as such underpinned state policy for almost two centuries and Ulster Protestant perceptions for even longer.

And out of that ancient hatred the Church of Rome beareth to the Reformed Religion . . . There hath been beyond all paralell of former ages, a most bloody and Antichristian combination and plot hatched, by well-nigh the whole Romish sect, by way of combination from parts foreign, with those at home, against this our Church and state; thereby intending the utter extirpation of the reformed Religion, and the possessors of it: In the room thereof, setting up that idol of the Masse, with all the abominations of the whore of Babylon.[72]

In an effort to persuade parliament to send help, Jones then detailed the atrocities, dwelling on particularly horrifying details such as reports of babies having been ripped from the womb and fed to the dogs. Jones took much of his information from the much-maligned 'Depositions' (taken from Protestant refugees who had reached Dublin), which are now housed in Trinity College, Dublin. To those of 1641–2 were added a further set of 1652, the main purpose of which was to acquire evidence against the rebellion's leaders. The hand of Jones, prime interlocutor on each of these occasions, is clearly visible, and there are good grounds for the centuries-old doubts about the reliability of the depositions.[73] Yet their more extreme claims provided the basis for a new English policy towards Ireland and in Sir John Temple's *Irish Rebellion* – an Irish equivalent of Foxe's *Book of Martyrs* – a formative influence on Protestant psyche. Jones and Temple were virulently anti-Catholic New English, whose understanding of Ireland would have been influenced by the timeless stereotypes of Giraldus Cambrensis.

The message of Temple was of heroic endurance against a barbarous infidel. He was the first to paint what was to become an enduring picture of the Catholic Irish as untrustworthy dissemblers. Their aim had always been the dispossession and extirpation of Protestants and such it would remain if they were given a chance. It confirmed Calvinistic belief in the Catholics as irredeemable and the message was reinforced in annual sermons on the anniversary of the rebellion which only ceased in 1784.[74] However propagandistic Temple may have been, such blanket reports of massacre became part of genuine belief among Irish Protestants generally in later centuries, a kind of 'occult force', informing Protestant consciousness particularly in times of crisis.[75] The cry of 'remember 1641' proved a powerful counter to would-be reformers in the next century. Incidents such as the discovery of bones of the reputed victims in County Down in the 1720s kept local traditions alive, and a century and a half later the United Irishmen failed to make headway in areas which had been the scene of killings in 1641. It was always at key political moments that the horrors of 1641 were recalled and manipulated by interested parties.[76]

More immediately the lurid accounts of cruelties, on which most of the popular English versions seized, transposed the centuries-old English perception of the barbarous Irish exclusively to the Catholics. Certainly many of the Cromwellian soldiers were fired by the accounts of the massacres into considering their campaign one of revenge. But the image of a religious crusade should not be carried too far, and ultimately Cromwellian policies towards Ireland were governed by fiscal, not punitive, concerns. If English Protestants had had more sympathy for the sufferings of their Irish co-religionists, the propaganda campaign mounted by the like of Jones and Temple would have been unnecessary. As it was, the entire parliamentary war effort in Ireland was funded by loans from speculators or 'adventurers', who would be repaid in Irish land. But much of the money was diverted to the English campaign and the soldiers in Ireland were left unpaid. Only in 1652 was Ireland finally subdued and Cromwell's campaign there was waged as much against Protestant (and Presbyterian) royalist as against the Catholic Irish. It was Cromwell's intention to crush support for Charles II rather than destroy either the Irish or their religion and by 1652 London was more inclined to moderation.

At that point Henry Jones resurfaced with an abstract of the 'barbarous . . . cruel, murders and massacres' in 1641. The four parliamentary commissioners sent to Ireland to arrange the terms of settlement later explained how he had overcome their 'temptation' to lenity. 'So deeply were [we] all affected . . . that we are much afraid our behaviour towards this people may never sufficiently avenge the same; and fearing lest others, who are at greater distance, might be moved to the lenity we have found no small temptation in ourselves', they sent a lengthy extract from Jones's depositions to deter parliament from making concessions.[77] Thus had Jones 'saved the settlement from moderation'.[78] It is the terms of the subsequent land settlement on which much of Cromwell's evil reputation in Ireland rests.

3. The Cromwellian settlement

Under Cromwell's land settlement those who had participated in the first stages of the rebellion or in the killing of civilians or who failed to surrender arms within twenty-eight days, together with 105 named persons (including Sir Phelim O'Neill, but also a large number of Protestants and leading Presbyterians like Viscount Montgomery of Ards), were exempted from pardon. All other landowners would be subject to partial forfeiture, depending on the extent of their 'delinquency' and required to move across the Shannon to Connacht or Clare. Forfeited lands in ten counties of the other three provinces would then be assigned to soldiers and adventurers. But the implications of 'blood guilt' on a national level were never carried through. Wives and children of 'delinquents' were to be allowed to retain up to a fifth of the confiscated estate, and 'Irish not guilty of blood' were to receive protection.[79] Cromwell was more worried by the radical Protestant sectaries in his own camp (who controlled the Irish administration) and his son, Henry Cromwell, sent to Ireland in 1655, became a moderating influence. The court set up to try those exempted from pardon (which, it has been estimated, could have encompassed as many as 80,000 people), was clearly designed to intimidate rather than to punish. We do not know how many were executed, perhaps about fifty. But many – including even key leaders – were acquitted or permitted to go into exile. Even Sir Phelim might have been spared had he not continued to deny that he received his commission from Charles I.[80] Some 34,000 swordsmen were permitted to enlist in the continental armies, and several thousand followed English and Scots royalists already transplanted to the new English colonies in the West Indies.[81]

The policy of transplantation to Connacht got under way in 1654 amidst confusion and uncertainty, and doubts remain as to how far it was actually implemented. No reliable survey of the acreage involved was completed until 1659, by which date the policy, though only partially implemented, had been abandoned. The commissioners, installed at Loughrea (County Galway) to parcel out the land in Connacht, were quickly overwhelmed and generally open to bribery. Cromwellian policy made a clear distinction between the people and their social leaders, and, under further pressure from Protestant land-lords who needed their Catholic tenants and labourers to work the land, only Catholic landlords and those tenants who chose to accompany them were subject to transplantation.[82] It took more than a generation for the Cromwellian land settlement to work itself out. Local government was not sufficiently restructured to ensure a smooth operation of such a potentially massive policy. Some officials in Connacht simply dispensed with paperwork and assigned land according to the number of cattle requiring grazing. Some Ulster Irish and Scots, due for transplantation, simply moved their cattle into the hilly areas of neighbouring County Leitrim.[83] Many Cromwellian soldiers had not wanted land and quickly sold their small portions, often to original tenants who were anxious to return. Of those soldiers who stayed (some 12,000) many inter-married with and became Catholics. Cromwellian ambitions to establish a resident Protestant yeomanry from the soldiery did not materialise. What it did achieve, however, was the virtual eradication of a Catholic landed elite, for despite original outlawry of certain Protestants, in the end only Catholic landowners were transplanted.[84] In their place the Cromwellian settlement established the backbone of a Protestant proprietary. The host of small grants to reluctant soldiers ensured a speculator's paradise. The vast estates of the Massarenes, Annesleys, Beresfords and Cootes, and many more who would dominate the country's political future, were accumulated in this manner.[85]

Historians seem strangely ignorant of the consequences of the Cromwellian settlement on the ground.[86] In fact, despite Jones's propaganda, Ulster suffered less than any other province, one of the reasons, possibly, why Cromwell is less a force of evil in popular tradition here than elsewhere.[87] The amount of land left in Old Irish hands had dramatically declined even from 1609 levels as a result of sales. This is why the map of Cromwellian confiscations for Ulster shows levels as low as 4 per cent for Tyrone, 11 per cent for Donegal, rising to a maximum of 41 per cent for Antrim and 43 per cent for Cavan (as against 77 per cent for Tipperary and 91 per cent for Galway). Moreover, although most Ulster landowners would have been royalist during the war, they were permitted to compound for their estates, so that fewer confiscations were necessary to pay the Cromwellian soldiers.[88] Of just under 2,000 landowners estimated to have been transplanted, around thirty were from Ulster. However, of the fifty-eight Gaelic Catholic landholders in 1641, only five retained their property in 1660, whilst Scottish and Old English Catholics generally fared better.[89] In fact, even some of the Ulster figures do not reflect the final outcome, for 'any lawful right, title or interest' to the forfeited lands were to be honoured before satisfaction of the adventurers' and soldiers' claims could be entertained. Efforts were made to prevent any precipitate land grabbing, while evidence of separate agreements made with individual leaders on their surrender suggests a large element of flexibility. Terms made with Philip O'Reilly, for instance, permitted his men 'enjoyment of their personal estates by such of them as desire to live in the nation', or freedom of sale if they go abroad, provided they had had no hand in murder or robbery.[90]

It was the confiscation of a third of the earl of Antrim's estates for distribution among some 800 soldiers which explains the disproportionally high figure for that county. This had been against the wishes both of Cromwell and his supporters in Ireland, since the earl had been instrumental in winning Ulster (and indeed the Papacy) over to the Cromwellian side in the last years of the war. In fact, only five adventurers and some 100 soldiers took up residence. Most of the soldiers quickly sold their small portions, often to Antrim's tenants, who were anxious to return or acting on behalf of the earl himself. The result was that some two-thirds of the earl's tenants remained either Irish or Scottish Catholics, and such indeed was the general picture all over the country.[91]

Sir Henry O'Neill of the Fews (son of Sir Turlough MacHenry) was not quite so fortunate. He had succeeded peacefully to his father's estates of 9,305 acres in 1639 and had studiously avoided involvement in the 1641 rising. He successfully contested the depositions against him, as witnesses confessed that their accusations were based on hearsay. However, all his children and kin were involved and he had supplied the Irish armies. He therefore lost his estates in Armagh and was partially compensated by two-thirds the equivalent in Mayo. In fact he only received a third, and this experience of receiving less land in compensation than initially promised was a common one throughout the country.[92] Maguire of Tempo alone of the Irish land-owners in Fermanagh remained. But it was the host of small Catholic proprietors created by the Ulster Plantation who lost most. Typical were the gallowglass families of MacDonnell in Armagh and Tyrone. They had received nine grants of land varying from 60 to 120 acres in the Ulster Plantation. By 1641 only two of the grants remained, and these were lost in the Cromwellian settlement.[93] Some were partially compensated in Connacht. Others went into exile, became outlaws or tenants.

But it was a decline that was accelerated rather than caused by the Cromwellian settlement. The vast majority of the Catholic population remained unaffected by the dramatic change in property at the top, and in many ways their position was a strong one because of the continuing acute shortage of tenants and the massive re-leasing of lands at low rents in the 1650s.[94] The Cromwellian settlement, unlike previous ones, did not involve any importation of large numbers of new tenants. The Ulster Catholics largely remained on their lands. In June 1652 the Magennises of Iveagh used a device which would become common under the penal laws of the eighteenth century, of conveyancing their lands to a friendly Protestant to be held until such times as they could be lawfully retrieved.[95] But, far more effectively than any of the plantations, the Cromwellian land settlement cemented the link between Protestantism and land ownership, prompting Lecky two centuries later to proclaim it as the originator of that 'lasting division between the proprietary and the tenants which is the chief cause of the political and social evils of Ireland'.[96] Lecky was writing at the height of the campaign to establish a peasant proprietorship. But he captured the essence of the Cromwellian settlement well enough. That it proved so complete and so enduring, however, owed as much to the thwarted efforts of the restored monarchy to reach a fairer settlement as to Cromwellian policies.

4. The Restoration settlement

One of the reasons for the foot-dragging over the implementation of the Cromwellian settlement was the heightened expectation of a change in the political situation. Hopes of a reversal of the Cromwellian land settlement ran high with the restoration of the Stuarts in 1660, though it is noteworthy that those petitioning for such did not question the original Ulster Plantation. At the outset the new king promised all things to all men. Protestants would be allowed to retain their lands and Catholics who had been loyal to the crown or deprived of their lands on the grounds of religion would be restored – prompting the duke of Ormond's cynical comment that the king would then have to discover a second Ireland to satisfy his promises.[97] Such promises nevertheless caused local skirmishing, some former owners simply seizing their old lands.[98]

But if Catholics thought a restoration of the Stuarts signalled a return to the *status quo ante*, they were to be rudely disabused. The Cromwellian settlement had established for the rest of the island what was already in place in Ulster: a new landed base of power which was firmly Protestant. Many Protestants had been royalist in the recent conflict. But the threat to land ownership posed by Charles II's court of claims united old and new Protestants as never before. It was this united Protestant front in the face of a still-divided Catholic elite which set the seal on the Cromwellian land settlement.[99] Even the Act of Settlement passed by the Irish parliament in May 1662, undertaking to look into the claims of 'innocent papists', was prefaced by a strongly anti-Catholic preamble which implied that an 'innocent papist' was a contradiction in terms. A court of claims commenced hearing cases in January 1663. But it was quite suddenly discontinued after only eight months, with less than a seventh of the claims heard. Some 540 Catholics over the whole island had been declared innocent, leaving over 7,000 claims unheard.[100] Although not all of these would have been major landowners, for widows and children were also allowed to petition, the entire 'scramble', as the Lord Lieutenant, the earl of Essex, described it, left no one satisfied. An additional act requiring adventurers and soldiers to surrender a third of their acquisitions was to have created land to compensate Protestants who had made way for innocent papists. But the uproar caused in the English parliament, and the unruly last session of the Irish parliament (December 1665) – where members confronted each other with half-drawn swords – revealed the depth of dissatisfaction also in this quarter.[101]

Again the situation provided many opportunities for sharp practice by speculators. So-called 'discoverers' were out searching for concealed lands. No one could feel secure. One public official writing in 1684 was very critical of the injustices created by the Restoration settlement. He was particularly critical of those with access to power who abused the system to the detriment of both the crown and the former proprietors:

For many years after the closing of the Court of Claims, those who had favour in Court got commissions of inquiry to look after concealed lands . . . And therefore these favoured grantees bought up unsatisfied debentures (which they might buy for a song) . . . It were to be wished that a considerable part of such money were distributed to those Irish families as have been notoriously disappointed of the good intended them by the acts, and by which their condition is most miserable, many of the English allowing some sort of gifts or poor subsistence to the old proprietors, who evermore haunt and live about those lands they were dispossessed of, and cannot forbear to hope and reckon upon a day of re-possession.[102]

The former proprietors in Ulster suffered particularly badly, not simply because of their support of the ultra-papal party in the recent war, though this was a factor, nor Charles II's bitterness at the eleventh-hour conversion of the Ulster Catholics to the Cromwellian side.[103] The main reason was the continuing disunity among the Catholic elite and the lack of influence by the Ulster Gaelic lords in the corridors of power. The outcome of the Restoration settlement was decided by influence and string-pulling. The position of the earl of Antrim in the pre-1641 power network, with all the contacts that brought, determined his restoration.[104] Likewise the influence of many Old English lords ensured that they would be the principal beneficiaries of any lands restored to Catholics and they made little effort to extend the operation of the court of claims once their own claims had been satisfied.[105] It was the claims of the small proprietors above all which were ignored and the bulk of the remaining Ulster Catholic proprietors in 1641 fell into this category. Another badly treated grouping were the so-called 'ensignmen' (perhaps as many as 30,000) who had joined the king in exile on the Continent. But since their claims were to have been considered only after the 'innocents' and Cromwellians, theirs remained largely unsatisfied.

Prominent among the losers was Viscount Magennis of Iveagh, County Down, one of the ensignmen, who ended up with only 2,000 acres out of an estimated 45,000. The Kilwarlin branch also suffered losses. In 1611 Brian Oge McRory Magennis alienated 5,204 acres of the Kilwarlin lands to Sir Moses Hill. Thus began a steady process of acquisition by the Hill family which was to see them become the most important landed family in Ulster by the next century. His son joined the Cromwellian forces and was rewarded with another 3,000 acres of the Kilwarlin lands in 1656. These he retained at the Restoration, contrary to the expectations of the Magennis family. Among those Magennises dispossessed was Father Patrick Maginn, chaplain to Charles II's queen (Catherine of Braganza, a devout Catholic), who was to remain a very influential figure on the Continent till his death in 1683. Nevertheless, despite a vigorous petitioning campaign by Maginn and his Magennis kin, the lands remained with the Hill family, the consequences of which would form an important element in the religious and political history of the area.[106] Phelimy Magennis and his son Ever were restored to their Castlewellan estates, Henry O'Neill of Killeleagh in County Antrim to his, as was Daniel O'Neill, son to Conn O'Neill of Clandeboye, who, though a Protestant, had used his strong familial ties among the Catholics to assist Charles II during Cromwell's time. But all were contested for many years, the latter two most effectively by the Presbyterian adventurer, Sir John Clotworthy, earl of Massarene.[107] The Scottish settlers Sir George Hamilton and his brother Claud, Lord Strabane, were restored in Tyrone, as was the Old English Patrick Russell to Killough in County Down. The chief line of the Savage family had become Protestant by this time and the main surviving Catholic proprietor in the family lost his lands as a Jacobite supporter in the Williamite settlement.[108] Colla MacBrian MacMahon of Tullyglass in Monaghan was restored, as was Miles MacSweeney in Donegal.[109] But such survivals were insignificant in the new power structure, for outside Antrim, less than 4 per cent of the land in Ulster remained in Catholic ownership.[110]

5. The Williamite land settlement

Dissatisfaction with the Restoration land settlement made its repeal the Catholics' main priority when Catholic James II became king in 1685. Under the Restoration Lord Deputy Ormond, with the benefit of direct experience through his many Catholic relatives, was irritated by Protestants' paranoia. After James II's accession, however, a wave of triumphalism swept through Catholic Ireland, particularly when his lord deputy, Richard Talbot, earl of Tyrconnell, was replacing Protestant officials with Catholics. Old prophecies were invoked to depict James as the saviour of the Gael, a 'sovereign sprung of their own most ancient royal race ... would forthwith restore ... to the natives their properties and estates of which they had been for so many years so unjustly despoiled'.[111] It was a triumphalism picked up in the most famous Protestant song of the period – 'Lillibullero' – a parody of Catholic hopes that their day had finally come.

> Now Tyrconnel is come ashore,
> Lillibulero bullen a la;
> And we shall have commissions gillore,
> Lillibulero bullen a la.

And he dat will not go to mass,
Lillibulero bullen a la;
Shall turn out and look like an ass,
Lillibulero bullen a la.

Now, now de heretics all go down,
Lillibulero bullen a la;
By Chreist and St Patrick de nation's our own,
Lillibulero bullen a la.[112]

Predictably, Talbot's activities raised fears of another 1641, and James himself infuriated his Irish supporters by suggesting them capable of such.[113] James's Irish parliament of 1689 had proclaimed Temple's book a seditious libel, which only increased its popularity among Protestants.[114] Catholic writers later accused Protestants of cynical manipulation of the religious issue to confiscate land.[115] But with James's ally Louis XIV ruthlessly suppressing Protestants in France and his Irish parliament attainting over 2,000 people on mere hearsay, there was good cause for concern.

It was, however, the land issue which was and would remain the main cause for that concern. Tyrconnell's actions had ensured an overwhelmingly Catholic return to the parliament of 1689 – only six of its 230 members were Protestants. It immediately repealed the Act of Settlement and sought to re-establish the court of claims, at a stroke providing the main justification for withholding political rights from Catholics over the next century.[116] Most land in Ulster was already in Protestant hands, and the actions of the 1689 parliament sent tremors through the province. This was 'the Irish summer', when former pro-prietors like Edmond Oge Magennis 'expelled, but without cruelty or effusion of blood, those whom Cromwell had introduced to his estates and replaced them by those who had been the ancient vassals of his house'.[117] These were the lands of William Waring – acquired by purchase in 1663 – and since he was not in arms against James, the Catholic MP for Newry, Rowland White, intervened on his behalf to secure continued ownership.[118] The ensuing war (1689–91) between James and William of Orange, more than any previous conflict, divided the province along religious lines. But the relatively generous terms granted to James's Irish army on its surrender at Limerick (leaving some 14 per cent of land in Catholic ownership, when Protestants called for total confiscation) determined the bitter mood in which William's first, totally Protestant, Irish parliament met in 1692. This was the parliament which passed the first of the penal laws. Several key clauses of the Treaty of Limerick, notably those extending its generous terms to everyone in areas under Jacobite control and granting religious freedom to Catholics, were omitted when it was finally ratified in 1697. But although the latter omission laid the ground for the penal laws, it made very little difference to the Williamite land settlement.

The vast majority of those outlawed by name in Ulster were Old Irish. Although a sizeable number of Old English were also outlawed (notably Savages, Whites and Russells), about one in three received pardons against one in seventeen Old Irish.[119] The last Catholic O'Neill proprietor (Sir Neill O'Neill of Killeleagh, County Antrim) had died after fighting on James's side at the Boyne (1 July 1690) and his Londonderry and Monaghan estates were confiscate. Cú Chonnacht Maguire (grandson of Brian Maguire of Tempo) died at the Battle of Aughrim (12 July 1691) on James's side. But the forfeiture of his estates was successfully contested by his widow and son. A string of County Down Magennises figure among King James's officers. One was killed at Aughrim, two more at Athlone; others, including Lord Iveagh, joined the Irish regiments on the Continent, though the bulk of Iveagh's Ulster regiment opted to transfer to William's forces. The exchange of letters between William Waring and the Magennises of Clanconnel during these fraught months suggests relatively friendly relations, and there is evidence that Waring gave some assistance to surviving members of the family who had fallen on hard times. This does not mean, however, that the loss of the land ceased to rankle with future generations, and the grandson of Bryan Magennis who was killed at Aughrim (John MacCartan) made another unsuccessful bid to recover some land early next century (interestingly claiming rights as a 'discoverer' of concealed crown property).[120] Ironically the largest forfeiture was the 9,861 acres of the Scottish Catholic, Claud Hamilton, earl of Abercorn, though it was later re-purchased by his Protestant nephew.[121] The earl of Antrim was restored, though initially outlawed. By the 1720s the Antrim MacDonnells had conformed to the established religion, as had other remaining Catholic landowners, sometimes under pressure from Protestant members of their own family.[122]

6. The Ulster Irish and the land at the end of the seventeenth century

Despite their loss of land, these formerly important Gaelic families retained 'gentle' status into the eighteenth century and did not marry beneath that. A history of the Magennises of Iveagh, written by a descendant at the height of the Catholic campaign of 1792, clearly illustrates this point. Successive generations had intermarried with other gentry families (of Irish and English descent) and were described as having retained the stature and manners of nobility even after their land had been lost.[123] Heads of families, though landless, still retained enough influence to raise large numbers of men from their traditional followers at the end of the seventeenth century.[124] The traditional Irish concept of status was to be a crucial determinant of identity through the next century, and the popular picture of an impoverished Catholic peasantry opposed to a Protestant elite does not survive close scrutiny.

It is equally true that the policy which had motivated the Ulster Plantation – that of curtailing the power of the overlords – continued into the eighteenth century, as Protestant landlords proved reluctant to let lands to leading Gaelic families.[125] And it is with these families that we must, first and foremost, seek the origins of the bitter traditions about the loss of the lands, never forgetting that the bulk of people adapted as they had always done.[126] It was such families that continued to supply successive generations of priests, now replacing the disappearing lords as social leaders. They were likewise the families who supplied most of the continental exiles and much of the bandit culture of south Ulster in particular. With the dismantling of the Gaelic warlord society early in the seventeenth century, vast numbers of masterless men remained in Ulster to haunt Stuart officials. Prior to 1641 some 32,660 were given British blessing to enlist in the forces of the continental powers (normally those of France and Spain). After each upheaval further contingents left and the turmoil of seventeenth-century Europe sustained the demand for troops. The geography of recruitment is telling. Gaelic lords tended to recruit from within their own kin, which explains the staggering number of O'Neills, O'Donnells and their relatives among the continental military class. It was difficult for such men to return to Ireland, but when they did, their influence was considerable. They were very largely based in Flanders, a key centre of the Counter-Reformation, and were militantly Catholic. They were fiercely resistant to recruiting for Protestant countries or fighting against Catholic ones and many defected from the levies raised for Sweden (1609–10) for this very reason.[127] In exile they preserved their former status, pride and territorial affinity with their birthplace, continental-born descendants citing their father's Ulster birthplace as their own and bequeathing their confiscated estates there.[128] They also retained their retinue of learned men (now usually clerics). In 1662 Captain Art O'Neill, upon applying for entry to one of Spain's highest military orders, called upon the family's hereditary genealogist, one of the Conrys, to prove his lineage back to the tenth century.[129]

Those military retainers who remained in Ulster in the early part of the century became the woodkerne who preyed on settler and Irish alike. Their more organised successors, the tories (from the Irish *toraidhe* or 'raider') and rapparees (*rapaire*, a form of pike), came to prominence in the Cromwellian period and continued intermittently until the middle of the eighteenth century. They operated in remote hilly and wooded districts in Cork, Kerry, south-west Connacht, but most notably in south-west Ulster and to a lesser extent in Donegal, the Sperrins in Tyrone, Londonderry and the Glens of Antrim.They have been seen by some writers as the dispossessed conducting an early nationalist struggle against the oppressor. Many were indeed survivors of such dispossessed families. The tories of Armagh and Tyrone, wrote Archbishop Oliver Plunkett to Rome in 1671, were 'certain gentlemen of the leading families of the houses of O'Neill, MacDonnell, O'Hagan etc . . . together with their followers';[130] while leaders in Leitrim were known to be men disappointed in their hopes of regaining their lands at the Restoration. Warrants issued in 1666 for their arrest in Counties Leitrim, Sligo, Londonderry, Down and Tyrone contain the names of almost all the leading Gaelic families in Ulster.[131] They also included those soldiers who managed to return from the Continent, and during the Williamite war they shaded into the Jacobite campaign as irregulars attacking Williamite forces. Old customs and traditions were not eroded overnight by the changes of the seventeenth century. Toryism in many respects was a continuation of the Gaelic order by other means. Successful cattle raids, feasting and accumulation of a personal following – all features of Gaelic lordship – remained the tory's route to leadership. There is too a territorial continuity in such activities, the Cavan O'Reillys for example continuing to raid into Louth, much as their ancestors had done in the past. In the sixteenth century areas like the baronies of Farney in Monaghan and the Fews in south Armagh and other wooded and boggy areas had been notorious sources of raiding parties into the adjacent Pale.[132] By the late seventeenth century they are identifiable frontier zones between surviving Gaelic and extending Scottish and English cultures.[133]

But nothing is ever quite so straightforward in Irish history and every attempt to look to the tories as an 'example of the passionate and indomitable resistance of the Celts to foreign despotism' is destined to be frustrated.[134] There is evidence of English and Scots amongst them, of 'settler' collusion in the black economy they operated, of men falling in and out of gangs according to their employment situation. Rather than protectors of Catholics, they robbed and murdered Catholic and Protestant alike and (usually) they were denounced by the priests.[135] What can be said with more certainty was that the folklore which developed around them helped generate the legend of 'Gentleman Robber[s]' and 'Protector[s]' of their people. The words are those of John Cosgrave's chapbook history of Redmond O'Hanlon (the most famous of all the tories), one of the most popular works of the eighteenth century. O'Hanlon had seen French service after his family had lost their lands in Armagh. Under the Restoration he became so famous for his exploits in Armagh and surrounding counties that he was a regular news item in the London press. He was eventually betrayed by another tory (a Franciscan friar) and murdered in 1681 by his foster-brother, under orders from the authorities. The story of O'Hanlon and his like would later inform nationalist traditions of the struggle of the dispossessed and betrayal by their own.[136] The traditions were particularly strong in the border zone of south Armagh, south

Down and north Louth – which were his major haunts – and the unfortunate descendants of those who had betrayed him were still being taunted by schoolchildren in the twentieth century.[137] The geography of tory and rapparee activity, whilst owing much to inaccessibility and deliberate concentration in those 'fastnesses' of old, also defines for the historian those areas where Gaelic ways survived longest. By the second half of the seventeenth century the upland areas had the heaviest concentration of people defined in official statistics as 'Irish' – places like the baronies of Omagh in Tyrone, Loughinsholin in Londonderry, Bannaugh and Boylaugh in Donegal, and the Fews in Armagh. It was in such areas that creaghting and lavish hospitality continued, practices which were part and parcel of bandit life. The Williamite officer George Story wrote in 1691, with barely concealed admiration, of the peripatetic lifestyle of these semi-militaristic bands in 'the wildness of the country between Newry and Dundalk'.[138]

It would have required superhuman qualities to have devised a just land settlement in the seventeenth century. It was not even clear cut who was the rebel, who the loyalist, and the Old English in particular claimed that the Catholics had been the only 'loyal subjects'.[139] The Restoration had recognised that much of the land had been legitimately acquired, or re-sold to new owners (many Catholic) who could not then be dispossessed. For most Catholics in Ulster the wrangles over the court of claims and the subsequent Jacobite attempt at reversing earlier land settlements would have been entirely academic. Both campaigns had been driven largely by Old English Catholics, and nothing points up the gulf between them and the Old Irish so much as the former's demands for a return to the situation as it existed in October 1641, by which time all but a few of Ulster's Gaelic Irish proprietors had disappeared. At the rate with which they were selling off their lands, little would have remained to them by the end of the century regardless of the political upheaval.[140] Even in the non-plantation county of Monaghan the Gaelic land-holding system had largely succumbed to more mercenary attitudes by the second decade of the seventeenth century.[141] In County Antrim, cushioned from the full impact of the century's land fluctuations because of the powerful position of its earl, only seven out of the hundred declared forfeit by the Williamite settlement had anything left to lose, and of these six were leaseholders, not outright owners.[142] Any of the sought-for changes in the second half of the century would have made very little difference to the existing proprietorship in Ulster. There was to be no return to the old Gaelic system.

The transformation of Ulster into a predominantly Protestant province in the eighteenth century would also contribute to Ulster Catholicism's distinctive qualities. In the seventeenth century Ireland became the receptacle of the largest movement of population in Europe. That it would have happened without official policies of confiscation and plantation is indisputable. Most land was lost unofficially to aggressive speculation, and the original British settlers of the Ulster Plantation also suffered because of progressive new immigration. The type and intensity of settlement also changed, jumping from 40,000 in 1630 to 270,000 by 1712. The influx of Scottish Presbyterians in the 1690s was to cause one of the most significant indents in what was still a substantially Catholic tenantry, with a massive re-leasing of lands to the new arrivals.[143] But the full impact of the land changes of the seventeenth century took generations to unfold and may not have registered fully with Ulster's Catholic tenantry till the sudden rise of population in the second half of the eighteenth century. The persistent shortage of good tenants would have placed existing ones in a strong position. Archbishop Oliver Plunkett noted this in 1671. 'The peasantry – those who cultivate the land – are all right and it is these who support the priests and friars; they even give some help to those who were once their masters.' But, he added, 'the gentlemen are completely ruined'. Only three had recovered their estates and all were in debt. 'All the others have difficulty in obtaining a lease of a part of their property, and it is regarded as a great favour when they succeed in this.'[144]

It would be difficult to exaggerate the social consequences of the seventeenth-century land settlements for the future of Ulster Catholicism. Only a handful of Catholic landowners survived into the eighteenth century and very soon these too disappeared, most conforming to the established church. The net result was to place the Ulster Catholics on a lower social level than their co-religionists elsewhere in the country. The Catholics of Ulster and adjacent north Connacht were generally the poorest in the country. This, and the absence of the kind of surviving Catholic gentry which sustained an institutionalised Catholic church elsewhere, dictated its different character in Ulster. Ulster never had a significant Old English class, an elite accustomed to the practice of power and politics. The absence of such a political tradition is still felt today. The Protestant gentry in Ulster never had to deal with equals, and the distance between them and the socially inferior Catholics bred unrealistic fears of subversion. The picture of an impoverished Catholic peasantry clinging to the hills is far-fetched. But they had lost their natural social leaders, they were to play little part in the eighteenth century's campaigns for Catholic rights until alerted to them by Catholics from the south and enlightened Presbyterians, and highly charged local resentments against those who got the land have festered to the present day.

5

THE MERGER OF 'IRISHNESS' AND CATHOLICISM IN EARLY MODERN ULSTER

That 'you may learn the sympathy between us modern Catholikes and St Patricke and the Primitive Christians; and on the contrary discover the discrepancy of the Protestants, not only with S. Patricke, whome I am sure they will discarde for a very superstitious papist, but from all the current of the ancient Catholiks, having no more alliance with them than truth with falsehood'.

Introduction to Fr. Rochford's 1625 *Life of Patrick, . . . Brigid . . . Columb* (Jennings, *Michael Ó Cléirigh*, 38)

Fionnuala O Connor's *In Search of a State* (1993) has a revealing interview with a woman from the working-class Catholic community of Ardoyne in north Belfast. She was speaking about the first stages of the Troubles in the early 1970s.

I was in Toby's Hall and a British foot patrol came in. Both sides exchanged insults. A glass was thrown. One soldier panicked and strafed the hall with bullets, leaving one of the crowd dead. Other soldiers outside – thinking themselves under attack – also started firing. When the shooting stopped somebody got up and started to sing an old hymn which was well-known in the Ardoyne. 'Faith of our Fathers'. I think it was to calm people down. Everybody stood and started singing it.

Recalling the incident over twenty years later, she could appreciate the incongruity of the situation.[1] And yet this nineteenth-century hymn was one of great political symbolism for northern nationalists on the eve of the Troubles. It linked fidelity to faith with the sufferings of ancestors. Though commemorating English saints and martyrs (a fact unknown to most Irish Catholics until recently), it had become something of a nationalist battle hymn: suffering, sacrifice and victimisation carrying with them the ultimate promise of victory.

> Our fathers chained in prisons dark,
> Were still in heart and conscience free
> How sweet would be their children's fate,
> If they like them could die for thee.
> Faith of our fathers living still,
> We will be true to thee till death.

The basic premises of later nationalism, of an ancient national faith, of unswerving fidelity and of ultimate triumph had already been laid by the end of the seventeenth century.[2]

Catholicism, like Presbyterianism, experienced intermittent persecution throughout the seventeenth century, the adherents of both projecting remarkably similar self-images as a persecuted people. Tacit if begrudging tolerance was, however, the norm – even under Cromwell. Indeed, it was arguments that Catholicism stood a fairer chance of toleration under Cromwell than under the exiled Stuarts which enlisted papal approval when the Ulster Catholics transferred their support to the Commonwealth.[3] But public displays of Catholic ritual were discouraged and the nascent church reorganisation crumbled. The result was the perpetuation of Ulster Catholicism's peculiarities – so persistently attacked by church authorities – into modern times. As in the eighteenth century so in the seventeenth, state penalisation of Catholicism most directly affected the elite and the social pressures to conform to the religion of one's class eventually eroded the few remaining Catholic gentry in Ulster. But lower down the social scale, traffic was often in the other direction. Although a relatively prosperous tier of Catholic tenants survived the land upheavals of the period, Ulster Catholicism was rapidly becoming the religion of the 'have-nots', mostly of Irish ancestry, but with a significant sprinkling of English and Scots.

Equally, Catholicism is unlikely to have survived at all without the connivance of some Protestant neighbours.[4] How such daily accommodations operated, how indeed the identity, religious or otherwise, of the Ulster Irish evolved in this period is now all but lost to history. The Irish language goes into rapid decline from the seventeenth century, not because of oppression but because the new legal system required the populace to come to terms with the English word and the written document.[5] Irish language culture's most accessible expression is still to be found in the poetry, although before the end of the seventeenth century it is an unsatisfactory source for the opinions of the people at large, and the interests of the patron who had commissioned the work would still have dictated the message. Katharine Simms warns: 'The bards are . . . professional wordsmiths paid to give the patron's desired public image a literary form. Thus a sharp change in tone from medieval warlike compositions of the late sixteenth century to pious preaching of Counter-Reformation morality and Catholic nationalism in the seventeenth does not necessarily reflect a sudden conversion of society at large, so much as the role of Counter-Reformation clerics as parsimonious substitute patrons, when the fall of the Ulster lords left many bards unemployed.'[6] The culture transmitted in these poems is that of a declining elite, for whom loss of land, status and the Gaelic order is a searing experience. Poetic language is often stark and exaggerated, concepts and images pared to their suggestive minimum. Yet the language of such poems had become stereotypical by the nineteenth century, and poets and priests were often one and the same.[7]

It is with these groups that an answer may be found to the question: why did Ulster Irish society not absorb the influx of new people in the seventeenth century as it had so often done in the past? State backing for the new Protestant culture is of course a major factor. But so also is the failure to accommodate the elite of the old culture as had been the original intention. For it was they who had created the pseudo-histories and genealogies to incorporate the *nouveaux arrivés* and had then transmitted such refashioned 'history' to future generations. In the seventeenth century these were the very groups against which most of the penalisation was directed. They were pushed down the social scale and their bitterness helped form the cultural identity of the future.

1. Who were the Catholics of Ulster?

Given the uncertainties of the seventeenth century, it should not surprise that the consequences of developments then were still only unfolding a century later. Nowhere is this more noticeable than in the area of religious identity. Little is known of the relationship between the various religious groupings before 1641. The extreme statements of sectarian identity produced by the events of that year played a formative role in emerging stereotypes. But they are not a reliable window on reality. Neither 'native' nor 'settler' would have had any clearly defined sense of religious identity before 1641.[8]

Nor should one assume that all the new arrivals were necessarily Protestant. Stories abound of Scots Catholics on the Inishowen peninsula of Donegal. They appear to have been on good terms with their Presbyterian neighbours, who by all accounts were just as superstitious – an accusation more normally made, then as now, about Catholics.[9] The religion of the tenancy on an estate was often dictated by that of the landowner. Thus, through the influence of the Catholic Sir George Hamilton of Greenlaw, the Hamilton and Abercorn estates in Tyrone continued to attract Scottish Catholic tenants well into Charles I's reign.[10] The MacDonnells in Antrim provided a haven for Scottish Catholics from the Highlands and the Isles. The Franciscan monastery at Bonamargy, near Ballycastle in north Antrim, was the focal point of a Catholic mission to convert the Scots and by 1640 was reputedly attracting five hundred Scots every year. By 1625 some 20 per cent of Scots settlers were Catholic.[11] Although the tendency was for greater distinctiveness by the end of the seventeenth century, by then there had been significant cultural and religious cross-fertilisation. The image of the Calvinist Scot introducing civilisation and the work ethic into Ulster was a nineteenth-century fabrication to explain the *status quo* then. In reality, the early Scots settlers were closer to their Irish counterparts, in dress, work practices and housing, than to the English.[12] We still do not know whether the new settlers included Gaelic speakers. But Scots – that regional dialect of English which has so affected the Ulster accent – had been present since the high Middle Ages, and was particularly strong in Donegal.[13]

The belief that Protestants were insincere in their religious beliefs, motivated by pure self-interest and reluctant to convert the Irish for fear of losing land and power, was first voiced in the seventeenth century.[14] *Ireland's Case Briefly Stated*, published in Louvain in 1695, by the Jacobite exile Hugh Reily, and popularised in numerous editions over the next century and a half as *The Impartial History of Ireland*, made the point particularly forcefully:

It was Saint Paul's sentiment that *Godliness is great Gain*, but the Reform'd saints of this Age invert the Maxim, and do rather conclude, that *Gain is great Godliness*. Upon this Godly motive it was, that our zealous Reformers went into Ireland to propagate their Gospel, where they took more pains to make

the land turn Protestant [than] the People; the confiscation of Men's estates
... being more beneficial, than the charity of saving their Lives, or reforming
their errors.[15]

In fact, the accusation was less appropriate for Ulster than for any
other province. The migration of people from Scotland in particular
would have occurred and did occur without either the official plantation or the Reformation, and the land transfer had already taken
place before the more overtly religious confiscations of the latter half
of the century. The accusation, however, was to become a central
element in Ulster folklore. Moreover, apart from the hiatus of the
1640s, there were regular attempts at conversion and criticisms of the
Church of Ireland for neglecting the spiritual welfare of 'the poor
Irish'.[16] Lamenting 'what small effect reformation hath taken in this
country', Henry Leslie preaching in Drogheda in 1622 attributed its
failure to 'custom and long continuance in error', 'fear of breaking
with their friends', 'busy trafficking of priests and Jesuits', 'want of
sufficient ministry' and 'miseducation of our youth'.[17]

The lack of Irish-speaking preachers and organisational infrastructure dogged the spread of Counter-Reformation Catholicism and all
but confined any successful Protestant evangelisation to the lowlands,
where native Irish were more influenced by the culture and language
of the settlers. The only Irish-language printing press in Ireland had
mysteriously disappeared – torn apart for heresy by the friars, so it
was rumoured.[18] A partial translation of the Bible was published in
1603, a full version in 1685, but little appears to have been done with
it and a general lack of knowledge of the Bible was one of the things
separating Catholic from Protestant, giving rise to the still-current
accusation that Catholicism is an unscriptural faith. Henry Jones's
antipathy may have been a contributory factor. During the Cromwellian period he was also provost of Trinity College, Dublin, where
Irish-speaking Protestant clergy were to have been trained. He
inherited the completed portions of an Irish translation of the Old
Testament, prepared by his predecessor, Bishop William Bedell –
a supporter of Irish language and culture – but did nothing with
them. Certainly the language problem is an important element in the
development of formal religion, as the respect of the Ulster Irish for

Irish-speaking Protestant divines like Bedell and Ussher illustrates. One might have expected Bedell's funeral in 1642, in the immediate aftermath of the 1641 rebellion, to have been a fraught event. Instead, the 'Irish of Cavan in considerable number' attended, including their main military leaders, respectfully observing the Protestant service and according the burial full military honours.[19]

'Conversion' presupposes some knowledge of the religion one is converting to. The vast majority of Ulster Irish had no knowledge of written language, Irish or English. This essential difference between Protestantism, a religion of text and the written word, and Catholicism, one of the spoken word and oral tradition, was fundamentally to affect the two religious cultures and goes a long way to explaining the failure of the Reformation in Ireland. Religious texts required oral explanation, usually by clergy. Although Ulster was better supplied with Protestant schools than elsewhere, most religious change came through cultural seepage and personal relations. 'Persecution, neglect and mixed marriages' were the causes adduced by the Revd James O'Laverty in his influential nineteenth-century history of Down and Connor to explain why Ulster Catholics turned away from 'the faith of their race'. And many did, large numbers reverting to Catholicism in 1641, and again after the Restoration, suggesting continued fluidity of religious affiliation.[20]

Intermarriage appears to have occurred at every social level and by 1639 Catholic clerics were discussing what provision to make for the children of mixed marriages.[21] Generally the tendency was for the remnants of the native landowning elite to intermarry with and conform to the dominant religion of their class, whilst lower down the social scale the drift was in the opposite direction. Thus the Clandeboye O'Neills, the Ardkeen Savages, the Tollymore Magennises intermarried with English or Scottish Protestants and the land descended through their Protestant heirs.[22] Such elite conversions did not mean an abandonment of Gaelic ways, however, and the Protestant descendants of a number of the Gaelic lords remained patrons of the poets into the eighteenth century. The new Cromwellian tenantry quickly succumbed to cultural pressures to conform to the practices of the society they had joined. The numerous references to Cromwellian soldiers marrying papist women and to widows of English extraction among the transportees to Connacht suggest as much.[23] It was those areas heavily settled by Scots and English that experienced the highest levels of bilingualism, conformity, intermarriage and participation in the new market-orientated culture by the Ulster Irish. In contrast the uplands, where the Irish progressively became concentrated, did not experience such levels of cultural seepage and remained strongholds of Irish culture. Although Gaelic culture would continue to suffuse Catholicism, there were enough English, Old English and Scottish Catholics and enough Ulster-Irish Protestants to make the claim of Catholicism as the religion of the Irish race untenable, even if that was the assumption (or more often the accusation) made by successive governments.

How and when did such fluidity change? The reorganisation of the churches played a part, but the real battle for the popular soul did not develop until the next century, and Presbyterianism, like Catholicism, experienced considerable organisational difficulties.[24] Of more immediate importance were the dramatic demographic changes in Ulster in the course of the seventeenth century. Although considerable numbers of settlers returned to Scotland in times of political tension – notably in the 1630s and 1640s – in the latter half of the century waves of immigration from Scotland (perhaps as many as 80,000 people in the 1660s and a further 50,000–80,000 in the 1690s) altered the religious makeup of the province.[25] This provided a youthful basis for population increase among Presbyterians, while there was a simultaneous decline in the equivalent Irish base with the exile of so many military men after James II's defeat in 1691. By 1732 Ulster had become the predominantly Protestant province of modern times, with an estimated 313,120 Protestants and 192,295 Catholics.[26] There was a corresponding shift of Irish into more marginal lands, concentrating the casualties of a rapidly changing economy. But the main effect of the demographic change was to place those Irish in areas of Scottish penetration in economic dependency on the settlers, for, as W. H. Crawford writes, 'a new layer of tenants had been slipped into the Ulster social pyramid so that most of the Irish paid their rents and duties not to the landlords but to substantial Protestant tenant farmers.'[27] The result was a transformation of Irish attitudes towards the Scots by the end of the seventeenth century. By 1679 Archbishop Plunkett was identifying the Presbyterians as the most anti-Catholic in his province:

The secular clergy have been granted a certain amount of toleration up to now, but in many places, and especially around Armagh, they are considerably harassed . . . so strict are the Presbyterians. The latter are very numerous in these parts . . . one could travel twenty-five miles in my area without finding half-a-dozen Catholic or Protestant families, but all Presbyterians, i.e. strict Calvinists.[28]

Thus in Ulster Irish did the word for Scot (*Albanach*) become that for Protestant, much as *Sasanach* (Englishman) did in Munster Irish. Likewise *Gael* and *Gall* (Irish and foreigner) had come to mean simply 'Catholic' and 'Protestant'.[29] The seventeenth century had thus set in place one of the essential ingredients of Ulster Catholic identity: its confusion between its local Protestant neighbour and some distant imperial state.

However, the image of the suppressed Gael stoking up thoughts of revenge is far-fetched. Participation in the new system, where permitted, was more likely. Poets sought patrons from all quarters. The presence of Ulster-Irish officials in the new legal and administrative system was such that it entirely collapsed in 1641 and that presence continued throughout the century, though in a steadily decreasing form. Even the father of the future Catholic archbishop of Armagh, Hugh MacMahon, acted as a tithe-collector for the Church of Ireland.[30] An awareness of religious difference was slow to emerge. It is most marked among the literate elite and it was they who provided its linguistic parameters.

2. The poetic tradition

The decline of the Gaelic elite brought in its train the disintegration of the bardic order, and it was within the Catholic Church that both dispossessed chiefs and learned men now sought social status. It is only when the main political families such as the O'Neills and the O'Donnells lost their lands that they entered the church in large numbers. They had not done so before. Priests and clerics were now hailed as saviours in a way once reserved for the Gaelic chiefs.[31] The coming together of these two classes of learned men explains the association of religion and dispossession which appears in many of these poems. The poets had long been part of the second league of landowners behind the main chieftains.[32] They were highly politicised as a class, but any new message in their poetry tended to be obscured by the standard themes and motifs of the bardic tradition. By the 1630s, however, the beginnings of non-professional poetry were already visible.[33] As the century wore on, the poets were of recognisably lower status. The metres of the poems changed. They became more comprehensible to the untrained ear and very often were set to music. The diplomatic veneer of the bards disappeared and often the language was stark and bitter. Much of this bitterness was economically driven, reflecting their own impoverishment. They tended to blame the new Protestant or English dispensation for the decline of their order, but were particularly resentful of those Irish who had prospered, thereby establishing a notable theme in future nationalism.

The five political poems from the mid-seventeenth century published by Cecile O'Rahilly in 1952 strike a new note. Only Munster and Ulster are represented – a reflection of the continuation of a literary Gaelic tradition in these regions alone. There is some suggestion that they were composed by continental-trained clerics, and, given their enormous popularity (with transcriptions being made far into the nineteenth century), they clearly had resonance far beyond their time – at least for the literary class. Only one, *An Síogaí Rómhánach*, is of Ulster origin; the other four are from Munster. All are highly propagandistic and politicised. The Munster poems reflect the bitterness of a dispossessed landowning class, the many English loanwords indicating dealings with the new legal system: King's Bench, Assizes, Exchequer, Court of Wards, all tending to the same end, 'the mangling of property'. Another, written on the morrow of the Cromwellian transplantation, reflects the searing impact it had on Munster in particular.[34]

Significantly, *An Síogaí Rómhánach* (c.1650) dwells less on the land than on religion, for little remained of Ulster's Gaelic landed elite. Members of the old noble families were joining the clergy in large numbers, particularly the Franciscans. Therefore when Ulster poets composed poems in praise of certain priests, they were often merely fulfilling their traditional obligation of praising a noble family.[35] *An Síogaí* is scathing of those who did not support Rinuccini's party during the Confederacy, and shows the consciousness of the Ulster clergy to have been far more Rome-centred than that of the rest of the country.

It is an early version of the emotional vision-poem, the aisling, which became the preferred format of the genre after the disappearance of the bardic schools. It tells of a vision of a beautiful maiden by the author as he lay on the tombs of O'Neill and O'Donnell in Rome. She bewails the fate of the Gaels. Why should they, alone of the race of Adam, they who had preserved the faith since Patrick's time, be punished by God, while the 'Saxon brood', the 'Lutherans', 'the heretics' who had 'scoffed at the Mother of the only son', were exalted? Most English monarchs were denounced, from the 'lecherous' Henry and 'whorish' Elizabeth, and the Stuarts fared little better. It is their attack on the mass and the Irish language which is singled out for particular scorn. Then Ulster arose to save them, first with Maguire and Mac-Mahon 'for love of the faith they would not forsake', then with Owen Roe (for whom *An Síogaí* is very much a praise poem). They failed because of the disunity of the Gael – the 'treacherous foreign Gaels [Old English]' – and those clerics who compromised with 'the heretic horde' and were cursed by the papal nuncio. The vision ends with a hope that the Gael will unite 'to drive out the strangers and set Ireland free'.

> Then none shall league with the Saxon,
> Nor with the bald Scot,[36]
> Then shall Erin be freed from settlers,
> Then shall perish the Saxon tongue.
> The Gaels in arms shall triumph
> Over the crafty, thieving, false sect of Calvin.
> . . .
> True faith shall be uncontrolled;
> The people shall be rightly taught
> By friars, bishops, priests and clerics.

Unlike the Munster poems, however, the poem ends on a passive note of despair – the poet is too weak, too alone to fulfil the maiden's dream. It is a theme which was to be a characteristic of Ulster poetry, a symbol perhaps of the passive nature of Ulster Catholicism which future commentators would note. Whereas the English are the over-arching threat, the poem speaks of the Scot with the petty jealousy of a neighbour. He is 'crafty', 'thieving', 'shitty', 'cowardly' – a significant shift from the early years of the century when some thought the plantation was a government ruse to sour relations between Irish and Scots 'who from ancient times were on most friendly terms . . . and to unite the Scotch and English against the Irish'.[37] The association of religion and culture, and the reduction of the generalised bardic theme of expelling the foreigner to the more specific English-speaking 'churl' and 'Luther's' and 'Calvin's brood', marks a significant break with the literary past. Hugh O'Neill does not figure prominently in popular oral tradition. It is quite the reverse with Owen Roe, who linked faith and fatherland and was represented as such in the poetry. It would take time to evolve into the embittered nationalism of Art Bennett's poetry in the nineteenth century, but the direct evolutionary link to the component themes is unmistakable.[38]

Although later versions of these poems are often criticised as unreliable, it is wrong to think their central themes twisted to suit later anti-English nationalism. There was no need to manufacture the bitterness of the elite at loss of land or religious persecution. Indeed, the early texts are far more insulting about the Protestant settlers. What the later versions have done is to remove most of the personal insults, the uncouth, scatological elements, thought to debase the noble message which the early nineteenth-century translators wished to convey. The intense regionalism (so prominent in seventeenth-century Ulster Irish), the dislike of the Scots as much as the English, have also been toned down and a more simplified message conveyed of the suppression of the Gael by the Saxon. The publication of *An Síogaí Rómhánach* in Hardiman's *Irish Minstrelsy* of 1831 was a landmark in this filtering process, since subsequent translations and transcripts tended to follow this version. Hardiman set out to portray Irish poetry as a dignified tradition destroyed by the English. The translations 'for the most part transmuted the originals into pallid imitations of Thomas Moore in an attempt to make them seem respectable by the standards of the day'.[39]

Transitional poets were the blind poet-harpist Séamus Dall Mac Cuarta (McCourt, c.1650–1733), born at Omeath in north Louth, and Patrick McAlindon (c.1665–1733), born in the Fews, south Armagh. Neither had yet fallen to the impoverished position of their immediate successors, and McAlindon appears to have been a prosperous farmer who gave hospitality and support to a host of lesser poets in the region.[40] Both were also accomplished harpists, ardent Jacobites and devout Catholics. McAlindon's home was regularly used for religious services and his most historically interesting works were often poems praising the clergy. Mac Cuarta's family had traditionally close links with the Franciscans and his devotion and sobriety were legendary. An analysis of the language used by poet and priest reveals the close identification which is occurring in these years (even if the priest who does not live up to the ideal continues to be the butt of satire). The use of the word 'heretic' as a blanket description for Protestants appears early in clerical material, matched by the equally prevalent use of 'papist' for Irish in Protestant sources. The beginnings of the '800 years of English tyranny' concept, traceable back to Henry II and the bull Laudabiliter, also appears in early seventeenth-century Ulster clerical and exile literature prior to its adoption by the poets.[41]

McAlindon's praise-poem for Hugh MacMahon, Catholic archbishop of Armagh, 1715–37, A Rí lér fuasclaíodh, contains the usual (by now) references to heretics and Luther and the association of Ireland's plight with that of the people of Israel.[42] He points to MacMahon's noble lineage, suggesting that this head of the church in Ireland has inherited the mantle of the Gaelic princes of old. McAlindon's clear support for Armagh, in yet another episode in the long-running controversy with Dublin over which episcopal see merited metropolitan status, reflects the strong provincial pride of these transitional poems. The steadfastness of Ulster is compared to the weakness of the south, which sold out on so many occasions, from Dermot MacMurrough's 'evil deed' in inviting in the Anglo-Normans in the twelfth century, to its refusal to assist Owen Roe 'in sustaining the faith of Christ against Oliver Cromwell'. The metre of a number of McAlindon's poems suggests that they were consciously written for popular consumption. Politically they are firmly Jacobite, but pessimistic about Ireland's ability to help herself.[43]

But beside such fatalism a powerful reorientation of popular culture was taking place. Keating's reordering of the past was part of an increasing identification of race and religion. It is epitomised in Mac Cuarta, the most religious of these transitional poets and undoubtedly the most popular. Lineage and rightful belonging is pitted against foreign possession, 'deceiving English law', and a heretic religion.[44] Mac Cuarta's poems deal with the apparent finality of defeat under King William. The bones of the true nobility lie scattered at Aughrim or in ruined castles, the very land itself abandoning them in the bleakness of defeat. As in bardic poetry, land and people have lost their vigour and bountifulness 'under the domination of the heretics' and 'the puffed-up New English'.[45] Houses which once provided hospitality to poet and cleric have adopted the new culture, language and religion. 'I cannot understand your Gaelic, so speak in the foreign manner', the returning poet is told, as he denounces the house's inhospitality and preference for 'prayers . . . explained in English' and a 'foreign Bible' over a clergy, with powers delegated from Christ, 'reading the passion' in Irish and administering the sacraments. Such refusal to change consigns your people to serfdom, responds the house. No, retorts the poet:

> . . . the English-speaking stock,
> it was who left the Gaels as serfs,
> their rents, their riches, their wealth, their property,
> it is you who have their value.

But like the Israelites in Egypt, such bondage will end: 'The saints and true clerics [my italics] say/ that the Englishry will be destroyed.'[46]

The numerous priests celebrated in Mac Cuarta's poems (even those of Old English extraction) possess 'the noble blood of the Gaels', reaching back to the Milesians.[47] And that true Gaelic blood has the imprint of Rome, linking them to the early church and a wider Catholic community on the Continent. His praise-poem for James O'Sheil, bishop of Down and Connor, 1717–24, also guardian of the Franciscan houses at Downpatrick and Dromore, is particularly significant, since O'Sheil was also involved in a public controversy concerning Catholicism as 'the only religion that is truly conformable to the express word of God'.[48]

> Your trumpet is sweeter in Rome
> and in Louvain of the orders amongst the clergy,
> than in Ireland to Luther and John,[49]
> who would extinguish the right by means of lies.

> Dear, wise Colm Cille,
> the good son of the king of Inis Fáil;
> your ancestry is the same as his –
> with Niall of the gold your lines separated.[50]

Nearly all the leading Ulster Catholic families appear in Mac Cuarta's poems as the unjustly deposed and rightful heirs of the true Gael. His litany also includes Gaelicised Scots like the MacDonnells, the O'Boyles and the MacSweeneys, and Old English like the Flemings of County Meath. Mac Cuarta lived on Fleming's Slane estate until it was lost under King William, so the poet felt the impact of the new Williamite dispensation particularly keenly.[51] But it is the O'Neills of the Fews and the Magennises of Iveagh who take pride of place – suggesting continued patronage of the poets by the descendants of both families – their priests and above all those who had gone into exile after the defeat of James II. Hope now lies with them and Mac Cuarta sets the tone for subsequent Irish-language poetry in his call for them to return with the hosts of Spain and France to free them from the foreigners:

> May I not retreat to the grave until I see hosts
> coming in victorious strength to pleasant Ireland;
> the kindred of Owen Roe in their ships [full] of true worthies
> who will place hundreds of foreigners in a new subjection.
> I'd be happy to be gazing
> on long-eared Britain running in terror from us;
> and the triumphant champion as leader of the hosts
> proclaiming a new battle against swarthy heretics.[52]

Mac Cuarta's poetry reflects the scale and finality of the defeat inflicted by the new order on the Jacobite cause and its Irish supporters, and the battle of Aughrim fought on 12 July 1691 – possibly the bloodiest episode of Irish history when over 7,000 were killed by the Williamite forces – haunts his verse. 'Aughrim of the slaughter' introduces his most popular poem: 'A lament for Sorley MacDonnell' (1691). A powerful poem which lists the members of the noble families who fell at Aughrim, it interlinks MacDonnell's death with the passion of Christ, the sufferings of the Christian martyrs, 'the only faith of Patrick', with Cú Chulainn and the people of the *Táin*. The poem is as elitist in content as the bardic poetry of old, for the lament is for the nobles who patronised the poets and clergy, but of its popularity there can be no doubt, for it survives in a staggering forty-one known manuscripts.[53]

However, in an exchange with another poet, Hugh MacGerrity, on whether the tories were the true descendants of the Gaelic nobility (as Mac Cuarta claimed), he comes off much the worse. To a small band of tories under their leader McDaid, Mac Cuarta attributes the standard virtues of the nobility: generosity to the poets, valour, vigour, comeliness, defying 'the men of England ... and all the greatest attorneys', holding the fort 'until the Gaels arrive with the prayers of the clergy/ on the waves from afar to liberate us'. Nonsense, responds MacGerrity, there is nothing noble about them. Their 'proper status' is 'applying their talents to the shovel'. 'Ugly churlish crouchers', 'setting themselves up as nobility', where were they when the true nobility was fighting with James? They wouldn't know how to read a letter or poem; they confront no enemy, but pass their time 'plundering the cattle of every tenant', and are scorned by 'the old women of Cooley and Carlingford'.[54] The tories, in other words, were committing that mortal sin of Gaelic society: getting above their station.

Many poems had already become popular songs by the end of the seventeenth century: 'infamous ballads ... bawled about the streets' composed by 'hired wretched scribblers' and prophesying the destruction of Protestantism.[55] By the time we reach Art MacCooey (*c.* 1738–73) and Peadar Ó Doirnín (*c.*1700–69) the remnants of the old poetic order have entirely disappeared. Although there are signs that Mac-Cooey was educated in one of the classical hedge-schools (and a very definite familiarity with *An Síogaí Rómhánach*), there are few literary flights in MacCooey. Most of his poems were written for singing and they were still being sung in the twentieth century.[56] MacCooey's poetry is rich in detail about the preoccupations of the Catholic poor. Indeed, he is the nearest we can get to a peasant poet. His family were small farmers in Creggan (Fews barony), south Armagh. But Art would have appeared to both Protestants and well-off Catholics as the archetypal feckless papist, drinking himself to an early grave, living from hand-to-mouth on odd jobs as a gardener, herdsman, or *spailpín* (a migrant harvest labourer), and praising (and expecting to receive) the old 'hospitality' to which poets traditionally laid claim. Although the most common theme in his poetry is a lament for the final destruction of the Gael at Aughrim and the Boyne (above all the O'Neills of the Fews), like other Ulster poetry in Irish, it is not a call to arms, but a nostalgic lament. Even his editor, the late Cardinal Ó Fiaich, thought his poetry 'a form of escapism'.[57] In his *Castle of Glasdrummond* (a former O'Neill castle), the ruined walls tell the poet:

> I shall not be restored in future, I will be swept away
> With all the loyal noble sons who won renown in me,
> They are under the slabs in Creggan and I'll not see them
> till death there.

Nor is there that mystical bitterness for the loss of land deemed to be naturally theirs, but the immediate problem of Catholics renting *any* land under the penal laws, particularly in the densely populated area of south Armagh. MacCooey speaks of 'the land sighing in sorrow/ our leases and our happiness yielding to the contemptuous brood'. Notable too is the way in which social, linguistic, cultural and religious loss are intertwined. Thus in his *Aisling Airt Mhic Cumhaigh*:

> My heart is shattered in a hundred thousand pieces,
> and even balsam will not ease my pain
> when I hear Irish all being abandoned,
> and a torrent of English in everyone's mouth,
> Wully and Jane are taking leases,
> on the lands of Ireland of the lovely golden spots,

and when I make enquiries I receive the reply:
'You're a Papist, I know not thee.'

The last line is in English in the original. Most of the English loanwords in other poems of the post-bardic era reflect similar insults, and Mac-Cooey was not the only one to express Catholic resentment at the word 'papist'.

His most bitter satire on the new Protestant culture is his allegorical dispute between the ruined medieval Catholic church at Faughart, County Louth, and the Anglican church at Forkhill – *Tagra an dá Theampall* or 'The Argument of the Two Churches'. In this the 'Foreign Temple' addresses the 'Roman Churchyard' in curt, abusive English. It is both 'Popery's vain devotion' and 'ignorant papist notions' which are responsible for the decay of its people's fortune and culture:

> My flock has estates, with land and demesnes,
> all riding in state in their coaches,
> while taxes arrears, and cesses severe
> upon your Gaedhelian broaches.[58]

The contrast he draws is that between the antiquity, nobility and cultured Roman faith and the novelty, worldliness and boorishness of Protestantism. MacCooey's poems contain all the stock references to Calvin, Luther, Henry VIII and Anne Boleyn, heretics, churls and foreigners.

However, one would be hard put to find in MacCooey some proto-type nationalist rebel. His resentments are often social rather than religious and the Catholic made good was the butt of one of his most vicious satires: 'The Churls of the Barley' – directed at the O'Callaghans, successful distillers and entrepreneurs in south Armagh. Much of his spite may have been caused by the failure of the *nouveaux riches* – unlike the gentry of old – to entertain the poets ('the breed and the seed of the vipers/ who threaten each day and never would pay/ a penny to poets or pipers'). But Art Bennett was to take up the theme from MacCooey and the O'Callaghans entered nationalist tradition as unpatriotic (a tradition totally without foundation).[59]

Also MacCooey, like so many other Ulster Irish, was not so

consumed with bitterness that he could not develop a *modus vivendi* with his Protestant neighbours. He was even married by a Protestant clergyman (a not uncommon event among Catholics, who resented the high level of priests' fees). Indeed, in one poem he suggests that he was even on the point of converting to Presbyterianism. His praise of the clergy (particularly the Franciscans), if from old noble (even Old English) stock, is unstinted. But those he considers upstarts receive the same verbal lashing as their secular counterparts, and his celebrated satire on Mary Quinn, the sister and housekeeper of the parish priest of Creggan, flailed the two for aping the new rich whilst fleecing the Catholic poor. The fact that the Revd Lawrence Taaffe, vicar-general of Armagh, had to intervene to defuse the situation is testimony to the power the poet could still wield as late as the 1760s. However, for a poet to so openly attack a priest in this way was highly unusual and he risked victimisation of his family by his community if he did so.[60]

All these key poets had come from old Oriel – the south Ulster/ north Leinster borderlands of Monaghan, south Armagh and Louth. Literary scholars have noted a greater bitterness in the poems of such Gaelic areas juxtaposed with more Anglicised areas.[61] This was an area where enough Old English landowners survived to act as patrons and protectors of poet and priest alike, and where the poets still thought of themselves as an elite.[62] The importance of such poetry cannot be overestimated, particularly that of the seventeenth-century transitional poets. It was known and admired by succeeding poets and scribes and set the tone and many of the themes for the future.[63] Their importance gathered pace as the poems began to be printed and translated from the end of the eighteenth century (feeding and inspiring Irish Romanticism). But what we are dealing with here are the 'hits' of Irish poetry, selected by the scribes, who did not usually concern themselves with the writings of lesser individuals. The corpus of the work of Simon Macken, a scribe and schoolmaster in County Fermanagh (active 1770s – 1820s) would have been typical. Among his transcriptions of popular medieval romance tales, various catechisms and continental devotional works, some tales and poems on death and the otherworld, humorous skits and burlesques, and the usual love poems and drinking songs, we find two poems attacking those who changed their religion, poems by Mac Cuarta (including his 'A Lament for Sorley MacDonnell') and MacCooey's *Tagra an dá Theampall* ('The Argument of the Two Churches'). No local folk poem or song is included. Macken, a linguistic purist, clearly despised such verse and is known to have transcribed only one during his lifetime.[64]

3. Persecution and 'political' Catholicism

In the first half of the seventeenth century Catholicism in Ireland did not experience major persecution. The oath of supremacy in the terms of the Ulster Plantation was not generally administered, the London companies even building mass-houses and receiving 'Popish priests' at their tables, as one aggrieved planter complained in 1631.[65] Active persecution returned under Cromwell, particularly in the initial stages of the military campaign (1649–50), when a number of priests and regulars were executed. The main difference during the first years of Cromwellian rule (1649–58) – and it was a difference commented upon by contemporaries – was that for the first time the laws could not be evaded.[66] Thereafter clerics were more likely to be exiled, and though the country was not entirely cleared of priests, their numbers were greatly reduced and the reorganisation of previous decades collapsed. Cromwell recognised the contradiction this posed to his general policy of liberty of conscience, and though 'popery' was not permitted such liberty and various acts of abjuration and discovery were placed on the statute book, there was a relaxation of official policy after 1654, and evidence of priests returning from exile. The persecution was short-lived, and, in the view of Monsignor Patrick Corish in what is the best short account of Irish Catholicism in this period, scarcely lived up to 'the national legend of Cromwellian ruthlessness'.[67] None the less, it helped establish the emotive tradition of the mass-rock and the hunted priest which until recently deterred dispassionate enquiry.[68] The effect on church organisation, however, was catastrophic. The synods held on the return to toleration at the Restoration (1660) record a reversion to 'superstitious' practices and widespread ignorance of the fundamentals of the faith.[69] It took over a century for church structure to recover.

For the next three decades tolerance and 'connivance'[70] was the norm. Political rather than religious conformity was the test, and most government officials recognised that, given the numbers of Catholics, their clergy required practical tolerance, 'since they must have Romish clergie whylst they are papists'.[71] For most of the seventeenth century private practice of Catholicism was tolerated, but public demonstrations or anything too ostentatious might provoke new restrictions. Responding to a complaint by the Spanish ambassador to London concerning recent edicts against Catholic clergy in Ireland, the future Charles I 'said he did not really know what prompted his father to issue such an edict, but he thought the occasion for it was a procession held by a bishop in Ireland with cross and lights etc.'.[72] Plunkett was irritated by those priests who drew attention to themselves by annoying the Protestants. Not until William and Mary's reign after 1688 did penalisation become systematic. How then can we explain the execution of Primate Oliver Plunkett in 1681, which was so out of character with the policy of the period, particularly since Plunkett was undoubtedly the most amenable Catholic bishop of the century where government was concerned?

The Ulster clergy (particularly the Franciscans) resented the appointment of an Old English outsider like Plunkett to the archbishopric of Armagh and they made innumerable complaints to Rome in ensuing years.[73] His absence from surviving Gaelic poetry (when nearly every other archbishop of Armagh was celebrated) is noteworthy. His preference for Protestant gentry and government supporters over his native Irish co-religionists was a particular charge made against him, and he would undoubtedly have attracted the taunt of 'Castle Catholic' – one who had gone over to the enemy or joined the system – had such a term of abuse then existed. There can be no doubt that his care to placate the authorities moderated government policy towards the Catholics and was appreciated by the higher clergy in particular.[74] Yet his bitter disputes with the Franciscans have given rise to a belief that they were responsible for his downfall. Certainly such internal bickerings were not unwelcome to the authorities. The Lord Lieutenant, the Earl of Essex, did not consider these friars the dangerous popish conspirators of English parliamentary propaganda. They 'alwaise have their little wrangles with the secular clergy', he wrote in his protest against the proclamation of 1673 banishing bishops and regulars.[75] He also made a personal appeal on behalf of Plunkett, 'who seems to me to be one of the best men of his persuasion . . . of a more peaceable temper and more conformable to government than any of their titular bishops in this country'.[76] Despite such disputes, however, and the presence of one renegade friar among the witnesses against him, the charges against Plunkett of plotting a French invasion were entirely manufactured in England. They were the Irish angle of the 'popish plot' devised by opposition English politicians to exclude the future James II from the throne. Plunkett was acquitted by a Protestant jury in Dundalk and the witnesses against him were utterly discredited. But a re-trial in London found him guilty of treason and he was executed at Tyburn on 1 July 1681.[77] His arrest and execution can only be explained by the rabid anti-popery of the English House of Commons, which even Charles II found impossible to control.

The authorities in Ireland had acquiesced in the implementation of security measures demanded by the discovery of the so-called 'plot'. A new proclamation ordered bishops and regulars to leave the country and a large number were arrested. Catholics were forbidden to keep weapons and mass-houses in towns were closed. But the English witch-hunt was not replicated in Ireland and, sporadic scares apart, the tendency to ignore inoperable laws and respect 'due process of the law' marked the entire penal era. Local magistrates seemed confused about the laws and the constant reminders suggest patchy implementation. In 1682 Franciscan vicar-general of Armagh, Bernard McGurk, defied the laws for the expulsion of regulars by taking the precaution of informing the local magistrate of any meetings held with his clergy and inviting official observance. This, and his acquittal of 'foreign jurisdiction' at successive assizes, highlights such confusion, and despite the high sheriff's determination to have him convicted, Lord Mountjoy ordered his release. He cannot simply be tried at one assize after another for the same offence, he argued: 'I believe this Maguirke a great rogue, but if he were a devil he must have right.'[78] He was to die in prison in February 1713 at the age of ninety, but his re-arrest the previous September gave rise to similar reminders that he had been acquitted of all charges at the earlier assizes. Nor were Catholics above taking their own priests before 'the Protestant tribunals' or themselves benefiting from the rewards offered for the capture of priests. Terence

Kelly, vicar-general of Derry, had used this very threat against successive primates to prevent his removal for misconduct.[79]

But if the measures against religion were easy enough to evade,
the political and material discrimination against Catholics had now
become part of the fabric of society. The historiography of the hunted
priest and the mass-rock tends to miss this point. Given the unformed
nature of Catholicism for much of the seventeenth century, the incursion of militant continental Catholicism with Owen Roe O'Neill and
Rinuccini gave a false impression of its political dimensions and cast a
long shadow over ecclesiastical and political relations. Not all the
Ulster clergy supported the extreme stance of Rinuccini; but most
did, and the northern province acquired a reputation for political
extremism thereafter. This was, and remained, the touchstone of anti-
popery: could Catholics be loyal to a Protestant state, given their
recognition of papal jurisdiction? Periodically acts were passed requiring Catholics to 'abjure' or renounce the Pope's temporal power, just
as the Black Act of 1639 had required the Presbyterians to renounce
certain beliefs before their political loyalty could be accepted. This
'foreign jurisdiction' or perceived political threat from international
Catholicism had already become part of New English propaganda;
but it was not fully developed as a popular war-cry until the Williamite
campaign of the 1690s introduced the full force of Dutch fears about the
progress of the Counter-Reformation.[80] The Jesuits certainly upheld the
right to depose an unjust ruler. Similar Presbyterian teaching put them
into the same category of potential traitors. But such conditional loyalty,
even if it was generally believed, and there is evidence of confusion about
papal authority even among the clergy themselves,[81] went against the
dominant political ethos of the seventeenth century. This presumed the
undivided sovereignty of the divine-right monarch, which required
religious as well as political loyalty. Even against such a background of
heightened religious tension, however, Catholic clergy resorted to the
time-old subterfuge of asserting that they were seculars or had been
ordained at home, and we find Ulster priests who had been attainted
in 1691 still registered for the same parishes in 1704.[82] Protestant
perceptions of Catholics as masters of subterfuge, dissemblers,
wheeler-dealers may well have had their origins in the daily accommodations which permitted a fragile religious tolerance.

The Old English had a long tradition of compromise with the English crown. The few remaining Old Irish gentry followed the same course. The difference was that the latter's almost total loss of political leadership gave excessive power to the clergy. The Old English would have been happy with tacit toleration. The Rinuccini party sought to make Catholicism the established religion and rejected the peace offered in 1646 by the Lord Lieutenant, the marquis of Ormond, which did not grant it. Rinuccini then excommunicated those who had subscribed to it, convincing Ormond that this was 'papal jurisdiction in action'.[83] But Rinuccini was an extremist. The Old English Catholics who dominated James II's Irish parliament of 1689 did not seek to create an established Catholic Church, or to deprive the Church of Ireland of its property. Rather they sought liberty of conscience for all, and the more moderate Catholic demands for religious and civil liberty were to remain the hallmark of Catholic relief campaigns for the next one hundred and forty years. The memory of the Rinuccini split in the Confederation and Ulster's role in transferring support to the Commonwealth dictated Ormond's religious policies thereafter, and he dominated the political scene until his death in 1688. Thus began a policy towards the Catholics which was pursued by successive governments until the nineteenth century: wooing those prepared to accommodate Protestant rejection of papal authority and playing upon internal Catholic disagreements to isolate the ultras.

Generally speaking, those areas which retained a Catholic gentry tended to be politically moderate. That gentry was usually Old English and disagreements over allegiance invariably fell along the traditional Old English–Old Irish fault lines, with the former quite ready to abandon the latter as they had already done over the Restoration land settlement. Since the Reformation had thrown the clergy into economic dependence on the richer Catholic laity, they too were similarly divided, supporting such gentry in areas where they had survived, remaining more politically 'turbulent' in areas like Ulster where they had not.[84] Issue was joined in 1661 when the Catholic gentry and some clergy proposed a loyal 'Remonstrance' to the restored monarchy, to prove that Catholicism was not incompatible with loyalty to a Protestant king.[85] In fact, many Catholics had little difficulty with declarations of allegiance or loyalty. But the issue of finding a satisfactory formula always foundered on Protestant belief that they could not serve two masters. Simple declarations, even oaths, of loyalty were deemed insufficient by the authorities, and, as with the Remonstrance controversy, specific rejection of any external papal power was required. The issue was clouded by continuing rifts left over from the Confederate War (1641–53). At the centre of the controversy was the archbishop of Armagh, Edmund O'Reilly, an ardent supporter of Rinuccini and mediator with the Cromwellians against Ormond, rendering him *persona non grata* with the restored Stuarts.[86] Against him was the Franciscan Peter Walsh, an opponent of Rinuccini. Following O'Reilly's lead, most of the clergy rejected the Remonstrance. Yet they accepted part of a compromise set out by the Sorbonne, declaring the king's divine right in temporal matters and rejecting the deposing power of the Pope, only to have it rejected by Ormond and the Pope alike. This very public confrontation simply perpetuated the notion of Catholic disloyalty and provoked leading Catholic laity to accuse the more ultramontane Ulster clerics of supplying the justification for continued persecution. In fact, there was a great lack of clarity throughout Europe about the relationship between the papacy and secular rulers of whatever denomination and some fifteen to twenty priests in Ireland took the 1708 oath of abjuration before the Pope's condemnation of it arrived.[87]

Dithering by the papacy only contributed to the confusion. Thus the Pope could reject the Irish compromise accepted even by O'Reilly, yet discipline the Franciscan author of a thesis at Louvain which asserted the Pope's supremacy over secular power. On the whole successive popes were anxious to avoid giving cause for persecution of Catholics. At the height of the Remonstrance controversy the Pope authorised a circular letter to the Irish clergy and nobility denouncing as malicious those who argued the impossibility of Catholics combining loyalty to king and pope.[88] James III's continued claim to monarchical rights to nominate Catholic bishops to Ireland encountered papal resistance for this very reason.[89] In essence this conflict between Old English Gallicanism (or acceptance of some state involvement in church organisation) and the ultramontanism (or unfettered papal authority) favoured by the Ulster clergy continued in some form until resolved in favour of the latter in the nineteenth century. But this was high church, high state politics, of little relevance to ordinary laymen, save those with any property left to lose. The way in which it dominates the printed literature is a further indication of the ecclesiastical dominance of Irish Catholic historiography over the past century. In this both Ormond and Walsh are arch-villains and even the late Cardinal Ó Fiaich succumbs to this overriding tendency by clerical scholars to back the anti-Remonstrants.[90]

4. The sacred and the secular in emerging Catholic identity

Free of the kind of control which made the Anglican Church in England and the Catholic Church in France extensions of state departments, free of the Inquisition to pull deviants into line with the Counter-Reformation, the Irish Catholic Church developed apart. Intermittent persecution – aimed most consistently at the hierarchy and papal jurisdiction – postponed Tridentine reforms indefinitely. The limited restructuring which had taken place under the first two Stuarts collapsed after 1641, and Plunkett had barely started to rebuild episcopal authority under the Restoration when it fell apart again under renewed persecution. Ulster was considered the most backward part of Ireland by ecclesiastical criteria. By 1704 only one bishop remained.[91] All the 'abuses' for which the Ulster church had been noted in the Middle Ages persisted, and the difficulties of the times reinforced existing tendencies for excessive interference by the laity. The tendency for the laity to regard the church as a localised family fiefdom had persisted since the arrival of Christianity, and 'lay' claims to the right to nominate priests continued to be made into the nineteenth century. In this the 'inferior clergy' were as much disputees with their superiors as the people, those of Inishowen developing an ingenious justification. 'The inferior clergy pretend to constitute their superior by their own election', wrote the parson of Inishowen to the Protestant Bishop of Derry in November 1682, 'and by this artifice and evasion think to secure themselves from the penalty of the law for extolling of and exercising foreign jurisdiction.'[92]

Poverty and persecution forced the clergy into even closer dependence on the laity, and both became common justifications for living among their relatives.[93] This was a laity, moreover, now devoid of its gentry class (amongst whom the Counter-Reformation had made most progress). Catholicism had become a religion of cabins, as Rinuccini dismissively referred to it.[94] It scarcely did much for a bishop's dignity, to be left wondering in his granary hide-out (as Plunkett did in 1674) whether he would be fed by his peasant protector or left to fast if his host drank away his earnings at the local market.[95] Poverty also adversely affected the quality of the clergy. By the beginning of the eighteenth century Ulster had the lowest number of continental-trained clergy in the country. The former gentry were too poor to fund their sons' education abroad, and bursaries at such seminaries were usually confined to families of the benefactors, which effectively restricted Counter-Reformation training to the elite and put the poorer Ulster students at a decided disadvantage. Archbishop O'Reilly even suggested the sale of hidden chalices in 1660 to fund such continental training.[96]

It clearly did not deter vocations, for if anything the Ulster church was oversupplied with clergy, and successive bishops complained about the inability of the Catholic laity to support them.[97] It was rather the quality of candidates which produced most criticism. The Ulster clergy's lack of education was legendary. Plunkett waxes lyrical about it. The Franciscans, still the most powerful element on his arrival, remained the butt of his criticisms, as they had done of all Old English clerics. It was also the topic of an extremely popular contemporary satire, *Mac Clave of Aughnamullen*, reputedly composed by the reforming Armagh cleric and poet, Owen O'Donnelly. He was typical of a number of priest-poets of the seventeenth century, his family having been Gaelic lords, closely attached to the Tyrone O'Neills, now producing dynasties of clerics. As evident from his verse, he had all the contempt of his class for the lowly born.

The satire concerns the advice given to 'Red Arsey Litis ... Sean son of Brian son of Fiachra son of Gloomy Donal son of Sean son of Turlagh etc.' on how he can change his miserable existence for the comfortable one of a priest, despite his lowly birth and lack of education. Simply 'pick up a little Latin from me ... [and] you can be a fully-fledged priest like the rest of them', he is advised. And as further inducement he is told the story of a low-born peasant, whose innumerable relatives push him forward to fill a vacant parish. His only qualifications are 'seven years a clerk of water and wafers' to the recently deceased incumbent, 'as well as that he is very plentiful with *amen* during Mass and likewise at a baptism or marriage'. The bishop cudgels him for his ignorance, which the ill-educated relatives mistake for ordination with his crozier and fall down on their knees to receive the blessing of the new priest. 'And he raised his hand cleverly and cleric-wise, smartly and pious over their heads and gave them general absolution.' The moral: you do not need a continental education to minister to the common people.[98] Certainly it would appear that the kind of religious instruction reaching the people was highly irregular. The low-born or worldly priest remained a common theme in poetic satire over the next century. But *Mac Clave* also captures that unquestioning reverence for the cleric which was such a feature of Ulster Catholicism.

Rigidly Tridentine in his separation of private and public religion, Plunkett seriously misconceived the nature of Ulster's Catholicism, in particular the strength of its societal and familial network. His comments bore many similarities to traditional English and Protestant criticism, a feckless church for a feckless people. He mistook the easy relations of the Franciscans with the local community for indiscipline. The ancient traditions of hospitality had always frayed into excess at the edges. But they were still strong in Ulster and there were clear expectations that the clergy should fulfil the role once held by the now dispersed gentry. Conviviality, drinking, meetings in taverns by the clergy all figure prominently in Plunkett's complaints. But there is a sense here of the 'outsider' of which the Ulster clergy complained, of the hierarchy standing apart from the people as they were to do in so many incidences over ensuing centuries, and it is hard at times to escape the conclusion that Plunkett was a social snob. He was most comfortable amongst the nobility – Protestant and Catholic alike – and, as was traditional for Catholic archbishops of Armagh, he resided in County Louth (where a Catholic gentry survived). There can be no doubt that his good relations with government officials moderated the application of penal legislation, and his mediation ensured that Ulster suffered less in this respect than Munster. It is equally true that the accusations of toadying to the Protestant authorities had much foundation in fact. Plunkett was highly sensitive to Protestant criticisms of popular Catholic religious practices. The Protestant and Catholic reformations had, after all, come from the same stable. The tight, centralised and controlled church which finally emerged in the nineteenth century was not a natural development from a society more accustomed to a highly localised and personal religion.

For most Ulster Irish, religious belief and practice had changed little from medieval times. The poems, like the ecclesiastical correspondence, reflect the concerns of the elite. There is little information on the interaction of people and clergy, and often no documentary evidence for priests who have nevertheless left their mark on folklore.[99] And yet it is with these clerics that the emerging identification of popular Catholicism with Gaeldom may lie. What knowledge we have of the lower clergy in Ulster reveals whole dynasties of former erenach and termon families or cadet branches of other leading Gaelic families continuing to supply most of the clergy.[100] It is clear that some of them adapted church teachings to local situations, as hinted at in the various ecclesiastical decrees condemning clergy who preached that the activities of the tories or thefts from Protestants were not sins.[101]

Plunkett was a very active primate and his many letters to Rome and to successive internuncios in Brussels are a mine of information on the state of religion in Ulster. But they only allow us to skim the surface, because they are largely regulatory, determined by an ideal of institutionalised religion that did not exist in reality. His early letters speak volumes for the collapse of ecclesiastical discipline: some 60,000 people unconfirmed in the archdiocese, tales of very old men in remote parishes who had never seen a bishop, and everywhere often untrained Franciscans administering the sacraments. The 'ancient custom' of questing for alms he found particularly offensive at a time when those Catholics with leases were supporting the now impoverished former nobles as well as their own and the established church's clergy (through tithes). And surely the practices of saying masses in private houses to increase fees or interrupting mass to inveigle alms from the congregation and cursing the ungenerous went against everything ordained at Trent?

There is hardly a Sunday in the Year that the Franciscans, Dominicans or Augustinians, etc., do not quest at the altar for barley, corn, lambs, geese, hens, onions, etc., and even the Franciscans of the Reform quest for money and put it in their pockets. They have an Our Father and Hail Mary said at the Mass for whoever speaks up first, and gives grain or a giulio, they hurl threats whenever the people are slow to give – they say 'may the devil close your mouths, your hearts and your purses!' In fine, it is a most indecent business.[102]

Drunkenness and worldliness were common failings in the clergy, and again the Franciscans came top of Plunkett's list of transgressors. 'Novices are taken in at random without any selection, and they are not trained as they should be . . . Certain friars do nothing else all day in those convents except scratch their tummies.'[103] What has become of 'the holy rule of Saint Francis', he lamented, when 'in your convents here hardly a priest is found who does not himself use a horse and have a servant on horseback', and many 'buy themselves, at considerable expense, rich clothing of French material . . . adorned with woven goffered fringes, and such like.'[104]

This was the Tridentine version of the Europe-wide diatribe against the worldly and dissolute friar, who became the synonym for Catholicism in the critical literature of the Enlightenment. It appears too in *Mac Clave* (unsurprisingly, since O'Donnelly was one of Plunkett's ordinands), as Arsey is intoned in the virtues of the ideal priest. 'As for the learned folk in your congregation, they will overlook your ignorance of Latin, your scarcity of learning . . . because they find you good, cheerful, and a fat mast-fed pig of Manannan in public taverns . . . stretching the neck of every bottle.'[105] Protestants, Plunkett writes, regularly pointed out such abuses to him in order to discredit the mass, and if they did so to him we can be sure they did so to others lower down the social scale. But his letters also highlight great variety in relationships between Ulster Catholics and Protestants: intermittent persecution and taunts on the one hand, but greater tolerance in Ulster than elsewhere in Ireland because of the liberality of the provincial president, Lord Charlemont, and, perhaps surprisingly, Protestants also paying alms to the friars and carousing at patterns.[106]

The practices condemned by Plunkett – burial in a monk's habit, excesses at wakes and holy places, primacy of burial places over any other physical representation of religion – reflect a continuation of medieval religion. But the problems were accentuated by the clergy's growing need for money. The destruction of the monasteries and churches (never in great supply in Ulster in any event) accentuated the tendency for a 'domestication' of religion. Cut off from continental developments to a greater extent than the rest of the island, Ulster remained immune to the growing emphasis on scripture in the Catholic Church.[107] Judgement Day, the torments of hell, the seven deadly sins, the passion of Christ and above all devotion to Mary remained the touchstones of both priestly and popular religion, aided by the popularisation of medals and above all of rosary beads – the pope's 'apish toys', as one Anglican divine described them, 'drugs of Rome, dregs of superstition . . . relics, hallowed beads . . . [which] Rome send[s] . . . to delude the people of this land'.[108] Religious verse is dominated by images of 'the pains of hell', and even in the eighteenth century there is little sense of Enlightenment-induced softening of such images of religious demonry. This is why Mary's protection, particularly at the hour of death, was such a part of popular devotion, why 'the habit of the saints'[109] was still considered a talisman of salvation, and why devotion to Rome as a semi-supernatural channel to the other world still figured so strongly in the religion of the people.[110] Nearly all the travel accounts of the period are very critical of the religion of the people, particularly in Ulster. But the criticism is based on textbook religion, by which standards most people of early modern Europe would have been found wanting. Even so, they pick up an unquestioning and instinctive religiosity focused on 'the Church of Rome'. 'The native Irish are very good Catholics, though knowing little of their religion', commented the French traveller Boullaye le Gouz in 1644, '. . . but their faith is great in the Church of Rome.'[111] It is a description echoed by another English traveller at the end of the century:

Ask many of them, what was the name of the blessed Virgin Mary, and 'tis ten to one, but they'll answer, it was Jane or Susan, and that St Patrick was her Godfather . . . so that if Ignorance be the true Mother of Devotion, the

City of Rome itself cannot produce such devout Catholicks, as those Teagues; and therefore it's a pitty but they should be transplanted into the Territories of the Holy Church, as being the most submissive Members thereof.[112]

Whatever the opinion some friars had of their archbishop, huge crowds came to hear Plunkett preach and to receive the sacraments during his visitations. The French traveller Jouvin de Rochefort reported in the 1660s 'astonishing' numbers 'travelling across the woods and mountains' to attend mass.[113] But the religious enthusiasm of the people was not church-based and it remained largely untutored until late in the eighteenth century, when the Catholic Church finally embarked on a programme of popular catechesis.[114] In the seventeenth century Ulster Catholicism would not have differed radically from that in continental Europe. Everywhere reforming bishops complained of ill-educated and wordly clergy, of lay interference and popular superstition; while Plunkett's complaints of a number of the Ulster clergy keeping mistresses and families could have been replicated throughout Catholic Europe. In France it was the female religious orders who first experienced Tridentine reforms. There were no female religious in Ulster until the eighteenth century, and Plunkett dismissed the handful he found in County Down as 'four Franciscan zealots'.[115]

Even so, judging from the content of some of the poetry, although regular sacraments are not yet the norm, there is a growing consciousness of what church-based religion expects. 'The general confession of Fiachra Mac Brádaigh', a Cavan poet, c.1700–55, is typical in this. It also reflects the social envy among what by now was a generally poor stratum of Ulster society.

> I commit pride, I break the Sunday holiday, . . .
> I am avaricious, too quarrelsome with the clergy
> and with gentle pleasant women who are married.
> I commit envy towards those with boots and coaches
> and anyone who is covered with coats, . . .
> I commit gluttony with no fast on Friday from meat,
> I do not enjoy the restriction of Lent, a soul-fast;
> I am often drunk from what I drink,
> and I swear against law and clergy . . .

> I love poems and songs,
> I am cosy in my bed when I should be
> Going to mass . . .[116]

Knowledge of canon law was largely irrelevant to this popular simpli-
fication of what differentiated Catholic from Protestant: mass and
Mary versus the Bible; poverty and the people versus wealth, materialism and empty churches. The evolution of Ulster Catholicism in this
period is a classic example of identity formation in opposition to traits
disliked in 'the Other'. Because 'that idol of the Mass', as Henry Jones
termed it, was so persistently attacked by Protestants, it was treated
with the same reverence as the priests, though its religious significance
was only dimly understood.[117] Although we know of regular social
dealings with Protestants, they were considered a damned breed, and
the Presbyterians were doubly damned.

> Twisted is their consciences, perverse their minds,
> they desire no bishop or cleric;
> they say no pater or creed . . .
> Fasts or feasts of the saints –
> bad is the whim – they keep them not;
> Mary is no more to them than a wisp,
> a rude breed unblessed by God.
> They hate baptism, cross and church,
> a treacherous stock; a pity, O God,
> is the decline of Patrick's faith . . .[118]

The 1641 rising was treated as a religious war by Protestant commentators and some accounts are suspect. But the account of the County
Monaghan priest Hugh O'Dugan Maguire converting forty to fifty
Protestants, then ordering them killed in case they lapsed, may not be
entirely apocryphal.[119] Such hostility was also triggered by the political
stance of Protestantism. The Bible was used as an anti-popish symbol
and political weapon. The 'Parliament of England', protested the
General Remonstrance of the Catholics of Ireland in October 1641,
had planned 'to send over the Scottish army with the sword and Bible
in hand against us . . . to supplant us and raze the name of Catholike

and Irish out of the whole kingdom.'[120] By then the Ulster Irish were displaying a marked antipathy to the Bible, and the depositions tell of attacks on it in 1641.[121] Mac Cuarta's Protestant house testing every Catholic belief against scripture was most likely a common experience, and it is in this period that the concept of the 'foreign Bible' enters popular tradition.[122]

Mary too has been politicised. She is now the protectrice exclusively of the Irish; the Saxons won't defeat her.[123] It is taken as read that one only converted to Protestantism for worldly pleasures, the convert priest rejecting Mary for sexual satisfaction in this world. Stories of priests becoming Protestant ministers abound in Ulster-Irish poetry and folklore, the most frequently related being that of two County Donegal brothers at the end of the seventeenth century, one a priest, the other a minister. The treatment of the Gael who converted to Protestantism is uniform: it is of Judas-like betrayal of people and religion, deserting them both when times got bad – 'a lopped off branch . . . far from your people' – his motives invariably the flesh or profit, his church opulent and empty, his earthly and heavenly mothers alike in sorrow.[124] In the standard histories written by clerics they are 'renegades' and 'apostates', an outlook which was to remain remarkably consistent among the clergy from the seventeenth century onwards.[125]

> O Manus dear, is the news true,
> which I heard yesterday in the neighbourhood,
> that you recently abandoned God's church,
> and the mighty Pope of Rome,
> and that you were reading your *recantation*
> in the Protestant church on Sunday?
> [to which Manus replies]
> Even if they go to God's paradise
> it's certain I'll be with them,
> my shining sword hanging by my side,
> and my lease in my pocket.[126]

The 'turncoat' Gael is even more heinous than the foreigner, or the Gael who anglicises his name (a practice which increases in the eighteenth century), in this case Phelim O'Neill of County Tyrone assuming the name Felix Neel:

> Scorning to spend his days where he was reared,
> To drag out life among the vulgar herd,
> Or trudge his way through bogs in bracks and brogues,
> He changed his creed, and joined the Saxon rogues
> By whom his sires were robbed. He laid aside
> The arms they bore for centuries with pride –
> The ship, the salmon, and the famed Red Hand,
> And blushed when called O'Neill in his own land!
> Poor paltry skulker from thy noble race,
> Infelix Felix, weep for thy disgrace![127]

Whatever the efforts made by Protestantism to proselytise through Irish speakers, it appears that these may have been even less acceptable than English-speakers:

> . . . false prophet of Conn's Half, . . .
> The stammerer of the senseless mishmash . . .
> you'll receive no respect from anyone descended from the gaels;
> coming to us with your babbling like the wheezing of a goose.[128]

The seventeenth century marked the beginnings of a composite tradition. It is not the loss of the land alone which is so resented in folk tradition; it is the loss of the land to Protestants – and those who 'turned' to keep it in the family are considered the worst villains of all. Such themes thread through many local histories, the minute listing of Old Irish family names against the new Protestant landowners in Father Éamon Ó Doibhlin's *Domhnach Mór* (1969) being a notable example. Forgetfulness would become a luxury not permitted to Ulster's Catholics. The Maguires of Fermanagh are considered 'traitors' in nationalist folklore. In 1978 in Blacklion, a village on the Fermanagh-Cavan border, between Northern Ireland and the Republic, Myles Dolan told Irish Folklore Commission collector, Michael J. Murphy: 'The people, our forefathers, was banished for their faith; they gave up their land and everything, and kept on to their faith . . .

And all the Maguires down about the banks of the Erne is all Protestants, because they turned their coats and stayed.'[129] In 1945 Murphy
was told in Hilltown, County Down, of O'Neill land going to Protestants when John O'Neill's sister married a Protestant lord. Her
offspring were then buried in 'Luther's Hole', the Protestant cemetery
of Rostrevor.[130] 'Thems not Irish at all', those that 'turned' to keep
their land, one of the most respected storytellers in Tyrone, and a firm
republican, commented in 1950.[131] And so indeed had Catholicism
become the prerequisite for Irishness.

These are the sentiments which have been part of Catholic sub-culture
over the past two centuries. They would not have been universally
shared in the seventeenth century. Moving in and out of different
religious denominations as practicalities demanded was not unusual
and no evidence has been found of contemporary ostracisation of 'land
Protestants' by their peers.[132] At first a middling group of Ulster-Irish
society benefited from the acquisition of long leases, but increasingly
as the century wore on the tendency was to re-let to Protestant tenants.
Religious persecution coincided with the beginnings of a modern
definition of property and wealth, by which political and social
status and power would be defined thereafter. By this new definition
even the great warlords of the sixteenth century would have been
found wanting. The demotion of this top tier of Ulster-Irish society
before this new definition entered into popular currency meant that
the remnants of that elite retained their status in the popular mind. It
was from this group, traditionally the producer of the clergy and the
learned men alike, and among whom there was already a much more
acute recognition of religious difference, that the sentiments which
were to become so instinctive to Ulster Catholicism first emerged.
Anti-Englishness and anti-Protestantism is largely absent from literature in Irish before the early seventeenth century.[133] By its close it is a
prominent theme and the two are usually intertwined. The fundamental point of departure was the religious persecution. It was never as
brutal or sustained as popular tradition would have us believe, and it
affected the elite more than the foot soldiers. But lay Catholics no
longer held positions of prominence. Power was Protestant. In such
circumstances the clergy emerged as the new social leaders and a

culture developed of separateness from a power structure which did not include them.

Historians of religion are divided over the issue of what constituted 'popular' or 'elite' religion and whether indeed the two can be legitimately separated.[134] The problem is even more acute when identifying at what point essentially secular notions were sacralised as part of a religious community's tradition. It was perhaps inevitable that a clerical elite would articulate them first. It is equally true that the centrality of the mass, with its message of sacrifice, and deliverance through suffering and victimhood, would already have provided the basis for the ready absorption of such ideas. The sense of occupying the moral heights against the victimiser, as expressed by the Ardoyne Catholics in the early 1970s, was a tradition which entered Catholic consciousness in the seventeenth century. Today's nationalists in Northern Ireland do not define their identity in anything other than cultural and political terms and are irritated by outsiders who more accurately portray it as religious. This is because that religion was so successfully subsumed into political culture over three hundred years ago.

6

LIFE UNDER THE PENAL LAWS

. . . the Scottish Calvinists, with whom the Province is swarming, put very serious difficulties in my way . . . Although all Ireland is suffering, this province is worse off than the rest of the country, because of the fact that from the neighbouring country of Scotland Calvinists are coming over here daily in large groups of families, occupying the towns and villages, seizing the farms in the richer parts of the country and expelling the natives . . . Prelates and regular clergy have, for some years, been proscribed by Act of Parliament, but the ordinary secular clergy are allowed to exercise their ministry . . . a difficult situation but not unbearable . . .

Bishop Hugh MacMahon, 1714
(Flanagan, 'Diocese of Clogher', 40–41)

The eighteenth century is the period when information about the Ulster Catholics is most scarce. They barely figure in the press; the records of the lower courts, which would have told us how they fared under the law, were destroyed in 1922; there are no *causes célèbres* to throw up information, no surviving landed class and even the continental archives contain little information, for the bulk of Ulster Catholics were too poor to send their sons to continental seminaries, and like the rural poor elsewhere in Europe, they do not make their mark on historical record until the end of the century. For some three hundred years after 1500 a process had been developing in Europe which historians call the emergence of polite society. This saw the gradual moving apart of the social classes from the shared rough lifestyle of the Middle Ages to the pursuit of refinement, good taste and social codes of restraint which would set the upper classes apart after the seventeenth century. The development coincided with the emergence of separate cultural and religious communities in Ulster. With no significant gentry class, few of the Ulster Catholics qualified for entry to this newly defined polite society and the modern stereotypes of social and mental inferiority were already well formed by the close of the eighteenth century.

Traditionally, it is the penal laws which have been held responsible for the disadvantaged situation of the Irish Catholics in the eighteenth century. 'This is the period of the Penal Code', reads a typical entry in a school textbook of the early twentieth century, 'when for more than sixty years, Ireland lay in helpless misery, ground down by an inhuman tyranny – the blackest known to history.'[1] It was a system, continues the traditional reading, designed by the 'Planter population' of Ireland with the backing of England to deprive the Catholics of their land, their civil rights and their religion. 'Priests were hunted, hanged, or banished', secretive penal day altars sprang up 'among the lonely mountains and in the quiet glens', and stories of priests gunned down at mass-rocks proliferate. Protestant 'discoverers' could deprive Catholics of their horses, arms and property; sons were encouraged to turn Protestant and disinherit their fathers; children were educated in hedge-schools because Catholics were banned from running schools. The penal laws lie at the heart of a composite reading of history in which the handful of clerical executions, the land confiscations of the seventeenth century and sectarian atrocities in the 1790s, have been subsumed into an image of biased authority, religious discrimination against an entire people and behind it all English domination. It is a popular image of such power that it has remained to the present day, undermining nascent Ulster Catholic trust when British governments, Unionist politicians and Orangemen seem to revert to type.

Little wonder that recent historians have been at pains to question this view. They argue that there was no systematic penal 'code'; that legislation was piecemeal and erratic, produced by genuine political crises and rarely fully implemented; that in terms of social relationships Ireland differed little from contemporary Europe; that far from being decimated, the Catholic Church actually flourished in the period. Nor was the political threat of 'popery in the gross' as groundless as the traditional reading makes out, for Jacobitisim dominated Catholic political thinking and Rome's ambivalence about Catholic loyalty to the state was real enough. Although historians accept that Ulster comes nearer than any other province to fitting the stereotypical image of the 'penal era', even here good neighbourliness was the norm.

All of this is indisputable and has gone a long way to defusing the explosiveness of the penal myth. However, it deals largely with the penal laws as cause and effect rather than symptom. The effects traditionally ascribed to the penal laws did not always materialise. But the penal laws were products of and enshrined a frame of mind about Catholics which continued long after their effectiveness had passed. It pervaded all aspects of civil society, affecting lower as much as higher social classes, and whilst it was honoured as much in the breach as anything else, it created an undercurrent of sullen Catholic resentment and swaggering, if insecure, Protestant imperiousness which would surface at times of crisis. Arthur Young, even though he was writing in 1776, at a time when religious penalisation was out of fashion, captures the situation perfectly. He had been staying with Anthony Foster, Lord Chief Baron of the Exchequer, who was famous for his improvements on his estate in County Louth. 'In conversation upon the popery laws', writes Young, 'I expressed my surprise at their severity: he said they were severe in the letter, but were never executed', which prompted Young to recall Edmund Burke's comment in the English House of Commons that ' "Connivance is the relaxation of slavery, not the definition of liberty".'[2]

1. *The Penal Laws*

The penal laws were passed in a brief period of heightened political tension between 1695 and 1707, after the reign of James II had shown how vulnerable was the seventeenth-century land settlement and when the Protestant succession to the English throne was by no means secured. The Irish parliament was angry at William III's generous terms in the Treaty of Limerick, and even before it was ratified it passed the first penal law. The 1695 acts prohibited Catholics from carrying arms, keeping horses valued at more than £5, sending their children abroad for education and teaching school. The aim was to prevent Catholics from assisting or communicating with the foreign enemy. In 1697 another act banished ecclesiastics and regular clergy. But there was considerable opposition in the House of Lords to measures against the Catholic religion itself – not least from a handful of senior Anglican ecclesiastics. Secular priests were given legal recognition in 1703, provided they registered and gave security for good behaviour; 1,089 over the whole country did so, though only 189 of these were from Ulster.[3] Another invasion scare, however, prompted the imposition of an oath of abjuration in 1709 on the registered clergy. This required the denial of James III's right to the throne. It was denounced by the Pope and only thirty-three priests took it, in effect rendering the whole Catholic Church illegal. But this was certainly not the original intention, and after a brief period of priest-hunting the authorities turned a blind eye.[4] Ironically the validity of priestly orders was accepted and Catholic marriages celebrated by a priest were recognised by the state. Presbyterians suffered greater inconvenience on these accounts, their ministers securing official recognition only in 1737.[5]

It was not that Catholics were being denied freedom of conscience. Indeed many Anglican divines made this very distinction and protested at measures that affected the ability of Catholics to practise their religion. *Raison d'état* might justify laws against the property and 'some moderate restraints' on the civil rights of those adhering to a religion so at odds with the ethos of the state, argued Edward Synge (future Bishop of Elphin) in an influential sermon preached on the 1725 anniversary of the 1641 rebellion. But this should not involve 'forcing men's consciences'. He pointed to France where Catholics had rejected papal claims to depose heretical princes and argued that such Gallicanism should be supported. 'All persons . . . whose principles in religion have no tendency to hurt the public have a right to a toleration.' Declaring their religious assemblies unlawful simply forced them underground, out of sight of the magistrates.[6]

After an initial period of persecution of the clergy, the actual practice of Catholicism was not interfered with. Mass-houses went up without protest. Cemeteries continued to be shared by Catholic and Protestant. Catholic patterns and pilgrimages were rarely disturbed, though prohibited under the 1704 Popery Act, and since the Catholic Church did not oblige clerics to wear distinctive dress until 1850, they did not always attract attention. It was a gap between public rhetoric and private practice which amused Arthur Young.

I must be free to own that when I have heard gentlemen who have favoured the laws as they now stand urge the dangerous tenets of the Church of Rome, quote the cruelties which have disgraced that religion in Ireland and led them into the common routine of declamation . . . I could not but smile to see subscriptions handed about for building a masshouse . . .[7]

Even so, the 1697 Banishment Act remained on the statute book throughout the century, notwithstanding various Catholic relief acts in the later decades. The legal position of the regulars remained perilous, old clauses against their very existence still being invoked as late as 1865, while each Catholic relief act – even the unsatisfactory one of 1829 – tended to reinforce petty and often insulting clauses retained from earlier laws. Not until Gladstone's act of 1869, disestablishing the Church of Ireland, were Catholic bishops finally permitted legal use of their titles.[8]

But the main target of the penal laws was property and its associated political power. Catholics were prevented from purchasing land or acquiring leases longer than thirty-one years; Protestant heiresses lost their claim on marrying a Catholic; Catholic estates had to be divided amongst the male heirs, unless the eldest turned Protestant, in which case he became sole owner, even during the lifetime of the father; Catholics could not act as guardians to minors; a Protestant 'discoverer' could acquire the Catholic's share in any transaction if he could prove any infringement of the 'Popery laws'. Faced with the loss of their land, most remaining Catholic landowners conformed. Honoria McManus, wife of Oliver O'Hara of Ballymena, County Antrim, raised her sons as Protestants, explaining that if she did not do so 'she might as well make tailors or shoemakers of them as their prospects in life would be destroyed'.[9] Such 'land-conformism' was generally accepted by eighteenth-century Catholics – whatever its notoriety in later folklore.[10] Some remained crypto-Catholics, a liberalising force against the passage of new penal measures and the application of existing ones. Indeed, the O'Haras retained their estates through occasional conformity, while continuing to marry Catholics.[11] Less acceptable was the Catholic who conformed to dispossess members of his own family and Paul MacLorinan of Ahoghill, County Antrim – killed in 1772, four years after conforming to acquire family land – cannot have been the only case of rough justice being meted out for doing so.[12] After 1693 Catholics were effectively debarred from sitting in parliament by the requirement of oaths against the Pope's deposing power and transubstantiation. But they could continue to vote if they took oaths of allegiance and abjuration, until that right too was removed in 1728.[13] Other measures debarred them from local government, the higher levels of the legal profession and from Ireland's only university.

The fears of the Protestant gentry for their land never entirely disappeared. It was these which made the Irish parliament, dominated by the country's major landowners, more anti-papist than the country at large. 'In a country where every man holds his estate and political consequence by dispossession of Catholics', one Lord Lieutenant, Lord Westmorland, in 1793 cautioned an English government inclined by then to dismiss Protestant fears, 'allowance must be made for even unreasonable apprehension.'[14] Affinity with the American colonies – to which as many as 150,000 Ulster Presbyterians had emigrated by 1775[15] – made Ulster particularly sensitive to the treatment of Catholic Canada. Correspondence to the *Belfast News Letter* linked the North American Indian threat to that of popery, 'as they are all Roman Catholicks', and the Quebec Act of 1774, granting toleration to Catholicism, prompted rumours that Catholic regiments would be used to crush the American colonists.[16]

The individual acts of the penal laws were not so-styled. Rather they were acts to prevent the growth of 'popery'. Protestants then as now had little difficulty separating the individual from the perceived concept and the less offensive term 'Roman Catholic' became more common in the second half of the century when fears receded. But fears of 'popery' as a political 'system' were never far below the surface. So embedded in Protestant consciousness was this spectre of popery that the ethos underlying laws passed to protect a ruling elite came to pervade all sections of Protestant society. Even reformers as sympathetic towards the Catholics as Henry Grattan and Theobald Wolfe Tone came to espouse Catholic emancipation only because they believed that 'popery' was withering.[17] What was this spectre of 'popery' and were Protestant fears justified?

'Popery' was political. It united a faith which was deemed corrupt, superstitious and persecutory to the foreign political threats of Jacobitism and absolute monarchy, and the image was sustained by frequent wars with the Catholic powers on the Continent. The Protestant archbishop of Armagh instructed his clergy in October 1745:

You are to raise in your people a religious abhorrence of the Popish government and polity, for I can never be brought to call Popery in the gross a religion ... Their absurd doctrines ... their political government ... makes it impossible for them to give any security of their being good governors, or good subjects in a Protestant kingdom ...[18]

The very concept of liberty as Protestant and embedded in constitution and state was part of popular Protestant psyche throughout Britain and Ireland. Morever, every state in *ancien régime* Europe considered uniformity of religion as part of state security and penalised those who did not conform. Certainly the Jacobite threat in Ireland was no illusion, even after the military defeat of Charles Edward, the Young Pretender, in 1746. Continued Stuart intrigues on the Continent, residual popular Jacobitism in Ireland, and the presence of huge numbers of Catholics training in continental seminaries or serving in continental armies – some 120,000 in the first three decades alone – sustained such perceptions long after the threat had evaporated. Moreover James III, the Old Pretender, resided in Rome, recognised by the Pope as legitimate monarch and continuing to exercise his right to nominate Catholic bishops until his death in 1766.

But the ultimate 'foreign jurisdiction' was the papacy itself. It was believed that the papacy exercised a temporal as well as a spiritual jurisdiction over Catholics, that it taught them not to keep faith with heretics and that 'princes excommunicated by the pope may be deposed or murdered by their subjects'. Fears were sustained by papal refusal to reject this medieval doctrine (even as late as the 1770s), to the dismay of Catholic reformers, lay and clerical alike.[19] Catholics were willing to swear a simple oath of allegiance and such an oath was agreed in the Treaty of Limerick. But oaths of abjuration, renouncing the Stuart succession and the deposing power of the pope, were another matter, and successive attempts to impose one foundered on papal disapproval. The Vatican temporised on these matters and scuppered various attempts at accommodation, because any concession to win toleration for Catholics in Ireland would open up the whole issue of church persecution of Protestants elsewhere in the world. Frederick Hervey, Protestant bishop of Cloyne, soon to become Bishop of Derry, was a prominent supporter of Catholic rights. Yet even he was baffled at the resistance to such an oath, as he explained to a Catholic friend in 1768.

Surely the *oaths and declarations* which I have myself drawn are such as any loyal subject would not scruple and any conscientious Catholic may safely swear. My object is to leave you your faith entire, but to secure your allegiance to the present government and to make you independent of all foreign jurisdiction whatever. For, depend on it that there is not an iota in the scriptures to warrant the least temporal jurisdiction in the Bishop of Rome . . . *penal laws* . . . can never take place against loyal subjects.[20]

The frequent re-issue of Hugh Reily's *Impartial History*, which asserted that Catholics were loyal subjects, was mirrored by the equally frequent re-issue of Temple's *Irish Rebellion*, testifying to continuing Protestant belief that they never could be.[21] Catholics were referred to as 'enemies' in the first decades of the century. Their clergy were 'dangerous', 'insolent', 'subtle', 'presumptuous'. Catholics could not be trusted. Their claims to loyalty showed their hypocrisy, for 'perjury' was 'a principle of the Popish religion'.[22] The range of insults reveals the mixture of fear and contempt for Catholics. Even though the impact of the penal laws was short-lived and the worst was over by 1730, Protestants preferred to keep them on the books as a form of security. Indeed, in 1762, on the very eve of their repeal, new acts were being passed to calm Protestants' fears for their property.[23] Wars and political crises invariably reactivated the law against the carrying of arms; and a century before they occurred in England, Ireland was obsessed with religious censuses, documenting any increase in the already overwhelming numbers of Catholics.[24] Nor did such attitudes retreat as the penal laws were repealed. The London Hibernian Society, with 326 proselytising schools in Ulster in the early nineteenth century, explained its crusade as follows:

The great body of the Irish wander like sheep, that have no faithful shepherd to lead them. Legendary tales, pilgrimages, penances, superstitions, offerings, priestly domination . . . abandoned practices, and all that shocks and disgusts in the mummery of the mass house, cannot fail to fix a mournful sentiment in the heart of every enlightened and pious observer . . . The hope, therefore, that the Irish will ever be a tranquil and loyal people, and still more that piety and virtue will flourish among them, must be built on the anticipated reduction of popery.[25]

Catholicism was believed to induce sloth and slavishness of mind in its adherents, making them incapable of liberty, virtue and entry to polite society. Catholic children reared in the Charter schools, where Protestant doctrine and practice were imposed, were paraded as examples of the association of Protestantism and cleanliness. If the effects of popery were so pernicious, why then was there such little effort made to convert its adherents to Protestantism?

Certainly the process of conversion was a deterrent in itself, and was meant to be so, particularly for those who nominally converted to preserve estates. The convert had to recant 'the errors of Rome' publicly, before an Anglican clergyman and his congregation at Sunday service. Great crowds would turn out to observe the occasion and very often the names appeared in the press.[26] In fact, the Protestant elite was as divided on the desirability of converting large numbers of Catholics as on many other issues. Many – including notable figures like the Anglican archbishop of Dublin, William King – would have liked an Irish-speaking ministry to explain Protestantism to the people, and in a much-quoted phrase from the Bible, he accused his co-religionists of preferring to maintain the Catholics as 'hewers of wood and drawers of water' rather than attempting to convert them through their own language.[27] The most notable campaigner for such was Dr John Richardson, rector of Belturbet, County Cavan, for he had experienced particular success in south Tyrone, Fermanagh, Donegal, and the Glens of Antrim – where Gaelic-speaking Scottish highlanders were rescued from their slippage to popery by Irish-speaking preachers. The Presbyterian Synod also sought to evangelise through the Irish language in the early years of the century, with seventeen preachers in the field by 1720. Such campaigns were not sustained, but persistent internal criticisms of the established church for failing to take its message to the Catholic people, and the success of Irish-speaking Methodist preachers in south Ulster at the end of the century, casts doubt on the view that the penal laws were entirely motivated by cynical materialism.[28]

The most sustained attempt at converting the natives was the establishment of the Charter schools. They were conceived by an enlightened group of gentry in the 1730s as a way of luring the poor from the perceived backwardness and indolence of popery by a mixture of proselytism, anglicisation and education into useful pursuits. The idea was to encourage poor Catholic families to send their children to these boarding schools, away from their home districts, where they might risk continued papist influence from their families and clergy. They would then receive some elementary education, particularly in practical skills (notably linen weaving in the Ulster schools), and above all religious instruction. Thereafter they would be apprenticed to Protestant families. The belief that the perfect recipe had been found for converting Ireland to Protestantism informs the initial crusading enthusiasm. By the 1750s ten such schools were functioning in Ulster (out of forty-seven for the entire country). At Killough in County Down, one of three schools in the county, Walter Harris (a Dublin man of letters) found '20 poor popish children trained up to useful labour and carefully educated in the principles of the Protestant religion'. He disapproved of the penal laws and thought the Charter schools a far more 'effectual and rational scheme' of winning the people from 'the superstitious and idolatrous worship of the church of Rome' and creating 'a race of honest and industrious Protestants'.[29] Harris's language deserves comment. It would have been instantly recognisable to Enlightenment thinking generally in eighteenth-century Europe, for it too saw Catholicism as backward, superstitious and oppressive, a dead weight on rational pursuits, improvement and prosperity.

However, sufficient Catholic poor were unforthcoming and from an early stage the original function of the schools was being diluted by the admission of poor Protestant children. A good deal of stigma also seems to have attached to those children reared in the schools.[30] The Charter schools acquired a villainous reputation in popular Catholic tradition, in which they became intertwined with the better-known proselytising activities of militant evangelicalism in the nineteenth century. By then attitudes had changed sufficiently for both the established church itself and the government to pronounce the aims of the schools offensive and self-defeating. The parliamentary report of 1825 into education in Ireland found considerable evidence of malpractice and cruelty in the schools, towards Protestant and Catholic children alike. 'But however great and numerous the instances of mismanagement and abuse which prevail in these establishments, it appears to us, that the main objection arises from the mistaken principles on which they are founded.'[31]

The Charter schools were not a success, even in Ulster. All but two of the ten had been closed by the 1770s, and in response to the damning report of 1825 the remainder were progressively closed. But other public charitable institutions such as almshouses also brought the children up as Protestants. This, and a number of well-documented cases of heirs being sent out of the country to Protestant guardians,[32] had already laid the basis for a long-standing belief among Catholics that Protestants targeted the innocent child to brainwash with their beliefs. The Catholic bishop of Clogher, Hugh MacMahon, refers to it as early as 1714. The context was the implementation of Church impediments against marriage to close relatives. If married before a priest, as required by the Church, this could be guarded against. But this clearly was not happening. He feared that if he were to enforce church law couples would simply 'pervert', or, if children were involved, they would 'fall into the hands of heretics who are always anxious to pick up children of this kind and have them reared as heretics'. Thus did marriage become one of the areas where the penal laws caused the church to compromise on its own teachings, for dispensations were regularly on offer.[33]

The friars caused as much concern to governments in the eighteenth as in the seventeenth century. But increasingly the reason was their rootlessness and their ability to wander freely. The Catholic Church shared such fears – coming to the aid of the state by suppressing the regulars' novitiates in 1751. As elsewhere, so in Ireland – this is the period of the 'Catholic Enlightenment', a time when sections in the Catholic Church were not only sensitive to Protestant criticisms but shared them. The efforts by the Catholic episcopacy and gentry to be accepted as part of the social hierarchy from mid-century onwards were not insincere. The British – if not the Irish – political establishment finally conceded such when a more potent threat to existing society than 'popery' emerged with Jacobinism at the end of the century.

Historians have struggled to find some clear intention behind the penal laws. But their researches into the labyrinthine processes of Anglo-Irish legislation reveal as much division as agreement among the law-makers.[34] Earlier tendencies to simply reproduce the acts themselves, or the descriptive heads of bills, have clouded understanding for almost two centuries. Some of the most influential accounts (Butler's

Digest of Popery Laws, 1792, Lecky's *History of Ireland,* 1892, Burke's *Priests in Penal Times,* 1914) did just that, and have been raided by scholars ever since. However, as in contemporary England, so in Ireland a huge gulf separated the practice from the letter of the law. In a society without a regular police force, the enforcement of the law depended on a level of popular acceptance. Attempts to arrest priests had to be abandoned, as they were regularly rescued by threatening crowds.[35] The folklore of innumerable priests killed at mass-rocks, usually at midnight mass, is largely unproven. In his detailed investigation of the clergy of Clogher, the Revd P. Ó Gallachair found such stories substantiated in only two cases, both in the seventeenth century, and one in the aftermath of 1641.[36]

There was also widespread Protestant collusion and connivance at Catholic evasion of the laws. The penal laws cut horizontally across the early modern concept of vertical social relations. Society throughout Europe operated along recognised lines of social division and responsibility, whereby elite paternalism and protection was repaid by deference and co-operation by the common people. The many relief and charitable schemes sponsored by the Protestant gentry carried no religious label. Irish Catholics had some power to make laws unworkable, which they did so effectively with the agrarian protest of the Whiteboys (1760s–1770s), mainly in Munster.[37] It would have been more difficult for Ulster Catholics to have engaged in such social protest, and in general they did not do so until towards the end of the century. Whatever their insecurities, many of the Protestant elite winced at laws which permitted inferior Protestants to challenge Catholics who were their social superiors. There are a number of cases of Protestant neighbours taking out leases or holding property in trust for Catholics, and stories of Protestants hiding Catholic clergy at times of persecution are legion. The Dickey family of Ballydonellan, County Antrim (who came from Ayrshire in the seventeenth century), was known to have sheltered priests and held land in trust for Catholic neighbours, and I have encountered a number of similar cases from Fermanagh, Donegal, Antrim and Down.[38] Ulster Catholics benefited less from the survival of a strong Catholic landed element which elsewhere mitigated the impact of the laws. Even so, many landlords tended to grant the longest leases permissible under the penal laws to their Catholic tenants. Although Protestant tenants were usually preferred, where Catholics of social standing remained they retained their leases and as often as not landlords who had converted from Catholicism to Protestantism remained favourably disposed towards their former co-religionists.[39] There are, of course, marked regional differences. The extreme Protestantism of the gentry in parts of south Down for example was to become legendary. Lord Hillsborough offered a reward in 1771 to every papist on his estates who would conform and declared that no papist in future would be given a lease.[40] However, until the 1780s Ulster society was very stable and landlords tended to use their rights of eviction sparingly.[41]

Priest-catchers, discoverers and sons conforming to disinherit fathers were as unpopular with the eighteenth-century legal system as they were to become in later Catholic folklore. Complaints by the chief law officers in England about the law being placed at the whim of 'an unfaithful wife, a disobedient child, an impatient heir and a common informer', were made in the more liberal climate of 1778.[42] But they could also have applied to the legal world earlier in the century. It was extremely difficult to disinherit Catholics under the penal laws. Judges and magistrates regularly stretched the law, and the legal establishment in Dublin, where property cases were dealt with by the higher courts, was frequently accused of being staffed by converts and crypto-Catholics. A case in point was brought by a Protestant 'discoverer' to the Court of Exchequer in 1749. Since the penal laws confined Catholics to leases of a maximum of thirty-one years, he challenged the leases for lives held in Monaghan by Nugent McKenna, who had inherited them from his father. A host of people (including the landowner and the sheriff) appeared for McKenna to prove that his father had been covered by the articles of Limerick (permitting certain categories to retain their land).[43] Nor, given the reservations of many Anglican divines, should it surprise to find the wills of Catholic bishops being registered unopposed in the ecclesiastical courts of the established church. Registered Catholic clergy were given legal status, and whilst bishops were not supposed to exercise ecclesiastical jurisdiction, a blind eye was regularly turned and magistrates, forced by the complaints of ultra-Protestants to arrest bishops in Ulster in 1739 and again in 1756, ensured that no further action was taken against them.[44]

Such incidents highlighted the unsatisfactory halfway house of the penal laws. They created a society attuned to evading the law. The 1704 Registration Act – by banning bishops from exercising ecclesiastical authority – failed to provide for a future priesthood and threatened to deprive Catholics of any religious direction whatsoever (not at all what the authorities, civil or ecclesiastical, had wished). In 1756 Lord Clanbrassil, a landowner in County Down, who had been sympathetic towards the Catholics since sitting as MP for Dundalk 1715–18, sought a new act to regularise their covert existence. The act was rejected by the English Privy Council and Clanbrassil's good intentions were denounced by the extremes of both religions.[45] But it highlighted the unsatisfactory nature of the legislation and was the immediate cause of the establishment of the Catholic Committee to campaign for its repeal.

Catholics were most likely to experience the penal laws in the workings of the law. The destruction of eighteenth-century assize records – apart from those for Antrim – makes generalisations difficult. The Antrim records till 1731 reveal surviving toryism in south-east Ulster, the Glens of Antrim and along the Derry/Tyrone borders. If caught, execution would be automatic, and, as in England, the heads of those executed were displayed as a deterrent to others. Even so, eighteenth-century Ulster was not a particularly violent society. Although there may well be other cases, now lost, in these surviving papers I have found only one case of a Catholic being accused of carrying arms against the law. This was Fergus McVeagh of Drumadoon in the Glens of Antrim, who terrorised the shopkeepers of nearby Ballycastle in 1725, threatening to burn their houses and hough their cattle if they appeared against him.[46]

As noted earlier, the higher courts tended towards relative impartiality – a cause for resentment among Armagh Protestants during the sectarian clashes of the 1780s and 1790s.[47] In the lower courts, however, although Catholics could serve on juries they could be challenged by a plaintiff or counsel in cases between Protestants and Catholics or those involving any aspect of the penal laws. The opportunities for prejudice were extensive. The United Irishman and magistrate in Tyrone, Thomas Russell, resigned from the bench for this very reason in October 1792, criticising his fellow JPs for asking plaintiffs their religion before trying the case.[48]

Certainly the opportunities afforded 'petty bigots' and the unscrupulous were legion. Under both English and Irish law, localities where crimes were committed could be made to pay the damages. In Ulster there are tales of the so-called 'Robbery Cut', whereby Protestants disposed of sickly farm animals, claimed they were stolen and had the costs levied from local Catholics by the Grand Juries.[49] In the last decades of the century, when Catholics were becoming more assertive, they put a stop to the rights apparently exercised by Protestant tenants of entering Catholics' lands to shoot fowl.[50] There were also times when the penal laws *were* enforced. Till mid-century every foreign war or political scare witnessed the arrest of priests and the seizure of arms from Catholics, and at such times sectarian tensions ran high.[51] Catholics were debarred from serving in the British army in Ireland until 1793 (and there were similar restrictions on Protestants until 1745), though in effect numbers of both were secretly enlisted. Nevertheless, the defence forces contained a disproportionate number of Ulster Protestants. Recruiting parties, troop movements and a knowledge of the use of arms were greater in the province than elsewhere. In 1756 106,295 Ulster Protestants joined the militia against just over 42,000 for all the other provinces together.[52]

A very full account of the position of the clergy in the more difficult times at the beginning of the century exists for the diocese of Clogher (covering much of south Ulster, including nearly all of parts of Fermanagh and Monaghan, and parts of Tyrone and Donegal). In this 1714 account Bishop Hugh MacMahon describes the great difficulty of functioning as a bishop in a province 'swarming' with Scottish Calvinists, of travelling in disguise, of his fear of being exposed by the 'incautious talk' of Catholic servants in Protestant houses, of priests hiding their faces from mass-goers to protect them if interrogated, of magistrates compelled to apply the oath of abjuration when previously they could be bribed. It was a year of particularly heightened tension after the death of Queen Anne and things were generally easier for the clergy after the succession of George I in 1714. By 1720 the worst of the penal laws were over. Even so, MacMahon's verdict that they made life 'difficult . . . but not unbearable' accurately summarises their general impact.[53]

2. Community relations

There is sometimes a tendency to read social relationships in Ulster back from the sectarian troubles of the 1780s and 1790s and to assume that it was ever thus. It would appear, however, that the eighteenth century was not a period of open religious conflict in Ulster. Territorial and linguistic segregation are part of the explanation. In 1744 Walter Harris reported only one Catholic living in Holywood, north Down. He was a coachman employed by a Mr Isaac, and when he first drove through the village people ran to their doors to see him, for most had never before seen a Catholic.[54] Where conflict occurred it was often because Protestants and Catholics invaded each other's recognised districts. Regular faction fights occurred between the inhabitants of Irish, Scottish and English streets in Armagh, Lurgan and Newry.[55] However, the famous incident in 1743 when Catholics burnt down a Presbyterian meeting house at Freeduff, south Armagh, was unusual. It came on the heel of the importation of Presbyterian tenants and the establishment of a Charter school in 1737 in this largely Catholic area. The meeting house was replaced by an enlarged one in 1760 (to cope with the expanding Presbyterian population) on the proceeds of fines levied on all the Catholic inhabitants for its destruction.[56]

Are we to assume then that Catholics settled down to co-existence with their Protestant and Dissenting neighbours? For the most part yes – awareness of difference should not be confused with bigotry – or they conformed. And Protestant, Catholic and Dissenter alike tended to conform to the majority religion in their area.[57] Social pressures to conform to the established church also eroded the small Presbyterian landed interest. Large numbers of Gaelic-speaking highland Scots turned Catholic in Inishowen and north Antrim, though in the north and east of the province, the religious traffic was in the opposite direction.[58] There is no record of any serious sectarian disturbance in Ulster before the 1780s. Though the Catholic clergy lamented the drunken tumult which generally accompanied funerals, there is no mention of inter-religious feuds at shared cemeteries. Lord Macartney's family of Lissanoure in north Antrim had been noted for their religious tolerance, and both he and other Protestant landlords in the area had contributed to the construction of 'a large handsome mass-house' nearing completion in 1789. But since the Catholics were refusing to pay tithe for the upkeep of the Protestant church, it had no minister and had fallen into ruin. As a result many 'Church people' now worshipped in the Catholic mass-house or Presbyterian meeting-house and were baptised by the priest 'for there is no other minister to do it'.[59] Indeed Macartney's informant thought this reflected the general situation throughout the country.

Mixed marriages were common, and wandering friars – so-called 'couple-beggars' – who earned a living from conducting them, drew scorn from the civil authorities and the Catholic Church alike, though only occasionally was action taken against them. In law a priest who conducted mixed marriages could incur the death penalty. This act remained in force till 1833, and was only repealed in 1870. But they were only illegal if they involved property, and all sides trod carefully. The Catholic bishops, anxious not to provoke the state, resisted promulgation of the papal decree *Tametsi* which required such marriages to be solemnised by a priest. Indeed, the 1766 case of the Catholic widow on the Abercorn estate in Tyrone – whose Protestant suitor tried to deny the validity of her marriage to an equally grasping Catholic by claiming that she had recanted and could not marry a Catholic – suggests that the lower orders entered mixed marriages without much hesitation, though it also shows the potential for mischief makers.[60] In the early 1800s, long after most of the penal laws had been repealed, the popular Catholic Tyrone writer (later turned Protestant) William Carleton was to meet a rather sorry degraded priest in Mullingar jail. 'His crime was the marriage of a Protestant and Catholic, and as it was a case in which there was property concerned, he had been prosecuted upon a statute dug up from the penal laws; while . . . the poor fellow knew no more about the property involved than I did.'[61]

In the English language at least, there was also a shared popular culture, particularly in the hedge-schools. Increasingly the hedge-schools were vehicles for the poor to learn English, and most of those children (Catholic and Protestant alike) who received any education in the eighteenth century received it in such schools – often together. The hedge-schools were irregular affairs, usually conducted in barns or disused farm buildings. Their staffing was equally irregular, many poets and scribes finding intermittent employment in such schools. They were not exclusively Catholic, whatever the folklore which has built up around them. Run on a shoestring, these hedge-schools had always used as readers whatever was available in cheap print. Chap-books and tales of romance and adventure doubled as school texts. Both Carleton and the Presbyterian controversialist Henry Cooke told of almost identical experiences as pupils at hedge-schools.[62] Carleton also recalled how the most popular play of the century, *The Battle of Aughrim*, was both used as a hedge-school 'reader' and attracted mixed religion audiences when staged in local barns. Although it celebrates 'the entire subversion of popery and arbitrary power' and contains most of the Protestant stereotypes of 'Romish tyranny' (Jacobitism, 'Romish worship', 'incense', monks, Jesuits, and the Spanish Inquisition), it distinguishes 'popery' from the defeated Irish, who are treated as a noble race. The central theme is the coming together of *Gael* and *Gall* in a Romeo-and-Juliet-style tragic romance.[63] Inevitably the flood of cheap literature put out by the United Irishmen in the 1790s also reached the hedge-schools – though never as universally as the authorities claimed.

Under the penal laws Catholics could not keep schools. But in practice they commonly did so. There is a reference in the 1731 *Report on the State of Popery* to 'straggling schoolmaster[s]' being threatened by churchwardens, but generally hedge-schools escaped penalisation. The same report details the numbers of 'popish' schools in each diocese and county: only six in Raphoe (Donegal), Armagh diocese with thirty-seven being at the other end of the scale. There is no sign of any clerical involvement in the schools – except in the case of Owen O'Gallagher 'an old fryer, [who] instructs a great many popish students' on the Fermanagh–Donegal border. The Catholic Church did not take an interest in schooling until the 1750s, and then only when prompted by anxiety at the activities of the Charter schools. The 1731 report cites only one case of Protestant children being 'taught to read together with natives'.[64] But unless there was a change in the course of the century, there must have been many more cases of this, for by the end of the century most hedge-schools would have been interdenominational, as were their teachers. An interesting case was reported from County Cavan in 1787, where the parish priest of Cress-stoney, Revd

Michael O'Reilly, had established a Sunday school where some four hundred children were taught reading and writing together, but given religious instruction by teachers of their own denomination.[65] In the more prosperous classical schools in the towns, catering for the sons of the middle class, it was the same story, but with clerical involvement more apparent. William Crolly, future Catholic archbishop of Armagh, attended such a school in Downpatrick in the 1790s, run by Dr James Neilson, a local Presbyterian minister.[66]

But although many hedge-school teachers may have taught through Irish, they were employed for their ability to teach classics, arithmetic and above all English. The surging demand for literacy lies behind these hedge-schools and that literacy was in English. It was a drive by the common people to advance themselves, for English was the language of everyday practicalities. Carleton was surprised at the 'number of books, pamphlets and odd volumes' that he found in the homes of Catholics in his parish in County Tyrone. Even if they could not read themselves – and half could not – such works were carefully preserved for the young relative who some day might do so. The ability to speak English had become a badge of status and in Carleton's *The Three Tasks*, when Jack Magennis moved up in the world through a pact with the devil, people marvelled at 'how high-flown and Englified he could talk'.[67] The poets might decry the English language, but they were usually bilingual and proud of it. In areas where Irish was declining, such bilingual speakers spoke English with a Scottish accent. Very few Irish speakers could either write or read their language and were becoming literate only through English.[68]

However, despite the general picture of good neighbourliness, mutual suspicions were easily aroused. There was a perception of Catholics as potential traitors, even on the most liberal of estates. In times of political tension, landlords would look to the religious makeup of their tenants and ensure that their Protestant tenants were well armed. In 1739 when war broke out between England and Spain some two hundred 'Protestant gentlemen' rode through Dundalk, beating drums and playing 'The Protestant Boys Will Carry the Day', and similar ceremonies occurred in Carrickfergus, Monaghan, Newry, Strabane, Belfast, Dromore and Enniskillen.[69] Election times also had the potential to underscore divisions, for although Catholics could still influence returns (much as the unenfranchised could in England) and landlords regularly ensured temporary conformity of tenants to increase the number of voters, opponents just as regularly campaigned to have such 'Catholic' votes discounted and at times Catholic tenants were turned out to create Protestant freeholders. Catholics could be trusty servants, but if even advanced thinkers like Mary Anne McCracken of Belfast hesitated on being asked if she completely trusted the family's Catholic servant, Betty, we can be sure that the sentiment was widespread.[70]

Statements in Irish were often more strident than those in English, much the same as in Northern Ireland of today Catholics and Protestants reserve different language for in- and out-groups. Awareness of difference expressed itself sometimes in mutual irritants, sometimes in mutual fascination. The firing of guns offended all sides and intentionally so. The Presbyterian wedding is a case in point, involving the ostentatious display of firearms in the pre-nuptial ritual. Describing the continuation of the ritual by Ulster emigrants in America, Edward Parker, writing in 1851, commented:

This practice it seems originated in Ireland, in consequence of the Catholics having been, after the Revolution, deprived of the use of firearms. The Protestants, proud of their superior privilege which they then enjoyed, made a display of their warlike instruments, on all public occasions.[71]

On the ground, jibes and insults about the inferiority of Catholics under the law would appear to have been commonplace and Catholics found the term 'papist' offensive. In *Adeir Clann Liútair* ['Luther's Children Say'] MacCooey contemplates the rewards of conforming:

> 'The children of Luther who are in court and in coaches say
> that I would have a vote in their own religion,
> cheap land and accurate guns,
> and my hat adorned with a cross-cockade;
> [i.e. able to join the army]
> . . .
> and wouldn't it be better for me to sign up with them
> than to be a waster in the Gaelic style?'[72]

However in such oral traditions Protestantism was deemed material-istic and acquisitive and woe betide any Catholic who rose in the world. The younger generation of the Gael, in their new prosperity, were becoming 'full of English pride', complained MacCooey.[73] One Donegal priest, Dominick O'Donnell (1700–93), who converted to Protestantism, was warned:

> It were better for you to be herding cattle,
> a stick in your hand and a blanket covering you,
> than to be seated under great windows,
> listening to the sounds of a minister.[74]

Catholics' belief in the antiquity, superiority and greater spirituality of their religion and traditions, however down on their fortunes, pervades the poetry – as it would do popular folklore in ensuing centuries – and we can be sure that it would have been given voice frequently, the jest veiling serious belief. However neighbourly, Catholics believed Protestants ultimately doomed. 'You must come over to our church,' Father Ned advised Andy Morrow in Carleton's *Ned McKeown*; 'you're a good neighbour, and a worthy fellow, and it's a thousand pities you should be sent down' – to which McKeown responded in agreement: 'It's a great thing entirely to be born in the true church – one's always sure, then.' There may too have been a peculiarly Irish version of the one-upmanship which poorer, older continental nobles indulged in against the newer, richer ones. The earl of Roden wrote to his sister in 1811:

There is a curious old woman here, a Mrs. Nugent one of the most decided Brogueniers you ever heard. She is of a very good Irish family, Mother to Count Nugent who is in the Austrian service, but she says she is not a Nugent at all but a McDonough who are a thousand years older than the Nugents. I told her to take care the Hutchinsons [whom Roden thinks 'decided Methodists'] did not convert her – she replied that there was no danger, if they talked to her she would tell them she was an *ould Papish* as their grandfather was, and would have nothing to do with their *fagairier*.[75]

183

As in every other rural society at the time, there is also a culture of outwitting the law and of celebrating those who did so. But one had to understand it first. Irish-language interpreters were available to the courts, but there is little evidence on their performance and a lot of evidence to suggest that monoglot Irish speakers were at a distinct disadvantage. In a Donegal folk song, the *Gall* taunts the *Gael*:

> What is your business at the sessions
> when you have no word of English?
> You'd not be given permission to speak there
> to plead any case.[76]

It is the priests, the educated men, who are celebrated for their understanding of the 'foreign' law and for protecting their people. A recurrent story in Ulster folklore is one where an eighteenth-century friar bottled the spirits of the local law officers, the site remaining an object of fear far into the nineteenth century.[77]

Although Protestant clerics who were not anti-Catholic were generally accepted by Catholics, Catholic youths were known to disrupt Protestant services of particularly anti-papist preachers. But they might also stay to listen, just as Protestants of all hues looked on with bemused fascination at popular Catholic practices – our people being as likely to join as condemn them, as one Protestant divine complained.[78] In the 1790s William Putnam McCabe, a United Irish leader noted for his impersonation skills, was able to turn this mutual fascination to good account in recruiting for the United Irishmen. He would spread word that 'a converted Papist would preach the Word in a certain barn ... and explain how he became convinced of the true doctrines of Presbyterianism', then recruit among the assembled mixed-religion crowd.[79]

Lough Derg in County Donegal had been a place of pilgrimage since medieval times. Although destroyed under Cromwell, it had been re-established and was undisturbed during the entire period of the penal laws, even though prohibited by the 1704 Act 'to prevent the further growth of popery'. With upwards of five thousand pilgrims converging on the south Donegal site every August, any interference risked popular tumult, and, like other penal legislation carrying such risks if implemented, this ruling was generally ignored. It was, after all, a tidy little earner for the local Protestant gentry who leased the island and a source of some fascination for the many more Protestant 'tourists' who came to witness Catholics act out their 'superstitious' beliefs.[80] Certainly the ritual demanded endurance of heroic proportions: the pilgrims fasting for up to nine days, traversing some fifty miles in bare feet over jagged stones, constantly reciting the rosary and finishing up being incarcerated in a cave or vault (the 'purgatory' proper). Here they neither ate nor slept for twenty-four hours, kept awake by clerical warnings that their soul would be seized by the devil should they succumb to weariness. Predictably the combined effects of sleep deprivation, fasting and religious ecstasy produced the many visions and hallucinations associated with the pilgrimage. Little wonder that Catholic people came to regard such pilgrims as having acquired saintly powers and the pebbles brought back from the lake as miraculous talismans. Lough Derg epitomised for Protestants the credulousness and superstition which they associated with the Catholic mind. For centuries it had been run by the Franciscans. But it too experienced the reforming sweep of a new breed of Catholic bishop later in the eighteenth century, when it was taken over by secular clergy and its primitive rigour considerably reduced. Even so, Carleton's courage failed him at the sight of the island early in the next century.[81]

3. Social status of Ulster Catholics

People of all denominations were poor in Ulster until the rapid expansion of the linen industry in the second half of the eighteenth century. The descendants of the Cromwellian soldiers in Monaghan, for example, subsisted on tiny, poor farms.[82] Catholic tenants were not always the poorest and if they were good tenants they were as secure as Protestants (though again it depended on the landlord). In the early decades of the century general insecurity made even Protestant tenants unwilling to take on long leases because of the contractual obligations. There is even a recurrent complaint of Catholics outbidding Protestants for leases.[83] The province was particularly badly affected by the series of natural disasters in the first decades – the terrible famine of 1741 alone thought to have brought the deaths of 300,000 people. The situation in Armagh inspired Swift's *Modest Proposal* of 1729 (in which he proposed the eating of the country's children to alleviate its poverty). The provision of churches, meeting-houses and schools was just as inadequate for Protestants and Dissenters as for Catholics, the discontent at tithes and ecclesiastical courts just as strong. The rewards of conformity were ideals which most Protestants could not aspire to. In the first half of the century firearms were generally in short supply because Protestants could not afford them and there are enough reports of firing at specifically Catholic celebrations to suggest easy defiance of the 1695 act.[84] Catholics were just as anxious to turn in malefactors to the law; landlords just as likely to use Catholic chapels as churches and meeting-houses to disseminate information among their tenants.

Under the Gaelic system the native Irish had not put much store on comfort, and later commentators noted a greater willingness by Catholics to endure hardship.[85] By the close of the century, however, most Catholics were prospering, linen-induced prosperity giving even the poorer a higher standard of living than their counterparts elsewhere in Ireland. Even if most Catholics were involved at its lower levels – spinning yarn, rather than weaving – the pace of change was such that marginal areas (traditionally dominated by Catholics) were being reclaimed and brought into production to feed a rapidly expanding population.[86] Landlords, still living in the castles and bawns of plantation times in the first part of the century, with all their overtones of division and insecurity, were building fashionable country mansions by the second half, planting new woods, laying out demesnes and deer parks, all alike providing new employment opportunities. In areas of linen prosperity landlords sought to increase their revenue by letting directly to the sub-tenants, granting secure leases to those who could pay and placing many Catholics, for the first time, in direct economic competition with Protestants. By the time MacCooey came to write his poetry in the second half of the century, leases for lives were the most coveted and the obstacles placed in the way of Catholics obtaining them had become live issues.

Despite the penal laws, the eighteenth century was a period of opportunity for Irish Catholics. There were no restrictions on the accumulation and transfer of non-landed wealth and a wealthy Catholic middle class emerged despite the laws. A sub-gentry also developed, largely consisting of original landowners who had survived as chief tenants and middlemen. However, Ulster diverges from this national pattern. The large Catholic merchant, strong farmer and middleman classes that came into existence elsewhere in Ireland, driving the rise of Catholic political power from mid-century onwards, are absent, as is a class of 'comfortable' Catholics at lower levels.[87] The top tier of Irish Catholic society, which survived to provide the base for upward mobility elsewhere in Ireland, had disappeared in Ulster. In the old O'Neill territories and in south Down there are even signs of reluctance to grant leases to old gentry.[88] The absence of Ulster from the early campaigns of the Catholic Committee is unmistakable. Financial contributions to its campaign were also lower from Ulster than from the other provinces. That campaign was urban-driven and Ulster's urban development was retarded until the second half of the century. Even then its urban culture remained largely Protestant. Few if any Catholics participated in the commercial end of the linen industry before the 1740s and when they settled in towns they tended rather to be publicans, grocers, small traders and shopkeepers.[89] By the 1790s, however, successful Catholic families – notably from County Down, where they had reached the top of the linen industry – were represented in the Catholic Committee's campaign, even though there were few from the other Ulster counties. Magennises, Savages, O'Neills and Teelings were among the Down representatives, Patrick Russell, Esq., represented Louth, Andrew MacShane, Esq., Donegal, Daniel Reilly Esq., Monaghan.[90] The Loinsigh (Lynch) family had been able to sustain a classical and Irish-language school at Loughinisland, County Down for generations.[91] A Catholic middle class was beginning to emerge by the end of the century, but it was tiny in comparison with the rest of the country.

However, the complexity of the Ulster situation has not yet been properly researched. It is not one of unrelieved social decline, and if we move away from the main families (who have fallen on bad times), we find enough examples of secondary lines remaining on the land and prospering. Where Catholics had a strong presence, they remained important figures, either as tenant farmers or small proprietors. This is particularly so in south Ulster: the Maguires of Fermanagh; McKennas, MacMahons, Plunketts and Murphys of Monaghan; O'Callaghans and O'Neills of Armagh; O'Reillys of Cavan; O'Neills, Magennises, Savages and Whytes (formerly White) of south Down. The O'Neills of the Fews in Armagh had retained some of their former status, Daniel being listed in 1766 as a 'yarn merchant' and manufacturer, with a number of weavers in his employment. In 1767 he was appointed petty constable for Creggan. His children intermarried with old Irish families of similar status.[92] The Coigley (Quigley) family of Armagh, with O'Neill and O'Donnelly ancestry, were also leading linen entrepreneurs by the last decades of the century.[93]

Likewise in south Down a number of old Catholic families retained positions of social importance. The Whyte family of Loughbrickland weathered the penal laws by a series of collusive trusteeships in the hands of Protestant relatives.[94] The O'Neills of Banvale, Hilltown (linear descendants of the Clandeboye O'Neills) prospered in the linen industry. John was owner of a bleach green and member of the 1792–3 Catholic Convention – 'old gentry' as Tone was to call him.[95] The MacCartans of Loughinisland are noted in the 1766 return of papists as employing seven servants. They also supplied large numbers of the local clergy, including a bishop of Down and Connor, Theophilus MacCartan (bishop, 1760–78) – who continued to reside in Loughinisland during his episcopacy. His will of 1777 goes some way to telling us why this small but powerful Catholic network survived. Not only did his family intermarry with the Magennises, O'Neills and Kellys, but they remained close to those Magennises and Savages who had conformed to the established church, and his grandnieces were warned that they would be cut out of his will if they married any 'base or inferior person'.[96] Another case of horizontal social relations between descendants of the old Gaelic elite and the new Protestant establishment is related in the account of a tour of Ireland made in 1752 by Richard Pococke (Protestant bishop of Ossory, 1756–65). At Castle Caldwell, on the Donegal/Fermanagh border, home of Sir James Caldwell, aide-de-camp to General O'Donnell in the Austrian service, Pococke, another Anglican minister, Sir James and the father of General O'Donnell dined together. O'Donnell 'they say is the head of that family descended from the Earl of Tyrconel and tho' he has only leases, yet he is the head of the Roman Catholicks in this country'.[97]

The most intriguing case of a once-important landed Catholic family retaining their status and prospering in the new linen industry is that of the Teelings. An Anglo-Norman family, in Ireland since the twelfth century, they had forfeited their estates in County Meath in 1657 and moved to County Louth, where they intermarried with another leading Catholic family, the Taaffes of Smarmore Castle. In the eighteenth century they had become linen merchants in Lisburn, County Antrim, also acquiring property in Dublin and amassing a fortune said to have been worth £30,000 by 1798. The then head of the family, Luke Teeling, figured prominently in Catholic politics. But his career and his business were ruined by the conflict of the 1790s and he was bitter at the continuing penal restrictions which barred Catholics like himself from a full participation in public life. As positions progressively opened up to Catholics in the nineteenth century, however, his descendants were found behaving like any members of the Irish upper class, some becoming officers in the British army and dying for it in World War I.[98]

The first real insight into this emerging tier of prosperous Ulster Catholics is in the Catholic Qualification Rolls.[99] To avail of the provisions of the Catholic relief acts after 1778 Catholics had first to take an oath of allegiance at the assizes in their county town. Apart from a small handful of Catholics appearing as gentry (the O'Rorkes, O'Haras and O'Neills of Antrim, the O'Neills and Savages of Down, the O'Callaghans of Armagh), there are some 111 undifferentiated merchants, a handful of linen drapers (7), distillers (11), and at the top of the linen industry 5 bleachers (Terence Hughes, Antrim, Michael McFall, Londonderry, Daniel McNeill, Antrim, Charles O'Hara, Randalstown, John Toole, Armagh). Although the vast majority describe themselves as 'farmer', there are also numbers of quite lowly Catholics (labourers, weavers, servants, shoemakers, carpenters) – a trend increased in the 1793–96 returns (1,899), and this when they actually had to pay to take the oath.[100] It testifies to the heightened expectations of change at the end of the eighteenth century among every class of Catholic.

Older wealth tended to enter the Church and there is usually a direct connection between those who became bishops and families who retained a landed base. Indeed the very existence of the Catholic Church in Ulster depended on the ability of such families to shoulder the expense of training their sons abroad. Ulster Catholicism is not an undifferentiated impoverished mass, as the supporters of Catholic emancipation at the end of the century tried to argue. 'If we drive the rich Catholic from the Legislature and from our own society,' argued pro-emancipist MP for County Tyrone, George Knox, 'we force him to attach himself to the needy and disaffected.' We shall admit him eventually, he predicted with more accuracy than he could have realised. 'But we shall withhold that admission so long, that at length we shall give without generosity what will be received without gratitude.'[101] There was a continuing undercurrent of disaffection among the poorer Catholics, which had all but disappeared from the Catholic elite. That elite argued that the very nature of Catholicism was conservative and far more likely to sustain the existing hierarchy in state and society than the Protestant sects.[102] There was little Catholic support in Ulster for any of the disturbances of the 1760s and 1770s, and some evidence that the uncharacteristic involvement of some Catholics was due to the temporary weakening of clerical control after the demise of the regulars. Likewise, at the end of the century even the by then radicalised Catholic Committee held back from association with the United Irishmen until pushed into it by the very rejection of which Knox had warned.

The case of Edmund McGildowney, younger son of a Catholic gentry family in the Glens of Antrim, was typical. A landlord in his own right, he also acted as agent to a number of prominent Protestant families (not least the Earl of Antrim) – which may have protected him from legal interference. He in turn seems to have protected his Catholic tenants from the worst effects of the penal laws. But he was also highly politicised. His papers reveal a knowledge of the arguments being put forward by the Catholic Committee for a relaxation of the penal laws. He took the Catholic qualification oath in 1782, became the representative for Antrim on the Catholic Committee in 1791, and a JP in 1797. At local level he had been active in promoting the welfare of the Catholic Church, and as an old man he was one of the organisers of O'Connell's campaign in Ulster.[103] Another highly successful Ulster Catholic was Armagh-reared Bernard Coile (1766?-1829), who was related to the Catholic bishop of Raphoe and who rose through the linen industry to become a cambric and muslin manufacturer. As with his friends the Coigleys, his success and prominence in Catholic politics attracted the wrath of the Orangemen, and his webs and yarns were destroyed in 1795. He went on to participate in the campaign for Catholic emancipation in the early decades of the next century. Again he is an example of good inter-communal relations at the higher social levels. Both his mother and aunt (who reared him) had converted to Catholicism on their marriage.[104]

At first there was little Catholic participation in the commercial side of the linen industry; and although this changed in the second half of the century, the most profitable side of the industry remained in Protestant hands. There are even signs of some resistance in Catholic areas to an activity being promoted by landlord importation of Protestant craftsmen.[105] By the 1780s, however, the market economy and the process of modernisation had reached even remote districts, and linen had opened up new opportunities unavailable through agriculture. As prosperity spread, so did 'polite' culture, the *Gael* (particularly the women) aping the fashions of the *Gall* and progressively abandoning the Irish language.[106] Surviving Irish-language scholars mistrusted print and Irish-language culture was becoming increasingly enclosed. There was a conscious shunning of Irish by the upwardly mobile, a trend reflected in the disappearance of large numbers of Irish-language manuscripts – stories surviving of them being found in rivers and fields and being used as wrapping paper in general grocers stores.[107] Surveys of Irish-speaking reveal continuing strength (50–70 per cent) in south Ulster, particularly in the main area of poetic activity (south Armagh, north Louth, east Monaghan and an isolated area around Newry), significant pockets in Tyrone and north Antrim (40 per cent) and the bulk of the populace in Donegal. But the trend was downwards, and within a century Irish-speaking had disappeared almost everywhere in Ulster apart from the extreme west and north of Donegal.[108] Irish-speaking becomes increasingly associated with the poorer labourer and the migrant *spailpín*.[109]

It would be difficult to exaggerate the impact of linen on the lifestyle of eighteenth-century Ulster. Although linen production was native to Ireland, it was the British colonists who began weaving the broad linen required for export. The Ulster Irish were slow at first to produce for the market, but were later won over by the higher prices it could command (particularly after 1743 when Britain placed a bounty on exports to the colonies). Between 1730 and 1790 exports of linen increased from 4 to 37 million yards. Since weaving and spinning techniques had changed little, the phenomenal expansion was the result of increasing numbers of spinners and weavers joining the industry. It was linen which paid the rent even on uneconomic farms, encouraging larger families, increased demand for food and a drive to bring even barren land into production. The result was 'a landscape of intensively cultivated small holdings reaching out into the bogs and up into the mountains, thronged by an industrious peasantry enjoying a higher standard of living than elsewhere in rural Ireland'.[110] Even before the repeal of the penal laws, such was the demand for linen that landlords were offering leases to weavers of any denomination. As competition for land intensified, Catholics outbidding Protestants for leases was one of the ingredients in the end-of-century sectarian troubles. The so-called 'Oultachs', who fled from Ulster to other parts of Ireland as a result of these troubles, were comfortably off, for it was mainly Catholic property-owners that the Orange gangs targeted. In the linen triangle (Belfast, Armagh, Dungannon) and the Newry–Drogheda axis, a recognisable Catholic middle class was emerging and belatedly joining the campaign of the Catholic Committee.[111]

Prior to the economic take-off of mid century, all denominations sought career outlets abroad. Dissenters left in large numbers for North America. According to Arthur Young, Catholics were less willing to leave: 'The Catholicks never went; they seem not only tied to the country but almost to the parish in which their ancestors lived.'[112] Emigration, he continued, was not an option for the very poor. But with the upswing of the economy Catholics too began to participate in the transatlantic flow. At one stage the apparent religious imbalance in emigration gave rise to fears that the country would be denuded of its Protestant population – 'the papists being already five or six to one, and being a breeding people', as archbishop King commented in 1718.[113] Traditionally Catholics had looked to the Catholic countries on the Continent, thousands joining the continental armies and seminaries in the period. Once considered a harsh consequence of the penal laws, this is now recognised as an important career outlet for the sons of Catholic gentry. The impact of those returning and the social and political consequences of such extensive family networks is only beginning to be investigated. Again Ulster's lower participation is commented upon. Yet, for a province whose upwardly mobile Catholics were starting from a lower base, it is significant enough.[114] Austrian and Spanish service hosted several generations of Ulster families, notably O'Donnells, Maguires, Plunketts and O'Neills, their absence lamented by the poets, but their status abroad sustaining the image of a surviving Gaelic nobility.

A survey of eighteenth-century tombstones in the ancient Fermanagh cemetery of Devenish is revealing. Every denomination still used it. Catholic tombstones reveal a number of old Gaelic family names (Reillys, Magraths, Gallaghers, Kellys, Cassidys, Maguires, Seerys (Ó Saoraigh), many displaying coats of arms. Indeed, the later eighteenth century witnessed an upturn in members of Gaelic-Irish families seeking to register their pedigrees prior to leaving for the Continent, and the Ulster (Heraldry) Office in Dublin Castle showed itself more than willing to collaborate with priests and Gaelic scholars to assist them.[115] The occupational history of a number of the families is recorded on these tombstones: the Cassidys, ancient physicians to the Maguires, still functioned as doctors and begat dynasties of priests. Edward Kelly is recorded as an Enniskillen merchant at the time of the death of his two daughters in 1793. The Maguire tombstones include those of Denis Maguire, bishop of Dromore, and Bryan Maguire, erected by his son, a captain in the Imperial (Austrian) service.[116] The Monaghan MacEnaneys, who left Ulster after the defeat of James II, had also found fame and fortune in Austrian service (Patrick MacEnaney becoming secretary of state, his son counsellor of state).[117] When the latter died in 1800, he left his fortune to his Monaghan relatives, suggesting the maintenance of ties in such dispersed families and no little contribution to the Catholic economy from those abroad.

The Cassidys are typical of other ancient professional families who continued their traditional calling. The Kernans became apothecaries and attorneys; the Hoods of Maghera – descendants of *ollamhs* to the O'Neills of Clandeboye – poets and schoolteachers;[118] the Quins – quartermasters to the O'Neills – owners of corn mills in Armagh.

Contrary to the accepted image, therefore, there is a nascent middle class in Catholic Ulster, its size underestimated because of the failure to take into account the large numbers entering and prospering in the church. But it is geographically confined (largely south and south-east Ulster) and does not dent the general image of the bulk of Catholics as an underclass. Even so, they form a potentially stronger support group than their Protestant equivalent, largely because of their group solidarity and close family ties with the clergy. Dr William Drennan (1754–1820), leading Presbyterian reformer and United Irishman, and, after early doubts, a lifetime campaigner for Catholic emancipation, was nevertheless to complain about the tendency of Catholics only to employ professionals of their own denomination – their group identity as Catholics overriding all others.[119]

4. The religious geography of eighteenth-century Ulster

However, such developments did not radically alter the religious geography of the province except in the few areas at the heart of the linen industry. Areas deemed native after the Ulster plantation remained so. The preoccupation with the religious make-up of the populace, mentioned earlier, took the form of a certain amount of social engineering in the first half of the century. At first many landlords went to great lengths to attract Protestant tenants in preference to Catholics, and the recent influx of Scots was reducing many Irish to the level of under tenants. Bishop MacMahon complained in 1714:

Although all Ireland is suffering, this province is worse off than the rest of the country . . . from the neighbouring country of Scotland Calvinists are coming over here daily in large groups of families, occupying the towns and villages, seizing the farms in the richest parts of the country and expelling the natives.[120]

There was too an economic motive as Protestant tenants were generally thought more likely to improve their lands and pay their rents. This attitude was to change as the economic standing of Catholics improved later in the century.

But the religious map remained much the same. Territorial segregation often kept the different religious communities apart. The 1766 religious census shows mixed communities to have been in the minority and a large number of predominantly Catholic juxtaposing predominantly Protestant areas. Areas where recognisably 'Catholic' territory bordered on recognisably 'Protestant' territory were to become traditional flashpoint areas. This was certainly the case in parts of south Ulster, on the Tyrone/Fermanagh border and the western shores of Lough Neagh and north Armagh (ancient O'Neill territory), where there was virtual parity in numbers of Catholics and Protestants and where the common eighteenth-century pastime of faction fighting first assumed a sectarian hue. 'In these parts, and in the adjacent parts of Cavan', wrote one commentator in the early 1790s, 'there reside numerous tribes of Presbyterians, called by the common people Scotch. Between these and the lower order of Catholics there has prevailed for many years an hereditary Animosity, and it is hard to say on which side preponderate ignorance and religious prejudices.'[121] The tories and rapparees of the early century successfully beat off Protestant incursion in the south of the province. The poorer terrain of Donegal, the Glens of Antrim, south Ulster and the Sperrin mountains of Tyrone and Derry proved unattractive to Protestant tenants until reclamation and population increase brought even these into the competition for space in this increasingly crowded territory.

By the second half of the century Catholics were in a minority in Antrim, Down and Derry, equal in numbers in Armagh and Tyrone, but in the majority in the other counties. Until then poverty, traditional immobility, lack of communications and surviving Gaelic culture – which, like its poetry, tended to be backward rather than forward looking – shut in traditional practices. With areas like the Glens of Antrim, almost totally inaccessible to wheeled vehicles and incapable of growing their own flax, these uplands came late to the linen industry, and in the case of the Glens not at all. In such areas, where the Protestant population was small, Catholics did have more chance of acquiring leases. But they could often only do so by joining with others in partnership groups, which would continue communal farming practices – giving a distinctive 'open' appearance to landscape which already contained large tracts of barren bog. This was subsistence farming; and whilst it protected vulnerable members of the community, it also curbed initiative and did not lend itself to improvement.[122]

In stark contrast to 'Protestant' landscape which was enclosed and neat – the model having been set by the late seventeenth-century English immigrants who reproduced their English landscape in the Lagan valley and north Armagh – this was seen as primitive terrain, avoided by the typical eighteenth-century traveller or traversed in trepidation. The Fews area of south Armagh – through which travellers from Dublin had to pass to reach Armagh city – was particularly dreaded. A landscape of 'very wild mountains', wrote Dr Thomas Molyneux of his journey in 1708, 'of a boggy, heathy soil, the road through them of a rocky gravel', scarce a house to be seen and no meadows or enclosures. After sixteen or seventeen miles of this, his relief was tangible as he left the mountains and entered 'pleasant, enclosed country' and 'new made roads to Armagh'.[123] It was still noted for bandits in mid-century, another traveller observing in 1750 that no one would risk a journey through 'the dreaded defiles' of south Armagh without an escort. It was an area which seemed to have stood still, its sparse population still ploughing by the tail.[124] In 1759 Chief Baron Willes likened the difficulty of journeying between Downpatrick and Newry through the Mourne Mountains of south Down to that through the Alps or Apennines:

Within these twenty years it was an absolute uncivilised country, and anyone who ventured to go among them did it at his peril, it being almost the inaccessible retreat of Tories and Rapparees and outlaws. But a good road being made . . . it is much civilised to what it was . . . it is the wildest and most mountainous country I have seen . . . The cabins one sees on the sides of the hills are the most miserable huts I ever saw, built with sods and turf, no chimney, the door made of an hurdle, the smoke goes all out of the door, the cocks and hens, pigs, goats and if perchance they have a cow, inhabit the same dwelling. They seem much upon a rank with the American savages, except that they have some notion about making the sign of the cross and stand much in awe of their priests. And yet there must be times when the master and mistress of the family are merry and jolly, for one sees the cabin doors crowded with little naked boys and girls.[125]

Until romanticism and the novels of Lady Morgan altered perceptions, this was unfashionable landscape. Towns, roads and canals were Protestant. The economy of whiskey, barley, black cattle and smuggling of the uplands was contrasted with that of linen in the lowlands. James McParlan commented in 1802:

In the mountain region, where the culture of barley, and use of whiskey . . . are suffered to predominate, industry and the habits of it are shamefully degraded. In the champain parts, where agriculture and manufactures employ the time of the peasant . . . industry and all its habits prevail; . . . in those parts of the mountain . . . where the linen manufacture is gaining ground, drunkenness and idleness are decreasing considerably.

He also noted Irish speaking generally in the mountains, but English with a 'Scotch twang' in the lowlands.[126] Although some of the mountainous districts, such as those on the Fermanagh/Donegal border, were still haunted by outlaws as late as the 1770s, there is a sense of the primitive rather than of actual danger in the many travel accounts. In the tenser atmosphere of the 1790s, however, awareness of Catholic concentration in 'the wild parts' once again caused alarm in adjacent Protestant areas.[127]

Nor was this religious tagging of the very land an exaggeration by outsiders. There was a heightened awareness of the location of ancient families' lands. In Carleton's *Poor Scholar,* the McEvoys, evicted from their farm by a Protestant land agent, look down from the barren hills where they now live to the fertile farms below. 'Look at thim . . . only look at the black thieves! how warm an' wealthy they sit there in our own ould possessions, an' here we must toil till our fingers are worn to stumps.'[128] The different habitats of the religious communities is thought accountable for their contrasting characteristics: 'The Catholic being, like his soil, hardy, thin, and capable of bearing all weathers; and the Protestants, larger, softer, and more inactive.'[129] This religious division of the economy can be pushed too far. The Scots were just as traditional in their farming methods as the Irish. Poorer Protestants also joined together in partnership leases.[130] But there can be no denying that different territorial allegiances and religious segregation had developed in the course of the eighteenth century and there was an acute awareness of who lived where. The process was accentuated by the very high mobility amongst Presbyterians and the reluctance of Catholics to move outside their immediate locality. The 1766 religious returns also show Protestants more resistant to living among Catholics than the reverse.[131] Little wonder that observers spoke of Catholics and Protestants inhabiting different districts and behaving and speaking like different peoples.[132]

John Gamble's invaluable tour of 1810 shows that the practice of seeking the stereotypical cues to identify one's religion – a practice ingrained in contemporary Northern Ireland consciousness – was already well established by the turn of the eighteenth century. Travelling through south Tyrone, he sought shelter from a rainstorm in a roadside cabin.

I stepped into a cabin, which by good luck was on the roadside. It was really good luck, for there was a large dunghill in front, which nearly hid it from view . . . 'ten thousand welcomes . . .', said the man of the house, starting up: 'Susy, draw his honour a creepy'. I knew now I was the guest of a Catholic. The dunghill was suspicious; 'your honour' was decisive. A Protestant never gives this appellation lightly, a Presbyterian never gives it at all.[133]

The incident (and there are many such in Gamble) shows that the old traditions of hospitality and deference had not been eroded by the bitter experiences of the 1790s – even if, as with Gamble, awareness of difference was probably rarely far below the surface.

5. Recovery of the Catholic Church

Despite the penal laws, the eighteenth century was a period of major recovery for the Catholic Church throughout Ireland. The penal laws had not destroyed church organisation, for there had been little recovery since the beginning of the previous century. Several Ulster sees had been vacant for much of the seventeenth century and by the new century there was widespread slippage among the faithful and a lack of clerical discipline.[134] However, from 1730 onwards episcopal succession was maintained. Despite the penal laws, the authorities had recognised the practical need for bishops to maintain discipline, and generally left them alone. By the second half of the century a succession of reforming ecclesiastics had laid the basis for the take-off of the nineteenth century. They were able to operate with a remarkable degree of independence, more indeed than their colleagues in countries where Catholicism was the established religion, and where state interference, the Enlightenment's attack on religion and growing religious indifference saw the church in retreat all over Europe. It is unlikely that the Catholic Church in Ireland would have become such a powerful institution had the Stuarts survived as Catholic monarchs. Under James II there had been tensions as he tried to assert the kind of state control which already existed in the other European monarchies. The long-term result was a more Tridentine, more severe, more conservative religion than elsewhere, a religion which, according to a leading Church historian, 'stood alone as a kind of affront to contemporary living in the West, even within the Church' until the second half of the twentieth century.[135] The drive for internal reform came mainly from Munster and south Leinster, Ulster and north Connacht clinging to old practices much longer than anywhere else. It took three forms: the restructuring of the visible church (notably the construction of mass-houses and chapels); the instruction of the faithful; and the imposition of ecclesiastical authority.

The preponderance of mass-rocks and other open-air places of worship in Ulster reflects the poverty of the people and the absence of a supporting gentry, much more than legal penalisation. Clogher was by no means the poorest of the Ulster dioceses. Yet even here Bishop MacMahon in 1714 reported the people 'in dire poverty' and unable to support their clergy. 'Indeed the sight of them would move one to compassion, as they go around unkempt, ill-clad, without companions, with no fixed abode, spending the night here and there in huts by the wayside . . . [celebrating] Mass in soiled or tattered vestments', using 'tin' chalices and cracked altar stones.[136] Pococke reports similar poverty from his tour of 1752. He was able to travel all over Ireland and was welcomed in the cabins of the poor. By now he was using the terms Roman Catholic and Papist interchangeably, with no sense of threat, and he comments on Catholic religious practice without any reference at all to the existence of the penal laws. Near Dunfanaghy, Donegal, he witnessed an open-air mass:

In the Side of one of them [the mountains] a Sort of Amphitheatre is formed in the rock; here I saw several hundred people spread all over that plain spot, the Priest celebrating Mass under the rock, on an altar made of loose Stones . . . I observed his Pontifical Vestment with a black Cross on it; for in all this Country for Sixty miles west & south as far as Connaught, they celebrate in the open air, in the fields or on the mountain; the Papists being so few & poor, that they will not be at the expense [sic] of a public building.[137]

In predominantly Protestant areas the provision of Catholic places of worship was worse. In 1764 the hearth-money collector for Carrick-fergus reported neither seceding Presbyterian nor Catholic places of worship in the area, but a priest, Phelix Scullion, saying mass in the fields in the summer, and in his parishioners' homes in the winter. In the nearby parishes of Templecorran and Kilroot mass had not been said 'in the memory of the oldest man living'.[138]

Ulster Catholicism had never been church-based and, in this drive of the episcopacy to restore the church's visible structures, it had to start from a much more undeveloped base than in much of the rest of Ireland. From at least the beginning of George I's reign (1721–27) mass-houses began to replace mass-rocks and other temporary structures. In some cases the sites were donated by Protestant landlords and they tended to appear in areas where relations with local Protestants were good. They were humble structures, resembling one-storey thatched cottages. Catholicism was not alone in this. Early Presbyterian meeting houses were remarkably similar and Protestant churches remained in a lamentable condition until the end of the century.[139] But the 1731 report into the state of popery shows Ulster and parts of north Connacht lagging far behind the rest of the country in the provision of mass-houses (though with neighbouring Louth the wealthiest in the country), and still dependent on itinerant friars.[140] The situation improved rapidly from mid-century, one commentator reporting as early as 1764: 'Till within these few years there was scarce a mass-house to be seen in the northern counties of Ulster; now mass-houses are spreading over most parts of that country.'[141]

Although Derry was registered as the poorest diocese in the country in 1731, and Philip McDevitt still found no churches there when he became bishop in 1766, by the time of his death in 1797 there were many churches and a seminary at Claudy near Strabane. His will reveals a man of comfortable means and social standing – a far cry from the fugitive priest at the beginning of the century.[142] But elsewhere the restructuring was slower and Carleton recalled of his south Ulster childhood that 'there was nothing in existence for the Catholics for the worship of God except the mere altar, covered with a little open roof to protect the priest from rain', and such mass-rocks figure prominently in his stories. But with no protection for the congregation he concludes 'that during the winter months the worship of God was . . . a very trying ceremony'.[143]

The church's teaching called for 'outward profession' of the faith, and after the early years of persecution, there were regular episcopal exhortations to construct mass-houses.[144] The kind of pragmatism which encouraged occasional conformity to retain family land was condemned by a new breed of bishop intent on tightening discipline and might explain why hostile folk traditions differ from contemporary acceptance of land conformism.[145] Mass-attendance was to become the cornerstone of such 'outward profession' and there has been considerable historical debate on this as a yardstick for Catholic practice.[146] In the absence of statistics, any analysis for the eighteenth century must remain impressionistic. In Europe generally, however, regular attendance was not expected, and there is no sign in these new religious texts that it was causing concern one way or another. Issues which *were* causing concern were the huge number of holy days (criticised by the state authorities for taking people away from their work and by the bishops themselves for the attendant drunkenness and bawdy behaviour); and above all the need to make the sacraments of penance and confirmation readily available. In all cases the aim was to impose church control, and on the issue of holy days – where the number was reduced but observance of the remainder made obligatory – they appear to have been successful, at least in the towns. 'This being Assumption-day, the shops were shut in every town,' remarked an English traveller, *en route* from Drogheda to Derry in 1804, 'and in the streets it looked like Sunday, as observed in the more remote and decent parts of England or Scotland.'[147] However, such was the continued shortage of churches in rural areas that in the south Ulster diocese of Kilmore the Bishop was conducting confirmation at the fairs and markets in the 1750s and 1760s – a period when an acute shortage of priests was depriving large tracts of the poorer districts of any ministry whatsoever.[148] It also gave rise to a practice known as 'stations', whereby once a month mass and confession was held in a private house in the parish.

Given Catholic Church teachings on the necessity of interpreting scripture for the laity – indeed, reading the Bible in the vernacular had been prohibited since 1559[149] – the absence of public places of worship in Ulster and the inability of most Catholics to read (in either English or Irish), were clearly major barriers to the Tridentine goal of instruction. Priests were obliged to provide instruction at mass. However, the considerable independence of priests in the eighteenth century made it difficult to enforce uniformity, and the extravagant praise heaped by the poets on those few clergy who provided instruction suggests that it was uncommon. An early eighteenth-century sermon in Irish, reputedly written by a Franciscan friar in Armagh, says as much:

The clergy don't consider it worthwhile to spend their time on catechism, but on great, highly-learned, ingenious sermons of which people don't understand the tenth part, and it is because of that, alas, that many have been listening to Mass and to sermons throughout their lives without much benefit and who are still ignorant of the faith of Christ.[150]

It was a complaint echoed by the Dominican Provincial in Ireland in 1730, who criticised clerical training at Louvain as too 'speculative' and called instead for instruction in matters 'of more use to this mission', particularly 'the subjects controverted between the Catholics and Protestants of this country'.[151]

It was in the eighteenth century that the Catholic Church began finally to address the issue of survival in a Protestant kingdom. In this, Ireland was not behind the times, for it was only in the eighteenth century that the Church throughout Europe accepted responsibility for giving sustained spiritual instruction to the laity. A new kind of bishop finally produced popular teaching texts and catechisms – texts which would define popular Catholicism into modern times and provide the basis for the Catholic publishing industry in the second half of the century. Two in particular, O'Reilly's catechism (c.1720s) and Gallagher's 1736 sermons, remained popular favourites into the twentieth century, notably in Ulster and Connacht. They undoubtedly played a key role in instilling that particularly authoritarian strain in Tridentine teaching into Irish Catholicism and in replacing the genuine affection for the friars with that fearful respect for the clergy which was cultivated by the Church in the next century. Both are extremely stern in tone, but their content would be recognisable to any Ulster Catholic who was a child before Vatican II. They also finally succeeded, where all their predecessors had failed, in destroying the power of the friars, and with it a more earthy, easygoing faith.

Michael O'Reilly (c.1690–1758) was born in County Cavan, trained in Paris, and served successively as parish priest of Cavan, vicar-general of Kilmore, bishop of Derry and primate of Armagh (1749–58). Kilmore and Derry had been without a bishop for fifty and one hundred years respectively before O'Reilly's arrival, and the resulting laxity of discipline would have had a major impact on his outlook. A 'rigid disciplinarian', he would arrive unannounced at Sunday mass and rebuke any priest who failed to provide instruction. His catechism was produced in phonetic Irish and English versions, the latter 'for the newly converted colonists'. It contains some two hundred simple questions and answers setting out the basic tenets of Catholicism. There are specific condemnations of drunkenness, 'carnal knowledge' outside marriage, and 'impure thoughts'. Those failing to confess and communicate at least once a year are to be debarred from divine service and denied a Christian burial. Readers are warned that there is 'but one true Church . . . the holy Catholic Church' and they should be prepared 'to suffer all hardships and extremities' rather than renounce it. This would be typical of the Irish hierarchy in the future, a tendency to reject any improvement in the lot of its adherents if it involved any weakening of church authority.

But if the English text is stern, the Irish is more so, with 'its tendency to multiply the heads in hell'.[152] O'Reilly was to stir up a hornets' nest in Ulster as he spearheaded its reform. But, Ó Doirnín apart, anti-clerical poetry is notably absent in Ulster; deference to the clergy and unquestioning acceptance of Catholic teachings remained a characteristic of Ulster Catholicism. Gallagher's sermons (1736) and Pulleine's catechism (1748) are likewise in phonetic Irish. The sermons of James Gallagher, bishop of Raphoe, were designed as clerical preaching aids, but by the nineteenth century they had become treasured possessions throughout Ulster, Connacht and Munster. Early this century Rose O'Doherty of Falcarragh, County Donegal, though illiterate and knowing little English, could recite entire sermons in Irish from Gallagher.[153] 'My father always had a few Irish books of his own, mostly on religion, the Irish catechism and Dr Gallagher's sermons,' recalled Patrick McGlinchey, Inishowen weaver (1861–1954). 'He could read the sermons well. There was a great sermon on the Day of Judgement ... Dr Gallagher's sermons were great reading. No one going now will be saved according to these sermons, for there's nobody living up to them.'[154]

The sermon which made such an impact on young McGlinchey was sermon II, 'On the Last Judgement', based on a reading of St Luke's Gospel. It presents a terrifying vision of the last day, the end of the world, and the 'Judge' taking 'vengeance on sinners': the lustful, the glutton, the drunkard, those who sold Christ 'for a bottle of whiskey', or the housewives selling their hanks of yarn in short measure. Women fare badly in these sermons, constantly measured up to the impossible ideal of Mary. These are the petty crimes of the common people. Other classes scarcely figure, giving some support to MacCooey's criticisms of the clergy. They are medieval in their vision and sternness: God is a terrible judge, Mary and the saints necessary intermediaries. There is considerable emphasis on sin, confession and communion (particularly at Easter), a suggestion that absolution was more often withheld than not and a consequent resort to 'a strolling priest [i.e. a friar]', or to a priest 'no longer in active service' or 'exiled from his diocese', and there is some evidence that O'Reilly himself often suspended priests.[155] As for any political message, there is none. Gallagher's message is typical of that coming from the hierarchy generally: the sufferings of the people of Ireland were brought upon themselves by their own sins and loss of piety.

Another, even simpler and very popular catechism in Irish (1748) is that by the Catholic dean of Dromore, James Pulleine. It is the earliest Irish-language catechism for children and is firmly addressed to the laity rather than the clergy.

The Council of Trent, sess. 24 c. 7 binds not only the Church, but also fathers and mothers, sponsors and teachers and all heads of hearths and homes to teach Christian doctrine to their families and charges so that the light of untarnished faith may shine in the hearts of the people in spite of all the storms of evil, in spite of every persecution or unjust power which is or may be ranged against them.

It also indicates an ability to read English far in advance of areas in the west, for the instructions on Irish pronunciation suggest that the reader was expected to have been able to read English, but not Irish. Irish speaking died out earlier in County Down than anywhere else in Ulster.[156]

In a county where Catholics were outnumbered by Protestants and where bitter memories of seventeenth-century events were vivid, it reveals a sectarian consciousness absent from Gallagher's and O'Reilly's works and a political message unusual to these new popular religious works. Like the chosen people in captivity in Babylon, the Irish are now 'under the yoke of slavery, under oppression and persecution at the hands of the foreigner', Down, Saul and Faughart, 'home of the saints . . . of Patrick, Brigid and Columcille', are now in spiritual ruin and the need for proper instruction was urgent.[157] The reason for this unusually strident tone is that something of a battle was being waged in south Down for the hearts and minds of the Catholic people. Three Charter schools had recently been established in the county at Killough, Ballinahinch and Moira, and another was planned at Donaghmore. Walter Harris, who described these developments in detail, hailed the progress of the linen industry, the spread of the English language and the decline of 'popery' in the area.[158]

The kind of proselytising literature used by the Charter schools was clearly having some impact in the area, for Pulleine only four years later was warning his readers 'not to place any erroneous or heretical book in the hands of your children, for the bad instruction and bad knowledge which they obtain from those books . . . ruins and pollutes them, and . . . will not easily leave them.' [p.vi] The catechism is a conscious effort to counteract such Protestant proselytising through the medium of Irish, and there is a suggestion that it was enjoying a fair degree of success, for the catechism contains specific detail about what distinguishes a Catholic from others. For Catholics the sign of the cross is 'a distinguishing sign between us and the Turks, Pagans, Gentiles, and every other accursed group that is without God and the church'.[p.7] 'What is the holy Catholic church? It is the general assembly of the faithful who . . . profess the law of God, under the rule and direction of the Pope . . . And just as none were saved at the time of the flood, except for those who were with Noah in the Ark; so nobody will be saved who is not in the Catholic church'.[p.13]

Part of Harris's crusade involved detailing every local atrocity carried out against Protestants, largely in 1641, and the local memory seems to have been extraordinarily vivid. Here we have two separate and antagonistic traditions of victimhood building up. Pulleine was also a minor poet, and in his *Óráid* or praise-poem for Owen O'Neill of Clandeboye, who died at Hilltown in September 1744, he detailed past atrocities against the Irish in remarkably similar terms to those of Harris. It is thought that Pulleine resided with O'Neill at Hilltown and acted as private chaplain, while serving as parish priest to the surrounding Clonduff parish. His *Óráid*, like the poetry of south Ulster generally, shows a detailed knowledge of the ancestry of O'Neill and ascribes to him all the noble virtues formerly associated with his forebears. It is bitter about the downfall of Conn O'Neill in the seventeenth century, who lost 'his country and his lordship' to 'the deceitful quarrel-raising Galls . . . by treachery, murder, and beheading of men', the remainder left 'wandering to strange foreign countries, leaving their land and their tribal inheritance . . . to strangers and to Scotchmen'. But Owen had been a constant 'surety' to his people, 'a protecting defensive branch between them and those who wronged them' and nothing could tempt him 'to forsake the Holy Catholic Church'.[159]

Pulleine is unusual, and although little is known about him he was almost certainly a friar. His catechism seems to have had a largely localised circulation, for O'Reilly dominated the rest of the province. Although 'the holy Catholic Church' is claimed as the 'one true church' in all these new catechisms, they tended to be less anti-Protestant than preceding ones. Most of the new breed of crusading clergy were acutely aware of Protestant criticisms and the need for clergy to be better prepared to answer them.[160] There is a drive to eradicate superstitious practices and excessive devotion to the saints. And it is the friars whom they hold most responsible for perpetuating such 'abuses'. Most of the secular diocesan bishops in Ireland were educated in France and brought back with them the Enlightenment's dislike of the regular orders, whose scandalous behaviour they blamed for the intermittent persecution in Ireland. They were more anxious to conciliate Protestants and the Irish government than the regulars, and O'Reilly's depoliticised catechism was typical. He also had personal reasons, having been replaced in Clogher by a younger Dominican on the recommendation of James III. Stuart nomination to bishoprics was another object of their attack, for it promoted too many regulars. O'Reilly was personally to debar the bishop-elect to Derry, John Brullaghan, notwithstanding Stuart nomination (1750), and he joined forces with other reforming bishops in their campaign against the friars. The outcome was the papal closure of the regulars' novitiates in Ireland in 1751. Henceforth numbers were to be strictly limited by the requirement to study abroad, few of whom could have afforded to do so.[161]

The crisis would point up the different nature of church organisation in Ulster and parts of Connacht from the rest of the country. 'The priests had no settled way upon them', McGlinchey recalled from stories circulating in his youth, 'wandering friars went about and said mass here and there among the hills . . . They were a droll lot of men, and I heard old rhymes about them arguing and bantering and joking with the people.' But that had all changed, he continued, sometime around the 1780s.[162] All the old accusations about questing at the altars, inadequate training and education and general scandalous behaviour resurfaced in the eighteenth-century campaign and there is an acute awareness that, with Protestantism's efforts to win the people from their popery, Catholicism needed to be better equipped to respond.[163]

In Carleton's rural Ulster the priest is the central figure of authority, and respect for the 'clargy' has become an eleventh commandment. In this the eighteenth-century reformers had been entirely successful.

Although problems of lay interference resurfaced into the nineteenth century – the Maguires of Tempo, though now Protestant, still claiming ancient rights of presentment – and further measures would be necessary to restrict excessive fraternisation between priest and flock, the trend, which would peak in the so-called 'devotional revolution' of the nineteenth century, had already begun. The dominance of the friars had disappeared. Those that remained were firmly under the authority of the parish priest. The mendicant friar who turns up at Carleton's *Shane Fadh's wedding* had been questing for alms – but only with the parish priest's permission, and there is clearly no love lost between them. Like Darby More in *The Midnight Mass*, he is fat and jolly, and closer to the people (in his vices as much as his virtues) – 'an admixture of fun and devotion, external rigour and private licentiousness, love of superstition and of good whiskey, as might naturally be supposed . . . [of] men thrown among a people in whom so many extremes of character and morals meet'.[164] The irony is that the superstition and foreign power which Protestants associated with popery were increasingly antagonistic, as the papacy and the episcopacy alike tried to rid Catholicism of such pagan leftovers.

O'Reilly's actions were very much in line with those of the hierarchy generally and accompanied the first stages of the campaign to prove to government that Catholics were loyal citizens. In Ulster, however, he had not had the support of all the bishops, the majority of whom supported the friars' claims that they had been grossly misrepresented. Ulster Catholicism had been dependent on the friars, and by the late 1760s there was a serious shortage of priests in rural areas – particularly in the province of Armagh, where the population growth was the highest in the country. Moreover, it was argued, the Protestant press had seized on the dispute to fabricate details of orgies in the convents, much as the continental press thrived on stories of lascivious friars. In 1769 eight Irish bishops appealed to Rome on behalf of the friars. Five of these were from Ulster, all (Denis Maguire of Dromore, Philip McDevitt of Derry, Philip O'Reilly of Raphoe, Daniel O'Reilly of Clogher and Theophilus MacCartan of Down and Connor) were from those Old Irish families which had traditionally supported the friars.[165]

Even after O'Reilly's death in 1758, turmoil continued under his successor, Anthony Blake, who raised a storm for his appointments, his overturning of old practices, his exactions and, above all, for his non-residence. A member of an Old English landed family in County Mayo, he resided for the whole of his primacy in Galway. But although he gave good cause for complaint, it was the old accusation of being an outsider (and of ignoring local opinion when making appointments) which surfaced most regularly in such complaints.[166] Blake's appointment in 1758 looked like a veiled censure of the Irish hierarchy, for he had stood aside from the attempt to devise a loyalty oath the previous year and his stance was known to have been regarded favourably in Rome. Rome made a succession of such appointments in later decades of the century – including that of the redoubtable Dr Thomas Troy to the Dublin archdiocese in 1786 and Richard O'Reilly as Blake's successor in Armagh in 1787. It was not that the papacy endorsed any political or civil discord. But it steadfastly opposed anything savouring of Gallicanism or diminution of its authority, and all of the oaths devised to prove Catholic loyalty (including that eventually adopted and signed by many clergy after 1774) involved rejection of the pope's temporal power. There is a sense that the quietude during the office of Richard O'Reilly (primate 1787–1832) was self-imposed after decades of turmoil. It goes part of the way to explaining the unusual turnaround in clerical political attitudes in Ulster and the overwhelming support for government during the crisis of the 1790s.[167]

More important, however, was the destruction of the power of the friars, traditionally far more politicised than the secular clergy. Although the papacy surrendered to pressure and restored the novitiates in 1774, they were now firmly under ecclesiastical control and they never recovered their former strength. Under the 1829 Catholic Emancipation Act, regulars were required to register. Only one appears to have done so in Ulster, a Dominican in County Tyrone, who had had no regular contact with the order for twenty-nine years.[168] The tendency for most priests to be secular was firmly anchored by the opening of the new seminary at Maynooth in 1795. Despite protests from Connacht and Munster, O'Reilly's stance was more representative of the Irish Church's desire for better relations with the government, and the papacy's 1769 conditions for reopening of some novitiates included a requirement to site them where they would give 'the least cause of suspicion' to government.[169] But the centuries-old attachment to the friars died hard, and they continued in the hillier, more Irish areas like south Armagh, Monaghan and Donegal.[170]

The penal laws had reversed the long-standing government policy of punishing the chiefs but helping the people. In the long term they performed the highly unusual process of cutting through class divisions to produce a common identity. Often it was those at the lowest levels who were affected most. And whilst those who did not draw attention to themselves got by well enough, the potential for 'annoyance' by 'some little local persecutor' was always there.[171] That potential was much greater in Ulster than anywhere else in Ireland. It helps explain why the province accommodated itself to the replacement of the friars by a more rigorous, distant and authoritarian clergy; why Ulster Catholicism lacks that earthy religious scepticism so common to rural Catholicism elsewhere in early modern Europe and why the central tenets of Catholic teaching were rarely questioned. Everywhere else people were straining at confessional controls and embracing new religious movements like pietism, evangelicalism and Methodism. Resentful, the Ulster Catholics certainly were. But the Protestants were simply another factor in life to be endured. Endurance and submission was part of Catholic teaching. Religion itself had come to the assistance of that medieval mindset which accepted evil as part of life. Protestantism tended to personalise evil and consider it capable of defeat. Protestants might be hopelessly lost to salvation in Catholic perceptions, but they were left to it and their places of worship were scarcely ever attacked. Protestant tendencies to see the Ulster Catholics as some kind of coiled rebellious spring were misconceived and such misconceptions were to produce some incongruous results in the last years of the century.

7

REFORM TO REBELLION: THE EMERGENCE OF REPUBLICAN POLITICS

A lamentable story dear people I'll tell you,
That happened in Armagh this very last year;
The landlord combined, with others they joined,
To plunder and rob us of all we held dear:
For as we were Catholics they vow'd to oppress us,
Because at elections we had not a vote;
But by St Patrick, as we can't get justice;
Before a year passes we'll alter their note!

United Irish song, 'Granu's Lamentation', 1797

The 1790s marked a watershed in Irish history and set the pattern which has not yet been broken. But there was nothing inevitable about its legacy of militant Catholic nationalism, despite the intensity of the religious suspicion. The decade opened optimistically. The French Revolution, with its message of religious and political equality, temporarily eroded old antagonisms. The main outcome was the Society of United Irishmen, founded in 1791 in the belief that old religious fears were things of the past. In their enthusiasm for the French Revolution, elements of Protestant patriotism and Presbyterian radicalism formed what many considered an 'unnatural' alliance with the new middle-class leadership of the Catholic Committee, and together they embarked on the political education of the Catholic masses. In the space of a decade the Catholic populace was exposed to the full gamut of contemporary political thinking. But French-inspired republicanism and counter-revolution, superimposed on the attitudes analysed in previous chapters, and the outbreak of war between Britain and France in 1793, caused underlying tensions to explode. The United Irish ideal of creating 'the common name of Irishman in the place of the denominations of Protestant, Catholic and Dissenter' was still-born.[1]

1. Catholic political awareness prior to the 1790s

For much of the eighteenth century, Ulster Catholicism seemed quiescent and de-politicised. In the first decades its poets and clergy, particularly the bishops, were as Jacobite as elsewhere in Ireland. There were periodic reports of recruiting for the Pretender until 1745[2] and the Jacobitism of poets like MacCooey and Ó Doirnín is real enough. But

Jacobitism was weaker in Ulster, and in the Jacobite scare of 1726 fewer troops were posted to Ulster than anywhere else in the country.[3] The Ulster poetry reflects a sense that the battle has been lost and the Stuarts themselves were responsible for the destruction of the Gael. Forgetfulness has already set in by the 1730s and, by the 1750s, the Ulster bishops were in the forefront of the campaign to prove the Catholics loyal. The Gael must shift as well as he can in the new system.[4]

> We lost the Boyne through superior strength that day,
> . . . King James – a cowardly king who took to flight, . . .
> leaving nine-fold affliction on the poor Gaels.
>
> . . .
>
> and it's easy for the churls who didn't see that time
> to speak most severely about James' boys.[5]

Yet behind such apparent fatalism lay sullen resentment and a conspiratorial ethos which excluded the stranger. The subversive message of deliverance and victory over the foreigner remained long after the Jacobite cause had been defeated. The metaphor of the Gael as the chosen people in captivity ran through much of the poetry and even today Jacobite songs form part of the repertoire of traditional musicians.[6] Mac Cuarta's 'Lament for Sorley MacDonnell' seemed as relevant to the new age as it had been at the time. The new Moses might have changed through time – from the Stuarts to the French revolutionaries, from Bonaparte to Daniel O'Connell – but the old message remained the same.

The penalisation of Irish language and culture was a thing of the distant past and for much of the eighteenth century the Protestant gentry not only participated in traditional Irish pastimes but promoted a major revival. But its conspiratorial nature for the in-group is already a feature of the poetry.[7] The prophetic twentieth-century threat 'our day will come' has a long antecedent. In conversation with the Hill of Tara – ancient seat of the High Kings of Ireland – Ó Doirnín (d.1769) laments the fate of Ireland. Worry not, replies the Hill, 'if the prophesy of the saints who have gone is fulfilled' the foreigners will be 'vanquished forever by Gaels . . . the Pope's faith will be held by every high prince ... and Martin's children will be put up without a saddle or reins'.[8] The theme was stereotypical of many poems and was not a call to action. The most traditionally Irish parts of Ulster were not prominent in the 1798 rebellion. But the Ulster Catholic was anti-Protestant before he was nationalist. Where the two merged – as they did in the Defenders (though only in certain areas) – it was not always clear whether the *Gall* to be got rid of was English rule or their Protestant neighbours. There was a linear connection between *An Síogaí Rómhánach* and the Defender who told the trial judge in 1794 that he and his like expected to knock the Protestants on the head and replace them in positions of power.[9]

But the train of events which brought the Ulster Catholic to such active resistance was not at all straightforward. Even at the height of penalisation early in the century, the Catholic Church urged 'endurance' on its flock.[10] The history of the Ulster Catholics in the eighteenth century was neither one of resistance nor even of open defiance, but rather a withdrawal into themselves and a tendency to cling onto old practices and values.

Even so, there is not the rush to placate government and display their political loyalty which characterises the Catholic gentry and clergy in other parts of Ireland.[11] Ulster displays little of the Gallicanism which dominated the Catholic campaign for recognition as loyal subjects. Is it because Ulster Catholicism had retained its traditional ultramontanism when the general trend throughout Europe and the rest of Ireland ran against it? Certainly there is an element of this and, as in other poorer areas, traditions were slow to change in Catholic Ulster. Earlier in the century Archbishop MacMahon had successfully resisted publication of the papal bull *Unigenitus* (1713) – which, though technically against the Jansenist movement within French Catholicism, sought to establish unquestioning obedience to papal authority. In France the monarch's insistence on implementing *Unigenitus* was a disastrous misjudgement, setting in train an attack on church and monarchy which would culminate in the French Revolution. MacMahon's judgement was sound in resisting it. He argued against drawing unwelcome attention and giving the excuse to their enemies 'to give the impression, as they usually do, that an attempt is being made to overthrow the government'. Besides he thought it unnecessary since the Irish catholics are very submissive in matters of religion, and believe on good faith anything which they are told, has been decided upon . . . at Rome; so there is no need to make a formal publication of such things . . . a homely instruction . . . is sufficient; the catholics in Ireland believe that the faithful of the whole catholic world are united by the same beliefs and by submission to the Holy See and that there is no contradiction among them; the bishops let them live this way in their simplicity, and do not bring disputed points to their notice . . . in case they might scandalize them in their weakness and because any other approach might do harm to their faith.[12]

Such statements would seem to justify Protestant perceptions about Catholicism's tendency to mentally enslave. Even Presbyterian radical Dr William Drennan, though a good friend to the Catholics, thought it a religion of 'faith' and 'trust' rather than reason: 'For the restless power of reason, once introduced, brings in doubt' – so he mockingly told his sister. 'Trust like a Papist, for if you doubt as a Dissenter, the same restless faculty that rejects the Athanasian Creed . . . will begin to nibble at the Incarnation, the Miraculous Conception etc.' He was impatient at what he perceived as Catholics' 'milk and water spirit', their 'slovenliness of mind', their clannishness. But he also thought their group identity as Catholics gave them a unity lacking in other religions; and he admired their clergy's total independence from the state and found his own clergy wanting in comparison.[13]

Ulster Catholicism also displays that distrust of government and its agents found in all poor societies. Even as the penal laws were being repealed, large swathes of Ulster did not take the oath which would have allowed Catholics to benefit. The Catholic Qualification Oath of 1774 permitted Catholics to swear their allegiance to the existing monarch. It also contained clauses renouncing the Stuarts, denying the temporal power of the pope and the whole notion that he could absolve Catholics from their loyalty to heretic princes. The oath split both the church and the Catholic Committee. But when the first major relief act was passed in 1778 and it was clear that only those who had taken the oath could benefit, large numbers, clergy and laity alike, came forward to do so. The pattern of acceptance was greater in the more anglicised and prosperous counties, with particularly powerful group-ings in Dundalk and Drogheda (both in County Louth), respectable showings in Fermanagh and Antrim, but tapering to only seventy-six in Donegal. Indeed although Lord Abercorn wished to place his Catholic and Protestant tenants on the same footing after the relief measures, his agent reported reluctance to register on his Donegal lands. The numbers of clergy are also well below those elsewhere in the country: six priests and one bishop in Fermanagh,[14] nine in Monaghan, one in Donegal.[15] The depth of suspicion amongst the poorer Ulster Catholics finds expression in the McCrackens' trusty Catholic servant who mourned when her son went into the army (after the Catholic Relief Act of 1793 permitted Catholics to enlist), not because she was losing him 'but his taking the oath that's so much against him'.[16] In contrast, the next phase of oath-taking after the 1793 act – which returned the franchise to Catholics – witnessed a steep increase, with some 667 coming forward in Down alone (a token of the rapid politicisation of Ulster Catholics in the interim).[17]

The lower social status of Ulster Catholics may have accounted for the slow uptake in the 1770s. Certainly, few people in Ireland would have had any direct experience of politics before the 1760s. Until 1768, elections occurred only on the death of the monarch and contests were largely urban events. The higher percentage of Protestants gave Ulster the largest electorate in the country, with County Down the largest single constituency. How far the hotly contested elections impacted on Catholics – though ineligible to vote – is difficult to say. But the opposing electoral interests of the major landlords in Armagh, and their mobilisation of election mobs in the 1753 election was certainly a factor in the deteriorating situation in that county over the next few decades.[18] Here intense dislike of the many payments required by the established church had brought cross-denominational protests earlier in the century.[19] Then they were landlord inspired. By July 1763, however, the unusual independence of the Ulster tenantry was a matter for comment, and in the Oakboys they organised their own protest. Starting in the linen-producing districts of north Armagh, the protest rapidly spread to most of south and mid-Ulster and within a few weeks gentry and law officers were intimidated into concession. The beating of drums and blowing of horns 'their martial music' – such a feature of the 1753 election contest – had by now become something of a permanent feature of protest in Armagh.[20] MacCooey's hero, Art Óg

O'Neill, was an Oakboy captain, and the Oakboys became folk heroes in Gaelic poetry – even though they were predominantly Presbyterian.

In areas which would see some of the worst of the sectarian outbreaks after the 1790s, it is tempting to see the absence of sectarianism in the Oakboy disturbances as unusual. Certainly Catholic involvement in riot was not common, and may well have owed something to the shortage of priests following the suppression of the friaries and resultant weakening of social control. It may also reflect the early stages of politicisation. There was enough common ground, for tenants of all denominations had shared grievances.[21] From at least mid-century there was a greater invasiveness by authority in the social and economic life of the people. Rents were rising as leases fell in and landlords tried to capitalise on an expanding Ulster economy. Tithes were increased as clergy too tried to cope with rising costs and more efficient collection was creating widespread discontent. The government was becoming more active in collecting taxes and as early as 1752 Pococke reported poor people around Lough Swilley simply abandoning their makeshift houses on news of the approach of the hearth-money collector.[22] But acts in 1774 and 1779 forbidding distilling except in towns and refusing licences to smaller stills soon brought poorer Catholics into direct conflict with the authorities. The net effect was to make illegal one of the most pervasive elements in the economy of Catholic districts. Illicit whiskey was everywhere, widely believed by the common people to be something wholesome – and the increasing raids on illicit stills from this time on became part of popular folklore. As taxes increased into the 1790s, so government agents became more aggressive in their collection. Hearth-money collectors and excise officials were regularly accompanied by military and bloody clashes became a feature in the increasingly tense atmosphere of the 1780s and 1790s, particularly in south Ulster and the north midlands.[23]

But timing and local situation is everything and in some districts sectarianism never disappeared. Thus in 1762 when Lord Hillsborough was mobbed and the Lisburn market suspended, the linen weavers and manufacturers in neighbouring Lurgan protested at such activities having disgraced 'this Protestant civilised country'. And ten years later the exclusively Protestant Hearts of Steel in Magherally, County Down, rejected accusations that theirs was a popish plot. We are loyal subjects, they wrote to the editor of the *Belfast News Letter* and 'will, with our lives and properties, defend his majesty's person and government against the unjust attempts of all popish pretenders to the crown of these realms ... Not one Roman Catholic is ever suffered to appear amongst us.'[24] After nearly two decades of intermittent disturbance in Ireland, France sent the American Edward Bancroft in 1779 to investigate news of discontented Presbyterians and Catholics coming together. He reported that they appeared to be 'too divided by the difference of their religions to be too jealous one of the other and of the designs which they imagine that foreign powers could have upon them to be able to unite in friendship, or to risk taking up arms even to obtain satisfaction for their grievances'.[25]

2. *The Armagh Troubles*

For most of the eighteenth century, a *modus vivendi*, based on recognisably different spheres, maintained the peace between Protestant and Catholic in Ulster. Paradoxically it was the breaking down of demographic, cultural and most of all political divisions which sparked the conflict of the 1780s and 1790s. The dramatic rise of population, more than doubling in Ulster between 1750 and 1790, involved significant encroachment on the kind of poorer, upland territory so often occupied by Catholics. This was particularly noticeable in Armagh – the most densely populated county in Ireland – where the success of linen and vastly improved communications were opening up more remote areas to outsiders. Catholics were belatedly entering the commercial end of the linen market, and the sight of successful Catholics outbidding Protestants for land, was a particular affront to the plebeian ascendancy of the lower-class Protestant. Another leftover from the Ulster Plantation was the unusually large number of lower-class Anglicans in Armagh and neighbouring parts of Tyrone.[26] A rash of chapel-building around this time would have further contributed to the image of Catholics as more visible, confident and organised. Worse still was the sight of Protestant gentry espousing the cause of the Catholics.

So-called Protestant or 'colonial' nationalism – whereby Protestant politicians saw themselves as the Irish 'nation' defending its rights

against the colonial power, with no recognition of the apparent contradiction when Catholics, and to some extent Dissenters, were excluded
from politics altogether – had been a feature of Irish politics since the
beginning of the century. From the 1750s it had flowered as the
'patriot' movement, with Ulster politicians in particular perfecting
an anti-Englishness which would have been inconceivable to future
generations. When war broke out in 1775 between England and her
American colonies (with whom Protestant Ulster had a particular
affinity), the patriots armed themselves as the Volunteers, ostensibly
to defend Ireland when most of the troops had been withdrawn for
the American campaign. At first the landed gentry were apprehensive.
Then, as so often in the future, they assumed leadership to assert
control, and the lower-class Protestants who later joined were satisfied
that the Volunteers were a further embodiment of the Protestant
nation. The Volunteers had originated in Ulster, and as they increasingly became the patriots' major prop, Ulster became the fountainhead
for the most extreme anti-government propaganda. For the first time
large numbers of Ulster people were exposed to a campaign denouncing British rule in Ireland. The timing of this campaign ensured a larger
audience for such ideas than ever before, for the war with America
had closed the safety valve of emigration, and increased prosperity
kept more at home thereafter.[27] The outcome was that thousands of
younger, more turbulent men – who would normally have emigrated
– remained in Ulster, and they included Catholics, for they too were
now emigrating in large numbers.

The significance for Catholics of this upsurge in political activity,
this Volunteer rhetoric about the rights of Irishmen, was not immediately apparent, for the Volunteers were as ardently anti-papist as the
early patriots. The process of repealing the penal laws had already
begun – with two acts in the 1770s permitting Catholics to hold land
on the same terms as Protestants. But they had been imposed by the
London government and the opposition in the Irish parliament from
MPs who were also Volunteers spoke volumes for the limits of their
reformism. Although reforming Protestants outside parliament came
to support the campaign for Catholic emancipation, the anti-popery
of those inside increased apace over the next two decades. In this they
represented the feelings of many Ulster Protestants, who viewed with

mounting concern Catholics now competing with them on equal terms for increasingly scarce land. Catholics were theoretically excluded from the Volunteers, because the law banning them from carrying arms remained in force until 1793. The Ulster Volunteers had been the most reluctant to accept Catholics into their ranks. Even in Antrim – one of the more enlightened counties – no company had more than seven Catholics serving. Louth – with its significant Catholic propertied class – admitted Catholics as early as 1780. Derry, Donegal and Tyrone admitted small numbers as privates. But although the Loughgall Volunteers in Armagh publicly rejoiced at the relaxation of the penal laws and welcomed Catholics joining, none had been admitted by the end of 1784.[28]

In areas of traditional tension such as Armagh, the very suggestion that Catholics be admitted was enough to increase tensions. Some Armagh gentry had been taking a relaxed attitude to arming their Catholic tenants for general agricultural purposes. Protestants were offended at the sight of numbers taking the oath of allegiance during the assizes. How could these people whom they had long been told were disloyal be welcomed into the system? Prominent among those who first showed their displeasure by raiding Catholic homes was a disgruntled group of Protestant tenants from the Cope estates at Portnorris, attracted to Mayo to start the linen industry only to run into controversy because of their displacement of existing Catholic tenants. Irritants multiplied. Protestants began to disarm Catholics, claiming to be enforcing the penal laws. Petty juries acquitted those Protestants brought to trial in consequence, much to the horror of many gentry who rightly thought such biased justice would further inflame the situation. A heated exchange between the parish priest of Armagh and the Protestant minister of Benburb unleashed old bigotry, which in the more tolerant climate of the 1780s few would have publicly owned. Attacks began on Catholic chapels and services, although, as our main source for all these events, John Byrne, commented, attendance at high mass in Armagh had become a great treat for all denominations in recent years.

This indeed is what strikes most about the troubles in County Armagh: how quickly very localised feuds and insults escalated out of control, how quickly neighbour turned on neighbour. 'It was lamentable to see poor, quiet peasants, coming to Armagh, every day,' comments Byrne, 'with grief painted in the emaciated figure of a poor old man, making a complaint against his neighbour, with whom he lived in peace and quietness since the days of his nativity.' It was a sentiment echoed by the prominent Whig magnate and Volunteer commander-in-chief Lord Charlemont : 'How strange is the inconstancy of the people! A few years ago I was compelled . . . to prevent the Protestants from ruining themselves and their country by giving up all to the Papists; and now I am forced . . . to prevent them from cutting each others throats.'[29]

The religious and occupational geography of late eighteenth-century Armagh was quite distinctive. A flat northern part was the centre of the most lucrative end of the linen industry. Here the dominant group was Anglican, with only a sprinkling of Catholics. In the middle, south of Armagh City, and where the gentle rise of the land created that pleasant vista so admired by many travel writers, Protestants were still in the majority, but here Presbyterians and Catholics were more numerous – even though the combined total put Protestants marginally in the ascendancy. Moving towards the south of the county, the landscape changed dramatically, with a band of mountains, stretching south-west from Keady's 600 feet (200 metres) to Slieve Gullion's imposing 1,894 feet (630 metres). This was in every respect a cultural barrier, with Catholics increasing dramatically, until, as the mountains dropped, the parishes of Creggan, Forkhill and Jonesborough, at the other side of the barrier, were almost exclusively Catholic and largely Irish-speaking. However, the erection of the Freeduff meeting house in 1734 marked the early stages of sustained Presbyterian immigration into this traditional Catholic area. The tensions created formed the backdrop to the Armagh troubles of the 1780s and 1790s.[30]

The troubles, which by 1785 had produced the Catholic Defenders and Protestant Peep O'Day Boys, had built on localised faction fights and party parades over the past two decades. Parading to Anglican or Presbyterian church services, in full military regalia, had been a particular feature of Volunteering, as had its public celebration of William of Orange. The map of the spread of the troubles reveals incidents radiating out from areas of mixed settlement (the Portnorris malcontents prominent in the second wave of 1786–7).[31] Outsiders were then attracted to the scene. By all accounts lower-class Protestants were the original aggressors. But very soon the Catholics returned like for like. Boycotts of traders of the opposing religion (by both Defenders and Peep O' Day Boys) extended the circle of malcontents. Parades and social events became factionalised. Fights at fairs increased. New regiments of Volunteers were raised on a purely Protestant basis. Neighbours began to withdraw goodwill from those of the opposite religion. Converts and those in mixed marriages became particular targets of Protestant rancour, and swaggering youths were to the fore in deliberately provocative actions. On Sunday 21 November 1788, one of the new, more lower-class Volunteer companies from Benburb marched to church at Armagh along the Eglish road. They planned to return by another road. However, their anti-papist comments and provocative drum-beating drew insults from Catholic countrywomen along the outward route. To avenge the insults of the morning, the Volunteers stocked up on arms and additional drums in Armagh and returned by the same route, 'playing tunes ['The Protestant Boys' and 'The Boyne Water'] which were an insult to Catholics'. Moderate negotiators failed to calm the young hotheads. At Drumbee stones were thrown, the Volunteers fired and two Catholics, one a Defender, were killed. Their funerals then became occasions for major shows of Defender strength and the following Sunday the Volunteers (reinforced by ex-soldiers from the American war) marched along the same road and cheered at the spot where the Catholics were killed. And so the situation rippled out of control, gathering pace as it spread farther afield.

By 1789 the troubles had reached more traditional Catholic territory in south Armagh and south Down. That year the traditional Drumbanagher pattern on St John's Eve was attacked by Peep O' Day Boys and Volunteers, and there were attacks on priests and chapels around Tanderagee and Portadown. The Defenders were already well-organised around Creggan, while at Forkhill an attack on the Protestant rector, Edward Hudson, was followed some days later by the destruction of the vestments and chalice in the Catholic chapel. This was Ó Doirnín and MacCooey territory and the language used by the Defenders suggests that old scores and historical grievances were fundamental to the escalating conflict.[32]

The landlord of Carrive and Forkhill had been attracting Protestant tenants on to wasteland which the Catholics had long thought their own. The same landlord left a hornets' nest in his will endowing Protestant missionaries in the area. It was rumoured that the will stated that 'whenever a Papist's lease was expired, that they should be banished their rocky habitations, and Protestants reinstated into the land of their fathers'.[33] The people were still largely Irish-speaking in these mountainous districts, and the situation was further enflamed by the replacement of an Irish-speaking schoolteacher in Forkhill – who had undertaken to teach forty children 'popish prayers' in Irish – by Alexander Barkely, the brother-in-law of an unpopular magistrate who was held responsible for the execution of a local Defender. On the night of 28 January 1791, Barkely and his family became the victims of the mounting tension in south Armagh. A group of Catholics, including the brother of the executed Defender, broke into his house and mutilated and cut out the tongues of himself and his family – wounds from which his wife later died. It was an act reminiscent of 1641, and in the years which followed the old belief that Catholics were out to massacre Protestants fuelled an upsurge in militant loyalism.

Virulent sectarian warfare was now sweeping south Ulster and north Leinster. Most contemporary accounts of the Armagh Troubles blamed the magistrates and local gentry for failing to nip them in the bud. Certainly contagion was prevented from spreading to neighbouring areas of Tyrone because of the impartiality of its gentry and clergy. The Armagh gentry were not at first partisan, though their Protestant tenants clearly expected them to be so, and those showing favour to the Defenders became particular objects of attack. But the petty juries consistently acquitted Peep O' Day Boys and convicted Defenders. And with landlord control challenged by both sides, it was all too easy to accept the invitation of the ultra-Protestants as a way of restoring control, at least over this section of the tenantry. Such a tendency was further prompted by the post-1793 war crisis and escalating domestic subversion. Ultimately many leading gentry added their weight to the unplanned, but ultimately welcome, graduation of armed loyalism from Peep O' Day Boyism to Orangeism.[34]

By now Armagh's sectarian troubles had spilled into Down, Louth,

Monaghan and parts of Tyrone, and a pitched battle between Defenders from all these areas and Peep O' Day Boys took place at the Diamond, near Loughgall, on 21 September 1795. The Defenders were routed and 'on the field of action' the victors drew up plans for 'a defensive association of Protestants', their resolution 'in no small degree excited by men . . . of very advanced age who had in the early period of their lives lived with those who . . . had been partakers in the War of the Revolution of 1688 and who had heard from the lips of those patriarchs of the Boyne and Aughrim of the sufferings which had driven them to the field in arms'.[35] The following 12 July Orangemen paraded through Lord Gosford's demesne at Markethill, where a decade earlier armed Catholic tenants had guarded his orchards. Gosford was the area's leading magistrate, and had been a friend to the Catholics. But increasingly Catholics felt they could expect little from the law. At least that is what the United Irish propaganda machine now told them, and Catholic refugees from these sectarian disturbances were singled out for their particular attention.

> A lamentable story dear people I'll tell you,
> That happened in Armagh this very last year;
> The landlord combined, with others they joined,
> To plunder and rob us of all we held dear:
> For as we were Catholics they vow'd to oppress us,
> Because at elections we had not a vote;
> But by St Patrick, as we can't get justice;
> Before a year passes we'll alter their note!
>
> The jails they are filled with your nearest relations,
> Your wives and your children are sorely oppressed;
> Your houses are burned, your lands desolated,
> By a band of ruffians with Orange cockades.
>
> The clergy and landlords they have oppressed you,
> Because that poor Ireland they wished to keep slaves;
> They bribed your own neighbours to ruin your labours,
> says they 'you are Papists, and so must be knaves'.[36]

When threatening notices signed 'Oliver Cromwell' were affixed to Catholics' homes, ordering them to quit or be burnt out, most chose to leave without question. Thousands of Catholics were thus intimidated out of Armagh and Down during 1795 and 1796, usually moving to known Catholic districts elsewhere. In 1945 Thomas Mulholland told of how his great-grandfather had thus fled from their ancestral home in Rich Hill, County Armagh, to Rostrevor in County Down. Later Donegal nationalist and writer, Seamas MacManus, told a similar story of his family fleeing to Donegal from Armagh. Others went as far as Tipperary, where they were still referred to as 'Oultachs' and still spoke 'Ulster Irish' in the twentieth century.[37] These so-called 'Armagh Outrages' sent hordes of Catholics into the United Irishmen. The government was fully aware of the possible consequences of thus alienating loyal Catholics and sought at first to curb such attacks by preventing provocative Orange marches.[38] But increasingly its emergency counter-insurgency measures seemed to give countenance to United Irish claims that such attacks on Catholics had government sanction. Certainly the United Irishmen later attributed the upturn in its membership to the Armagh Outrages. There can be no doubt that their alliance with the Defenders was made good that year as the United Irishmen mounted a major recruiting drive among the Catholics.[39]

The sectarian disturbances in Armagh were to set the tone for future politics in Ulster. But at the outset they were highly unusual and spread only to similar cultural frontier zones such as south-west Down. Here recognisably Protestant and Catholic territories abutted, and clashes between Defenders and Peep O' Day Boys prompted a joint Catholic Committee-United Irish peacekeeping mission in 1792. They were told, by the Whig peer, Lord Moira, among others, of how the notorious anti-popery of some of the local gentry was creating the image of biased authority. The main landlord (Lord Annesley) in the worst-affected area around Rathfriland and Castlewellan, was widely held to be 'a mere brute' with a 'trick of knocking down the Catholics on the roads or wherever he meets them for his amusement'. The Defenders could expect little mercy from him at the assizes, for he would always find another charge even against those acquitted. His naked sectarianism was a worry to the authorities – still at this stage convinced that the Catholics were infinitely more loyal than the Presbyterians. But Annesley was not alone. Lord Downshire – governor of County Down, head of the Hill family and one of the most powerful magnates in Ulster – shared his anti-popery and was noted too for his intense dislike of the Presbyterians. He had been barely civil to the Catholic Committee delegates and made no secret of his belief that they and the illegal Defenders were one and the same. They had more support from Catholic leaders, like the O'Neills of Banvale and the O'Hanlons of Newry, and the priests undertook to read out statements urging calm on the Defenders. But opposition from the Protestant gentry ensured a hostile reception when they returned in the autumn.[40]

Downshire was not representative of the gentry even in Ulster – many of whom supported the Catholic case for total repeal of the penal laws – and the hostility between such Anglican magnates and the Presbyterians was an additional factor in the latter's espousal of the Catholics' cause. But Downshire did speak for a large number of the most influential people in the country, who now increasingly defined themselves as a 'Protestant Ascendancy'. Although the London government was in favour of Catholic relief, each new measure had to be wrenched from the Dublin parliament which made its opposition known in increasingly strident terms.

3. The United Irishmen and the education of public opinion

Given traditional Catholic teaching on subordination and deference to authority, the hierarchy's gradualist approach had dominated Catholic Committee dealings with government since its formation in the 1760s. But to a new breed of middle-class Catholic leader educated into the politics of 'natural rights', such traditional deference increasingly looked like grovelling. In 1791 these had finally replaced the conservative gentry at the head of the Catholic Committee in a widely publicised coup, and thereafter conducted an aggressively radical campaign for Catholic emancipation. The new mood among these middle-class Catholics was the backdrop to the formation of the United Irish Society, for it had been the belief that Catholics were not yet ready for admission to political life which had split the reformers in the 1780s.

Certainly this was a key theme of Tone's *Argument on Behalf of the Catholics of Ireland* of 1791. It was largely directed at the northern Presbyterians, since their reservations about the Catholics had prevented the inauguration of the Society of United Irishmen the preceding summer. It argued that Protestants were themselves victims of unscrupulous governments because their fear of Catholics was the ultimate deterrent to reform. The government knew it and played upon it. Protestants had denied Catholics education, then complained of their ignorance; persecuted their religion, then wondered why they drew together with their priests; and having shut off every avenue of improvement, they then claimed that they were incapable of liberty. 'We plead our crime in justification of itself.' Proclaiming the *Rights of Man* and the downfall of tyranny sat uneasily with the degradation of three million Catholics. The choice was clear : they must admit the Catholics into their demands for reform, or abandon it altogether.[41]

Such fears Tone saw as based on stereotypes, and he dismissed each in turn. He might have found them more difficult to dismiss had he examined lower-class Catholic culture, with its pervasive resentment. But this as yet had found no political outlet and he was right in his assessment of the propertied and middle-class Catholics, who would have repaid their re-admission to political rights by bringing their brethren with them, rather than giving a head to that resentment. Their 'weapons', commented Tone, were still those of 'constitutional loyalty', even if 'sulky' and 'complaining'. Such was the topicality of the issue that Tone's pamphlet became an instant bestseller. However, since the stereotyped Catholic was as alive in Ulster Protestant imagination at the end of the twentieth century as it was in the eighteenth, it should be no surprise that Tone continued to encounter it. His journals recount 'a furious battle' at a private dinner in Belfast, where the Whig reformers (mostly Presbyterians alike with those setting up the United Irish Society) stated their objections to Catholic emancipation :

1st. Danger to true religion, inasmuch as the R[oman] C[atholics] would, if emancipated, establish an inquisition. 2nd. Danger to property by reviving the Court of Claims . . . to substantiate Catholic titles. 3rd. Danger, generally, of throwing the power into their hands, which would make this a Catholic government, incapable of enjoying or extending liberty ... Sad nonsense about scavengers becoming members of Par[liamen]t &c.[42]

But the newly radicalised Catholic leaders were just as suspicious of the Presbyterians. Tone's gentle mocking of their mutual suspicions, during a historic visit of the former to Belfast in 1792, makes for amusing reading. But the suspicions were never entirely removed. The bulk of the rural Catholic populace did not join the United Irish Society until after 1796, when fears of Orangeism drove them to the only other body likely to provide protection. Although the northern United Irish Society would remain largely Presbyterian, and had a significant presence among Presbyterians in the Laggan area of east Donegal, outside Antrim and Down lower-class Presbyterians commonly became Orangemen, reinforcing traditional Catholic suspicion of Presbyterians generally.[43]

Once again, the religious geography of Ulster is crucial to understanding what happened in the 1790s. In areas of ancient animosities the alliance between Dissenter and Catholic was weaker, though even here it rather depended on which form of Presbyterianism prevailed. South Ulster in particular witnessed a dramatic spread of revivalist evangelicalism in the 1790s, the anti-Catholicism of the Methodists noticeably to the fore.[44] The different varieties of Presbyterianism also had different perceptions of the Catholics. The 'New Light' Presbyterians were concentrated in the wealthiest areas and in the towns, particularly Belfast. These were the more radical and libertarian, who believed in freedom of conscience and dominated the early United Irishmen. But the Seceders and Covenanters – who were more rigidly Calvinist and anti-papist – were more likely to be lower class and resident in those areas like south Armagh and west Down, where Catholics were perceived as a threat. They more than doubled their congregations towards the end of the century.[45] That some, nevertheless, found their way into the 1798 rebellion has been explained in terms of a peculiarly Presbyterian form of millenarianism which would have been just as exclusive as the anti-Protestant variety which propelled many rural Catholics into it.[46]

The message of the Catholic clergy throughout the 1790s remained the traditional one of non-involvement in politics and the number of

Ulster priests caught up in the 1798 rebellion was the lowest in the country.[47] In a telling statement Archbishop Troy denounced the idea of state payment of priests as holding out a 'danger that the people would become Presbyterians, Methodists or politicians'.[48] The Catholic Church had good reason to fear the United Irishmen, for they actively spread Presbyterian belief in the primacy of individual conscience and an end to priestcraft. 'The Catholics of Ireland', proclaimed the United Irish newspaper the *Northern Star,* 'are now beginning to look to the position of free men and cast away that indolent disposition which tied up their senses and made them insensible as it were of their debasement.'[49] That newspaper's satirical column, 'Billy Bluff and the Squire', has the Catholic priest proposing the toast: '*Every man his own road to Heaven.*'[50] The Catholic hierarchy had always argued a natural affinity between Catholicism, a naturally hierarchical and conservative religion, and the *status quo* – an argument which the London government had largely conceded by 1793. Eighteenth-century Catholic culture may have aspired to a Catholic victory, but it was not particularly anti-government and was entirely antithetical to the notions of democracy and individual rights unleashed by the French Revolution. Indeed, early overtures from the United Irishmen to the Defenders seem to have foundered for this reason. The Defenders 'looked to France, in the earlier period of her Republic, with a two-fold feeling of alarm, alike regarding the invasion of the altar and the throne . . .' wrote Charles Teeling, one of the architects of the union between the two movements. 'Indeed, they rather prided themselves, as being the descendants of men, whose devotion to monarchy had long been proverbial; though their fidelity was badly requited!'[51] How then can we explain the rapid radicalisation of the Catholic populace and its almost total alienation from government as a result?

The Volunteer movement had become split on the issue of further Catholic reforms. But a sizeable element in Ulster (including Armagh) continued to espouse the principle. There was a long tradition of suspicion of government in Ulster Presbyterianism and its attempt to kill reform by playing upon religious divisions was all too obvious. The belief that the mass of Catholics were still in thrall to a tyrannical religion, unthinking and as yet 'unfit for liberty', held many advanced reformers back. It was the more benign wing of a very general Protestant fear of 'popery'. But the dismantling of Catholic absolutism in France and the religious tolerance of the early French revolutionaries caused many to rethink such traditional stereotypes. If the government would not change, then, as in France, the reformers would bring the weight of the people into the fray. The United Irish Society was formed in 1791 'for the promotion of constitutional knowledge, the abolition of bigotry in religion and politics, and the equal distribution of the rights of man through all sects and denominations of Irishmen'. It saw its role first and foremost as creator and educator of public opinion, and to do so it brought together one of the most formidable gatherings of talent in Irish history.[52] Although the tactic of mobilising traditionally unpoliticised sectors of the populace had already begun with the Volunteers and the Anglo-Irish 'patriots' of the previous decade, the scale and character of the United Irish propaganda machine was quite unprecedented and it impacted on a Catholic populace just emerging into political awareness and experiencing the greatest surge of Catholic literacy that century.

The United Irishmen fostered an explosion of print, subsidising key texts like Paine's *Rights of Man*, Tone's *Argument*, Butler's *Digest of Popery laws*, which were run off in tens of thousands, many United Irishmen exhausting private fortunes in the process. 'Such writers were extensively put into the hands of the people', Henry Cooke later testified; 'it was very common to drop them on the road, and leave them at the door of the poor man, or push them under the door.'[53] The Catholic Committee's nationwide elections – based on the organisational unit of the parish – set a precedent. United Irish broadsheets were affixed to chapel doors or nailed to nearby trees. Handbills were distributed to mass-goers and United Irish newspapers read to huddled groups after the service. The United Irishmen capitalised on that traditional reverence for the printed word and the learned man so notable among the rural Irish. Most of the society's declarations were printed as handbills, in simple language which made the most sophisticated political ideas accessible to the common man.[54]

Their main propaganda weapon was song and satire, both threading through the reports from Europe, the letters, the polemical editorials, the serialised radical works which were the standard fare of the enormously popular *Northern Star* newspaper. Established in Belfast at the end of 1791 by that same group of middle-class Presbyterians which had set up the Society of United Irishmen some weeks earlier, the newspaper became the society's main mouthpiece till its suppression in 1797. It was frequently distributed *gratis*, and its popularity so worried the government that it hounded its printers and proprietors and gave free licence to a number of military attacks on its offices. 'At every cabin around us you will see them reading the *Northern Star* (a paper which has sharpened them all for rebellion)', commented an English visitor to Ulster in 1797, 'and I often meet Sir John's labourers walking to work, and reading this paper as they move along.'[55] It utilised every aspect of popular culture which could be turned to propaganda purposes. Its songs were set to popular tunes, so that the most common-place came to have the kind of double, subversive meaning so beloved of the poorer people; and their popularity is attested by the frequent re-issue of the United Irishmen's most notable song collection, *Paddy's Resource*. 'They dispersed liberty-songs composed for an Irish climate', complained one Protestant minister from the Armagh–Tyrone border.[56] And so they did: songs in the Scots dialect for the Presbyterians, songs that used the themes and style of Gaelic verse for the Catholics. The United Irish leaders shared the enthusiasm for the patriotic antiquarianism of the 1780s which produced Charlotte Brooke's influential *Reliques of Irish Poetry* (1789). But they ignored (if indeed they recognised) the strident sectarianism of the Ulster poetry and instead they told of Ireland's ancient glories, when freedom prevailed, until treachery and disunity let the 'foreigner' in.[57]

At first the pro-French songs spoke of abstract rights, of equality versus tyranny, of the cause of the French being the cause of mankind. But increasingly – particularly as the war crisis after February 1793 brought repression and economic hardship – the songs identified with the plight of the poor. By 1797 – as the military clampdown intensified – the theme of Ireland as 'Granu' or the 'Shan Van Vocht', a suffering old woman, prophesying help from overseas, became more common. Thus did the United Irishmen erode the Catholics' traditional deference and direct their vague sense of grievance to the entire structure of government.

Typical of such tactics was the skit 'Billy Bluff and Squire Firebrand', which first appeared as pseudo-letters in the *Northern Star* (May to

December 1796). It was published as a pamphlet that same year and freely distributed among the peasantry. The liberal Presbyterian divine, the Revd Henry Montgomery (1788–1865) recalled the peasantry of south Antrim committing it to memory and such was its popularity that it was still being reprinted in 1840. It was this kind of propaganda which helped reduce traditional Catholic suspicion of the Presbyterians. The writer 'A Presbyterian' or 'R' – in reality the Revd James Porter, Presbyterian minister of Grey Abbey (County Down) – is worried that he will be prosecuted for shaking hands with a priest, because his neighbour Squire Firebrand has ordered his tenant Billy Bluff to spy on him. Firebrand and his immediate superior Lord Mountmumble were satires on the Earl of Londonderry and the magistrate and agent the Revd John Cleland. The two were prime movers in the campaign against the United Irishmen in north Down and through them Porter represented the entire Ascendancy, on which the government relied, as stupid and intolerant. Firebrand is scandalised by the idea that Presbyterians and Catholics might sink their old animosities. The new rights granted to the Catholics were upsetting his notions of the proper ordering of society, for R was encouraging them to register their freeholds [i.e. to vote, after the 1793 Catholic Relief Act restored the franchise to Catholics] 'filling their head full of notions and setting them all a thinking'.

D — m thinking, Billy, 'tis putting the world mad. O, what a happy world we had before men turned their thoughts to thinking! Catholics thought nothing but just getting leave to live, and working for their meat; Presbyterians thought of nothing but wrangling about religion and grumbling about tithes; and Protestants thought of nothing but doing and saying what their betters bid them; and the gentlemen thought of nothing but drinking and the game laws. O! how times are changed, and all for the worse. Your Catholic college – your Catholic schools – your Catholic emancipation . . . your book societies, your pamphlets . . . all turning the people's head and setting them a thinking about this, that, and t'other.

And as for those songs – and the whistling of them was even worse – his own tenants were singing them and ballad-singers were carrying baskets full of handbills and seditious tunes. A poor Catholic, Bryan

O'Carolin, whose home had been burnt and son murdered by Orangemen, came to seek justice from the Squire, but was subjected instead to a torrent of perverted reasoning such as could have come from Voltaire's mock-philosopher Dr Pangloss. 'Did you resist?' asks the Squire. 'We did, please your Worship,' answers Bryan. 'You resisted, that is, you defended. Are you a Defender? I would like to defend myself. I thought so. I am sorry you come under the act against Defenderism. Let me see again; you had firearms and you are a Catholic? Worse and worse. I am sorry Bryan, I must commit you; my duty demands it as a Magistrate.'

The series ends – like the many heroic tales so beloved of the eighteenth-century public – with a moral. R is damned by the Squire for his 'reading, and thinking, and talking, and planning'. 'I make use of plain understanding, Sir, and compare the promises of the GREAT with their performances . . . when their own wickedness has brought them into danger . . . they throw the blame on the innocent and unoffending, should they dare to complain.' F: 'You drink with the priest . . . And yet you are a Presbyterian . . . And your fathers persecuted the Catholics . . . And now you are friends . . . D-n-n to such friendship, so new, so unexpected, so *unnatural*!' R: 'They persecuted each other . . . we are wiser than our ancestors . . . our absurd dissensions were the cause of our national poverty, ignorance, degradation, and slavery.'[58]

The early success of United Irish tactics was remarkable. The outbreak of war with France in 1793 met with almost immediate grumbling from ordinary people, and soon they were refusing to pay their debts in expectation of some major upheaval. Thomas Russell was told that the

great majority of the people [were] in favor of the French in the mountains [of Cavan, Fermanagh and Leitrim] where you could not conceive that any news could reach . . . Know of the abolition of tythes in France and infer therefrom. Few republican. Fond of the King. Hate the gover[n]ment. Angry at the King's ent[e]ring into war agains[t] France. Strong for reform.[59]

It is an extraordinary mixture of sentiments which Russell's informant attributes to these mountain people, who would almost certainly have been Catholic, and his information almost perfectly mirrors the conflicting messages of Defender oaths. It is the hatred of government which is so new and it was not simply the outcome of United Irish propaganda. Such hatred started with the public exposure of the depth of anti-popery in the top echelons of government. It had always been there. But the general body of Catholics would have been unaware of it. As the penal laws were gradually repealed, it became more strident, particularly since repeal was evidently being forced on Irish politicians by the British government. And both the reconstituted Catholic Committee and the United Irish Societies – there was common leadership – had a vested interest in disseminating information about their resistance. Thus were the bitter parliamentary debates on the Catholic Relief Bills of 1792 and 1793 publicised as never before.

4. The Catholic Convention, 1792–3

Ireland was unfortunate to have been governed by a succession of weak Lord Lieutenants in one of the most crucial decades in its history. As a result, the opinions of her ultra-Protestant officials at Dublin Castle came to prevail, and British rule in Ireland was tarred with their prejudices, even though they were unrepresentative of Protestant political opinion as a whole. It was the Catholic Committee's interference and perceived threat to Protestant social control which had so incensed men like Downshire and Annesley in the summer of 1792. But in demanding the traditional submissiveness from the Catholic Committee the Irish government miscalculated the public mood. Initially the credibility of the Catholic gentry and prelates with their people was severely damaged and there is a noticeable turning away from the leadership of the priests in these years. Tone feared 'that the Catholic clergymen are bad friends to liberty'. But he noted that when the parish priest of Saintfield preached against the United Irishmen and warned his parishioners not to join, he was publicly rebuked in his chapel by one of the congregation.[60] The Catholic Committee and United Irishmen were providing defence lawyers (and very often material help) to the families of arrested Defenders, and in a masterly publicity campaign in the summer of 1792, the Catholic Committee effectively became the real director of Catholic opinion in the country.[61]

In the 1792 Irish parliamentary session – in which London sought to have a bill passed to extend to Irish Catholics concessions recently made to their English co-religionists – petitions in favour of the Catholics were treated with an unprecedented contempt, and insults were showered upon the Catholic Committee. In response the Committee launched a country-wide election (based on the principle of universal manhood suffrage – a revolutionary departure), which would copper-fasten its truly representative character. Members were to be elected for each town and county to sit on the existing Dublin Committee. The whole body of 233 would then meet in a Convention in Dublin to draw up a petition to the King. The Catholic parish was the base unit of organisation for the election. Committee members had stumped the country that summer, drumming up support and flooding it with propaganda. There had been a split in the Committee the previous year, with a number of clergy and gentry (particularly from Munster) seceding. This was now mended. However, the Catholic bishops and gentry largely shared government distaste for the radicals and were to spend most of the rest of the decade recalling Catholics to their old habits of deference.

The elections and Convention (meeting but a short walk away from the Irish Parliament building) were perceived as a threat to the whole structure of government as it had existed since the 1690s. But the strident anti-popery which had informed it sounded out of place in the new mood of the 1790s and only served to further discredit government in the eyes of Catholics. Commencing with the Grand Jury of London-derry, grand juries throughout the country proclaimed the Convention a threat to 'Protestant Ascendancy'. The attacks (and the continued insistence of the Castle on traditional submissiveness) incensed the Catholic delegates and gave the radicals an unusual (though short-lived) victory. The Convention decided to go over the heads of the Dublin administration and make a direct plea to the King for complete emancipation. The delegates chosen to take the petition travelled via Belfast, pushing home the message that the 'Ascendancy' could no longer rule by dividing. Here the leading Convention member from Ulster (Luke Teeling) had forged a close working alliance with the

United Irishmen and it was he who had argued the case for demanding total emancipation. En route through the town, the Catholic delegates were greeted by supporters, who insisted on removing the horses from their carriages and drawing them over the bridge across the River Lagan. 'To those who looked beyond the surface, it was an interesting spectacle', commented Tone, '. . . to see the Dissenter of the North drawing, with his own hands, the Catholic of the South in triumph through what may be denominated the capital of Presbyterianism.'[62]

That the Convention members endorsed such radical action was a symptom of how far they had been goaded by government. But it was out of character. Fewer than thirty of its members can be identified as United Irishmen and Tone would later fume at their docile acceptance of the partial concessions of the 1793 act.Two of the Ulster representatives, Edmund McGildowney of Ballycastle, County Antrim, and Owen O'Callaghan of Cullaville, County Armagh, would have been typical – successful entrepreneurs, anxious to participate in the establishment rather than overturn it. Both were to hold public office soon after the 1793 act permitted them to do so. The Ulster county representatives reveal a high level of participation by old families: Philip, Constantine and Terence Maguire for County Fermanagh, John O'Neill, Hugh and Thomas Savage and John Magennis for County Down, Terence O'Neill of Ballybawley, Tyrone and a number of McLaughlins and McShanes for Donegal and Derry. Only in Antrim and Down did Convention members later emerge as republican leaders. One of the three representatives of County Antrim was Luke Teeling, linen bleacher and wine merchant in Lisburn, whose influence also extended into Down, Armagh and Louth. He was the richest and most prominent Catholic in Ulster and his son, Charles, was treated with considerable deference by Lord Castlereagh, even as he was in the process of arresting him. Luke Teeling was already in close contact with the Belfast United Irish leaders in 1792 (though he never became a member) and his family (particularly his two sons Bartholomew and Charles) were to play a central role in republican organisation in Ulster. John Magennis, also a successful linen dealer, and a representative for County Down in the Convention, was Teeling's son-in-law, and with the youthful Charles Teeling was instrumental in bringing the Defenders into alliance with the United Irishmen.[63]

In north Down and most of Antrim (including Belfast) relations between Catholic and Dissenter were good, and Down would become the strongest United Irish county in the country. The county had produced the most advanced Presbyterian supporters of Catholic political rights during the 1780s, even after their co-religionists elsewhere were beginning to pull back, and the many chapels erected during these years – Belfast, Lisburn, Dromore, Saintfield, Ballynahinch, Saul, Ballee, Portaferry – were all built with substantial Protestant, and particularly Presbyterian, assistance.[64] Sectarian tensions would weaken the movement almost everywhere else in Ulster and provide government with its most important informers. But it was the perceived spinelessness and 'popery' of some of the Dublin-based Catholics in the United leadership which turned a Newry Presbyterian and United Irishman, Samuel Turner, into an informer. The Teeling brothers he appears to have respected, sharing their militancy and mistrust of the Dublin moderates, whom he accused of betraying the Ulstermen.

The Catholic delegates were favourably received in London and many believed that full emancipation would be forthcoming. War was declared between England and revolutionary France in February 1793 and, in a sharp exchange with the Dublin government, ministers in London insisted on concession to the Catholics. A Catholic Relief bill was forced through the Irish Parliament on Britain's instructions, but traditional government supporters made no secret of their distaste – and this at a time when anti-popery was very much on the decline, and when a Catholic reading public now took note. All the old stereotypes of Catholics being incapable of loyalty to a Protestant power were raked up, prominent government supporters taking a lead in the accusations. The most vociferous attack came from Dr Patrick Duigenan, Judge in the Prerogative Court, who, although (or perhaps because) he had been twice married to Catholics and had a Catholic mother, plundered history to show the Catholics as incorrigible traitors, whose real objects were 'power and the recovery of the forfeited estates'.[65] A riposte from the Catholic hierarchy denying such accusations only worsened matters. The upshot was the imposition of yet another Catholic loyalty oath requiring any Catholic wishing to benefit from the new concessions to deny papal infallibility and recognise the Protestant establishment in property and politics.

Certainly the concessions were substantial: the franchise was restored, civil and military offices opened up (with some exceptions); Catholics could now take degrees at Dublin University and, most controversial of all, could carry arms, subject to a property qualification and the taking of the new oath of allegiance. But the concessions were permissive rather than obligatory and a newly awakened Protestant Ascendancy chose as often as not to withhold them. As late as 1836 a government report on municipal corporations found that no Catholic had ever been a member of Bangor corporation, its provost, seemingly unaware of the 1793 change in the law, still thinking that only Protestants qualified.[66] Moreover the withholding of the right to sit in parliament, having granted everything else, seemed petty and was interpreted by the newly politicised Catholic populace as final proof that the existing government was their natural enemy. That year – one torn by an escalating crisis and riots against the embodiment of a new militia – demonstrated more than ever before that even lower-class Catholics had renounced the time-old Catholic principle of patience and endurance. Indeed, reports from Donegal told of a turning away from the priests – one was even accused of being a Protestant for advising subordination.[67] The local elections to the Catholic Convention had particularly unnerved Protestants in areas of ongoing sectarian tension and a new 'insolence' among lower-class Catholics was being reported.[68] 'The clergy, who formerly misled the minds of the Catholic body', wrote Leonard McNally, United Irishman and Dublin Castle's most talented spy, in December 1794, 'have within a few years lost all influence over the better sort and retain very little authority over the lower classes.' He held the distribution of Thomas Paine's works by the northern United Irishmen responsible. 'One consequence of these publications is a strong union between the better classes of Papists and Dissenters. They have been brought to think alike.'[69]

5. Defenderism

Defenderism was the prototype for the pervasive secret societies which were to become so common in Ireland in the next century. It reflected the communal values of its locality, its bitter anti-Protestantism in its south Ulster/north Leinster heartland, shading into more agrarian concerns in Munster and Connacht (where it was generally weaker) and more political ones in United Irish strongholds. Its mix of oaths and sign language gave its members a sense of importance and belonging at a time of major dislocation. In this it had much in common with freemasonry, which was everywhere in late eighteenth-century Ireland, as it was elsewhere in Europe. But its stated aims seemed so contradictory and nonsensical that they baffled the government of the day, as they have done so many later commentators. They are entirely comprehensible, however, if we remember that Defenderism flourished in a deeply conservative, semi-literate (sometimes illiterate) society, where the values expressed in the oral poetry were widely shared, and where the intensification of sectarian attacks by Peep O' Day Boys and Orangemen would have unleashed existing undercurrents of anti-Protestantism. Just like the poetry, so in Defender oaths, Biblical imagery is mixed with the idea of deliverance, of the restoration of 'the true religion ['the true Catholic church'] . . . lost at the reformation', of obtaining the conditions of Limerick, of help from France. But there is confusion in the nature of that assistance and the end to be achieved. The very many references to French revolutionary symbols and institutions, to fraternity and equality, to pulling down 'the British laws', show that the significance of post-1789 events and ideas have made an impact. Against this, however, is the apparently contradictory belief that the Stuarts were somehow involved, for it is the Stuart 'duke of York [who] will save us', and an apparent allegiance to the British monarchy. The Monaghan-born Gaelic League scholar Énri Ó Muirgheasa (Henry Morris) collected the following song in the Rosses of Donegal, where it was and has remained popular:

> Oh rise up you finest of men
> and put a pike on top of every shaft,
> strike them down, the evil-hearted ones,
> and establish French law.

> And O woman of the house, what's your trouble? . . .
> we'll have land without rent from this year forth;
> . . .

the Duke of York has army enough,
the Frenchman and the Spaniard are on the seashore[70]

However, Charles Teeling later denied that the Defenders were highly politicised or revolutionary at this stage – and he should have known as he was to play a lead role in their political education – arguing that they had retained the largely defensive role of their origins.[71] Certainly the often incongruous language of Defender oaths and statements bears the hallmark of Carleton's part-educated rustic, impressing his compatriots with high-sounding phrases and snippets of Latin. His own account of being sworn in 1814 into the Ribbonmen (the new name for Defenderism) could have applied equally in the 1790s. Ribbonism, like Defenderism, like the United Irishmen, were societies of young men. Peer pressure made it difficult (and at times positively dangerous) not to belong. The nineteen-year-old Carleton noticed a certain coolness among his acquaintances as he failed to respond to their signs and passwords. Eventually, at an open-air dance, and in between several glasses of poteen, he found himself and many more young men sworn in by Hugh Roe McCahy. 'He was one of those important individuals who make themselves active and prominent among their fellows, attend dances and wakes, are seldom absent in fair or market from a fight.' He insinuated that Carleton should be ashamed at his ignorance of 'what is going on ... over the whole country', and almost before he knew what was happening, Carleton was sworn in, with 'dexterous rapidity' of language, on a Catholic prayer-book. Although McCahy was illiterate, he kept some works of Catholic theology in his home and had committed to memory lengthy Ribbon oaths and catechisms.[72] He was typical of the petty godfather which enclosed cultures, alienated from authority, tend to throw up. Among the Defenders there was much talk of getting rid of the heretics, massacring the Protestants, and taking their places, similar to the wishful thinking of the poetry. However, the widespread attacks on Protestant homes in south Ulster and north Leinster in the winter of 1793 were for arms, almost certainly for defensive purposes, and nearly all the casualties were the Defenders themselves. Even so, such talk fed the old Protestant fear of popish massacre and dispossession. Protestants fled to the towns for safety and – as the Catholic Committee had feared – gave substance to the ultra-Protestant attack in the Irish Parliament.[73]

The year 1793 was the most violent that century and set the tone for the remainder of the decade. With the outbreak of war, the government began a series of measures against the radicals. Belfast was ransacked by troops and warrants issued for the arrest of the proprietors of the *Northern Star*. A House of Lords secret committee report lumped the Defenders, United Irishmen and Catholic Committee together in an alleged Catholic conspiracy, and over the next year key Committee members were targeted for prosecution. A Convention Act made it impossible for a body like the Catholic Convention to convene again. A stringent Arms Act suggested that the right of Catholics to carry arms given with one hand in 1793 (and very reluctantly so) would be whipped away with the other. A new Militia Act was deeply unpopular, for it involved compulsory balloting to replace regular troops withdrawn for the war against France. A new wave of Defenderism sweeping through south Ulster and north Leinster in the winter of 1792–3 was met with an unprecedented show of force by the authorities. In Meath the Defenders were routed in a botched bid to rescue a captured colleague. Forty-seven were killed and nearly all the remainder captured in this one incident alone, and at the ensuing trials the authorities sought to make a dreadful example by handing down the death verdict on twenty-one Defenders and transporting a further thirty-seven. The *Northern Star* made much of the 'summary justice' meted out to the 'deluded Defenders', intertwining its reports of the hostile debates on the Catholic bill with accounts of the new security measures to show that the country was being rushed to 'arbitrary government'.[74]

In fact, at this stage, the Defenders were still a mirror image of those in Armagh and south Down, a deeply sectarian defence force. But their systematic arming was now unmistakable. The anti-militia riots which swept through the country in the summer of 1793 were initially unconnected, and they were worse in more rural counties where neither the United Irishmen nor the Defenders had penetrated. But a general alienation from government was evident and a recognition that the Catholic Relief Act had been granted with ill grace. There is evidence too that ordinary Catholics were looking to their secular leaders rather than to their clergy – a decline in respect intensified by the role of the priests in drawing up lists of their parishioners for the militia ballot.[75] Predictably, trouble in Ulster was mainly in areas where the Protestant gentry were already considered enemies. After eight weeks of riots, five times as many casualties had been sustained as in the previous thirty years, even though such years had witnessed persistent agrarian trouble.[76] The old *modus vivendi* between rulers and ruled, which had underpinned stability throughout *ancien régime* Europe had entirely broken down in Ireland. The rupture was the background to the development of militant republicanism in succeeding years.

6. The alliance between the United Irishmen and the Defenders

In the spring of 1793 when a United Irishman, Joseph Cuthbert, was sentenced to an hour in the pillory and twelve months' imprisonment for attempting to seduce the soldiers from their loyalty, some 25,000 people converged on Belfast for the event, and a rescue attempt was only prevented by military saturation. Belfast was considered the fount of all sedition in the country, and General Whyte, the military commander in Ulster, thought his lot comparable to that of General Gage in Boston on the eve of the American Revolution.[77] But Belfast and its hinterland in Antrim and Down was unusual. In these non-plantation counties, where Catholics were very much in the minority, a libertarian spirit had long existed and Charles Teeling was later to reflect with affection on the enlightened spirit in which he had been nurtured in the 1780s and 1790s.[78] The handful of upwardly mobile Catholics in these two counties were ready to identify their own cause with that of the advanced political reformers. Thus in 1795 when they were thwarted once again with the sudden removal of the emancipationist Whig Lord Lieutenant, Earl Fitzwilliam, and revelations that the King himself opposed Catholic emancipation, they publicly threw in their lot with the United Irishmen. In a meeting of the Belfast Catholics on 29 March 1795 at St Mary's Chapel, they proclaimed their cause the same as that of their Protestant brethren in the United Irishmen.[79] Further meetings took place in Antrim, Down and

Drogheda, with a final angry one in Dublin pronouncing the end of the Catholic Committee.

Shortly afterwards the decision was taken by the United Irishmen to seek an alliance with the Defenders, the secretary of the Belfast Catholics, the attorney's clerk Daniel Shanaghan, acting as intermediary. But the two most important Defender–United Irish axes were those centred on the linen triangle (involving the mediation of the Teelings and the priest, James Coigley) and the south Down–north Louth area, notably around Rathfriland, Newry and Carlingford. In this latter area Louis Cullen has traced a particularly high number of Catholics among the most radical United Irishmen, and those in Newry seem also to have spearheaded the reorganisation in Leinster.[80] These Catholics involved in the enlistment of Defenders appear to have already been United Irishmen, a 'junto of d–d United Papists [which included the Magennises] . . . instilling into the minds of a numerous banditti of cottiers under them, that you are only entitled to a chiefry upon the lands, and cannot dispossess them', as Downshire's agent claimed.[81] They were, however, concentrated in the east, and generally in the wealthy linen areas. Ulster has always been a patchwork of highly localised regions. Presbyterians only tended to join the United Irishmen in areas where Catholics were in a minority. In poorer rural areas, areas where old sores from confiscation persisted, or those where Catholics predominated or where they equalled Protestants in numbers, Presbyterians tended not to join the United Irishmen. Yet even in mid- and west Ulster, where Catholics had been relatively quiescent, a very sudden change had occurred by spring 1797, and Abercorn's agent began also to suspect the Catholics, though until then he had considered them ten times more loyal than either the Presbyterians or the Methodists.[82] The main reason was the upsurge in Orange attacks.

In July 1796 – in response to a government request for advice on how to extinguish animosities – John Ogle, high sheriff of County Armagh, warned Dublin Castle to avoid the mistakes of the past in failing to control Orange aggression. Catholics claimed as their excuse for turning equally aggressive that the Peep O' Day Boys had always been acquitted by Protestant juries. 'As this have been so or not, their minds were strongly impressed by it, & with the alledged oppression of their sect & having no cordiality toward a Protestant Government when they broke out under the style of the Defenders they became a ready prey to any sort of miscreants, whether United or Disunited Irishmen.' He had not known the Catholics to show any discontent at their exclusion from political power until enflamed by this Peep O' Day Boy turned Orange 'Protestant banditti', with their 'absurd bravados', not satisfied 'with the security & advantages they possess unless they may be allowed to bawl out Protestant ascendancy, as in the 12th Instant [July, when the Orangemen paraded through Lord Gosford's estate]'.[83] As late as 1797 even the Armagh gentry had been anxious about appearing to countenance the Orange Order. But as disaffection spread in 1796–7 and their inability to control their own areas became all too evident – to say nothing of the persistent French threat of invasion – they came increasingly to depend on the ultra-loyalists. The march through Gosford's estate was highly symbolic. This was the Orangemen reasserting the concept of the Protestant state, which the recent Catholic legislation had so obviously weakened. With the embodiment of a yeomanry force in September 1796, which would become a predominantly Orange institution, despite the recruitment of some Catholics, the reassertion of Protestant supremacy seemed complete.

The yeomanry was a part-time policing force, organised by the gentry for local service. But it could – and increasingly was – used like a regular army at times of crisis. Fitzwilliam had hoped to embody such a force as part of a Catholic emancipation package, uniting the propertied of all denominations, who would then be expected to enrol their own tenantry. But he was concerned at the prospect of a yeomanry recruited on a purely Protestant basis. At first his successor, Lord Camden, Lord Lieutenant 1795–8, shared such fears. But, in the absence of Catholic emancipation and given the escalating security threat, Fitzwilliam's fears were realised. Outside Ulster, Catholics did enrol in the yeomanry. In Ulster, however, there was fierce resistance to admitting Catholics. Entire Orange lodges were recruited, and, as time progressed, and rebellion and invasion seemed ever more likely, increasingly with the Castle's tacit blessing. The bulk of the yeomanry were located in Ulster, their local knowledge and Orange sympathies adding to the perception that they were arrayed against 'papists' rather than rebels. A 1798 version of the popular loyalist tune 'Croppies lie down' had the chorus changed to 'Papists lie down'.[84] The predominantly Catholic militia was particularly targeted. On 12 July 1797 in Stewartstown, County Tyrone, an affray occurred between the Kerry militia and a crowd sporting Orange ribbands, leaving a number killed on both sides. The following day the yeomen and fencibles took their revenge, attacking another group of Kerry militia and killing three.[85] The militia remained a politically suspect force and increasingly the authorities came to depend on a mixed force of yeomanry and fencibles to contain the rising tide of Ulster's disaffection.[86] Both forces were heavily infiltrated by Orangemen, ostentatiously displaying Orange emblems as they disarmed people in disturbed areas. The fear of Orange attack became the main reason for a sudden Catholic influx into the United Irishmen after 1796.

This growing ascendancy of Orangeism in the mechanics of counter-subversion was frowned upon by many who were not necessarily anti-government, and the action of General Lake (the British military commander in Ulster) in reviewing huge gatherings of Orangemen and yeomen in Belfast and Lurgan on 12 July 1797, was thought singularly inappropriate.[87] Nor was the spirit of radical reform entirely dead – many leading Protestants and Dissenters still calling for Catholic emancipation and parliamentary reform.[88] Ultimately however, even critics had to admit that Orangeism was a necessary evil to combat disaffection, which had got entirely out of hand. Even so, a French traveller, the chevalier de Latocnaye, moving through Ulster towards the end of 1796, found reports of sedition there greatly exaggerated. When he returned the following year, however, the situation had entirely changed.[89] A failed French invasion attempt on Ireland in December–January had exposed the country's vulnerability. The military forces at government disposal were inadequate and London refused to send reinforcements. The French attempt had boosted disaffection in the north and at the spring assizes no juries could be found to convict those arrested. A terrible change had come over Ulster. In Tyrone and Donegal whole baronies which had been quiet in January were in a rebellious state only weeks later, the United Irishmen having successfully spread among 'all religions'. Elsewhere new mansions, recently built in the heyday of Protestant confidence, were bricked up for defence. In County Down Lord Londonderry had to be guarded in his home by soldiers, though his father had rarely bolted his windows.[90] United Irish agents in France assured the French government of widespread support among the country's defence forces and there is no denying that they were having things very much their own way in the early months of 1797.[91]

In March 1797 government decided on a crackdown in Ulster. Martial law was proclaimed and the populace required to surrender arms and take an oath of allegiance. Infected militia units were purged and exemplary punishments meted out to militiamen who had taken the United Irish oath. Four Catholics from the Monaghan militia stationed near Belfast were executed beside their coffins in a macabre showpiece *pour encourager les autres*. Their fate was immediately immortalised in a popular ballad.[92] For the first time in a century Ulster was exposed to the full rigours of martial law. House burnings and floggings became routine and prison ships were anchored off the coast to accommodate the large numbers of those arrested. De Latocnaye found Ulster given over to military licence, the 'poor peasant' suffering the brunt of the military campaign, the real rogues 'very careful themselves to stay behind the curtain'. He found the people in the mountainous areas near Newry had suffered far more than their neighbours, their houses routinely burned to extort information about arms. Here the most notorious fencibles' regiment, the Ancient Britons, was quartered. Certainly south-east Ulster seems to have experienced particularly harsh treatment – even the noted government supporter John Giffard observing that the Ancient Britons' route could be traced by 'the smoke and flames of burning houses and by the dead bodies of boys and old men'. Since such atrocities were aired in the English parliament by Lord Moira they have become the stock of every historical account of the period. But even Lecky – a noted critic of government – warns that the authorities were obliged to take strong measures, such was the seriousness of the situation in the north. The existence of a formal United Irish assassination committee was roundly denied by its leaders. Certainly when told about it by one of its most useful informers – Edward Newell – government effectively incorporated it into its propaganda campaign. But a number of informers and active magistrates met violent deaths in these months and, as Nancy Curtin has shown, Ulster was in the grip of both republican-inspired terror and government counter-terror in the year before the 1798 rebellion.[93]

Not every county experienced the lash of the Ancient Britons. In those areas which underwent the worst military licence, however – notably Down, Antrim and adjacent areas of Derry – there was major Catholic involvement in the rebellion. Although even peaceable Protestants were abused, it was the poorer Catholic populace which suffered most in the disarming of Ulster. For the first time they joined the United Irishmen in great numbers, intensified efforts having been made to woo them via specifically Defender oaths.[94] The suddenness of this transformation among the Catholics from passive loyalty to active subversion was a matter of comment. The final date to surrender arms was 25 June 1797 and a great flurry of activity was noticeable among the United Irishmen as they attempted to bring about a rising before their undoubted strength was eroded. The attempt highlighted the traditional animosities between Ulster and Leinster, for the leaders in Dublin (many Catholic or pro-Catholic) opposed a rising before French help arrived. However, nothing separated the Catholic United Irish leaders in east Ulster from their Presbyterian counterparts, and people like the Teelings, the Revd James Coigley, and John Magennis were among the leading militants attempting to bring about a rebellion and a French invasion.

Catholics, however, also came forward in large numbers to take the oath of allegiance and to subscribe to the flood of declarations of loyalty orchestrated by their parish priests, while the Revd Patrick MacCartan, the parish priest of Saul, was prominent among those trying to woo their flocks away from subversive activities. The Catholic hierarchy had finally won its long campaign to convince the government that it was a force for conservatism, and that government's establishment of a Catholic seminary at Maynooth in 1795 saw them firmly on the side of the authorities throughout the crisis of 1798. Only one Irish bishop (Thomas Hussey, bishop of Waterford and Lismore) was to speak out against Orange and military atrocities, and the Ulster bishops – under Archbishop O'Reilly's firm anti-political lead – were the most silent of all. It is no accident that fewer Catholic clergy were involved in the 1798 rebellion in Ulster than anywhere else in the country. O'Reilly's excommunication of the Defenders, however, made little difference and the declarations of loyalty still accounted for a tiny proportion of Ulster Catholics (though it looks as if most of the Catholic middle class were among them). The United Irishmen had urged their adherents to take the oath and surrender some arms to prevent worse damage and we have the evidence of Abercorn's agent that, quite out of character, Catholics by 1797 had no reservations about perjuring themselves.[95] There was nothing unusual in Catholic tradition of the faithful ignoring the priest who stepped outside his community and there was no denying the widespread disaffection of the Catholic populace by 1798.

7. The 1798 rebellion in Ulster

In such a conservative society, whose world had been literally turned upside down, millenarianism was rife. Defenderism made public the kind of visionary expectations so common in the poetry. Old prophecies spread rapidly; those of the thirteenth-century Thomas the Rhymer, the seventeenth-century Scottish Covenanter, Alexander Peden, and the sixth-century Colum Cille, converged in foretelling deliverance at the hands of the French. A widespread belief in cataclysmic change was the backdrop to the dramatic, almost trance-like atmosphere of the years 1796–8.[96]

But the power of prophecy, particularly in times of distress and dislocation, and particularly in poorer rural communities, lies in its ability to foretell whatever the community wants it to. And whilst it served to unite at the height of United Irish confidence, ultimately it fed the increasing sectarian polarisation. The Defenders operated at many different levels, their chameleon character and transmutation over time confounding historical efforts at explanation. In their south Ulster heartland, however, they acted as the bridge linking the prophetic vision of the poetry with the political ideas of the 1790s. The idea of a French saviour picked up the old Jacobite message and translated it for a new age. In a contemporary poem in Irish, the Messiah was the French rather than the Stuarts, but the message of a radical overthrow of the existing order was the same.

The French at this time are relegating rank,
and there'll be no prince over them but a pure new régime;
Germany and Flanders will be subject to them in that state,
and I suspect that Scotland and Ireland will be in the bloc.

There'll be no Louis or any other king from now on
in the countries forever oppressing each fine son;
people will be full of wisdom, unfettered, unthreatened,
and the children of Milesius will have free will
        and prosperity until Judgement Day.

Remember the conditions the Gaill gave you at Limerick, my woe!
you were betrayed, and no mistake, since the time of King William
which left your poor children in distress, without property but in pain
like a blind beast running for a prize while the one guiding it has no reins.

Not by inheritance did Luther or anyone of the descendants obtain
all the bright new courts from Limerick to the Boyne
a scourge will come on these boors from the Gaels in battle
and they'll have no estate or fortress in Ireland any more.

The province of Munster is controlling its multitudes sensibly
and every famed man among the victorious Leinstermen is happy
the mighty, active Ulstermen will be defending the hosts
as they rout the race of Luther, and may they not escape them.[97]

French help would 'get [them] the conditions of Limerick', their followers were told; 'that the Protestants had the power of the country
long enough, and that they would have it as long more'.[98]

The main United Irish leaders and the Catholic middle class (however radical) distanced themselves from the increasingly sectarian readings of the prophecies. But many others were not averse to playing on
fears of Orangeism and hopes for a reversal of the land settlement as
a means of recruiting Catholics. The United Irish press became much
more shrill after the destruction of the *Northern Star* in May 1797.
The prophecies of Colum Cille foretelling a dreadful massacre of the
Catholics, which had circulated in 1641 and would again in the next

century, gained particular currency. Catholics in Antrim, Derry and Donegal were reported to have fled to the hills because of the prophecy.[99] In Armagh de Latocnaye thought such prophecies had been spread by Orangemen to force the Catholics to flee to the west.

The poor folk, who are after all the most timid and credulous of the universe, with their families and small remains of furniture, started in crowds to put themselves in safety on the other side of the Shannon. I myself have met often these wandering families moving to the line of safety . . . It was in talking to some of these on the road that I learned of the prophecy of St. Columba.[100]

At first widespread intimidation swelled the ranks of the United Irishmen – 'designing men who buzzed in our ears Catholic emancipation, and the danger of being massacred by Orangemen', as the parishioners of Arboe, County Tyrone, told their priest in June 1797.[101] Certainly the ease with which Ulster was disarmed suggests that many had enlisted through fear rather than commitment. Neighbours were now perceived as potential murderers where once they had lived in peace. Even converts to Protestantism were suspect. Thomas Macan, who converted in 1751, was a Volunteer captain and sovereign of Armagh until 1794. But he retained a liberal attitude towards the Catholics. His son Arthur succeeded him as sovereign and was a yeomanry commander. He was nevertheless nicknamed 'Papist Macan' and it looks very much as if his departure for India in December 1797 was for his own safety.[102]

By 1798 the prophecies were intensifying the sectarian polarisation of Ulster. After spring 1797 Ulster was effectively a military camp, and many of the troops were billeted on the people. The other provinces did not experience martial law till the spring of 1798 and the terror induced was a major factor in the outbreak of the rebellion. As a result of military repression and sectarian polarisation, little of the United Irish movement survived outside Antrim and Down by 1798. The United Irishmen still expected support from parts of Donegal and Derry, but in the event only Antrim and Down rose in June 1798, an attempted turn-out at Maghera, County Derry, collapsing on news of the approaching troops.

By the last week in May 1798, nearly all the main United Irish leaders were in prison, and confusion reigned in Ulster, when the planned rebellion finally erupted in Dublin on 23 May and spread to the other counties in Leinster. The entire country had been proclaimed at the end of March and as the floggings, torture and houseburning made infamous by the disarming of Ulster now spread south, affected counties witnessed a similar upsurge in sectarian tensions. Reports of anti-Protestant activities by the rebels in the southern counties – coming through in late May and early June and peaking with the brutal massacre by defeated rebels on 5 June of some 184 prisoners at Scullabogue in Wexford (all but 10 to 15 of them Protestants) – further dampened support for the United Irishmen.

I am happy to be enabled to assure your Lordship', wrote Abercorn's agent in Strabane on June 3, 'that the zeal and loyalty of almost all ranks in this part of the North have of late been increasing in proportion to the disaffection of the South. The Presbyterians (however late) now plainly see that the disaffection to government which originated with their party, must, without a speedy check, end in the total annihilation of them, in common with the church establishment ... they will now fight in earnest to keep down the Catholics.

He now looked upon the Catholic populace as the most disaffected – only months after he had reported the exact opposite – and apprehended 'a rising of the Catholics in the wild parts of Donegal ... [where they were] as numerous as sand', to say nothing of the 20,000 or so then gathering at Lough Derg only sixteen miles from Barons Court (Abercorn's seat). News of the rising in Antrim and Down on 7 June came as a shock: 'So long as it appeared a Catholic business I was quite easy about the North, but Antrim is quite a Protestant county.'[103]

On 5 June the Down commander, the non-subscribing Presbyterian minister of Portaferry, the Revd William Steel Dickson, was arrested. Down's succession of United Irish leaders friendly towards the Catholics (Russell, Dickson and finally Henry Munro) maintained an unusual unity right through the tensions of 1797–8. In Antrim, the last-minute assumption of command by Henry Joy McCracken would have had the same effect and assured a high Catholic turnout. Along with Russell, McCracken was one of the few highly placed United

Irishmen who was popular with the common people. A telling instance of this occurred days before the rebellion, as he was leaving Belfast. In Hercules Street (today's Royal Avenue), then a Catholic enclave, he was rescued from a group of yeomen by a woman wielding a huge knife – almost certainly one of the Catholic butchers operating in the area. McCracken had been central in the United Irish–Defender alliance, reputedly chosen by the Defenders shortly before the rising as their deputy for communication with the United Irish Society.[104]

But the omens were bad. Many of the Antrim colonels refused to act, and it was younger men, occupying positions of less social prominence, who were pushed to the fore. Martial law had been intensified and spies at the very heart of the United Irish command were supplying the military commander, General Nugent, with accurate information about their plans. A vital letter to co-ordinate the movements of the Antrim and Down rebels was secreted by the key informer, Nicholas Magin, a Catholic farmer from north Down and member of the United Irish provincial committee. The Antrim rising began on 7 June, with perhaps as many as 22,000 turning out in battles at Randalstown, Antrim and Ballymena, and countless skirmishes in almost every other town and village.[105] But the rebels were ill armed and poorly led, and after early victories they succumbed to Nugent's forces. When one of the military commanders offered an amnesty, McCracken's rebel army melted away.

Much has been made of religious dissensions among the rebels. Indeed, given the atmosphere of the time, their absence would have been unusual and there was much greater dissension among the rebels generally. But most of the incidents reported come from the pens of two hostile writers, the loyalist politician Sir Richard Musgrave and the former yeoman Samuel McSkimin, and should be treated accordingly. The early stages of the Antrim rising had a carnival atmosphere. Old banners, flags and ensigns were resurrected (many from former volunteering days); columns sang the *Marseillaise* en route to the battlefield, and in his excitement, Larry Dempsey, an army deserter from Munster, exclaimed: 'By J—s, boys, we'll pay the rascals this day for the Battle of the Boyne.' The story is McSkimin's and is plausible given the bad relations between the Orangemen and southern soldiers noted earlier. 'The great Orange fear' of 1798 tended to assume greater proportions the further removed from Ulster itself. But threading through McSkimin's account is a suggestion of separate Defender forces, often involved in dissensions with the rest.

As the largely Presbyterian leadership began to fall apart, there is some evidence of escalated recruiting among Catholics – United Irishmen capitalising on the Orange scare by using specifically Defender oaths to entice them to join. James Hope, the Presbyterian weaver from Templepatrick (and still something of a folk-hero in those parts), was McCracken's closest aide in the recruitment of Defenders. 'Charles Teeling was labouring . . . to unite the Defenders and Catholics of the smaller towns of Ulster', he later told the historian of the United Irishmen R. R. Madden, 'and joining in sworn brotherhood, they became United Irishmen. At a later period, Henry Joy McCracken advised and assisted in the special organisation of a body of seven thousand men, *originally* of the Defenders, to act as a forlorn hope, in case of necessity, out of the twenty-one thousand that were returned fighting men in the county of Antrim.'[106] This is an intriguing passage suggesting a later strategy in tune with reports of separate recruiting of Defenders. It receives further endorsement from the account of events in these crucial early days of June from one of the commanders in north Down, David Bailie Warden – a young Presbyterian schoolmaster and trainee minister. On 3 June he was present when an express arrived from Antrim announcing: 'That the Colonels of United Irishmen in the County of Antrim were averse to action but that the Defenders were 5,000 all ready for action.' On 1 June, the Ulster commander-in-chief, Robert Simms – one of the few original leaders still at liberty and, along with most leaders of that vintage, adamant against rising without the French – resigned. On 2 June, as the remaining commanders still vacillated, when faced with demands from the inferior officers for immediate action, McCracken was raised to the command, his elite force of Defenders apparently becoming part of the argument for action.

However, the image of Catholics and Presbyterians fighting under different banners can only be taken so far. When the so-called 'regenerated Defenders' emerged after the collapse of the United Irish rebellion, it is clear that their leaders had been United Irishmen in the rebellion year.[107] Catholics only seem to have coalesced in separate Catholic divisions when the demography of their particular area was exclusively Catholic and such would have been the case in parts of County Down. Predictably it is from here that the main case of religious division is reported, for more than any other county in Ulster, huge numbers of County Down Catholics joined the standard of rebellion.

In the split of 1797 over the timing of the planned rising, a meeting was reported to have taken place near Newry at which over 1,000 were said to have attended. Prominent among those calling for an immediate rising were leading Catholics John Magennis and Alexander Lowry, and they appear to have won their case, for it was a minority (some 300) who withdrew in protest.[108] Thereafter the same group took the initiative in Ulster in support of a militant faction within the Dublin leadership. Their immediate strategy, short of avoiding arrest – a distinct possibility for warrants were out against them – was to organise supporters in Britain and France. They were joined by Coigley, Bartholomew Teeling, Anthony McCann from Carlingford, and Patrick and John Byrne from Dundalk. By now Down was the United Irishmen's most organised county and the most vocal in pushing for rebellion.[109] With most of the main leaders either out of the country or in prison, it is difficult to keep track of the vicissitudes among the leadership. Yet even after the great Orange scare which immediately preceded the rising, Catholics were well represented among the United Irish leadership – a list of six colonels of April 1798 included three Catholics: Patrick McDonnell, the priest Bernard Magennis and Hugh O'Hanlon of Newry.

Down and Antrim were to have risen on the same day, but McCracken's message had not arrived and most of the Down commanders had been arrested. The rising in Down started belatedly with an attack on Saintfield on Saturday 9 June. Warden, 'having gone through several stages of promotion' in one day, was made commander of the Ards brigade. By the following day the Ards peninsula was in rebel hands. But Warden could barely contain the disposition among his ill-trained men to flee, arms and all, at the slightest rumour of attack. The insubordination escalated en route to the main rebel camp. This had been established at Creevy Rocks – just south of Saintfield on the road to Ballynahinch – but as yet it had no overall commander. On Sunday Henry Munro appeared and was 'appointed by acclamation, to the chief command'. Munro was a young linen draper from Lisburn with an established reputation as a reformer. Ironically he was a direct descendant of the same Major-General Munro who had been sent to quell the 1641 Ulster rising, and who introduced Presbyterianism to Ireland.[110]

The rebellion in County Down had been a largely Presbyterian one until now. But the Ards men hoped to cross Strangford Lough to link with the Defenders in an attack on Downpatrick. The main battle occurred at Ballynahinch on 11 June. On its eve, 'the mutinous disposition . . . [and] spirit of insubordination', which Warden found among the footsoldiers from the outset, had reached such a height, that entire units, officers and all, threatened to decamp and return home. The rebels were poorly armed and ill equipped and Munro hesitated. Troops converging from Belfast and Downpatrick could be tracked by the plumes of smoke on the horizon, for towns taken by the rebels were torched and a statement put out by General Nugent offered a choice of clemency on surrender or utter destruction. Whether it was this or clear indecision among the rebel command which caused it, there can be no doubt about the hundreds defecting on the eve of battle. The twelve-year-old James Thompson watched the battle from a neighbouring hill, where his family had sought refuge, and in later life left a vivid account of the day's proceedings. 'The chief injury sustained by the rebels . . . consisted in the gradual desertion of a great part of their army . . . we distinctly heard their more determined fellows shouting to stop the runaways . . . during every hour of the night fugitives were seen passing our station.'[111] Musgrave claimed these were Catholics.[112] But this cannot be proved. Nor can the continuing speculation that John Magennis had returned on the eve of the rebellion and that it was he who had argued with Munro and withdrawn with the Catholics from Ballynahinch.[113] Such were the stories still circulating in 1834 about the defection of the Catholics, that Hope felt compelled to confront them. He told Madden:

A party, which was assembling near Rathfriland, was advised to disperse by John O'Niel, of Eight-mile Bridge; they did so and traitors represented them as Catholics who had deserted the people. There was another false report that was industriously spread, and which is current to this day, that Maginnis had gone to Ballinahinch, with a body of Catholics, but in consequence of a dispute with Munro, had abandoned the people, and taken away his party with him. Maginnis was not there at all, nor any body of men, exclusively Catholics; the Catholics that were there were mixed with the Dissenters, and fought side by side with them, in a common cause ... the Killinchy people were the men who deserted, and they were Dissenters.[114]

The story first surfaced in information given to the Revd James Mac-Cary – a Dominican priest who had been compromised by the information of another priest into informing. He had it from a Felix Conroy or Converoy from Armagh, who had it from a Lisburn innkeeper and cotton manufacturer named Clarke, said to be one of the rebel commanders at Ballynahinch. Clark blamed the defeat on 'an ambitious and religious contest' between Munro and a Magennis. The dispute over who should lead the forces was decided in Magennis's favour by the toss of a coin. But Munro drew his sword, crying out that 'his intentions was[sic] to establish a presbiterian independant Government' – unlikely, since he was a Protestant of the established church – and called to his side all who supported him. Magennis did likewise and that night they left the rebel camp. Several hundred Catholics who were to have joined the camp the next day heard of Magenis's departure and failed to turn up.[115]

In the south of the county a military council was held to decide whether to march north to join Munro at Ballynahinch, or to capture Newry, extend along the Armagh–Louth border and cut Ulster off from Dublin. After much time was wasted, the latter strategy was adopted. But before it could be implemented, news arrived of the defeat at Ballynahinch. It may well have been from this group of United Irishmen that young Charles Teeling escaped into the mountains of south Ulster, his journey charting the widespread military licence and destruction which had occurred since the previous year. But about sectarian quarrels among the Down rebels, Teeling is silent. Catholic rebels also set out from Monaghan to join the Down men,[116] and, as with the Derry United Irishmen who tried to reach Antrim, others too may have been stopped in their tracks by news of the swift suppression of the rising in the two counties. It is difficult to know what to make of the Magenis story, for Clark was clearly no bigot and seems to have used his business dealings to spread the United Irish system among the Defenders of Connacht. It does not at all square with what we know of Munro. Yet there is a possibility that it was rather Bernard Magennis or another relative, Roger, who took part in the Down rebellion, for they were arrested after the battle of Ballynahinch.[117] A far more reliable witness – David Bailie Warden – blamed their defeat on a failure of command, 'the arrestment of most of our principal officers – the neglect or ignorance of the next superiors [all accounts agree on Munro's courage and honour, but absence of military acumen], the disordered embodyment of the people and the too great eagerness in General Munro for engaging – together with some improprieties committed at Ballynahinch'. In his long account of the Down rising, he does not single out religious dissension as a major factor in its failure.[118]

Hope may be guilty of special pleading in what he told Madden. But in the aftermath of 1798, there was no shortage of those trying to shift the blame on to the other side and the tendency was actively promoted by government supporters. Indeed, the Ballynahinch incident, like so many from the events of 1798, was exaggerated to suit party purposes. Frank Wright was told of it by some Protestants in Newtownards in the late 1980s. The point of such stories, he reflected, 'is that they create a picture of a United rising that really had very little to do with the Catholics, and which was anyway seen as a mistake later ... They dispose of the romantic rubbish about how the 1798 Republicans were 1916 rebels little over a hundred years before their time.' To paint the 1798 Ulster rebels as somehow deluding themselves until Wexford had alerted them to the real threat of Catholic power, concluded Wright, is 'to accept uncritically the claims of later political actors who wanted to destroy the very idea that there might be any unity of purpose between Protestant and Catholic'.[119] The reality was that in those areas where the rebellion did erupt, Catholics were too few and too insignificant to appear in any other guise than the victims of military and Orange atrocities, and on the whole those Catholics were beholden to the Presbyterians who had given such support to the campaign for Catholic rights in recent years.

Government had long sought to drive a wedge between Catholic and Dissenter. The withdrawal of the propertied Presbyterians on the eve of the Ulster rising caused intense bitterness among lower-class Catholics throughout Ireland. Their action, Hope reflected, 'gave our enemies an opportunity of shaking the confidence of our countrymen in the other provinces, by constantly reminding them how the Dissenters of the north began the business, and in the time of need were the first to abandon it'.[120] The truth, as ever, probably lies somewhere in between. The Catholic Church in Ulster was almost totally united in its condemnation of disaffection and barely half a dozen Ulster clergy out of seventy for the entire country were involved. The *Belfast News Letter* took comfort from the inaction of the bulk of Ulster Catholics during the rebellion:

The different character maintained by the Catholic of the north and the Catholic of the south is well understood by everyone acquainted with Ireland. God be praised the former has better information than the latter and has we believe a degree of liberality with which the other is unacquainted.[121]

Given the religious demography of the rest of Ireland, it was inevitable that the foot soldiers of the rebellion there should have been largely Catholic. The possible consequences of this clearly worried some United Irishmen. The Antrim leader James Dickey's oft-quoted declaration, immediately prior to his execution, 'that if the *north* had been successful, they would have had to fight the battle over again with the Catholics of the *south*',[122] echoes Turner's suspicions the previous year.

The propertied of all denominations had steadily withdrawn from the United Irishmen after Lake's disarmament, and lack of leadership and continued military licence, more than any dissension, was responsible for the steady stream of defections. Disillusionment was widespread. James Orr, the Ulster-Scots folk poet of Ballycarry, whose entire village was 'out' in '98, graphically described the feelings in the main rebel camp at Donegore Hill in Antrim. Many were half-hearted:

> Repentant Painites at their pray'rs,
> An' dastards crousely craikin',
> Move on, heroic, to the wars
> They meant na to partake in,
>   By night, or day.

And when the soldiers appeared, they took flight:

> For Nugent's red-coats, bright in arms,
> An' rush! the pale-fac'd randies
>   Took leg, that day.
>
> The camp's brak up. Owre braces, an' bogs,
> The patriots seek their sections;
> Arms, ammunition, bread-bags, brogues,
> Lye skail'd in a' directions;
>
> Come back, ye dastards! – Can ye ought
> Expect at your returnin',
> But wives an' weans stript, cattle hought,
> An' cots, an' claughin's burnin?
> Na, haste ye hame: ye ken ye'll 'scape,
> 'Cause martial worth ye're clear o';
> The nine-tail'd cat, or choakin' rape,
> Is maistly for some hero,
>   On sic a day.
> Better he swing than I, on
>   Some hangin' day.

What might have been, asked Orr, 'Had they no been deserted'; but flesh is weak and:

> In tryin' times, maist folk, you'll fin',
> Will act like Donegore men.[123]

We may never know the exact number who lost their lives during the rebellion. But when Lord Cornwallis arrived as the new Lord Lieutenant in late June he was shocked by the military licence, the Catholic militia to the fore in an effort to counter previous charges of disaffection. The military had given no quarter in the aftermath of battle, bodies were left hanging from trees at Antrim, others stripped and buried in shallow graves on the shores of Lough Neagh, while rebels fleeing from Ballynahinch were cut down in the surrounding

1a. Belfast from the River Lagan. Cave Hill in the Distance, 1863.

1b. West Belfast Peace Wall separating the Loyalist Shankhill Road and Nationalist Falls Road, 1994. One of seventeen such barricades still separating Belfast Catholics and Protestants – usually at their own request – often physically dividing streets in apparently 'mixed' areas.

2a. Aerial photograph of Emain Macha (Navan Fort). Emain Macha in Armagh is believed to have been the capital of ancient Ulster, the centre of the Ulaid dynasty until its demise in the fourth to fifth century AD, and location of many of the legendary exploits of Cú Chulainn.

2b. Statue of Cú Chulainn, republican plot, City Cemetery, Brandywell, Derry. Legendary youth warrior of Ulster as depicted in the medieval Ulster Cycle tales, Cú Chulainn was reinvented by late nineteenth-century nationalism, his death (depicted here) becoming the key inspiration in the 'blood sacrifice' tradition of Patrick Pearse and twentieth-century Irish republicanism. Ironically he has also become a symbol for Ulster loyalism, because of his mythical role as defender of Ulster against the south.

Tullahoge was the inauguration site of the O'Neills, the most powerful Gaelic lords in Ulster. It was destroyed by the Elizabethans in 1602, symbolically ending O'Neill power.

3a. *The Dartmouth College Map of the North East of Ireland*, Map 25, *c.*1586. Detail showing Tullahoge, County Tyrone.

3b. Aerial photograph of Tullahoge Fort.

A   *Now when into their fenced holdes the knaues are entred in,*
     To smite and knocke ths cattell downe, the hangmen doe beginne.
     One plucketh off the Oxes cote, which he euen now did weare,
     Another lacking pannes, to boyle the flesh his hide prepare.
C   *These theeues attend vpon the fire for seruing vp the feast,*
B   *And fryer smelfeast sneaking in, doth preace amongst the best.*
     Who play'th in Romish toyes the Ape, by counterfetting Paull;
     For which they doe award him then, the highest room of all.
     Who being set, because the cheere is deemed little worth,
     Except the same be intermixt and lac'de with Irish myrth.
D   *Both Barde and Harper is preparde, which by their cunning art,*
     Doe strike and cheare vp all the gestes with comfort at the hart.

4. *The Chief of the MacSweeneys seated at Dinner* by John Derrick, 1581.
Derrick's engravings, though typical of the anti-Irishness of the Elizabethans,
nevertheless provide a contemporary image of the importance of the bards,
musicians and friars in the retinue of the Gaelic lord (in this case the
MacSweeneys of Donegal).

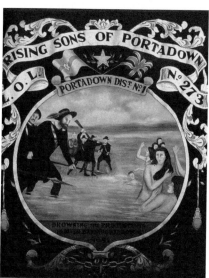

5a. Hedge Row School Mural, Ardoyne Avenue, Belfast. A romantic portrayal of a hedge-school in this late 1990s mural in a nationalist estate of north Belfast (note the depiction of the Cave Hill in the background, identifying it with the locality). The caption in Irish translates 'speak the Irish language to me'.

5b. Orange banner, Loyal Orange Lodge 273, Portadown No. 1 District – representing the drowning of Protestants by Catholics in the River Bann during the Ulster rising of 1641. The events of 1641 are regularly retold by some Ulster Protestants as an example of Catholics' inherent treachery.

6a. Mural of a Mass Rock, Ardoyne Avenue, Belfast. Late 1990s mural in nationalist North Belfast, near that of the Hedge School, this represents the most common nationalist image of the eighteenth-century penal era: the Catholic priest, saying mass in secret and hunted by the 'red-coats' (British military), in the distance.

6b. Mural of the Virgin Mary, Berwick Road, Ardoyne, Belfast. This 1990s mural in a North Belfast nationalist estate (Holy Cross Catholic church depicted in the background) is also something of a shrine, with an altar and monthly rosary meetings announced in an attached plaque.

THE STATION.

7a. 'The Station'. Before the so-called 'devotional revolution' of the nineteenth century, the 'station', whereby the priest would periodically visit the house of a selected parishioner to hear the confessions and give communion to Catholics in the parish, was a significant part of Catholic devotion in rural areas.

7b. *Cabins, Mourne Mountains, Co. Down* by R. J. Welsh, *c.* 1900. Though a later photograph, these cabins would have been inhabited since the eighteenth century.

8. *Battle of Ballynahinch, 13th June 1798*, (detail) by Thomas Robinson, *c.* 1798/99.

9a. *Cardinal Paul Cullen*, artist unknown, nineteenth century – redoubtable leader of the Catholic Church in Ireland between 1849 and 1878, he is largely credited with fashioning modern Irish Catholicism.

9b. *At Doon Holy Well, Kilmacrenan* by R. J. Welsh, 1912. Devotions and 'cures' sought at holy wells have been a feature of 'popular' religion in rural Ireland since early Christian days. Denounced by successive generations of clergy for the excesses which often accompanied the gatherings, some, like Doon Well in southwest Donegal, have nevertheless survived and been incorporated into the Catholic Church's devotional calendar.

The Great Famine of 1845–9, when over a million people died from starvation and disease, came to feature prominently in Irish nationalism's attack on British rule. The more polemical and unfounded accusation of genocide by Britain has been a feature of republican propaganda. But the bitterness at such suffering (well represented here) is real enough, even among nationalists who denounce violence.

10a. *An Gorta Mór: 'Britain's Genocide by Starvation'.* Mural of the Great Famine, Whiterock Road, Ballymurphy, Belfast.

10b. *An Gorta Mór: 'They buried us without shroud nor coffin'.* Mural of the Great Famine, Ardoyne Avenue, Belfast.

11a. *Rioting in Sandy Row, Belfast*, 1864, artist unknown. Belfast was torn by regular sectarian riots in the nineteenth century, often centred on the Protestant Sandy Row/Catholic Pound districts, the Boyne Bridge (pictured here) marking the interface.

11b. *Riots in York Street, Belfast*, 1922. Severe inter-communal violence marked the birth of the Northern Ireland state, 1920–22, claiming the lives of 453 people in Belfast. York Street, just north of the city centre – a district of internal segregation between Protestant and Catholic streets – was one of the flashpoint areas.

12a. *Walker's Pillar, Walls of Londonderry*, drawing by W. H. Bartlett, engraved by R. Wallis, *c.* 1825/1840. The walls of Derry/Londonderry hold a special place in Protestant tradition because of the walled city's resistance to the forces of James II in 1690. The Walker Pillar (commemorating the joint-governor of the city in 1690) was erected in 1826. It was intended as a symbol of Protestant dominance and considered so by the Catholic Bogside area over which it towered. It was blown up in 1973.

12b. Parliament Building, Stormont, Belfast – the massively imposing seat of the Northern Ireland Parliament, built in 1932. Situated in Protestant East Belfast, and transferring its name to the entire period of Unionist rule (1920–72), it was considered another symbol of Protestant dominance by most Catholics.

13a. Terence O'Neill with Councillor Robert Hart after opening O'Neill Road. This photograph was reproduced by Terence O'Neill in his *Autobiography* as an example of his constant taunting by Paisleyites (in the background) during his premiership (1963–9).

13b. *"Biased!! How dare you, you long haired Fenian agitator."* Martyn Turner – best-known caricaturist of the Troubles in Northern Ireland – capturing (in *Fortnight*, May 1971) Catholic perceptions of discrimination.

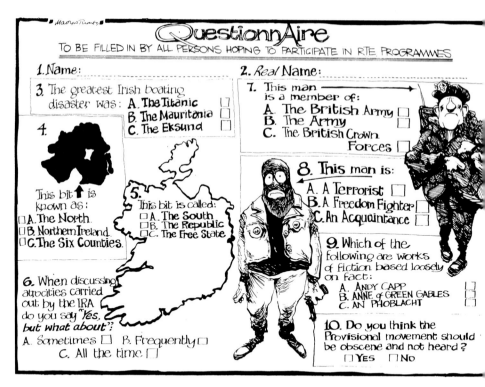

14a. *Questionnaire* is Turner's satire on the verbal ambivalence associated with Northern Ireland – usage of certain terms identifying the religious and political leanings of the speaker – and first appeared in the *Irish Times* where he has worked since 1976.

14b. Residents leaving Divis Street, in West Belfast in August 1969, after their homes were destroyed in sectarian riots.

15a. *'Free Ireland'* 1916 commemoration mural, Beechmount Avenue, Belfast – reproducing Patrick Pearse's 1915 oration at the grave of the Fenian, O'Donovan Rossa.

15b. *Bobby Sands' Funeral, 1981.* The funeral of Bobby Sands – first and the most famous of the republican hunger strikers to die in May 1981 – was attended by some 100,000 people.

16. Last rites by Father Alex Reid said over the body of one of the two British Army corporals killed at Andersonstown, March 1988.

woods. The leaders were executed shortly afterwards, their heads displayed on market-house spikes throughout the affected counties. The Revd Robert Magill was a child in 1798, 'I particularly remember . . . the awful spectacle of human heads fastened on spikes and placed on the Market-house of Ballymena,' he later recalled, '. . . the hair of the heads waving to and fro in the wind.'[124] The physical scars also would have remained, the towns burnt by Nugent's forces, the Catholic chapels burnt to the ground, their sites continuing to be used for services until passions calmed and they could be rebuilt. It was a reversion to an uglier past, wiping from memory the many gains that had been made in the interim.[125]

Another casualty was the Irish parliament itself. An unusual combination of loss of faith by the British government in its capacity to cope with the security situation and its willingness to buy off vested interests, radical and republican contempt for a reactionary, aristocratic institution, and confidence by the Catholic establishment that London would reward its support by granting emancipation, produced the abolition of the Irish parliament by the Act of Union of 1800. But the King's implacable opposition to Catholic emancipation thwarted Catholic expectations (largely encouraged by Pitt) that further reforms would reward their support and nearly three decades were to pass before emancipation finally came.

8. The Fall-out

The sufferings and horrors of the 1798 period seemed a world apart from the euphoria of 1792, and all sides had cause to pause and reflect. The fact that most Ulster Catholics remained uninvolved and their clergy conspicuously loyal was soon lost in the return of the belief that, given the chance, Catholics would always behave as they had done at Scullabogue. Religious stereotypes were already well formed by the 1790s, and the decade provides an awful example of how the underlying fears of Protestants and resentments of Catholics were allowed to become a self-fulfilling prophecy. Even without the anti-Catholic propaganda circulating in the aftermath of the rebellion, former Presbyterian rebels needed little persuading that they had been snatched from the jaws of a popish conspiracy. Presbyterian radicalism did not die in 1798. James Orr's continued support for Catholic emancipation well into the nineteenth century was not untypical, though, as his editors suggest, it might not have survived its link with O'Connellism, which for Ulster Presbyterians came to symbolise the kind of Catholic tyranny forecast by Turner and Dickey.[126] As long as the possibility of French aid survived – which it did, at least theoretically, until 1815 – government feared the 'few Protestant traitors' still active around Belfast.[127]

Within months of the collapse of the Ulster rising the main flow of disaffection was into revived Defenderism. 'The word "Protestant", which was becoming obsolete in the north,' commented the Revd Edward Hudson in a graphic description of the new polarisation, 'has regained its influence, and all of that description seem drawing closer together.' He considered the spread of 'the Orange mania' the main culprit. It had been introduced to his area by a corps of yeomanry in the aftermath of the rebellion, and those, like himself, who tried to stop it were denounced as 'Catholic lovers'. It was said to be countenanced by the government and notices began to appear carrying 'the old inscription: "To hell or Connaught"'. United Irishmen were joining the Orangemen to hide themselves, and these he considered the most violent against their former Catholic associates. These in turn began to inform, and suspicions that the Catholics had betrayed the popular rebel commander at Antrim, George Dickson – captured and executed in May 1799 – contributed to the growing religious gulf.[128]

For Presbyterians 1798 has left a much more confused legacy than for Catholic nationalists, for whom it holds out the simplified vision of Ulster Protestantism once again accepting 'the common name of Irishman'. Even after the religious and political transformations of the late nineteenth and twentieth centuries, which saw Presbyterianism fully integrated into a common Protestant unionism, there was a residual pride that their ancestors had been 'out' in '98. But this could only be sustained through the Catholic nationalist 'hi-jack' of the United Irish story by adopting the myth that the Ulster rising had been a Presbyterian one, quite different in character from that in the rest of the country. The story of *Betsy Gray and the Hearts of Down* was once a favourite with the people of Down, Catholic and Protestant alike. It was immortalised in the 1896 novel of W. G. Lyttle, a liberal newspaper editor in Bangor, north Down. The short novel became a minor classic and I remember my father retelling the story as late as the 1960s and 1970s. It is the story of Elizabeth Gray, who had joined her brother and lover at the battle of Ballynahinch – all three being killed by yeomen in the aftermath of the defeat. Far into the nineteenth century the descendants of these yeomen were shunned at the Anahilt Protestant church and their children stoned at school. But when Catholics and Home Rulers tried to use Betsy's grave for the 1898 centenary celebrations, local loyalists smashed it to pieces to prevent its takeover by nationalists. Ballynahinch loyalists turned out on 13 June to parade in honour of the victory by royal troops in 1798, placing union jacks on the courthouse and the hills overlooking the battle site. Nationalists, thwarted in their desire to lay a wreath at Betsy Gray's grave by the destruction of the headstone, moved to the grave of another rebel only to find that the owner of the land had called in the police to block them. The following month a 'monster' Orange demonstration on Edenavady hill was addressed by the Revd L. A. Pooler. Why Catholics should want to celebrate '98 anyway, he could not understand. 'They had little or nothing to do with it. The night before the Battle of Ballynahinch the Roman Catholics deserted . . . They decorated the grave of Betsy Gray, but they had not the courage to fight beside her', and were she alive today, she would be a Unionist.[129]

The events of 1797–8 had indeed transformed relationships in Ulster. For the first time that century the bulk of lower-class Catholics were disaffected, the bulk of lower-class Protestants and Presbyterians were loyalist. Lord Castlereagh, always an astute observer of long-term trends, described the transformation which had occurred in popular politics:

The Protestant dissenters in Ulster have in a great degree withdrawn themselves from the Union, and become Orangemen. The Northern Catholics always committed in feeling against the Presbyterians, were during the early period of the conspiracy loyal – the religious complexion of the Rebellion in the South gradually separated the Protestants from the Treason, and precisely in the same degree, appear'd to embark the Catholics in it – defenderism was introduced, and it is principally under that organization . . . that whatever there is of Treason in the North, is at present associated. They are destitute of Leaders, and the people of substance, manufacturers as well as farmers have withdrawn from them.[130]

Normally suspicious Catholics had been taught by the likes of Henry Joy McCracken to accept leadership from sympathetic Presbyterians and Protestants, and a turning away from the priests has already been noted. But as the Presbyterians in particular drew back, Catholics felt they had been misled and then made the scapegoats. An anonymous correspondent writing to the military under-secretary at Dublin Castle, warned that although not all Catholics had been rebels, nevertheless they now believed 'that they had been first misled, then forsaken, and lastly betrayed by the leaders of the Rebellion'. Even so the actions of the Orangemen kept them disaffected. 'Being made to believe that these outrages are committed on them under the authority, and sanction of government, their antipathy against it and against the Orange party is exactly the same: for they conceive on this account Government to be the real source of all their real or ideal sufferings.'[131] When Thomas Russell came north to organise the Ulster part of 'Emmet's Rebellion' in 1803, he found little support, except from 'the lowest order of the Catholics', even if their clergy again organised loyal addresses against the latest attempt.[132]

Catholics were now profoundly alienated from the state, where once they had looked to England as a better friend than their Protestant fellow Irishmen. Such alienation was deepened by the continuing influence of Orangeism over the forces of law and order. In the new century, the suspect Catholic militia was progressively whittled down, the numbers of British troops and yeomanry simultaneously increased (reaching 21,000 and 31,000 respectively by 1823).[133] The countenance given by government to the Orange takeover of counter-insurgency in 1797–8 proved difficult to shake off – even though almost every government thereafter sought to do so. Orangeism did not always attract support from higher social orders, and most of its history has been a continuation of Armagh's lower-class sectarianism, just as Ribbonism (the direct descendant of Defenderism) perpetuated lower-class Catholic sectarianism into the nineteenth century. The enemy for Catholic Ulster remained the Protestant and above all the Orangeman. Ribbonism, like the early Defenders, was a largely reactive force and when the Orange Order was temporarily dissolved and parades ceased (1836–45) Ribbonism likewise declined.

But for the future character of Ulster Catholicism, perhaps the most important casualty of these years was the sudden curtailment of that secular Catholic leadership which had started to emerge. Many like to think of the 1790s as one of the great might-have-beens of Irish history, when Catholic, Protestant and Dissenter came together. But the union was only really successful at the leadership level – a coming together of the excluded middle class. The great might-have-been was not that they could have realistically carried out a revolution without exacerbating existing sectarian divisions but that a secular Catholic leadership might have been peacefully incorporated into the state, pre-empting the emergence in the nineteenth century of the kind of clerical nationalism which so fed Protestant terrors of political Catholicism. The claims of repentant United Irishmen that they would have been satisfied with such a move (accompanied by a measure of parliamentary reform) have been dismissed as an attempt to distance themselves from the catastrophe of 1798. However, it was such rejected middle-class Catholic leaders who effected the alliance between the Defenders and the United Irishmen, and whilst it is likely that sectarian animosity would have persisted in some form, both the 1790s and the subsequent history of Ribbonism showed that lower-class Catholics were as status-conscious as ever and as willing to follow the leadership of their own kind or, (as in Antrim and Down) even of sympathetic Protestants and Presbyterians. Dr Haliday writing to Lord Charlemont from Belfast at the close of 1791 caught the mood of a Catholic middle class no longer willing to grovel for recognition:

I understand that the Catholic members of the Belfast United society . . . have . . . insisted on their Protestant associates pledging themselves to go all lengths with them in that business of franchise . . ., and he warned that the Whigs could not afford to alienate 'a body who are likely to rise into prominence'.[134]

The awful experiences of 1798 had done nothing to weaken this new mood. An attempt to secure an oath of allegiance from Luke Teeling in return for his liberation in December 1798 produced the stinging retort that it was 'contrary to honour and religion, and, therefore ought not to be required. It is unreasonable to expect, and dishonourable, in any person who is not of the established religion, to swear that "he will, to the best of his power, support the laws", when one law (without going further) degrades and taxes his mode of worship, and is contrary to the free will which God has given to man.' He believed that his only crime lay 'in being considered the head of the Catholics in this county and active in their cause at the time of our convention', and in no uncertain terms he denounced the 'faction' in the Irish government for its 'mysterious policy . . . of arming and inflaming the minority against the majority, who were distinguished for loyalty and peaceable behaviour'.[135] For the Ulster Catholics a sense of rejection by the state, the apparent takeover of state apparatus by Orangeism, and a reassertion of Catholic church authority (so shaken in these years) were ultimately more important legacies from the 1790s than republican nationalism.

8

THE REVIVAL OF 'POLITICAL' CATHOLICISM

'To be a Catholic is still a political thing . . . [Catholics] have an affinity with the Church which has to do with its history in Ireland . . . the Church was part of the people's struggle.'

Gerry Adams, speaking in 1992
(O Connor, *In Search of a State*, 291)

There is a belief held by some Ulster Protestants that Catholics are under the domination of their priests and that those priests teach them biased politics and history.[1] Such beliefs represent a continuation of the fears of 'political popery', present in Protestant psyche since the Reformation and acquiring a new stridency in the nineteenth century. However, like all stereotypes, this one is only partly true and is largely based on developments elsewhere in Ireland. The Ulster Catholic clergy have traditionally been averse to political involvement. Attuned to operating in a climate of sectarian sensitivities, they have been much less aggressive than their southern colleagues. However, Catholicism and Protestantism in Ulster – particularly the militant varieties – have always fed off each other. The two communities' identities owe far more to sectarian awareness than to any Irish or British nationalism. It should not be surprising therefore that in the period when those identities were acquiring their modern form, it was the extreme representations which dictated the pace.

1. The 'Second Reformation' and the re-organisation of the Catholic Church

By the close of the nineteenth century the Catholic Church had acquired almost all its modern characteristics: a highly visible organisational structure, a disciplined clergy, a high level of religious instruction and practice, church control of Catholic education and social activities, and visible allegiance to Rome. The revival and restructuring was already in progress by the end of the eighteenth century. None the less the term 'devotional revolution' to describe developments within

Catholicism in the nineteenth century – however much it has been criticised and modified since it was coined by Emmet Larkin a quarter of a century ago – still seems an appropriate description for such a remarkable transformation, in particular the activities of the redoubtable bishop and cardinal, Paul Cullen.[2] In Ulster the pace was dictated by equally dramatic developments within Ulster Protestantism and Presbyterianism. There were similar religious developments throughout the western world in the nineteenth century, as papal authority revived after the shock of revolution in the late eighteenth century. 'The essence of their creed', writes Hugh McLeod in the best short overview of such developments in the western world, 'was the combination of a highly dogmatic and anti-rationalist theology with a warmly emotional piety, and a preference for life within a Catholic ghetto, where the faith of the masses could be preserved from Protestant or rationalist contamination.'[3]

Until mid-century (and beyond that in Belfast), the Ulster Catholic hierarchy continued in the O'Reilly mode, preferring a *modus vivendi* with Protestant society and keeping as low a political profile as possible. Church building – such a feature of the Catholic revival – lagged behind in Ulster, because of the continuing poverty of most of the Catholic people. In the western rural areas – where mass-attendance was significantly lower than elsewhere in the province – there was a distinct reluctance to subscribe.[4] Belfast, in Corish's analysis, was 'a disaster area' in this period, in its shortage of places for public worship – a judgement which the Halls even in the 1840s would have fully endorsed, for they found Catholics had but two chapels, ' one large and commodious . . . in Donegal St [sic – i.e. St Patrick's]; and the other, a dingy brick building, in Chapel-lane' [St. Mary's].[5] Even so, the appearance of such visible signs of 'popery' still caused tensions in traditional areas of conflict like Armagh. But since the land was predominantly in Protestant hands, the Catholic Church in Ulster remained heavily dependent on Protestant goodwill and generosity for sites and financial assistance. Provided Catholicism appeared as unthreatening as it did in Ulster in the early 1800s, liberal Presbyterians, particularly in the towns, remained supportive. But the prognosis was not good. Developments in Catholic politics elsewhere in Ireland and within Ulster Protestantism suggested that neither had changed their spots, and the middle ground was steadily eroded.

Daniel O'Connell's campaigns for Catholic emancipation (notably 1824–9) and the repeal of the Union (1832–47) raised the old spectre of political popery, and eroded much of what was left of Presbyterian liberalism. Many former United Irishmen continued to support Catholic emancipation, as did the Presbyterian Synod. But even they came to accept the Union as immutable. To leading Catholics, their betrayal by the government after the Union, the insistence by successive British governments that Catholic emancipation should be accompanied by some form of 'securities' – notably a veto over episcopal appointments – and the known hostility of successive monarchs did not inspire confidence. As successive bills were defeated, so statements from the Dublin-based Catholic Association became more aggressive, so the temperature rose in Ulster. Even though he accepted limited emancipation, the fiery Presbyterian minister Henry Cooke caused a furore in 1825 by revisiting stories of atrocities in 1641 and other past examples of popery's attack on liberty and religion. Although he was denounced by leading Presbyterians, all the signs were that Cooke was speaking for a growing tide of lower-class opinion, Presbyterian and Anglican alike.[6]

Faced with the same begrudgery as the campaigners of the 1790s, O'Connell too resorted to mass mobilisation and again utilised the best network available: the priests. But there the comparison with the Catholic campaign of the 1790s ceases. The priests were mobilised not for one election, but as organisers of the Catholic rent – the scheme under which individual Catholics paid a penny per month in support of the campaign's activities. This, it has been argued, with perhaps pardonable exaggeration, did more than anything which had gone before to create a nationwide Catholic community.[7] The sums raised were then mobilised to fund Catholic legal expenses, education and political activities. It prefigured the future by facilitating alternative Catholic social and political structures. But it was undoubtedly O'Connell's mobilisation of the Catholic vote which made demands for 'Catholic emancipation' irresistible. It was finally granted in 1829, when the right to sit in parliament, belong to corporations and hold high civil and military office, was restored to Catholics.

Support for O'Connell's campaign had been muted in Ulster. The low returns for the Catholic rent may have reflected relative poverty (as it did in Connacht).[8] But there was also considerable clerical ambivalence about its wisdom. The bishops were anxious about its effect on the always delicate community relations in Ulster, and cautioned those priests who became too publicly involved. One of those cautioned was Edward Maginn, parish priest of Inishowen, later bishop of Derry (d.1849) – a highly politicised priest and ardent supporter of O'Connell. He was no revolutionary, and was as critical of agrarian outrage as his predecessors. But he argued that if England expected loyalty, then Catholics expected justice.[9] A more moderate figure was bishop Crolly of Down and Connor, who had carefully nurtured relationships with Belfast's liberal Presbyterians and was particularly worried about O'Connell's antagonistic statements. Knowing little about Ulster, O'Connell spoke of it almost as a foreign country, and that is how his deputy, John Lawless, behaved in the one effort made to mobilise the province. In September 1828 Lawless announced the 'invasion of Ulster'. Great crowds joined him as he advanced through Meath and Louth, and in a mood of incautious triumphalism he pre-announced his plans to enter Ballybay, a Presbyterian enclave in Monaghan. It was a time of heightened sectarian tension. Both sides were spoiling for a fight and Orangemen called in their brethren from neighbouring counties. The local military commander persuaded Lawless to retreat, as did the Catholics of Armagh – his next venue. Lawless's conduct was condemned by the Catholic clergy and liberal Protestants as 'foolish and improper'. But the Orangemen of south Ulster viewed his retreat as a major victory and marched in triumph through Armagh, prompting the liberal *Northern Whig* to comment sadly on the apparent bias of the law in preventing one side's triumphalism, but not the other's.[10]

The O'Connellite campaign was only one element in the atmosphere of heightened religious tension in the 1820s, 1830s and 1840s. The so-called 'Second Reformation' not only added a new tier to persistent anti-popery, but forced the Catholic Church to rethink its pastoral role. In these early decades of the nineteenth century a number of evangelical societies set out to convert Irish Catholics to Protestantism. In doing so they activated an alarmed Catholic clergy, whose successful fight back in many other parts of Ireland effectively concentrated the proselytising campaign in the north – notably in the densely populated south Ulster counties. The activities of the evangelicals were based on the fundamentalist Protestant perception of Catholicism as a backward, superstitious, even unchristian religion, and of its adherents as in thrall to a crafty priesthood. Catholics were bombarded with leaflets outlining the errors of their church. At its worst, the campaign assumed apocalyptic proportions, a final effort to rescue Catholics from the abyss of resurgent political Catholicism. Catholic clergy were challenged to theological disputations, children taken aside secretly by itinerant preachers, and a kind of missionary paternalism operated whereby Protestant landlords offered Catholics material rewards for conversion. To the fore was Lord Farnham of Cavan, who in 1828 claimed a total of 428 converts, mostly from his own estates.[11] There was, moreover, a distinct correlation between such evangelical landlords and Orange sympathisers, and there can be no doubt that the movement heightened religious tensions.

Such abuse of landlord power over their tenants was not widespread. But it left a lingering sore in Catholic tradition, for it became the 'souperism' of the Great Famine, 1845–9, when as many as a million people may have died of starvation and disease, and when a few districts experienced the trade of food for conversion to Protestantism. Even in Donegal – where responses to the 1945 Irish Folklore Commission's famine questionnaire did not throw up strong memories of 'souperism' – the word evoked stories of the proselytising schools, the *Cait Bhreaca* (literally 'speckled cat', the bi-lingual primer used in such schools) and the *Bíobla Gallda* (literally foreign but doubling too for Protestant) Bible. The Donegal writer, Seamas MacManus (1870–1960), recalled a brother and sister who gave themselves airs and despised the common people. These 'were the children – the cursed children, everyone agreed – of a turn-coat father, one of the very few who traded their religion for the land with which a proselytising Protestant landlord would bribe them'. A country ballad mocked the father for his action and the son was taunted as 'Orange' by local boys.[12]

Art Bennett was inspired by the activities of the Revd Henry Young around Forkhill, County Armagh (1846–58), to compose a bitter attack on proselytisers' use of the Irish language. 'I went to the Post

Office of Forkhill on Good Friday last', he explained to Father Patrick Lamb in April 1852, 'and there I seen *(sic)* a large multitude of the most wretched fugitives trudging after Mr Young to church. Each of them had an Irish Bible. I was told that they attended that synagogue every day during that week, and received their communion. Those shameful doings set the feathers on end upon me, and prompted me to give vent to my feelings [in the attached poem].' The poem traced the history of the use of the Irish-language Bible to 'seduce' and 'bait' 'our people'. But it is the 'dregs' of the people who are enticed by offers of food and drink.

> It was shame enough, on Holy week, the vile lunatics
> who were gathered from all directions around the foreign church, each
>   with his Bible,
> there's not one of the party who didn't receive a piece of cake and a little
>   drop of wine
> for insulting the Pope and the Virgin of graces and the Church of Christ

As far as Carlingford and Dunleer in County Louth, Bennett accused Young of seeking out every donkey-man, bag-man, street-sweeper and woman carder. But they are 'weeds' whom the church can do without. In death no priest will come near them and their 'bribes and prizes and their false Bible' will not save them from damnation on Judgement Day.[13]

Although both Irish-language poetic and scribal traditions were in rapid decline in the nineteenth century, surviving poems register the bitterness of some Catholics at the activities of the proselytisers in Irish-speaking areas. 'Do you hear me, O children of the Gaels?' went a poem still recited in Ulster in the twentieth century. It warned the Gael not to exchange his religion for worldly wealth. It is not natural for the Gael to take on the language and religion of the foreigner, for the foreigners will go to hell and the Gael to eternal happiness.[14] Many Irish-speaking poets found employment with the Bible societies. But the poems of Hugh McDonnell (Aodh Mac Domhnaill), like those of Bennett, suggest a good deal of cynicism on their part. McDonnell was employed as a Bible teacher in Meath, Cavan, the Glens of Antrim and later in Glenties, County Donegal. He tells of how he was recruited to the Presbyterian Home Mission by Henry Cooke, who showed him 'the Bible written in Irish' and of how he, like the other teachers, made inflated claims about the numbers of pupils to obtain more money. These inflated figures were published in good faith by the Home Mission, till exposed as a fraud by the Catholic Church in 1844. His poems tell of the activities of the societies in Cavan, particularly Lord Farnham's teacher, Francis Brennan, 'arranging schools on bogs and on mountains' and seducing the ignorant with miraculous claims:

> 'And O beloved Mary, isn't he the spouter of lies!
> I don't believe any more in the lies of the traitors
> since my eyes have seen every deceit and wrong.'[15]

McDonnell was dismissed from the Antrim mission when his daughter was discovered to have called in a Catholic priest during an illness. Indeed Antrim – after Cavan – witnessed much of the sectarian skirmishing in Ulster during the second quarter of the nineteenth century. One magistrate addressing the 1835 parliamentary enquiry into Orange Lodges in Ireland attributed much of the trouble in the Ballymena-Broughshane area to the evangelical fervour created by local preachers.

I saw at one time, 2,000 or 3,000 children brought for many miles to march in procession, each child holding a bible in its hand, and there ... were trumpets to go before each party ... I saw this Revd Mr McClelland ... trying to break into a [Catholic] chapel at the head of all these children ... and when he was not admitted, I saw him ride out of town ... followed by 10,000 well-dressed respectable persons.[16]

MacClelland was later condemned by the Presbyterian Synod and such activities were denounced by very many Protestants. But the 'Second Reformation' ultimately had more impact on Ulster Protestantism than on Ulster Catholicism, infusing it with a new fundamentalism which would steadily erode Presbyterian liberalism and, in time, paper over the cracks which divided the various Protestant denominations. It also heralded a tradition of fiery populist preachers, stretching from Henry Cooke to Ian Paisley, tarring the whole of Protestantism in Catholic eyes with their anti-popery. In a highly symbolic gesture, the statue of perhaps the most prominent exponent – the Revd Hugh Hanna (1821–92) – was blown up in Belfast in 1970, at the beginning of the Troubles.

The intensity of this sectarian strife in the years before the Famine saw a revival of the old prophecies which had also been circulating before the 1798 rebellion, particularly those attributed to Colum Cille. In Ulster they were claimed to have foretold the massacre of the Catholics by the Protestant clergy, but that the Catholic nations would intervene to destroy Protestantism and restore the Gael. Such prophecies were widely believed among the Catholic lower classes, though they were embarrassing to those of the Catholic middle class trying to make their way in politics. One of McDonnell's best poems – 'On the prophecy of Colum Cille son of Phelim' (*Ar Thargair Cholmcille mhic Féilim*) – probably accurately reflects popular belief. It tells of how Colum Cille had predicted the English 'swarm', the massacre of Islandmagee in 1641, the loss of the Irish parliament in 1800 and the Famine; of how 'the descendants of the Gael' would take their parliament back from England, which would 'incite the dogs to murder through the north'. But then the Spaniards would come, Britain would be split, Wully (England) and Sandy (Scotland) gnawing over the bone, and Ireland would be freed. McDonnell had been a fervent O'Connellite and a large number of his poems are devoted to O'Connell. But 'On the prophecy of Colum Cille' reflects the disillusionment at the defeat of repeal in 1843: 'It isn't the Repealers who'll relieve the distress/ or who'll give their land to the Gaels', but the 'mighty champion' from Spain.[17] It is a reminder that the same gulf existed between the Catholic poor and the Catholic political leadership as in the time of the Defenders, even though the power of that leadership to harness the poor's more militant tendencies remained strong, provided it continued to play to their traditional prejudices.

The 'Second Reformation' also intensified denominational divisions in another way. The good relations between Protestant and Catholic clergy early in the century distintegrated from the 1820s because of the proselytising campaigns. The Catholic hierarchy – thoroughly alarmed by such proselytism – took up the challenge, and for the first time mobilised the kind of religious instruction which the Council of Trent had called for three hundred years earlier.[18] Denominational education now became the key dividing issue. Despite their initial anxiety about the Charter schools the previous century, the Catholic hierarchy had not given much priority to Catholic education below that required for educating the priesthood. But the activities of the Protestant missionary societies in the early nineteenth century coincided with an increasing desire for education among the populace. Increasingly unable to afford even the traditional hedge-schools, poorer Catholics (and Protestants) were being attracted to the free schools offered by the proselytising organisations. By 1818 the London Hibernian Society alone was operating 194 schools in rural Ulster (almost as many as for the rest of the country put together) and the Irish Society – with its emphasis on Bible study in the Irish language – was targeting predominantly Catholic areas.

The Ulster hierarchy – more accustomed to mixed denominational teaching – did not respond to the perceived threat as early as those elsewhere in the country. In Belfast Catholics still attended mixed Sunday schools until the early 1820s. But as signs of proselytism grew, even Crolly became worried, opening a Catholic Sunday school in 1822 and the first Catholic day school in Belfast in 1830. But his problems in financing even such small beginnings were symptomatic of Catholic education generally, and this venture only got off the ground through generous Protestant subscriptions. The establishment in 1831 of state-funded National schools was a godsend, and they were very generally welcomed by the Ulster clergy. Crolly's Belfast school was among the first in the country to join the national system. Protestants continued to attend National schools in the first years of their existence, and those in Antrim and Down were generally of mixed religion. In effect, however, the religious demography of Ulster meant that large numbers of such schools were one religion from the outset. At this stage the hierarchy was prepared to tolerate common religious teaching. But Presbyterians and especially Anglicans were not. Cooke conducted a heated campaign against the schools, claiming that they were channels of popery. The Anglicans founded the Church Education Society to rival the commissioners of national education. Groups of angry Protestants in Counties Antrim, Down and Tyrone forced the closure of a number of National schools after daubing them with anti-papist graffiti.[19]

Catholic opposition came not from within Ulster, but from the anglophobe archbishop of Tuam in Connacht, John MacHale. Having effectively split the hierarchy on the issue, banned the schools from his own archdiocese (much to the mental impoverishment of his own people, as was later admitted), and all but destroyed the scheme entirely in the eyes of the papacy, it was the reasoned arguments of Crolly and his like which won the day. The Catholic people simply could not afford the education for which they clamoured. Without such state support, they would take it where they could and many would fall victim to proselytisers. The papacy accepted such arguments, and by 1840 was prepared to delegate judgement to the local bishops. Control of education was one of the earliest campaign issues in the Catholic Church's revival and its resistance to interdenominational education would be long-lasting.[20] However, in the first half of the nineteenth century it was the withdrawal of Presbyterians and Anglicans, and their refusal to permit priests in their schools, which brought about the development of exclusively Catholic schools. The religious teaching orders, like the Christian Brothers, were to play a vital role. But until the 1860s, the vast majority of Catholic children, who were receiving education in Ulster, did so in the National school system.

However, the move towards separate denominational education was proceeding apace in all the religious groupings and archbishop Crolly's final years were darkened by the row over the Queen's Colleges. After his elevation to Armagh in 1835, he and his successor at Down and Connor, Cornelius Denvir (bishop, 1835–65), and the equally accommodating archbishop of Dublin, Daniel Murray (bishop 1809–52), were already being bypassed within the hierarchy because of their support for the Charitable Bequests Act of 1844. Although genuinely intended by government as a conciliatory measure (opening up to Catholics public offices hitherto monopolised by Protestants), the act contained some anti-Catholic restrictions and in a heated attack the three bishops were accused of gullibility in their relations with government.[21] The dispute over the same government's establishment of non-denominational colleges in 1845 caused Crolly and Murray to become even more isolated. It was perhaps not unreasonable for the government to think that the colleges would mirror the success of the National schools. But opinion had hardened since the 1830s.

O'Connell's repeal campaign had failed, leaving nationalists embittered. His denunciation of the colleges was an important factor in the mustering of Catholic opinion against them. Pointing also to the increase of religious indifferentism produced by such 'secular' higher education in Prussia and elsewhere in Germany, the *zelanti* among the Irish bishops, following MacHale's lead, and now including Cullen, persuaded the Pope to issue condemnations in 1847–8. Their case was that without a Catholic professor of theology and Catholic appointments in sensitive subjects like history, logic, metaphysics, moral philosophy and geology, the religion and morals of Catholic students would be undermined. Many Anglicans and Presbyterians had made the same point for their students. Given the influence of Cooke's brand of Presbyterianism in Belfast, Crolly always knew that the establishment of the College there would draw episcopal opposition, and he had campaigned for its establishment at Armagh. Unlike the Colleges at Cork and Galway, that in Ulster would always have been predominantly Presbyterian in any event, since these were colleges designed to educate the middle classes, and Ulster's Catholic middle class was still insignificant. Crolly had had no problem with Catholic students attending what passed for a university till then – the Royal Belfast Academical Institution, a Presbyterian foundation. But his was a minority voice among the Irish bishops, and after his sudden death from cholera in 1849, the Synod of Thurles in 1850 formally condemned the colleges as dangerous to faith and morals. It was the first national synod to have been held since 1642, and it marked the arrival of Paul Cullen as Crolly's successor at Armagh, and with him an entirely new era in Catholic church development.[22]

Cullen had spent most of his life, since the age of seventeen, in Rome. These were the years of a resurgent papacy and Cullen was to stamp the Irish Catholic church with its ultramontanism. For nearly a century the Ulster bishops were generally known for their political quietism. Cullen claimed that this had made Crolly and his like too uncritical of government, and during his long reign as effective head of the Catholic Church in Ireland (1849–78), he appointed bishops in his own image. By the 1860s Cullen's own anti-Englishness and anti-Protestantism had made such quietism a thing of the past. His arrival had coincided with an unseemly and unnecessary furore –

sparked off by the British Prime Minister's anti-papist scare-mongering – over the restoration of a Catholic hierarchy in England. But the fall-out was largely felt in Ireland, where it brought nationalist feeling in behind the church and undermined the spirit of accommodation which had marked its relationship with the state for over a century. Shortly after Cullen's arrival at Armagh, an incident occurred which symbolised the changing climate. The Protestant archbishop called to pay his respects. He was told that Cullen was not at home and such niceties were never repeated.[23] It is, however, important to put this in the context of the heightened religious suspicion of the day, and even Cullen could distinguish a liberal or apathetic Protestant from a bigot. He was also quite prepared to work with reforming English politicians in pursuit of Catholic policies and did so very effectively with the emerging Liberals.[24]

Cullen was very critical of the state of religious practice in Ulster. His own appointment was a token of things to come. The Ulster clergy were just as resistant to the appointment of outsiders to the see of Armagh as they had been in Oliver Plunkett's time. But Cullen was appointed over the heads of the local candidates, and in his drive to impose internal church discipline, he would steadily erode Ulster's long-standing claim to lay control of clerical appointments. Like those continental clerics who visited Ulster at the time, Cullen remarked on the extreme neglect of the externals of religious devotion. 'The exterior ceremonies of religion', he reported in 1851, 'are very neglected, and matters proceed as in the time of persecutions.' By the following year he had already introduced some of the Italianate devotions which would become such a feature of the Irish church generally, adding further credence to the attack by Ulster's newly evangelised Protestantism on popish idolatry. 'The people are beside themselves with joy at seeing processions, functions etc. [during Holy Week]', wrote Cullen, 'which formerly were not to be seen.'[25] Over the next few decades 'missions', where thousands would come for spiritual renewal, benediction, new devotions to the Sacred Heart, exposition of the Blessed Sacrament, novenas, and other services little known to the easy-going ways of the past, became permanent features of Ulster Catholicism. Superstitious practices, rowdy festivals, patterns and wakes, were already under attack at the time of the ordinance survey of 1834.[26] By the close of Cullen's life, most were a thing of the past as the Catholic Church was transformed by the new puritanism of Victorian middle-class morality. New religious orders were introduced to Ulster: the Redemptorists, the Passionists (opening in 1877 the first monastery in Belfast since the Reformation), the Sisters of Mercy (establishing convents in Belfast 1854, Downpatrick 1855, and six more the following decade), and the Christian Brothers (1856). By 1920 some sixty convents had been established in Ulster, all but two or three of them since 1840.[27] Progressively education and a number of other social and medical facilities were transferred from lay to clerical hands, as the church came to dominate Catholic community life. By the turn of the century Catholics and Protestants were operating in separate social spheres.

The new bishop of Down and Connor, Patrick Dorrian (bishop, 1865–85), though critical of the quietism of his predecessors, admitted that had he been bishop in the 1830s he too would have welcomed the National schools. Indeed he continued to support them for the benefits they brought to Catholics. But as the communities became increasingly polarised, the concern of the Catholic clergy at covert proselytism and inbred hostility to Catholic practices grew apace. There were too many signs of Catholic pupils still attending scriptural education in school hours, their parents too illiterate, too poor or too intimidated to exercise their right to withdraw them, as permitted under the National school system. Even the books in use for general education had a Protestant ethos. By the 1860s a more confident episcopate was more prepared to challenge the government's claims of fair play. A special commission established in 1868 investigated their complaints and many reforms followed. The introduction of fully denominational education in Ulster did not occur until 1923, but even before then the trend was unstoppable. By the time of the Powis Commission of 1868–70 the bishops had already formulated a philosophy of Catholic education which went far beyond protection against proselytism, a philosophy which is still in place today. Dorrian explained this to the Commission in 1868. He did not think that secular and religious education could be separated and since information was received as much through the senses as the intellect, the surroundings, religious symbols and general tone of the place were as important as its teaching.[28]

Above all Trent had finally arrived in Ireland. The 1834 data collected by the parliamentary commissioners into public instruction in Ireland revealed very low levels of formal religious practice in Ulster (alike with parts of Munster and Connacht). Churches were still in short supply, the ratio of priests to population was unfavourable, and poverty, particularly in the western counties, all played their part. The church was not yet at the centre of religious life. Cullen made this one of his central missions: the transfer of religious practice from the home to the church, by increasing the number of church-based devotions and masses on offer. From mid-century new churches were to have baptismal fonts and confessionals with grilles. Administration of the sacraments in private houses, particularly in the form of the so-called 'stations' – so open to abuse by the clergy, and the topic of one of Carleton's most revealing satires on the avaricious priest[29] – were progressively discontinued. Priests themselves were better educated and set apart from their parishioners as holy men (black clerical dress being widely adopted for the first time after the 1850 Synod of Thurles). There would be far less criticism of the negligent or scandalous priest in the nineteenth than in any previous century. Regular religious education of the laity also appears to have been achieved. Admittedly it was the regular religious education through the National and new religious schools which brought this about.

But even Carleton's peasants had the basics of modern Catholicism. Gallagher and his like had already secured this. The 'Second Reformation' also spurred the Catholic clergy into a frenzy of print. Alarmed at the dissemination of Protestant bibles, the Antrim and Down bishops alone had 308,600 Douay Bibles printed between 1817 and 1852 and the Catholic Book Society produced five million books in its first ten years of existence (1827–37).[30] Certainly commentators noted a new sobriety and sharp upturn in religious practice among Catholics at the end of the century. The new public rituals, the display, the new array of religious aids and decoration of churches, picked up the emotionalism of nineteenth-century romanticism and seemed to supply the need previously met by folk ritual. Moreover, under Pius IX (pope, 1846–78) indulgences came back into vogue, proving as popular as they had done in the Middle Ages. There is an Ulster folk tradition that the 'Big Wind' of 1839 banished the fairies. Another version has the angelus bell doing away with them at the time of the Boer War (1899–1902). Thus did memorable events come to be associated with the changes wrought on Catholic society by the 'devotional revolution'.[31]

An associated factor was a wave of Catholic triumphalism – for which Cullen has been much criticised. Its main physical legacy was the great nineteenth-century Gothic churches, with their towering spires and heavy ornamentation. There was already more than a hint of sectional rivalry in the surge of new church-building in the first half of the century.[32] But they were often great empty structures, unadorned through either lack of money or lack of will. In many cases, however, they were knocked down and replaced with far more elaborate buildings, costing six or seven times as much as the original.[33]

Developments in Belfast (even though its Catholic population was far less wealthy than urban Catholics elsewhere) were typical. Bishop Dorrian was a Cullenite expansionist. His predecessor, Denvir, had been a bishop in the old mould, keeping a low profile and pursuing a policy of quietism. Dorrian, in contrast, oversaw a massive expansion of Catholic church organisation in Belfast. As co-adjutor in Down and Connor since 1861, Dorrian's frustration at the lack of amenities for Catholics had been sharpened by his knowledge that some 1,000 Catholics a year were converting to other religions. During his term as bishop the ratio of priest to people jumped from 1:5,000 to 1:1,600. He invited the Christian Brothers and a number of other teaching and charitable orders to Belfast, their schools, orphanages and convents springing up in all the Catholic districts. He purchased land for a new Catholic cemetery at Milltown in west Belfast (after a row with the corporation over separate provision), he orchestrated the building of a host of new churches (including the replacement of the old St Mary's and St Patrick's along the Gothic lines outlined above), and in 1883 a hospital, the Mater Infirmorum. Almost the entire physical structure of modern Catholicism in Belfast was in place by the time of his death. By then Belfast's 70,000 Catholics were served by twenty-eight priests, twelve Christian Brothers, seventy nuns and seven churches.[34] The Catholic Church had become the main provider of needs for the Catholic populace and with that Catholicism had become a community, not just a church.

Although it is traditional to trace the authoritarianism of twentieth-century Catholicism to this period, the Catholic Church could never force a reluctant Catholic people in a direction of which they did not approve. The new devotions were popular. It was the first injection of confidence for several centuries, and by all accounts ordinary Catholics were thrilled at the new profile and public display of their Church. The magnificent pomp attending the opening of St Peter's pro-cathedral on the Falls Road in Belfast in 1866, just after Dorrian took over, had Cullen and twelve other bishops celebrating high mass, to the music of a full orchestra. Dorrian had none of his predecessor's inhibitions about offending Protestants with such displays.[35] Such developments already had a basis in widespread respect for the priest as the learned man of the community. The absence of visible church structure before this period by no means should be assimilated to irreligion. Quite the contrary; although Carleton was to become a Protestant in his adulthood and worked for the proselytising societies, this is not apparent in his fiction, because, as he states himself, respect for the priest and the rudiments of Catholicism were part and parcel of the simple people's lives which he was celebrating. There is not even a hint of a lapsed Catholic in his stories.[36] A particular feature of peasant devotion in his fiction is the saying of the rosary, and he remembered his father constantly with his beads in his hands.[37] Significantly this was one of the items in established popular devotion which the church did not jettison.

Nor should one carry too far the image of the newly authoritarian church at war with the more superstitious beliefs of its people. Rather it was part of the process of civilising and taming which was such a part of middle-class culture everywhere in Europe. Although the Ordnance Survey Memoirs of the 1830s reveal considerable progress by the Ulster priests in curbing popular excesses, the main success came later in the century and owed as much to changing social conditions and outlook as to priestly intervention. Most important were the decimation of the cottier class in the Famine, growing urbanisation, changing work-patterns and modes of behaviour, and the prevalence of Maynooth-trained priests among the clergy, thereby providing a lower middle-class leadership to nineteenth-century Catholicism. The pursuit of respectability which was implicit in the 'devotional revolution' also involved priestly damnation of the rowdier and irreverent side of Catholic culture. The novels of the Donegal writer Patrick MacGill expose the snobbery of the Father Devany character, the scourge of country dances and popular pastimes, whilst admiring the 'polite' gatherings of the 'quality'. It was a trend which was not confined to Catholic society, for the removal of country dances from the cross-roads was also a product of the new fashion for ballroom dancing.[38] The seriousness and prudishness which infused extreme nationalism and which saw the sentimental songs of Thomas Moore replace traditional singing and storytelling, owed not a little to this triumph of lower middle-class morality within the Catholic Church.[39]

The new puritanism of the Catholic Church was also a response to developments within Protestantism. In many ways the 'devotional revolution' was Catholicism's equivalent of the Second Reformation. It was partly initiated by fears of proselytising and tended to focus on those aspects of Catholicism most criticised by the Protestant reformers. The churching of folk religious practices was the main response to attacks on superstition, rowdiness and excessive drinking. But the Church went even further: it founded the Pioneer Total Abstinence Association in 1898 and effectively destroyed the illicit distillation of poteen – something of an industry in Donegal in particular – by declaring it a reserved sin which only the bishop could absolve.[40] Predictably it would be a sanitised version of the Irish Catholic peasant which became the ideal of the Gaelic revival. Don't by your drunkenness give Ireland's 'enemies' the excuse to sneer, Matthew Russell, a Jesuit priest from County Down and editor of the popular Catholic periodical, the *Irish Monthly*, appealed to the Irish peasant in June 1894:

> Dear Irish peasant, brave and pure and true,
> Ah! let this scandal rest no more on you
> Honest, contented with your scanty score,
> And Catholic, aye to the very core;
> Yet why let Pharisees their eyebrows lift
> At your intemperance and lack of thrift?
> If by no nation are ye left behind
> In generous qualities and gifts of mind,
> Why not do justice to your creed and race
> By stamping out this vulgar, vile disgrace?[41]

The 'devotional revolution' was, moreover, a continuation of the clergy's long-standing campaign against practices which might reinforce hostile Protestant stereotypes of the Catholics.

The wakes and even some patterns at holy wells remained, but shorn of their former excesses. The priest himself became the master of ceremonies, leading the faithful in prayer. In the early decades of the twentieth century Ó Muirgheasa plotted the location and history of holy wells in Donegal. He found over a hundred, many having gone out of usage or declined in importance – notably at the end of the previous century – but others having been adopted officially by the church. St Patrick's well, at Inishowen, was actually re-opened and re-dedicated by clergy from Derry City, while the 'most frequented' well in Donegal – Doon Well, near Kilmacrenan – was relatively modern, having been founded by one priest and blessed by another. Although some older inhabitants remembered patterns on St John's eve and May eve, and many of the older wells listed by Ó Muirgheasa celebrated aspects of the Colum Cille legend, by the early twentieth century most ceremonies had been transferred to 15 August (the Feast of the Assumption of the Blessed Virgin Mary).[42] The 'missions' – Catholic versions of the renewal and emotionalism of Protestant evangelical revival meetings – came to supply a demand once met by the patterns, but again now firmly under clerical control. Just as in the early centuries of Christianity, so in the nineteenth and twentieth centuries, localised saints' cults and relic veneration were replaced by cults formally approved by the Church itself. Cults to the Sacred Heart and Mary, and to the relics of the 'True Cross' would dominate Catholic popular devotionalism into modern times – as well as a small number of 'legitimised' cults (St Anne, St Jude, St Joseph and later the Little Flower and St Martin de Porres). Anthropologist Lawrence Taylor, whose *Occasions of faith* provides one of the best local studies of the changing nature of popular Catholic devotional practices, comments on this process in relation to holy places formerly associated with local saints. 'It is difficult to find poor Brigid among the Marian images and Sacred Hearts . . . Then again, that is probably no more than what Brigid herself did to whatever goddesses preceded her . . . one is tempted to conclude that the once wild pilgrimage so often condemned by the clergy is now but an extension of the church.'[43]

Religion is woven into the fabric of Michael MacGowan's Donegal childhood in the 1870s. En route to the hiring fair in Letterkenny, his mother insisted on doing the 'station' at Doon Well. Nearby they stayed with friends, for whom extensive prayers were part of the evening cycle. Fifteen decades of the rosary were succeeded by 'the little prayers'. 'The old woman prayed for seven generations that preceded her, for the neighbours and for those who were away in foreign parts, for protection against sickness, against devils of the earth and air, against any other harm that might be hanging over us.' Young Michael regarded this as excessive piety. But nightly rosary and Sunday mass were part of Donegal Catholic life in the 1870s and were carried to the Klondike by the Irish Catholic miners.[44]

Mrs MacGowan's list of 'intentions' is a reminder that the 'magical' – such a feature of poorer rural societies everywhere – was not eradicated in the 'devotional revolution'. Indeed, there appears to have been quite a mix of clerical attitudes towards such non-Christian customs. There are signs of adaptation by the clergy of those supernatural elements in popular belief which could be 'churched', and leaving well alone those which could not. The belief that Catholic priests possessed magical powers remained strong, even in the twentieth century. Although a survival from pagan times, it continues in the popular belief that priestly exorcism is the only effective remedy against satanic possession. The idea that the Catholic sacrament of extreme unction or 'last rites' held the passport to heaven not only made it the most important rite of the Church for Catholics, but has informed a rich folklore tradition of converts to Protestantism reconverting at the time of death. A visit to the priest for the 'cure' was commonplace – a special power more traditionally attributed to the unfrocked priest.[45]

But again, just as the holy wells had acquired rituals legitimised by the church, so the 'cures' now sought were often in the context of Catholic devotionalism. There is, writes the folklorist Linda May Ballard, a tendency for Ulster Protestants to think of folklore as something peculiarly Catholic, thereby leaving them a convenient excuse to reject aspects deemed undesirable.[46] The belief that Catholics may well have a better link to both folk customs and the supernatural has remained extraordinarily durable throughout Europe. Gamble comments on it in his travels in Ulster in 1812; whilst in 1992 Dr Bob

Curran recalled similar experiences from his childhood at the edge of the Mourne Mountains in County Down. His grandmother, 'a staunch Ballymena Presbyterian', losing faith in conventional medicine's remedies for her grandson's ringworm – which had all failed – took him (much against her will, he suspected) 'to an old Catholic woman who lived in the Dromara Foothills and who was supposed to have had "a cure" given to her by the fairies for sickness and irritations'. The old woman passed some 'sally-rods' over the skin, muttering something which his grandmother thought 'very Catholic' and Dr Curran remembered as the Apostles Creed. The 'cure' worked, but in the 1950s when his grandmother was reminded of the visit, she was clearly embarrassed, trying at first to accommodate it within the non-denominational concept of faith-healing. 'Catholics, on the other hand, believed that such things came from fairies. Their priests both encouraged and reinforced this view to keep them servile. As long as they believed in the supernatural – fairies, cures, visions and miracles – the priests had them in their grip.'[47]

Despite such disclaimers, all the evidence shows that Ulster Protestants were just as superstitious as Catholics. Indeed, some practices appear to have been entirely Presbyterian in origin. Father James O'Laverty was at pains to detail these Scottish-imported 'superstitions' in his 1884 *History of Down and Connor*, particularly when such 'charms' did not work or needed the addition of Catholic prayers to do so.[48] The difference was that Protestant culture located religion and the supernatural in different spheres, whereas Catholic culture intertwined them. And while some Protestants could be supercilious about yet another sign of Catholic inferiority and some Catholics could be overly defensive about it, it also informed Catholics' self-perception that theirs was an older, more organic culture. Protestants were uninterested in the souterrains, one north Antrim Catholic told Ballard in 1976, because they knew they were earlier than their time. Hence they had less respect for the fairies: 'A fairy thorn had no time in a Protestant field.'[49] This idea of sacred landscape and Catholicism as organically linked with it is commonplace, a tradition of sacred landscape at least traceable to the early Christian compilers of the heroic tales.[50] This was also the view promoted by the Gaelic revival, in which the priests played a major part.

However, the fairy-lore associated with specific features of the landscape and belief in the fairies as the sources of everyday misfortunes proved less adaptable to official Catholic devotionalism. Why Irish Catholic folk-beliefs do not subscribe to the witchcraft mania which affected Protestant and Catholic countries alike in the early modern period has never been adequately explained. Aside from a famous Kilkenny trial in the fourteenth century, accusations of witchcraft since the seventeenth century have been largely confined to the east Ulster Presbyterian community, suggesting some foundation for the apparently prejudiced Catholic view that it was brought from Scotland.[51] It may be that the fairies – believed to be the angels who had fallen with Lucifer – provided quite adequate explanation for evil. The most prevalent and long-lasting of such traditions were those of the fairy thorn and the changeling. Fairies could express their displeasure in all manner of ways and could even replace humans, particularly children and young women, with changelings. Unsurprisingly, less orthodox beliefs remained strong in rural Ulster, where the friars held sway for so long, where Irish speaking locked in tradition and where the Catholic populace remained largely peasant and rural. 'Official' Catholicism had always been more successful in richer areas and in the towns.

Certainly clerical denunciations of fairy beliefs did not deter a County Tyrone man in the twentieth century from having his wife's body exhumed because he believed her death in childbirth to be a case of fairy abduction.[52] 'My native place was a spot rife with old legends, tales, traditions, customs and superstitions', recalled Carleton of his early youth in south Tyrone; 'even beyond the walls of my own humble roof, they met me in every direction.' His father's 'unrivalled' stock of tales and legends consisted of 'all kinds of charms, old ranns, or poems, old prophecies, religious superstitions, tales of pilgrims, miracles and pilgrimages, anecdotes of blessed priests and friars, revelations from ghosts and fairies'.[53] And lest we think the 'devotional revolution' made any significant dent in this aspect of rural belief, listen to Seamas MacManus's account of the 'fairy faith' in his late nineteenth-century upbringing in Donegal:

My Mother's faith in the Good People wasn't just static but missionary. She brought up her children to reverence all fairy haunts, the Mount, the raths, their playgrounds on many a Glen Ainey hilltop, their *sciog* [from *sceach* – whitethorn or hawthorn] bushes from which one mustn't break a twig, any more than they'd break a Commandment. She taught the youngsters always to pray, 'God bless you!' when anyone sneezed – the fairies having, for that instant, power over the victim. Her children from her learned, no matter how hungry they'd be at quitting the table, never to finish their portions – to leave . . . the fairy bit – a modest offering which reassured the watching Good People that they were not forgotten by anyone in *her* house.

She had twice heard the banshee cry and claimed to have seen the white-clad figure 'raising her blood-curdling lament for one of the family about to leave the world'. She told salutary tales of the fate of those who had doubted the fairies' power. The half-Scottish Bab McClay, 'scorning "fairy superstitions", built his house on a fairy rath which everyone else respected, and suffered the consequences in the deaths of his livestock and failure of his crops.[54]

The prevalence of lone thorn trees and undisturbed mounds in the middle of so many Irish fields indicates that Mrs MacManus's belief in the power of the fairies was widely shared. Thus were ancient raths preserved from plough or spade, as Gamble noted early in the century, because people thought them fairy forts.[55] Although most people will claim not to believe such old superstitions, yet there are still those who will not pick the whitethorn, just in case. The tradition of the sacred or magical tree goes back to pre-Christian times, their association with royal sites a feature of the *Ulster Cycle* and other ancient legends. They were particularly associated with inauguration sites, leaving their traces in placenames like Lisnaskea (or 'whitethorn fort', the Maguire place of inauguration in Fermanagh). Like much else, the tradition was christianised in early medieval times, when they also became associated with local saints and ecclesiastical sites. It was, however, the association with the supernatural which was to be most enduring, and tales of misfortune befalling those who interfered with the thorn-trees were still told in the twentieth century.[56]

2. The Catholic Church and the development of nationalist politics

Did the Cullenite 'revolution' amount to the political Catholicism which Protestants so feared? Certainly until the 1890s there seemed little leadership of the Catholic community in Ulster other than clerical. But this is not the same as clerics promoting nationalist politics – which the fear presupposes – and the relationships between rising nationalism and even the newly aggressive Cullenite Catholicism is by no means clear cut. Crolly's nervousness about political campaigns was generally true of the Ulster hierarchy throughout the nineteenth century, and militant nationalism in particular continued to be denounced from the altar.

The religious polarisation of the late nineteenth century occurred also in politics. Catholics and Presbyterians traditionally voted Liberal before the rise of Parnell in the 1880s. But whereas Catholics regularly voted for Protestant Liberal candidates, Protestants did not reciprocate if the candidate was Catholic, a trait which the clerical-backed *Ulster Examiner* noted with some resentment.[57] Protestant politicians making interdenominational gestures were given a rough ride by their constituents. The basis was already there for Ulster politics to divide into separate religious blocs, but there was no specifically Catholic political leadership until the end of the century and when it first arrived it was largely imported from the south. The development of Ulster Catholic political consciousness in the nineteenth century is still one of curious apartness from the rest of the island. Few had the vote until the major electoral changes of the 1880s. Although the stereotype of the Ulster Catholic as a natural rebel continued unabated into the modern era, the Catholic population was not highly politicised. The frequent use of the terms 'invade', 'invasion' of Ulster by successive nationalist movements is telling. Organised nationalism took a very long time to gain a foothold in Ulster, and when it did it was solidly constitutional. Militant republicanism held little attraction. The amnesty campaign for Fenian prisoners secured emotional support throughout Ireland, some 30,000–40,000 turning out in Belfast in September 1867 for the funeral of a Fenian who had died in jail there. While in the summer of

1872, a mass demonstration for the release of prisoners gathered some 30,000 at Hannahstown on the western edge of Belfast, and set off another round of sectarian riots.[58] Even so, Fenianism itself was weaker in Ulster than in any other province. As Parnell's movement was beginning to make an impact on Ulster in the 1880s, Catholics remained more concerned about local Orange parades than about national politics.

The key to all this, ironically, was the Catholic clergy. Protestant perceptions of the sinister role of the priests, brainwashing their people and bent on a popish political tyranny, have never entirely disappeared. But the true picture of clerical involvement in nationalist politics is very far from the stereotype. Throughout the century the Catholic Church performed a delicate balancing act of damning violence, without losing the support of the mass of the Catholic people. By the second half of the century its politics were decidedly nationalist, but above all it sought to protect Catholic church interests. The pursuit of non-denominationalism in any body affecting those interests was frowned upon and increasingly crushed. In this the Church undoubtedly played a major role in squeezing out the Protestant voice in Irish nationalism. Such was the identification of Catholicism and nationalism by the end of the century, that both the state and successive national movements had to recognise the Church's special position and to consult it. No nationalist movement could hope to survive without clerical support. Acceptance of this spelt the end to the concept of an Irish nationalism which espoused all creeds, 'except for rhetorical purposes'.[59] However, the clergy were rarely initiators or leaders of political movements.

O'Connell's campaign for Catholic emancipation – involving as it did the mobilisation of the Catholic clergy as agents and collectors of the Catholic rent – created the illusion of the political priest. O'Connell became a particularly heinous figure for Protestants, to the extent that the sectarian riots of 1864 in Belfast were sparked off by the unveiling in Dublin of a statue to his memory. And yet O'Connell was entirely constitutional in his politics, a Whig for most of his political life, utterly loyal in terms of seeking justice for Catholics within the British connection. In as much as the Catholic clergy had a consistent political approach in the nineteenth century, it was O'Connellite. Even the highly politicised and nationalist Dorrian was loyal to the British crown and utterly opposed to republicanism – which returned the compliment by retaining the anti-clericalism of its founders (a trait largely absent from constitutional nationalism). Indeed, the papacy was against *any* political activities by clergy and issued frequent declarations to that effect throughout the century. Nevertheless the Ulster clergy did eventually become heavily involved in nationalist politics (more so than those in the rest of Ireland, largely because of the absence of any significant lay leadership in Ulster) and their involvement both alienated the handful of Protestant nationalists and established the dominant Catholic ethos of modern Irish nationalism. But they were also a moderating force, and they ensured that on the eve of the 1916 rising Ulster nationalism remained overwhelmingly constitutional.

Despite their inherent distrust of secular politics, the Catholic clergy had no problem involving themselves in campaigns seeking justice for Catholics. In this they usually followed rather than led and Dorrian responded to the Pope's attacks on the Land League by warning that priests would lose all influence with their people if they did not stand by them in their sufferings:

The exasperation of our people at the neglect of the government and want of sympathy of those who ought to be their friends, alienates many and drives our people to Fenianism . . . priests and people must keep united and I hope nothing shall induce the Holy Father to interfere against the friends of the distressed and famishing poor.[60]

Between the death of O'Connell and the rise of Parnell, although the clergy still intervened to defend Catholic interests (on poor law boards, for example), there was no strong national lead and clerical politics too became 'fragmented'.[61] In 1864 the establishment of the National Association of Ireland to press various Catholic demands, drew a very mixed response from the hierarchy. Five Ulster bishops refused to endorse it. Even Archbishop Cullen hung back. But Dorrian believed that if nothing was done for the Catholic people by constitutional means they would turn to Fenianism, and he persuaded Cullen to sign up. Dorrian was also among the earliest supporters of Parnell. But the Home Rule campaign initially caused great confusion among the Ulster clergy. In its early stages suspicion of initial Orange support and the predominance of Protestants among electoral candidates caused the Ulster bishops to trust more in Gladstonian reforms. The Home Rule movement's first foray into Ulster politics at the 1874 general election was a failure – returning only two of the twenty-nine Ulster seats, though holding most of the seats outside Ulster.[62] It was perhaps inevitable, therefore, that it had to become more 'Catholic' to succeed, for, given the growing strength of conservatism among the Protestant populace, only the Catholic Church had the organisational structure to increase the nationalist vote on the ground. By 1885 Parnell's parliamentary party had won the full support of the Catholic hierarchy in its promotion of specifically Catholic aims (notably denominational education). That year it nominated candidates only in constituencies with Catholic majorities, held its meetings in Catholic church halls and schools, and publicly involved the clergy on its political platforms. Predictably early Protestant support faded and the Liberal party (which for decades had secured Catholic and Presbyterian backing) was eliminated.

After 1885 Ulster electoral politics were almost entirely denominational, Catholics voting Nationalist, Protestants voting Conservative or Liberal Unionist. Till then Catholics had little political clout. But the 1884 Franchise Act (establishing household suffrage) brought many thousands of lower-class Catholics and Protestants into politics for the first time. This – combined with clerical mobilisation and effective Nationalist central organisation from Dublin – transformed the political map. Nationalists won over half the Ulster seats (17) on a massive turn-out of 93 per cent. There had been no Catholic MPs in Ulster in 1868. In 1885 there were sixteen. In the rest of the island Nationalists swept the board, taking 68 seats against only two conservatives. With the bulk of non-nationalists representing Ulster constituencies, the differences between the province and the rest of the island had never seemed greater, even if the Ulster Catholics were now visibly part of an island majority.[63] But Ulster Catholicism was anti-Protestant before it was anti-English. Such leanings would have to be reversed before Ulster Catholicism's traditional apartness could be overcome and there was little evidence of the newly powerful clerical lead doing so. Rather they were much less worried about Protestant sensitivities than they were at the beginning of the century.

It seemed as if clerical domination of Ulster Catholic politics was complete. Even then, however, the clergy did not set the pace, and it was not until the Nationalist Party itself had decisively rejected Parnell after the O'Shea divorce that they too became anti-Parnellite. The weakness of an alternative Catholic leadership and that tendency to close ranks against possible Protestant criticism, caused the bulk of the Catholic vote to swing in behind them. In the 1892 elections Ulster was much more anti-Parnellite than any other province. In the four constituencies contested by both factions of the Irish Nationalist Party, the anti-Parnellites obtained 97.8 per cent of the combined vote, and in thirteen other constituencies anti-Parnellites stood without opposition. The Catholic clergy played a highly visible role against the Parnellites, even to the extent of swallowing up the Parnellite Catholic newspaper, the *Belfast Morning News*, into the new anti-Parnellite *Irish News*.[64] However, Ulster clerical support for the Irish Parliamentary Party returned after 1900, when it was reunited under John Redmond. Militant republicanism continued to find few supporters among the Ulster clergy and they were unprepared both for the 1916 rising and for partition.

Protestants, however, might be forgiven for not seeing in the prospect of Home Rule or independence anything other than submergence in Catholic culture – given the espousal by Irish-Irelanders of everything in Irish culture which they had traditionally considered popish and backward-looking – though Catholics too could be forgiven for now seeking to enhance everything in their own culture which had been so maligned for the past three centuries. And yet, however 'popish' the undoubted authoritarianism of the Ulster hierarchy in these years, theirs was actually a much more 'Ulsterish' approach than their critics recognised. Their chief concern remained – even in the dramatic climate of 1916 and afterwards – the defence of Catholic interests in the predominantly Protestant society of Ulster.

But there emerged at the turn of the century a new kind of Catholic, whose political base was the Catholic ghetto and who was less welcoming of clerical politicking than the old elites. In the 1860s an attempt to establish a Catholic Institute outside clerical control had been effectively crushed by Dorrian. 'Some of our Catholics in the North have been imbued with too much Presbyterianism', he claimed in this failed effort at what he considered 'lay dictation'.[65] However, in 1899 to 1905 when a similar contest occurred under another bishop of Down and Connor, Henry Henry, this time the leader of lay Belfast nationalism was the legendary Joe Devlin. In a foretaste of those tensions between a predominantly middle-class constitutional nationalism and a working-class republicanism – still apparent in Ulster nationalism in the late twentieth century – Devlin challenged Henry's efforts to control nationalist politics. Henry had set up a local political association in Belfast in opposition to the Parliamentary Party and totally devoted to local Catholic interests. Although an exaggerated version of the Ulster hierarchy's tendency still to view national trends through their localised view of the Protestant peril, such overt and aggressive political involvement was not the norm and disquiet at Henry's political activities within the Church itself helped in Devlin's successful challenge. Yet even Devlin's brand of Ulster nationalism – shorn of clerical domination – could not divorce itself from Catholicism.[66] Secular nationalism in Ulster still had to be seen to defend Catholic interests, for by now there was no other constituency to court and although Ulster nationalism did identify with that in the rest of the island, it retained distinctive features. The old Irish Nationalist Party remained the main political voice of Catholics in Ulster, even as Sinn Féin was sweeping nationalist support elsewhere, and most notably it expressed itself in the Ancient Order of Hibernians, whose core strength, under its president, Joe Devlin, was in Ulster.

The AOH was a mirror image (if never as strong) of the Orange Order in its sectarian identity and its mesmerisation with parades. Also, like the Orange Order, it was largely working class. Even though it functioned as a friendly society throughout Ireland, it was considered too sectarian and it never quite gained the hold which it did in Ulster – where, by 1909, it was the main nationalist organisation. Although it traced its lineage back to the Defenders and Ribbonmen, it was firmly constitutionalist in its activities.[67] The AOH looked after its own kind within existing sectarian politics and the headlong rush of Catholics and Protestants in apparently opposite directions in these years disguises one very important fact: it brought about a measure of stability. With their separate social, educational, religious and political institutions, both communities could feel a certain kind of security.

Until the outbreak of the First World War the Irish Parliamentary Party under Redmond seemed to be regaining some of its former strength. The next decade, however, witnessed a crisis in Ireland which ended in partition, and the form it took was about the worst of all options for Ulster Catholics. It was the Catholic bishops, fearing for the future of Catholic education in a Unionist state, who foresaw this far more clearly than the politicians and desperately tried to urge unity on them. The Third Home Rule Bill, giving limited autonomy to Ireland, was passed shortly after the outbreak of the First World War, and was due to be put into effect when the war ended. But the Ulster Protestants were already preparing to resist, some 471,414 having signed up to the principles of the Solemn League and Covenant, and 90,000 having joined the paramilitary Ulster Volunteer Force. Partition had already been discussed before the war, the Ulster Unionists demanding that the nine counties of Ulster be excluded from the scope of the bill. Eventually it was accepted that Cavan, Monaghan and Donegal, with their overwhelming Catholic majorities, must be included. The fate of Tyrone, Fermanagh and Derry City, with small Catholic majorities, was less easily resolved. By 1916, however, the six-county option – Antrim, Down, Armagh, Tyrone, Fermanagh and Derry (both city and county) to be excluded from any home-rule scheme – had emerged as the Unionists' minimum demand.

Redmond and Devlin believed such exclusion would be temporary and tried to recommend the scheme to their followers on that basis. They also believed that the excluded counties would continue to be governed from London and rejected as 'absurd' claims that the excluded area would have its own government. In June 1916 they addressed a stormy meeting of Nationalists in Belfast, when 776 delegates from all over Ulster packed into St Mary's Hall. Although a majority of 475 to 265 voted in favour of the scheme, the result was reached only through Devlin's deft management and Redmond's threat to resign. Only Belfast, Antrim and Down – reflecting Devlin's standing in the north-east – fell in behind them. Nationalists west of the Bann remained anti-partitionist and this east–west split in Ulster nationalism was to endure after partition. Delegates included a priest from every parish in Ulster. Significantly most of the clergy supported the anti-partitionists. Foremost among them were the bishops. Both the bishops and the constitutional nationalists were far more worried about the treatment Catholics would receive in such a state than about partition itself. All the Derry clerics had voted against the resolution and the city's bishop, Charles McHugh, had been a powerful spokesman for those fearful of the consequences of partition. Asked by Redmond two years previously to intervene against a march by the Irish Volunteers, which might have added fuel to Unionist criticism, the bishop – normally no friend to the militants – nevertheless made clear his mistrust of extreme Protestantism in power:

The Orange Order is never done crying out intolerance and publishing what they would suffer under home rule, but there is not a word about what the Catholics and nationalists would suffer if the Orangemen got control and what they have already suffered at their hands. The great object of the [Volunteers] meeting was to give the liberals to understand that the nationalists have their rights and that while agreeable to making concessions, they were not prepared to accept a state of things that would be worse than if they never stood up for home rule.[68]

The Irish Parliamentary Party had sent delegates to all the Ulster bishops to try to win them over, but found them totally opposed to any solution which would give extra administrative power to a devolved Belfast administration. 'What a prospect for Ulster Nationalists to be put under Belfast Orange Rule', McHugh wrote in a letter to the press. 'Unionist bigotry will then have full control over the lives and liberties of Catholics.'[69]

The Nationalist leader in County Tyrone, John McGlone, had warned the Belfast meeting: 'Catholics would again, after years of heroic struggle for equality of rights, be subjected to an odious oppression, and become the hewers of wood and drawers of water which the Unionists thought good enough for the papists.' Experience of sitting with Unionists on the new county councils for the past sixteen years, he continued, showed how intolerant they were and unwilling to co-operate when in a majority, and nationalists would be betraying their forefathers if they yielded to such an 'ascendancy' party.[70] After a century of reform, often extracted with difficulty, but of late accelerated to the point where a reversal of roles was a distinct possibility, here were Catholics like McGlone faced with the possibility of a return to the bad times of the past. Historic resentment prevented them from recognising their own double standards, for they were unwilling to concede the kind of separate identity to Protestants which they were claiming for themselves.

A bewildering array of political bodies claimed to represent nationalists by now, and militant nationalism was on the upturn. The 1916 rising received as little support in Ulster as it did elsewhere in the country and the Catholic hierarchy was caught off-guard. But the ensuing arrests and executions – as Pearse had foreseen – popularised militant republicanism and in the elections of 1918 Sinn Féin swept the board. Only six members of the old Parliamentary Party were returned – four of them from Ulster. But although Sinn Féin had begun to make headway in Ulster, particularly among the young, its success should not be taken as proof that the Ulster Catholics had abandoned their long tradition of constitutional nationalism. For the Ulster bishops – in time-honoured tradition of avoiding division in the face of Protestantism – had stepped in to force some pragmatism on the warring nationalist factions, who were in danger of splitting the Catholic vote and ensuring an Ulster Unionist landslide. The outcome was a shareout of winnable seats. A remarkable personal victory for Devlin in Belfast Falls – where he defeated the Sinn Féin leader Eamon de Valera by 8,488 to 3,245 votes – prefigured the future split in nationalist politics between east and west Ulster, and there were significant tensions too in south Down and south Armagh.[71]

But Sinn Féin's abstention from Westminster all but handed the Unionists a victory in any event. As the fine details of partition were being debated, the once-filled benches of the Irish Nationalists were empty, apart from the dispirited rump of Parnell's party, six in all, including the four Ulstermen – Devlin, Patrick Donnelly (south Armagh), Jeremiah MacVeagh (south Down) and Thomas Harbison (north-east Tyrone). And yet they still represented the bulk of Catholic opinion in Ulster – both lay and clerical – and with much justification they chided Sinn Féin for allowing partition through by their abstention. Sinn Féin used its landslide victory in the 1918 election to set up their own parliament in Dublin the following year, the first Dáil. Thereafter the party's attention was fully absorbed in its pursuit of an independent republic.[72] For the moment – the critical moment – it had little time for the partition issue, and northern nationalists felt increasingly abandoned.

The preferred option of the constitutionalists, including the archbishop of Armagh, Cardinal Logue, was that of dominion status for the whole of Ireland within the British empire. If the outcome was permanent partition, under a home government in Ulster, they would prefer to return to the *status quo ante* of rule from London. But with a weakened Nationalist presence at Westminster and an increased Ulster Unionist one in Lloyd George's Conservative government, and against a backdrop of the worst sectarian troubles for over a century, partition and home rule for Ulster became a reality in December 1920. The Boundary Commission – thought by Ulster nationalists to hold out some prospect of renegotiation – came to nothing. Ironically, despite Catholic bitterness, the 1918 election result had turned out to be a false dawn for Sinn Féin. The bulk of the hierarchy had been wary of republicanism, and, as on previous occasions when republicanism revived, clerical influence waned. Militant republicanism continued to be weaker in Ulster than elsewhere in Ireland and after 1922 nationalist politics settled back into its stable constitutional nationalist mould, in alliance with the Catholic clergy.

The partition of Ireland and the emergence of a Northern Ireland state with a sizeable Catholic minority had come about almost accidentally, and owed as much to the southern politicians' disinterest as to Unionist intransigence. At crucial moments southern nationalists were too preoccupied with attaining 'independence' for their part of Ireland to resist partition, and the balance of power at Westminster slipped from the pro-nationalist Liberals in 1914 to a pro-Unionist Conservative government which decided the details of the fourth Home Rule Bill in 1919–20. The resulting Government of Ireland Act (December 1920) provided for two Irish parliaments and administrations for the north and south, and a Council of Ireland to consult on common interests. As the rest of Ireland then became embroiled in civil war over the form of government to be established there, the northern state was able to settle into early permanency. By the time the civil war ended and the Boundary Commission finally came into existence (November 1924) most Irish people – even in the south – had become accustomed to the border. The final report involved tinkering rather than major changes – and most of the Catholic areas of Tyrone, Fermanagh, Derry City and south Down would have remained within Northern Ireland. Even so, 31,000 people would have been shifted into the Irish Free State and 7,500 in the other direction. By now even the Dublin government thought it better to concentrate on consolidating what they already had and to leave the border unchanged. The Boundary Commission report was shelved, much to the distress of its chairman, and one Irish cabinet member felt that the Ulster Catholics might with some justification think that they had been sold down the river.[73] However, such were the levels of mistrust on both sides by the time of partition that neither Nationalists nor Unionists showed any understanding that their fears of being ruled by parliaments dominated by the other religion (whether in Dublin or Belfast) were mirror images of each other.

9

THE FAMINE AND AFTER: CATHOLIC SOCIAL CLASSES IN NINETEENTH-CENTURY ULSTER

But if there survived in high station in this place champions of old,
    Mac Cumhaill and the son of Dáire not to mention King Conchobhar,
Cú Chulainn, Conall Cearnach and all who were vanquished in battle,
    it wouldn't be long before Wully [Protestants] were dumped in the
    slime.

But since they've gone without trace, the bands who trained in our country,
    and we have nothing in their place but want, hunger and thirst,
    warbling and singing on the branches isn't heard in the valleys,
and there are no trout in the stream as is normal in the Island of Saints.

There's no man in the land of Fál, or woman and suckling baby,
    there's no strapping youth or elegant stately woman,
there's no beggar in the street whose lament isn't tortured and deep
    since the plague came upon the potatoes . . .

> Hugh McDonnell, *Milleadh na bPrátaí*
> (The destruction of the Potatoes), 1846
> (Beckett, *Aodh Mac Domhnaill: Dánta*, 46)

In time the growth of Catholic organisations outlined in the preceding chapter opened up new career opportunities for a small Catholic middle class. But the trend for Catholics to be disproportionately represented in the lower social levels reinforced the kind of stereotype which became the standard fare of the evangelical preachers. The Ulster Catholics, the Revd Henry Cooke claimed in 1825, 'are generally inferior in point of education; they are greatly inferior, generally, in point of farming . . . they are not generally so industrious as the Protestants; they put up with far less comfort'.[1] Even as late as 1861, Catholics, though 51 per cent of the Ulster population, supplied only 15 per cent of the professions and 22 per cent of the merchant class. Catholics had no monopoly on suffering and disadvantage.[2] Even so, the rural crisis which hit Ulster in the nineteenth century disproportionately affected Catholics, who predominated in the areas worst affected – south and west Ulster, with Cavan and Monaghan suffering most, followed by Tyrone and Armagh.

1. The Famine

As early as 1776, Arthur Young had foreseen the rural crisis which hit Ulster in the early nineteenth century.[3] The expansion of domestic linen had produced excessive sub-division, exhaustion of tiny plots of land and a dangerous reliance on the potato. Archaeological excavations in the Sperrins on the Tyrone/Derry border have shown potato cultivation spreading far into hitherto uncultivated, mountainous land during the eighteenth and early nineteenth centuries.[4] In predominantly Catholic areas social observers noted a particular tendency to sub-divide among children – a side-effect of that reluctance to leave the land noted earlier. Successive slumps, partial harvest failures and most of all the collapse of the domestic linen industry after 1815 had already weakened the once flourishing Ulster rural economy when natural disaster struck with the Great Famine (1845–9).[5] Much has been made of British government laissez-faire economic policy which allowed grain ships to sail from Ireland at the height of the Famine. But increasingly it is recognised that the underemployment of the huge agricultural labourer and cottier class when the Famine struck meant that few had the resources to buy other foodstuffs when the potato failed.[6]

Henry Glassie in his study of Ballymenone in Fermanagh discovered that the two issues which recurred most often in folk memory were the Famine and 'the days of the landlords'. Although cases can always be found to match the stereotype, the image of the tyrannical Irish landlord has been largely discredited along with that of the feckless absentee. Indeed nationalist literature often ignored the petty tyranny of the large Catholic tenant farmer or shopkeeper, because it was largely written by them or their offspring.[7] But it is notable that stories of bad landlords and evictions in the folklore records come mainly from south Ulster, where the disappearance of rural weaving was almost complete by 1841. Social commentators noted a listlessness and sense of hopelessness among the rural poor.[8] The terrible suffering of Ireland's Great Famine would become the centrepiece of Catholic nationalist tradition, driving a further wedge between the rest of Ireland and Ulster (for not suffering enough), and permitting extreme Protestants to claim the heavy losses in the south as yet another token of Catholic fecklessness. Beneath all the propaganda, it was easy to forget that Protestants also died in the Famine.[9]

The Great Famine, which started with the first potato blight of 1845, was drawn out over a number of years, successive potato blights, bad weather and the failure of other crops leaving the most vulnerable sectors without seed and without the income to purchase other food-stuffs at soaring prices. Fever and disease followed. Emigration soared. Ireland lost an estimated 1 million people through starvation or disease, another 1.2 million through emigration, and the trend of demographic decline continued until the end of the century. Ulster's population declined less than that of the rest of Ireland in the Famine decade of 1841–51 – 16 per cent against 20 per cent for Ireland as a whole. Even so, that 16 per cent accounted for 374,000 people and it disguises considerable regional variation. Thus while Antrim lost 10 per cent of its population, Cavan and Monaghan lost 30 per cent, with Tyrone and Armagh falling into the next worst-affected areas.[10] The Famine, in other words, had hit most in those areas least able to cope. On the very eve of the first potato blight, the Devon Commission reported the cottiers in Monaghan as largely unemployed. And yet no Ulster county escaped, even in prosperous Newtownards the soup kitchen was distributing 100 gallons of soup per day by 1847.[11]

Although the misery of the Famine was very widely shared in Ulster, and there are many oral traditions of decent Protestant landlords and clergy, there can be no doubt that in the long term the experience further soured communal relations. Prominent in these oral traditions of the Famine was that of the heartless landlord, the image of Prot-estants doling out soup to Catholics, proselytism, people dying in the open and the demeaning experiences associated with relief. Unsurpris-ingly the bulk of such stories come from areas where communal relations were already poor and overcrowding and poverty already extreme.

In general, Ulster landlords appear to have been rather better than their southern counterparts at remitting rates and rents for distressed tenants, though each county threw up examples of the best and the worst.[12] Both Derry and Donegal benefited from improving landlords such as Sir George Hill in Dunfanaghy – who actively flouted stringent government guidelines, by selling Indian meal early and cheaply. Indeed, the hate figures in Ulster folklore were not the grandees, but the middling farmers.[13] There were also counties in which criticism of the absentees like Lords Londonderry and Waterford were most heated. In fact the likes of Londonderry – who had estates in Antrim, Down and Derry – were more guilty of insensitivity than tyranny, and other landlords dreaded his tendency to air his 'mischievous' private opinions publicly.[14] His agent on the County Down estates, John Andrews, was representative of a particularly narrow-minded approach, which although untypical, came to be associated with Tory Ulster's reponse to the national disaster. As the crisis deepened, successive relief schemes – imports of Indian meal, public works, inside relief in the workhouses – all proved insufficient to cope, and by 1847 the government belatedly instructed the Poor Law Guardians to offer outdoor relief. Antrim, Belfast and Down were the only Poor Law unions in the country to refuse it. Andrews had viewed the Famine as a way of 'civilising' the country, of weaning the people of the south and west in particular from that lethargy and indolence which he thought resulted from the culture of the potato. It was the 'discipline' and the 'cleanliness' of the workhouses which they disliked, he claimed, and outdoor relief would simply give them 'the means of enjoying petty luxuries in their own filthy cabins'.

Andrews and his like were lambasted even by the Protestant press.[15] However, the outcry with which the so-called rate-in-aid scheme was met in Ulster was a token of things to come. In 1849 London decided to levy a rate on the more prosperous poor law unions to subsidise the impoverished ones in other parts of Ireland. The outcry from the north was not specifically anti-Catholic. Indeed, most protests were based on the belief that the rest of the British Empire should be sharing the cost of Famine relief, not foisting it all on Irish property. But many complaints were tinged with the kind of stereotyping of Irish poverty which often served as shorthand for Catholicism. Thus the Lisnaskea board of guardians in County Fermanagh told the Poor Law Commissioners:

it is with indignation we learn it is recommended . . . to impose a rate-in-aid on the peaceable and industrious inhabitants of the North of Ireland for the support of the lazy, vicious and indolent population of the south and west of the kingdom who neither fear God, honour the queen nor respect the laws of the land.[16]

It was this kind of mentality which eventually produced what Frank Wright called Ulster's collective amnesia of the Famine, denying memory even to the many Protestants who died or emigrated in it (a third of the population of Lisnaskea workhouse itself throughout the Famine being Protestant).[17] Many landowners were ruined by the Famine, as tenants could not pay rents and some 50 per cent of the total costs for relief was levied on Irish property. Catholics too protested at escalating rates. In truth everyone could have done better during the Famine; and if Lord Londonderry attracted criticism for lavish expenditure on Mount Stewart at the height of the Famine, the Catholic Church too was still trying to raise money for its ambitious building programme during it – one priest was even accused of levying contributions on the meagre earnings of his parishioners from public works.[18] However, the Famine would have been a good deal worse without the clergy's efforts, and many died in the process.

Given the heightened religious tensions of the previous decade, it is the co-operation of all the churches in relief schemes which is most impressive. When the workhouses were collapsing under the strain, increasing numbers being evicted for non-payment of rent and destitute people having to walk miles for any kind of relief, clergy of all denominations, like those in Cavan, joined to appeal to the poor law commissioners.[19] In Antrim, particularly in the Glenarm area, the churches had been co-operating on relief since the shortages of 1817 – and were early in establishing soup kitchens – the most effective of all the relief measures adopted during the Famine.[20] Before the end of 1846, soup kitchens were already in operation in Belfast – and clergy of all denominations were involved in the Belfast Relief Fund (which raised money not only for Ulster, but for Cork and Mayo). The rate-in-aid controversy should not be overplayed.

With such widespread co-operation by the clergy, why is 'souperism' – proselytising activities attending food relief – such a vibrant memory? Oral traditions throw up a number of memories of Protestant evangelicals using the weakened state of Catholics to trade food for conversion. But, in contrast to the south and west of the country – which saw a concentration of such missionary efforts – the few modern histories which pay any attention to Ulster do not give much prominence to this during the Famine period. What seems to be happening – as so often in folk memory – is a compression of stories over a longer period of time. These then become associated with the Famine period because of sensitivities about the general image that Catholics more often than not were those coming to the soup kitchens and Protestants more often than not were those administering them. Traditions of such occurring are very strong in north Antrim, where earlier proselytising activities had already aroused such hostility. 'Taking the soup' meant turning, taking soup for proselytism, and the families who did so were still remembered when folklorist Michael J. Murphy visited in the 1950s.[21] The Donegan family of Ballintoy spoke in 1956 of traditions of 'a soup kitchen run by people named McKinnan in the townland of Cloughcur. They called them the "Brockan-men" [from *brachán*, porridge or stirabout, associated with the Indian meal used during the Famine]. It was porridge they would give if you would change your religion . . . The children would bless themselves before they would ate; and these ones would have their hands tied behind their backs so's they couldn't bless themselves. . . . And another thing I hear them tell, they would offer to give you brogues and a top coat if you would ate bacon on a Friday.'[22]

Other stories of intentional usage of meat in the soup kitchens on Friday come from Cavan, and were particularly associated with Lord Farnham's continuing activities. It was said that a number of Catholics 'turned' for the food, only to return to Catholicism when the Famine was over. But they were not allowed to forget that 'they ate Lord Farnham's bacon', and there is a tradition that Catholics so enticed through sheer necessity were denounced by their priests.[23] Certainly a series of embittered letters from both Farnham and local priests to the *Freeman's Journal* in 1848–9 suggests very bad relations and a perception of religious discrimination operating in the evictions which followed the Irish Poor Law of 1847. 'There never was perhaps a more terrible persecution carried on against the poor than at the present moment', wrote Matt McQuaid, parish priest of Killsherdany, County Cavan.

There seems to be a hellish rivalry among some agents as to who will banish the most. . . . It is not enough to drive out the mother and flock to tumble their cabin, wound their feelings and see their tears, but it is said some of these monsters grinned at their victims' devotions and mocked them . . . Everyone knows that the mere Irish are being banished from some estates and Protestants substituted for them on long leases.[24]

Similar traditions survive from the Armagh–Monaghan borders. 'Of course it was all Planter Protestants about,' Robert McAlester of Crossmaglen, speaking in 1945, recalled of his grandfather's stories of the Famine, 'an' they had the soup kitchens of course, trying to convert ... the Catholics.' They had to go to Castleblayney, where 'big Hamilton, a Protestant of course ... could afford to boil a big pot'. People were dismissive about the ingredients and composed a rhyme about it.

> Oh, Mister Hamilton, you're big an' your [sic] fat;
> With plenty of grease on top of your pot.[25]

Such traditions were particularly associated with bad landlords – the soup being stigmatised with black humorous names such as 'Benson's gravy' or 'Downshire's porridge', and those who took it chided as 'turncoats' long afterwards. Several of these landlords and their agents, including the Catholic O'Callaghans of Armagh, Monaghan and Louth, who had evicted tenants during the Famine, became objects of retaliatory attack by Ribbonmen.[26] Although there is considerable folklore material on the good Protestant landlord, I have found no recognition of the genuine philanthropy which often co-existed with such missionising, particularly in the women's branches of the evangelical movement. Indeed, the dropping of tracts by these women on routes to the soup kitchens are a feature of the bitter memories.[27] There is not much criticism of government in these accounts. Again the cause of the suffering is much closer to home and invariably the shame of it all involves resentment of the Protestants who (as the more prosperous) figured prominently in the relief schemes.[28]

Most of the workhouses in Ulster had only recently been built when the Famine struck. Given that the Irish Poor Law of 1838 forbade public-financed relief outside the workhouse, many thought the new buildings ill-attuned to Irish needs. The Ulster-born Young Irelander John Mitchel – despite his typically melodramatic language – captured some of this in his dismissal of the Glenties (County Donegal) workhouse as 'rearing its accursed gables and pinnacles of Tudor barbarism, and staring boldly with its detestable mullioned windows as if to mock those wretches who still cling to liberty and mud cabins ... like the fortress of Giant Despair, whereinto he draws them one by one, and devours them there.'[29]

There was certainly a great reluctance among the Ulster poor to enter the workhouse and the preponderance of females and children amongst the inmates undoubtedly reflected male emigration or migration for work, but may also reflect the shame attached to males (of all religions) entering. Likewise with the soup kitchens. The *Newtownards Independent* recalled:

Oh to see those emaciated and half-famished souls surround the dog kennel where the soups was distributed. How to get a shawl, or cape or an old petticoat to envelop the head and fit to be seen, even at a dog kennel, was a question difficult to answer. And for the men to go with a can or jug was out of the question.[30]

The 'wee tin cans' carried along the roads for the daily ration while the soup kitchens operated made it hard to disguise one's plight.[31] 'If the parliament has gone without returning to this nation', the proselytising Irish Society's teacher Patrick Brady taunts the poet in Hugh McDonnell's *Agallamh idir Brádaigh an spiadhóir agus Bard Gaeilge* (A conversation between Brady the spy and an Irish poet):

> don't you have there in its place English schools
> and a prison building [the workhouse],
> where your women will receive more than a quart
> of mutton broth,
> drugget and an apron to cover their shame . . .[32]

Many soup kitchens and other direct relief schemes were financed directly by private charity, landed families like the Leslies of Monaghan, the Adairs of County Antrim, the Gwynns of south Down, along with the Quakers and innumerable clergy, emerging as heroes of the hour.[33] Even so, it was generally in the houses of Protestant landlords or in Protestant churches that the soup kitchens were set up.

It would be some time, however, before the sufferings of the Famine era came to reinforce pre-existing grievances and resentments. There is little evidence of attachment of blame at the time. Mitchel's attack on England for having 'slain' the Irish in the Famine finds little echo in oral memory, and where it does it is directly attributable to later printed sources – notably the immensely popular A. M. Sullivan's *The Story of Ireland* (1867).[34] In Monaghan – by far the worst-hit county of Ulster – its most recent historian, Patrick Duffy, has found that it 'left no trace in the collective memory'.[35] Something similar to the suppression of memories too awful after 1798 may be happening in the case of the Famine and there was a very general shame at death from starvation.[36] South Armagh and north Antrim (neither so badly hit) and south Down (which, like south Ulster generally, suffered most) may well be throwing up such bitter memories because a tradition of such was already well established before the Famine. South Down too became the area where many evicted from neighbouring counties settled. There is, however, some evidence in McDonnell's poetry of talk about the Famine being part of England's plot against the Gael – a precursor of a trend in later nationalism. But this is rare and may reflect the concentrated bitterness of the many migrants to Belfast, where McDonnell was living at the time of the Famine.[37]

2. *Seasonal Migration*

Predominantly Catholic counties continued to register the greatest decline in population in the latter half of the century, Ulster's Catholic population declining from 50.5 per cent in 1861 to 43.7 per cent in 1911, while all other denominations increased.[38] The rural decline meant that the hiring fair and seasonal migration, often to Scotland and England, became increasingly important to poor rural communities. By all accounts those experiences were often demeaning, and hiring fairs continued in Ulster into the twentieth century – long after they had disappeared elsewhere in Ireland.[39] Michael MacGowan's autobiography vividly recalls the typical experience of the rural poor in the nineteenth century. One of twelve children brought up in County Donegal, he was first taken by his mother to the hiring fair at Letterkenny at the age of nine. He was hired as a herd for six months to a kindly Catholic family at Glenveagh. By the time he was fifteen he had gone through five or six seasons of the hiring fair, having good and bad experiences. At ten he was taken on by a Presbyterian brother and sister at Drumoghill, five miles from Letterkenny. 'In my day, it was all "Scotsmen" who were there, but I heard that it is much changed and that some of our own people were now [1941, when his story was written down] getting the places that their forefathers had been driven from.'

MacGowan's account of his stay with the Presbyterians tells us more of inter-communal relations than any statistics. It should also raise a question mark over many of the stereotypes about the manner in which the different communities lived, for Michael, though coming from an overcrowded three-roomed cottage, was shocked by the personal and domestic slatternliness of the couple. The floor of the house was thick with dirt, food for the pigs and human food cooked side-by-side, and chickens scratching about on the floor. Their stinginess about food and money he saw as a characteristic of their people. But despite the acute awareness of difference, there is absolutely no prejudice on either side. Young Michael came to respect and like them, and although he clearly expected ill will towards Catholics – and there is a suggestion that there was enough of it around – he found none in Sam and Jane. On Sunday they made sure he went to mass and when their own minister came around for a 'lesson' he was never compelled to stay. He also found them just as superstitious and fond of storytelling about the fairies as 'our own people'. Michael was an Irish speaker, with just a smattering of English picked up the previous season. At first there were communication difficulties as he could scarcely understand their Ulster-Scots dialect. Another Irish-speaking Donegal migrant – Aodh Ó Domhnaill – had similar difficulties after he was hired at the Letterkenny fair in 1867. But he too experienced kindness, when the farmer and his wife brought in another Irish speaker to help him communicate.[40] However the initial difficulty in communication would have underscored the gulf between the Protestant and English-speaking culture of the richer areas, and the Catholic Irish-speaking one of those supplying the labour. Early last century Ó Muirgheasa collected in Donegal a poem still recited and thought to have been written a century earlier. 'The Gael amongst the Gaill' tells of the loneliness of the young Irish-speaking worker going to the English-speaking Protestant district (almost certainly the Laggan district in east Donegal):

The day that I went north through Barnesmore Gap
there was a coldness and a great tiredness on my shoulders,
my cheeks were wet with loneliness and I was crying,
such a pitiable man I've not yet met with in the province of Ulster.

When I was at home with my father and mother,
I did nothing for them, and they were no better off for my work;
but now I'm overcome and I'd prefer to be with them,
and if the day was a month long I'd be glad to be working.

It's I who am tormented and I'm not ashamed to recount it,
for since I left home many is the day that I spent,
listening to voices, Oh! such as I was not used to,
bleating on Sundays like a cow to its calf.[41]

The hiring fairs remained the fate of many rural poor in west Ulster until the Second World War – by which time they were confined to Omagh and Strabane in Tyrone. This was 'the slave market' in Patrick MacGill's *Children of the Dead End*, where boys and girls 'stood huddled together like sheep for sale in the market-place'.[42] In Tyrone Colm Tóibín was shocked to discover how powerful were the memories and resentments about the fairs as late as 1986. Few wanted to talk of their experiences because of the stigma attached, and Irish speakers from Donegal felt conscious that their very language singled them out in Tyrone as having come in to be hired. Rose McCullough told of her experiences in the 1920s when she first went to the hiring fair at Strabane aged thirteen, and of how she and her sister cried with homesickness as they stood in the snow. She remembered harsh treatment and inadequate food for the six years that she was hired out. 'They were all Protestants, the farmers', but the hiring included permission to attend mass every fortnight.[43]

When at the age of fifteen MacGowan first joined the very large numbers of seasonal migrants from Donegal to Scotland, the communication problems were even greater. There was no difficulty getting work and he regularly encountered 'great hordes' of people from Donegal 'on the "tramp"' like himself. By all accounts it was not a pleasant experience. 'Nothing was thought of the Irish in Scotland

those days and as well as every other ill-usage they received, they
certainly weren't paid in any way commensurate with the work they
did.' He does not recount in detail any incident apart from general
hardship. But the old people spoke of a village on their route through
Scotland where they were regularly attacked. Carrying their own
sickles and wearing the distinctive Irish homespun greatcoat, they were
easily recognisable as Irish migrant workers.[44]

Migrant experiences differed greatly. In general conditions were
worse for those migrants travelling to other parts of Ireland, and better
in England than in Scotland, where resentments against the Irish were
greater than anywhere else – and where more Ulster migrants went than
from any other province. Within Ireland there was a keen awareness of
the religion of the employer. There is some folklore evidence of bad
employers creating difficulties about workers observing Sundays and
holy days, and serving up meat on Fridays. However, Protestants –
even in areas of traditional sectarian tensions – were generally considered better employers than Catholics and were more concerned
with 'fair play'. Indeed, workers from Dromintee in County Armagh
did not attend the hiring fair in Dundalk, County Louth, since the
southern Catholic farmers did not have so good a reputation for
attention to the comforts of their workers as the northerners.[45]

After some fifteen years in America, Michael MacGowan returned
to his Donegal home of Cloghaneely in 1901. On arrival at Derry he
was told of the great changes which had come over the area. In the
first place he would no longer have to walk to his home, for a railway
now ran from Letterkenny to Burtonport.

A Board was set up called the Congested Districts Board and some years ago
a man named Balfour visited your parts. He enquired about the condition of
the people and when he had done that, he conferred with people in authority
about schemes to help the poor districts that stretch from here westwards to
the sea. As a result of that, the railway . . . was started. . . . Changes there are
. . . and the people down by the sea where you live can be thankful to this new
Board for many of them. They've done well for the fishing all around the
coast; roads and bridges were built; grants were given to poor people to help
them to build new houses; they're helping home industries and the
weavers are very busy now making bawneen. There are twenty ways in which

THE FAMINE AND AFTER

they're trying to help the people, late and all as it is. But better late than never.[46]

MacGowan is the human face of economic and social trends in post-Famine rural Ulster. The continued decline in rural population after the Famine was largely due to increasing emigration, delayed marriage and urban expansion. The net outcome by the early twentieth century was the kind of improvement in rural conditions noted by MacGowan on his return home. By then peasant proprietorship was almost complete, the old rundale system had largely disappeared as farms were consolidated and 'the days of the landlords' were a thing of the past. Indeed, MacGowan himself became one of a growing class of strong Catholic farmers, having bought his house and 150 acres from the landlord who had been in financial difficulties for some time.

3. Tenant Right

Return emigration with 'Yankee' money, however, was unusual and, until the government-inspired improvements of the late nineteenth century, rural poverty remained a factor of life. The letters of small tenant farmers (Catholic and Protestant alike), written in the 1860s, 1870s and 1880s and analysed by David Fitzpatrick, show the same insecurities, the same long hours, the same meagre diet, the same watchful eye on the potato 'Since the year of the Failure', the same fear of expropriation in lean years, the same extended emigrant network.[47] These subsistence farmers could not have survived without the traditional help of neighbours often across the religious divide, however important the cultural and religious differences. Indeed, it would be difficult to explain the very high levels of religious co-operation in Ulster in the various land campaigns of the nineteenth century, and the lower levels of agrarian violence, except in the context of such shared grievances or perceived grievances.

By the early twentieth century the land acts of successive governments had created peasant proprietorship and effectively removed the land problem from Irish politics, except as an emotive memory. The passing of landlordism was not achieved in the rest of Ireland without considerable violence – notably during the Land War of 1879–82 – and in the more traditionally Catholic areas of south and west Ulster there were sufficient similarities in the campaign to create a community of interest. But in Ulster generally the land campaign was waged with remarkably little violence. This was partly the result of rather better landlord–tenant relations than elsewhere (with some glaring exceptions), but also of the interest of a powerful Presbyterian tenant interest, which politically the landlords could not ignore. The main social development in Ulster Catholicism in the second half of the nineteenth century was the massive influx into the towns. But the bulk of Catholics continued to live in the predominantly rural parts, and although they still tended to occupy smaller holdings than Protestants, there was enough antagonism between Presbyterian tenants and Anglican landlords to create a community of interest between Catholics and Presbyterians – even after the recognised Nationalist–Catholic/Unionist–Protestant polarisation that occurred after 1886. Brian Walker, in his study of the religious make-up of the different social groupings in Ulster between 1868 and 1886, highlights considerable diversity within the overall picture of Protestants at the top end of rural life (owning some 72.5 per cent of the land), Catholics at the bottom (some 57.3 per cent of agricultural labourers, 63.1 per cent farm servants). Protestants of all denominations also accounted for a considerable portion of the poorest. The landowner class was dominated by Anglicans, wealthier tenants by Presbyterians, with Catholics making up a significant portion of medium-sized farmers.[48]

The campaign for Tenant Right came to the fore in the 1850s. Essentially it sought to legalise the so-called Ulster Custom (which was just that, a 'custom', not always generally practised, even in Ulster where it was traditionally thought to be the reason for the rather better landlord–tenant relations than elsewhere in Ireland). Although there was considerable confusion over its interpretation, essentially it gave outgoing tenants the right to compensation for improvements or for the remaining 'interest' in their property, which they could sell to the incoming tenant. During the Famine, its operation was particularly important in helping to finance emigration. What it did not do was give any guarantee against eviction.[49]

The problem then and since was the belief that Catholics should have been the natural inheritors of the land which had once belonged to their ancestors. It had sufficient weight even among Protestant tenants for them to vote with the landlords.[50] The task of getting them to identify with the largely Catholic tenant-right campaign elsewhere in Ireland seemed an almost insurmountable challenge. The editor of the Presbyterian *Banner of Ulster*, Dr James McKnight, assumed the challenge and presented an intriguing interpretation of the Ulster Plantation. By this the original undertakers were simply trustees rather than outright owners. Their tenants had carved out their estates from uncultivated wastes. The landlords only had the right to the rent of the 'raw' earth and not the inflated rates of the land improved by the tenants themselves. The argument found a ready audience among Catholics. There are intriguing echoes of it in the Revd James O'Laverty's history of the *Diocese of Down and Connor* (1878–95), where the Gaelic chieftains are also included among those who had no right to the land separate from the people who farmed it.[51] The tenant-right campaign soon ran foul of the anti-popery generated by the restoration of the Catholic hierarchy to England and the ensuing Ecclesiastical Titles Act (1851), which prohibited Catholic bishops from including a British or Irish placename in their titles. The landlord interest fanned the flames of sectarianism to defeat the popular challenge. But for a short while the campaign had the backing of both Catholic and Presbyterian churches. Even in areas of acute religious tensions, like Ballybay in County Monaghan and the Downpatrick area in County Down, priests and ministers shared platforms. There were also some signs of Catholic–Orange co-operation on the ground, which became even more prominent at the time of the Land League.[52]

McKnight was also editor of the *Londonderry Standard*, and his stand was undoubtedly influenced by the Donegal experience – the one part of Ulster where the stereotype of the tyrannical landlord found supportive examples. When MacGowan went to herd cows for the old Presbyterian couple of the Laggan, he found a police barracks oddly situated in the middle of nowhere. It had been built in 1861 to protect the landlord John Adair at the time of the notorious Glenveagh evictions. After the murder of his agent and the loss of many of his sheep, he took revenge by evicting hundreds of his tenants and pulling down many of their houses. McKnight, through the *Standard*, made the harrowing scenes an international scandal.[53] Simultaneously McKnight was conducting a campaign against the landlord from hell: the Third Earl of Leitrim, whose activities on his large north Donegal estate, from the 1850s till his murder in 1878, would rival any fictional account of aristocratic antics in *ancien régime* France. No one mourned his demise, not even the authorities. 'He was what we call a bad land Lord', wrote the Fermanagh small farmer and Methodist William Fife, whose letters to his emigrant daughter in Australia reveal the continued community of interest on the land issue across the religious divide.[54]

The tenant-right issue went into abeyance during the post-1850 economic recovery. But it was fanned into renewed activity in the late 1860s by Gladstone's disappointing Land Act of 1870 and by the agricultural depression of the late 1870s, which spelt disaster for the poorer farmers, particularly in the hilly areas. Again it produced some highly unusual alliances: Catholics voting for Conservatives who promised land reform (Tyrone by-election, 1873), where traditionally they would have been Liberal,[55] and again Orange–Catholic co-operation, even as Fenianism was contributing to the tensions which would see political polarisation reach new dimensions in the following decade. In the 1880 election the Orange Order in County Armagh refused to endorse any candidate who did not support tenant right, but repudiated the ultra-nationalist Land League which made its first appearance in Armagh that same year.[56]

The most surprising and notable example of this was Catholic support for the ultra-Protestant William Johnston of Ballykilbeg near Downpatrick, most remembered for coining the phrase 'Home Rule is Rome Rule'. Johnston's writings and speeches bristle with all the traditional anti-papist stereotypes of the fundamentalist Protestant. But, whilst never abandoning his Orangeism, he seems to have been sufficiently affected by the sufferings of the Famine to have decided that he had a destiny to take on the landlords and the government, and he was returned as an independent Conservative MP for Belfast in 1868 with significant Catholic support. There were similar stories from County Antrim, where the strongly pro-tenant-right Ballymoney was the first of any Ulster town to elect a Catholic to the town commission. Ulster Liberalism was paying the price of complacency about the Catholic vote, just when more and more Catholics were becoming enfranchised and resentful of continuing Protestant dominance of the party. Over the next decade organised nationalism under Parnell was able to sweep their vote, sending even radical Protestants back to Conservatism. Although tenant right continued to occupy rural voters of all denominations in Ulster – and initially the Land League recruited considerable Protestant support there – by 1885 renewed sectarianism had confined the tenant-right campaign to mainly Catholic areas.[57] The passage of a number of other Land Acts in the 1880s (particularly beneficial to the hill farmers) followed by the Wyndham Act of 1903 effectively removed tenant right as a common grievance.

4. Belfast

Although Catholics still tended to live predominantly in rural areas – they were 53 per cent of the farming population in 1871, though only 48.9 per cent of the Ulster population as a whole[58] – the nineteenth century witnessed a dramatic increase of Catholics in the towns, notably from internal migration by rural Catholics. The experiences of Catholics in Victorian Belfast in particular played a major role in shaping Catholic identity on the eve of partition. By 1911 40 per cent of Ulster's population was town-based. Most dramatic of all was the growth of Belfast. By the end of the nineteenth century, Belfast, in its size, economic activities and social problems, had more in common with Glasgow and Liverpool than with any town elsewhere in Ireland, Dublin included. It had grown from 19,000 in 1801 to 349,180 by 1901. Increasingly Ulster people were urban-dwellers, while the population on the rest of the island remained largely rural. In the 1780s Catholics formed only 8 per cent of Belfast's population. By 1808 their numbers had jumped to 16 per cent, by 1834 to 34 per cent. This represented a five-fold increase over twenty-six years.[59] The arrival of increasing numbers from rural areas was already causing tensions in this predominantly Presbyterian town, and in 1813 it experienced its first sectarian rioting.

It was the mechanisation of the textile industry which both ruined the rural industry and attracted increasing numbers to the town.

Already by the 1840s, the huge mills – still a feature in the 1950s – were defining the skyline. Mr and Mrs S. C. Hall in 1842 commented approvingly of the sense of bustle and full employment which they gave to the city: 'Such an "aspect" of business; a total absence of all suspicion of idleness in contrast to the south, that we thought we were in clean Manchester.'[60] The numbers employed in the Irish linen mills and factories increased ten-fold between 1839 and 1917 and the industry was almost exclusive to Ulster. But within Ulster the regional focus shifted dramatically eastwards. As early as the 1830s Belfast had ten steam-powered spinning-mills, four of them in the already recognisably Catholic Falls Road. By 1861 there were thirty-two mills and the port had begun its legendary expansion to accommodate the textile trade.

Belfast's sectarian geography was already being defined by these mills. Rural Catholics, seeking employment, tended to move in family groups and settled near each other. Despite the upsurge in the number of Catholics, in 1861 they still only accounted for a third of Belfast's population and only a quarter by 1911. Belfast remained very much a Protestant town. Thackeray, visiting in 1842, found theatre-goers damned from the pulpits of meeting-houses and churches, and the bookshops stuffed with evangelical literature. 'I was not very sorry to leave the town behind me, and its mills and its meeting-houses, and its commerce, and its theologians, and its politicians.'[61] The tiny Catholic middle class felt uncomfortable with their social peers and increasingly channelled their activities into Catholic social organisations. The changing nature of organised Catholicism in Belfast in the second half of the nineteenth century was also a response to this upsurge in the Catholic population. The building of chapels, convents and other social institutions further defined the Catholic areas and increasingly provided a social outlet for the often dreary lives of the Victorian working class.[62]

Thackeray was as impressed as the Halls by the huge mills and bustle of Belfast. But his main observation concerned the large numbers of young females in the city. He noted 500 in Mulholland's mill alone working twelve hours a day 'in huge long chambers, lighted by numbers of windows, hot with steam, buzzing and humming with hundreds of thousands of whirling wheels'.[63] What Thackeray did not note was that 60 per cent of the employees in Mulholland's mill were children, many as young as eight; that the average age of death in Belfast was said to be nine; that the employers resisted many of the reforms of workers' conditions imposed from Westminster; that Belfast Town Council (on which only three Catholics had sat that century) was notoriously resistant to providing any social amenities for its working class, even to the point of rejecting a bequest to provide Sunday music for the workers in the parks.[64]

Ten years after Thackeray's visit the Revd W. O'Hanlon – a Congregationalist minister, originally from Lancashire – conducted his famous walks among the poor of Belfast. Among Catholic and Protestant working class – inhabiting the rookeries and airless 'courts' in its centre – he found wretched poverty, strangers sleeping seven to a room, few practising any religion (though they knew what religion they were born into, and occasionally priests were invited in for specific needs). Drunkenness was rife and public houses proliferated. It is a reminder that a Protestant underclass also existed – though heavily disguised by Protestant and Catholic myth-making deeming such a thing inconceivable.[65]

Even so, the structural disadvantage of Catholics – there since the seventeenth century – assumed new and more visible proportions in Belfast. In 1853 they constituted 48 per cent of workhouse inmates. Fifty years later they still accounted for 46 per cent, though only 24 per cent of the population. Moreover economic developments and discrimination ensured that they remained clustered in the lower levels of the labour market. There is a perception among Ulster Protestants that Catholics are culturally pre-conditioned towards arts-type disciplines and averse to the 'useful' sciences and technology. But this – if proven – may be because they had little choice. All the commissions and surveys of the nineteenth century show low percentages of Catholics in the skilled trades and among the middle classes. In the second half of the century, the activities of the Harland & Wolff shipyard began to define the employment profile of more and more male workers, just as the mills had done that of females. But few Catholic workers were employed (only 225 out of 3,000 in 1886), and when they were, they were unlikely to figure among the skilled workers. At the end of the century Catholics accounted for 41 per cent of the dockers but only 7 per cent of the shipwrights. Battles between the two groupings became a feature of Belfast's sectarian rioting, and intimidation seems to have played a part in the decline in the proportion of Catholic shipyard workers from perhaps as much as 20 per cent in 1861 to 7 per cent in 1901. In 1886 only one of the town's large employers, the Combe, Barbour and Combe foundry in North Howard Street (today's interface between the Falls and Shankill Roads) had a religious balance, with 40 per cent of the workforce Catholic. This may have been because of the mixed religious makeup of the area, and Catholic employers in Catholic areas seem to have been equally discriminatory in employment practices. Sectarian rioting (at its height in the period 1857–86) accelerated segregation in both the workplace and housing. And – just as in rural areas landlords preferred to let to co-religionists of an outgoing tenant – so managers and foremen were simply taking the 'line of least resistance' to maintain the peace: 'Where one community dominated a workplace, its position was allowed to drift towards exclusivity.'[66] Belfast's Catholic population did not occupy an inferior position in relation to the overall workforce in the United Kingdom. The key point is that the Protestant population had secured a particularly privileged position.

Worst of all in employment practices were the public bodies, particularly local government, where Orange political influence was in the ascendant. The Belfast Riots Inquiry of 1886 found that only five of the ninety-five officers of Belfast Corporation were Catholics, on a salary only half that of Presbyterian officers. By 1911 only 9 per cent of those employed in local government and poor law administration were Catholic. In municipal elections the £10 household franchise had discriminated against Catholics who tended to be amongst the poorest. But increasingly they had allies in Dublin Castle and at Westminster. Central government employment of Catholics in Belfast was nearly proportionate to their numbers. In 1887 a special extension of the British household franchise to Belfast, and in 1896 Westminster's creation of two new wards (Falls and Smithfield) for these predominantly Catholic areas, resulted in the automatic election of eight Catholic councillors.[67]

By the end of the nineteenth century some 91 per cent of west Belfast was Catholic, and the trend throughout the century was one of increased religious segregation. The Falls area of west Belfast had developed from the Catholic districts of Smithfield, Hercules Street (now Royal Avenue), Millfield, and the Pound. It was in west Belfast that competition for employment and territorial rivalry was most intense from early in the century. For the expanding Catholic population was pushing up against the Orange weaving districts of Brown Square and Sandy Row. Until the Famine, Protestant Orangemen and Catholic Ribbonmen or Repealers were equally aggressive. The upsurge in Catholic numbers, the ascendancy of O'Connell, the banning of party processions, 1832–45, the distancing of the gentry from the plebeian Orangemen – all seemed to give the Catholics the edge on triumphalism, and in the 12 July riots of 1843, thousands of Catholics marched along the edge of the Protestant enclaves, just as the Orangemen had always done to Catholic areas. After the Famine, however, the tide had turned decisively, with the decline of Catholic numbers from pre-Famine heights, the re-entry of the 'respectable' classes to Orangeism, the accession of Protestant working-class strength from the expansion of the shipyards and the addition of anti-popish street preaching and newspaper coverage to election campaigns.

The 1852 riots – sparked off by shots fired from the Sandy Row area into the neighbouring Catholic one – witnessed the first extensive use of firearms and the intimidation of families out of mixed areas. Thereafter, each successive riot marked an intensification of previous ones – 1857, 1864, 1872, 1880, 1884, 1886, 1898, 1901, 1907, 1909 – the four months of rioting on the defeat of the first Home Rule Bill (1886) resulting in 32 deaths and 371 injuries. Most of the riots were still confined to the Sandy Row/Pound, Falls/Shankill interface, with conflict between Protestant shipwrights and Catholic dockers becoming a regular feature. The Royal Commission investigating the 1857 riots could not understand why Orangemen felt such a need to incite Catholics in a town that was predominantly Protestant. But the rise of organised Catholicism and nationalism in the second half of the century, and Gladstone's Home Rule Bills fed traditional Protestant belief that political popery was in the ascendant. All the more so since Catholics were emulating them and insisting on their right to march. Sybil Baker describes the trend at the end of the century: 'Marches to

Hannahstown by the Ancient Order of the Hibernians; torchlight processions by the '98 Centenary Clubs; [fundamentalist Protestant preacher] Trew's anti-ritualist demonstrations; Twelfth parades; Lady Day [15 August] excursions ... bands with their followers playing nightly through the town – Belfast's mobs had never exerted with such tireless vigour their right to parade the streets.'[68]

The persistent riots and intimidation had made safety among one's own a priority for the working class of Belfast. By 1901 over two-thirds of Catholic householders lived in Catholic areas, the 'tribal map' of the late twentieth century already recognisable: the Falls Road/ Smithfield area, New Lodge Road, Markets, Ardoyne, with smaller groups in Dock and Greencastle. But the percentages of Catholics living in one-religion areas jumped to 75 per cent among manual workers and Belfast-born Catholics. The rural influx had stopped. A specifically Belfast working-class culture was developing and the trend towards separate cultures grew apace. By the beginning of the twentieth century most Catholics could attend exclusively Catholic educational establishments, exclusively Catholic public houses, shops and parks and often even exclusively Catholic workplaces. It suited most Protestants and Catholics alike and was an important factor in the increasing role of the Catholic Church in Catholic social life.[69]

Here was a world very different from the rural one of MacGowan, where the agricultural cycle and relative isolation did not permit the development of such antagonistic identities. However, Tony Hepburn has identified segregation also between towns, all the main industrial centres becoming more Protestant in the 1861–1911 period, establishing the enduring perception of towns and localities as predominantly of one ethos or the other. Thus in Portadown – though registering a percentage population increase as great as that of Belfast – the proportion of Catholics fell by 12 per cent and there were similar falls in Larne, Ballymena and Lisburn. Even in Derry City – whose Catholic population, drawn mainly from neighbouring Donegal, outnumbered Protestants by 1850 – there was a 2 per cent decrease during the period. Whilst net increases of 7–12 per cent occurred in perceptively Catholic towns like Downpatrick, Newry and Strabane, Lurgan experienced a 67 per cent Catholic increase, with a 149 per cent Protestant increase in neighbouring Portadown. Of course the religious segregation and polarisation were already intense in this historic flashpoint area, and there was a pre-existing Catholic linen-weaving population in Lurgan to act as a magnet.[70] But the development of different religious cultures in the neighbouring Armagh towns of Portadown and Lurgan was setting fast the area's historic divisions.

5. Catholic social classes

The structural disadvantage of Catholics in Ulster even impeded genuine attempts at reform. Protestant domination of the magistracy continued because traditionally its members were taken from among the major landowners.[71] Magistrates had to be of sufficiently independent means and standing so that influence could not be brought to bear on them. The problem was that, although there were many Catholics among medium-sized farmers by the late nineteenth century, the landowners were still largely Church of Ireland and the numbers of magistrates in 1884 – 72.6 per cent Church of Ireland, 14 per cent Presbyterian, 8.5 per cent Catholic – was a fair reflection of the social situation. Among the middle class, Catholics continued to make slow progress, though more among its lower than its upper levels. Thus, although their share of the legal profession increased from 14.1 per cent to 22.3 per cent between 1871 and 1891, it was in traditional areas of Catholic employment like the retail and drinks trades that they came to dominate – some 55.5 per cent of hoteliers or publicans being Catholic in 1871. Lest one think that this rising social class would emerge as lay champions of their fellow Catholics, however, it is important to remember that they were part of that reviled breed of gombeenmen, small retailers who sold on credit, then exacted a high price, often the forced sale of smallholdings, for unpaid bills.[72]

Significantly, other areas of employment in which Catholic numbers soared were closely connected with the expansion of Catholic social organisation. Thus the growth in Catholic schooling is reflected in a Catholic percentage of 39.5 per cent of teachers by 1871, while the number of Catholic clergy by 1891 accounted for 31.7 per cent of clergy in the province. Thereafter they continued to increase, reaching a ratio of 1:1,276 in Belfast by 1926, up from 1:4,601 forty years earlier.[73] This picture of social advancement within their own community marks an important change of outlook among Ulster Catholics. Even in O'Connell's time the ambition of those who prospered was to join the existing social and political system. And whereas the old, small elite tended to live outside the exclusively Catholic areas, this new middle class did not. These would become the leaders of nationalist politics in Ulster. They also produced the clergy, since they alone could afford the costs of clerical training. Given the greatly expanding power of the Catholic Church by the end of the nineteenth century, it was very much the values of this lower middle class which came to infuse the modern Church.[74]

This is not to say that religious identity had totally overtaken that of social class. Indeed, in Belfast the rivalries between the Christian Brothers (imported to cater for the education of the working class) and the more elitist St Malachy's College, run by the diocesan clergy, was a factor in organised Catholic life until the second half of the twentieth century. But inter-denominational class identity was severely impeded and indeed discouraged. The Catholic Church did not approve of socialism. Trade union organisation among teachers was specifically banned in the Armagh archdiocese. The activities of the Society of Saint Vincent de Paul, and the organisation of sodalities, evening classes and early morning religious services to accommodate the mill-workers were more typical of the kind of self-help culture fostered by the church.[75]

Such ghettoisation greatly assisted the expanding power of the Catholic Church. But Ulster Catholics showed little resistance. They had always been less anti-clerical than their co-religionists elsewhere and, by the end of the nineteenth century, there was none of the resistance to church payments, which had been such a feature of earlier times. There were some wealthy Catholics. Bishop Dorrian, assessing the prospects on the eve of the remarkable expansion of church building during his episcopate, thought there were between seventy and ninety in Belfast who could spare £100 each for church purposes. Prominent among these were John Hamill, the landowner, whose home (Trench House on the Falls Road), was later donated to become the Catholic teacher-training college; William Watson, the property developer in west Belfast; George Murney, the shopkeeper and tobacco importer; William Ross, owner of the Clonard flax mill; and the Armagh-born Bernard Hughes, who began his apprenticeship as a baker in 1827, later starting a bakery empire which was still a significant Catholic institution in the 1960s.[76]

Despite their generosity, however, it was the Catholic people as a whole who funded the second wave of major church building in Ulster (in the 1870s and 1880s) and the acquisition of buildings for Catholic social institutions. The door-to-door collections, the charity sermons, special appeals and bazaars became a significant feature of Catholic life. Accounts published by the parish priest of Ballymoney in 1881 show that the funds for a new church, reading room, schools, parochial house and offices had been raised very largely from parishioners' subscriptions, collections, charity sermons and a bazaar.[77] On the whole Catholics were proud of such external displays of new wealth and status by their church and were anxious to donate to it.[78]

But in predominantly Catholic areas – lacking the potential for priests to pull critics into a common Catholic line against local Protestants – there may well have been tensions. The most publicised case of such was that of Canon James MacFadden of Glenties, County Donegal, an arrogant and authoritarian figure, whose political militancy became an embarrassment to his superiors. His extensive building programme on behalf of the church in the 1890s was typical. But his lavish expenditure on his own parochial house, often extracted from the poorest of his parishioners, while he 'hobnobbed' with Catholic gombeenmen, earned for him the savage 'image' as Father Devany in the autobiographical novels of Patrick MacGill – for which the young author was denounced by MacFadden from the altar.[79] Seamas MacManus remembered a similar priest in Kinawley (County Fermanagh), though he lived at Swanlinbar, County Cavan. Father Tom O'Reilly chased drinkers from the public houses and loiterers from the street with his stick, and would publicly shame any parishioner who did not put the weekly halfpence into the Sunday collection box.[80]

However, wealthy Catholics seeking to run their own denominational bodies outside the control of this newly powerful church were quickly pulled into line. The most notable example of this was Dorrian's dispute with the businessmen founders of the Catholic Institute in Belfast. In 1859 they bought property on the edge of Hercules Lane to serve as a kind of residential club for the Catholic middle class. Dorrian distrusted such 'Catholic' institutions outside episcopal control – citing the 1864 *Syllabus of Errors* to underscore his claim that no one should be running Catholic societies whose religion and character did not have his approval – and feared its possible use for political purposes. It is a significant commentary on the changed times that such wealthy Catholics (Hughes among them) did not attempt to put him in his place as their social peers on the Catholic Committee would have done at the beginning of the century. The Protestant press, picking up on the dispute and portraying it as proof of Romish priestly tyranny, simply rallied Catholic opinion behind Dorrian – an early example of how Ulster Catholics would suppress internal differences in the face of hostile Protestant attention. Joe Devlin was later to win his contest against the autocratic Bishop Henry, in part because Henry had broken this widely accepted rule of Catholic politics.

This confessional basis of northern nationalist politics caused predictable problems to trade union and labour organisations. Although the leader of the 1907 Belfast dock strike, James Larkin, was a Catholic – a factor which the employers used to great effect to play on sectarian tensions among the strikers – he was a Liverpool Catholic. Joe Devlin, despite his impeccable working-class credentials, did not appear on strike platforms till very late in the day and then largely to take up traditional nationalist complaints about the activities of the police and the army. The difference was that Catholic workers were far less likely to turn on employers of their own denomination than Protestant workers. 'Catholic workers viewed the Protestant ruling elite as their chief agent of oppression', writes John Gray, historian of the 1907 strike, 'and were thus far less likely to develop specifically working-class opposition to their own middle class which, whatever its faults, was in no sense a ruling class in the north.'[81] Nor did the early stages of Labour politics in Belfast inspire confidence among Catholics. Working-class Protestants had invariably demanded traditional anti-popery from their candidates, and even William Walker, champion of the unskilled in the shipyard, and Labour candidate for North Belfast in the elections of 1905–7, seemed more than happy to defer to their expectations by agreeing to oppose any Catholic succeeding to the monarchy, resist Home Rule and always place the interests of Protestantism above those of party. Needless to say, the Catholic electorate deserted him and Ramsay MacDonald despaired at the failure of socialism to surmount Belfast's traditional sectarianism.[82]

10

ACROSS THE DIVIDE: COMMUNITY RELATIONS AND SECTARIAN CONFLICT BEFORE PARTITION

[The Catholics'] fires are kept up in a kind of party spirit, in contradistinction to the British and Caledonian settlers, who, principally on that account, annually commemorate by bonfires on the 1st and 12th of July their delivrance from Popish domination, by the victories gained by their ancestors at the battle of the Boyne and Aughrim in 1690 ... The descendants of these primitive [the old Irish] and more modern British and Caledonian settlers ... have not yet assimilated, so as to form one general character; this in a great measure may be attributed to the difference of their religious tenets ... [they] are extremely jealous with the British and Caledonian settlers, whom they are taught to believe are intruders and foreigners.

[John Donaldson, *Historical and Statistical Account of the Barony of the Upper Fews* (1838)]

By the time of partition Ulster Protestants and Catholics had acquired separate political identities. But they were simply superimposed on long-established communal and religious differences. They were identities which fed off one another. This is why sectarian and highly localised Ribbonism was never replaced in Ulster by the avowedly non-sectarian Fenianism, and why it ebbed and flowed in response to levels of Orange activity. Outsiders were (indeed, still are) surprised at how apart Protestants and Catholics were in Ulster, when racially, culturally and linguistically they seemed so similar. The resurgent Catholic Church and increased papal authoritarianism, the greater Catholic visibility as they poured into the towns, outnumbering Protestants in their original city (Derry) by the end of the century, the growing confidence and political assertiveness of Catholicism – all had the effect that every sign of Catholic assertiveness had in the past: Protestants of all denominations closed ranks and liberalism faded. Catholics saw this as conforming to type, Protestants thought them inferior and would always try to dominate, given the chance – and so the simplified stereotypes were reinforced.

1. Across the divide

What all this produced was a mutual wariness merging into hostility at the extreme, and always a sensitivity about name calling or mockery from the other side. But local situations ensured wide variations. In the second decade of the nineteenth century Dr John Gamble, a native of Strabane in County Tyrone, made a number of tours on foot through the north of Ireland. The impression is of roads full of human traffic, of walkers invariably seeking companionship, of hospitality to excess. He was particularly interested in how Catholics and Protestants viewed each other. He too commented on how alike they were. But Protestants were very anxious to assure him that they were not papist – particularly if they had Catholic-sounding names. Near Larne he spoke with an innkeeper named O'Sullivan: 'He was very anxious to assure me that he wasn't Catholic, despite the name, but descended from a Huguenot' – 'a zealous Protestant would as soon call his son Judas as Pat.'[1] The lesser gentry he found particularly anti-papist. His host in Omagh regaled him with a typically lurid commentary on the 'scarlet whore' of Rome because he thought Gamble had 'a good Protestant face'. 'You don't know *thim* as I do', he confided, having drawn his chair near; 'you *hivn't* lived amon them, and can't tell what sort of *varmin* they are: why, man, my own *sarvants* would murder me in my bed, if they durst.' Certainly a young male Catholic servant whom he met on the road a day or so later showed scant respect for the gentry and expressed a hope that the 'croppies' would have their day. 'Emancipate the Catholics to make friends of them', his host continued [for Gamble supported Catholic emancipation]; 'J–s, what fools our great people be! if they were to give them the crown of England today, they would be quarrelling for the diamond (that I'm *tould* once dropped out of it) to-morrow' – a traditional Protestant complaint still made today – that Catholics would never be satisfied.[2]

Further along the road to Omagh, Gamble found a parish priest lodging with a Presbyterian landlady. He thought it unusual enough to query. Catholics were good customers, she told him, and the priest in particular. Their pounds were the same as Protestant ones, and who's to know they might not be right in the end! Gamble thought such comments unrepresentative and he was right. Friendships between individuals there were – particularly in rural areas – but the idea of 'popery in the gross' was as strong as ever and one is struck by anti-papist perceptions unchanged since the Reformation, now riveted in popular Protestant consciousness. As in all societies, the school-children reduced such perceptions to their simplest expression. The future Young Irelander, Charles Gavan Duffy, attended a classical school in Monaghan in the late 1820s and early 1830s, where he was the only Catholic. At first the boys were resentful about a 'papist' joining them. The resentment did not last and Duffy made close friends. But he found books like Foxe's *Book of Martyrs* circulating among them. One lad was particularly steeped in the lore of popish atrocities, which he regaled to his school-mates during recreation, his favourites being the old tale of popish priests absolving murderers of Protestants.[3]

At the other end of the century nationalist playwright Seamas Mac-Manus told a similar tale of the largely Protestant model school in Fermanagh, where he went as a teenager. But the intermingling brought tolerance and he too built strong friendships, particularly with John Irvine. Though 'a loud Orangeman', and drummer in an Orange band, he was nevertheless warm-natured and developed such a liking for 'the Fenian' that he taught him Orange tunes which he drummed on the school's revolving globe, while MacManus tried to beat out the pink patches that marked the British empire.[4] A Protestant perspective from Downpatrick-born writer Lynn Doyle (1873–1961) shows that no side had a monopoly on sectarian awareness. At his overwhelmingly Catholic National school there were frequent after-school fights provoked by religious taunts and, even during class, protagonists would flash scrawled slogans on their slates: 'To H– with the Pope', 'To H– with King William'. One day the Catholic master caught the Catholic culprit and he was caned for his 'unchristian' action. The master was respected as a fair man, but even he could not help adding, besides, 'It's . . . *unnecessary.*' 'One dogma, maintained equally firmly by Catholic and Protestant when I was a boy [was] – the eternal damnation of all adherents of the opposite faith.'[5]

The ease with which all creeds resorted to stereotypes was noted too by Gamble – though the Catholics' imagery was impoverished by contrast. King Billy came too late to attract the purple prose of the Reformation era. On the road to Ballymena, Gamble was rescued from some disorderly farm animals by a kindly Catholic. He surmised as much, for the good Samaritan did not recognise his biblical allusions. 'Of course then you are not a Presbyterian,' commented Gamble. 'No; I thank God,' replied he, 'I don't belong to the black-hearted breed.' However, when asked why he called them such, he was at some loss to explain. 'Why, – why,' said he, somewhat puzzled, 'because I always heard them called so.' And when urged further for some rational explanation, none was forthcoming, save that they had sold their king for silver (i.e. Charles I) and abandoned the Catholics in 1798. Gamble found this opinion pretty general amongst Catholics.[6]

The nineteenth century was a defining time for such prejudices, because of the developments in politics and organised religion discussed earlier, and sectarian conflict was on the increase. But it was still locally confined and the experiences of Duffy and Doyle would have been the norm: heightened mutual awareness, suspicion and, at times, fear, tempered by genuine friendship and neighbourliness and an ability to laugh at their prejudices. Doyle reflected:

Yet none but an Ulster man can fairly criticise Ulstermen. The foreigner, looking at the surface of things, judges both sides too hardly. There was a good deal of convention in our attitude towards each other in those days . . . In theory we hated one another bitterly, but practise did not follow at theory's heels, in country districts at least. Our childish freaks apart, in all my boyhood I never knew of anyone being insulted on account of his religion. . . . We possess in the North one great corrective of bitterness, that dry sense of humour that is so often infused with self-criticism. We are conscious of our bitterness, and see the ridiculous side of it now and then.[7]

Nor was he the first to comment on the tendency for people from Ulster, when thrown together outside the province, to make sport of their mutual feud. It is also crucial to recognise that even in the worst of times Ulster communities were never totally polarised. The Catholic grandfather of William McComiskey (b.1875) emigrated to America from County Down, boarding a Liverpool-bound ship at Warrenpoint. Nearly all aboard were from the south of Ireland and 'he didn't have much to do with them'. But there was an Orangeman from Derry called Walker on board; they recognised each other's Ulster accents and stayed together the whole voyage. Mass was said on board every morning. But when the captain tried to stop it the Irish all rose and captured him and the Orangemen took their side.[8] At its edges, sectarianism shades into that particular brand of Ulster black humour, so appreciated by natives, so appalling to outsiders. Hugh McEnhill told of the local landlord in late nineteenth-century Tyrone taunting the Catholics with a chamber-pot carrying a picture of the pope at the bottom. 'But he wasn't a bad man,' he continued. And unlike his wife, he never gave himself any airs and graces. He walked everywhere and would always treat them to breakfast at Omagh fair.[9]

A degree of local accommodation was normal when political issues did not intervene and an awareness of what might offend (or give others the excuse to do so) often smoothed over potentially divisive situations. The difficulty of finding neutral venues – such a feature of late twentieth-century Ulster – was already a problem a century earlier. It was particularly noticeable during the cross-community tenant-right campaign of the early 1850s in south Ulster, where the large number of evictions after the Famine and resultant agrarian incidents exacerbated persistent sectarian tensions.[10] Lynn Doyle's tales of *Ballygullion* – his fictional Ulster village, with its equal numbers of Catholics and Protestants – charts the perennial efforts of the more moderate to surmount communal tensions, and they make for hilarious reading. Even the setting up of a creamery society in the town seemed doomed to be thwarted by petty sectarianism. Disputes over the location of the initial planning meeting nearly scuppered the project at the outset, for how to choose between Orange or Nationalist halls. Even if both were used in rotation, one would necessarily be first, and there were far too many who would not concede even that to the other community. Very well, responded the priest – one of the community leaders called upon to mediate – let there be two creameries, a Catholic one and a Protestant one. 'The only thing that bothers me . . . is the difficulty av doin' it. It's aisy enough to sort out the Catholic farmers from the Protestant; but what about the cattle?' – a variant on the standard theme in humorous Ulster writing: nobody and nothing could be anything other than Protestant or Catholic.[11] Stories of good neighbourliness and genuine friendship are legion, from the MacManuses in Donegal leaving payment for the apples they had picked from their Methodist neighbours' orchard – because they could not trade on Sundays – to the Brennans of Drumcullen in Fermanagh sponsoring the passages to Australia of their Methodist friends, the Fifes, between 1859 and 1865.[12]

Even so, it was friendship *across* the divide. Generations of friendship between the Presbyterian Hamiltons and the Catholic Floods in Tyrone did not lead to any greater religious understanding. May Brunt, née Hamilton, speaking of her childhood friendship with one of the

Floods in the early twentieth century, recalled that they could never agree on religion and she still thought theirs 'a peculiar blend of religion, politics, and superstition under the domineering influence of their church and its lust for power'.[13] The greater visibility and assertiveness of the Catholic clergy in the nineteenth century were finally giving substance to such ancient perceptions. It can be found even in the works of a sympathetic Protestant novelist from Fermanagh, Shan Bullock (1865–1935). Sarah and Felix are poor Protestant farmers in his *Dan the Dollar* (1906). They had taken in the orphaned children of distant relatives and they became like their own. But young Mary was a Catholic, and a particularly devout one at that. Sarah could not quite reconcile Mary's undoubted goodness with her fervent Catholicism. She 'fasted and did penance, prayed to the Virgin and the Saints, confessed to a priest, knelt to idols. Such practices in Sarah's eyes were abominable.' Mary too had all the stereotypical traits of a Catholic. She was utterly guided by and uncritical of the priests, whatever evidence was put to her of their worldliness. Despite her goodness, she still felt herself unworthy. Her excessive humility and sense of guilt is commented upon by the other characters, as if being miserable was a Catholic duty. Mary, for her part, was always aware of Sarah's dislike for her Catholicism – however much they loved each other – and she was convinced her religion was at peril if she married a Protestant (even a lapsed one like Dan, Sarah's son). Another theme is the perceived Catholic disdain for comfort and their tendency to live in run-down and ill-kept houses. The stereotypical Catholic lack of domestic comfort and cleanliness may have made a virtue of necessity, for, as noted earlier, the majority of Ulster Catholics were generally to be found in the lower social categories. For their part Catholics viewed materialism as a vice associated with Protestants.[14]

Whilst rural life imposed necessary mixing and co-operation, denominational cultural spheres were becoming increasingly separate. The practice of sharing at least some cemeteries seems to have continued for much of the nineteenth century.[15] National schools were still mixed in rural areas till the end of the century, but at the secondary level Catholics left in droves from mid-century on, given the choice of denominational education.[16] However, it is in the thorny area of 'mixed marriages' that the intimate social tensions caused by religious difference are most apparent. The very term raises eyebrows outside Ireland, where it is understood as mixed race. And yet in Ireland, and more especially in Ulster, the cultural taboos and impediments have been just as strong. Neither Catholic nor Protestant clergy or laity liked them. The Catholic Church progressively tightened up its controls until its notorious *Ne Temere* decree of 1908 insisted that all children of mixed marriages be brought up Catholic – where the tradition had been for sons to be raised in the faith of the father, daughters in that of the mother – and banned the couple from remarrying before another clergyman. But although it made many couples' lives unnecessarily difficult and delivered a major propaganda weapon to anti-popery, pressures from the Protestant churches were equally effective. Such marriages were treated as popish in any event, and in sectarian rioting mixed-religion couples were hounded out of Protestant areas, just as Protestants who married Catholics were dismissed from the Orange Order. Nor should the churches be held entirely responsible. As D. H. Akenson observes in his investigation of inter-communal relationships, *Small Differences*, no church could impose restrictions which its adherents did not endorse.[17] It looks as if the mixed marriage between Mary Brennan and Joseph McKee of north Down compelled the couple to emigrate. Certainly their letters from Australia (1865–76) reveal little evidence of friendly relations between the families at home.[18] Once out of the country, they were not so inhibited by communal pressures.

Relations were undoubtedly becoming more strained from quite early in the century. The rapid growth of population – particularly in the poorer sectors and traditionally Catholic districts – was creating tensions beyond the purely economic. If Gamble noticed it, then others less tolerant would also have done. Catholics were tolerated if an unthreatening minority. To this was added the economic stereotyping underpinned by the Ulster Catholics' concentration in the unskilled and labouring end of the employment market. David Fitzpatrick's analysis of the 1901 census figures for one parish in north Down reveals only Protestants employing domestic servants, and all those servants were Catholic.[19] Such was the limited experience of the rural poor that, when they moved for work to more prosperous areas, they could appear backward. H. A. Lafferty recalled the Donegal servant girls on his father's farm at Ardstraw, County Tyrone, coming down stairs backwards because their only experience of a second storey was climbing by ladder into the loft of their single-storey houses.[20] Many of the lower-class Protestants who still dominated Orangeism in the nineteenth century were just as underprivileged, but eagerly accepted the rhetoric of superiority *vis-à-vis* the Catholics. After the Union the anti-Catholicism of English politicians was less disguised by the presence of an Irish parliament, and the thirst for political news created by the United Irishmen did not evaporate. The Catholic emancipation issue dominated debate for much of the first three decades. In the end, emancipation had to be extracted from a reluctant parliament and, as before, the concession did not meet the high expectations. But in the process O'Connell had mobilised a Catholic movement of staggering power. Tory politicians were not slow to play on the anti-papist paranoia which it gave rise to, particularly among Ulster's lower-class Protestants.

Irish-language poems are awash with references to 'Luther's breed' and Protestant 'heretics' – with particularly scathing references to Elizabeth I – and such poems were still being recited in Armagh in the twentieth century.[21] Indeed, the last bardic contention to have taken place in Ireland, at Dundalk in 1822, had as one of its themes: 'The faith which Christ left a while ago . . . now under a cloud since the greed of the *Gaill* began; but . . . near is the hour when Clan Luther will be exhausted and weak.'[22] But it is resentment at Protestant slights which most comes through. Ó Muirgheasa collected an Irish-language prayer in Monaghan dated 1824:

O loving Mary, O gentle virgin . . .
send down your heavy blow and rudely fell the heretics of Ireland;
expel the English language from our country, and leave the dear Irish in
    its place,
the children of Luther it was who left us without life, like an old faggot
    you'd find in a hedge.
Give a heavy damaging blow to the deceitful children of blind Calvin,
it's the Scots I mean, lay your hand down on them fiercely.[23]

A poem composed by Hugh McDonnell in the 1840s picks up the dismissive language being employed by the teachers of the proselytising societies.

> O heedless lackey who never puts aside
> nonsensical chatter,
> stuff up the throat which won't stop your mouth
> from talking about oppression
> . . . layabouts of your nation,
> poets and druids,
> who'd normally go without shelter or shade,
> or a place to spend the night.[24]

An early nineteenth-century sectarian doggerel also collected by Ó Muirgheasa in Donegal – 'The Orangeman' ('*An tOrangeman*') – dreams of the Orangeman 'ploughing the land for us'.[25] At the Belfast meeting of June 1916, McGlone's choice of phrase in the heat of the moment to express Catholic resentment at being presumed inferior by Protestants is entirely representative of Catholic opinion: give Protestants the chance and they'll reassert their old ascendancy over us and treat us like 'hewers of wood and drawers of water'.[26] The Revd John Tohill, a professor at St Malachy's College, Belfast, said much the same during the 1887 Belfast Riots' Inquiry. He complained of 'an aggressive Protestant ascendancy' being exercised by all classes of Protestants, and of Catholics being 'treated as if they were an inferior and conquered race'.[27] Catholics were generally very aware that Protestants thought them inferior and that for much of the century they still held most of the state power. 'The Protestants are generally of higher rank and pride themselves on being Protestants and freemen,' Gamble concluded. 'The Catholic is depressed and dispirited; he hates the Protestant, but fears him for the party to which he belongs . . . which he thinks is supported by the magistrate and the state.'[28]

In fact, as the century wore on, the state was making considerable efforts to ensure impartiality in policing and the administration of justice. Although Belfast and Derry retained borough police forces until 1865 and 1870 respectively (both of which were regularly accused of anti-Catholic bias), a new centralised police force was established for the entire country, which became the Royal Irish Constabulary in 1867. Many Catholics were recruited into this, and a system of stipendiary magistrates was introduced from 1836 onwards. Evidence to the numerous riots commissions in the second half of the century show the beginnings of a greater trust among Catholics in the central government's desire to ensure equal justice. A Protestant doctor who ministered to the working-class Catholics of Derry told the 1870 commission: 'I know that party [the Catholics] are very much inclined to accept the protection of the law, if they have any expectation of it.' Indeed, the Catholic clergy had dissuaded their people from clashing with the loyalist Apprentice Boys of Derry the previous year, on the understanding that the government commission would indeed introduce reforms.[29] However, although government enquiries regularly rebuked Orange magistrates, the belief among Catholics and often the reality was that the forces of law and order were inherently anti-Catholic, even Orange. The tendency for such magistrates to see Orange parades as legitimate loyal displays and nationalist meetings – however constitutional – as rebellious, becomes particularly marked during the Home Rule campaign. The problem, as always, about such imperiousness and lack of generosity was that it created the very evil which it claimed to prevent. It also disguised the legitimate concerns of many Protestants.

2. Parades and sectarian riots

Lower-class Protestants were unnerved by Daniel O'Connell's often inflammatory rhetoric and heeded warnings that Catholic emancipation would adversely affect their community.[30] Orangeism witnessed a phenomenal growth in the early decades of the nineteenth century. Gamble found it everywhere. 'Beyond all other things, Orange processions are become offensive to the Catholics; they remind them forcibly of their ancient misfortunes, and what they think their present degradation. They regard them not only as injuries but insults, and writhe at the sight of them.'[31] 'We did not know much of history', Gavan Duffy recalled, 'but we got . . . "object-lessons", to keep it alive in our memory. The Orange drum was heard on every hill from June till August to celebrate the Boyne and Aughrim . . . To be a Protestant of any sort was a diploma of merit and a title to social rank . . .'[32] In time the Orange parades became part of popular Protestant tradition and Lynn Doyle remembers the little boy's ambition to participate in the flute bands. But for much of the nineteenth century Orange parades were aggressively and provocatively anti-Catholic and were central to Catholic complaints throughout the century.

It was at this time too that such parades became Protestantism's most cherished symbol of a fading Protestant ascendancy. Until the end of the Napoleonic war in 1815, the security policy of successive governments was still dependent on the yeomanry (20,000 of its total force of 30,000 being Ulstermen), which had always been highly susceptible to Orange infiltration, and Orangeism still had many friends in high places. After 1815, however, the yeomanry increasingly fell into disfavour. The reorganisation of the police and the introduction of stipendiary magistrates began to challenge respectively the yeomanry's role and that of the local Orange gentry who occupied the bench. One of these new magistrates – John Hancock – waged such a campaign against the Orangemen of County Armagh that his home came under armed attack.[33] By the 1820s the movement seemed under siege. O'Connell's campaign, however – particularly Lawless's ill-advised 'invasion' of Ulster – brought about a major revival. The yeomanry was needed to cope with a serious 'tithe war' in the Irish midlands (1830–33) and it was re-armed. Its 'new' arms now began to feature prominently in an upturn in sectarian clashes. This did not mean a renewal of government approval. On the contrary, Orange processions continued to be frowned upon and were banned under the first Party Processions Act in 1832; while a major parliamentary enquiry in 1835 was so critical that the Grand Lodge of Ireland voluntarily dissolved itself the following year, even though the local lodges continued their activities.[34]

But in areas of traditional confrontation, notably County Armagh, they clearly had, and expected to have, the side of the law. A map of Orange lodges in 1836 reveals a very heavy concentration in the old linen triangle, centred on north Armagh and south Tyrone. Since the 1790s both the yeomanry – and to all intents, the justice system – seemed to be entirely under Orange control. Colonel William Blacker was a yeomanry commander with impressive Orange credentials: he had been present at the Battle of the Diamond, was the Grand Master of County Armagh and had been Deputy Grand Master of all Ireland. He was also chairman of the petty sessions. Orangemen were confident he would take no action against them. The parliamentary report of 1835 into Orange Lodges concluded likewise, and he and several other Orange magistrates were stood down. The Portadown, Tanderagee, Lurgan area is the prime example of the kind of league between Anglican gentry, clergy and labourers which gave the latter such a sense of 'owning' the system. Lord Mandeville (owner of the Tanderagee estate) and the Revd Dean Carter were known to have kept up Protestant fears by prophecies of popish plans to massacre Protestants and dark references to a 'Sicilian vespers'.[35]

A number of liberal landlords and legal men were encouraging Catholics to complain to the government and from the late 1820s it took action to curb such activities. But by then a pattern of behaviour had been established. 'For most of the year', one Protestant witness told the 1835 enquiry, people are usually good neighbours, 'but prior to the 12 of July in every year, say for a month, the people become estranged from each other as if they were foreigners.'[36] Although Carleton had become a Protestant by the time he came to write his autobiography towards the end of his life (he died in 1869), he recalls with some bitterness the early nineteenth-century Orange ascendancy in County Tyrone and how Protestant neighbours could so easily turn on respectable Catholics to show they were in control:

This [early nineteenth century] was the period of Protestant, or rather of Orange, ascendancy ... Every yeoman with his red coat on was an Orangeman. Every cavalryman mounted upon his own horse and dressed in blue was an Orangeman. ... Merciful God! In what a frightful condition was the country at that time. I speak now of the North of Ireland. It was then, indeed, the seat of Orange ascendancy and irresponsible power. To find a justice of the peace not an Orangeman would have been an impossibility. The grand jury room was little less than an Orange lodge. There was then no law *against* an Orangeman, and no law *for* a Papist.

These yeoman were in the habit – especially when primed with whiskey, or on their way from an Orange lodge – of putting on their uniform, getting their guns and bayonets, and going out at night to pay domiciliary visits to Catholic families under the pretence of searching for firearms; and it is painful to reflect upon, or even to recollect, the violence and outrage with which these illegal excursions were conducted.

He went on to relate a night-time raid on their house by a group of Orangemen, all of whom were their neighbours.[37] Protestant friends and neighbours turning aggressive during the marching season would have been a common experience for Catholics – particularly at the lower end of the social scale. Lynn Doyle's Catholic narrator of Bally-gullion claims:

I'm no party man, myself; but whin I see William Robinson, that has been me neighbour this twenty years, goin' down the road on the twelfth av July wi' a couple av Orange sashes on, me heart doesn't warm to him as it does av another day. The plain truth is, we were bate at the Boyne right enough; but some av us has more than a notion we didn't get fair play at the fightin'; and between that and hearin' about the batin' iver since, the look of ould Billy on his white horse isn't very soothin.[38]

Groups of young men would roam the countryside playing party tunes, attacking their opponents, organising 'drumming parties' outside the homes of liberal magistrates or clergy – who would be damned as 'papists', 'a term they deem very offensive'. Huge parades would take place on 12 July – 10,000 parading at Tanderagee in 1831 – fed by long marches from other areas.[39] Drink would be taken and Catholic areas attacked on the homeward march. Catholics would retaliate and very often end up convicted by Orange juries. The following year during the marching season, anniversaries of 'incidents' would draw even greater numbers. 'Orangemen' or 'Ribbonmen' became generic terms of abuse – even though neither represented the majority of either community. However, it is clear that the Orangemen still believed that they were defending the interests of a Protestant state against rebellious Catholics, and in 1831 attacks were reported on Catholic houses in the Portadown area by young labouring Protestants who believed that Catholics were still not entitled to keep arms.[40]

In fact the 'Protestant state' *was* being slowly dismantled – too

slowly to attract Catholic gratitude, but too quickly for Ulster Protestants. Again O'Connell's campaign, however constitutional,
enflamed a raw nerve, and it coincided with the kind of Protestant
revival which depicted popery as a disease in need of cure. One incident
in County Monaghan gives some idea of the communal bitterness of
these years in areas of long-standing conflict. On the night of 13
February 1828 in Drumswords churchyard, four miles from Clones,
the body of David Burke was disinterred and hung from a nearby tree.
It seems to have been an area of long-standing religious conflict and
was the scene of a massacre of Protestants in 1641.[41] Burke was
master of Drumanan Orange lodge; a yeoman and a leading figure in
suppressing rebellious activities in 1798, he was considered also as a
scourge of the local Catholic population. Of late the area had witnessed
a number of clashes between Orangemen and Ribbonmen, including
one over whether a Protestant convert to Catholicism should be buried
in a Catholic graveyard. One press report described it as the action of
'Dan's [O'Connell's] worse than savage pupils'.[42]

Catholic emancipation brought little immediate benefit to the average Catholic. But it did wonders for him psychologically and from
1829 onwards Orange parades were challenged at every level. At its
crudest it involved Catholic youths challenging the marchers. A notable
example of this occurred at Mackan in Fermanagh in July 1829. The
marchers seem to have attacked a group of youths who had jeered
them on the outward march that morning. That evening the Catholics
gathered with their pitchforks and billhooks and took revenge, killing
three of the Orangemen. Four Catholics were later capitally convicted
for the killings. They claimed to have acted in self-defence, that none
of the original perpetrators had been called to account, and that they
could not expect a fair trial because of the notoriety of the Orange
juries in the area – a claim the Lord Lieutenant seemed to accept, for
he later commuted the sentences to transportation, though too late for
one of the men, who was hanged at Enniskillen.[43]

Like so many more local affrays, that at Mackan gave rise to strong
local traditions, which were embellished over time. By the last decades
of the century, the hanged man had died 'for God and Ireland', for
'faith and fatherland'. By the next century it had entered a composite
picture of a time when the Catholics were enslaved and the Protestants

in control – though none of those who related the tale to Henry Glassie were particularly militant. One of the commemorative songs incorporates the kind of insults which the Orangemen would have used:

> On the 13th of July,
> Of the year of twenty-nine,
> Being the time of these bloody No Surrender,
> They were cheering loud and shrill,
> To they came to Mackan Hill,
> For the face of a papish pretender.
>
> Where they drew up their lines,
> In square and rank and file,
> The cry was for No Pope or No Surrender.
> But with steadfast hope,
> They who consmate [sic] the Pope,
> All his nuns and crucifix pretenders.[44]

As the affrays grew worse, the respectable people began to abandon the Orangemen, and Catholics made their feelings clear to government that 'they will not suffer themselves to be insulted, or their feelings outraged by these senseless parades, of what they have hitherto considered a domineering faction'.[45] Certainly once government clamped down on the marches (Party Processions Act of 1832), there was a visible relaxation in tension for almost three decades and the propertied Protestants remained aloof from Orangeism until the 1880s.

When the Party Processions Act lapsed in 1845, there was an immediate resurgence of Orange parades. Catholic clergy called for re-routing and urged Catholics not to react – but to no avail. Ribbonism was reactivated. Invariably the Orangemen were better armed. A famous incident occurred at Dolly's Brae near Castlewellan in County Down. Communal relations in the Rathfriland–Castlewellan area had long been fraught and an incident earlier in the century had convinced residents in the largely Catholic Dolly's Brae area that no more Orange marches would be permitted to pass. A new road skirting below the pass of Dolly's Brae allowed Catholic clergy and local magistrates to ensure a peaceful resumption of marches in July 1848. But local Ribbonmen treated the failure to go through the pass itself as a great victory and celebrated it as such in printed songs. Predictably Orangemen rose to the challenge the following year and succeeded in marching through the pass itself. But tensions were high. They had been taunted by Catholic women along the way with threats that they were walking into a trap. In fact, although the Ribbonmen had been potting shots all day to show that they were armed, their threat was to prove something of an illusion. The Orange parade had marched through the pass to their grand master's (Lord Roden's) estate at Tollymore. There they were told of how recent measures by the government had placed the Protestant constitution in jeopardy and of how their loyalty was needed to defend it. On the route back some shots were heard – whether from the Orangemen or Ribbonmen on the hill no one could later ascertain. A general affray ensued. But the Orangemen emerged unscathed, while at least thirty Catholics were killed and Catholic homes in the area fired. The descriptions of attackers and assailants in the government report into the incident shows the deadly nastiness of these sectarian feuds among the underprivileged. The armed Orangemen had fired on children fleeing across the fields, shot domestic animals and strangled chickens.

But the report singled out those in higher places for particular censure. The two local priests were praised for their efforts to keep the peace, but criticised for then formally blessing the Ribbonmen as they knelt on the hill – a gesture the commissioner felt gave unintended legitimacy to the Ribbonmen's actions. But his major criticism was reserved for those magistrates (including Lord Roden), who, though aware of 'a population consisting of two contending bodies, whose prejudices and feelings are inflamed against each other from old recollections and religious differences', nevertheless – because they were leading Orangemen, had failed to stop what he regarded as an unlawful march.[46] Once again propertied Protestants took flight from Orangeism. The government reimposed the Party Processions Act (1850) and added a Party Emblems Act in 1860. But lower-class Catholics might have been forgiven for not appreciating that the authorities were no longer the Orange supporters of the past, for the local magistrates had again shown themselves partial (and three, including Roden, were stood down after a government enquiry). Moreover, the event entered Orange mythology as another great victory over popery.

> Twas on the 12th day of July, in the year of '49,
> ten hundreds of our Orangemen together did combine,
> In the memory of King William, on that bright and glorious day,
> To walk all round Lord Roden's park, and right over Dolly's Brae.
> . . .
> And as we walked along the road not fearing any harm,
> Our guns all over our shoulders, and our broadswords in our hands,
> Until two priests came up to us, and to Mr. Speers[Beers, a magistrate]
>   did say,
> 'Come, turn your men the other road, and don't cross Dolly's Brae.'
>
> Then out speaks our Orangemen, 'Indeed we won't delay,
> You have your men all gathered and in a manger lay;
> Begone, begone, you Papist dogs, we'll conquer or we'll die,
> And we'll let you see we're not afraid to cross over Dolly's Brae.'
>
> And when we came to Dolly's Brae they were lined on every side,
> Praying for the Virgin Mary to be their holy guide;
> We loosened our guns upon them and we gave them no time to pray,
> And the tune we played was 'The Protestant Boys' right over Dolly's
>   Brae.
> . . .
> Come all ye blind-led Papists, wherever that ye be,
> Never bow down to priest or Pope, for them they will disown;
> Never bow down to images, for God [you must] adore,
> Come join our Orange heroes, and cry 'Dolly's Brae no more'.[47]

Orangeism to Catholics represented hatred of their religion and insulting dominance, and they were increasingly unwilling to stand for it. But their own assertiveness, the growing visibility and power of the Catholic Church, and the renewed dogmatism of the papacy exacerbated the fears which translated into a murderous sectarianism at the lowest levels of Orangeism. Many Protestants frowned on Orangeism – notably the Presbyterians, who disliked its overwhelming

Anglicanism. But evangelicalism and revivalism were bringing the different Protestant denominations closer together and the development of nationalism reacted upon centuries of tradition about political popery to make the Home Rule campaign of the 1880s the deciding moment in consolidating a common Ulster Protestant identity. That identity was firmly rooted in anti-popery and in a belief that their very religion made Catholics inferior, disloyal and persecutory.[48] This is why Ulster Protestants never made a distinction between so-called moral-force and physical-force nationalists. It was their 'popery', not their methods, which threatened the Protestant way of life. Orangeism witnessed a remarkable revival in the 1880s – in response to the growth of organised nationalism – and provided much of the organisational basis for developing Unionism. Both communities, accordingly, approached the Home Rule crisis in the belief that the other would persecute and tyrannise if successful. 'Home Rulers to my childish mind were a dark, subtle, and dangerous race,' Lynn Doyle recalled of his childhood in County Down; 'they were ready to rise, murder my uncle, possess themselves of his farm, and drive out my aunt and myself to perish on the mountains ... in my aunt's stories it was on the mountains we always died.' Later he reflected on how such fears could co-exist with the friendship and trust which his family felt for a number of Catholics. He also learnt that the young Catholic maid in his house was as fearful about going near Orange Lodges as he had been of the nationalists' meeting places.[49] By the 1870s the Government's ban on marching had become unenforceable because of widespread civil disobedience and was replaced with a policy of equal marching rights within confined areas.[50]

Lynn Doyle characteristically put a humorous slant on the way the marching season impacted on the smaller villages. In Ballygullion, where 'although we're just about half-an'-half, nationalist an' Orange ... we can live side by side friendly enough until both of us begin to make ready for the party processions in the summer time. But from the first blatter on an Orange drum comin' up to the Twelfth of July, ill-will an' bitterness sets in like the flowin' tide, an' only ebbs with the last wallop of a Nationalist drumstick on the night of the fifteenth of August.' By the early twentieth century, party quarrels had become so bad during Ballygullion's marching season that the police had confined the parades of each side to that half where their own religion predominated. But no occasion for annoyance was let pass. On the Catholic side a priest's ordination was made the excuse to bedeck their area with 'such a flyin' of flags as never had been in Ballygullion before', arousing predictable ire from the other side and leaving the sorry Protestant grocer serving the Catholics in a quandary about what to do. His efforts – helped by a Catholic friend – to find some flag which would offend no one, and the impossibility of such, forms the core narrative.[51]

But in the towns, where social intercourse between working-class Protestants and Catholics was increasingly disappearing, such sectarian stereotyping left a dreadful legacy. Belfast in particular became a by-word for sectarian riots, in which more people died in the nineteenth century than in rioting in any other European city. 'I had not the least idea that religion could cause such rancour between people until I came here', John O'Donovan wrote during his ordnance survey visit to Belfast in 1834. 'It is principally fomented by clever men, who are well acquainted with the nature of the human mind, and whose interest it is to paint the failings of other sects in the strongest lights possible.'[52] In Belfast Orangeism, Ribbonism and the Ancient Order of Hibernians found their main strengths, and new waves of rural migrants came prepared. In 1864, Sandy Row Protestants attacked the Catholic Pound area in protest at the great rally in Dublin to unveil a statue to O'Connell. Mrs Mullins prepared to defend the Catholic enclave. Her husband had taught her to use a gun when they first came to Belfast. 'When she heard the Protestant shipwrights were coming, she put her three children in the piggery at the back of the house, loaded her gun and went off to defend the church.'[53] The riots had started out with the crowd from Sandy Row conducting a mock requiem mass and funeral for O'Connell within sight of the Pound, and continued with groups of Protestant shipwrights and Catholic navvies terrorising the city. It was a particularly nasty attack by the navvies on a Protestant school in Brown Square, Millfield, which mobilised the Shankill Road crowd to attack Mrs Mullins's church on the Falls Road. Repeated armed attacks by Protestant gangs on Catholic churches and convents had Catholics arming and rallying to their defence.

The emergence of a common Ulster Protestant identity firmly

anchored in anti-popery was also accelerated by a series of demagogic open-air preachers – particularly in Belfast. They played to the lowest form of anti-popery and were tremendously popular with lower-class Protestants. Indeed, the Revd Thomas Drew's inflammatory sermons were said to have sparked off the 1857 riots. On the evening of 12 July he regaled the Sandy Row boys – who had marched to church with their Orange regalia secreted under their hats, the ban on such parades being still in force – with terrifying images of papal prisons paved with human blood and hair and of wicked Catholic prelates in bygone times dabbling in the gore of Protestant women being tortured on the rack. Popery's wiles were traced from James II's reign through to the contemporary outrage of 'Romanists' actually occupying state office and 'Jesuit intrigues' polluting 'our Protestant Universities'. Britain's mission ought to be one of 'Protestantizing the world' and Protestants were urged to vigilance against 'the arrogant pretences of Popes and the outrageous dogmata of their blood-stained religion', with its 'detestable machinations of the Confessional, of Jesuitism, and of the Inquisition'.[54] Drew's church was situated at the corner of Durham Street and College Street North, at the end of Sandy Row, and therefore on the interface between working-class Protestant and Catholic areas, a traditional location of confrontation around the 12 July. As opposing mobs gathered outside Drew's church, it only took the prank of a tipsy Catholic youth waving an Orange lily to set off a week of rioting. The subsequent parliamentary enquiry criticised both sides, for they had been preparing for conflict, and the mobs included entire communities, men, women and children – even little girls singing sectarian street-rhymes. However, it laid particular blame on the Orange Order and on preachers like Drew. 'The feeling which leads to the separation of these districts in July . . . is a feeling of dominancy and insult on the one side, and of opposition to its display on the other.' It attributed the origins of the riots to the celebration of 12 July, 'a festival which is used to remind one party of the triumph of their ancestors over those of the other, and to inculcate the feeling of Protestant superiority over their Roman Catholic neighbours'.[55]

The parliamentary enquiry also found a near monopoly of 'insulting language' on the Protestant side. Betty Donohue lived on waste ground between the Pound and Sandy Row, a widow with four children, who sold eggs and milk from her cows and poultry. Early one morning she was confronted behind her home by a gang of youths who tried to get her 'to curse the Pope'. Catholic mill-girls walking to Grimshaw's mill near Sandy Row were stoned, told the water being poured on them was 'holy water', that they were 'Papish whores', that their attackers 'had burned Dan O'Connell [a straw man having been burnt as such], and that they would burn the Pope, and . . . the Blessed Virgin'.[56] Some of the language reveals the continuing belief that Catholics were disloyal. A militiaman went through the Protestant streets calling on the people to arm against 'the rebels coming down the Blackstaff' [the river running between the districts], whilst Catholics being intimidated out of their homes during the night were called upon to 'rise up and surrender'.[57] The commissioners were dismissive of the Orange Order's justification that it was arming in self-defence against the Ribbonmen. They thought the latter organisation nearly gone from Belfast, and anyway such measures were hardly needed in a town where Protestants were in the majority.[58]

The 1857 riots were localised to the Sandy Row/Pound areas, with ripples in neighbouring frontier zones, Shankill Road/Peter's Hill/ Millfield areas, and, as with the late twentieth-century Troubles, people in other districts could live almost unaffected by them, except through heightened press coverage. Those intimidated out of their homes told of good neighbourliness before 1857 and of friendly acts even at the height of the riots. One Protestant woman in Quadrant Street was seen to point out the houses of her Catholic neighbours. But very many more covered up for them. Anne Cummins – one of the mill-workers at Grimshaw's – heard her landlady deny that she had a 'Papist' lodger when they came to turn her out. Betty Donohue told of how a Protestant woman from Sandy Row had brought her to the police for protection in 1854, when her house was wrecked, while another Protestant neighbour had carried out the repairs without charge. In 1857 she was finally forced out, but the Presbyterian neighbour who had alerted her had been a family friend and the warning was 'friendly intended'.[59] However, a pattern had been set and the intimidation of Catholics and Protestants (and those in mixed marriages) from working-class areas would be a prominent feature of all future riots.

Drew's sermons were an embarrassment to his religious leaders. He was banned from open-air preaching and shortly afterwards moved away from Belfast. But his brand of fundamentalism was popular and the *Belfast News Letter* saw his silencing as putting Belfast on the same level as 'Romish cities' like Cork or Limerick, where Protestant ministers risked stoning or murder from priestly mobs.[60] The arrival of Catholic convents also added to the reactivation of popular Protestant stereotypes of popery. Just like the confessional, here again was priestly power destroying the family and using the helpless female as its instrument, and calls were regularly made for inspections to ensure the nuns were not being held against their will.[61] Another Orange preacher, the Revd Hugh Hanna, called on Protestants to unite against this same threat from political popery which had confronted their forefathers three centuries earlier and even less messianic commentators on the threats of Home Rule were to take the same line.

The right to 'walk' was vigorously exercised by Belfast Orangeism throughout the recent bans, which had heightened their sensitivities on the issue of marches. The repeal of the Party Processions Act was followed in 1872 by huge Orange displays all over Ulster. It was unusual for Catholics to insist on marching. But this year on the Feast of the Assumption (15 August) they planned to march from Carlisle Circus, just north of the city centre and the site of Hanna's church, to Hannahstown, west of the town. It was the first occasion on which a Catholic procession sparked off major rioting, for Hanna had assembled a huge crowd of 5,000–10,000 to stop it.[62] No one could remember a Catholic parade in Belfast that century. But increasingly Catholics emulated the Orangemen, and 15 August vied with 12 July as riot seasons – particularly when AOH lodges organised seriously. The growth of Orangeism and the Hibernians in the city was truly phenomenal in these years – the Orange Order up from 1,335 in 1851 to 18,800 in 1913, the bulk of the AOH's 60,000 membership being based in Belfast and County Tyrone by 1909. Both had a grip on their respective religious ghettos and it would have been difficult for the working class to find employment outside these sectarian organisations. Orangeism came to have a particular stranglehold on the Belfast shipyard, to the extent that the seventh Belfast district of the Orange Order was concentrated there.[63] In Belfast, writes Sybil Baker,

A century of Orange and Green rivalry had conditioned its communities to violent confrontation. The influence of the lodges upon Belfast's working classes had always exceeded their numerical strength, for they reflected much wider circles of family, neighbourhood, and trade, and crystallised much sectarian competition and ethnic enmity. Their indoctrination fed prejudice. Their disciplinary codes enforced chauvinistic intolerance. Their celebrations taunted the opposition to retaliation. Their ballads perpetuated an impassioned urban folklore where victories on seventeenth-century battle-grounds and nineteenth-century brickfields [open ground on the Falls/Shankill interface] were entwined. Separate education began ethnic isolation: the culture of the lodges turned it into ethnic alienation.[64]

After further riots in Belfast in 1864, the Government criticised the anti-Catholicism of the Town Council and abolished the largely Orange police force which had been under its control. Replacing it with the largely Catholic (and militarised) RIC, however, set the scene for the 1886 riots – the worst of the century. The 1885 parliamentary election had delivered virtually the whole of Ireland to Parnell's Nationalists, decimating the Liberals and leaving Ulster (with sixteen Conservative-Unionists and seventeen Nationalists) as the only province registering any significant opposition to Home Rule. Ulster had voted along almost exclusively denominational lines, Belfast in particular returning Conservatives for all four of its constituencies.[65] There had been a closely fought contest in west Belfast – which also included the Protestant Sandy Row and Shankill Road. After Gladstone introduced his Home Rule Bill in April 1886, tensions ran high, particularly in the shipyard, which drew most of its skilled workers from Protestant districts.

On 3 June word went out that a Catholic navvy in dispute with a Protestant one had claimed that under Home Rule none of his sort would get leave to work.[66] The story was clearly embellished in the telling, but the next day the Protestant shipwrights descended on the Catholic labourers and forced them to swim for their lives. One was drowned, and his funeral cortège from his home in Ballymacarrett in east Belfast to Milltown cemetery turned into a huge nationalist demonstration. But the defeat of the Home Rule Bill on 8 June caused the ensuing riots to merge into Protestant victory celebrations, and Catholic-owned public houses and grocery stores in Protestant areas were wrecked. So many Catholics were put out of work that the Catholic Church organised a diocesan collection for their relief.[67] Disturbances continued through the marching season and Catholic and Protestant mill-girls turned on each other – the former now giving as good as they got, cries of 'Fenian whore' and 'Orange whore' echoing through the streets, and the segregated map of working-class Belfast growing apace. The term 'Fenian' (from the republican movement of the 1860s), and its association with political disloyalty, had now become the preferred term of abuse for Catholics. The old battle-fields surfaced again: the interface between the Shankill and Falls Roads, the Falls Road and Sandy Row, the Catholic enclave of Carrick Hill and the Old Lodge/Clifton Street area, York Street, and Ballymacarrett, near the shipyard. Thirty-two were killed, 371 injured and over £90,000 of damage was sustained in the riots.

Another commission was severely critical of the borough corporation – not one Catholic officer serving on it, nor on its police committee. But once again it was the parades, processions, and party music which was deemed to keep religious tensions alive – prompting the president of the Commission, Mr Justice Day, to comment that perhaps music in Belfast should be restricted to the more neutral barrel-organs. Certainly the parading of Orange bands had got out of hand. Even the Sunday-school parades to the Revd Hanna's church and school at Carlisle Circus were accompanied by them, attracting crowds of 'roughs' who would then attack Catholic property. Michael Kernan was a publican on the corner of Carrick Hill and Clifton Street. His property was attacked by such crowds on almost every significant political occasion (the Prince of Wales's visit in 1885, Lord Randolph Churchill's in 1886) and on numerous occasions every year during the school parades. Certainly the commissioners concluded that 'the principal actors in the rioting were what is known as the Protestant mob'.[68]

Derry escaped the repeated sectarian riots of Belfast until later in the century. Residential segregation there was. But the predominance of Catholics in the Bogside was the result of geography, not sectarian confrontation – it was situated on the Donegal side of the city, from which county most of the Catholic families had originated. In predominantly Catholic Donegal there was not the history of sectarian conflict of the counties further east. Possibly because of the largely lower-class nature of Derry's Catholic population, the Catholic Church exercised considerable moderating control, encouraging its members to seek political remedies from the Liberals rather than from Fenian revolutionaries. Apart from the years of Edward Maginn's term as bishop of Derry (1845–54), the hierarchy tended to divert activities into internal Catholic organisation. Certainly Derry Catholics were still voting for Protestant Liberals as late as 1913 and a significant number of Presbyterians – irritated at the Tory–Orange dominance of local politics – joined them. One of these, Dr James McKnight, addressing the 1870 Commission of Inquiry into the riots and disturbances in Derry the previous year, thought the people would live peaceably together were it not for parades stirring up animosities.

Whenever these periodical displays are intended as a commemoration of the victories of one political party in the State over another they tend inevitably to perpetuate the original feud . . . in the city of Derry and throughout the north of Ireland, every celebration of that kind, both historically and otherwise, is regarded by [the] conquered party as a triumph of the representatives of the opposite party over them; and in some of our platform oratory . . . I am sorry to see a wish repeatedly expressed to fight the battles of Aughrim and the Boyne over again.

He cited the annual commemorations by the Apprentice Boys of Derry of the shutting of the gates in 1688 (18 December) and the lifting of the siege by James II's forces in 1689 (12 August). He queried their claim to long tradition and condemned in particular their ritual of choosing that part of the city walls which overlooked the Catholic populace below, 'and firing in practical triumph over the heads and houses of these people'.[69] He might have added the presence on the same spot of the 90-foot-tall monument to the Revd George Walker – joint governor of Derry at the time of the siege – built at the height of the Catholic emancipation campaign in the 1820s. Thereafter it became the focal point of Orange celebrations, a reinforcement of the seventeenth-century fortified walls to keep out popish pretenders. It was fiercely resented by local Catholics and was blown up in 1973.[70]

Although poor Protestants also lived outside the city walls by this stage (largely in the Fountains area), the Apprentice Boys – with the support of significant numbers of the city authorities and police – viewed the walled city area as peculiarly their own and one to be defended at all costs against Catholic incursions. From the 1860s Catholics began to challenge this by organising their own parades and the young hangers-on were just as provocative as those who followed the Orange parades.[71] The various riots suggest that a definite territorial battle was in train. As the Home Rule campaign became more aggressive and a monster nationalist rally was planned for St Patrick's day in 1883, the Apprentice Boys of Derry called on Orangemen to come from all over Ulster (the extension of the railways bringing in thousands of Orangemen to controversial venues) 'to oppose this renewed attempt to erect the standard of rebellion on sacred historic ground . . . and from her [Derry's] walls declare your firm determination to oppose treason and the dismemberment of the empire.'[72] Some months later, the Apprentice Boys seized Corporation Hall in the Diamond and raised their flag over it to prevent another nationalist meeting. Nationalists were diverted by police into the Bogside. That night there were armed clashes between the two factions. Catholic leaders complained of 'an insolent minority' who controlled civic office and thereby the instruments of the law, a complaint which was largely upheld by the various Royal Commissions.[73] However, the growth in Catholic numbers (which had already made Catholics a majority by 1861), and the rise of Catholic political organisation and aggressive nationalism after the 1880s was bringing about the same kind of Protestant realignment in Derry as elsewhere in Ulster.[74]

It is worth noting that the many reports of sectarian riots in the nineteenth century may give a false picture of communal relations. They are also geographically confined, largely concentrating on Belfast and to a lesser extent on Derry. However, they highlight already well-established patterns of conflict and the tendency for each side to turn on those within their own community who tried to remain neutral or worse, who actually helped victims of the other religion.[75]

A notable feature of the 1886 riots was the sustained attacks by Protestants on the police. RIC reinforcements had been brought in from other counties in Ireland and there was a belief among the

Protestant working classes – actively fanned by some of their political and religious leaders, notably Hanna – that they were brought in to subdue the Protestant populace. There was also considerable irritation among the Protestant magistracy at any hint that 'loyal' Belfast might be subjected to the Coercion Act, just like disturbed counties in the south and west.[76] A pamphlet, sponsored, if not actually written, by Wesley De Cobain (former Orange Grand Master and independent Conservative MP for East Belfast) depicted the riots, whatever the evidence to the contrary, as having been produced by priestly tyranny. Had priests not been seen talking to those who later joined the riots and to the police (those 'Royal Irish' [RIC] – with obvious stress on the assumed incongruity of the two terms), who then fired on Protestants, and weren't those same police those big, stupid 'southern' Catholics, from the 'poteen making and poteen drinking districts' who talked funny, with their 'foinest' southern accent? And since all papists were 'poor credulous fools . . . brought up and trained in a church founded on lies', they would believe anything their priest told them. The pamphlet is a meandering, gossipy and often prurient piece of propaganda, a suggestion that convents were in reality prisons for young girls to satisfy priestly wiles continuing Drew's imagery. It reproduced the boast reputedly made by the Catholic navvy that when Home Rule came, no Protestant 'would get leave to earn a loaf of bread'. 'In fact', observes the writer, 'I believe that the Papists – poor mortals that they are – under priestly rule, and thereby not enjoying anything like true liberty themselves, neither would know or could know how to give liberty to others.'[77] It was the old Protestant belief, prevalent since the seventeenth century, that given half a chance Catholics would prove just as persecutory and triumphalist as themselves.

3. The refining of Catholic nationalist identity

Protestant culture had subsumed Elizabethan stereotypes of the Irish and transposed them to the Catholics. Popular folklore even in contemporary Northern Ireland holds that Catholics and Protestants can distinguish each other by appearance and speech. The Belfast Police Committee Chairman, Samuel Black, claimed as much before the 1865 Commission.[78] At its most extreme, ultra-Protestantism thought the assumed mental oppression of popery was reflected in the demeanour of its adherents. 'Contrast the Protestant and Romish physiognomy,' Thomas Drew told his audience, 'and say where you will find such depressed, saddened, drooping-looking men, as the poor, oppressed, mentally aggrieved Romanist.'[79] History books written by Catholic clerics, which appear in great abundance in the later nineteenth century, are steeped in resentment at these attitudes and it has left its legacy in the Ulster Catholic's heightened sensitivity about the potential 'put-down'. Catholics still dislike the 'Roman' prefix, for the emphasis had always been put on that in the past. The historian of Monaghan, D. C. Rushe, thought the prefix only became common among Protestants in the nineteenth century: 'And the bigots rumbled the word Roman round their mouths with a spice of contempt, which is still noticeable.'[80] The Revd Ambrose Coleman who in 1900 produced a Catholic version of James Stuart's 1819 *Historical Memoirs of the City of Armagh*, was pleasantly surprised at the absence of bigotry in this future editor of the *Belfast News Letter*. But communal relations had deteriorated since then and Coleman systematically replaced Stuart's 'Roman Catholic' with 'Catholic'.[81] The Revd James Connolly, who delivered a highly emotional centenary sermon at St Mary's church in Belfast in November 1883, spoke at length of 'the taunt and insults', 'the scorpion sting of calumny', 'the withering sneer of scorn' endured by the Ulster Catholic.[82]

Out of that resentment developed a specifically Catholic reading of history, in which the Catholic is always the underdog, the victim. To a remarkable degree Ulster Catholic culture became one of grievance, each new grievance copper-fastening all those which had gone before. 'It is impossible, without a sinking of the heart', Gamble mused, 'to think of the fate of these generous and warm-hearted, though often misguided and misled people, of their sufferings, their proscriptions, their expulsions, and when actual violence had ceased, of the contempt which unceasingly pursued them – the brutal scorn, the idiot laugh, the pointed finger, . . . which has made past recollection almost predominate over future hope.' The past, he noted, held an unusual sway over their imagination, with present grievances sustained by the memory of past ones.[83]

Modern commentators note similar victim psychologies in contemporary northern Protestants and Catholics alike. These outlooks have lengthy roots, Jacqueline Hill identifying 'beleaguered Protestant' and 'long-suffering' Catholic readings of history from as early as the seventeenth century.[84] Ulster's Catholics and Protestants had long been equally sectarian, with one very fundamental difference. The latter had been in the seat of power for several centuries. Liberal Protestants only tended to support Catholic causes when Catholics were unmistakably the underdogs or when they had a common purpose. However, with the steady rise of Catholic nationalism in the nineteenth century, the Catholic clergy were markedly less concerned about Protestant sensitivities than their predecessors.

The Gaelic revival of the late nineteenth century and associated political developments did not create the notion of the Catholics as the Irish nation proper. That was already a widely held Catholic belief. But it made it fashionable and politicised it in an unprecedented way. It coincided with an explosion of Catholic print-culture and a dramatic increase in literacy as a result of the expanded education system, and it ensured that future Catholic readings of the past would be based as much on the heroes and villains in the popular histories, novels and plays of this period, as on accurate memory.[85] In William Johnston's evocative image of 'Home Rule' being 'Rome Rule', Protestant Ulster expected triumphalistic Catholicism to be in the driving seat of Gladstone's Home Rule Ireland.

The perception of Protestants as foreign usurpers is a long-standing feature of Ulster Catholic mentality. John Donaldson writing in the *Newry Register* for 1818 of the Upper Fews barony in south Armagh, could still speak of the different religious groupings as separate peoples: they 'each . . . retain a portion of their national customs, manners etc . . . [and] have not yet assimilated, so as to form one general character . . . [the Catholics] are extremely jealous with the British and Caledonian settlers, whom they are taught to believe are intruders and foreigners'.[86] The theme was a common one in Watty Cox's racy *Irish Magazine* (1807–15), as was that of the Catholics as the nation proper.[87] Protestants felt sensitive and insecure on the topic, however much they tried to attribute loss of land to Catholic fecklessness.[88] As the Home Rule campaign belatedly got under way in Ulster, its posters calling for 'the land' to be 'restored to the people' – though in reality calling for agrarian reform – were deemed particularly inflammatory by the Orange leaders. Lord Rossmore, county Grand Master of Monaghan, depicted such publicity as 'separatist' and 'communistic' and was only narrowly prevented from orchestrating a bloody counter-demonstration at Rosslea in County Fermanagh (1883).[89]

The common belief that Protestants are somehow un-Irish, not just Protestants, but 'British' Protestants and symbols for all England's wrongs against Ireland, becomes standard in the writings of Catholic priests in the late nineteenth century. But it was simply proclaiming publicly, in a time of more confident Catholicism, a view which had long been held in private. The Young Irelander and editor of the *Nation*, Charles Gavan Duffy, tells of how the senior curate in Monaghan taught him Irish history as a child. He told of religious persecution, of the dispossession of the native princes 'who were Catholics' by Scots and Englishmen; of how the natives were almost 'exterminated' when they tried to reclaim their lands; of how after the Boyne there were passed 'laws designed to exterminate the Irish race', after which they became 'serfs' on the land; of how they were denied education, their priests liable to be hanged for performing religious functions; of how their churches were taken away from them, and of how their humiliation was celebrated in annual processions and 'insulting celebrations'.[90] One of Art Bennett's most bitter poems 'O Gentle Cleric' ('*A Chléirigh Cheansa*'), tells 'of the unrelenting cruelty exercised over conscience by English rulers in order to annihilate Catholicity'. It paints a picture of frightful slaughter, listing the names of clergy who actually did lose their lives and suggesting that no member of any religious order was left alive. It was addressed to Bennett's friend Fr Patrick Lamb of Lower Creggan, and it would be unlikely for him to have presented such a picture, had he not believed that the priest shared his sentiments.[91]

When Ulster Protestants accuse the priests of teaching their people biased history and hatred of Protestants, they have a point, even though their own clergy had been doing likewise for much longer.[92] The post-Cullenite priest was in a powerful position to dictate the shape of emerging cultural nationalism. Anthropologist Lawrence Taylor tells of just such a priest in the 1870s, who, quite against the facts, was able to define himself and the Church as the defender of the oppressed against the *Gall*. John Magroarty, parish priest of Glencolumbkille, County Donegal, was a particularly litigious priest, who engineered his own eviction by his Protestant landlord, and then created his own legend of 'An Sagart – the heroic priest', fighting the cause of the Irish Catholic against the foreign Protestant. 'The discourse', Taylor concludes, 'managed (and still manages) to link a comfortable clergy to the outlaw prophets of Penal times, and keeps class-conscious anti-clericalism at bay.' In other words, the existence of Protestant power allowed the clergy to set up a competing power structure and defeat anything like internal criticism. Taylor encountered a similar situation a hundred years later with another parish priest of Glencolumbkille, who denounced critics from the altar, squeezed them out of employment in Catholic schools and then also portrayed himself as the father of his people in his memoirs.[93] It is important to recognise, however – and he does – that the theme of oppression of the *Gael* by the *Gall* was one widely held by all Catholics. It did not need to be created, even if it could be manipulated.

The world-wide campaign of the Catholic Church against secularism and modernism at the end of the century also added yet another vice to England's villainies, whilst the Catholic Irish had clung heroically to their faith. Father Connolly's centennial sermon at St Mary's made much of this.

Look across the sea at that country which for centuries trod under foot our most sacred liberty – liberty of conscience – and put forth its giant strength to impose upon the people of this land an alien faith at the point of the bayonet, and what a sorry spectacle, religiously speaking, it presents before the nations of the world to-day! England is now a battle-ground for sects, her people, robbed of their priceless inheritance of Catholic Faith, are running after every form of human error ... But you – you, children of Catholic Ireland, you, Catholics of Ulster, you still hold in your midst the sacred and untarnished deposit of Catholic faith.[94]

Likewise O'Laverty's *History of Down and Connor* is replete with comments about the heroism of the people clinging to 'the ancient faith of their race' and assumptions that all Orangemen would come to a sticky end.

In a sophisticated attack on the Catholic ethos of modern nationalism and republicanism, Conor Cruise O'Brien argues that the lip-service paid to Tone's ideal of a 'common name of Irishman' has allowed both to appear non-sectarian and all-inclusive, whereas they are anything but. He points in particular to cultural nationalism's most talented propagandist, D. P. Moran (1872–1936), and draws a direct link to the belief of modern-day Sinn Féin that once you 'de-anglicise' Ireland, Unionists will fall into line and become good Irishmen. He finds too in Moran's newspaper *The Leader* – 'the journalistic flagship of Irish Ireland' – that belief common to all shades of Ulster Catholic opinion, that only Protestants are bigots. 'Just as black racists in modern America think that only whites can be racists, so *The Leader* thought that only Protestants could be bigots: "Why should Irish Catholics try to prove their tolerance when they have never been intolerant? Let those who have been intolerant prove that they have given it up." '[95] By the turn of the century Protestants were no longer welcome as members of the 'Irish-Irelander' wing of the Gaelic revival.[96]

Admittedly Conor Cruise O'Brien's agenda is informed by his conversion to Unionism from a nationalist background, and the main Northern Ireland nationalist leader of contemporary times, John Hume, accuses him of 'paranoia' in this book. In a similar mould is the critique of contemporary republicanism by Ulster journalist Malachi O'Doherty. But both are courageous efforts to draw to the attention of non-militant nationalists the kind of brainwashing behind their own culture which made them unwitting accomplices to republican atrocities. Both single out Catholic education for criticism, particularly as it has been delivered by the Christian Brothers. In the nineteenth century I do not find popular Catholic emphasis on Ireland as an organic whole, divinely ordained to nationhood. Rather there is considerable local pride in Ulster. In the works of both Art Bennett and Hugh McDonnell (Aodh Mac Domhnaill) there is still a sense of competition with the other provinces and a feeling that the Ulster men have always been let down by them. Gavan Duffy also feels himself an 'Ulster man' first and foremost, and rejects the common perception of Ulster in the south as 'the enemy's country; a territory where Nationality could only appear under some decent disguise'.[97] O'Doherty recalls how the largely southern Christian Brothers who taught him 'sneered' at such local and regional identification.[98] It is this regional identity which is sublimated to the national one in nationalist literature and so successful was that change of emphasis that after partition few Ulster Catholics could conceive of a specifically 'Ulster' identity outside the whole island context.

It is the popular school histories of the Christian Brothers which are usually credited with finely tuning the Catholic nationalist reading of Irish history. The early National school readers were very sanitised histories. Indeed, the teachers were supposed to avoid political controversy. This did not stop teachers such as Seamas MacManus imparting their nationalist readings of the past in the 1880s and 1890s. It was from him and his successor as teachers at Kinawley National school in Fermanagh that the local storyteller who provided Henry Glassie with much of his material learnt of the Mackan fight and the time when the Catholics *'were slaves'* and the Protestants *'in control'*.[99] The Christian Brothers' texts were assertively Catholic, Irish and anti-English. Their works were central to the Irish-Ireland movement, glorifying Ireland's Gaelic past and culture. Their literature was by no means confined to use in their schools. Their *Our Boys* magazine (launched in 1914) sold outside the churches and was still regularly taken by Ulster Catholic homes for much of the twentieth century. Their motto of 'faith and fatherland' tripped easily from the tongue of those educated in their schools, as did their dismissal of the more middle-class Catholic schools for not being nationalist enough.[100] Although they sent a number of ex-pupils into the 1916 rising, the Christian Brothers, like the Church generally, were neither militant nationalists nor particularly anti-Protestant. Besides the anti-English rhetoric, there was much of that romantic nationalism which remained the dominant strain in that of Ulster, even after partition, and there is much in Conor Cruise O'Brien's contention that the Catholic Church endorsed and developed the intensely Catholic nationalism of the cultural revival as an antidote to the more inclusive but anti-clerical varieties of both Parnellism and the Fenians.[101] There is an equally compelling explanation voiced earlier by Cardinal Cullen that if you did not give the people constitutional outlets for voicing their discontent, they would drift to unconstitutional ones.[102]

However, the clergy had a somewhat ambiguous relationship with the Gaelic revival. The majority of the bishops, for example, opposed the Gaelic League's campaign for compulsory Irish in the schools.[103] The history of the Irish language in the nineteenth century was one of dramatic decline. By 1851 only 6.8 per cent of Ulster people could speak it; by 1911 only 2.3 per cent (very largely in Donegal and Antrim) – though there were small pockets of Irish speakers in Counties Armagh, Londonderry, Cavan, Monaghan and Tyrone. The clergy themselves played a significant role in its decline and children were punished at the National schools for speaking it.[104] It came to be seen by the people as a badge of inferiority. It was, one elderly lady in Tyrone told the folklorist Michael J. Murphy, equated with 'low intelligence, social backwardness and ignorance, a verbal emblem which an inferiority complex compelled them to treat with derision and contempt'.[105] The Gaelic League was to have more success in the towns than in the rural areas where such attitudes were rife. Francis McPeake, of the famous Belfast family of traditional Irish musicians, remembered Ulster Protestant Gaelic Leaguers – Bulmer Hobson, F.G. Bigger, Roger Casement, Alice Stopford Green – initiating the Gaelic revival in the city. They were in a long tradition of Presbyterian and Protestant Irish-language speakers, which included James McKnight, editor of the *Belfast News Letter*.[106] However, when news of Roger Casement's execution reached the Falls Road in 1916, Paddy the local tram-driver said to McPeake's father: 'Ach we're better without them people anyway' – by which he appears to have meant upper-class Protestants – '. . . you never can trust them.' McPeake's grandfather was not an Irish speaker. But the likes of Bigger and Casement travelled around 'to tell the people that they were Irish in the North', and at Bigger's home in north Belfast there were lantern slides on the O'Neills and the O'Donnells 'because the ordinary people didn't know anything about it'. The Gaelic League succeeded in rescuing the Irish language from its terminal decline. It taught people how to write their names in Irish. But its later republicanism and involvement of some of its prominent members in the 1916 rising began that association of the language with rebelliousness in the minds of Unionists. One Falls Road coal-man painted his name in Irish on his cart, and was arrested.[107]

It had been several centuries since Irish culture was perceived as subversive. For a while after 1798 there was a similar reaction – the blind harpist, Art O'Neill, who had always been patronised by Catholic and Protestant alike, was chided on his journey to Tyrone in 1803 by 'illiterate loyalists' who saw his harp.[108] But on the whole Irish culture was not used for political purposes in the nineteenth century. Nor was the turn-of-century Gaelic revival intended to be. But its aim of de-anglicising Ireland was a perfect fit for militant republicanism. The attempt to de-couple the Irish language from this association with extreme nationalism continues to the present day.

The celebration of Irish peasant culture at the heart of the Gaelic revival firmly associated Catholicism with Irishness. Local priests both transmitted the central ideas of the new nationalism, but also virtually made loyalty to that ideal 'a moral obligation'.[109] The linkage infused the penny pamphlets of the newly formed (1899) Catholic Truth Society of Ireland and made the increasing Protestant rejection all but inevitable. The Gaelic revival sanitised the Gaelic past, discarding anything deemed vulgar or crude. And this pursuit of 'respectability' continued into the collections of the Irish Folklore Commission (established 1935).[110] The Gaelic League and associated Gaelic Athletic Association (which banned English sports) increasingly fell under the control of the Catholic clergy and the association of Protestantism with foreignness becomes a standard in clerical writing.[111] 'Irish' culture had become 'Catholic' culture. 'There is an assumption among locals', the folk-collector Michael J. Murphy was told in Tyrone in the 1950s, 'that only Catholics [were] able to speak it [Irish] and it's subconsciously seen as their own particular code.'[112] Catholics had finally, it seemed, found their own form of 'ascendancy' with which to belabour Protestants and members of their own community who did not sign up to the 'Irish-Irelander' philosophy in its entirety. It was perhaps, as Roy Foster suggests, 'the logical response to generations of English and Anglo-Irish condescension towards "priest-ridden", "backward" Ireland'.[113]

11

CATHOLICS IN NORTHERN
IRELAND 1920–2000

Not since the foundation of Ulster [*sic*] have they been prepared
to contemplate assimilation. They rejected the concept of the state
from the beginning and refused to participate in its institutions
... The inevitable consequence has been that they have drawn
to themselves the very antagonism and suspicion of which they
complain.   Harold Jackson, *The Two Irelands*
                                 (Minority Rights Group, 1971)

It all turns on the question of 'loyalty' ... The Six Counties is a
'loyal' area and it is natural sometimes that 'disloyalists' should
get hurt ... [and] fail to get jobs. And so on. 'Well, they must
expect it if they are "disloyal",' says the outsider. But then the
outsider does not know that the words 'loyalist' and 'disloyalist'
have a meaning all their own in Northern Ireland.

                        'Ultach', 'Orange Terror', 1943

1. Birth of the new state

The state of Northern Ireland came into being in 1921 amid confusion and violence. The continuing IRA campaign provoked similar paramilitarism on the 'loyalist' side, largely in the form of the hastily recruited Ulster Special Constabulary (USC or 'Specials'). But most of the confusion was on the nationalists' side. They remained as split after 1920 as before, and had no contingency plans to deal with the new situation, short of recurrent appeals for help to Dublin. 'Surely this cannot be happening' just about sums up their reaction to partition, and all hopes were centred on the Boundary Commission to rescue them. In the meantime they embarked on a policy of passive non-recognition of the Northern Ireland state. Because of the continuing hostilities in much of Ireland (first with the brutal Anglo-Irish war 1919–21, then with the civil war in the Irish Free State, 1922–3) and the delay in the report of the Boundary Commission, a sense of insecurity and impermanence prevailed. Although the boundary imposed by the Government of Ireland Act of 1920 put some 90,000 Protestants in the largely Catholic southern state, the size of the Catholic minority left in Northern Ireland was far more problematic (430,000 against a Protestant majority of 820,000). In June 1920 local government elections were held under new proportional representation (PR) regulations. As a result Fermanagh, Tyrone, south Down, south Armagh and Derry City returned local councils with Catholic majorities, and they promptly voted their allegiance to the Dáil and the republican government in Dublin.[1]

Protestants in these areas felt vulnerable. Their fears were confirmed by the triumphalist speech of Derry's first Catholic mayor in 230 years, in which he asserted Ireland's right to decide its own destiny whether the Ulster Protestants liked it or not.[2] At the same time the other three provinces were engulfed in the Anglo-Irish war – largely consisting of guerilla IRA activities against the RIC – and while the northern IRA was not as organised as it was elsewhere, its intermittent attacks on RIC barracks (particularly along the border) and other public buildings added to a sense that the embryo northern state was under siege. It also further contributed to the image of Catholics as generically 'disloyal'. In fact, although Joseph MacRory, Catholic bishop of Down and Connor, made a number of highly provocative statements at this time, the clergy and Catholic middle class were opposed to violence and were instrumental in bringing Nationalist abstention from the Northern Ireland parliament to an end in 1925. Even so, reprisals now assumed a familiar pattern. Militant Protestantism, having long seen the institution of Catholicism itself as the enemy, took revenge for IRA attacks on Catholic civilians and church premises. This was 'the doctrine of vicarious punishment,' MacRory declared in his 1922 Lenten pastoral, 'according to which the Catholics of Belfast are made to suffer for the sins of their brethren elsewhere.'[3]

There had already been severe sectarian rioting in Derry City in April and June 1920, and the July funeral in Banbridge of an RIC commissioner shot in Cork sparked off a series of expulsions of Catholics from their homes and workplaces. In Lisburn the shooting of another RIC inspector was followed by the mass burnings of Catholic business premises and the expulsion of almost the entire Catholic community from the town. But predictably it was in Belfast – its traditional lines of conflict already so well mapped – that sectarian violence was worst. Over the next two years sectarian conflict resulted in 453 deaths (37 members of the security forces, 416 civilians – 257 of them Catholic), the expulsion of between 8,700 and 11,000 Catholics from their places of work and 23,000 from their homes – a quarter of the entire Catholic population of Belfast. In addition, some 500 Catholic-owned businesses were destroyed. Very many innocent Protestants also lost their lives, but since Catholics formed only 25 per cent of the city's population, they figured disproportionately among the casualties. In Catholic consciousness it became known as the Belfast 'pogrom' and it left a terrible legacy of bitterness to the new state.

In the charged atmosphere of the time, the inflammatory speeches of the Unionist politicians on 12 July 1920 may well have lit the fuse. On the first full day back at work after the holiday, the 'disloyal' Catholic workers were expelled from the shipyard. Once again many had to swim for their lives, and those who returned to collect valuable tools, or wages owing to them, were brutally beaten. Similar expulsions took place from other traditionally Protestant firms, where Catholics had acquired jobs during the war. Catholic enclaves in predominantly Protestant districts were then attacked and looted. St Matthew's Catholic church and convent in Ballymacarrett experienced semi-permanent siege over the next two years. It was bombed six times and worshippers attacked and murdered.[4] But the incident which has survived longest in Catholic folklore was the killing of the McMahon family in north Belfast. During the night of 24 March 1922, the house of Owen McMahon, a wealthy Catholic publican, was broken into by a group of men reportedly in 'police uniform'. The male members of the family, and a barman who lived with them, were lined up in the sitting-room and shot. The murders were thought to have been in retaliation for the killing of two 'Specials' the previous day. No one was ever brought to justice, but District Inspector J.W. Nixon was rumoured to have been involved with the murder squad. Certainly he was thought too extreme by James Craig's Unionist government, and was dismissed from the police two years later – only to remain a thorn in Craig's side as Independent Unionist MP for Woodvale in the Northern Ireland parliament (1929–49).[5] There were claims that police and military often protected the anti-Catholic rioters and even perpetrated some of the worst outrages. Certainly the image of a police force dominated by extreme Protestants, particularly after the RIC was replaced by the RUC (Royal Ulster Constabulary) in June 1922, was copper-fastened in these years. Police raids on Catholic homes singled out prayer-books and religious objects for particular scorn and Catholic members of the security forces often found themselves objects of attack.

The terrible events of 1920–22 form the backdrop to Michael McLaverty's 1939 novel, *Call My Brother Back*. The MacNeill family has moved from Rathlin Island to Catholic west Belfast after the death of their father. Colm, the young narrator, makes his perilous school journey from west to north Belfast through snipers' bullets and police searches. It is a nightmarish picture: people pinned in their houses by gunfire and curfew, the night-time sounds of armoured cars rushing through the narrow cobbled streets, shuddering the small houses, the screams of victims, the neighbourhood cries of 'Murder, murder', the sight of IRA men shooting from their streets into the neighbouring Protestant ones, the police raids. The MacNeill household is 'done' one night. The British soldiers are courteous. But the policeman is convinced they are hiding guns and when he cannot find any, he smashes the republican pictures. The eldest brother, Alec, is a soccer supporter. But he gives up the football after persistent sectarian riots at the matches and joins the IRA. His mother disapproves. He is a zealot and contemptuous of the 'spineless Hibernians' (the constitutional nationalists in the AOH) who won't talk to the republicans.

The surrounding hills and beautiful views afforded over the city provide a stark contrast to the murderous hatred unfolding in the streets below. At first Colm is startled at the sectarian conflict, which was entirely absent from Rathlin. But as he reads the papers, with their lists of those killed the previous nights, he falls into the Belfast habit of identifying them as Protestant or Catholic. It is instinct rather than prejudice. But his mother is appalled at the change which has come over him since their move to Belfast.[6]

The provisional government in Dublin, alarmed at the attacks on Catholics in the north, did not help matters by partially re-arming the IRA and supporting a boycott of Belfast goods and businesses. Thus was the image reinforced of the new northern state under siege, and the already deteriorating economic plight of Catholics as well as Protestants exacerbated. In the early months of 1922, Michael Collins (chairman of the provisional government in Dublin) seemed to be coming round to recognising the Northern Ireland state in return for measures to involve and protect the Catholic minority. This was increasingly the thinking of moderate nationalists, particularly in Belfast, and their influence helped fashion the second Craig–Collins pact between the London, Dublin and Belfast governments in March 1922. The most significant clauses implicitly recognised the particular plight of the Catholic minority in Belfast. The police there would be reorganised, with Catholics joining the Specials, mixed Catholic–Protestant patrols operating in mixed areas and Catholic ones in Catholic areas.

A Catholic police advisory committee would recommend recruits, a joint Catholic–Protestant Conciliation Committee would investigate outrages and try to prevent melodramatic reports in the press. Even the Belfast IRA seemed disposed to give the pact a trial.

But the opportunities offered by the pact were lost, for the extremes on both sides soon made it unworkable. The final split in the IRA in the south (between supporters and opponents of the Anglo-Irish Treaty and the provisional government), and the onset of civil war saw a re-imposition of the Belfast boycott by the anti-Treatyites. Collins was anxious at Craig's slowness in implementing the pact and his refusal to investigate a particularly brutal set of murders of Catholic civilians in Belfast in April 1922 when, in retaliation for the shooting of a colleague in the vicinity, uniformed police raided Catholic homes in Stanhope and Arnon Streets, killing five people, including a child, and wounding several more. He therefore sought to keep pressure up by sanctioning a renewal of IRA attacks in Northern Ireland in May. Predictably this provoked further reprisals against the Belfast Catholics, making May and June 1922 the bloodiest months of the two years of inter-communal violence and prompting the moderate nationalist *Irish News* to lash out at extremists on their own side for giving the excuse to others to terrorise innocent Catholics.[7] The northern IRA campaign collapsed the following month. Vastly outnumbered by security forces, it had always been ill-equipped and poorly armed, and was nicknamed 'the Rag man's army' in border areas.[8] The bulk of the northern IRA remained firmly pro-Treatyite in its support of Collins. His death in the civil war on 22 August 1922 removed the Ulster Catholics' most powerful protector. Thereafter, the attention of the Irish Free State turned inwards. A peace of sorts descended on the north. But it was one of exhaustion and disillusionment on the minority's part. The Craig–Collins pacts had held out the prospect of peaceful collaboration by the minority with the northern state. Not until the Sunningdale agreement of 1973 was another such effort made.[9]

It would be difficult to exaggerate the damaging impact of the sectarian attacks of 1920–22. Father Hassan, curate of St Mary's in Chapel Lane, and author of the fullest contemporary account of the Belfast 'pogrom' of those years, absolved the city's Protestant population generally from any part in them.[10] For they too now felt the need to move out of areas dominated by people of the other faith and there were large numbers of agreed exchanges of houses between Protestants and Catholics caught in such areas. But the movement had been overwhelmingly that of Catholics into the already bulging Catholic ghettos and when things calmed down after 1922 the mood was one of sullen resentment and introversion. The moderate Patrick Shea, arriving in Belfast for the first time in 1926 to take up a post as one of the very few Catholics in the Northern Ireland civil service, found the city still bearing the scars of the recent troubles:

The Catholics, large numbers of them crowded into streets along the Falls Road, were cowed and dispirited; they had seen riots and death, the burning of homes and business premises, the violent expulsion of their men from the shipyards and factories and building sites. They had stories of murder and cruelty, of the wild exploits of the Special Constabulary, the bigoted outbursts of political leaders. The Protestants had something to say about the involvement of the IRA in the city's troubles but the Catholics discounted any allegations that blame lay on their side. They feared their Protestant neighbours with the anger of people who had been subdued by force and left without any means of retaliating against their persecutors.[11]

The civil war south of the border took much of the pressure off the Northern Ireland government. It moved quickly to abolish proportional representation in local elections, a move so against the terms of the Anglo-Irish Treaty and so blatantly directed against nationalists, that Lloyd George's government withheld approval until obliged to do so by Craig's threats of resignation. This, the imposition of a declaration of allegiance upon local authorities and the redrawing of the local electoral boundaries, halved the number of councils left in nationalist hands. Londonderry County Borough, where Catholics were in the majority and where boundaries were repeatedly redrawn to create a Unionist majority on the council, acquired particular notoriety. Powers of allocating houses and jobs now became heavily biased in favour of Unionists and whilst Nationalist-controlled councils acted in a similarly biased fashion, as David Harkness concludes, 'there were not only more Unionist authorities, but more than there ought to have been'.[12]

Collins told Churchill that such measures to alter the outcome of local elections were designed to convince the Boundary Commission that nationalist areas were unionist. There can be no doubt that the delay of the Boundary Commission simply copper-fastened the uncertainties and divisions in the new state. Catholics fully expected a redrawing of the border which would bring those areas with Catholic majorities, Tyrone, Fermanagh and the border areas of Armagh and Down, into the the Irish Free State, and thereby render the rump state unviable. Patrick Shea recalled such certainty in nationalist-dominated Newry that a Newry unionist had exchanged his house with that of a republican businessman in Warrenpoint.[13] Unionists felt besieged and the pattern of calling and fighting elections on the one issue of 'the state in danger', which would characterise Northern Ireland's elections for the rest of the century, was first established by Craig in 1925. It was only in that year that the delayed Boundary Commission reported, by which stage even the Dublin government, battling with its own post-civil-war difficulties, had lost interest. The leaked report of October 1925 left most of the existing territory of Northern Ireland intact (including Newry, Derry City, Tyrone and Fermanagh). But it also proposed the transfer of small portions of territory from the Irish Free State, chiefly from east Donegal, and since the leak itself caused such a furore, Cosgrave's government in Dublin acquiesced in the ultimate suppression of the report. The border would remain as it was in 1920. The Catholics in Northern Ireland had been abandoned.[14]

2. Securing the state

But with such a large Catholic minority, and such entrenched sectarian fears, Craig's government felt little incentive towards generosity. The police proposals in the second Craig–Collins pact had been put together by a group of Catholic businessmen, led by two supporters of Joe Devlin, shipbroker Raymond Burke and Hugh Dougall, owner of a substantial carrying business.[15] At this stage the terms on which the Catholic minority might work with the new state were still negotiable. Since the pact was never implemented, however, it was in the area of security more than any other that Catholics were made to feel they did not belong.

A third of the RUC was to have been Catholic. In the event only 400 Catholic RIC men transferred to the new 3,000-strong force. At first Catholics were quite well represented among the senior officers (17.1 per cent by 1936), because of the transfer from the RIC. But such transferees encountered a prejudice in the new force which had not existed in the old one. As they gradually retired, fewer Catholics came forward to join and the proportion of Catholics had dropped to 11 per cent by 1963. The force became visibly more 'Protestant' as Specials were given favourable entry conditions, accounting for between a quarter and a third of recruits to the RUC, until the Specials' disbandment in 1970. Increasingly it came to be seen by Catholics as a partisan force, soft on the Orangemen, hard on the Catholics when they clashed.[16]

But it was the Ulster Special Constabulary, established in 1920 and numbering some 48,000 by the end of 1922, which effectively policed the new state. And here lies the problem, for not only were they exclusively Protestant, but they were built from a base of loyalist paramilitaries, the UVF (Ulster Volunteer Force), various Protestant vigilante groups and the Ulster Protestant Association (a loyalist group responsible for many sectarian murders in Belfast).[17] In part it was the authorities recognising the inevitable and gaining some control over the persistent tendency for unauthorised loyalist paramilitaries to take matters into their own hands. Although the IRA was weaker in Ulster than in the other three provinces, it still had 4,500 members in 1921, and, when set against a backdrop of IRA violence in the rest of the country and the withdrawal of British forces to deal with it, the growing sense of Protestant vulnerability is easier to understand. Protestants in border areas, in Tyrone, Fermanagh, Derry City and parts of Armagh, were particularly active in the demand for increased protection. Although the full-time A Specials were disbanded in 1926, the larger part-time force, the B Specials, continued until 1970. They restored to popular Protestantism that supremacy over Catholic neighbours (notably in the rural areas) so threatened in recent years. By mid-1922, over half the adult male Protestant population of Fermanagh had joined the Specials and similar figures were reported from other areas bordering the Irish Free State and where Protestants were outnumbered by Catholics. In addition to a number of revenge murders

of Catholics which they were thought to have carried out, petty intimidation and harassment of Catholics were part and parcel of the history
of the B Specials and their activities tainted the entire police force
in Catholic minds. Moreover, because the force was financed from
London, the impartiality of British justice was seriously affected. In
fact, the very existence of the USC and its blatant lack of discipline
gave such cause for concern in England that an attempt was made in
1922 to bring it under British military supervision. By then, however,
the kind of militant popular Protestantism which it represented was
essential for Ulster Unionist survival, and the notoriously bigoted
Unionist Home Affairs Minister, Richard Dawson Bates, ensured that
the critical reports of the British Military Adviser sent to investigate
the USC were suppressed.[18]

Sir Arthur Hezlet's favourable history of the B Specials, whilst
conceding that the USC was exclusively Protestant, points to Catholic
political and religious bodies actively discouraging Catholic recruitment into the force. This indeed has always been a factor deterring
Catholic recruitment into the police, and in the ghetto areas the IRA
made it positively dangerous to join. The requirement of the oath of
allegiance was another deterrent. Certainly such resistance gave an
excuse to those who never wanted Catholics to join anyway. Selection
committees discouraged Catholics and Protestant Specials refused to
train with them. Thus did the loyalist ethos become established at a
very early stage in the police force. Even the Catholic businessmen,
who had once encouraged their co-religionists to join, now dismissed
it as sectarian. Although the B Specials never again reached the
numerical strength of the 1920s, they did tend to be called out at times
of sectarian disturbances, IRA campaigns and general border scares,
thereby reinforcing the image that they were mobilised against the
Catholics. Their role was often that of mounting road-blocks, check-
points, patrols and searches, giving ample opportunity for that petty
harassment for which they became notorious in Catholic circles. Certainly as early as the summer of 1922, a senior English civil servant,
sent to Belfast to report on the breakdown of the Craig–Collins pact,
was profoundly disturbed by the reputation which the Specials were
acquiring. 'Catholics', he stated, 'regard them with a bitterness
exceeding that which the Black and Tans' – British ex-soldiers recruited

temporarily into the RIC in 1920–21, who gained a reputation for brutality – 'inspired in the south', and even some leading Unionists warned him that 'this purely partisan and insufficiently disciplined force was sowing feuds in the countryside which would not be eradicated for generations'.[19]

Patrick Shea's autobiography shows that not all Unionist ministers were the villains of Catholic imagination. Craig had every intention of ensuring the impartiality of the law.[20] But he let himself be constantly overruled by his Ministry of Home Affairs, where the tendency to defer to Orangeism was all prevalent. Moreover, the emergency situation which had necessitated the Specials also produced the Special Powers Act and this too became a permanent feature of Northern Ireland until its repeal in 1973. This gave the Minister of Home Affairs, and through him the police, extensive powers to detain without warrant, and suspend civil liberties altogether when he thought it necessary. Similar emergency powers had been assumed by the provisional government in Dublin, and it proved far more brutal in suppressing the IRA than did the Northern Ireland government. The difference was that the Special Powers Act and the accompanying internment tended to be used routinely and more severely against Catholics, more 'circumspectly' against Protestants. Between May 1922 and December 1924, the overwhelming majority of the 728 men interned were Catholic, whilst of the twenty-one flogged in prison in 1922 – to the outrage of nationalists and the embarrassment of the London government which tried to persuade Craig to remit the sentences – only three were Protestants.[21]

As John Whyte warned, in his impressive 1983 overview of Unionists' treatment of Catholics, Northern Ireland was not a police state. But he, along with nearly every other scholar who has attempted a dispassionate analysis of security under the Northern Ireland state, found this area the most difficult of all to arrive at the truth. This is because of the maddening pettiness which has always infused everyday attitudes and behaviour in Northern Ireland and pettiness is not well documented. But, as the bitter popular traditions of the penal era show all too well, it is the petty oppressions rather than outright tyranny which impact most on a community. 'Baiting business', was how Daniel Mageean, Catholic bishop of Down and Connor, referred to police activities in 1942, 'multiplied instances of petty persecution, the perpetual pin-pricks of the "where's-your identity-card-from-the-same-policeman-four-times-a-day" variety'.[22] Recalling the beginning of the 1969 Troubles in his home town, Downpatrick, Maurice Hayes, one of the few Catholics to reach the top echelons of the Northern Ireland civil service, observed 'the build-up of aggro' between local youths and the B Specials. 'What you had really was two groups of louts, defined by religion, one lot of whom had uniforms and guns and the power to stop and harass the others on their way home from dances late at night.'[23] The experience of very many Catholics of policing in Northern Ireland consisted of this kind of petty, one-sided harassment by the B Specials. Both the Cameron Commission (1969) and the Scarman Tribunal (1972), reporting on events at the beginning of the Troubles, rejected the more hostile assessments of police activities. But they did find evidence of 'long-standing' sectarianism and lack of impartiality in the force. There had been a progressive improvement of police attitudes after the Second World War. Even so, Whyte concluded that for most of the century the police force in Northern Ireland was 'teetering uncertainly between impartiality and partisanship'.[24]

3. Discrimination

Nationalists boycotted the new Northern Ireland parliament when it opened at Belfast City Hall on 22 June 1921, as they did every other state body including the crucial Leech and Lynn Committees (set up to decide on the future structure of local government and education). This policy of abstention was disastrous, particularly in these early days when things were still open to change. It also absolved the Unionists from blame for the developing bias, since they could legitimately claim that Nationalists had been given the opportunity to influence developments, but refused, and by so refusing simply proved their disloyalty.[25]

The assumption that all Catholics were rebels was to permeate Unionist thinking for the next fifty years. In the violence and uncertainty of the 1920–22 period, emergency measures to protect the embryo state were understandable, as was the ambivalence of very many Catholics towards a state which might not have lasted. However, most Catholics did not actively work against the Northern Ireland state, even though they disliked its political leaders, and there were times like the late 1930s or the 1950s when increasing numbers would have accepted integration into the state had they been given any encouragement. But such a gesture of goodwill had to await the premiership of Terence O'Neill and, just as with many other liberal Unionists in the past, it proved his undoing. With monotonous regularity it was the Unionists with impeccable anti-Catholic credentials who rose to leading positions. It was the one issue on which they were sure of retaining popular Protestant support, and throughout the period 1921–73 urban working-class Protestants continued to vote into power big landowners with whom they had little else in common. Nor is the dismissive epithet 'Orange State' such an inaccurate description. Not all Protestants were Orangemen; indeed many, notably the professional classes, considered the Orange Order an embarrassment. But for Unionist politicians membership was almost mandatory and, as a result, Orangeism exerted a quite disproportionate influence on government.[26] Orange complaints about 'disloyalists' in public employment were made regularly to ministers and were just as regularly taken seriously.

Charges of state discrimination against the minority Catholic community have been the central theme of northern nationalism. Certainly the belief in blanket discrimination produced a highly sensitised victim psychology among Catholics, which has not yet disappeared. Fear of rebuff eventually stopped them applying for certain jobs and those who did risked the old accusation of 'selling out' or of becoming 'Castle Catholics'. Invariably, it was that ever-impeded Catholic middle class that was caught in between. That Catholics were more likely than Protestants to suffer discrimination in Northern Ireland is no longer in doubt. Even pro-Unionist historians accept this. Working-class Protestants, feeling the pinch of unemployment since the 1970s, as their traditional industrial base has collapsed, have been resentful at the implication that all the suffering and all the victimisation has been one-sided. 'We know that things were not right under Stormont and we can never return to that,' one highly respected community worker in the Protestant Shankill Road told the Opsahl Commission in 1993, 'but if we say so, all the wrongs of the past are heaped on our shoulders.'[27] Since the belief in systematic discrimination gave rise to the civil-rights campaign of the 1960s, the immediate background to the Troubles, and still survives in a streak of resentfulness, prickly defensiveness and reluctance to forgive among many Catholics, particularly in the republican community, it is vital to establish how far the accusations are sustained.

John Whyte, one of the most dispassionate writers on Northern Ireland before his untimely death in 1989, examined all the available literature on the issue. His conclusions largely, though not universally, sustain the charges made against the Unionist government that it discriminated against Catholics. Claims that gerrymandering and the abolition of proportional representation disadvantaged Catholics in parliamentary elections are upheld only in the case of Fermanagh and possibly Armagh. In local government elections, however, the Unionist record was bleaker. Here the number of councils in Nationalist hands declined from twenty-three – and two shared equally – to eleven, and these were less important than those held previously. Foremost among the losses was Londonderry County Borough, which had a substantial Catholic majority, and where boundaries were repeatedly redrawn to ensure Unionist control. The usual Unionist defence was that boundaries reflected rateable value of property as much as population. Owners of business premises also had a double vote, and since these were more often Protestants, and since Catholics were traditionally poorer, the outcome was predictable. This Whyte dismissed as a 'dubious defence', for democratic politics does not accept the rule of the rich over the poor and in general he found gerrymandering in local politics 'one of the clearest areas of discrimination' in the history of the state.[28] The Cameron report of 1969 also looked at the traditional Unionist explanation and dismissed it. 'Such validity as this argument ever possessed is one which is rapidly losing any force ... universal adult local government suffrage has for long been the rule in the remainder of the United Kingdom.'[29] A bad-tempered and highly unsatisfactory debate over reputed discrimination against Catholics took place between two American-based academics in the 1980s. Perhaps the only valid point to emerge was the reminder that Catholic families were larger, the stark statistics ignoring the fact that as children many of the Catholics would not have had the vote in any event. Whilst accepting some of these arguments, however, Whyte still reaches the conclusion outlined above.[30]

In 1938 the British government was sufficiently concerned at de Valera's accusations of discrimination against the Catholic minority in Northern Ireland to order an internal investigation. It found the accusations of gerrymandering in the Tyrone and Fermanagh local councils and discrimination in public employment generally substantiated, thought the Northern Ireland government had 'emerged with little credit' in recent cases involving the Special Powers Act, doubted the fairness of educational legislation, and expressed concern at the nature of Unionist party domination of the state.

It is everywhere inimical to good and impartial administration where Government and Party are as closely united as in Northern Ireland. In the South, Mr. de Valera was at one time largely dependent on the I.R.A. for support, but he has been able to throw off his dependence on that body – in a way in which the Government of Northern Ireland have not been able to throw off their dependence on the Orange Lodges. If the Government of Northern Ireland wish partition to continue, they must make greater efforts than they have made at present to win over the Catholic minority, just as on his side Mr. de Valera, if he wishes to end partition, can only do so by winning over the Northern Protestants. At present both sides are showing a lamentable lack of statesmanship and foresight.[31]

It was common knowledge that the gerrymandering also underpinned poor housing and employment opportunities in certain areas. Northern Ireland's housing record was generally poor. Unionist authorities – dominated by deeply conservative rural landlords – were not favourably disposed towards public housing schemes. The government preferred to leave the initiative to private enterprise and this proved woefully inadequate. Until the setting up of the Housing Trust in 1945, public housing schemes accounted for under 8,000 new houses since the foundation of the state. The first housing survey to be conducted in Northern Ireland in 1943 revealed an urgent need for some 200,000 new houses, existing shortages having been exacerbated by the German bombing of Belfast in 1941. The target still had not been met when the Troubles erupted in 1969. It was not so much the appalling shortage of housing which lay at the heart of nationalist complaints, however, as their politically motivated allocation. Indeed, it was the persistence of bad practices into a new era when more public housing was becoming available which fuelled much of the discontent in the 1960s.[32] 'Council housing policy has also been distorted for political ends in the Unionist-controlled areas to which we specially refer [i.e. Londonderry County Borough, and Omagh and Dungannon Urban Districts]', concluded the Cameron Commission. 'In each, houses have been built and allocated in such a way that they will not disturb the political balance . . . There have been many cases where councils have withheld planning permission, or caused needless delays, where they believed a housing project would be to their electoral advantage.'[33] The Cameron Commission's case-histories were taken from areas which had generated most complaints, and not all councils were at fault. But those were areas west of the Bann where Unionist-dominated councils often controlled Catholic majorities, and Whyte, like Cameron, found the case against them largely proven.

Whyte's analysis of discrimination in public employment is equally damning. Since the establishment of the Fair Employment Agency in 1976, a series of reports have shown that Catholics were twice as likely to be unemployed as Protestants. These figures are disputed by many working-class Protestants. They sometimes see Catholics as inveterate whingers and scroungers on the state, perfectly happy to live on the dole. In fact, research has shown that Catholic attitudes to work differ little from those of Protestants.[34] In the past other variants have come into play: lower educational achievements by Catholics, demographic concentration in areas far removed from urban industry, reluctance to apply for jobs in Protestant-dominated sectors such as the shipyard. Even so, Whyte found that discrimination did play an important part in Catholic disadvantage, even though, by the time he was writing, 1983, it was in decline.[35]

Discrimination against Catholics was particularly acute in public employment. A quick glance at the religious breakdown of public service employees reveals a Catholic percentage broadly in line with overall population breakdown. A close look, however, reveals the traditional bunching of Catholics in the lower levels – with 40 per cent of labourers employed by local councils being Catholics in 1951, but only 11.8 per cent in senior posts. Another survey in 1969 found little change. Catholics were also under-represented on other statutory bodies, the more educated finding it particularly difficult to break into the system. 'We are satisfied', the Cameron Commission concluded, 'that all these Unionist-controlled councils have used and use their power to make appointments in a way which benefited Protestants.' Even at the level of school bus-drivers, over 90 per cent were Protestant in counties like Fermanagh where Catholics were a majority. Cameron did find that Nationalist-controlled Newry Urban District employed very few Protestants.

But two wrongs do not make a right; Protestants who are in the minority in the Newry area, by contrast to the other areas we have specified, do not have a serious unemployment problem, and in Newry there are relatively few Protestants, whereas in the other towns Catholics make up a substantial part of the population.[36]

Many reasons besides discrimination have been put forward for the under-representation of Catholics in public employment, and there can be no doubting a definite antagonism within the Catholic community against those who entered public service. 'It was my experience', recalled Patrick Shea, 'that some Catholics, and especially those in Belfast where, I had been told, the Bishop had advised them against seeking Government employment, looked with suspicion on Catholic civil servants. We had joined the enemy.'[37] Unionists told Cameron that there were fewer Catholics in public employment because they did not apply – a claim that was still being made in the 1990s. 'No doubt that is factually true', concluded Cameron, 'but the answering comment, which is made with force and supported in evidence, is that from experience it is realised that an application made by a Catholic would stand no real prospect of success.'[38] Whyte, after examining all the evidence on both sides and accepting some of the Unionist explanations as partly valid, still found the case for discrimination overwhelmingly proven. Patrick Buckland, though he had started out broadly sympathetic to the Unionists in researching his *Factory of Grievances* (1979), reached the same conclusion and argued against ever restoring devolved government to the region.[39]

Even had there not been active discrimination against Catholics, the many sectarian public pronouncements by government ministers and officials would have been enough to deter applications. Much of the surviving evidence on discrimination was not the product of dispassionate government inquiries, but of investigations of numerous complaints from loyalist organisations about 'disloyal' elements in public employment. Protestant pressure groups, particularly the Orange Order, wielded a dominant influence on the structures and policies of the state. It was virtually impossible to be a Unionist politician without being an Orangeman. Every prime minister of Northern Ireland has been an Orangeman and between 1921 and 1963 only three cabinet members were not Orangemen upon election.[40] Orange complaints and delegations were readily received and acted upon, when nationalist ones were dismissed. In 1933 an allegation that the majority of the porters at Stormont were Catholic prompted John Andrews, minister of labour and a future prime minister, to investigate. He was then able to proclaim that of the thirty-one porters he had found, only one was a Catholic and he was only temporary. The following year a Catholic gardener at Stormont was dismissed because of Orange claims that he was a Sinn Féiner, despite his British army record and personal service with the Prince of Wales. Most famously, Home Affairs Minister Dawson Bates refused to have Catholics in his ministry and in 1934, upon learning 'with a great deal of surprise' that a Catholic telephonist had been appointed in Stormont, he refused to use the phone for important business and the telephonist was transferred. James Kelly, remembering his early days as a reporter with the Catholic newspaper the *Irish News*, recalled that one editorial writer's particular task was to scour the Ministry of Home Affairs' Gazette for details of the application of the Special Powers Act: 'A nationalist meeting banned, or another local anti-unionist served with an "exclusion order" . . . an obscure publication or patriotic gramophone record banned.' Bates was said 'to sleep with the Special Powers act and a revolver under his pillow'.[41]

The belief that Catholics stood little chance of entering public employment is well chronicled. The headteacher of the Christian Brothers' school in Newry, attended by Patrick Shea, had stopped entering his bright boys for the Northern Ireland civil service examination for this reason. But Shea applied in any event and no one was more pleased when he succeeded than the same headmaster. The story epitomised Catholic attitudes towards the Northern Ireland state – shunning state employment for fear of being shunned. Shea's lifetime experience in the civil service would confirm some, but by no means all, of the stereotypes. He did indeed, as a Catholic, find himself in a tiny minority within the Northern Ireland civil service.

To many of my colleagues Catholics were strange animals of which they had astonishingly little knowledge . . . I learned of their beliefs about the power of the Pope and his clergy and no words could persuade them that I was not subject to malevolent direction by black-robed priests to whom Rome had entrusted its master plan for world domination. I was astonished to meet youths of my own age who had never met a Catholic until I appeared in the office, who believed, as one of them told me, that in the event of their coming under a Nationalist government the Pope would require his obedient Irish flock to banish the Protestants from the land.[42]

Certainly Shea experienced discrimination and his promotion was impeded because of his religion, only coming under the more relaxed regime of Terence O'Neill in the 1960s. But he also learnt that the discrimination came from the politicians and angered and embarrassed the career civil servants. He singles out Sir Wilfred Spender in particular for his integrity. An Englishman and head of the Northern Ireland civil service until 1944, he is on record as protesting at the anti-Catholicism of the politicians and he particularly disliked Bates. He personally recommended Shea for promotion, but it was rejected by the 'political advisers' because of Shea's religion. Spender (and the other senior civil servants who had supported the recommendation) was angry. 'I thought it only right I should tell you about this,' he said. 'I can only say that I am surprised and disappointed and very sorry.' Shea was happy in the civil service. He found much 'native kindness' there and many in senior positions who would have liked more Catholics appointed. But he felt 'a cuckoo in the nest', Protestants wondering how he had 'got in', and Catholics, particularly those in Belfast, suspicious that he had. 'I was probably a "bad Catholic", perhaps secretly a Freemason . . . [I] had gone over to the "other side".' But although critical of Catholics for being fatalistic and for not always using opportunities that existed, he nevertheless believed that 'very serious discriminatory practices' operated against Catholics in public employment and that both Unionism and the Northern Ireland government were in thrall to the often 'malevolent' influence of the Orange Order. Only then could one explain 'how men for whom one could feel genuine respect could have acquiesced, even participated in, illiberal practices which, in the end, brought discredit on fifty years of government'.[43] Certainly the percentage of Catholics in the civil service had declined since partition and remained at 6 per cent between 1927 and 1959, while only one Catholic achieved the status of permanent secretary before Terence O'Neill's premiership. This was A.N. Bonaparte Wyse, permanent secretary at the Ministry of Education 1921–39, who had transferred from Dublin Castle after partition and travelled back to his Dublin home at weekends.[44]

Cameron was told by one local council that it only employed 'loyal' citizens. This belief that no Catholic could be loyal was the bedrock of Unionist thinking till the 1960s and was deeply resented by Catholics. It was at the heart of Ultach's damning indictment of Stormont in a series of pamphlets in the 1940s and of numerous *Irish News* reports. Ultach's challenge consisted of case after case in which leading Unionist figures, up to and including successive prime ministers, declared Catholicism as incompatible with allegiance to the state.[45] The fact that many of the public statements were made to massed Orangemen on 12 July further endorsed Catholics' sense that Northern Ireland was an 'Orange State'. The most famous of such claims was made by Sir Basil Brooke (Lord Brookeborough, Prime Minister of Northern Ireland, 1943–63). On 12 July 1933, Brooke, then Minister of Agriculture, spoke at Newtownbutler, County Fermanagh:

There were a great number of Protestants and Orangemen who employed Roman Catholics. He felt he could speak freely on this subject as he had not a Roman Catholic about his own place . . . Roman Catholics were endeavouring to get in everywhere. He would appeal to Loyalists, therefore, wherever possible to employ good Protestant lads and lassies.[46]

The speech became notorious and was retold by countless Catholic parents to their offspring. But Brooke refused to retract a syllable when publicly criticised. 'I recommended those people who are loyalists not to employ Roman Catholics', he told the Londonderry Unionist Association the following March, 'ninety-nine per cent of whom are disloyal.' When called upon to dissociate himself from the speech, the Prime Minister (created Lord Craigavon in 1927) simply dug deeper by stating that 'there is not one of my colleagues who does not entirely agree with him'.[47]

'Ultach' cites many instances of such attitudes at every level of the political and justice system and he blamed such 'inflammatory speeches from responsible public men' for the anti-Catholic riots of 1935, a criticism also made by the Belfast City Coroner. The public face of Ulster Unionism did a great disservice to the Protestant community generally, creating the illusion that all Protestants were victimisers and all Catholics were victims. Such 'injudicious public utterances [by Unionist leaders]', commented a 1938 brief to the British Home Secretary, 'seem to have been stored up by the Nationalist propagandists year after year and are constantly being brought forward again.'[48] The internal inquiry into the treatment of Catholics, of which the brief was part, concluded – after consulting the marquess of Dufferin – that 'there was nothing approaching persecution', but Dufferin 'did consider that gerrymandering . . . had taken place and that the attitude of the Northern Ireland Government towards the minority had been illiberal . . . He thought that many Ulstermen shared his view and were uneasy about the attitudes of their Government which had the effect of perpetuating a division which a more enlightened policy might close.'[49]

Though descended from the O'Neills of Antrim and spending long periods at the ancestral home, Shane's Castle, Terence O'Neill was brought up and educated in England. When he came to Stormont as MP for Bannside in 1946, he had a wider British view of Northern Ireland's constitutional position and was shocked at the parochialism of its politics. Predictably that parochialism often took the form of Unionist resistance to British-inspired legislation which might also benefit Catholics. In 1956, efforts were being made by some in the Unionist party to have him unseated as minister of finance, because it was rumoured that he was admitting more Catholics into the civil service. By that stage, however, relations between the two major traditions were improving. There were enough Unionists to support him and his threat to reveal the reasons for a smear campaign against him caused the conspirators to back down. He was particularly critical of Lord Brookeborough, 'a man of limited intelligence', who would never have been a minister in London. O'Neill thought that Brookeborough treated the whole business of government and politics as of secondary importance to hunting and fishing in Fermanagh; 'the tragedy of his premiership was that he did not use his tremendous charm, and his deep Orange roots to try and persuade his devoted followers to accept some reforms . . . [He] played safe. In twenty years as Prime Minister he never crossed the border, never visited a Catholic school and was never received or sought a civic reception from a Catholic town.'[50] This is why, perhaps, he assumed that all Catholics were out to overthrow Northern Ireland by force and why he felt the need to reiterate his views in opposition to O'Neill in 1969.[51]

The provocative statements of the Unionist politicians in the 1930s fed the rising tensions caused by the revival of militant Protestant evangelicalism in the Ulster Protestant League (founded 1931). In 1934 Brooke's call to boycott Catholic businesses was denounced by Nationalist MPs as inviting reprisals. 'Are we to take it', asked Alex Donnelly, Nationalist MP for Tyrone West, 'that it is but a prelude to another pogrom?'[52] Certainly there were ominous hints of renewed sectarian trouble in Belfast. Poverty and unemployment had briefly drawn the Protestant and Catholic poor together in the outdoor relief strike of 1932, when the huge numbers of unemployed in Belfast demanded adequate poor relief outside the workhouse. But this was highly unusual and a build-up of sectarian incidents in north Belfast's Dock ward saw both sides preparing for trouble when the factories closed for the 12 July holiday. As 40,000 Orangemen paraded back to Belfast on the evening of the 12th, there was mutual taunting and riots erupted. Many of the Orangemen had come from outside the area for the annual celebrations and it was a group of Glaswegian loyalists who led one of the most sustained attacks on Catholic houses in the area. For nine days the riots continued, leaving 10 dead, 83 injured and 2,500 intimidated out of their homes.

In the event it was the Catholic populace in mixed areas who suffered most, accounting for some 85 per cent of those displaced. Once again Belfast's sectarian map was redrawn, once again those in mixed-religion relationships were the object of loyalist attack. Catholic families intimidated or burnt out of York Street, the Old Lodge and Donegall Road areas, crowded into refugee huts on the Falls Road and a half-built housing estate (Glenard) adjoining Ardoyne. On the return to work on 22 July, thousands of Catholics were expelled from the mills and the shipyard. This time the employers, who tried to protect their workers, were absolved from any charges of sectarianism, and it was mobs at the gates to the shipyards, rather than fellow-workers, which were responsible for the expulsions. There were also attacks on Catholic enclaves near Portadown. But a number of retaliatory attacks on Protestants in the Irish Free State weakened the Nationalist argument that Protestants encountered no discrimination there. Not all Catholics were forced out of Dockside, for Fred Heatley remembered a return to neighbourly relations during his childhood in the 1940s.[53] But few political lessons were learnt. Indeed, it is hard not to sympathise with the Catholic bishop of Down and Connor, Daniel Mageean, in his dismissal of Ultach's 1943 recommendation that Britain be asked to intercede, for the Bishop had sought political action from London, Dublin and Stormont alike in 1935, but to no avail. Craigavon had taken himself off on holiday to Scotland and virtually ignored the Bishop's protest. De Valera was anxious to improve relations with Britain and made no more than consolatory noises, which Mageean was at much greater pains to excuse than what he considered the predictable lack of action from the Northern Irish and British authorities. The British Government continued its conventional reluctance to interfere in Northern Ireland, despite considerable English pressure to do so and the deployment of British troops during the riots – for the first time since 1922.[54] There had been no significant paramilitary involvement, though the IRA experienced a surge in membership in the aftermath. The combustible potential of Belfast's ethnic frontier zones had once again been demonstrated and once again reinforced, as had the 'ostrich'[55] mentality of the statesmen.

4. *Nationalist politics during the Stormont years*

One of the most fundamental and baffling aspects has been the apparently ineradicable tendency of the minority to attract discrimination. Not since the foundation of Ulster [sic] have they been prepared to contemplate assimilation. They rejected the concept of the state from the beginning and refused to participate in its institutions ... The inevitable consequence has been that they have drawn to themselves the very antagonism and suspicion of which they complain.[56]

So concluded a Minority Rights Group report in 1971, in an atmosphere where old-style nationalism was generally under attack. It is a token of how people can live in open harmony, yet never talk about what really concerns them, that Richard Rose could find 74 per cent of Protestants in 1969 believing that no discrimination against Catholics existed in Northern Ireland and exactly the same percentage of Catholics declaring that it did.[57] Only such a gulf of understanding can explain why the early civil-rights movement was perceived by Unionists as an IRA plot, long before it became just that. There was a terrible circularity of argument in Northern Ireland's political rhetoric, entrapping both communities, Nationalists saying 'we cannot give allegiance to the state because it is anti-Catholic', Unionists 'we cannot give them a stake in the state because they are disloyal'. Here were two absolutes, to which variations were inadmissible. How can the 'ascendancy party' defend its policies to England, asked 'Ultach' in 1943, for by then many Catholics considered England something of an honest broker and were baffled that it did not interfere more forcibly to ensure fair play.

Examine almost any 'defence' ... It all turns on the question of 'loyalty' ... loyalty to the King of England, to the flag, and to the Empire. The Six Counties is a 'loyal' area and it is natural sometimes that 'disloyalists' should get hurt. Riots break out in 'disloyal' areas. 'Disloyalists' fail to get jobs. And so on. 'Well, they must expect it if they are "disloyal",' says the outsider. But then the outsider does not know that the words 'loyalist' and 'disloyalist' have a meaning all their own in Northern Ireland.

He then reproduced endless quotations from Unionist politicians and Orangemen showing that for them '"Disloyalist" and "Catholic" are synonymous'.[58]

So how 'disloyal' were Catholics after partition? It is certainly true that not until the 1960s were Catholics prepared to accept the legitimacy of the Northern Ireland state. But neither did they actively try to subvert it. An IRA campaign of sorts continued intermittently throughout the first forty-five years of the state's existence, though on nothing like the scale of the post-1969 Troubles. However, the bulk of northern Catholics remained, as they had always been, conservative, clerically-dominated, but utterly constitutional nationalists. Until the Boundary Commission reported in 1925 uncertainty reigned in nationalist politics, particularly in those areas thought likely to be transferred to the Irish Free State. Some Nationalist-controlled councils swore allegiance to the Dáil and were dissolved. Others were happy to vote temporary allegiance to the Northern Ireland government. For a while large numbers of Catholic teachers (as many as 50 per cent in Tyrone) were supported in their non-recognition stance by continued payment of their salaries from Dublin. But this was discontinued after Collins's death in 1922 and the Irish government then urged Catholics in Northern Ireland to recognise the Belfast regime.[59] Nearly half a century was to pass before the bulk of Catholics recognised that the border was not simply a temporary and unnatural imposition and demanded their rights as 'UK citizens'. Until then their ambivalence towards the state simply played into the hands of the ultra-loyalists.

For a while in the 1920s there was a co-operative mood among some Nationalist MPs. Backed by the leading nationalist press, most of the Catholic clergy and the Dublin government, the members for Belfast and Antrim decided that abstentionism was no policy at all and took their seats in the Belfast Parliament after 1925. Joe Devlin had been the first to take his seat, and his pragmatism, charisma and experience made the years before his death in 1934 the most favourable for any constructive relationship between Nationalists and Unionists. Most republicans continued to favour abstention and remained antagonistic towards Devlin. But his old Sinn Féin opponent, Cahir Healy, MP for Fermanagh-Tyrone, joined him in restructuring the Nationalist Party. By 1927 it had ten MPs in the Northern Ireland Parliament, leaving two republicans still abstaining. The revamped party promised conciliation and co-operation whilst pursuing nationalist aims. Devlin got on well with Craig. There were even some minor government gestures towards the Nationalists, most famously Craigavon's visit and concessions to the Catholic Mater hospital in Belfast in 1930. But the abolition of PR for parliamentary elections in 1929 was more symptomatic of the new political reality. Sick and disillusioned, Devlin saw himself going in directions which his whole career had fought against. Discrimination and the constant need to pursue purely Catholic issues made him realise that he was leading a Catholic party (and this when he had always been cold-shouldered by the local bishop and cardinal). Finally he led his followers out of the Northern Ireland parliament in May 1932, after delivering a bitter verdict on the Unionist government's treatment of the Catholic minority:

You had opponents willing to co-operate. We did not seek office. We sought service. We were willing to help. But you rejected all friendly offers. You refused to accept co-operation ... you went on on the old political lines, fostering hatreds, keeping one third of the population as if they were pariahs ... and relying on those religious differences and difficulties so that you would remain in office for ever.[60]

Thereafter the Nationalists became part-time MPs, abstaining more often than not, and remaining almost totally absent during the period of the Second World War. They sank into an already well-worn rut of sulkiness and whinging. For this they were to be criticised by northern nationalists in the 1960s and 1970s.[61] With constitutional nationalist politics so directionless, it cannot surprise that the party failed to develop any new vision. After Devlin's death it was deeply conservative, middle class and clerically driven. T. J. Campbell (Nationalist leader 1934–45), was a barrister and former editor of the *Irish News*. His successor, the MP for Mourne, James McSparran (1945–58), was another barrister with *Irish News* (and therefore clerical) connections, and as he handed over the leadership to his successor, East Tyrone MP and publican Joe Stewart (leader 1958–64), he was thanked for upholding 'Catholic and Nationalist interests'.[62] None have left their mark on the history books – although this is also a product of the historical neglect of northern nationalism, with the notable exception of the works of Michael Farrell, Eamon Phoenix and Brendan Lynn.

Within this political world of largely rural and conservative Catholic nationalism, Devlin's former Belfast constituency sat uneasily and after his death working-class areas with sizeable Catholic populations voted for a range of socialist and labour candidates. But these candidates also had to be anti-partitionist, and when the Northern Ireland Labour Party officially accepted partition in 1949, it lost its Catholic support to the newly formed Irish Labour Party. Then, as later, it proved impossible to build a labour movement drawing support from Catholics and Protestants alike.[63]

Catholics in the mid-twentieth century, however, were as conservative and predisposed to authority as they had ever been. Why then should they have so vehemently opposed the very existence of the Northern Ireland state? Why did it take so long for the disappointment and frustration at the time of partition to abate? Part of the answer lies in the continuing territorial link between those predominantly Catholic areas in the western and southern parts of Northern Ireland with the three Ulster counties that had become part of the Irish Free State. Few here would ever have travelled to Belfast. Belfast was the seat of the enemy. Belfast Catholics reconciled their residence in Unionism's capital by a kind of spatial alternative thinking. Protestant Stormont, east Belfast, the shipyards were worlds apart from the other world over the ring of hills – Colin Mountain, Black Mountain, the Cave Hill, which edged the Catholic areas.[64] Elsewhere, the mental world moved slowly from the local parish, to Dublin, to Rome. The regional nationalist press reflects all three. Northern nationalism was extraordinarily confused. Just as their religious leaders would have preferred continued rule from Britain to partition, so territorial unity was more important to northern nationalists than Irish national self-determination. The declaration of a republic by the Irish Government in 1948 was a shock, a token of southern rejection. It was the first time, recalled a retired Catholic academic in conversation with Fionnuala O Connor in 1992, that he and his like recognised that they would have to reconcile themselves to life in the northern state. Until then, they were totally convinced it would not last.[65]

Intermittently Nationalist MPs, when pushed to the limit, would seek permission to sit in Dáil Éireann in Dublin (always unsuccess-fully); would accept political funds from the south (usually counter-productively, as with the disastrous 'chapel-gate election' of 1949, when southern politicians organised collections after Sunday mass to assist anti-partition candidates in the north, thereby providing a propaganda gift to their Unionist opponents); and would further iden-tify themselves with the southern state by sporting the Irish tricolour. Because so many nationalists believed (or, rather, wanted to believe) the political rhetoric in the south claiming an overwhelming desire to unite the six Ulster counties with the republic, they began culturally to think of it as home. Of course it was not and never had been. But above all they wanted to belong to a state and their rejection of and by the northern one caused the identification with the southern state to become a necessary crutch. This was the essence of romantic nation-alism – a psychological need. However, their experience was often one of rejection. Northern Catholics were treated as troublesome and embarrassing by the south, at best lumped together with all the other 'black northerners', at worst treated as far more problematic than the Unionists (the latter tendency predominant after the onset of the Troubles). Certainly Fionnuala O Connor found that those Catholics who still nourished the idea of a united Ireland in the early 1990s 'had inherited a powerful sense of betrayal and rejection by the southern state', often from parents who had grown up in the 1930s and 1940s. 'We are the bastard children of the Republic', the Nationalist leader Eddie McAteer told civil-rights campaigner Dr Conn McCluskey in the 1960s; 'sometimes they must needs acknowledge us, but generally speaking they try to keep their distance'.[66]

But the Unionists were the old enemy, and they held exclusive power for over fifty years after the foundation of the state. Just after Devlin's departure from the Northern Ireland parliament, it was re-housed at Stormont in Protestant east Belfast. Even today it seems entirely over the top, a magnificent, over-sized Portland-stone mansion, completed in 1932 at a cost of some £1,150,000 at the height of the Depression. Craigavon now had his Protestant parliament for his Protestant people, commented the *Irish News*.[67] It was a reference to a speech delivered by Craigavon to Orangemen at Poyntz Pass in County Armagh on 12 July 1932, when he declared, 'Ours is a Protestant government and I am an Orangeman.' He was to reiterate the claim in the Northern Ireland parliament on 22 April 1934.[68] In Catholic mythology the parliament buildings became another symbol of Unionist domination. Nationalists duly boycotted the opening ceremony by the Prince of Wales. And yet the sequel had all the hallmarks of good old one-upmanship. After the opening of Stormont, the Prince of Wales paid a visit to the Mater Hospital in north Belfast. The crowd which gathered was, the *Irish News* boasted, the largest attending any of the events during his stay in Northern Ireland and the hospital's chapel the only place of worship visited by him.[69] For most nationalists, denials of the legitimacy of the state sat incongruously with a desire for participation and recognition. Although the nationalist press reveals an intense dislike of the Union flag as a symbol (largely because of its usage by some Protestants to denote exclusivist loyalism), attitudes to the British monarchy were respectful. In the 1980s and 1990s resistance to the playing of the British national anthem became common among younger, often republican-minded nationalists. But their more con-servative forebears were far more restrained. Catholic councillors were angry at being excluded from the City Hall lunch to welcome Queen Elizabeth to Belfast in 1953. One complained:

The Nationalist people of the city . . . paid more than lip sympathy to this young woman. Their wishes towards her were sincere and good . . . it is a damnable thing and most insidious thing to say we would attempt to insult or injure the Queen. We don't recognise her. But the British people are entitled to have monarchy if they want it.[70]

Civil rights campaigner in the 1960s, Dr Conn McCluskey, recalls being hurt that many Protestants assumed Catholics would not rise for the national anthem: 'My kind of Catholic would never dream of offering a discourtesy to the Queen.'[71]

MPs, local councillors and all other public employees (including teachers) were required to take the oath of allegiance. Nationalist MPs duly took the oath on George VI's accession to the throne in 1936. But it was one of the many areas where nationalists were not pressed too hard. As Maurice Hayes recalls his experience of taking it in the 1940s and 1950s, most Catholics did so, but squared their consciences by taking it before a Catholic JP. His own experience suggests that Protestant JPs were anxious not to offend. With all 'the pomposity' of the young graduate he wanted nothing to do with such double standards. He sought out a Protestant JP, took the oath and declared that were he ever to withdraw his allegiance he would return to inform him.

He looked at me with mounting horror and said he did not think that would be necessary, that it was no part of his function and that, in such a case, he would be better not knowing. We had a pleasant discussion about the novels he remembered from his Edwardian schooldays, and the proprieties had been attended to.[72]

Thus did daily life in Northern Ireland function between the apparent absolutes.

In the end the old Nationalist Party had no role except to 'maintain a protest'. It had no proper party organisation, no policy beyond that of ending partition and defending Catholic interests. In the mid-1950s it was thought to be on its last legs. In the elections for the Westminster parliament in 1955, when the party did not field candidates, there was a major transfer of the Catholic vote to Sinn Féin, not because Catholics necessarily supported the IRA, but because they appeared to be the only candidates able to sustain 'the traditional protest'.[73] The essential parliamentarianism of the Nationalist Party ensured a welcome for Terence O'Neill's conciliatory gestures, and for the first time since partition it agreed to act as the official opposition. It also caused it to misread the signs in refusing to respond to calls for civil disobedience just months before Northern Ireland was swept by civil-rights demonstrations. Eddie McAteer, leader of the Nationalists, was defeated by the civil-rights candidate, John Hume, at the next election for the Northern Ireland parliament in 1969.[74] By then, increasing numbers of Catholics were disillusioned with the politics of old-fashioned nationalism. But it had reflected their interests accurately enough for much of the century.

These then were the 'disloyalists' of Unionist rhetoric. Pure rhetoric it sometimes was and Unionist leaders respected some of the Nationalist MPs. But the Nationalists had put themselves in an impossible situation. They made no secret of their dislike of the state and ultimate ambition to see its demise. This allowed Unionists to dismiss charges that they were penalising the Catholic religion as such, and to assert that their quarrel was with nationalism in its 'political sense'.[75] To some commentators in the 1960s and 1970s it seemed incomprehensible that it had taken nationalists till then to accept the constitutional position of Northern Ireland.[76] However, they were hardly encouraged to do so. What would have happened had that encouragement been forthcoming must remain speculation. Moreover, Unionists were given every reason to think nationalists a threat. Even though most nationalists did not seek to overthrow the Northern Ireland state by violent means, they shared the religion and traditions of those who did: the IRA. Indeed, an IRA campaign of sorts had continued since partition. After 1942 it was largely directed at Northern Ireland and entirely so by the 1950s.

5. The IRA

The post-partition IRA was the direct descendant of the anti-Treatyites, completely dedicated to overthrowing partition by force. It was antipolitical and those who chose a political path, from de Valera to the so-called Official IRA of the 1970s, tended to withdraw and change their name. Once independence had been established, the new Irish state took a far more vigorous line against the IRA than either the British or Northern Irish governments: some seventy-seven members were executed between November and May 1922–3; internment was introduced by successive Irish governments; IRA hunger-strikers were more likely to be left to die in Irish than in British or Northern Irish prisons; and after 1957 the tough measures of de Valera, once one of their own, effectively decimated the IRA in the south of Ireland. He was particularly incensed at their bombing campaign in England in 1939, since he was then involved in delicate anti-partition negotiations. Their meetings were banned and the leaders rounded up under a new Offences Against the State Act, June 1939. The IRA was denounced by the Catholic Church throughout the twentieth century, much as it had denounced previous violent movements. The success of the suppression south of the border shows how limited was the support for the IRA there.[77] But with bombs and volunteers being transported over the border and IRA funerals turning out thousands of followers, the Northern Ireland authorities might be forgiven for not entirely recognising the change of mood in the south.

The northern IRA was marginalised from the national leadership by the 1930s. But so long as sectarian tensions persisted, it played a traditional role of defending the Catholic community against attack, notably during the parading season around 12 July. This was particularly the case in Belfast and it was the attacks on Catholic homes in 1968–9 which effectively recalled it into existence. The riots of 1935 played a similar role and by 1938–9 it had a Belfast membership of 800.[78] The terrible economic conditions of the 1930s produced common suffering and considerable co-operation among working-class Catholics and Protestants. Peadar O'Donnell, the prime mover in taking some members of the IRA in the Irish Free State to the political left, thought only their sectarianism prevented the Ulster republicans from winning working-class Protestants to their cause. He recalled attending a 1916 commemoration in Belfast – traditionally held by republicans at Easter. He had persuaded some Protestants to come along. But when stopped by the B Specials: 'The whole republican procession flopped down on its knees and began the rosary. My Orangemen could have afforded to risk getting their heads cracked with a baton, but they couldn't kneel on the Belfast streets to say the rosary.' The Belfast IRA, he concluded, was no more than 'a battalion of armed Catholics'.[79]

The Belfast IRA developed a new, younger command structure, far more aggressive than that in Dublin. During World War II they ran a republican radio station out of west Belfast, organised symbolic burnings of gas-masks and were partly blamed for assisting the Belfast blitz by refusing to obey black-out orders. The IRA was in negotiation with Germany at this stage and collecting information on British military bases. There were a number of isolated attacks on the RUC and one IRA man was hanged in September 1942 for killing a policeman in Belfast. Internment was re-introduced for the duration of the war, with 243 interned by 1942.[80] In that mental framework which has ever been a part of Irish republican tradition, the IRA blamed the erosion of their campaign on traitors and informers. But the war was a time of shared suffering, particularly in Belfast: bomb attacks by the German air force on Protestant and Catholic working-class districts indiscriminately killed over 1,000 and wounded hundreds more, destroying workplaces and 53.5 per cent of the city's housing. Clonard Monastery gave refuge alike to people from the Shankill and the Falls. Once-crowded areas seemed eerily silent as an estimated 100,000 fled to the countryside.[81] The arrival of 120,000 American servicemen in 1942 brought jobs on their bases and excitement as international stars like Glen Miller and Bob Hope came in their wake. It was more difficult to depict the war as England's difficulty when such a friendly nation was involved. By the late 1940s the northern IRA had almost totally disintegrated. The support in the Catholic community, on which it relied, no longer existed.

Paddy Devlin, one of the founders of the SDLP and a future minister in the 1974 power-sharing executive, was an IRA man in this earlier period. His was not a particularly republican family. Indeed, his mother was an ardent supporter of Joe Devlin and he remembered fisticuffs between nationalists and republicans. But they lived on that ethnic frontier zone between Protestant and Catholic enclaves of west Belfast. There were family traditions of attacks from Protestants dating from the nineteenth century and more recent ones from the 1920s and 1935. Paddy Devlin joined the Fianna, a republican youth movement. These were a form of ideological boy scouts, which aspired to transform basic ghetto-defensiveness into a kind of spiritual martialism along the lines of the mythical ancient hero, Cú Chúlainn. Membership (which Paddy had from the age of eleven) raised even the most puny boy's prestige. Classes indoctrinating the boys in a particular brand of Irish history were punctuated by real drilling after Sunday mass. When war broke out in 1939 their teenage commanding officer, with all the pomposity of youth, told them that their time had arrived, for England's difficulty was Ireland's opportunity. They were ordered to daub the gables with suitable slogans. Paddy lied about his age and gained admittance to the IRA at fifteen. Contrary to Unionist belief in Catholic 'disloyalty', he found the IRA very generally disliked in west Belfast and people all too ready to give information to the police, who still walked the beat there.[82]

By early 1942 the Belfast IRA had all but faded away. In the post-war period the benefits of the British welfare state were progressively implemented in Northern Ireland, adding a new propaganda weapon to the Unionist case for partition – and one which Catholics found increasingly difficult to answer. These were the 'Quiet Years' and the historian Jonathan Bardon criticises the Unionist government for not taking the opportunity to offer some concessions to the nationalist population.[83] But it was matched by equal intransigence in the south, for with de Valera out of power after 1948, all political hues vied with each other to show their patriotism on the issue of partition. In the north the early 1950s witnessed a number of skirmishes over parades and flags. The result was a new series of Public Order Acts and the 1954 Flags and Emblems Act. This was to prove a long-running sore with nationalists, since it gave special protection to the Union flag, heightening the sense that its sometimes provocative use had state approval. A restive IRA group had broken away, and its leader, Liam Kelly of Pomeroy, County Tyrone, had built up a sizeable personal following. The climate was perfect for an IRA comeback. However, the fate of their renewed campaign (1957–62) showed yet again that the majority of northern Catholics eschewed violence.

But this would not have been immediately apparent to the authorities. There had been a number of small IRA raids and explosions and a noticeable increase of tensions along the border. It was partly to control such actions by splinter groups that the IRA launched its 'Operation Harvest' on 11 December 1956, with attacks on public buildings all over Northern Ireland. Over the next five years the newspapers regularly carried reports of IRA attacks. This time Belfast figured hardly at all, most IRA activity being confined to Tyrone, Fermanagh and Armagh. The campaign was a total failure, though characterisitically republicans tried to pull some kind of moral victory from defeat. Notable was the attempt on New Year's Eve (1956/7) to bomb Brookeborough police barracks and the consequent deaths in an exchange of fire of IRA men from the Irish Republic, Sean South from Limerick and Fergal O'Hanlon from Monaghan. Their deaths became immortalised in a popular song and massive crowds turned out for their funerals in the south. Taoiseach John Costello publicly denounced the IRA attacks and lost the support of some members of his unstable coalition government as a consequence. But outrage greeted the murder of an RUC constable at Forkhill, County Armagh, the following July. De Valera, Costello's successor as Taoiseach, re-introduced internment and swooped on IRA men in the south. In 1957 internment was re-introduced in Northern Ireland. By 1961 there was only a hard core of some thirty to forty IRA men still active. The northern campaign had continued intermittently, but was sufficiently low-key for the last of the internees to be released in the south by 1959, and in the north two years later. Even so, there had been some 600 'incidents', considerable destruction of property and a significant number of deaths. It had sustained the image of the Catholics as murderously disloyal and provided the backdrop to the rise of Paisleyism.

In fact, this IRA campaign of 1956–62 had failed largely through lack of Catholic support. The IRA admitted as much in its statement calling off the campaign on 26 February 1962:

TO THE IRISH PEOPLE

The leadership of the Resistance Movement has ordered the termination of the Campaign of Resistance to British Occupation launched on December 1956 ... Foremost among the factors motivating this course of action has been *the attitude of the general public whose minds have been deliberately distracted* from the supreme issue facing the Irish people – the unity and freedom of Ireland.[84]

The IRA campaign had been condemned all along by the nationalist press and by the Catholic bishops, the bishop of Clogher perceptively catching the essence of the dilemma when the campaign opened in 1957:

That there is obstinate and subtle discrimination against Catholicism and Nationalists in the separated counties we are painfully aware. Nevertheless the opposing elements in our nation ... constitute the people of one indivisible country, and nothing short of extreme provocation would justify a resort to violence ... The border is not merely a geographical division. It is a spiritual division of minds and hearts which physical force cannot heal, but only aggravate.[85]

6. The O'Neill Era

There is a tendency to think of the premiership of Terence O'Neill (1963–9) as one of the great might-have-beens of recent Irish history – like Grattan's Parliament two centuries before, a regime apparently moving to heal its religious divisions, being derailed by the extremes on both sides. There are indeed many parallels, and no regime is so vulnerable as when it is reforming itself, for it raises expectations unlikely to be met in their entirety and the subsequent falling out sends the regime back into its shell. Despite Terence O'Neill's plummy accent and nervous, haughty ways, his arrival as Ulster's Prime Minister (after Brookeborough's resignation in 1963) seemed to match the mood of the sixties. Not only did he embark on an apparent whirlwind of regional development, but for the first time a Unionist Prime Minister made religious reconciliation part of government policy. Catholics had never forgiven Brookeborough his anti-Catholic statements of the 1930s and many came to see O'Neill as some kind of saving hero. That was his problem. It was hardly traditional Unionism and it left too many Unionists uneasy and ultimately hostile.

The legislation that established the welfare state in post-war Britain came to Northern Ireland in the various health and insurance acts of 1946–8. There was still some Unionist reluctance to share all its benefits with Catholics. The Health Services (Northern Ireland) Act of 1948 did not contain that clause of the 1946 British National Health Service Act, whereby hospitals with religious links could maintain their character within the health service. The Catholic Mater Hospital in Belfast was accordingly excluded from state funding. Such reluctance was also evident in the abortive attempt to reduce family allowance to larger (more typically Catholic) families in 1956. In education there was some Unionist grumbling at the apparent generosity of the 1947 Education Act towards Catholic voluntary schools. The following year the liberal Unionist Education Minister, Colonel Hall-Thompson, was forced out of office in favour of the former socialist, but now virulently anti-Catholic populist Unionist, Harry Midgley, to the dismay of civil servants in his department.[86] Even so, things were getting markedly better for the average Catholic. Northern Ireland's chronic housing shortage was beginning to be addressed, and the scrupulous fairness of the Housing Trust (established 1945) in allocating housing has been recognised in every social survey. Sadly, the new mood was not also reflected in the housing record of all local councils, one of the main reasons for the emergence of the Northern Ireland civil-rights movement in the late 1960s. Some 125,000 new jobs had been created in Northern Ireland between 1950 and 1969, many in the service industries, a traditional area for Catholic employment. Ominously, this made little difference to unemployment which was always higher than in Britain, for the industries on which Ulster had built its reputation – engineering, shipbuilding and textile manufacture – were in decline.[87] These were traditionally Protestant areas of employment and, unfortunately for O'Neill, there was no Protestant working-class 'feel-good factor' to match that of the Catholics during his premiership.

When he came to power, however, the omens were good. The IRA had just called off its campaign and admitted its failure to win Catholic support. The reforming papacy of John XXIII, the presidency of John F. Kennedy (the first Catholic, and one with Irish ancestry, to reach the White House), placatory gestures by the new Wilson government in London and a change of political opinion in Dublin were all adding to growing Catholic self-confidence. The media also played an important role in changing public perceptions. In retrospect critics like to see BBC Northern Ireland's early productions as anodyne. But this was simply making a policy of Northern Ireland's unwritten rules of social engagement: never raise controversial topics in mixed religious company. Its coverage in these years was scrupulously balanced. Northern Ireland's main daily newspaper, the *Belfast Telegraph*, had been moving steadily from its traditional Unionism to a centrist position. The young Cal McCrystal, later to become a top political reporter with the broadsheet press in England, recalled his appointment in the 1950s to its staff straight from Belfast's prime Catholic school, St Malachy's. He could tell that the interviewers genuinely wanted to appoint him. But his very Gaelic-sounding name (Cathal) appearing on its political columns would raise traditional Protestant hackles. So he was gently nudged to spell the name as it was pronounced and was duly appointed.[88]

O'Neill saw reconciliation as a fundamental part of his modernisation policies. He already had something of a reputation as one of the few Unionist ministers who would not block the promotion of Catholics. Patrick Shea finally won promotion under O'Neill, after waiting fifteen years for it.[89] O'Neill sent condolences to Cardinal Conway on the death of Pope John, visited a Catholic school, opened a civic reception in a nationalist town, invited two Irish premiers to Stormont, starting with Seán Lemass in January 1965. Nothing like this had ever been done by a Unionist leader. Nationalists took note. For the first time since the foundation of Northern Ireland the Nationalist Party agreed to assume the role of official opposition. The *Irish News*, after generations of anti-Unionism, swung behind O'Neill's efforts. In the general election of November 1965, some Catholics voted Unionist for the first time.[90] Surveys of voter behaviour in Belfast the following year showed Catholics more prepared to accept existing political arrangements than ever before. But although most Unionists seemed to favour the new conciliation, their words did not translate into actions. Nothing was being done to involve nationalists' representatives in existing institutions. Indeed, for four successive years one of the most moderate of Nationalist aldermen on Belfast City Council, Charles Daley, had been refused a chairmanship on its least important committee.[91] Richard Rose's 1967 pilot survey for his exhaustive 'Loyalty Survey' of the following year found respondents confused about O'Neill's policies.[92] Moreover, O'Neill's 'modernisation' programme contained some remarkable blunders. Most of the new economic development was going to predominantly Protestant areas in the east. Three issues in particular showed considerable insensitivity towards nationalists: the 1965 siting of a new university in the small Protestant town of Coleraine, rather than the predominantly Catholic, economically-depressed second city, Derry, which already had in Magee College the nucleus of a university; the naming of a model new town in County Armagh after Craigavon the same year; and the equally insensitive suggestion of 'Carson' – Unionist leader at the beginning of the century, closely associated with the threat of militant opposition to Home Rule – as the name for the new bridge over the Lagan.[93]

But the main challenge to O'Neill's concilation policies came from within his own camp. He had not been the Unionist party's first choice as leader and his most bitter recriminations after his downfall were reserved for Unionist rivals, notably Brian Faulkner.[94] His aloof, English manner alienated many, as did his reluctance to jeopardise his conciliatory policies by discussing them in advance with his party. Outside Stormont Ian Paisley was playing on traditional Protestant fears. Today the Revd Ian Paisley is a senior politician, commanding a huge popular vote at every election. But many hold him personally responsible for wrecking almost every attempt at fair government in Northern Ireland since the 1960s. His fundamentalist Protestantism sees Catholicism as the supreme evil, every drift towards conciliation part of popery's evil plot. His is an apocalyptic vision whereby Protestantism is fighting its last stand in Ulster. His Old Testament biblical imagery, and lurid images of popish persecution, appeals to that part of the Protestant psyche which genuinely fears the Catholic Church and the Irish Republic, with its claims over the whole of Ulster (only abandoned in 1999) and its dominant Catholic ethos. The decline of the Protestant population south of the border from 11 per cent before partition to 4 per cent by 1961 was used as irrefutable evidence of the end product of political popery.[95] The normally ultra-compassionate Dervla Murphy was shocked by the messianic violence of Paisley's sermons when she visited his church in 1976. She felt she had encountered pure evil. The only other occasion on which she experienced similar feelings was in the presence of an older, relatively prosperous guru of the Provisional IRA (the militant breakaway group in 1969, which went on to dominate the movement and was largely responsible for IRA activities throughout the Troubles).[96] Paisley came to symbolise for Catholics all that was wrong with the Northern Ireland state; whilst the Provisionals or Provos became the living symbol of Paisley's claims about the murderous threat of political popery.

Paisley first came to public notice in the 1950s, founding his own Free Presbyterian Church in 1951, 'rescuing' a young Catholic girl (Maura Lyons) from the popery of her parents in 1956, participating in the activities of the ultra-Protestant organisation 'Ulster Protestant Action'. The combination of the new ecumenism of the 1960s and O'Neill's invitation to southern leaders brought the Unionist prime minister into Paisley's gallery of enemies. His followers stalked O'Neill, waving placards: 'O'Neill must go', 'O'Neill the Real Enemy of Ulster', provoking riots and demonstrations not only against O'Neill but any other public figure or organisation guilty of ecumenism or dealings with 'popery'. The authorities clearly did not quite know what to do with him. Convicted in July 1966 of unlawful assembly and breach of the peace, he welcomed imprisonment and relished the martyr status which it gave him. As ever, the extremes fed off each other. Widespread republican rallies for the fiftieth anniversary of the 1916 rising produced Paisleyite counter-demonstrations and excessive deployment of armed police. That summer a young Catholic barman was murdered by the revived UVF, in an attack that was seen by Paisley's critics (and admitted by one of those convicted) as the direct outcome of his sectarian rhetoric. O'Neill was forced to invoke the Special Powers Act against Protestants, an action which further contributed to growing Protestant nervousness.[97]

One wonders if O'Neill would have survived had the traditional Catholic endurance continued through this period. As it was, Catholic restiveness at the slowness of reform took far longer to materialise than the Protestant backlash and in many ways was provoked by it. As Charles Carter wrote in 1972, when revising his and Denis Barritt's path-breaking study of ten years earlier, Catholics at first held their breaths on O'Neillism. This was not the Unionism they were used to and as the Paisleyite backlash gained momentum 'evidence suggested that there was little change at the grassroots of Unionism: that, whatever Captain O'Neill might say or do, the reality of what would happen would in the long run be nearer to what were then considered to be the wishes of the Revd Paisley'.[98]

In the western parts of Northern Ireland, where Catholics were more numerous, there was little to show for O'Neill's modernisation. In February 1967 unemployment in Derry City was 20.1 per cent, against a British average of 2.6 per cent and a Northern Ireland one of 8.1 per cent.[99] Some Unionist-controlled local councils had a record of neither building nor allocating houses in Catholic areas. O'Neill had begun an overhaul of local government which would eventually undermine such local Unionist autonomy. But a new breed of professional Catholics, frustrated by the negative whinging of traditional nationalism, had already started to demand equal rights within the state. Dr Conn McCluskey, a Catholic GP in Tyrone, who with his wife, Patricia, founded the Campaign for Social Justice (CSJ) in 1964, tells of older nationalist leaders dismissing their new approach, finding it incomprehensible that they could actually trust Unionists to deliver. Indeed, as they set about gathering statistics, wooing journalists, and most of all ensuring that English MPs were kept informed, they found the same traditional nationalists critical that they had so far accepted the system as to actually use the name 'Londonderry', instead of 'Derry', as preferred by nationalists![100] The instruction of the British political establishment had vastly improved with the election of the charismatic Gerry Fitt as Republican Labour MP for west Belfast in 1966. Lord Cameron criticised the authorities in his 1969 enquiry for misreading the CSJ and later civil-rights movement as somehow dangerously political:

These organisations concern themselves with immediate social reforms, such as opposition to housing and job discrimination by Unionists, support for universal adult franchise in local government elections and fairer electoral boundaries in local government. They are not concerned, as organisations, with altering the constitutional structure of Northern Ireland, and in this sense represent a quite new development among Catholic activists.[101]

In 1967 the McCluskeys' low-key efforts developed into the Northern Ireland Civil Rights Association (NICRA). As Lord Cameron was later to conclude, it arose largely because of the failure of normal politics in Northern Ireland. It had started out in the early 1960s with Patricia McCluskey's campaign to secure even low-standard prefabricated publicly-funded housing for needy Catholic families in the Dungannon area, where the two Unionist-controlled councils had a reputation for discrimination against Catholics and where efforts to secure redress through normal legal channels had proved fruitless. It was on the housing issue that the civil-rights campaign first broke through to attract widespread media attention. In June 1968 Austin Currie – Nationalist MP for East Tyrone – squatted in a council house in Caledon village to highlight the injustice of its allocation to the young secretary of a local Unionist candidate, when large Catholic families, living in squalor, had been repeatedly refused council housing. The media attention focused on these events at Caledon provided the impetus for the public marches which came to mark the civil-rights campaign and which started symbolically in Dungannon that August. This after all was 1968. The demand for 'civil rights' was mobilising vast crowds from Czechoslovakia to Mississippi.

But marching was never a neutral activity in Northern Ireland. Home Affairs Minister William Craig was already making the usual Unionist assumption that NICRA was a front for the enemies of the state (a claim which Cameron utterly dismissed). When the Apprentice Boys of Derry called a counter-march to that planned by the civil-rights campaigners on 5 October, Craig banned the latter. Why the authorities so consistently opposed these early peaceful demonstrations baffled many, even the Presbyterian Church in Ireland asking as much.[102] The 2,000 making their way to Dungannon in August dispersed when stopped by a police cordon. Now in Derry some of the original civil-rights leaders, including the McCluskeys, wanted their march called off.But this was the most economically depressed, most gerrymandered city in Ulster. The civil-rights campaign had unwittingly stirred up the resentment of centuries; 'we're not going to take this any more' just about summed up the mood, and the march went ahead. Even Eddie McAteer, leader of the Nationalist Party, joined the march, as did Gerry Fitt and three Westminster MPs, John Ryan, Russell Kerr and Anne Kerr.[103] Inexperienced at handling such situations, their manpower low after successive cuts, the police over-reacted, batoning and beating the unarmed demonstrators and spraying powerful water-cannon even over innocent bystanders. But the image flashed not only around the province that evening, but around the world (the first time international media attention had been focused on Northern Ireland) was of blood pouring from Gerry Fitt's head and vivid examples of police brutality.

Huge numbers became politicised overnight. The new term was just starting in Queen's University in Belfast, a relatively placid, even politically apathetic institution till then. But within a few days some 3,000 – including a number of academic staff – had mobilised for a peaceful protest march from the university to Belfast city centre. A short distance from the university the lawful student march was re-routed by police to avoid a counter-demonstration by Paisleyites, and then brought to a standstill within sight of its destination by the same

Paisleyites. For three hours the students sat in the rain as police and Paisleyites continued to block their route. It was one of the many occasions when police were noticed to stand with their backs to the loyalist protesters, while facing the peaceful and legal marchers. That evening those who had made it back to the university formed People's Democracy, from which emerged sociology student Bernadette Devlin as its most charismatic leader. Initially, People's Democracy was a radical extension of the civil-rights movement, but its tactics eventually played into the hands of those most anxious to destroy the movement altogether.

By now Northern Ireland was becoming badly destabilised. Civil-rights protests were continuing despite Craig's ban on 'non-traditional' (i.e. non-Orange) parades, and Paisley was mobilising increasing numbers against them. O'Neill was summoned to Downing Street and told to speed up his reform programme. On 22 November 1968 he announced a programme of reforms which granted most of what the civil-rights campaigners had been demanding: Londonderry's gerrymandered local authority was to be replaced, local authorities were to adopt a fair points system in allocating housing, an Ombudsman was to be appointed. On 9 December in a widely-viewed television broadcast, O'Neill appealed for the space to carry out further reforms without the increasingly provocative demonstrations. The response was overwhelming, some 150,000 messages of support and the media across the border in the republic voting him man of the year. NICRA called off its campaign and even his critics in the Unionist party seemed supportive. But a small portion of People's Democracy decided to keep up the pressure, against the wishes of most of its student supporters. During the Christmas vacation PD activists decided on a march from Belfast to Derry, in the belief that the Unionists could not be trusted to continue the reforms without such pressure. Certainly it would be another three years before O'Neill's promised reforms were forthcoming. But in the event this small, bedraggled group of student protesters helped destroy emerging Catholic confidence in O'Neill, because the excessive loyalist reaction did indeed seem to prove that Paisley and not O'Neill was still the authentic voice of Unionism.[104]

About eighty students set off from the City Hall in Belfast to march to Derry on the morning of 1 January 1969. Craig did not think the march sufficiently dangerous to ban. But all along the way it was harassed by loyalists, and at Burntollet Bridge outside Derry it was subjected to an orchestrated and bloody attack, in which, as subsequent inquiries proved, off-duty B Specials took a prominent part and the RUC seemed more in sympathy with the attackers than the victims. Attacks continued when they arrived in Derry and the RUC rampaged through Catholic areas in the city. As violence increased, moderates retreated into their traditional corners. O'Neill tried desperately to rally the middle ground in a snap election in February 1969. He was returned, but his mandate was not large and Paisley had fought a damaging campaign against him in his own constituency. A contemporary analysis of the election found traditional party structure very fragmented, but 'the sectarian divisions' unshaken. Anti-O'Neillism among Unionists was strongest in those areas where the Catholic presence was greater and in Protestant working-class constituencies, which would have lost most from civil-rights reforms. Although votes cast for pro-O'Neill candidates were more than double those for his opponents (pro-O'Neill twenty-four Unionists, anti-O'Neill twelve Unionists and three independent Unionists), Catholics had not been won over.[105] It was too small a mandate to go on forcing unwelcome reforms on his party and, when a number of explosions took place, many were convinced that Paisley and Craig had been right after all and that the civil-rights campaign was simply a Trojan Horse for the IRA. Later revelations showed the explosions to have been the work of loyalists determined to bring O'Neill down. They succeeded all too well and O'Neill resigned on 28 April 1969.

By then almost all the demands of the civil-rights movement had been granted and O'Neill himself admitted that its campaign had produced the kind of reforms which normally it would have taken government a decade to produce. He had also established the Cameron Commission to report on the reasons for the 1968 disturbances. There were queues outside Her Majesty's Stationery Office on the morning of 12 September 1969 when it reported.[106] The report was well disposed towards the civil-rights movement, generally absolving it from accusations that it was a cover for republicanism. Whilst it recognised that the RUC was in no way as sectarian as the USC, it nevertheless found it guilty of 'grave misconduct' and 'malicious damage' in Catholic areas in Derry. But most of all Cameron, in the words of O'Neill himself, 'blew sky high' 'the faithful [Unionist] Party line' that it did not discriminate against Catholics.[107] The Cameron Report found all the claims of discrimination made by the civil-rights movement to have been substantiated and, significantly, it found very many 'responsible' Protestants recognised this 'and called urgently for remedy'.[108]

The genuineness of O'Neill's reformism has been doubted by some commentators.[109] Others think Brian Faulkner, a more talented politician, should have succeeded Brookeborough. But all of this is to overlook the contribution of O'Neill to a real climate of hope in the 1960s which allowed many Catholics to identify with Northern Ireland, often for the first time. Here was a decent man who did not play the Orange card for political gain. It would have taken more time than was available to O'Neill to entirely remove Catholic mistrust of Unionists. But some Catholics did join the Unionist party in his day and there are few moderate nationalists who do not remember the O'Neill era without nostalgia. His problem was that despite his genuine Ulster roots – he really could claim descent from the ancient O'Neills – he never quite seemed to belong, never quite recognised the niceties and pitfalls of intercommunal living in Ulster. Even some republicans, however, credited him with trying. One Belfast IRA man told Dervla Murphy in 1976:

'We couldn't wait forever while O'Neill was pussy-footin' about trying to keep Paisley calm. He was a fool of a Prime Minister. Brave enough though, I'll say that for him. There was a time back in the sixties when a whole crowd of his own lot were itchin' to bump him. But he stuck with his principles, for all the good they were to anyone. Too much namby-pamby Eton carry-on. That kinda crap's no good in Belfast. He always went on like he was in London. Paisley could knock him flat with a look – and often did.'[110]

7. The Troubles

Whatever people at the time thought of the 'Burntollet' march – it had been opposed by the main civil-rights movement and many student supporters withdrew in its aftermath – it had achieved what some of its more radical leaders had sought. It had shown the bankruptcy of the Northern Ireland state and was a preliminary to its swift disintegration. In 1969 all the undercurrents which had gone to create that fearful and suspicious part of Ulster mentality suddenly exploded.

In Derry the battle between the police and the Catholic Bogside had continued intermittently since the beginning of 1969 – each case of over-reaction by a desperately overstretched police force (and there were a number of them) adding to the emotional time-bomb. By the time the traditional 12 August Apprentice Boys march passed along the walls overlooking the Bogside, the riots which ensued could have been predicted. Nothing had been done to take the heat out of the 'marching season' and there had already been ugly incidents elsewhere. There were hooligan elements spoiling for a fight. But the trigger seems to have been the tossing of pennies by Apprentice Boys, though a longstanding tradition, from the walls on to the Bogsiders below. It symbolised hundreds of years of Protestant contempt, and the area exploded. For three days a running battle was fought with police and there were supportive riots right across the province. In Belfast they assumed the all-too-familiar pattern. The *Sunday Times* Insight team reported:

In Derry a Catholic victory was always possible, for the Catholics have a local majority. In Belfast, on the other hand, the Catholics are outnumbered and hemmed into their ghettos: traditionally, the Belfast Catholics have seen themselves as hostages for the good behaviour of their co-religionists elsewhere.[111]

And so indeed did subsequent events enter Catholic folk-memory: another 'pogrom' on the Catholic ghettos, just as in the past, and again one in which the forces of the state seemed to have sided with their attackers. But this underestimates the real sense of fear and uncertainty which often lies behind the undoubted bully-boy tactics of elements of loyalist paramilitarism. That they really do fear and hate Catholics is beyond question. But they had been told by their political leaders that Catholics were out to destroy all that they stood for and the civil-rights movement was just another cover for the IRA. For years they had been experiencing their own economic recession, as the industries which had traditionally employed large numbers of Protestants, notably ship-building, went into terminal decline, while Catholics seemed to be getting better off. The demoralisation of the police in these months reflected that of their community. The misfortune is that both acted as if all Catholics were rebels.

In good civil-rights fashion, several hundred marchers had set off up the Falls Road to the Springfield Road RUC station on the evening of 13 August to present a petition against police action in Derry. But the inspector on duty refused to accept it, sending them instead to a station near Divis Street, at the lower end of the Falls, from where they had come in the first place. As they arrived at Divis Street, hooligans on the Catholic side stoned and petrol-bombed the police station, although the protest had been largely peaceful until then. But by all accounts the police panicked and unleashed armoured cars, armed with machine guns, on the area. The following day the B Specials were deployed. Not only did this action incense nationalists, but it created an impression on the neighbouring Protestant Shankill Road that the Divis Street riots were the prelude to a republican invasion of their area. That evening Catholic hooligans taunted the massed Protestants, waving tricolours and chanting the Irish national anthem the 'Soldier's Song'. Protestant mobs then invaded, torching Catholic houses in the streets connecting the Falls and Shankill. In the mêlée the RUC machine-gunned the Catholic Divis Flats and killed two innocent bystanders. There was similar police muddle in the north Belfast enclave of the Ardoyne, where Catholics were also being burnt out of their homes. The following night another Catholic street on the traditional frontier zone between the Falls and the Shankill – Bombay Street, near Clonard Monastery – was burnt out, the Protestant mob believing, with some justification, that they were being attacked by gunmen from within the monastery's precincts. It was the start of several years of intimidation which forced between 30,000 and 60,000 out of their homes in Belfast, further increasing the sectarian division of the city. An estimated 80 per cent of these were Catholic. Not all such intimidation during the Troubles was by 'the other side' and a distinctive feature of later years was increasing intimidation by paramilitaries within their own community. But there can be no doubt-ing the importance of such early intimidation to republicans' self-image as protectors of the Catholic community.[112] In the first days of the Troubles Catholics expelled from mixed areas elsewhere in the city poured into the already over-crowded Falls district – most with no possessions but the clothes they wore. Not all became IRA supporters, but such suffering explains the ambivalence of large numbers of ghetto Catholics towards the IRA (particularly in the first decade of the Troubles), for they might be needed again as defenders – at least that is what they were told by the emerging Provos.

There was no IRA organisation in Belfast at this time. The old – soon to be called the 'Official' – IRA had abandoned 'the armed struggle' and become socialist. They had recognised the legitimacy of the Belfast and Dublin parliaments, sought reform rather than revolution, and were largely content with the way the civil-rights movement was operating. Against accusations that NICRA was a front for the IRA, Cameron generally absolved the recognisable IRA members from any role in the riots.[113] In 1969 the IRA was called back into existence as the traditional defender of the Catholic ghettos. As slogans 'IRA – I ran away' appeared on gable walls, those leaders who had been discontented at the way in which the organisation had been moving took over. The people in these Catholic ghettos, some of the poorest areas in Northern Ireland, had little time for Marxist theorising by the Officials. The 'Provisionals', as they were now called, offered the traditional right-wing, pious national-ism and quite simply good old-fashioned defence. The feud between them and the Officials continued for several years. Amazingly, security intelligence was so poor in these early years of the Troubles that the military targeted the Officials rather than the emerging Provisionals, effectively undermining the former and recruiting for the latter. The Provisionals also found covert support from within the Irish Republic's Fianna Fáil government. Agriculture Minister Neil Blaney and Finance Minister Charles Haughey were sacked (May 1970) and later tried (September 1970) for alleged involvement in an illegal attempt to send arms to Northern Ireland.

The British army, when first deployed in Derry and Belfast in August 1969, was welcomed by the Catholics, in whose eyes the police had been totally discredited. Indeed, after further investigations the B Specials were disbanded in 1970, and the RUC disarmed and placed under the control of the military commander. This had provoked riots in the Protestant Shankill, which seemed to justify Catholics' complaints about the partiality of the police. But sending young, heavily armed soldiers, with little local knowledge and no experience of civil disturbance, into ghetto areas, with existing social tensions and high male unemployment, was a recipe for disaster. Being roughed up at the point of a soldier's rifle was more often than not an initiation rite into the IRA. Paddy Devlin, since February 1969 Northern Ireland Labour Party MP for Falls, watched with dismay as such tactics recruited for the Provisionals. Interestingly he spoke highly of the local RUC officers at this time, who were increasingly becoming the scapegoats for the army's mistakes.[114]

Several disastrous security decisions were taken after a Conservative election victory in England in June 1970 ushered in a more hard-line approach. That no effort was being made to curb provocative Orange parades for a second year running further enflamed the situation. During the last weekend of June, Orange parades from all over Belfast converged on the troubled Shankill Road–Crumlin Road area, some passing the recently burnt-out Catholic streets. There were gun battles between the two sides and riots all over the city. The army retaliated some days later by placing the Lower Falls under curfew. For an entire weekend the area was cordoned off by the army; homes systematically raided, often with gratuitous violence, and large amounts of CS gas utilised. An arms' haul was indeed made. But otherwise the exercise was a disaster. There were five civilian deaths, seventy-five injuries, 'outright communal hostility' against the army in the whole Falls area and an eight-fold increase in Provisional recruitment by the end of the year. The Lower Falls had been one of the few remaining strongholds of the less threatening Official IRA. When the curfew was over two Unionist ministers – one the son of Lord Brookeborough – were toured round the devastated Falls by the army. If anything else was needed to convince people that this was a replay of Unionist and security force collusion to crush the Catholic ghettos, this was it. Future Northern Ireland Ombudsman Dr Maurice Hayes, who held the post of Chair of the Community Relations Commission at the time of the curfew, writes with unconcealed anger at this event – a stupid decision, conducted by stupid leaders, political and military – which he sees as one of the disastrous turning points in the Troubles.[115]

It now became a vicious circle – misguided security decisions feeding the IRA machine. The most disastrous of these was the introduction of internment in August 1970. Both police and army commanders were against it. But the IRA had now resorted to what was to become their preferred weapon – the bomb – and the security chiefs could offer no alternative. Internment had been used before, most successfully by the Dublin government, but so recent was the upswing in recruitment into the Provisionals that sound intelligence was lacking. Accordingly it was largely old IRA members and their relatives who were initially taken. Between 9 August 1970 and 5 December 1975, 2,158 were interned. Very many internees emerged hardened republicans and as word leaked of torture of internees (for which Britain was later condemned by the European Court of Human Rights) another wave of riots and violence was unleashed. Thousands more were put out of their homes, this time many Catholics fleeing over the border to be housed in camps made available by the Irish army.

It was one of the many anti-internment marches which produced 'Bloody Sunday' in Derry (30 January 1972). Although, as I write, there is yet another public inquiry under way to establish exactly what happened on that day, it looks as if the soldiers may have over-reacted to the taunts and missiles of a youthful Catholic crowd and shot dead fourteen unarmed civilians. It was incidents such as this which recruited for the IRA and deterred Catholics from standing up to its hoodlum activities in their own community. 'Bloody Sunday' became one of the defining movements for a younger generation of republicans. That the IRA went on to become the most ruthless, callous and efficient terrorist movement in modern times should not detract from the early mistakes made by the authorities which helped it on its way. Notwithstanding bombing campaigns in England, the main theatre of the Troubles remained those same crowded streets of Belfast that had witnessed the main sectarian disturbances in the past. Over the next thirty years two frightened, defensive and resentful working-class communities systematically terrorised each other. In the first twenty years of the Troubles, there were 924 fatalities in north and west Belfast (586 Catholic, 338 Protestant) almost four times as many as in Derry or Armagh/Newry – the next in scale – and over a hundred times as many as in neighbouring north Down. By 1993 working-class north

Belfast, with some 600 fatalities, had become the blackest spot in Northern Ireland for sectarian murder.[116]

After 'Bloody Sunday' the British government suspended Stormont and imposed direct rule (March 1972). Working-class Protestants believed they had been on the losing side since the beginning of civil-rights movement. They saw nationalist areas – many for the first time – flashed on their television screens. They had long been told they were better-off than the Catholics. Now they saw housing which was no worse than their own, their traditional industries declining, low levels of educational achievement, the population of working-class Protestant areas declining whilst neighbouring Catholic ones were bursting at the seams.[117] In addition they saw their traditional protectors, the B Specials and the Stormont regime, vilified and then abolished. The vacuum created after 1972 (and there were similar occasions in the 1980s and 90s) produced some of the bleakest moments of the Troubles. Random and brutal sectarian murders made ghost towns of city centres after dark. Places of amusement closed down, and mass fear trapped people (particularly those young men most likely to be both the recruits and the victims of the paramilitaries) in their own areas. And yet, even in the very first years of the Troubles, the fundamental lesson had already been learnt: no stability could exist in Northern Ireland till the nationalist community was brought into the political system. The state of permanent opposition had bred a sense of alienation and frustration among the old nationalists. It was this sense of powerlessness (even when times seemed to be getting better) which lay behind the violence.

8. Nationalist politics 1970–99

The civil-rights movement was the first experience very many Catholics had of participatory politics. In 1970 it spawned a coming together of constitutional nationalists and other non-Unionist groups in the Social Democratic and Labour Party. The old Nationalist Party slowly withered. The initial leadership of the SDLP brought together a formidable array of talent. The two most experienced politicians were Paddy Devlin and Gerry Fitt. Both were working-class Belfast men, with strong socialist leanings and republican roots. Indeed, Devlin had been interned as a member of the IRA in the 1940s, but had long since renounced violence. They were both popular with British politicians for their gutsy, down-to-earth approach, and Gerry Fitt, as West-minster MP for West Belfast since 1966, had played a major role in breaking down the convention that Britain should not interfere in the internal affairs of Northern Ireland. Austin Currie was Nationalist MP for East Tyrone, credited with kick-starting NICRA's campaign of direct action. Paddy Wilson was a Republican Labour Senator. The other three had emerged through the civil-rights movement: Paddy O'Hanlon, Ivan Cooper (the only non-Catholic among the founders) and John Hume.

The SDLP was an unprecedented alliance of rural and urban consti-tutional nationalism. The product of the new mood of the 1960s, its policy was to work within the existing structures and its MPs were to be full-time politicians, unlike the old Nationalist Party. But in the disintegration of political structures and rapid communal polarisation caused by the Troubles, the kind of political participation by Catholics sought both by the SDLP and by successive British governments proved more and more elusive. The problem was further compounded by a dilemma at the heart of the new party's stand on the constitutional issue. Despite some flirtation by the SDLP with the idea of a negotiated independence for Northern Ireland, its aim of Irish unity by consent has remained one of its most consistent policies. However, this necessarily involved participation in and recognition of the legitimacy of the Northern Ireland state, a dilemma only resolved with the acceptance of power-sharing in 1973.[118]

Britain's policy after partition had been to steer clear of embroilment in Northern Ireland. Terence O'Neill recalled the British Prime Minis-ter's surprise that he should have expected to talk about anything other than the weather. At the outset of direct rule from London there was appalling ignorance of the niceties of the situation, and throughout the Troubles too great a tendency to see it merely as a security problem. But as time went on, information improved as did the calibre of the teams of politicians and senior civil servants sent over. Sadly – in retrospect – the most exciting initiatives came in the very early days of direct rule. In October 1973 Maurice Hayes (the first Chairman of the

Community Relations Commission) was called in for advice by Ken Bloomfield – then under-secretary at the Northern Ireland Office. He was told that the NIO was opening negotiations with the SDLP, but knew nothing about them. He wanted to learn. Hayes reflected:

Here were people, elected members of parliament, some of whom . . . had been around for years, yet they had rarely, in the days of government at Stormont, met government ministers or senior civil servants . . . This might be said to reflect their failure as an opposition. More seriously it reflected the failure of successive governments to accommodate, much less encourage a responsible opposition.

For the next two hours they spoke about the different strands of opinion in the Catholic community and the 'politics of accommodation'. The SDLP were being looked upon as 'the spokesmen of an oppressed people, as the best bet to avoid a descent into anarchy . . . and as men whose time had come'.[119] And so indeed it appeared. In elections for a new Northern Ireland Assembly in June 1973, and with proportional representation restored, the SDLP, with 22 per cent of the vote and eleven seats, had emerged as the dominant voice of nationalism in Northern Ireland.[120]

The Hayes–Bloomfield conversation was one of the opening moves in what became the Sunningdale Agreement and the power-sharing executive of 1974. The Heath government in London recognised that no solution was possible without recognition of the so-called 'Irish dimension' – nationalists' desire to involve the Irish government in some way – whilst the Dublin government in turn recognised, for the first time that century, that there could be no re-unification of Ireland without the consent of the majority of people in Northern Ireland. Both were major shifts in policy and the concept of power-sharing with an Irish dimension has remained the bedrock of British policy ever since. It was on this basis that, in January 1974, nationalists entered government in Northern Ireland for the first time. The six SDLP ministers made a point of choosing portfolios in those areas which had exercised the civil-rights movement, and reforms were on the way which might, in time, have transformed some of the more contentious elements of northern life. Potential investors were clearly impressed at being greeted by both a Unionist chief executive (Brian Faulkner) and an SDLP deputy (Gerry Fitt), whilst John Hume as minister of commerce had made a successful start on what was to become his own particular mission: transforming Irish-America's misguided support for the IRA into investment in the Northern Ireland economy. Indeed, the teamship and professionalism of the power-sharing executive surprised even themselves. Brian Faulkner, its leader, had been something of a hate figure among Catholics, as the hardline Unionist who had forced Orange marches through Catholic areas in the late 1950s and later engineered the demise of O'Neill. Yet he now won the respect of the SDLP, and many in retrospect recognised him as the most talented politician Northern Ireland had ever had. Paddy Devlin, by his own admission a rough diamond, developed a particular fondness for Faulkner. He recognised that Faulkner was being asked to swallow too many nationalist demands at once and might not be able to bring his party with him.[121]

In fact, a unified Unionist party was no more, with the largest number of unionist people now supporting an array of anti-Sunningdale splinter parties. Like Ian Paisley, now leading his own Democratic Unionist Party, most wanted a simple return to majoritarian rule and disliked sharing power with nationalists. But the Council of Ireland, which was to give the Dublin government a share of executive power in Northern Ireland (without any corresponding concession on those clauses in the Irish constitution which laid claim to its territory) was simply unacceptable to the general body of Unionists. Faulkner's supporters were heavily defeated in a general election, called unexpectedly by Prime Minister Edward Heath on 28 February 1974. The timing was disastrous – before the executive had time to prove its worth. The final coup came in a most extraordinary display of loyalist strength – the so-called Ulster Workers' Strike of May 1974. It was orchestrated by loyalist paramilitaries, but with the support of large numbers of Protestant workers. The directing committee also contained a number of Unionist politicians: Ian Paisley, Harry West and Bill Craig. The strike succeeded in bringing Northern Ireland to a standstill, much to the satisfaction of the IRA, which, according to Brian Faulkner's memoirs, was actually assisting the Ulster Workers' Strike by intimidating the largely Catholic workforce at the Derry power-station and preventing them going to work. Progressively all the essential utilities were closed down, roads blocked, businesses forced to close. When its organisers threatened to swamp the cities with raw sewage, Faulkner resigned. The leaders of the strike later admitted that it would never have gathered momentum had the security forces been moved against it. Ironically, security was one of the areas reserved to London under direct rule and the recently arrived Labour Secretary of State for Northern Ireland, Merlyn Rees, chose not to confront the leaders of the strike – even though Brian Faulkner had asked him to do so.[122] Certainly the whole episode marked an appalling abdication of responsibility by Wilson's Labour government. But lessons were learnt, and when another strike was tried in 1977, swift military action brought it to a premature end.

Politically – although many efforts have been made since – no one has come up with a better answer to Northern Ireland's difficulties than that found in 1974.[123] The Good Friday [Belfast] Agreement of April 1998 involves the same principle of power-sharing with an Irish dimension. Because it is operating in a climate of relative peace, it just might succeed. If Sunningdale could have delivered peace, it too might have lasted. But its failure added yet another element which would have to be accommodated – paramilitary politics. The SDLP and Unionists can now work constructively together. But the failure of the first power-sharing experiment created a political vacuum from which Sinn Féin in particular emerged to threaten the constitutional nationalists.

In time direct rule from London came to be accepted as the least unpleasant of all the options, if rarely anyone's first choice. But it gave Northern Ireland politicians no direct responsibility for the running of the state and no opportunity whatsoever of participating in any change of administration in London and inevitably spread the irresponsibility of permanent opposition to all Ulster politicians, nationalist and Unionist alike. The demoralising effect of this on the foot-soldiers – those who did the constituency spadework, but with little chance of rising to any position themselves – was becoming particularly notice-able in the SDLP, as a revived Sinn Féin (the political wing of the IRA) began to eat into its natural constituency. The success of Sinn Féin can be traced to the political outcome of the 1981 hunger strikes by republican prisoners in Northern Ireland, in which ten died. Even supporters of the IRA had shown that they did not like mindless killing or civilian casualties and the new strategy – proclaimed at the Sinn Féin *ard fheis* of November 1981 – of the 'Armalite' and 'the ballot box' was popular. But they were never again able to mobilise the emotional Catholic support which they had done during the hunger strikes. Indeed, very many Catholics were angered by the clear 'moral blackmail' which they had exercised at that time and far more bitterness existed between Sinn Féin and SDLP supporters than between any of the groupings on the Unionist side.[124] But after the hunger strikes, the thought of Sinn Féin becoming the voice of northern nationalism was enough to frighten London and Dublin alike into rescuing the SDLP from the doldrums. The outcome was the New Ireland Forum of 1983–4 (which involved a wide-ranging rethink of Irish nationalism's response to the problems of Northern Ireland) and the Anglo-Irish Agreement of 1985, involving the Irish government in the search for a solution. Needless to say, both provoked Unionist anger. But they had achieved one of their key purposes in restoring credibility to constitutional nationalism.

The SDLP had started out with southern financial backing; this and its tendency to see its natural partners as successive Dublin governments had always provided a hostage to Paisleyite rhetoric about the 'pan-nationalist' threat to the very existence of Northern Ireland. But although the Forum still endorsed re-unification as nationalism's ultimate goal, and the Anglo-Irish Agreement recognised the Irish government's role by actually giving it an executive presence in Northern Ireland, both marked a major alteration in nationalist thinking about the majority Protestant population in the north. No longer was the central problem seen to be partition or the British presence, but rather the conflict of two identities, which would have to be resolved before any change in Northern Ireland's constitutional status could take place. It also restated the 1974 position on power-sharing. It was a great victory for John Hume and over the next few years it helped restore the SDLP to its position as the main voice of northern Catholics. Peter O'Hagan, an SDLP councillor in Lisburn, remembered its impact on the moderate Catholics whom he represented. He had been involved in civil-rights activities since the early 1960s, one of 'the "poor bloody infantry" . . . who has slogged through the Troubles at the SDLP's grassroots, and occasionally come close to despair . . . "Give-up time was the '79 to '85 period". But then came the Anglo-Irish Agreement. It was "unbelievable".'[125]

The Troubles divided Catholics in Ulster as never before. Hume has often baffled and infuriated some of his followers. Indeed, Fitt and Devlin were lost to the SDLP at an early stage because of its apparent retreat backwards to old-fashioned nationalism, for which Hume was often blamed. Brian Faulkner found the Belfast SDLP less 'Dublin-orientated' than its rural (and Derry) supporters. Derryman John Hume he described as 'a formidable political thinker with great personal integrity but a sometimes exasperating dogmatism'.[126] Republicans disliked the SDLP as too middle class and too church-orientated. John Hume denounced them as 'whingers', wallowing in their victimhood. As the Troubles polarised people according to religion, and the old Labour vote (notably in Belfast) collapsed, Sinn Féin became the voice of the Catholic working-class ghettos. But the SDLP – and particularly John Hume – has given most Catholics what they so desired: respectability, recognition and political clout. The fall of the power-sharing executive in 1974 had shown that the involvement which they had so craved would never be conceded unless there was peace. Time will tell whether John Hume's high-risk strategy (embarked upon in 1993, but with a precedent in 1988) of bringing Sinn Féin out of the political wilderness, will pay off. Power-sharing is now on the books again, only this time with the potential for finally neutralising the physical force tradition in nationalism, for it also encompasses the 'men of violence'. But it was already neutralised in the 1960s and it is hard not to reach the conclusion that the awful trauma of the last thirty years – which has so fortified that tradition – need never have happened.[127]

I2

A RESENTFUL BELONGING: CATHOLIC IDENTITY IN THE TWENTIETH CENTURY

[A] man of about fifty, poorly dressed . . . began to air all the old obsessions . . . 'I could tell you where the land that was ours is, away below in the Co. Down – and rich planters gettin' fatter on it every day and talking all the time about the lazy Taigs who wouldn't work for a livin' but go drinkin' on the dole!' . . . It was impossible to unhook Gerry from the past; he seemed to need his grievance, to have built his whole personality around it . . . so much resentment – generations of resentment, forming the very marrow of his soul.   Dervla Murphy, *A Place Apart* (1978)

Since the outbreak of the Troubles, society in Northern Ireland has been analysed as never before. These studies make bleak reading. They confirm how attitudes developed several centuries ago have become fixed. Religion is a very public weapon. In the 1961 census only 384 in a population of 1.5 million did not accept a religious identity. There has been a decline in weekly church attendance among Catholics, from the 95 per cent in 1968, to 86 per cent in 1989, and overall an increasing number of people willing to admit 'no religion'. Even so, in 1994 scarcely anyone from a Catholic background professed to having no religion.[1] Converts are not easily integrated into their new community, for they carry the cultural baggage of their upbringing. Yet the studies also show great variety within the underpinning religious and cultural categories, and above all a widespread recognition of shared prejudice. This explains the black humour which is such a feature of Northern Ireland and the following of comedy acts like the Hole in the Wall Gang, a group of four Queen's University graduates, whose humour is based on Northern Ireland's stereotypes and obsessions. At some of the bleakest moments of the Troubles it has allowed us to laugh at ourselves. Dervla Murphy caught this aspect of Ulster life perfectly in the mid-1970s, a time of particularly acute fear.

It is impossible to be gloomy for long in Belfast. I was feeling rather depressed one afternoon when I turned a corner and saw on the gable-end the familiar NO POPE HERE. And underneath, in different coloured paint, LUCKY OLD POPE![2]

Likewise within hours of the issue of the Patten Report on policing (September 1999), North Belfast's gable-wall artists were at work.

Overnight 'Disband the RUC' murals became 'Disband NIPS' – the setting up of a Northern Ireland Police Service being Patten's key recommendation – confounding those not in the know, amusing those who were.[3] Comedy indeed has been one of the few areas which uses sectarianism to rise above it, one of those 'modes of reassurance' that emphasises 'shared or interchangeable experience'.[4]

1. Northern Ireland stereotypes

In March 1993, David McKittrick, one of Northern Ireland's most respected journalists, produced a startling report on the levels of segregation in Northern Ireland. He found that half its residents lived in areas which were over 90 per cent one religion (often reflecting a three-fold increase during the Troubles), that less than 110,000 of its 1.5 million populace lived in truly mixed areas and that even these might be divided by the so-called peace-lines (twenty-foot-high reinforced walls to keep Catholic and Protestant – at their own desire – apart).[5] The Opsahl Commission, which reported that same year, found ample evidence of such self-imposed segregation in working-class areas, with young males in particular fearful of travelling outside their own community, even to take up much-needed employment.[6] There are also considerable communal pressures deterring people from selling property to members of the opposite religion, thereby intensifying spatial segregation.[7] Direct intimidation there undoubtedly has been. There are particularly high levels of intolerance in predominantly Protestant areas to Catholics living there. The attempt, at the beginning of the Troubles, to intimidate Mary Beckett's fictional 'Belfast Woman' out of her home in the Falls/Shankill frontier zone, simply followed a pattern already set in 1921 and 1935. Her fictional account finds ready evidence in reality, though this particular feature of Belfast is not always replicated across the province.[8] But direct intimidation is only part of the story. More often it is the anticipation of such that sends families to the perceived safety of their own communities. They are influenced by the stereotypical view of how the other side will behave.

Catholics are very quick to sense a slight. It is a touchiness developed through centuries of being considered and treated as inferior. Mrs McFadden, recalling her youth in early twentieth-century west Belfast, told of how she was sent by the 'Boru' (the labour exchange or job centre) to a job in a mill in Protestant north Belfast. It was little over two miles from her home, but it was foreign territory. When asked by her new employer 'what are you', she defensively replied 'an RC', when the man had simply wanted to know whether she was a fine or coarse spinner.[9] At the other end of the century, Martha's emotional support for the IRA in Mary Beckett's *Give Them Stones* (1987) had come from her hope that in a united Ireland 'the Catholics wouldn't be despised any more and we could have a bit of confidence in ourselves'.[10] Since there was a long history of Catholics being deemed inferior in Ulster, it is not surprising that such attitudes should have become part of the fabric of the post-partition state. The anything-but-extreme Patrick Shea – after a lifetime in the Northern Ireland civil service – recalled the patronising of Catholics by Unionists:

The Catholics of Northern Ireland did, of course, benefit in many ways from the Government's progressive legislation; any fair-minded person would be bound to admit that in material things they would not have fared so well in a united Irish Republic. But when Unionists point to these benefits and ask why Catholics did not more actively support the Government, they talk as though the Protestant community has been sharing its wealth with the less well-deserving. (This attitude was outrageously typified by the comment of a schoolmaster in my presence; "We should never have given them Maynooth'.) [Catholic seminary, founded 1795 by the exclusively Protestant government.][11]

It was a sentiment echoed as recently as 1996 by a member of the Northern Ireland Conservative Party, who complained about 'this lawless and ungrateful minority', who had been in receipt of 'the largesse of our country'.[12] Little wonder then that the advent of the welfare state and attendant educational reforms should have increased this tendency. Protestants, particularly poor Protestants, tended to view these as gifts from *their* state, the British state, to which Catholics were most reluctant to give allegiance. The sight of all those Catholic university students on civil-rights marches touched a raw nerve among working-class Protestants with no tradition of sending their children into higher education: 'They'd taken the State's money for grants to get themselves educated at university, and repaid it by fomenting trouble', an unemployed loyalist from Londonderry complained in 1993.[13] This sector of Northern Ireland's Protestant population is embittered. They feel they have lost out through the anti-discrimination measures, fair-employment legislation and a host of other reforms arising from the civil-rights campaign. All this talk of discrimination working-class Protestants consider as typical Catholic whinging. They do not believe the statistics which show that one is still twice as likely to be unemployed if Catholic. Whilst Catholics and Protestants are more alike on a range of social issues, Catholics are more likely to attribute social evils to 'injustice', Protestants to 'laziness', 'drinking' and 'too many children'.[14]

The historic Protestant stereotype of Catholics was reinforced by developments in the twentieth century. This is what Ken Heskin, in an intriguing early study of the Troubles, has called the concept of the 'negative reference group', against which Protestants and Catholics alike define themselves in Northern Ireland. But it is the Catholic Church and religion itself which is the most common 'reference' point in an otherwise diverse Protestant community. Anti-Catholicism is an important defining element in Protestant identity, as it was throughout Britain. The fears of 'political popery' are still very much alive, the fragmentation of northern Protestantism exaggerating the view of Catholics as an undifferentiated and threatening mass, in thrall to their priests and pope. At its extreme it has produced the 'religious pornography' of the Paisleyite *Protestant Telegraph*.[15] Even the more highly developed community activity among Catholics, though envied by some community workers in working-class Protestant areas, is perceived as part of this herd instinct.

A series of focus groups were organised in 1992 as part of the Opsahl Commission. In Belfast and Counties Derry, Tyrone and Armagh, every group, whether Catholic or Protestant, expressed an over-riding desire for peace. Even so, every Protestant group had the same perception of the power of the Catholic Church. It was the Church, they believed, which dictated the size of Catholic families and taught 'perverted history' and 'hatred of Protestants', and whilst these

Protestants supported integrated education, they feared Catholic teachers might inculcate their views 'in subtle ways'.[16] Catholics were disloyal. Through their church they were linked with a Catholic state south of the border, whose territorial claims over Northern Ireland were enshrined in its constitution.[17] Predictably it was border Protestants (including those in Derry City) who subscribed most to such views of Catholics during the Troubles. And with an undoubted IRA campaign to murder and intimidate Protestant farming families out of their properties, they had good reason to think that this was 'political popery' in action.[18]

Like majorities living beside sizeable minorities elsewhere in the world, Ulster's Protestant population has always been very sensitive to demographic change. The widespread publicity accorded the 1991 census in particular had horrific consequences. To a Protestant working-class community visibly in decline in Belfast, whilst Catholic areas were bursting at the seams, media reports conveyed the news that such had been the percentage increase in Catholics over the preceding twenty years that it was only a matter of time before Catholics became the new majority. Although such conclusions were later discredited, they fuelled a terrifying escalation of murders, particularly of Catholics, in the years preceding the first ceasefires of 1994.[19]

The fear of being outbred by Catholics feeds continuing Protestant horror of the mixed marriage, for such are the pressures from the Catholic Church, that the offspring are as likely as not to be reared as Catholics. The Catholic Church's *Ne Temere* decree of 1908 – which required that children of mixed marriages be raised as Catholics – has been largely enforced until very recently. The result has been a steady erosion of the Protestant population in the south (from 11 per cent to 4 per cent between 1911 and 1961) and a reinforcement of Ulster Protestant stereotypes that 'popery' is out to destroy Protestantism. There are signs, however, that this decline is about to be reversed, a 1993 report showing 40 per cent of mixed-religion couples in the Republic opting to raise their children as Protestants.[20] Currently it is only the Catholic partner who has to make such an undertaking. But in a society as divided as Northern Ireland still is, such an undertaking could only be fulfilled with considerable strain on the other partner. In fact, *all* churches in Northern Ireland discourage mixed marriages and, because of the quite separate socio-religious networks operating, such partnerships frequently encounter difficulties. Couples often feel compelled to move away from their communities; either they cease formal religious practice entirely, or the children go one way and the other partner cuts links with his or her kin. There is a heady folk-lore – based on reality – of the outrage caused when the widow (for usually it was) had her dead husband buried in her cemetery, away from his community.[21] 'I've got a Protestant girlfriend', a 16-year-old Catholic from the Falls Road told Tony Parker in 1993, 'but I wouldn't like my parents to know that, and she hasn't told hers.' Little wonder that his ambition was to get away to England or America, or that doomed love across the divide should be such a feature of contemporary Northern Ireland fiction. A loyalist song of 1970 takes up the theme:

> Come gather round kind Protestants.
> A tale I'll tell you all
> Of deeds and recent happenings
> In the town of Donegal
> When my sister to a rebel wed
> And broke our happy home
> To live in fear and darkness
> With a popish son of Rome.[22]

A survey of 1986 showed that 98 per cent of Protestants and 95 per cent of Catholics married within their own religious grouping. By 1993 the equivalent figures were 91 per cent and 83 per cent.[23] 'Fear and hatred of Rome are instilled into the [Protestant] children from their earliest days', wrote 'Ultach' in 1943. 'They are taught that the [Catholic] Church has a specially-trained troop of sirens to bewitch young non-Catholics with their insidious charms and lure them into the dreaded mixed marriage, so that the children may be reared Catholic and the non-Catholics gradually swamped. (This, notwithstanding repeated condemnations of mixed marriages from Catholic pulpits.)'[24]

The reverse of Protestant self-perception as an honest, hard-working, straight-talking and law-abiding people is theirs of Catholics as devious, untrustworthy, lazy, slovenly, happier to 'diddle' the state and whinge, than turn an honest penny. 'Rebels beware', proclaims a loyalist mural featured in the 1943 pamphlet by 'Ultach', painted on a wall near a Catholic Church. 'To Hell with Popery. Where Popery Reigns Poverty Remains. God Save Our King.'[25] Catholics are alternatively hurt and amused by all of this. They tell self-mocking jokes about beating the system and of nationalist areas devoid of television licences.[26] This Ulster version of the 'Protestant ethic' explanation of economic development is of considerable vintage, and, as earlier chapters have demonstrated, it was frequently reinforced by real situations. In 1989 a sociologist, Leo Howe, examined two working-class housing estates, one in Protestant east Belfast, the other in Catholic west Belfast. In the latter he found over 56 per cent unemployment, no tradition of skilled industry and a reluctance to travel into Protestant areas, where almost all the major industries have been traditionally located. It was not only fear which was the deterrent, but a belief that Catholics do not get the jobs anyway – hence the greater readiness (and indeed necessity) to 'do the double' (drawing unemployment benefit whilst involved in casual work). It then becomes a way of life, accepted by a community traditionally averse to 'informing' and hostile to DHSS inspectors operating in the area. All of this only reinforces Protestant stereotypes of Catholic laziness and lawlessness and Catholic stereotypes of a system which discriminates against them and thereby deserves to be 'diddled'.[27] In many ways it had all been culturally and demographically determined even before partition. Most of the traditional engineering industries were located in Protestant areas and Protestants came to see such jobs as 'theirs' by right. So although in 1989 there were also high levels of unemployment in Protestant east Belfast (26 per cent) and many cases of real hardship, there was nevertheless an expectation that they would eventually get back to work. The weakness of a black economy, the greater ability of inspectors to operate and willingness of people to 'inform', endorsed Protestants' image of themselves as honest, hardworking and law abiding, and of Catholics as totally the reverse. This was notoriously epitomised in 1991 when, in response to a complaint by nationalists that their voice was not heard on Belfast City Council, DUP councillor Sammy Wilson retorted: 'Taigs don't pay rates.'[28]

This is why it is so important to ascertain the religious affiliation of the other person before serious conversation is engaged. There are topics which are best left alone, lest they reveal the stereotypes which inform most people's attitudes in Northern Ireland. Since there really are two mind-sets behind the apparent similarity of Ulster people, there are so very many areas where offence can be inadvertently caused unless the 'off-switch' is triggered by the stereotypical cues. One's school, name, place of residence, pronunciation and use of certain words are the most obvious clues. Some claim an ability to identify Catholics or Protestants from their very appearance and most have developed a sixth sense for such niceties. The random sectarian killings, which were such a feature of the Troubles in Belfast in particular, were very often preceded by this sectarian identifier process. Bernard MacLaverty uses it as the theme of his 1994 story 'Walking the Dog'. The hero (apparently Protestant) is picked up on a lonely road by two loyalist terrorists posing as IRA men in order to entrap and murder a Catholic. The grilling included all the set questions: name, school, how he pronounced the alphabet, where he worked, whether he could say the Hail Mary. Fortunately for him he passes the test and is let go. It is a chilling – and all-too-true – version of how the everyday social codes of Ulster so easily adapt themselves to terror. Frank Burton's 1978 study tells of a Quaker social worker, with an address in a Catholic block of flats, wrongly identified by a loyalist assassination gang as Catholic and murdered as such.[29] In one of the better analyses of the Troubles by a foreign journalist, Rian Malan, a South African, commented in 1993 on how finely tuned such indicators had become. He found Belfast a place 'full of people with nervous tics and trembling hands and eyes that gleam paranoically at the most innocent of questions. They can't tell the enemy by looking at him, so they've invented all these obscure codes and arcane riddles to distinguish friend from foe.'[30]

In fact it is an unthinking feature of everyday life, triggered as much by a desire to avoid offence as anything more sinister – at least that is what we like to think. It is why there has been such a tendency to patronise shops, businesses, professional practices, social gatherings and sporting fixtures sponsored by members of one's own religion – for only then can the guard come down. In Catholic-owned shops, one is likely to find newspapers from south of the border, Catholic news-sheets, Catholic charity boxes, mass-cards and produce advertised on the southern radio stations – preferred listening in many Catholic households. This is why mixed marriages can cause such discomfiture in a society which has only been prevented from falling apart by mutually agreed distance between the communities and where most social visiting occurs within the kin-group, which by the same unwritten rules tends to be of the same religion.[31]

The stereotypes are frequently reinforced and there are limited opportunities for re-assessment through direct experience. Although there is a small and growing number of children in integrated education (and in Belfast at least a trend for some middle-class Catholic parents to send their children to state – in effect Protestant – schools, because of the better facilities offered), the vast majority of children in Northern Ireland attend either Protestant or Catholic schools, soaking up quite different cultures in the process. Since very many social activities tend to revolve around the churches and schools, even here there are few neutral venues. Sociologists warn against attaching too much blame to the schools and churches, for the stereotypes and heightened awareness of difference are inherited. Sectarian street-rhymes have always come naturally to children, as generations of Ulster's children 'skipped to songs of cheerful hatred'.[32]

Catholics like to think that only Protestants are bigoted and in a purely religious sense they have a point. They certainly have no equivalent of the anti-popery so readily resorted to by every rank of Protestant, and their lexicon of insults is impoverished by comparison.

> I am Ulster, my people are an abrupt people
> Who like the spiky consonants in speech
> And think the soft ones cissy
>
> . . .
>
> Anything that gives or takes attack,
> Like Micks, Tagues, tinker gets, Vatican.
> An angular people, brusque and Protestant,
> For whom the word is still a fighting word,
> Who bristle into reticence at the sound
> Of the round gift of the gab in Southern mouths . . .'

(W. R. Rodgers, Ulster poet of Presbyterian background 1909–1969)[33]

Catholics are not obsessively hostile to Protestant clerics in a way that Protestants are to Catholic clergy. Because most of the pressure is on the Protestant partner to conform, Catholics have fewer problems living among and inter-marrying with Protestants than the reverse, and no problems with ecumenism. But Catholics *are* obsessed about the political ramifications of Protestantism in the Northern Ireland state, the Orange Order and the excessive displays of loyalism to Britain, its flag and its monarchy, and they are far more resistant to being educated with Protestants than the reverse. Ironically the situation in the Irish Republic today is quite the reverse, a high proportion of pupils in Protestant schools being Catholic, except in Ulster Counties Cavan, Monaghan and Donegal where the situation resembles that in Northern Ireland.[34] The reason for such apparently contradictory positions is the same. Catholic culture and identity is far more secure and all-embracing than that of Protestants. It has suffused – some might say 'hi-jacked' – 'Irishness' and, with the essentials of Catholic church teachings, Catholic schools also deliver what amounts to a nationalist 'ideological package deal'.[35]

2. A grievance culture

The anti-Catholicism (or more accurately the anti-popery) which underpins Ulster Protestant identity is rarely admitted. It is indeed difficult to articulate (even if recognised) in a largely secular age, which sees Ian Paisley as antediluvian. In a 1997 survey of the press in Northern Ireland, John Brewer found this Protestant fear of 'political popery' to be alive and well – anti-Catholicism underpinning Protestant identity generally, even though at different levels of intensity. As Heskin had concluded in his earlier study, 'Protestants object primarily to Catholics as Catholics, but not as people.' And whilst Catholic attitudes to Protestants changed in reaction to political events (in general mellowing during the Troubles), Protestant attitudes have proved more deeply-rooted psychologically and more unchanging.[36]

Complaints by groups of 'concerned residents' in the late 1990s that Orange insistence on marching through Catholic areas is simply to 'maintain an ascendancy over us', echoes down through the ages, sustained by a host of popular songs and literature of oppression and suffering. This culture of grievance and self-perception as the victim, the underdog, has united Catholics in the past (and to some extent still does). 'Discrimination' was the ready explanation for all manner of wrongs – and certainly the main reason evoked for unemployment and poor housing conditions, even if not always the real reason. During the Troubles petty verbal abuse by young soldiers and policemen of residents in Catholic ghettos fed this long-standing tradition of victimhood. Such suffering became something of an entrance requirement for full membership of the ghetto community. Those who prospered no longer conformed to the identikit and became an easy target for republican sarcasm.

At the outset of the Troubles, Richard Rose found Catholics less willing to use violence in pursuit of their political aims than Protestants. This surprised him. And yet, as I have argued throughout this book, Ulster Catholics were not natural rebels. Certainly the IRA campaign – particularly when it became more ruthless and, ironically, more successful – caused a major dilemma for Ulster's Catholics, for it lost to them the moral high ground. 'The perception of Catholics as rebels is the trap into which the Provos have fallen,' Monsignor Denis Faul told the Opsahl Commission in 1993.[37] How could Catholics continue to proclaim themselves victims, when the IRA were carrying out dreadful atrocities in their name? Even one Sinn Féin councillor admitted to nearly giving up republican politics after the IRA bomb in Enniskillen in 1987, which killed eleven and injured sixty-three of those attending the Remembrance Day ceremony, for it had taken away the 'moral dignity' of being the oppressed.[38] Just as the bullied become the bullies, so the victims of the Northern Ireland situation had become the victimisers and in the process they destroyed the legitimacy of their cause. Psychiatrist John Mack writes:

The egoism of victimisation is the incapacity of an ethno-national group, as a direct result of its own historical traumas, to empathise with the suffering of another group. [They] have little capacity to grieve for the hurts of other peoples, or to take responsibility for the new victims created by their own warlike actions. Victims kill victims through unendingly repeated cycles that are transmitted from one generation to another, bolstered by stories and myths of atrocities committed by the other people, and by heroic acts committed . . . by one's own.[39]

As the reforms called for by the civil-rights movement started to come through, middle-class Catholics in particular began to turn the old Unionist complaint about Catholics as scroungers and whingers on to the republicans. The Troubles shattered that Ulster Catholic identity, based on a common sense of grievance and a tailored version of history. Many found themselves in the same moral dilemma as the woman from County Tyrone who told her tale to Fionnuala O Connor in 1993. She had gone to England in 1972, but as IRA killings mounted, she found herself in tears of frustration as she tried to explain to English friends her Catholic view of the underlying historical reasons for the conflict. To them it sounded like justification for IRA actions. 'For years I had a very idealistic thing about nationalism and the rebellion against British domination. Emotionally, I don't want them [the IRA] to be bad guys.'[40]

Like her, the only way that constitutional nationalists could salvage their traditions was by treating the Provisional IRA as distinct from the 'noble' republicans who had gone before. 'We were fightin' a decent clean war and killin' on'y the Queen's men,' an IRA man from a previous generation told some Provos in a west Belfast republican shebeen in 1977, 'not blowin' up women and babies an' anythin' else that happens to be around.' But it was only a criticism of their methods, for he went on to talk about 800 years of 'torment' by 'the Brits', land which belonged to his forebears taken by 'rich planters' who then berated the 'lazy Taigs' for 'drinkin' on the dole'. It was impossible to divert the speaker from his rendering of the past, as Dervla Murphy (who witnessed the episode) recalled: 'he seemed to need his grievance, to have built his whole personality around it . . . so much resentment – generations of resentment, forming the very marrow of the soul.'[41]

It was a persona which the majority of Catholics in Northern Ireland would have identified with before the Troubles. The bitterness at centuries of patronising and contempt by those considered 'blow-ins' and usurpers became a peculiarly northern thing in the twentieth century, shared even by successful Catholics with little sympathy for republican separatism. Few recognised how much they themselves

subscribed to republican readings of history until the Troubles. Bernadette Devlin came from a strongly republican household – at least on
her father's side. Her early introduction to Irish history was in bedtime
stories, rebel songs and the actor Micheál Mac Liammóir's rendering
of the speeches of Patrick Pearse and Robert Emmet. Her father was
typical of the working-class Catholic unable to find work except in
England, yet blaming the English that he should have to do so. At her
convent grammar school the Reverend Mother was so pathologically
anti-English that she tore posters representing events in English history
from the walls and stamped upon them. Even Bernadette thought
this extreme and accused the nun of bigotry.[42] My own childhood
memories of the 1950s and 1960s, of Catholic families and friends in
north and west Belfast, are of stirring tales about nationalist heroes,
fortified by films about the fight for Irish independence such as *Mise
Éire, Saoirse* and the Hollywood rendering, *Shake Hands with the
Devil*. All of which would be interspersed with stories of sectarian
attacks in the 1920s and 1930s, the McMahon murders, the attacks
on pilgrims to the 1932 Eucharistic Congress and the ever-present
villain: the B Special. None of these families had republican backgrounds. Most were and remained romantic nationalists. Yet even
amongst these, it was Pearse's messianic republican message which
was favourite.

Whatever one thinks of Patrick Pearse, his power as a propagandist
beggared that of any of his predecessors – even his heroes, the United
Irishmen. A devout Catholic and consummate Gaelic scholar, whose
children's books were often the stock of Irish-language classes in the
Catholic schools, Pearse combined the visionary elements of Gaelic
poetry with Catholic themes of endurance and sacrifice to produce a
new republican theology which remains the dominant inspiration in
militant Irish republicanism. The theme is of a pure Gaelic Catholic
race finally being restored to what is rightfully theirs, not by overnight
victory, but by endurance and sacrifice, notably the ultimate blood-
sacrifice of 'dying for Ireland'. From the examples of the mythological
Cú Chulainn, to Robert Emmet and the Fenian O'Donovan Rossa, he
preached 'redemption' through 'death', the perfection and 'Christ-like'
nobility of the ultimate blood-sacrifice. The hopeless rising of 1916
(as Pearse himself had envisaged) drew triumph from failure, when he

and fourteen other leaders were executed by a British firing squad. Thus was he added to the pantheon of glorious dead, who – in the words of one of his most famous speeches, his 'Oration' at the grave of O'Donovan Rossa – could never be taken away and whose inspiration would eventually triumph. The idea of 'dying for Ireland' – much as it appears in the refrain of Frank McCourt's Ulster Catholic wastrel father – now seems pathetic and ludicrous.[43] And yet, just as with Malachy McCourt, that principle had been enunciated by generations of constitutional nationalists and militant republicans alike as somehow giving meaning to otherwise insignificant or intolerable existences. Many constitutional nationalists admit to paying lip-service to it at some time or another. It is why bungled actions such as that in 1956 which brought about the deaths of Fergal O'Hanlon and Sean South could be turned into hugely popular rebel songs and draw massive crowds to their funerals. It is why the sense of betraying the patriot dead can still prove such a major obstacle to the inching of republicans towards consensual politics. It allows republicans – with more success than nationalists care to admit – to pull at their guilt strings with taunts of 'selling-out', 'collaborating', 'shoneen' [seoinín, toadying to, aping English ways], 'West Briton', 'Brit-lover'. It is why the IRA hunger strikes of 1981 presented nationalists with such a dilemma.

Until very recently Catholics generally would have been reluctant to accept the forces of law and order as impartial. In return soldiers and police were more likely to consider Protestants as friends and Catholics as suspect.[44] Many Protestants considered these attitudes tantamount to supporting the Provos, and said as much. In February 1993 I watched a generally good-humoured sixth-form debate in Belfast fall apart and polarise along the traditional religious divisions on this very issue. The Catholic teenagers – male and female alike – commented on how often they were stopped by the security forces and how they feared the police, even though they had done nothing wrong. This triggered in some of the Protestant pupils the traditional assumption that all Catholics supported the IRA in their hearts, which in turn incensed the Catholics, prompting even those who had been critical of Catholic culture to draw together with their co-religionists. On core issues they were voicing inherited values and the girl from west Belfast who had sparked it all off was exasperated: 'I am thoroughly disgusted the way we are behaving . . . just like . . . the older generation.'[45] And so indeed had been the experience of the 'older generation' – they knew why the Provos had arisen, they worshipped at the same altar of romantic nationalism, they distrusted the security forces controlled by a Unionist state. But if they said so they risked being taken as apologists for the Provos. And so it joined those many 'no-go areas' of mixed-company conversation which is such a feature of Northern Ireland society.

This troubled silence, where once there would have been righteous indignation aimed exclusively at Unionists and Protestants, is part of the confusion into which the Troubles have thrown the once secure Catholic identity. In many ways it is only the extreme republicans who have retained that old identity, and they blame everyone but themselves for the widespread questioning of the myths which once gave meaning to real sufferings. The Dublin intelligentsia and present-day historians have been favourite targets. They 'tell people they can't be satisfied with what they came from', Gerry Adams commented in a 1993 interview. 'That's putting things you thought of as constants under attack: the effect's like a family trauma, like discovering you've been adopted.'[46] Those readings of their past were a necessary crutch for the bulk of Ulster Catholics after partition. Like all crutches they provided relief from suffering, but scarcely an inducement to move on. Even so, Adams was right in identifying them as such an integral part of Catholic culture that to deny the relationship between this past and the IRA campaign is self-delusion. There is no need to seek banned publications or republican declarations for such readings of history. They were the constant drip-feed of the Catholic press and other Catholic writings for much of the twentieth century.

The most widely read Catholic newspaper, the *Irish News*, and its Unionist counterpart, the *Belfast News Letter,* have moved a long way in recent years from their past sectarianism, and both have been instrumental in producing the current peace process. In this change the *Irish News* has reflected readership opinion. But for much of the twentieth century that opinion would have been virulently anti-Unionist. The *Irish News* accordingly (and its weekly spin-off, the *Irish Weekly*) thought partition unnatural and the term 'Ulster' – because truncated – incorrect usage for the political entity of Northern

Ireland. The editorials and commentary sections were highly polemical, and the tendency to blame Britain for everything was a regular
theme. Partition was the old policy of 'divide and conquer'(1932), the
ills that stem from it the product of 'alien rule' (1953). 'British hypocrisy' was a favourite theme, and the 'causes' opposed by Britain (India,
Franco) received automatic endorsement. There were still too many
Catholic ex-British-army soldiers around in the 1930s for the *Irish
News* not to have commemorated Armistice Day, and the relevant issue
in 1932 carries a reverential editorial and a half-page advertisement
for the poppy appeal.[47] But increasingly Catholic ex-soldiers were
marginalised. At an early stage Unionists had subsumed the ceremonies
into their own blood-sacrifice mythology; whilst the imperialist overtones of the Remembrance Day ceremonies and downright opposition
from republicans sidelined them within their own communities.[48]

However, just as with today's republicans, the belief that Unionists
would recognise their Irish identity if Britain pulled out, and a nostalgia
for the 1790s when their ancestors did so, was never reconciled with
the persistent tendency to see Protestants as blow-ins, planters, with
no history and an inferior religion.[49] Assertions that they would have
nothing to fear in a united Ireland were contradicted by the most
abiding theme of the nationalist press: that Irishness and Catholicism
were one and the same. Distasteful as this may now seem, however,
it is important to recognise such attitudes as fundamental to the
self-protective mechanism developed by generations of Catholics in
response to traditional 'put-downs'. In post-partition Ulster the protective myths of Catholicism as the one true faith, indelibly bound up
with the 'Irish struggle', seemed all the more necessary. In recent years
the once highly politicised Catholic clergy of the late nineteenth and
early twentieth centuries have, with a few exceptions, become very
nervous of politics. Republicans are bitter and confused about the
critical attitude of the Catholic Church, since they usually come from
working-class areas where traditionally conservative Catholicism has
been strongest. Moreover, they still see Catholicism as an integral part
of their political identity. 'To be a Catholic is still a political thing,'
Gerry Adams told Fionnuala O Connor in 1992; 'it identifies you as a
Fenian, a Taig. People are killed for being Catholic . . . And they have
an affinity with the Church which has to do with its history in Ireland,

echoes of the penal days, punishment by death for being a priest or a bishop – the Church was part of the people's struggle.'[50] And who can deny that this is exactly the picture promoted by the Catholic Church since at least the seventeenth century?

It is no accident that among the 'cultural' rapidly replacing the 'armed struggle' murals in post-ceasefire republican Belfast will be found that most stereotypical image of the penal laws: the priest at the mass-rock, the crown forces closing in.[51] The message is hardly a conciliatory one. It is also false, since it was never unlawful under the penal laws for a priest to say mass. However, this image was a central part of Ulster Catholic culture in the twentieth century. Editorial attacks by the Catholic press on Unionist politicians sometimes alluded to their ancestors' persecution of priests in the eighteenth century. Clerical sermons published by the press regularly referred to religious persecution in the past.[52] The hedge-schools, which had not been exclusively Catholic, were also appropriated as part of the story of persecution, endurance and superior culture, linking penal-day persecution to the fight to retain separate Catholic education under Stormont. 'Can't you see a ring of eager little faces, with eyes that looked up at him [the hedge-schoolmaster] with all the clear bright courage of a great race?' the Revd Francis Connolly S.J. wrote in a full-page article in the *Irish Weekly* for 15 March 1958.

Can't you hear him as he starts one of the old-time songs about Granuaile . . . or the Dark Rosaleen calling for her Sarsfield to come back from over the sea to ransom her? . . . Besides, what can great souls do when they are chained and crushed to the earth by force – what can they do but sing . . . here was a whole people ground down and destitute for centuries, who never lost their urbanity, their spirit of gaiety, their consciousness of obvious superiority . . . in the darkest days of penal times. If it was the martyred and fugitive priests who kept the soul of Ireland alive, it was the Hedgemaster who kept its eyes open.[53]

The 1932 Eucharistic Congress – attracting a million pilgrims to the mass in the Phoenix Park in Dublin and a number of other events – was proclaimed the 'Triumph of Catholic Ireland' by the *Irish News* in a prominent feature article on the Revd B. McLaverty's sermon at

St MacNissi's Church in Larne. The Congress, he said, represented 'the triumph of Catholic Ireland over 750 years of persecution such as even the early Romans or the Jews had not endured'.[54] Thirty years later (1962, the year in which the second Vatican Council began its transformation of worldwide Catholicism) the theme remained unchanged in the nationalist press. 'The Irish people are rightly proud of their country's stand for the Faith throughout fifteen hundred years,' ran the *Ulster Herald* editorial for 10 March 1962 – praising the Catholic bishops' Easter pastorals – 'a stand that endured the longest of the persecutions known in European history, proud that, with Spain, our land was the one territory in which the "Reformation" failed to gain even a foothold ... the valiant souls of the Penal Days who rejoiced to suffer and endure that our land might hold its religious heritage.'[55]

Throughout Northern Ireland every county and sizeable town had separate Catholic and Protestant newspapers. Such was the difference in tone and news items that readers might as well have lived in different countries. Even the successful middle-class father in Brian Moore's (1965) novel *The Emperor of Ice-Cream* looked to the *Irish News* in the 1930s and 1940s to reinforce his prejudices:

[He] read the newspaper as other men play cards, shuffling through a page of stories until he found one which would confirm him in his prejudice. A Jewish name discovered in an account of a financial transaction, a Franco victory over the godless Reds, a hint of British perfidy in international affairs, an Irish triumph on the sports field, an evidence of Protestant bigotry, a discovery of Ulster governmental corruption: these were his reading goals.[56]

Given such acculturation over many generations, it is little wonder that the IRA hunger strikes of 1981 posed such a dilemma for Ulster Catholics. The IRA's claim that they were fighting a war rather than mounting a terror campaign found partial recognition in the special-category status of their prisoners until 1976. This was removed under the Thatcher government's 'criminalisation' programme. They immediately mounted a campaign to secure the return of their 'political status', of which the hunger strikes were the culmination. Bobby Sands was the first to refuse food on 1 March 1981. His family, burnt out of the Rathcoole housing estate on the northern edge of Belfast in 1972, had moved to the Twinbrook estate in Catholic west Belfast. There Sands joined the Provisional IRA at the age of eighteen, eventually becoming commander of its 'active service' unit on the estate. At the time of the hunger strikes, he was five years into a fourteen-year prison term for possession of firearms. In prison he had become a republican intellectual, learning Irish and orchestrating a brilliant public-relations campaign. The IRA prison protest had been making little progress. Now Margaret Thatcher's famous intransigence provided the perfect foil to the image being built of the noble rebel, battling against insurmountable odds. It was Pearse's vision all over again and Sands recognised it. A failing movement would emerge re-fortified when Britain fulfilled its traditional role in republican mythology. Granting leave to wear civilian clothes would have pre-empted the hunger strikes. But by October 1981 ten men had died, beginning with Sands on 5 May. By then he was a Westminster MP, having stood as a protest candidate in the Fermanagh–South Tyrone by-election on 9 April. The IRA had been given new life.

The election of Sands in Fermanagh–South Tyrone capitalised on previous divisions among the nationalists and republicans which had let Unionists win this predominantly nationalist constituency. In a highly emotional atmosphere, in which the republican campaign centred on the need to save Sands's life (rather than on the IRA prisoners' campaign for political status), intense pressure and 'moral blackmail'[57] secured the withdrawal of the constitutional nationalists, and victory (though by a small margin) for Sands. A hundred thousand people attended his funeral in west Belfast some weeks later. Members of the SDLP, Fianna Fáil ministers and TDs from the Irish Republic, Catholic bishops and even a special papal legate tried to mediate between government and hunger strikers, but to no avail. They were being pulled by their own past into being the apparent spokesmen for a tradition of violence which they abhorred. Moreover, the officiation by Catholic priests at the often elaborate republican funerals of the dead hunger-strikers seemed to confirm the most extreme loyalist vision of 'popery'. Ambivalence about the use of violence, and a tendency to view its use by the 'others' as worse than by 'one's own', has been common to all sides in the recent Northern Ireland conflict.

Even so, there has been what Dervla Murphy termed 'a massive muddle' in the Catholic mind about this – particularly before the rules for the use of firearms by the security forces were tightened up.[58] Even non-violent Catholics tended to have less sympathy for members of the security forces killed during the Troubles – particularly since Protestants have traditionally considered the security forces as part of *their* community – than for Catholics killed in sectarian attacks.[59]

The discomfiture and helplessness of constitutional nationalism during the hunger strikes was palpable. How could it denounce what the hunger-strikers were doing without also damning the traditions of Tone, Emmet and Pearse – the 'good' republicans of the past who had laid the basis for the Irish state? Moreover, the results of a series of elections over the next eighteen months saw Sinn Féin capturing 30–45 per cent of the Catholic vote in Northern Ireland. The constitutional nationalists in the SDLP seemed to have nothing to show for their years of condemning IRA violence, and the hunger strikes had touched all the right nerves in Catholic consciousness. The SDLP needed a lifeline. It came in the form of the New Ireland Forum report of 1984 and the Anglo-Irish Agreement of 1985. The 'poor bloody infantry' of constitutional nationalism, who had come close to giving up at the time of the hunger strikes, seemed at last to have been rewarded.[60]

3. Catholicism as cultural and political identity

However critical republicans were of the Catholic Church, their criticism had to be muted, so intertwined had Catholicism and Irish nationalism become. For Catholics their religion *was* their political identity, and the Church provided all the necessary institutional infrastructure. This is why secular nationalist institutions, including the Nationalist Party itself, remained so weak in Northern Ireland. There was no need for them.[61] This is why, in contrast to the unionist press, the nationalist press was so dominated by Church matters, and why the presumption that nationalism depended on Catholicism for its survival is such a common theme in Catholic statements (both lay and clerical) throughout the twentieth century.[62] A friend recently told me of his memories of reading the *Irish News* in the 1960s. 'It was the most appallingly bad daily paper for news I ever read. It was noted for reports of greyhound races and priests' funerals.' As I look through its past issues in the Belfast Newspaper Library the prevalence of Catholic Church news and pictures of priests in the *Irish News* stands out, as does the association of Catholic religious practice with often quite extreme nationalist sentiments. The highlight of the republican year – the commemoration of the 1916 Easter rising – was intertwined with the Church's liturgical calendar. Indeed, public religious practice by Catholics became something of a defiant political act after partition. Whatever the hierarchy's traditional denunciation of violence, priests regularly led the recitation of the rosary in Irish at commemorations of the 1916 rising. Crowds of Catholics, falling on their knees and reciting the rosary when blocked by police from attending republican demonstrations, were a common occurrence, and recital of the rosary was still a feature of republican demonstrations in the 1970s and 1980s.[63] In 1957 public recitation of the rosary was the chosen form of defiance by the crowd outside the Enniskillen morgue where the bodies of South and O'Hanlon were laid.[64] Why it should have been the rosary which became the traditional form of protest is not entirely clear, but it may have developed from the recognition of how much it was disliked by Protestants. The Catholic Truth Society of Ireland had been founded in 1899 and became part of the Church's armoury against modern evils such as socialism and communism. Sales of the CTS booklets in Down and Connor alone amounted to 174,937 in 1957, with Ardoyne, Clonard, St Peter's and St Mary's – at the heart of working-class Catholic Belfast – accounting for over a third of these.[65] Ash Wednesday provided many a Catholic child the opportunity for his or her first gesture of political defiance, as the black ash on the forehead was flaunted and preserved long after the day itself. Ulster Catholicism had now become a defiant religion, which emphasised difference.

It was much the same with symbols of Irishness: Irish games, Irish dancing, Irish language. As in the rest of Ireland, Irish-speaking had gone into terminal decline by the early twentieth century. Even before partition, only 2.3 per cent of Ulster people were Irish speakers.[66] In the nineteenth century the Catholic clergy had been willing assistants in the decline of the Irish language.[67] But after partition, they were prominent in Gaelic League activities, which were in decline everywhere else in Ireland. As the Free State drained revivalist enthusiasm by making the language a compulsory part of Irish identity, Unionist condemnation of it had the opposite effect in Northern Ireland. In the years immediately preceding partition, the British government had been according the Irish language an increasing place in the schools' curriculum.[68] But loyalist claims that Irish language and Irish history were subversive secured a progressive attack on their funding and timetabling. In their efforts to produce highly qualified Catholics to disprove the Protestant stereotype, the Catholic schools progressively abandoned the subjects. State exams did not require the formal teaching of Irish history, so it was often picked up from amateurs and enthusiasts outside the school system.[69]

Protestant interest in Irish language and culture did not entirely disappear after partition. Jack O'Rourke – a traditional piper who came to live in Belfast in 1940 – recalled people from the Protestant Shankill Road and Sandy Row at *céilís* (Irish dancing events), and cross-religious enthusiasm for Irish music, particularly from people he termed 'old Presbyterians', by which he seems to have meant the old United Irish type. It was, he claimed, the Troubles which finally destroyed such interest.[70] In 1992 Dr Bob Curran, a teacher in Portrush, County Antrim, remembered his Protestant grandfather from south Armagh as a fluent Irish speaker and traditional musician. But his Ballymena grandmother's reaction would have been more typical.

My grandfather was frequently told to 'stop filling the child's head with nonsense' and I was told . . . he had come from 'a Catholic part of the country' and that the traditions which he held were 'very Catholic'. There were many good Catholics, she insisted . . . but 'they had a very different culture to us' and it was best not to have too much to do with that.[71]

Successive ministries of education after 1921 had to combat the dominant Unionist prejudice and paranoia towards Irish language and culture. Even Craigavon was persuaded that outright suppression would be ill advised. But most of his party considered the language subversive, and cited the prominent role of Gaelic League members in the 1916 rising as proof. *Any* official sanction was tantamount to supporting 'an anti-British and disloyal faction', protested the Loyalty League in 1928. 'As loyal subjects . . . we strongly resent this pandering to a cunning foe.' It would 'enable rebellious spirits to propagate sedition . . . The language is of no practical utility, but may be of much value to incipient traitors.'[72]

Like so much in Northern Ireland, Unionist association of rebelliousness and Irish culture became a self-fulfilling prophecy. The Irish language became something of a Catholic code, since only Catholics were presumed to speak it. Inability to do so often meant a double marginalisation, particularly for Catholics outside traditional Catholic areas, where classes and *feiseanna* tended to be located. Ever since the foundation of the Gaelic League in 1893 there have been tensions between those supporting the revival of Irish for scholarly or preservationist reasons, and those who use it for political ends.[73] In Northern Ireland the language came to be used as a weapon by the more republican-minded – brief statements in Irish, usually rejecting the 'sassanachs' [sic *Sasanaigh*], marking the appearance of IRA men in courts, which they otherwise refused to recognise.[74] 'Every word of Irish spoken', claimed a prominent Sinn Féin member in the early 1980s, 'is like another bullet being fired in the struggle for Irish freedom.'[75] In prison republicans often studied the language for the first time and the current revival owes much to the increased numbers of prison 'graduates' in the Catholic community. It has also provoked internal tensions in that revival. The various community ventures which have produced a number of Irish-language schools in west Belfast and other educational projects, have invariably involved such republicans and just as invariably attracted 'political vetting' in the allocation of funds.[76] Although the 1991 census recorded a large increase in interest in the language, and new bodies such as the Cultural Traditions Group (1988) and the Ultach Trust (1989) are promoting an apolitical approach, its public face has tended to be that of militant nationalism. 'In the North the IRA has all but appropriated the Irish language,' wrote the writer Sam McAughtry in 1993,

and the other Catholic Irish speakers are silent on the issue; Fianna Fáil politicians at their conferences have made the language elitist; the Gaelic

Athletic Association's ban on the army and the RUC is seen as sectarian; the task of persuading Protestants to encourage the growth of Irish culture, never mind embracing it to themselves, is a huge one. But Catholics can help. Already there is support within the GAA for the removal of the Ban ... Irish-speaking Catholics should ease the concerns of Protestants by condemning politicians who use the language for political ends.[77]

Many Irish-language speakers and most Catholics would like to depoliticise the language issue, but given recent tensions about bi-lingualism in the new Northern Ireland Assembly – when Sinn Féin and some SDLP members conducted proceedings in Irish, some Unionists mocking and most insisting on equal rights for Ullans or Ulster-Scots – a resolution still seems a long way off.[78]

An awful piety infected northern nationalism and the Irish-language movement for much of the twentieth century, both alike infused with the puritanism of post-Cullenite Catholicism. 'Canoodling' in the Donegal Gaeltacht was the most heinous of crimes and treated as such in the Catholic schools. Cal McCrystal recalls priests patrolling the roads and hills in the 1940s Gaeltacht in search of courting couples. He also recalls the time in 1955 when his Irish-speaking father was denounced from the pulpits, forced out of his twenty-year chairmanship of the Gaelic League in Belfast, and dropped as a regular columnist in the *Irish News* for flouting that other taboo of Catholic cultural nationalism then, consorting with dangerous leftist movements. As a life-time socialist, he had led a cultural delegation to Moscow that year.[79]

The *fáinne*, a gold or silver tie or lapel pin, signifying levels of proficiency in the Irish language,was one of the most respected symbols of such nationalism. It often accompanied an array of other pins and motifs in a defiant gesture to the majority Protestant culture: the Pioneer Total Abstinence Association, the Legion of Mary, the Sodality of the Holy Name and sometimes an Irish tricolour pin too. The use of the tricolour, however, had a chequered history and symbolises the largely reactive nature of such displays. Its usage, though often in a relatively unobtrusive way, sparked a considerable overreaction by the authorities, culminating in the Flags and Emblems Act of 1954 and the Paisleyite attack on the flag in Sinn Féin's Belfast office in 1964. Predictably such action produced the opposite result to that intended, and for a while the tricolour became the main emblem of nationalist defiance. Bernadette Devlin recalled being prompted to flaunt a tricolour pin as a teenager by the knowledge that it was banned by the 1954 act. But when a policeman simply laughed good-humouredly at her impudence, she lost interest and ceased wearing it.[80] The act was repealed in 1986. The adoption of Gaelic forms of names was another way of expressing separate identity and defiance of Unionist pettiness. They marked the bearer as Catholic just as much as the name Patrick had done a century earlier. As such they acted as an effective bar to Catholic employment in certain areas. As late as 1984 the Ulster Unionists' annual conference could treat the numbers of Róisíns and Séamuses in the local media with a mixture of contempt and fear that they somehow posed a threat to Ulster's Protestant heritage.[81]

The kind of ascetic pious nationalism encapsulated in the array of symbols noted above is typical of the defensiveness of embattled minorities. It was the underlying theme of Irish-language school textbooks, printed south of the border, and of the Gaelic revival generally. The promotion of rural values as the ideal of Irishness struck a particular chord with northern nationalists, who had long dignified their inglorious lot with the conviction that they were Ulster's native sons. Little wonder that after partition the Gaelic League's most missionary elements should now be in Ulster. The Irish cultural revival was also espoused by the Catholic Church as a channel for promoting a more wholesome culture against the perceived atheism and immorality coming in from England. *Céilís* were often the only dances permitted in parish halls and the only ones permitted by the Gaelic Athletic Association until 1973.[82] The GAA epitomises the best and the worst of such Catholic cultural nationalism. The increase in the number of clubs in Ulster after 1920 was politically inspired. However, sporting success gave large numbers of Catholics the opportunity to participate in team games and the GAA's cultivation of local pride sometimes brought Protestant support for team victories. But the organisation was dominated by priests and country school teachers, who conducted organisational meetings in Irish, played 'Faith of Our Fathers' and 'The Soldier's Song' at fixtures and generally acted as 'cultural policeman and gauleiter'[83] of the Catholic community, particularly in rural areas. It policed its ban on 'foreign [for which read English] games' by

sending vigilantes to patrol the gates at soccer matches and came
to symbolise the new political correctness of Catholic nationalism,
lampooned in a satirical song of the 1960s.

> Come all you boys that vote for me, come gather all around,
> A Catholic I was born an' reared an' so I'm duty bound
> To proclaim my country's misery and express our Papish hope,
> To embarrass all the Orangemen an' glorify the Pope.

> Our allegiance is to Ireland, to her language and her games,
> So we can't accept the border boys, as long as it remains,
> Our reason is the Gaelic blood that's flowin' in our veins,
> An' that is why our policy is never known to change.[84]

This parade of stereotyped 'Irishness' was both unwelcome to and
unwelcoming of Protestants, and its political overtones, notably the
GAA's exclusion of members of the security forces, tarred all those
involved with the stigma of 'disloyalty'. *Céilí*-goers, Irish-speakers and
GAA members often attracted hostile attention from the police (and
latterly from loyalist terrorists), thus reinforcing Catholics' self-image
as a persecuted people, with right on their side. Catholics claim that
their Irish culture rather than their religion is the key to their identity.[85]
But the time has not yet arrived (at least not in Northern Ireland) when
Catholicism, Irish culture and political nationalism can be disen-
tangled, for they have been consciously intertwined for centuries. This
was the 'package deal' from which Catholics deviated at their peril. It
had played an important social function before the recent Troubles,
often dignifying the lives of those who genuinely were victims. But it
also set up an internal elitism, unaccepting of Catholics who did not
subscribe to or fit the composite image of Gaeldom. It was a total
identification of religion and culture which, whilst it could just about
accommodate Catholics from other European countries as part of the
auld alliance against England, found 'British' Catholics discomfiting
and something of a contradiction in terms. There was a story told
in Tyrone about a Scottish Catholic family who had moved there
towards the end of the Second World War and whose celebration of
things British, including the flying of the Union Jack, met with such

thorough disapproval from local Catholics, that they eventually had to move.[86]

4. *Catholicism as religion*

In 1993 I listened to some Catholic teenagers in Belfast argue for an ideal future in which their faith could be separated from the traditions associated with it. By this they inferred its traditional association with political nationalism, and, at its extreme, militant republicanism. Certainly the Ulster hierarchy has attempted to do just this in its consistent condemnation of the IRA. As a result it has incurred the wrath of republicans, particularly since it has been more reticent in its condemnation of state violence. In this it has reflected the opinions of the vast majority of its adherents. Even so, it has embittered and confused a significant number of Catholics who vote for Sinn Féin, particularly in working-class areas, where there has been a noticeable drop in religious practice. This is because Catholicism and nationalism have traditionally been one and the same thing. For much of the twentieth century the clergy have been the real political leaders of the Catholic populace. Republican leaders recognise the connection and are careful not to offend the religious sensibilities of their followers. When Gerry Adams accuses the Church of going back on its own traditions in its criticism of republicans, he has a point, even though he conveniently ignores that other longstanding Church tradition – opposition to violence.[87]

In the absence of effective nationalist politics under Stormont, the clergy were expected to be the main voice of the Catholic people. Nationalist politicians could not survive without their endorsement. So much coverage was given by the Catholic press to their statements, sermons and pastorals that critics could be forgiven for thinking them penned by the same people. In these writings the debt nationalism owed the church was a regular theme as was the idea of St Patrick as 'ours'. Indeed, Cardinal MacRory – a dominant influence in the Catholic Church in Ulster, first as bishop of Down and Connor, 1915–28, then as archbishop of Armagh, 1928–45 – declared the Protestant churches to be no part of the church of Christ, took great exception to

Protestantism using the name 'Church of Ireland', and sought to have a clause inserted in the new Irish constitution of 1937 declaring Catholicism the true faith established by Christ. De Valera was too astute a statesman to accept this and cultivated the papacy in successfully resisting it.[88] MacRory was supported by his successor in Down and Connor, Daniel Mageean (bishop, 1929–62). Their formative years were the traumatic ones of post-partition Ulster and like the rest of the older clergy they carried their scars and prejudices into the early 1960s. They rarely made representations to government on behalf of their community other than on educational matters, and it is perhaps unsurprising that they lacked any civic culture. Even in towns like Downpatrick, with a Catholic majority on the council, there was no easy relationship, and Protestant clergy turned up to civic occasions more readily than their Catholic counterparts.[89] Since the Catholic clergy had not been made welcome at state functions in any event, and had alternative administrative and welfare systems, their parishes remained their essential administrative units. There was little internal challenge to the authority of the Catholic Church as long as Catholics generally felt themselves excluded from the state.

The main impact of church authority on Catholic lives has been in the field of education. The prevalence of devotional symbols distinguishes Catholic from state schools, and preparation for the sacraments takes place in school hours. The Catholic Church is passionate in its defence of separate Catholic education, believing that 'the faith is caught as much as taught'.[90] 'We stress that Religious Education', wrote the Ulster bishops in 1988, in a strongly-worded protest at new government education proposals, '. . . is *the* foundation on which all aspects of the curriculum in the Catholic school are based. For that reason we must demand that Religious Education be given its rightful place *before* the other "foundation subjects"'.[91] Bishop Farren of Derry had put it more forcefully in the 1950s – the Church 'required' Catholic parents to send their children to Catholic schools to preserve the faith of the next generation, otherwise the children of those attending non-Catholic schools would be 'perverts'.[92]

However, what once was a justifiable reaction to Protestant proselytism has solidified into dogmatism. Catholic parents going outside the Catholic school system encounter considerable hostility from their clergy when they seek help to prepare their children for the sacraments.[93] The Catholic Church's opposition to integrated education takes the same line, and were it not for the more charitable approach of the religious sisters and brothers, Catholic children in integrated schools would be deprived of such instruction. In this stance the Church is out of step with a majority of lay Catholics, who approve of integrated education in principle.[94] This does not necessarily mean that they are correspondingly critical of the Catholic educational system. Catholic parents are generally content for their children to receive their religious instruction during school hours. But since those who were closest to the Church's official hostility to integrated education were Sinn Féin and the IRA (organisations which the hierarchy disliked intensely) – largely because of the nationalist which accompanies the religious ethos in Catholic schools – it should at least have caused the Church some unease. However, since Sinn Féin's Martin McGuinness took over the Education ministry in the new (1999) devolved administration in Northern Ireland the party's public pronouncements on integrated education have been more positive.

Educational surveys from the 1960s to the 1990s reveal percentages in the high nineties of children in totally segregated schools. Although there is a steadily-growing integrated school movement in Northern Ireland, it accounts for only 4.5 per cent of the school population. One of the best accounts of the early debate on integrated education is that by the Revd Eric Gallagher (former President of the Methodist Church in Ireland) and Stanley Worral (former headmaster of Methodist College in Belfast). It shows educational segregation to have been such an everyday 'fact of life' that few gave much thought to it and the high numbers registering support for integration did not translate into pressure to achieve it. The fact is that Northern Ireland society generally supports denominational schooling. Gallagher and Worrall's study also suggests that the Catholic Church's declared opposition has allowed the other churches to avoid taking a stand on the issue. 'As long as Catholicism insists on its special role in education, the others are absolved from any requirement to develop their apparent or alleged call for radical change.'[95]

The court is still out on the role that separate education may have played in the problems of Northern Ireland. Yet the very ethos in maintained (religious, mostly Catholic) and state (Protestant) schools must surely have been a factor. John Whyte concluded in his study published in 1990 that segregated education *was* divisive 'not so much because of what was taught, but because of the "hidden agenda", the values – political more than religious – which are informally put across to the pupils'.[96] In Catholic schools children were more likely to pick up negative attitudes to the state and civic society. Until quite recently, it was believed that Catholics had little chance of employment in a range of public services, and so everything in this area might be the subject of unfavourable comments by teachers.[97] Similar perceptions of the Union flag as a symbol of dominance were also transmitted, while in some schools there was a tendency to shun British and Imperial history in favour of Irish history and sometimes a particularly national-istic version of it.[98] In addition, most Catholic religious brothers and sisters – a significant element in Catholic education, particularly in boys' schools – were trained south of the border. Indeed, in 1962 Barritt and Carter found only two of the forty-three teachers at St Mary's Christian Brothers' School in Belfast had been trained in Northern Ireland.[99] The differences in school curricula, however, had narrowed by the 1980s. As elsewhere, the Troubles have caused a questioning of what was being taught and today one is as likely to learn Irish history in state as in Catholic schools.

The story of how Northern Ireland's educational system became almost totally segregated is not a pleasant one. Indeed, D. H. Akenson chose to call his pioneering study of the issue *Education and Enmity* (1973). The proselytising activities of fundamentalist Protestants in the nineteenth century had made the Catholic clergy wary of education over which they did not have control, and even before partition they were already blocking government reforms. The MacPherson Bill of 1919 would have introduced education authorities and rate support for schools. But it was denounced by the Catholic Church, often in shrill anti-English and anti-Protestant language, and had to be withdrawn. By the time of partition, the entire educational system was overdue for reform.[100] The establishment of a central Ministry of Education (such as happened in 1922) had already been advocated by educational reformers. But the required transfer of schools to its authority was resisted not only by the Catholic Church but by some

Protestant clergy also. Indeed, it was the extremism of many Protestant clerics rather than the difficulties created by the Catholic bishops – though there were enough also of these – which turned the state system into a Protestant one and brought down the enlightened regimes of education ministers Lord Londonderry in 1926 and Hall Thompson in 1949.[101] The religious sensitivity of the educational issue was recognised, and, with the possible exception of the deeply anti-Catholic Harry Midgley (1950–59), successive ministers of education were to prove remarkably ecumenical in their approach.[102]

Even so, the Catholic Church's early opposition to educational reform threw away its main chance of negotiating equitable treatment for Catholic pupils, and Catholic children have remained relatively deprived to this day. The refusal of the church to co-operate with the Lynn Committee (established in September 1921) and of about a third of Catholic elementary schools to recognise the new ministry's responsibility – until October 1922 their teachers were being paid from Dublin – were political gestures that made it more difficult to argue a religious case. Indeed, the political nationalism of Catholic clergy in the twentieth century often confused religious and political issues, both in their own minds and in those of their opponents. It was unfortunate that Sir Robert Lynn's Orangeism and distinct hostility towards Catholic cultural values should have provided an additional excuse for non-co-operation, for it was not until the mid-1920s that the Unionist party abandoned its efforts at non-sectarian government. But with political leaders in the Irish Free State beginning to use the schools as the channel for their vision of a de-anglicised and Gaelic new order, and the Lynn Committee equally bent on a school curriculum that would inculcate British civic values, the future of Irish education was being decided in a highly intolerant atmosphere.[103]

The 1923 Education Bill sought to make primary education free, compulsory and largely secular. The secular aspect of such provision was incompatible with Catholic practice of providing religious instruction as part of the curriculum. The Bill therefore accepted a category of schools totally independent of local control. Teachers' salaries and half the running expenses of the schools would be paid from public funds, but no capital costs. Education Minister Lord Londonderry had tried to be impartial, and rewrote the Lynn Committee's proposals on religious education to ensure that the fully-funded state sector did not provide denominational religious education in school hours. But a heated campaign by Protestant clerics won concessions on Bible instruction which made state schools Protestant in all but name. Continuing agitation by the Protestant clerics finally roused the Catholic bishops. A concession of 50 per cent capital funding to Catholic schools was granted under the 1930 Education Act. This was increased to 65 per cent in 1947, and 100 per cent by 1992 – a level of public funding for denominational schools much more generous than that provided in the Irish Republic.

But this point could have been reached much earlier had the bishops accepted the middling route offered under the 1923 Act. By this, schools with committees composed of four members of the original owners (i.e. the clergy) and two lay representatives of the new authorities (who would certainly have been Catholics) would have received substantial capital grants. Understandably Catholic authorities were most reluctant to grant any influence to the gerrymandered local authorities. But Akenson argues forcefully that this obstacle could have been surmounted and that it was rather the Catholic clergy's insistence on maintaining control (even against their own laity) which condemned generations of Catholic children to antiquated and inferior school facilities. A number of retired Catholic teachers concluded as much in their interviews with Fionnuala O Connor in 1992.[104] Bishop Farren of Derry had argued in 1945 that the government's requirement of lay members was spurious, since the clergy were always accepted by the Catholic people as their natural representatives. When in 1968 capital grants of 80 per cent were offered if voluntary schools accepted government representatives on to their committees (essentially the middling route offered in 1923) almost all the Catholic primary schools came over.[105]

Such relative deprivation was also reflected in the secondary sector. There was no free secondary education at the time of partition. Indeed, only 6,237 pupils of all denominations were receiving secondary education in 1921. Real progress in this area only came in 1947, when the government – following the 1944 Butler Act in England – extended compulsory education to the age of fifteen. It was only in 1951 that a means test was abolished for grammar school pupils (selected through the eleven-plus examination) and it took over another decade for the real benefits to filter through. Even then Catholic schools struggled to provide enough places for those qualified, and they levied a small fee to help make up the deficit in the capital grant – a real hardship for the larger number of poor parents among the Catholic population.[106]

As with other matters in Northern Ireland no side could claim the moral high ground. Immediately prior to partition a largely denominational system of state-funded education was already in place and the Catholic bishops were nearing victory in their long battle over education. Now they were faced with a state whose ethos and school system exuded anti-Catholicism. Any gesture of more generous funding of Catholic schools by government invariably raised Protestant ire. Protestant clerics were regularly invited on to the boards of management of 'state' schools. Catholic clergy never were. Advertisements sought Protestant staff for state schools, even in school kitchens.[107]

Much the same battle was engaged over teacher training. On the eve of partition there were seven teacher-training establishments in Ireland. The Marlborough Street College in Dublin was intended to be non-denominational, but effectively operated as a largely Presbyterian establishment. The other colleges were entirely denominational. Only one was based in Northern Ireland, St Mary's in Belfast, for Catholic women. The new northern Ministry of Education accordingly had an immediate problem to resolve: how to ensure continued facilities for male students generally and Protestant students in particular. It tried to reach an arrangement to continue training in the southern colleges, but its overtures were rejected. Indeed one of the Irish Free State's first actions was to close the Marlborough Street College, thereby depriving Presbyterian students of any training facility whatsoever. The northern government accordingly established Stranmillis [Training] College in Belfast, and initially Catholic men also attended. But when, in 1925, the government rejected the hierarchy's demands for the establishment of a separate Catholic establishment for male students, the bishops reached an arrangement with a Catholic training college in England (St Mary's Strawberry Hill) and informed Catholic students at Stranmillis that if they did not transfer, it would seriously jeopardise their chances of obtaining employment in Catholic schools in Northern

Ireland. Thereafter Stranmillis effectively became a Protestant college, although that had not been the government's intention.[108] It is at the very least some tribute to the Northern Ireland Ministry of Education, whatever about the known discriminatory policies of other ministries, that it continued to subsidise Catholic students who attended Strawberry Hill in England. The Catholic bishops were opposed to *any* state control over areas traditionally considered the church's domain, and since three had dioceses which straddled the border, they would have been acutely aware of the Irish Free State's acceptance of undisputed ecclesiastical supervision in matters educational.[109]

The Ulster bishops were also ambivalent about the extension to Northern Ireland of the British welfare state after 1946, which involved unprecedented interference with their role as a voluntary provider of social services. As in southern Ireland, they tended to see the increasing role of the state as smacking of socialism and communism and, from recent experience with state agencies, they had good reason to think the new system would interfere with Catholic social teaching.[110] In 1951 the Catholic bishops' objection to limited state welfare in the south helped bury Noel Browne's 'Mother and Child' scheme (to provide free medical care to mothers and children under sixteen), and they had already resisted nursery schemes which would have assisted the many Catholic women employed in the mills of Derry and Belfast.[111] It was an extra stigma on poor communities that their women went out to work while their men were idle, and the Catholic clergy and Unionists were unlikely allies in treating it as such.[112] Although the activities of Catholic welfare societies such as St Vincent de Paul had been praised by social reformers, there is evidence that poorer Catholics preferred the anonymous state to the shame of relief from the better-off in their own community.[113] The very real benefits which the welfare state brought to the traditionally poorer Catholic population in Northern Ireland soon made the quality of life very different from that in the Irish Republic, where church influence had positively conspired against the less well-off.

But one running sore remained: the position of the Mater Hospital in north Belfast. At the outset run largely by Sisters of Mercy, this small hospital has always catered also for the needs of the largely working-class Protestant population in the area. It had good relations with the Queen's University and was a recognised teaching hospital. But, although provisions had been made in British legislation for protecting the ethos of such voluntary hospitals within the welfare state, the Northern Ireland Act of 1949 left the Mater out of the system. The Catholic Church had objected to the proposed transfer of the Hospital to state control as a form of 'theft', and it continued to function on voluntary assistance until 1972. In many ways Catholics have been disproportionately the beneficiaries of the welfare state, having started from a lower economic base. Indeed, the benefits of the welfare state played a major role in the softening of many Catholics' attitudes towards continued inclusion in the United Kingdom. But there can be no doubt that the limbo status of the Mater left a running sore. Again there was fault on both sides and the normally balanced study by Barritt and Carter had considerable difficulty reaching a conclusion on where the main fault lay. Their suggestion that the Minister should have made more effort at accommodation had also been made by more traditional supporters of the state, including the *Belfast Telegraph*.[114] Denied consultancies in the National Health Service, Mater Hospital doctors were to the fore among the rising Catholic middle class which spawned the civil-rights movement.

This absence of full state funding for Catholic educational and medical institutions became part of the Catholic folklore of unfair discrimination. The northern state's 'penalisation' and 'persecution' of Catholic education was a recurrent theme in the nationalist press and in clerical sermons and homilies, particularly during school renovation ceremonies or fund-raising events. Such fund-raising was woven into the pattern of everyday life for generations of Catholics, binding their identity ever more closely to that of an apparently embattled church. The YP pools, which helped fund the Mater Hospital, were collected on Friday evenings, giving pin-money to many a Catholic teenager and demarcating Catholic households which subscribed in mixed areas. The 'white babies' and 'black babies' collections in aid of the Catholic orphanages and missions, the imaginative 'buy-a-brick' school-building-fund schemes involved even those on the lowest income in that culture of 'supporting your own', which Catholics were nurtured on. Necessity shaded into defiance, school-building campaigns built up fighting funds to deter government interference. 'All our days were spent organising concerts or raffles or draws or competitions to raise more money to get equipment for the lab,' recalled Bernadette Devlin of her convent grammar school's 'struggle to do without government help and interference'.[115] Eamonn McCann, journalist, writer and former civil rights activist, recalled the high profile of such fund-raising activities in his working-class Derry community and their role in bonding church and community. 'The collection of money and articles for sale and the selling of tickets for weekly functions kept every household in almost daily contact with the church, provided the occasion for constant, repeated renewal of commitment to it.'[116]

A long tradition of necessity and self-help made Catholics adept at community organisation – a feature increasingly recognised in recent years by community workers in deprived Protestant areas. The drawback was that it created the image (and frequently the reality) of a grasping church. Stories abound of favouritism towards the children of publicans, bookmakers and the like in Catholic schools. Because of their estrangement from the dominant culture in Northern Ireland, Catholics have generally been reluctant to criticise their church in public. It is highly significant, therefore, that in the otherwise highly sectional-minded rural community of south Tyrone, analysed by Rosemary Harris in the 1950s, she should have found Catholics preferring to seek financial advice from a Protestant minister, rather than reveal their financial circumstances to their parish priest.[117]

Such communal self-help also intensified authoritarian tendencies within the Catholic Church and its resentment at Mother Teresa's interference in 1973 and most of all at Sinn Féin activities during the recent Troubles had much to do with its perceived role as sole arbiter of Catholic community projects. Maurice Hayes is a prominent lay Catholic. His lifelong experience of working closely with the Catholic Church involved some time training for the priesthood. He found that the most talented and spirited clergy tended not to be promoted and the limited experience and training of the others simply reinforced old stereotypes by returning priests to their communities in positions of leadership but without any new thinking.

The Down and Connor priests tended not to serve abroad. They were drawn from closed communities, educated within them in a segregated system, propagated in a sort of enclosed clerical hothouse, and returned straight to the community again in a position of status and leadership, where their views were not questioned or challenged. This was a recipe for the continuous reinforcement of values – the bad as well as the good. In a good sense, it meant that the clergy might be closer to the people, but the system also induced a lack of vision, an unwillingness to take risks, and an inordinate dwelling on old sores.

As chairman of the newly established Community Relations Commission in 1969, he found that the Catholic clergy had a highly developed sense of working within their own community, but none whatsoever of cross-community contacts.[118]

Until recent years there has been a sense of a repressive culture in the Catholic press, where clerical views were faithfully reproduced and never criticised, where communism, materialism and 'impurity' were regularly and hysterically denounced. The Catholic Church syllabus for religious instruction in second-level schools (in place until 1966) was particularly concerned about 'the subversive influences of the age'.[119] Little wonder that the faddish addition of a CND pin to a lapel in the 1960s was grounds for severe disciplining in the Catholic schools, or that Vatican II came as such a shock to most of the Irish hierarchy. Indeed, there are many well-educated Catholics in Northern Ireland today who still carry the same psychological scars of their education as those articulated to Fionnuala O Connor in 1992. Besides the wanton violence in some Catholic boys' schools, one university lecturer recalled his schooling in the late 1950s and early 1960s as one of 'ferocious humiliation and destruction of the personality'. Others remembered the victimisation of those from working-class backgrounds and favouritism towards the rich.[120]

It is an ethos most famously depicted in the fiction of Brian Moore, in his life-long critique of his native Belfast, the Catholic Church and (but thinly disguised), St Malachy's College, the Catholic boys' grammar school attended by Moore himself. It is a school where even the teachers are victims of its repressive violence and sexual puritanism [The Feast of Lupercal]. Judith Hearne had found meaning to her loneliness and suffering in the teachings and devotions of the Church. But as she loses her faith, the unsympathetic priest, to whom she turned for solace, was incapable of dealing with those who did not conform unquestioningly [*The Lonely Passion of Judith Hearne*]. And just as with Gavin in *The Emperor of Ice-Cream*, her questioning involves stark reappraisal of the ever-present holy statues and pictures, when stripped of their devotional significance – the Infant of Prague becoming a nagging little martinet, the picture of the Sacred Heart retained simply because it was familiar, part of the furniture.[121]

But Moore wrote at a distance. For most Catholics in the 1950s, when Moore's writing career started, the idea of criticising your own was unthinkable. It still is. Many of those talking with Fionnuala O Connor in 1992–3 asked for the tape-recorder to be switched off when they criticised the Church. Catholics, even lapsed ones, recognise Catholic culture as part and parcel of their identity. To attack it is to play the Protestant card. Catholic culture south of the border is altogether more confident and unthreatened. But in Northern Ireland the Church is still protected from internal criticism by that Catholic sixth sense of saying nothing which would feed anti-Catholicism. When Protestants claim that Catholicism is an authoritarian religion, which crushes debate and individualism, they have a point. But when they carry that criticism through to an assumption that Catholics are an unthinking herd, they entirely miss the real reason for such apparent lack of critical instincts within northern Catholicism. The same person who keeps mum in mixed company is as likely as not to let rip in the company of fellow Catholics.

Nor should one confuse internal criticism of the clergy with a rejection of the faith, still less of the community defined by it. Many commentators have noted a qualitative difference between Protestant and Catholic bigotry in Ulster. As noted earlier, Protestant bigotry seems to be more against the Catholic religion itself, whereas Catholics do not see Protestantism as threatening. This is because of a belief in the superiority of their religion and the time-old Church traditions of triumph through suffering and endurance: 'the Church suffering', 'the Church militant', 'the Church triumphant' were regular refrains. Maurice Hayes recalls the in-talk of his friends at the Catholic school in Downpatrick, of ghostly monks and bells below the river Roughal awaiting the reversal of the Reformation and return of property stolen by the Protestants.[122] Eamonn McCann tells of childhood pilgrimages to a rock near Buncrana, where the 'redcoats' were said to have murdered a penal-day priest, of other stories about the penal laws and the English offering food during the Famine if the people would 'turn' – 'but through it all the people stayed faithful'. 'An essential part of the Irish Freedom for which patriots had fought through the centuries was, we understood, the freedom to be Catholic.' There were daily reminders of the threat from red communism: the church attacked in Spain (prior to the 'Catholic victory' of Franco), in Mexico, in Yugoslavia, in Hungary, in China. The plight of Cardinal Mindszenty (Hungarian prelate, imprisoned by the Communists) was known to every Catholic schoolchild in the 1950s. 'That, one gathered, was what communism was about. The church was persecuted everywhere. The fact that it had survived was proof positive of its divine mission.'[123]

This sense of being part of a world-wide community was reinforced by references to the internationalism of the Latin mass, and many felt that something had gone out of their lives when the vernacular replaced it after Vatican II. The 'devotional revolution' reached its apogee in the twentieth century as daily lives revolved around the church's liturgical calendar. Aside from family rosary, daily mass and weekly confession, there was an extraordinary array of Catholic devotions on hand, recalled Maurice Hayes of his childhood in the 1930s and 1940s.

There were novenas for this and that which meant nine evenings on the trot, and nine Fridays, which involved mass and communion every Friday for nine weeks in succession . . . November Devotions and May Devotions and Lenten Devotions and Advent and Saint Patrick's Day and Corpus Christi and Sundays and Holy Days of Obligation and almost anything else anybody could think of, and the Men's Confraternity once a month and the Women's sodality and Perpetual Novena every Friday night so that there seemed to be few days in the year on which we did not go to church.[124]

Added to this were the large number of Catholic societies and committees to which one might belong. In 1939 tributes to the new bishop of Derry, Neil Farren, came from bodies ranging from the Knights of St Columbanus, the Irish National Foresters, the Ancient Order of Hibernians and St Vincent de Paul to St Columb's Past Pupils Union, the Derry Catholic Club and the Catholic Ex-Combatants

Association.[125] There would have been little time for social activity outside such a densely packed Catholic timetable. Catholicism provided a great big comfort blanket for its adherents, and far from repressiveness at this level, most remember a communal togetherness, crowded services, a place to meet friends and a sense of well-being in the dimly lit warmth of the perpetually open chapel.

There was too the pomp and pageant. In addition to the great processions for the feast of Corpus Christi and the thousands who would turn out for the various confraternities, investitures or funerals of bishops were like alternative state occasions. The Congress of the Catholic Truth Society of Ireland held in Belfast in 1934 attracted 120,000 to its pontifical mass. Tens of thousands lined the streets of Derry for Dr O'Kane's funeral in January 1939 and those of west Belfast for Dr Mageean's funeral in January 1962. Figures of 10,000 and 6,000 were estimated to have processed with the male and female confraternities to Clonard monastery in west Belfast in June and July 1958, whilst the golden jubilee of the Holy Family Confraternity had attracted 40,000 to the services at Clonard and accompanying street festivities in 1947.[126] But it was the activities surrounding the 1932 Eucharistic Congress which provided the most stunning example of triumphal pageantry and Catholic devotionalism as a leisure activity. An estimated 100,000 Catholics travelled south for the Phoenix Park ceremony, and a special high mass was said in Corrigan Park in Belfast for another 80,000. Numbers were further swollen by pilgrims disembarking at Belfast from other parts of the world. Open-air shrines and arches appeared all over Catholic Belfast and the press was full of pictures of the crowds who participated in the street devotions. It was, proclaimed the *Irish News* in bold headlines, the 'Triumph of Catholic Ireland', and so indeed it was treated by gangs of loyalists who stoned the trains as they departed.[127]

5. The Catholic Church and the Troubles

The post-war years saw a more conciliatory approach by the Catholic Church to the state. But in 1962 when William Philbin, bishop of Down and Connor, sought to pay a courtesy call on the Lord Mayor of Belfast – the first bishop of Down and Connor to do so since partition – he was snubbed, and a meeting between a Unionist Prime Minister and the head of the Catholic Church did not occur until 1970. An invitation to appoint a chaplain to the Northern Ireland parliament first came in 1968. It took the bishops three years to concede. By then the Troubles were already under way and there was some pressure from radical priests for the appointment to be suspended until the Stormont regime had reformed itself. Such internal criticism was highly unusual. Cardinal Conway could afford to ignore it. But the Troubles shook the Catholic Church – as they did the entire Catholic community – in a way not experienced since the 1790s.

When the civil-rights movement got under way, the Archbishop of Armagh was Cardinal William Conway, a Queen's University-educated Belfast man. He and Bishop Philbin had arrived within a year of each other in the early 1960s and in outlook were quite different from their recent predecessors. Both were intellectuals who had participated in Vatican II. Though religiously orthodox, they brought to the hierarchy a political reticence unthinkable since the time of the 'devotional revolution'. The civil-rights movement, with its call for reforms within the state, matched this new mood precisely, and there was considerable involvement by the clergy in its early stages. When violence erupted the bishops followed tradition by condemning it, Philbin personally intervening in 1972 to have the barricades removed in Catholic 'no-go' areas. As such they increasingly ran foul of the emerging republican movement.

Although many accuse the Catholic Church of having partly assisted the rise of the Provisional IRA – as an antidote to the socialist Official IRA – a survey made in 1986 could identify only three priests as having had any sympathy for the Provos, and *they* were ostracised. Likewise barely nine showed any inclination to vote Sinn Féin.[128] The northern church, whilst it has remained as thoroughly nationalist as before (or, more correctly, as anti-Unionist), has been solid in its condemnation of IRA violence. This has often placed it in an ambiguous situation, which critics have been all too ready to exploit. It sought to explain the apparent contradiction of supporting past rebels, whilst condemning present ones, by depicting the Provos as something entirely different. But its lack of moral certainty on a range of associated issues laid it open to attack in a majority culture so attuned to seeing priests as the real enemy. Whatever its public condemnations, it has not actually deprived the IRA of any of its theological services or sacraments, continuing to bury IRA men and refusing to bend to pressures to excommunicate them. In fact, history was on its side, for such actions in the past were counter-productive. Even so, its explanations sounded unconvincing to outsiders. Its refusal to denounce the hunger-strike deaths as suicide revealed its theology to be compromised by its nationalism and occasioned something of a rebuke from Cardinal Hume, then head of the Catholic Church in England.[129]

There can be no doubt that the clergy has walked a tightrope in its attitudes to republican activities, sensing they would be damned if they did and damned if they didn't. At times it has been near impossible to argue church teaching on Catholic funerals, when they have been made such occasions for republican propaganda. The clergy also recognised that any criticism of the state, when before the Troubles they would have had no such inhibitions, would be twisted to insinuate that they were Provo sympathisers. In 1969 one priest, Father Denis Faul, was publicly criticised by Cardinal Conway for his attacks on the judiciary. His subsequent campaign with another priest, Father Raymond Murray, to highlight injustice and misbehaviour by the security forces, also caused embarrassment to his superiors.[130] Promotion was a long time in coming. But even among many lower clergy there was concern in these early years that their church was not speaking out against state violence. It has to be said that as IRA violence (and even more so the political threat from Sinn Féin) increased, most clergy fell in behind their bishops. Although many, in protest at internment, had refused co-operation with the 1971 census, none supported the republicans' campaign against the next census in 1981.

The position of the Catholic Church has been an unenviable one during the Troubles. Its tendency to discourage internal debate at a time when it was never more necessary has weakened it. But the awful position of many clergy, at the centre of a bloody vortex, partly produced by their own predecessors and largely centred on their own community, must surely be epitomised by that terrifying picture of Father Alex Reid, despair in his face, as he prayed over the semi-naked body of the dead British soldier, battered to death in west Belfast in the spring of 1988. He subsequently became a key player in bringing about the IRA ceasefires of 1994 and 1997.

The Catholic Church had already become more accommodating towards the state even before the Troubles and was broadly supporting an internal power-sharing rather than an anti-partitionist constitutional solution. But just like the constitutional nationalist politicians, particularly after the downfall of the power-sharing executive in 1974, it had little to show for its denunciation of republican violence. In a moving interview with Fionnuala O Connor, Bishop Edward Daly of Derry spoke of the almost impossible position of the clergy during the Troubles, every incautious word pounced upon by one side or the other. Born in south Fermanagh, with impeccable nationalist credentials, Daly had been a popular priest in Derry and was the priest most associated with his community at the time of Bloody Sunday (1972). One senses that his promotion to the bishopric of Derry in 1974, at the young age of thirty-nine, was an effort by the Church to stem the flow of recruits to militant republicanism, as was the elevation of Tomás Ó Fiaich to Armagh in 1977.

Ó Fiaich was a charismatic, generous and plain-spoken man, whose historical studies of his native Armagh were masterly. His ten-year 'reign' as head of the Irish Church was nevertheless a mixed blessing for the northern Catholics. Popular with republicans, because he called for Irish unity and British withdrawal, he aroused mixed feelings in other Catholics. They sometimes admired his outspokenness on issues where they were traditionally reticent. But this native of Cullyhana in south Armagh, near Crossmaglen, who had spent most of his adult life outside Northern Ireland, did not always observe those unspoken conventions by which northern Catholics and Protestants regulate social interaction. When, with the best of intentions and genuine emotion, he apologised on behalf of the entire Catholic community for the 1987 bombing of Enniskillen by the IRA, many Catholics were outraged that he should have so identified them with republican atrocities.[131] His misfortune was to have been leader of the Catholic Church in Ireland at the time of the hunger strikes. His own ultra-nationalism and open support of the prisoners' cause both hardened theirs and the British government's resolve, where a more neutral figure might have had more success in securing concessions.

The successor to Cardinal Ó Fiaich could hardly have been more different. It was as if the Church had gone on the offensive against the growing strength of republicanism after the hunger strikes. Dr Cahal Daly was from County Antrim and had been bishop of Down and Connor since 1982. His was the most anti-republican of all the clerical voices. Politically a nationalist, like all the clergy, he nevertheless adopted the line that the future lay in respect for both traditions in Northern Ireland, and unification, if it ever came, could do so only with the consent of all. On the ground he began seriously to combat the growing challenge to church authority posed by the rise of Sinn Féin.

Catholic voluntary social activity – aside from that of the St Vincent de Paul Society and the Legion of Mary – was underdeveloped, as was the Church's communication with the providers of state social funding.[132] Philbin and Conway had a rather better record than their predecessors in this area. Even so, the fact that the Church itself sought and became the main channel for government funding to job-creation schemes in Catholic west Belfast by the 1980s was quite a reversal of previous practice and owed much to the new bishop's crusade to combat the growing community activity of Sinn Féin. Mass attendance had dropped alarmingly in some west Belfast communities, falling as low as 33 per cent in one parish by 1983. The increased communal involvement by the Church, notably by the nuns, brought the figures up again, though there has been no return to Richard Rose's findings in 1968 of 95 per cent Sunday observance in such areas. The bitterness of republican response was some measure of the Church's success, one outraged republican declaring of a competing church-run community centre that it had even called in the police to deal with trouble![133] The sum total of such accusations was that the Church had joined the enemy, and indeed this is one of the most fascinating, though rarely-noted,[134] aspects of the church-republican battle. Since the clergy have rarely been out of touch with the pulse of popular acceptability, such a very public stance against the IRA speaks volumes for general Catholic opinion. The decline in Church influence in working-class areas is undisputed. But for the first time it now has considerable influence both within the state and a range of other opinion and policy-forming bodies. The ghetto church has gone.

Has the Catholic clergy been as profoundly changed by the Troubles as the laity? On religious issues, and above all on education, it still seems profoundly authoritarian. The 'pick-and-mix' or 'café' Catholicism of so many of its flock today evokes little sympathy and it is significant that the most innovative thinking is coming from the religious orders or from clergy who have come to Northern Ireland from the south. Traditional Catholic reluctance to criticise one's own was reinforced by the Troubles and the northern Church has been spared the rethinking which criticism by a more confident Catholic populace in the Republic has produced. Edna Longley, professor of English at Queen's University, is critical. 'The Northern Catholic Church, still locked into a nineteenth-century relationship with nationalism, is also pursuing its own interests, in that Northern Catholics can be kept thirty years less liberal than their Southern counterparts.'[135]

However, there would need to be a significant decline in the anti-Catholicism of the majority community in Northern Ireland for such Catholic revisionism to take hold. In the most comprehensive survey of northern clerical attitudes this century (Gerald McElroy's questionnaire of 1986), there was a significantly higher rate of response from religious orders than from diocesan clergy (58.5 per cent – rising to 100 per cent in Derry – against 31.7 per cent). Even so, McElroy's findings do reflect internal debate within the Church, even if it has not yet erupted on to the public arena. From 232 responses, he concluded that, whilst respondents were uniformly nationalist in political orientation, they were almost exclusively constitutional nationalists. Younger, urban-based priests tended to more flexibility on the issue than older or rural-based ones. They also were more aware of the need to accommodate Protestants than their southern counterparts, as many as 50.4 per cent of the respondents favouring the liberalising of church attitudes either on divorce or mixed marriages (and in this they reflected Ulster Catholic lay opinion at the time). Again it was the younger clerics and the religious who were more willing to criticise their church on a range of issues associated with the Troubles: failure to condemn state violence, to help the poorer communities, to encourage inter-communal reconciliation. All were broadly happy on the Church's denunciation of republican violence. The only area on which the clergy were discovered to be out of step with lay Catholic opinion was that of education. The bulk of northern-born clergy (as against the southern-born) were opposed to integrated education, 67.2 per cent and 39.7 per cent respectively, the figures for those accepting that it would reduce Northern Ireland's problems: 14.5 per cent parish priests, 31.2 per cent curates, but 66.1 per cent religious. These findings largely correspond with the conclusions of the Opsahl Commission in 1993. Significantly it was the religious sisters, who do not appear to have been included in McElroy's questionnaire, who were then more prepared to comment on the shortcomings of their church. The dramatic post-Vatican-II transformation of the role played by nuns in Northern Ireland still awaits research.[136] During the Troubles they were certainly instrumental in reversing the mounting criticism of the clergy in deprived communities.

As I complete this final chapter, Ulster Catholic identity is in transition. The Troubles have shattered many of the old certainties and for a number of years the resulting confusion eroded much of that nascent Catholic confidence so noticeable in the civil-rights movement. 'This is the reason for the withdrawal into private life and apparent apathy of so many Northern Ireland people', I concluded in 1993, 'the fragmentation of the old identities, the abuses to which they have given rise, but the inability to arrive at anything new which carries the same clarity.'[137] The Troubles have completed the clergy's withdrawal from vocal nationalist politics, a process also hastened by the emergence of a strong nationalist party in the SDLP and latterly in Sinn Féin. Although the Troubles witnessed periods when political Catholicism retreated into traditional moulds – notably at the time of Bloody Sunday (1972) and the Hunger Strikes of 1981, the aspirations of the civil-rights movement for justice and equality within Northern Ireland have remained the dominant political aim of a majority of Ulster Catholics. This, and the recognition that an aspiration to eventual unity is a legitimate aim, if pursued by peaceful means, is enshrined in the Belfast-Good Friday Agreement of April 1998. Anti-discrimination laws, job-creation schemes, the Parades Commission, reforms within the RUC and more to come following the report of the Patten Commission, have gone some way to bringing Catholics into a sense of legitimate belonging in Northern Ireland.[138] Seamus Mallon, in that black humour so characteristic of Northern Ireland, has called the 1998 Agreement 'Sunningdale for slow learners'. The humour only barely disguises the tragedy that similar arrangements were on offer a quarter of a century ago.

Certainly the literature coming out of Northern Ireland in the past twenty-five years, particularly its fiction, makes bleak reading. The sectarianism is so prevalent that it is almost a caricature. Authors are still recognisably from one community or the other. Inevitably, as the largest concentration of population, Belfast has been the setting for the majority of such fiction. Often presented in monotones, fated to its grimness and violence as much as to its climatic wetness. It was in itself such an accepted stereotype that, as Edna Longley amusingly observes, camera crews, arriving to make the equally stereotypical Troubles thriller, were reluctant to film a sunny Belfast.[139] Seamus Deane's semi-autobiographical *Reading in the Dark,* shows an equally bleak Derry, where the countryside across the border in County Donegal serves the same function of escape to another world as that of the Cave-Hill for Belfast writers. Here is a parable of a community carrying the scars of the 1920s and nurturing its grievances into the 1960s. The result blights their own families and community as much as the society around them.

This is a feature of late Troubles novels by Catholic writers: a recognition of the imperfect past which helped produce the Troubles, but a bafflement at the outcome. In Deane, as in others, England is the conqueror who should get out of Ireland, but also a place of refuge and freedom for escapees from the claustrophobia of charity-less Catholic vendettas. And when the enemy appears as the mourning Yorkshire miner father of the soldier son shot by an IRA sniper, even Deane's staunchly republican family is moved to pity.[140] Mary Beckett's Belfast working-class Catholic heroine in *Give Them Stones* (1987) also carries the experiences and rhetoric of the past into the present, but again it provides an awkward fit. 'The IRA [of which her father had been a member in the 1940s] would never hurt ordinary people', comments Martha, 'only the system they were going to pull down. And the border would disappear and we'd all be one united country with our government giving fair play to everyone' – at least this is what they were supposed to do, 'not fighting Protestants'.[141]

'Catholic' writing, like Catholic identity, is in transition.[142] There is little romanticisation of the past, little left of the belief in the old panaceas of 'freeing Ireland', and a recognition that the problem like the solution lies with the two communities themselves. A plague on all your houses, is the most extreme version of this in Robert McLiam Wilson's *Ripley Bogle*. Catholic west Belfast in upbringing, and thrown on the streets as an adolescent by his mother – for dating a Protestant – the young male anti-hero blames his fate on the traditions of his blighted upbringing and the 'senseless sentimentality' of stock Irishness. The reality inspires some of the most unromantic descriptions of IRA activity to appear in any Troubles-inspired fiction. Here they are petty, jumped-up young hoods – their leaders aping leadership by sporting cheap suits and gangsterish hairstyles – their fight for Ireland consisting of stripping and tarring a young girl for consorting with the army.

The Troubles have been a dehumanising trauma, with the very communities which produced the paramilitaries at the sharpest receiving end of their violence. The New Ireland Forum of 1983–4 published a demography of the violence in Northern Ireland showing a heavy concentration in nationalist areas. 'In other words the IRA was causing greater damage to those it was supposed to be defending.'[143] People in Catholic west Belfast felt treated as outcasts, assumed to be Provo supporters simply because of their religion and location. One Catholic man at the Falls Road session of the Opsahl Commission hearings in February 1993 was dismayed at the 'set' pieces and resort to the time-worn themes of old nationalism. 'All the new thinking is among the Prods . . . All the old thinking is among the Taigs. We're stuck,' he lamented. It was hard not to sympathise with his sense of frustration, after listening to the presentation and discussion that had provoked his outburst and which had argued that the Northern Ireland situation was a 'colonial' problem.[144]

There are still some in Northern Ireland who will reiterate the old orthodoxy of 800 years of British misrule as the root cause of the Troubles and its removal as the ultimate solution. But even Sinn Féin is inching away from this – however belatedly. Too often it transferred the blame elsewhere, and disguised the ethnic nature of Ulster Catholic nationalism. In this the successful transformation of a religion into an all-encompassing culture may yet prove quite an obstacle to harmonious communal relations. Catholics are startled by the continuing anti-popery of political Protestantism, at the insults to their clergy, at the attacks on their churches. Even the newly successful members of the Catholic middle class carry scars of prejudice encountered. Many Ulster Catholics are indeed still 'stuck', still the prisoners of their past, or what they have been told is their past. They are deterred from constructive criticism both of their Church, because their culture is so entwined with it, and of their culture, because it is still under attack. The workings of the eighteenth-century penal laws and seventeenth-century Ulster Plantation have been partly misunderstood and consciously used for partisan purposes. But they did happen. They represented defeat for a way of life and later injustices gave them added value. It is largely among an older generation and committed republicans that such historic bitterness remains strong. But that such respected community leaders as Paddy Doherty in Derry can still view them as dictating the fate of a people, can still speak of 'settlers' and 'natives', that nationalists can still polarise at election time, that even the growing Catholic middle class is still reluctant to give full allegiance to the state testifies to the continuing burden of the past.[145] There is a view that Ulster Protestants are not really interested in Irish history because they will always be depicted as the victimiser, the 'blow-in', the 'planter', and blamed accordingly. Indeed, it is baffling the extent to which they have thus subscribed to nationalist historiography and accepted both the 'settler' category and the predominance of the land issue. The ethnographer Henry Glassie spent the late 1970s studying the rural community of Ballymenone, not far from the Fermanagh/ Cavan border. Basic neighbourliness within this mixed (though largely Catholic) small farming community was predominant. Even so he found knowledge of local history confined entirely to Catholics. 'Protestants say they are not interested in history, and Catholics say that is because they cannot be; Irish history is filled with the mistreatment of Catholics'.[146]

Intellectuals in the Republic of Ireland have spent several decades questioning the anti-English underpinnings of their nationalist past – often in a language which shocked the greener nationalists. But the debate, even the shock-therapy, was a necessary prerequisite to the emergence of the now confident Irish state as a player in world politics. The Troubles embarked nationalists on a more painful process of self-examination. It was easier for the republic to exorcise the ghost of the long-absent British. In the north, however, the people held responsible for the land confiscations and persecutions are one's neighbours. Orange marches through Catholic areas still have the potential to open half-healed sores about territoral conquest.

The acceptance of Northern Ireland as home, warts and all, has been a feature of recognisably Protestant writing. It has not been prominent in Catholic writing, though in reality intense local pride (or defensiveness) has been common to both communities. Mary Beckett's short story, *A Belfast Woman,* is a more mature writer's reflections on how working people negotiated their lives in those bleak streets of Belfast. The central character, Mary Harrison, had been intimidated out of her home twice before (1921 and 1935). But when the threatening notice came in 1972, she decided this time to stay. She had been the only Catholic in a Protestant street. Her husband's people had been Protestant; but he had been raised a Catholic in accordance with his dead mother's wishes. It took Mary some time to get used to the Protestant street, where neighbours kept themselves to themselves. They had been good neighbours none the less, and when they in turn were intimidated out and Catholic families moved in, she found the Catholic expectations of constant sociability and open doors hard to take. Her daughter had moved to Canada and wrote of how ashamed she was of those at home. Mary was stung. 'It's not right to put the blame on poor powerless people. The most of us never did anything but stay quiet and put up with things the way they were', and they warned the young ones that went on marches that it would all end in 'shooting and burning and murder'. One day a salesman came trying to sell Venetian blinds. But she told him she liked to see the sunset behind the Divis Mountain. He agreed that if through the smoke and dirt and pollution of Belfast you could still have sunsets like that, 'then there's hope for all of us'.

This pride of place is (and always has been) widespread in Ulster. But it is rarely heard above the political rhetoric, and the mutual mistrust of Protestant and Catholic is too ingrained to be easily overcome. However, it is high time that we 'poor powerless people' stopped blaming everyone else for what has happened and took control of our future by accepting responsibility for our past. For several centuries Catholics have felt no sense of ownership of Ulster and their rejection even of the name 'Ulster' since partition was part and parcel of an extraordinary nihilism and communal fatalism which thankfully appears to be coming to an end. There was little forgiveness in the past for the Unionist takeover and redefinition of the ancient Gaelic territory. The future of the peace process in Northern Ireland may yet be determined by the ability of all to agree on what 'Ulster' means. Until then 'Irishness' and 'Britishness' will remain the fig-leaves disguising the underlying local quarrel. The structures set up under the Good Friday Agreement involve something of a forced marriage of normally antagonistic parties. But it is the first time in history that Catholics and Protestants have been placed on an equal footing, with political structures to match, and the more the militant wings of the two traditions can be tied into constitutional procedures which work, the more they will decline.

I have argued throughout this book that it is a myth to see Ulster Catholics as natural rebels. Even today, their dislike of the Union flag derives not from any particular wish to overthrow the state, but rather from its aggressive (and very widespread) intimidatory usage by loyalists. There is no corresponding attachment to the Irish tricolour, except by republicans. Nor is there any immediate desire for Irish unification, except as an aspiration. A significant number of Catholics (ranging from 16 to 31 per cent in the 1990s) are content with the British connection, and the overwhelming majority support the current constitutional arrangement based on majority consent.[147] This is not to say that dissident republicanism does not have some power to destabilise this fragile consensus. But militant republicanism requires some communal support to flourish, and today the bulk of Catholics want decommissioning of weapons just as much as Protestants do. Moreover, republican violence during the Troubles badly shook nationalist self-confidence. There has been a noticeable return of such confidence since the Good Friday Agreement. There has, unfortunately, been a corresponding decline in confidence among Protestants – conditioned to think that Catholics can only prosper at their expense. A certain amount of republican and nationalist triumphalism is contributing to such Protestant insecurity. But I would suggest that such confidence may be no bad thing, for their new-found 'place in the sun' is firmly located in Northern Ireland. A sense of 'belonging', without the resentment, may yet prove to be the most important legacy of the Good Friday Agreement.

Notes

Short titles for books and abbreviations for journals are used in the notes. Please refer to the Bibliography for full references to the books and the following list of abbreviations for the journals.

Anal. Hib.	*Analecta Hibernica*
Archiv. Hib.	*Archivium Hibernicum*
BL	British Library
BNL	*Belfast News Letter*
Cal. S.P. Ire.	*Calendar of the State Papers relating to Ireland*
Coll. Hib.	*Collectanea Hibernica*
E.H.R.	*English Historical Review*
FDJ	*Faulkner's Dublin Journal*
FJ	*Freeman's Journal*
Hist. Jn.	*Historical Journal*
Ir. Eccles. Rec.	*Irish Ecclesiastical Record*
IFC	Irish Folklore Commission, University College, Dublin
I.H.S.	*Irish Historical Studies*
Jn. Med. Hist.	*Journal of Medieval History*
CKS	Centre for Kentish Studies, Maidstone
NAI	National Archives of Ireland, Dublin
NICH	*Northern Ireland House of Commons Debates*
NLI	National Library of Ireland
NS	*Northern Star*
NUI	National University of Ireland
Proc. R.I.A.	*Proceedings of the Royal Irish Academy*
PRO	Public Record Office, London
PRONI	Public Record Office of Northern Ireland
QUB	Queen's University, Belfast
R.S.A.I. Jn.	*Journal of the Royal Society of Antiquaries of Ireland*
UFTM	Ulster Folk and Transport Museum, Cultra
U.J.A.	*Ulster Journal of Archaeology*

I FROM CÚ CHULAINN TO CHRISTIANITY

1 Duffy, 'Geographical Perspectives on the Borderlands', in Gillespie and O'Sullivan, eds., *The Borderlands*, 11, shows this to be 'the most extensive drumlin belt in western Europe'. See also Mallory and Hartwell, 'Down in Prehistory', in Proudfoot, ed., *Down. History and Society*, 1–31.

2 De Paor, *The Peoples of Ireland*, 20–21, and O'Kelly, *Early Ireland*, 85–7; Aalen, *Man and Landscape in Ireland*, 52; Mallory and McNeill, *The Archaeology of Ulster from Colonization to Plantation*, 8–10, 20–21.

3 Piggott, *The Druids*, 55; but see Waddell, 'The Question of the Celticization of Ireland', *Emania*, ix, 5–16.

4 O'Rahilly, *Early Irish History and Mythology*, though pioneering and exerting much influence on later writings, many of his findings are now dismissed as speculation.

5 Notably Adamson, *The Identity of Ulster*; Buckley, ' "We're Trying to Find Our Identity" ', in Tonkin, McDonald and Chapman, eds., *History and Ethnicity*, 183–97.

6 Mallory and McNeill, *Archaeology of Ulster*, 176–9.

7 Mitchell and Ryan, *Reading the Irish Landscape*, 255; McCormick, 'Farming and Food in Medieval Lecale', in Proudfoot, ed., *Down. History and Society*, 34–38.

8 O'Kelly, *Early Ireland*, 305; Aalen, *Man and Landscape*, 86–7.

9 Norman and St Joseph, *The Early Development of Irish Society*, 60, 68–72.

10 Kelly, *A Guide to Early Irish Law*, 36.

11 Kinsella, trans., *The Tain*, 58–60, 157–8; what O'Riordain, *The Gaelic Mind and the Collapse of the Gaelic World*, 117–18, calls 'the Cuchulainn factor': generosity, valour, immortality.

12 O'Rahilly, *Early Irish History and Mythology*, 291–2 (also taken up in one of Moore's melodies).

13 See Gantz, *Early Irish Myths and Sagas*, 15.

14 O'Rahilly, *Early Irish History and Mythology*, 289–90.

15 Livingstone, *Monaghan Story*, 14–16.

16 Moody, Martin and Byrne, eds., *A New History of Ireland*, viii, 13, 15.

17 Kinsella, trans., *The Tain*, 86.

18 Rogers, 'The Folklore of the Black Pig's Dyke', *Ulster Folklife*, iii, 29–36, and see response in *ibid.*, iv, 75.

19 O'Kelly, *Early Ireland*, 322; Livingstone, *Fermanagh Story*, 4; Mallory and McNeill, *Archaeology of Ulster*, 150–153.

20 On the debate over the origins of the 'Irish' language and the whole problem of 'Celticization', see a number of contributions to *Emania*, ix, notably by Waddell (5–16), Raftery (28–32) and Mallory (53–8).

21 For later interpretations of the Celtic past see: Bjersby, *The Interpretation of the Cuchulainn Legend in the Works of W. B. Yeats*; Flower, *The Irish Tradition*; Hill, 'Popery and Protestantism, Civil and Religious Liberty: The

Disputed Lessons of Irish History 1690–1812', *Past and Present*, 118, 96–129; O'Halloran, 'Irish Re-creations of the Gaelic Past: The Challenge of MacPherson's Ossian', *Past and Present*, 124, 69–95; MacCartney, 'The Writing of History in Ireland, 1800–30', *I.H.S.*, x, 347–362; Jeffares, 'Place, Space and Personality and the Irish Writer', O'Driscoll, 'Return to the Hearthstone', both in Carpenter, ed., *Place, Personality and the Irish Writer*, 11–40 and 41–68 respectively; Vance, 'Celts, Carthaginians and Constitutions: Anglo-Irish Literary Relations, 1780–1820', *I.H.S.*, xxii, 219–22; Dunne, 'Haunted by History: Irish Romantic Writing, 1800–50', in Porter and Teich, eds., *Romanticism in National Context*, 68–91; Rafroidi, 'Imagination and Revolution: the Cuchulain Myth', in MacDonagh, Mandle and Travers, eds., *Irish Culture and Nationalism, 1750–1950*, 137–48; Green, *History of the Irish State to 1014*; MacNeill, *Celtic Ireland*; Comyn and Dineen, eds., *The History of Ireland by Geoffrey Keating*, 4 vols.

22 Mallory, ed., *Aspects of the Táin*, 33, 58–62, 111–13; Jackson, *The Oldest Irish Tradition: A Window on the Iron Age*; but see critique of Jackson in Aitchison, 'The Ulster Cycle: Heroic Image and Historical Reality', *Jn. Med. Hist.*, 13, 87–116; also McCone, *Pagan Past and Christian Present in Early Irish Literature*, 4, on the proper context for understanding early Irish literature being the early Christian period, despite assumed oral origins; and Ó Cathasaigh, 'Early Irish Narrative Literature', in McCone and Simms, eds., *Progress in Medieval Irish Studies*, 58. However, Murphy, *Saga and Myth in Ancient Ireland*, 43, accepts 'the general historicity of their background', a similar conclusion to that of Mallory and McNeill, *Archaeology of Ulster*, 167–71.

23 Mallory, ed., *Aspects of the Táin*, 29–30; Green, *History of the Irish State to 1014*, 93–4; O'Grady, *History of Ireland*, 22.

24 Cited Hyde, *A Literary History of Ireland*, 592.

25 O'Grady, *The Heroic Period*, 25.

26 Flanagan in Vaughan, ed., *A New History of Ireland*. v, 515–20. On Cú Chulainn in modern folklore see Murphy, *Tyrone Folk Quest*, 69; Murphy, *At Slieve Gullion's Foot*, 17; Murphy, *Ulster Folk of Field and Fireside*, 83–4, 151–2; Murphy, *Rathlin: Island of Blood and Enchantment*, 6, 174–5; Livingstone, *Monaghan Story*, 10–11; Livingstone, *Fermanagh Story*, 1–3.

27 See, however, Sharpe, 'St Patrick and the See of Armagh', *Cambridge Medieval Celtic Studies*, 4, 33–59 on the debate surrounding Patrick's association with Armagh; also Binchy's seminal study, 'Patrick and his Biographers, Ancient and Modern', *Stud. Hib.*, ii (1962), 7–173.

28 Kelly, *Early Irish Law*, 60; Etchingham, 'Early Medieval Irish History', in McCone and Simms, eds., *Progress in Medieval Irish Studies*, 127; Hanson, *Saint Patrick*.

29 Gerald of Wales, *The History and Topography of Ireland*, translated by O'Meara, 115–16.

30 Linenhall Lib., NI Pol. Coll., P. 1740, *The Rise of Papal Power in Ireland* (London and Cork, 1983), P. 3479; Griffin, *Anglican and Irish*; Linenhall Lib., Joy MSS, 8, 113–35; Ussher, *An Epistle Written by the Rev. James*

Ussher, Bishop of Meath, Concerning the Religion Anciently Professed by the Irish and Scottish (Dublin, 1631); Mason, *The Testimony of St Patrick against the False Pretensions of Rome to Primitive Antiquity in Ireland*; Hamilton, *Letters Concerning the Northern Coast of the County of Antrim*, 50–70. For an excellent survey of the eighteenth-century debate on the nature of the early Irish church see Hill, 'Popery and Protestantism', 96–129.

31 See good discussion in Corish, *The Irish Catholic Experience, A Historical Survey*, 8–10, also his 'The Early Irish Church and the Western Patriarchate', in Ní Chatháin and Richter, eds., *Ireland und Europa, die Kirche in Frühmittelalter*, 9–15; Richter, *Medieval Ireland*, 62; Hanson, *Saint Patrick*, 203.

32 For the ongoing debate on the nature of early Irish ecclesiastical settlements see Etchingham, 'Early Medieval Irish History', 137–8; Etchingham, 'The Implications of Paruchia', *Ériu*, xliv, 139–62.

33 For the survival of such claims by the leading Gaelic families, see Ó Doibhlin, 'The Deanery of Tulach Óg', *Seanchas Ard Mhacha*, vi, no. 1, 141–82; Martin, 'Derry in 1590: a Catholic demonstration', *Clogher Record*, vi, no. 3, 597–602; Faulkner, 'The Right of Patronage of the Maguires of Tempo', *Clogher Record*, ix, no. 2, 167–86. This proprietorial outlook by the coarbs and erenachs (as the successors were called) extended to the relics and religious artefacts; see, for e.g., IFC, MS 1215/44–76, the bell of Drumragh in Tyrone, said to have been in the keeping of the McEnhill (MacConchoille) family for eleven hundred years.

34 Ryan, *The Monastic Institute*, 49–50.

35 See Binchy, 'A Pre-Christian Survival in Medieval Irish Hagiography', in Whitelock, McKitterick and Dumville, eds., *Ireland in Early Medieval Europe*, 165–178.

36 Ó Corráin, 'Nationality and Kingship in Pre-Norman Ireland', in Moody, ed., *Nationality and the Pursuit of National Independence*, 13–19.

37 Binchy, 'Opening Address', Mac Niocaill, 'Christian Influences in Early Irish law', and Ó Corráin, 'Irish Law and Canon Law', all in Ní Chatháin and Richter, eds., *Irland und Europa*, 4, 151–6 and 157–66; all three see native traditions and laws as transforming Irish Christianity rather than the reverse. In the same collection, Ó Cathasaigh, 'Pagan Survivals: The Evidence of Early Irish Narrative', 291–307, examines the heated controversy over the contribution of oral native traditions to the early church. See also McCone and Simms, eds., *Progress in Medieval Irish Studies*, 62, 124–6.

38 Flower, *The Irish Tradition*, 1–23 and 74–5; the *Annals of Ulster* are traditionally seen to have originated with Colum Cille's community in Iona, then continued probably at Armagh and Clonard, see Richter, *Medieval Ireland*, 82–4. See also Hamlin, 'The Early Church in County Down to the Twelfth Century', in Proudfoot, ed., *Down. History and Society*, 47–70.

39 Glassie, *Irish Folk History*, 32; for the strength of local tradition on Colum Cille, see also Murphy, *Rathlin*, 3; O'Laverty, *An Historical Account of the Diocese of Down and Connor, Ancient and Modern*, 5 vols., ii, 11–20; IFC, MS 102/25–30, 42–6; UFTM, Field Recording, R80.55, and Transcript 7/

28–9, Tyrone traditions of Colum Cille; also Lacy's accessible *Colum Cille and the Columban Tradition.*

40 IFC, MS 1364/36, 120/55–6, and UFTM, R85.10, traditions of Colum Cille's association with curses; O'Laverty, *Down and Connor*, i, 126; Gillespie, *Devoted People*, 138.

41 See Corish, *The Christian Mission*, 4–5. Colum Cille is frequently seen as Ireland's first exile; see Ó Laoghaire, 'Irish Spirituality', in Ní Chatháin and Richter, eds., *Irland und Europa*, 73–5, on how this notion of wrenching from country appeared in very early writings. Also de Paor, *Peoples*, 62. See Livingstone, *Fermanagh*, 8–19, on the royal lineages of the early saints and the rich folklore attaching to them.

42 Hennessy, ed., *Annals of Ulster*, 4 vols., i, 377.

43 Byrne, 'Tribes and Tribalism in Early Ireland', *Ériu*, xxii, 128–66, 160–66; though see McCone's attack on the idea of 'cosy' tiny kingdoms before the Viking raids in *Pagan Past and Christian Present*, 8ff.

44 *Annals of Ulster*, i, 323. Livingstone, *Monaghan Story*, 38–9, gives good account of local consequences of these developments.

45 *Annals of Ulster*, i, 433, see also entries for 899 and 917.

46 de Paor, *Peoples*, 75; Simms, *From Kings to Warlords*, 10–11; though see Etchingham in McCone and Simms, eds., in *Progress in Medieval Studies*, 141.

47 Gillespie and O'Sullivan, eds., *The Borderlands*, 33; Byrne, 'Tribes and Tribalism', 156.

48 See for e.g. Livingstone, *Fermanagh Story*, 23–4; Ó Corráin, *Ireland before the Normans*, 15.

49 Cited Byrne, in Cosgrave, ed., *New History of Ireland*, ii, 39; also Ó Corráin, *Ireland before the Normans*, 172.

50 Corish, *Christian Mission*, 86–7; Etchingham, 'The Early Irish Church', 99–118.

51 Hughes, 'Sanctity and Secularism in the Early Irish Church', in Dumville, ed., *Kathleen Hughes*, 21–37.

52 Hughes, *The Church in Early Irish Society*, ch. 20.

53 Doherty, 'The Use of Relics in Early Ireland', in Ní Chatháin and Richter, eds., *Irland und Europa*, 95: Livingstone, *Monaghan Story*, 24–8; O'Laverty, *Down and Connor*, i, 248–53; *Fermanagh Herald*, 9 September 1981 (Holy Wells).

54 Glassie, *Irish Folk History*, 21.

55 Philip Dixon Hardy, *The Holy Wells of Ireland*, iv; Ó Muirgheasa, 'The Holy Wells of Donegal', *Béaloideas*, vi, 141–62; Doherty, 'The Use of Relics in Early Ireland', 89–101. O'Laverty finds holy wells in almost every townland, *Down and Connor*, iii, 419–20, 443; also IFC, MS 102/62–31, for holy bells and their traditional custodians.

2 GAELIC ULSTER: LAND, LORDSHIP
AND PEOPLE

1 There is some confusion over respective usage of the terms Anglo-Norman or Anglo-Irish during the two centuries following the 'invasion'. The practice here is that suggested by F. X. Martin: Anglo-Norman for the period up to 1216, Anglo-Irish thereafter (Cosgrove, ed., *New History of Ireland*, ii, li–liii). Medieval historians now tend to play down the 'invasion' as some kind of turning point, see Cosgrove, 'The Writing of Irish Medieval History', *I.H.S*, xxvii, 97–111. For a comprehensive survey see McNeill, *Anglo-Norman Ulster*, also his chapter in Brady, O'Dowd and Walker, eds., *Ulster: An Illustrated History*, 44–76.

2 Though see Seán Duffy's argument for a Cumbrian origin of John de Courcy, 'The First Ulster Plantation: John de Courcy and the Men of Cumbria', in Barry, Frame and Simms, eds., *Colony and Frontier in Medieval Ireland*, 1–27.

3 See e.g. in the case of Monaghan – Livingstone, *Monaghan Story*, 42–4 – how the MacMahons established their ascendancy under the mantle of the Anglo-Normans; also Simms, 'The O'Hanlons, the O'Neills and the Anglo-Normans in Thirteenth-century Armagh', *Seanchas Ard Mhacha*, ix, 70–94; idem, 'The O'Reillys and the Kingdom of East Breifne', *Breifne*, vi, 305–19; idem, 'The Medieval Kingdom of Loch Erne', *Clogher Record*, ix, 126–41.

4 Frame, *Colonial Ireland, 1169–1369*, 26–32.

5 *The Ancient and Noble Family of the Savages of the Ards*, compiled by G.F.A., 121–3, 154–5, 161; Davies, 'A Discovery of the True Causes Why Ireland was Never Entirely Subdued', in Morley, ed., *Ireland under Elizabeth and James I*, i, 304.

6 Frame, *English Lordship in Ireland 1318–1361*, 137; Simms, 'Nomadry in Medieval Ireland: the Origins of the Creaght or *Caoraigheacht*', *Peritia*, v, 383.

7 Aalen, *Man and Landscape*, 113; Simms, ' "The King's Friend": O'Neill, the Crown and the Earldom of Ulster', in Lydon, ed., *England and Ireland in the Later Middle Ages*, 214–36.

8 See the discussion of Domnail O'Neill's famous 'Remonstrance' to the Pope in *c*.1317 by Phillips, 'The Irish Remonstrance of 1317: An International Perspective' *I.H.S*, xxvii, 112–29. Among other things, this complained that the English had abused the grant of Ireland in the papal bull *Laudabiliter*. But the complaint was against the English colonists, not the king. Simms, 'Gaelic Lordships in Ulster in the Later Middle Ages', 545, shows that Aedh O'Donnell had little sympathy with O'Neill's call for Irish unity to expel the English and indeed that such unity was illusory. See also Duffy, *Ireland in the Middle Ages*, 138.

9 Andrews, 'Geography and Government in Elizabethan Ireland', in Stephens and Glasscock, eds., *Irish Geographical Studies*, 186; Davies, 'A Discovery', in Morley, ed., *Ireland Under Elizabeth and James I*, i, 268, 288; Frame, *English Lordship in Ireland*, 74–84.

10 Brady *et al.*, eds., *Ulster*, 63–4.

11 Hore, ed., 'Marshal Bagenal's Description of Ulster, Anno 1596', *U.J.A.*, 1st ser., ii, 153–4; Davies, 'A Discovery', in Morley, ed., *Ireland under Elizabeth and James I*, i, 304. Anglo-Irish interest in the area was sustained through landed acquisitions of the descendants of Janice Dartas, which passed through Alice Fitzeustace to the Great Earl of Kildare. See Curtis, 'Janice Dartas', *R.S.A.I. Jn.*, lxiii, 182–205.

12 Gillespie, *Colonial Ulster*, 17.

13 Simms, 'Gaelic Lordships in Ulster', 277–8.

14 McCall, 'The Gaelic Background to the Settlement of Antrim and Down, 1580–1641', 14, on the importance of their Gaelic culture; Walsh, *Leabhar Chlainne Suibhne*, xvii–x.

15 See Simms, 'Gaelic Warfare', in Bartlett and Jeffery, eds., *A Military History of Ireland*, 108–10.

16 Moody, Martin and Byrne, eds., *A New History of Ireland*, iii, *Early Modern Ireland, 1534–1691* (Oxford, 1978), 522; Hayes-McCoy, *Scots Mercenary Forces in Ireland*, 27–35; Cunningham and Gillespie, 'The East Ulster Bardic Family of Ó Gnímh', *Éigse*, xx, 106–14; Walsh, *Leabhar Chlainne Suibhne*, especially i–xliv.

17 Brady, 'The Failure of Tudor Reform', in Brady, O'Dowd and Walker, eds., *Ulster*, 90.

18 Hayes-McCoy, *Scots Mercenary Forces in Ireland*, 146; Simms, *From Kings to Warlords*, 124; Morgan, 'The End of Gaelic Ulster', *I.H.S.*, xxvi, 16–17.

19 Cosgrove, ed., *New History of Ireland*: ii, 332; Simms, 'Nomadry in Medieval Ireland', 379–91.

20 Livingstone, *Monaghan Story*, 44.

21 Spenser, *A View of the State of Ireland* [1596], in Ware, ed., *Ancient Irish Histories*, i, 23.

22 Davies, 'A Discovery', in Morley, ed., *Ireland Under Elizabeth and James I*, i, 374.

23 Mahaffy, 'Two Early Tours in Ireland', *Hermathena*, xl (1914), 9. There is another translation in *The Medieval Pilgrimage to St Patrick's Purgatory: Lough Derg and the European Tradition*, ed. by M. Haren and Y. de Pontfarcy (Enniskillen, 1988).

24 Patterson, 'Housing and House Types in County Armagh', *Ulster Folklife*, vi, 9–10; Robinson, 'Vernacular Housing in Ulster in the Seventeenth Century', *Ulster Folklife*, xxv, 1–28. See also O'Danachair, 'Representations of Houses in Some Irish Maps of 1600', in Jenkins, ed., *Studies in Folk Life. Essays in honour of Iorwerth C. Peate*, 101–2; Evans, 'The Ulster Farmhouse: A Comparative Study', *Ulster Folklife*, iii, 14–18; Simms, '"Warfare" in the Medieval Gaelic Lordships', *Irish Sword*, xii, 102–8.

25 Simms, 'Guesting and Feasting in Gaelic Ireland', *R.S.A.I. Jn.*, 108, 91; idem, 'Gaelic Lordships in Ulster', 699–700; Bergin, *Irish Bardic Poetry*, 129–32, 271–3, good poem on this from Maguire's poet; Livingstone, *Fermanagh*, 33–4.

26 Cited Cullen, *Life in Ireland*, 46.

27 See Quinn's summary of the elements of sixteenth-century English cultural nationalism in *The Elizabethans and the Irish*, 7–11, 62–3.

28 *Cal. S. P. Ire.*, 1598, 440; also Patterson, 'Housing and Housing Types in County Armagh', 9.

29 Cosgrove, ed., *New History of Ireland*, ii, 329–30; Knott, ed., *The Bardic Poems of Tadhg Dall Ó Huiginn*, I, li.

30 Hore, 'Bagenal's Description of Ulster', 139; also Bergin, *Irish Bardic Poetry*, 129–32, 271–3 for poem by Maguire's poet, Ó hEódhasa, 1595, in celebration of the gathering of Maguire's hosts.

31 Bergin, *Irish Bardic Poetry*, 9–10, 231–2; Morgan, 'End of Gaelic Ulster', 23; Simms, 'Gaelic Lordships in Ulster', 568.

32 Spenser, *A View of the State of Ireland*, i, 86–8.

33 Hore, 'Bagenal's Description of Ulster', 152; Morgan, 'The End of Gaelic Ulster', 23–4.

34 Quoted Hore, 'Bagenal's Description of Ulster', 139; Livingstone, *Monaghan*, 59.

35 McErlean, 'The Irish Townland System of Landscape Organisation', in Reeves-Smyth and Hammond, eds., *Landscape and Archaeology in Ireland*, 315–39; Graham, 'Rural Society in Connacht', 195–9.

36 Simms, 'Nomadry in Medieval Ireland', 379.

37 See e.g. McCourt, 'Surviving Openfield in County Londonderry', *Ulster Folklife*, iv, 17–28.

38 Simms, 'Nomadry in Medieval Ireland', 379–91; Story, *A True and Impartial History*, 15; Graham, 'Rural Society in Connacht', 199. See also Quinn, *Elizabethans and the Irish*, 125–6; Spenser, *A View of the State of Ireland*, i, 247, 258–9; and *A Historie of Ireland Written in the Yeare 1571 by Edmund Campion*, in Ware, ed., *Ancient Irish Histories*, i, 19, for Tudor criticism of such practices.

39 Walsh, *Leabhar Chlainne Suibhne*, 51, 73.

40 Hayes-McCoy, 'The Making of an O'Neill', *U.J.A.*, xxxiii, 89; see modern-day photographs of the site in Mallory and McNeill, *Archaeology of Ulster*, 239–40, and Donnelly, *Living Places*, 74.

41 Information on the inauguration ceremonies is taken largely from Simms, *Kings to Warlords*, 21–40 (the fullest account); idem, 'Gaelic Lordships in Ulster', 4–35; Livingstone, *Monaghan Story*, 46–7; idem, *Fermanagh Story*, 479; also Nicholls, *Gaelic and Gaelicised Society*, 28–30; Watt, in Cosgrove, ed., *New History of Ireland*, ii, 320–22; Morgan, *Tyrone's Rebellion*, 85–6.

42 Murphy, *Ulster Folk*, 7.

43 Nicholls, *Gaelic and Gaelicised Ireland*, 23, thinks the term obsolete by the twelfth century in its original sense as a political unit, though clearly still being used as a notional measurement in north-east Ulster in the early seventeenth century (see Gillespie, *Colonial Ulster*, 18–19).

44 Glancy, 'The Primates and the Church Lands of Armagh', *Seanchas Ard Mhacha*, v, no. 2, 375; for Gaelic landholding generally see O'Dowd, 'Gaelic

Economy and Society', in Brady and Gillespie, eds., *Natives and Newcomers*, 125–7; Nicholls, 'Gaelic Society and Economy in the High Middle Ages', in Cosgrove, ed., *New History of Ireland*, ii, 425–6, 430–32.

45 Davies, 'A Discovery', in Morley, ed., *Ireland under Elizabeth and James I*, i, 372 (also 291).

46 Butler, 'Irish Land Tenures: Celtic and Foreign', *Studies*, xiii (1924), 530.

47 Spenser, *A View of the State of Ireland*, i, 227–8; Livingstone, *Fermanagh Story*, 59; Graham, 'Rural Society', 200, on local definitions of 'gentleman'; Watt in Cosgrove, ed., *New History of Ireland*, ii, 329; Gillespie, *Colonial Ulster*, 113–20.

48 Nicholls, *Gaelic and Gaelicised Ireland*, 11; Simms, 'Gaelic Lordships in Ulster': Toirdhelbhach O'Donnell had eighteen sons by ten women, late fourteenth to early fifteenth centuries (p. 563), and land hunger may have contributed to the disputes in families with a large number of sons (p. 492).

49 Simms, *From Kings to Warlords*, 31.

50 Duffy, 'Geographical Perspectives on the Borderlands', 7; Hore, 'Bagenal's Description of Ulster', 149–50; Ó Dufaigh, 'The Mac Cathmhaoils of Clogher', *Clogher Rec.*, ii, 44–45.

51 O'Dowd, 'Gaelic Economy and Society', 141; Simms, *From Kings to Warlords*, 55, 58–9.

52 McCourt, 'Surviving Openfield in County Londonderry', *Ulster Folklife*, iv, 19–28; Graham, 'Rural Society', 198–9; see also Currie, 'Field Patterns in County Derry', *Ulster Folklife*, xxix, 70–80.

53 Andrews, *Plantation Acres*, 11; Simms, *From Kings to Warlords*, 39–40; Hore, 'Bagenal's Description of Ulster', 362, also 370. Hugh Maguire was found to have used mainly mercenaries in the recent rebellion, leaving most of the freeholders in Fermanagh unscathed.

54 Simms, *From Kings to Warlords*, 32; the O'Friels of Kilmacrenan fulfilled the same role for the MacSweeneys (Walsh, *Leabhar Chlainne Suibhne*, 51).

55 Hore, 'Bagenal's Description of Ulster', 363.

56 Andrews, *Plantation Acres*, 13.

57 Quoted in Simms, *From Kings to Warlords*, 2.

58 Gillespie, *Colonial Ulster*, 17–20; Duffy, 'Patterns of Landownership in Gaelic Monaghan in the Late Sixteenth Century', *Clogher Rec.*, x, 314–17, when the modern county of Monaghan was created in 1585, the five baronies into which it was divided were the traditional territories of the various branches of the MacMahons. Andrews, 'Geography and Government in Elizabethan Ireland', 178–91, shows how they were unwilling to invest in proper surveys and simply accepted old territorial units. O'Laverty, *Down and Connor*, ii, 450–61: certain ancient standing stones (this at Mallusk) still marked territorial boundaries till the early nineteenth century, while certain modern names derive from old family territorial units.

59 Aalen, *Man and Landscape*, 138; also McCoy, *Scots Mercenary Forces in Ireland*, 257.

60 Glancy, 'The Primates and the Church Lands of Armagh', 375.

61 Duffy, 'Geographical Perspective', 146, n. 16.

62 Canny, 'Hugh O'Neill, Earl of Tyrone, and the Changing Face of Gaelic Ulster', *Stud. Hib.*, x, 27–32.

63 Spenser, *A View of the State of Ireland*, i, 16.

64 O'Dowd, 'Gaelic Economy and Society', 125–6.

65 Simms, 'Late Medieval Donegal', in Nolan, Ronayne and Donlevy, eds., *Donegal*, 191–3; Hamilton, *Elizabethan Ulster*, 152–3; Canny, 'Hugh O'Neill', 13–14; Davies, 'A Discovery', in Morley, ed., *Ireland Under Elizabeth and James I*, i, 294–5; McAfee, 'The Population of Ulster, 1630–1841: Evidence from mid-Ulster', 73–4.

66 See Alexander, ed., 'The O'Kane Papers', *Anal. Hib.*, xii, 94–6: in the deanery of Derry Donald O'Cahan was rector of four different churches, Dermot O'Cahan erenach of five and p. 101 shows extraordinary complexity of who had what rights on church lands; Ó Doibhlin, 'The Deanery of Tulach Óg', *Seanchas Ard Mhacha*, vi, 141–182, notably 157–9, identifying the erenach families, the O'Loughrans, O'Conlons, McGirrs, O'Cullens, Mac Kathmaylls (Mac Cawell, McCall or Campbell) in this future Barony of Dungannon; Simms, 'Frontiers in the Irish Church – Regional and Cultural', in Frame *et al.*, eds., *Colony and Frontier in Medieval Ireland*, 177–200 *passim*.

67 Mooney, *The Church in Gaelic Ireland*, 10–15; a detailed case history in Glancy, 'The Primates and the Church Lands of Armagh', 370–96; Simms, 'The Archbishops of Armagh and the O'Neills, 1347–1471', *I.H.S*, xix, 38–55.

68 Reeves, ed., *Acts of Archbishop Colton in his Metropolitan Visitation of the Diocese of Derry*, 5n. Ó Doibhlin, 'Deanery of Tulach Óg', 167–75, reproducing findings of the 1609 and 1620 Inquisitions.

69 Reeves, ed., *Acts of Archbishop Colton*, particularly 5–7, 10, 12, 16, 19–21; Hamilton, *Elizabethan Ulster*, 152–3; Canny, 'Hugh O'Neill', 13–14; Robinson, 'Settlement in Tyrone', 61. See excellent map in Simms, 'Frontiers in the Irish Church', 179.

70 See e.g. McCall, 'The Gaelic Background to the Settlement of Antrim and Down', 69 and 81; Gwynn and Hadcock, eds., *Medieval Religious Houses. Ireland*, 268–74; Ó Doibhlin, 'Deanery of Tulach Óg', 179–82. See Morley, ed., *Ireland Under Elizabeth and James I*, i, 364–8, for Davies' survey of Church lands, 1607.

71 Harris, *The Ancient and Present State of the County of Down*, 35.

72 Walsh, ed., *Leabhar Chlainne Suibhne*, 39 – the MacSweeneys had been inaugurated by Colum Cille's successors.

73 Binchy, cited in Nicholls, *Gaelic and Gaelicised Society*, 44; but see Simms' critique of this view in 'The Contents of Later Commentaries on the Brehon Law Tracts', in *Ériu*, xlix, 23–40.

74 Morley, ed., *Ireland Under Elizabeth and James I*, i, 368–71.

75 For recent overviews of the debate see McCone and Simms, eds., *Progress in Medieval Irish Studies*, 211–15; also Caball, *Poets and Politics; Reaction and Continuity in Irish Poetry, 1558–1625*, 7–12.

76 Cunningham and Gillespie, 'The East Ulster Bardic Family of Ó Gnímh', *Éigse*, xx, 106–14; also Cunningham, 'Native Culture and Political Change

in Ireland, 1580–1640', in Brady and Gillespie, eds., *Natives and Newcomers*, 148–70.

77 Simms, *From Kings to Warlords*, 16–17; idem, 'Bards and Barons: the Anglo-Irish Aristocracy and Native Culture', in Bartlett and Mackay, eds., *Medieval Frontier Societies*, 188–94; Stalley, 'From the Twelfth Century to the Reformation', in de Breffny, ed., *The Irish World*, 97; O'Riordain, *Gaelic Mind*, particularly pp. 3–8, 22–3, 37, 131–3 (though see Ó Buachalla's critique of O'Riordain in 'Poetry and Politics in Early Modern Ireland', *Eighteenth-Century Ireland*, vii, 149–75.

78 Spenser, *View of the State of Ireland*, i, 62–63; but see Simms, 'Bardic Poetry as a Historical Source', in Dunne, ed., *The Writer as Witness*, 58–75. I am deeply grateful to Dr Simms for her advice on these issues.

79 Though see Ó Cuív, in Moody *et al.*, eds., *New History of Ireland*, iii, 537. Popular folk tales seem to have consisted of the ageless romantic tale and cast doubt on the average person's interest in high politics.

80 Ó Gnímh, hereditary poet to the Magennisses, quoted by Bergin, *Bardic Poetry*, 120.

81 Simms, 'Propaganda Use of the Táin in the Later Middle Ages', *Celtica*, xv, 142–9; idem, 'Gaelic Lordships in Ulster in the Later Middle Ages', 711–20.

82 Campion, *Historie of Ireland*, i, 19. On the poets' claims to druidic antecedents see Simms, 'Literacy and the Irish Bards', in Pryce, ed., *Literacy in Medieval Celtic Societies*, 250.

83 Quinn, *The Elizabethans and the Irish*, 44; Brian Ó Cuív, 'The Irish Language in the Early Modern Period', in Moody *et al.*, eds., *New History of Ireland*, iii, 514.

84 Cunningham, 'Native Culture and Political Change', 152; O'Riordan, *Gaelic Mind*, 120–22, 141; Breatnach, 'Metamorphosis 1603: Dán le hEochaidh Ó hEódhasa', *Éigse*, xvii, 171.

85 Simms, 'The O'Hanlons, the O'Neills and the Anglo-Normans', op. cit.; Bergin, *Bardic Poetry*, 120–23, Ó Gnímh's poetry; Simms, 'Propaganda Use of the Táin', 144–6.

86 Martin, in Cosgrove, ed., *New History of Ireland*, ii, l.

87 Morgan, 'The End of Gaelic Ulster', 30; Simms, 'Gaelic Lordships in Ulster', 711, also shows how successive generations of O'Neills could make a distinction between the crown and the Anglo-Irish.

88 Brady, 'Sixteenth-century Ulster and the Failure of Tudor Reform', in Brady *et al.*, *Ulster*, 77–103; O'Dowd, 'Gaelic Economy and Society', 132–4; idem, *Power, Politics and Land*, 32–5, 50–53.

89 Davies, 'A Discovery', in Morley, ed., *Ireland Under Elizabeth and James I*, i, 259–75; Hamilton, *Elizabethan Ulster*, 151; and see O'Dowd, 'Gaelic Economy and Society', 144–5, on the lower sectors of Gaelic society who prospered from the process. Also Canny, *Reformation to Restoration*, 118–19. However, there was only a limited extension of the machinery of English law, and it was not introduced into the main lordships of Tyrone and Tyrconnell until after their defeat in 1603.

90 McCarthy, 'Ulster Office, 1552–1800', 21–3.

91 See O'Sullivan, 'The March of South-East Ulster in the Fifteenth and Sixteenth centuries', in Gillespie and O'Sullivan, eds., *The Borderlands*, 64.

92 As suggested by Canny, 'Hugh O'Neill, Earl of Tyrone, and the Changing Face of Gaelic Ulster', *Stud. Hib.*, lx, 33.

93 See e.g. Morgan, 'The Colonial Venture of Sir Thomas Smith in Ulster, 1571–1575', *Hist. Jn.*, xxviii, 261–78.

94 Davies, 'A Discovery', in Morley, ed., *Ireland under Elizabeth and James I*, i, 335.

95 For an excellent account of the lead-in, see Morgan, *Tyrone's Rebellion*, particularly 139–66.

96 Nicholls, in Cosgrove, ed., *New History of Ireland*, ii, 426–7, sees this happening by the sixteenth century.

97 See e.g. Chart, 'The Break-up of the Estate of Con O'Neill, Castlereagh, County Down', *Proc. R.I.A.*, xlviii, sect. C, 119–45.

98 See Canny, 'The Treaty of Mellifont and the Re-organisation of Ulster, 1603', *Irish Sword*, ix, 249–62.

99 Davies, 'Letter to Robert, Earl of Salisbury', in Morley, ed., *Ireland Under Elizabeth and James I*, i, 352.

100 Falls, *The Birth of Ulster*, 111–14, 148.

101 Davies, 'Letter to . . . Salisbury', in Morley, ed., *Ireland under Elizabeth and James I*, i, 359–60; Falls, *The Birth of Ulster*, 145.

102 Simms, ' "Warfare" in Medieval Gaelic Lordships', *Irish Sword*, xii, 98ff.

103 See G. Mac Niocaill, 'The Contact of Irish and Common Law', *N. Ireland Legal Quarterly*, 23 (1972), 16–23. Campion writing in 1571 recounts the tale of a northern 'gentleman' attending confession with a travelling monk, asked if he committed homicide, said he never knew it was such before – Campion, *Historie*, 21–2; and when, under Lord Deputy Fitzwilliam's term of office (1571–5), a sheriff was to be sent to the new county of Fermanagh, Maguire asked to know beforehand his 'eric' or price of his head, 'that if my people cut it off I may cut the ericke upon the country', Davies, 'A Discovery', in Morley, ed., *Ireland Under Elizabeth and James I*, i, 290.

104 Simms, 'Gaelic Lordships in Ulster in the Later Middle Ages', 801, points out that even in the Middle Ages it was not the chieftains (who adapted to new conditions after the Anglo-Norman invasion) who were backward-looking, but the poets and preservers of tradition. See also O'Riordan, *Gaelic Mind*, 117–18, on the way Gaelic society could accommodate even those who had been militarily victorious, but not the increasing presence of such an expansionist and culturally different social grouping.

3 RELIGION IN ULSTER BEFORE THE REFORMATION

1 Moryson, *Itinerary*, ii, 274–5.

2 Canny, in Foster, ed., *Illustrated History of Ireland*, 128.

3 The point is that the church in Irish areas remained integrated into the

traditional kinship structure (see Watt, in Cosgrove, ed., *New History of Ireland*, ii, 335).

4 Costello, *De Annatis Hiberniae*, xix, Primate Octavian writing in 1508.

5 Simms, *Kings to Warlords*, 27–8.

6 Bruford, *Gaelic Folktales and Medieval Romances*, 24–6.

7 Reeves, ed., *Acts of Archbishop Colton*; also Corish, 'Two Reports on the Catholic Church in Ireland in the Early Seventeenth Century', *Stud. Hib.*, xxii, 141.

8 Mahaffy, ed., 'Two Early Tours in Ireland', *Hermathena*, xl, 13; Monter, *Ritual, Myth and Magic in Early Modern Europe*, 6; Watt, 'The Papacy and Ireland in the Fifteenth Century', in Dobson, ed., *The Church, Politics and Patronage*, 133–43. And yet under Henry VIII senior ecclesiastics in Gaelic areas accepted the early states of the Reformation, see Canny, *Reformation to Restoration*, 53–4.

9 Bradshaw, *The Dissolution of the Religious Orders in Ireland under Henry VIII*, 37; Costello, *De Annatis*, xviii–xix.

10 Mahaffy, ed., 'Two Early Tours', 10, 13; Watt, *Church in Medieval Ireland*, 193.

11 See e.g. account of Culdees in Armagh, Cathaldus Giblin, 'The Processus Datariae and the Appointment of Irish Bishops in the Seventeenth Century', in Franciscan Fathers, eds., *Father Luke Wadding*, 540–41. Murray, 'The History of the Parish of Creggan in the 17th and 18th Centuries', *Louth Arch. Soc. Jn.*, viii, no. 2, 134. In Creggan parish, South Armagh, the name Killyloughran (O'Loughran's church) recalls the fifteenth-century prior of the Armagh Culdees, John O'Loughran.

12 Campion, *Historie of Ireland*, i, 19.

13 Mhág Craith, *Dán na mBráthar Mionúr*, ii, poem no. 27, pp. 58–67, verse 66; O'Dwyer, *Mary*, 187; O'Duffy, *The Apostasy of Myler Magrath, Archbishop of Cashel*, 5 – this translation from Irish has him bartering his faith for flesh on Fridays.

14 Murray, 'The History of the Parish of Creggan', 131–2. Local folklore in Donegal, for example, is rich in stories and folk memory of their haunts and refuges, see Mooney, *Franciscan Donegal*, 13, 17–18, 33; also Millett, *The Irish Franciscans 1651–1665*, 74.

15 Costello, *De Annatis Hiberniae*, 49–50; Gwynn and Hadcock, eds., *Medieval Religious Houses*, 254; Walsh, *Leabhar Chlainne Suibhne*, 69: in 1516 Maolmhuire and Maire MacSweeney built a Carmelite monastery at Rathmullan because one of his sons was buried in the church there.

16 Murray, 'The History of the Parish of Creggan', 130–31; Murray and Gwynn, eds., 'Archbishop Cromer's Register', *Louth Arch. Soc. Jn.*, viii, 44, 179, in the early sixteenth century a typical penance is for the offender to be obliged to perambulate the cemetery in white linens on successive Sundays; Walsh, *Leabhar Chlainne Suibhne*, lvii.

17 John Derricke, *The Image of Irelande*, 54, plates III, IV.

18 Gwynn and Hadcock, eds., *Medieval Religious Houses*, 10, 240–47, 263–6.

19 Canny, 'Why the Reformation Failed in Ireland: *une question mal posée*', *Jn. Eccles. Hist.*, xxx, 423–50; Bottigheimer, 'The Failure of the Reformation in Ireland: *une question bien posée*', ibid., xxxvi, 196–207; the fullest account of the Reformation in Ireland is Ford, *The Protestant Reformation in Ireland, 1590–1641*.

20 Cameron, *The European Reformation*, 12–19.

21 Bergin, *Irish Bardic Poetry*, 93–100, 254–7, a good thirteenth-century example of this; O'Dwyer, *Mary*, 91, 100, 106, 289; Simms, 'Frontiers in the Irish Church', 200. In the Middle Ages the saints were seen in same light as the king or overlord, honour-bound to avenge his vassals; Giraldus Cambrensis also had noted the peculiar vengefulness of the Irish saints.

22 Quoted in Mooney, 'The Irish Church in the Sixteenth Century', *Ir. Eccles. Rec.*, xcix, 111; the foregoing from 'A Discourse for the Reformation of Ireland [1583]', in Brewer and Bullen, eds., *Calendar of the Carew Manuscripts Preserved in the Archiepiscopal Library at Lambeth*, ii, 1575–1588, 367.

23 Cited Simms, 'Gaelic Lordships in Ulster', 477; O'Reilly, 'Remarks on Certain Passages in Capt. Cuellar's Narrative of His Adventures in Ireland ... 1588–89', *Proc. R.I.A.*, iii, 211 and 201; Costello, *De Annatis*, xiv, xviii.

24 'Archbishop Cromer's Register', *Louth Arch. Soc. Jn.*, ix, 41; Simms, 'Frontiers in the Irish Church', 197; Canny, ed., 'Rowland White's "The Dysorders of the Irishery, 1571"', *Stud. Hib.*, xix, 155.

25 *Cal. S.P.I.*, 1611–14, 430.

26 Costello, *De Annatis*, xxi, 46–7; 'Archbishop Cromer's Register', *Louth Arch. Soc. Jn.*, viii, 44, 322.

27 Campion, *Historie of Ireland*, i, 23.

28 Watt, 'The Papacy and Ireland in the Fifteenth Century', 142–3; Corish, *Irish Catholic Experience*, 97–8.

29 Reeves, *Acts of Archbishop Colton*, 12n, 16n.

30 Watt, 'The Papacy and Ireland in the Fifteenth Century', 136–7; Simms, 'Gaelic Lordships', 485–90.

31 Simms, 'Frontiers in the Irish Church', 200; idem, 'Women in Gaelic Society', in MacCurtain and O'Dowd, eds., *Women in Early Modern Ireland*, 32–42.

32 Shirley, ed., *Original Letters and Papers in Illustration of the History of the Church in Ireland*, 117.

33 Mahaffy, 'Two Tours', 14.

34 Campion, *A Historie of Ireland*, i, 21 – he also admitted to never having received communion. K. Simms tells me this tale may have originated in the preface to the Vision of Knight Owen.

35 Mooney, 'The Friars and Friary of Donegal, 1474–1840', in O'Donnell, ed., *Franciscan Donegal*, 9.

36 See for e.g. the Franciscan manual for preachers, Little, ed., *Liber Exemplorum*, British Society for Franciscan Pubs., i.

37 Burrows, 'Fifteenth-century Irish Provincial Legislation and Pastoral Care', in Sheils and Wood, eds., *The Churches, Ireland and the Irish*, Studies in

Church History, no. 25, 55–67; Watt, *The Church in Medieval Ireland*, 210–11; Jones, *The Counter-Reformation*, 37. See also Mooney, 'The Friars and Friary of Donegal', 7, 13, the O'Donnells holding important meetings in the Franciscan Abbey which they had endowed.

38 Campion, *A Historie of Ireland*, i, 19.

39 See Scribner, 'Interpreting Religion in Early Modern Europe', *European Studies Review*, xiii, 89–105, and particularly 94, for a survey of findings on popular religion in Europe.

40 Flower, *The Irish Tradition*, 119–29; Cosgrove, ed., *New History of Ireland*, ii, 704, 722–6.

41 Ó Maonaigh, ed., *Smaointe Beatha Chríost*; O'Dwyer, *Mary: A History of Devotion in Ireland*, 140–54.

42 Walsh, *Leabhar Chlainne Suibhne*, xliv–lviii, 37, 67–9; Walsh, *Irish Men of Learning*, 179–80.

43 Lennon, 'The Counter-Reformation in Ireland, 1542–1641', in Brady and Gillespie, eds., *Natives and Newcomers*, 76; see also Monter, *Ritual, Myth and Magic*, ch. 2.

44 Where a vigilant mayor and deputy-governor secured funds to rebuild the church and compel attendance, so that by 1605 most of the priests were said to have taken the oath of supremacy, see O'Laverty, *Down and Connor*, iii, 101–2; Bradshaw, *The Dissolution of the Religious Orders in Ireland*, 97, 121, 142; White, ed., *Extents of Irish Monastic Possessions, 1540–1541*.

45 Mooney, 'The Friars and Friary of Donegal', 11: in 1588 the soldiers attacked Donegal friary, destroying statues and pictures; Murray, 'Franciscan Monasteries after the Dissolution', *Louth Arch. Soc. Jn.*, viii, 275–82: in 1589 the large monastery in Monaghan was reduced to rubble, the Guardian and five friars put to death.

46 *The Ancient and Noble Family of the Savages of the Ards*, 176: in the 1570s the O'Neills burned the abbeys of Moville, Bangor and Holywood in a campaign against Sir Thomas Smith; Simms, 'Gaelic Lordships', 794, 1455, conflict between Arch. Mey of Armagh and the O'Neills for making territorial claims on church lands; O'Laverty, *Down and Connor*, iii, 60; the unnamed author of *Les martyrs de la Province dominicaine d'Irlande*, 71, tries to argue that the deaths of friars at the hands of Sorley Boy MacDonnell (sixteenth century) must have been instigated by the English.

47 Shirley, ed., *Church in Ireland*, 117–18. Moryson, *Itinerary*, in Falkiner, *Illustrations of Irish History and Topography*, 319: 'In christenings and like rites of religion they use generally the rites of the Roman Church, the which they persist with obstinacy, little care having been taken to instruct them in the reformed doctrine.'

48 Ford, *Protestant Reformation in Ireland*, 53–7; Clarke in Moody *et al.*, eds., *New History of Ireland*, iii, 210.

49 Cameron, *The European Reformation*, 311–13; see Steven G. Ellis, *Ireland in the Age of the Tudors*, 205–42, for the most recent analysis of the Reformation in Ireland.

50 See e.g. Shirley, ed., *Church in Ireland*, 90–91: extract from Queen Elizabeth's 'Instructions', 1559; Sir John Davies' similar belief that they could plant true religion 'among these rude people, who are apt to take any impression', in Morley, ed., *Ireland under Elizabeth and James I*, i, 378.

51 There is a useful survey of the literature on the Reformation in Ireland in, 'The Church of Ireland: A Critical Bibliography', Part I: 1536–1603, by James Murray, and Part II: 1603–41, by Alan Ford, *I.H.S.*, xxviii, 345–8.

52 O'Dwyer, *Mary*, 221.

53 Bossy, 'The Counter-Reformation and the People of Catholic Ireland, 1596–1641', in Williams, ed., *Historical Studies*, viii, 155–69, and idem, 'The Counter-Reformation and the People of Catholic Europe', *Past and Present*, no. 47 (May, 1970), 51–70.

54 Scribner, 'Interpreting Religion in Early Modern Europe', *European Studies Review*, xiii, 89–105.

55 Hagan, ed., 'Miscellanea Vaticano-Hibernica, 1580–1631', *Archiv. Hib.*, iii, 284; Jones, *The Counter-Reformation*, 37–8.

56 Murray, 'Franciscan Monasteries after the Dissolution', 275–82; Giblin, ed., 'Catalogue of Material of Irish Interest in the Collection *Nunziatura di Fiandra*', Vatican Archives: Part I, vols. 1–50, *Coll. Hib.*, i, 57. Franciscans administering the sacraments in Ireland; Gwynn and Hadcock, eds., *Medieval Religious Houses*, 11, for papal permission to hold mass in places other than churches.

57 Hagan, ed., 'Miscellanea Vaticano-Hibernica', 285; Clarke in Moody *et al.*, eds., *New History of Ireland*, iii, 210; O'Laverty, *Down and Connor. The Bishops*, 369–71 – he resided in Tyrone after his appointment, protected by the O'Neill family.

58 Silke, in Moody *et al.*, eds., *New History of Ireland*, iii, 629.

59 O'Laverty, *Down and Connor. The Bishops*, 404–11.

60 *Ibid.*, 411–14.

61 Cunningham, 'Native Culture and Political Change in Ireland, 1534–1641', 162–3; also Silke, op. cit., 628–9.

62 'The O'Kane Papers', *Anal. Hib.*, xii, 79–111; Morgan, 'The End of Gaelic Ulster', 28. Miler Magrath names twenty monasteries still operating in Ulster in 1594.

63 *Cal.S.P. Ire., 1611–14*, 431; Maxwell, *Irish History from Contemporary Sources, 1509–1610*, 150–51; Lodge, ed., *Desiderata Curiosa Hibernica*, i, 394–6.

64 *Cal.S.P. Ire., 1611–14*, 429–31.

65 Gillespie, 'The Transformation of the Borderlands, 1600–1700', in Gillespie and O'Sullivan, eds., *The Borderlands*, 86–8.

66 Bossy, 'Catholicity and Nationality in the Northern Counter-Reformation', in Mews, ed., *Religion and National Identity*, Studies in Church History, xviii, 285–96; also Cunningham, 'The Culture and Ideology of Irish Franciscan Historians at Louvain 1607–1650', in Brady, ed., *Ideology and the Historians*, Hist. Studs., xviii, 11–30.

67 Giblin, ed., 'Catalogue of Material of Irish Interest … Part I', 61,

63; Lucian Ceyssens, 'Florence Conry, Hugh de Burgo, Luke Wadding and Jansenism', in Franciscan Fathers, eds., *Father Luke Wadding*, 295–331; O'Rahilly, ed., *Desiderius, Otherwise Called Sgáthán an Chrábaidh*, by Flaithrí Ó Maolchonaire, ix–x.

68 On MacCaghwell see Ó Cuív in Moody *et al.*, eds., *New History of Ireland*, iii, 526–7, 562–3; O'Laverty, *Down and Connor. The Bishops*, 398–401; Tomás Ó Cléirigh, *Aodh Mac Aingil Agus an Scoil Nua-Ghaeilge i Lobháin* (Dublin, 1935).

69 Jennings, *Michael Ó Cléirigh: Chief of the Four Masters and His Associates*; Ó Briain, 'Three Friars of Donegal', in O'Donnell, ed., *Franciscan Donegal*, 82–92; Ó Cuív, op. cit., 531–2; Walsh, *Four Masters*, 34.

70 These points are also made in Cunningham, 'The Culture and Ideology of Irish Franciscan Historians at Louvain', especially 20–21.

71 Quoted in Jennings, *Michael Ó Cléirigh*, 38.

72 Ó Cuív, op. cit., 533.

73 Ó Buachalla, 'Poetry and Politics in Early Modern Ireland', *Eighteenth-Century Ireland*, vii, 149–75; idem, 'Na Stíobhartaigh agus an tAos Léinn: Cing Séamas', *Proc. R.I.A.*, 83, sect C, 4–129.

74 Gillies, 'A Poem on the Downfall of the Gaodhil', *Éigse*, 13, 203–10; Ó Buachalla, 'Cing Séamas', 90–91.

75 Hardiman, *Irish Minstrelsy*, i, 102; Hyde, *Literary History*, 522.

76 Ó Buachalla, 'Cing Séamas', 85.

77 Leerssen, *Mere Irish and Fíor Ghael: Studies in the Idea of Irish Nationality, Its Development and Literary Expression prior to the Nineteenth Century*, 220; Cunningham, 'Native Culture and Political Change', particularly 165–70; Millett, in Moody *et al.*, eds., *New History of Ireland*, iii, 568–9. Hyde, *Literary History*, 517.

78 Spenser, *View of the State of Ireland*, i, 254–5.

79 Hagan, ed., 'Miscellanea Vaticano-Hibernica', 260–64: 'Brief of Paul V to the Irish People', c.1607; Corish, *The Irish Catholic Experience*, 95.

80 Bruford, *Gaelic Folktales and Medieval Romances*, 58–63; Breatnach, 'Early Modern Irish Prose', in McCone and Simms, eds., *Progress in Medieval Studies*, 195–6; Hyde, *Literary History*, 558–9; Cunningham, 'Native Culture and Political change', 165–7.

81 Ó Buachalla, 'Foreword' to Geoffrey Keating, *Foras Feasa ar Éirinn, The History of Ireland*, ed. by Comyn and Dineen (London, 1987), 5.

82 There is considerable disagreement over what messages can be taken from the poetry in this period. See Cunningham, 'Native Culture and Political Change', 164; Knott, *Bardic Poems*, xxxiv, arguing against reading too much into bardic conventions regarding the foreigner etc.; Ó Buachalla, 'Poetry and Politics in Early Modern Ireland', *Eighteenth-century Ireland*, 7, 149–75; idem, 'Jacobitism and Nationalism: the Irish Literary Evidence', in Michael O'Dea and Kevin Whelan, eds., *Nations and Nationalism: France, Britain, Ireland and the Eighteenth-century Context* (Oxford, 1995), 103–16. But see Simms's sensible overview of the controversy in McCone and Simms, eds., *Progress in Medieval Irish Studies*, 210–15.

4 THE LOSS OF THE LAND:
PLANTATION AND CONFISCATION IN
SEVENTEENTH-CENTURY ULSTER

1 Lin. Lib., Opsahl Comm., no. 184.

2 See Bernadette McAliskey, in O Connor, *In Search of a State*, 364, also her article explaining why republicans rejected the Downing Street Agreement, *Guardian*, 28 December 1993; Donegal writer Seamus MacManus, *Rocky Road to Dublin*, 131–2, the descendants of 'the hard-headed Scottish planters whom James I loosed upon Ulster, to grab everything in sight', being shunned in modern Donegal; see also Brewer with Higgins, *Anti-Catholicism in Northern Ireland, 1600–1998*, 86, showing how, by the twentieth century, 1641 is being raked up for purely political reasons. However, Clayton, *Enemies and Passing Friends*, particularly ch. 2, portrays present-day Ulster Protestants as retaining their 'settler' mentality.

3 Mac Suibhne, 'Canon James McFadden (1842–1917)', in Moran, ed., *Ten Radical Priests*, 173, shows that the *seanchas* of Donegal depicted the O'Donnells as 'harsh overlords who coerced labour to build roads and a castle', quite unlike the image created by later cultural nationalism.

4 UFTM, School Textbook Coll., E2/61/13: Mrs Stephen Gwynn, *Stories from Irish History*, 108.

5 Davies, in Morley, ed., *Ireland under Elizabeth and James I*, 276–81.

6 *Ibid.*, 379.

7 See e.g. map of population density in 1660 in Smyth, 'Society and Settlement in Seventeenth-century Ireland', in Smyth and Whelan, eds., *Common Ground: Essays on the Historical Geography of Ireland*, 66.

8 Harkin [Maghtochair], *Inishowen*, 74–6.

9 Robinson, *The Plantation of Ulster*, 45–52.

10 Chart, 'The Break-up of the Estate of Con O'Neill', *Proc. R.I.A.* xlviii, sect. C, 119–51; Perceval-Maxwell, *The Scottish Migration to Ulster in the Reign of James I*, 49–52.

11 Quoted in Ohlmeyer, *Civil War and Restoration in Three Stuart Kingdoms*, 83–4.

12 *Ibid.*, 25–40.

13 Perceval-Maxwell, *Scottish Migration*, 58–67.

14 O'Laverty, *Down and Connor*, ii, 137; Reeves, ed., 'The Irish Itinerary of Father Edmund MacCana', *U.J.A.*, ser. 1., vol. ii, 55.

15 *Report of the Lough Foyle Fishery Case ... tried ... at Omagh, 1856* (London, 1857).

16 Hunter, 'The Ulster Plantation in the Counties of Armagh and Cavan, 1608–41', 33–4; Robinson, *Plantation*, 201.

17 Walsh, *Leabhar Chlainne Suibhne*, xxx–xxxi; Hugh O'Neill scarcely figures in popular Irish poetry, see Ó Muirgheasa, *Céad de Cheoltaibh Uladh*, 192.

18 Gillespie and O'Sullivan, eds., *The Borderlands*, 61, also 84–5; Ó Fiaich, 'The O'Neills of the Fews', *Seanchas Ard Mhacha*, vii, 55–6; Robinson,

Plantation, 199. See also Moody, ed., 'Ulster Plantation Papers, 1608–13', *Anal. Hib.*, no. 8, 214–15, a host of lesser grants in Tyrone to the smaller allied septs, the O'Quinns, O'Devlins, O'Hagans, O'Mellans, O'Corrs, etc.

19 *Cal. S.P. Ire.*, 1608–1610, 68.

20 Hamilton, *The Irish Rebellion of 1641*, 99–101; Livingstone, *Fermanagh Story*, 61–2; George Hill, *An Historical Account of the Plantation of Ulster*, 109–10, 411; Gilbert, ed., *A Contemporary History of Affairs in Ireland*, vol. i, pt. 1, xx–xxi.

21 Moody, ed., 'Ulster Plantation Papers', 206–7.

22 Hamilton, *Rebellion of 1641*, 98–9; Robinson, *Plantation*, 200.

23 Hunter, 'Ulster Plantation', 52–78; Davies, in Morley, ed., *Ireland under Elizabeth and James I*, i, 384; Ó Gallachair, '1622 Survey of Cavan', *Breifne*, i, 60–75; Robinson, *Plantation*, 201.

24 Davies in Morley, ed., *Ireland under Elizabeth and James I*, 371–2; see also Ó Doibhlin, *Domhnach Mór*, 97ff, for the jurors at Dungannon; Hill, *Plantation*, 153–90, lists all the jurors involved in the 1609 commission's enquiries – also very good outline of the difficulties over termon and erenach lands.

25 Robinson, *Plantation*, 86; Hill, *Plantation*, 218, 311, 410–11, 569; Moody, Martin and Byrne, eds., *A New History of Ireland*, ix: *Maps, Genealogies, Lists*, 142.

26 Robinson, *Plantation*, 89–90.

27 Perceval-Maxwell, *Scottish Migration*, 210–14; see Hill, *Plantation*, extensive notes to pp. 454, 456, 480, 487, 490, 518 for yearly leases, but also examples of life leases, 533, and substantial tenancies, 503 and 535.

28 IFC, MS 976/167 and 1215/212; Gillespie and Sullivan, eds., *Borderlands*, 80.

29 Hunter, 'Ulster Plantation', 41, also 240; 1622 survey sees Armagh with almost twice the number of British settlers as Cavan (1,200 against 765).

30 Robinson, *Plantation* (his tables), 87.

31 *Ibid.*, 97–100; Macafee, 'The Population of Ulster, 1630–1841', 56.

32 Moody, 'The Treatment of the Native Population', 63.

33 Hunter, 'English Undertakers in the Plantation of Ulster', *Breifne*, x, 483; Moody, *Londonderry Plantation*, 327–31.

34 Hunter, 'Ulster Plantation', 149–53, 248.

35 Gillespie, *Colonial Ulster*, 140–41; also in *Natives and Newcomers*, 195.

36 Quoted in Gillespie, *Conspiracy*, 29.

37 Walsh, *Leabhar Chlainne Suibhne*, xxxv–xxxvi.

38 Buckley, ed., 'A Tour in Ireland in 1672–4', *Cork. Hist. and Arch. Soc. Jn.*, 2nd ser., x (1904), 89.

39 Gillespie, *Colonial Ulster*, 114.

40 *Ibid.*, 118–19; Hill, *An Historical Account of the MacDonnells of Antrim*, 61–2, 236.

41 Gillespie, *Conspiracy*, 31–3.

42 McCarthy, 'Ulster Office', 172.

43 Marshall, *History of the Parish of Tynan in the County of Armagh*, 42–3; Hill, *Plantation*, 207–10, 217.

44 Hunter, 'Ulster Plantation', 545–8, 574; Glancy, 'The Primate Lands . . . Armagh', 387, the 1714 list of the sub-tenants on these former erenach lands registers that decline.

45 Cited Flower, *Irish Tradition*, 167.

46 Cunningham, 'Native Culture and Political Change in Ireland', 161; Gillespie, *Colonial Ulster*, 150–51.

47 Williams, ed., *Pairlement Chloinne Tomáis*.

48 Macafee, 'The Population of Ulster', 52–4.

49 See Gillespie in Mac Cuarta, ed., *Ulster 1641*, 109.

50 Hunter, 'Ulster Plantation', 324–5 – 25% to 19% in Armagh, 22.5% to 16.5% in Cavan in the period between the plantation and 1641.

51 Kennedy, 'Eagla an Ghallsmacht. The Religion and Politics of Irish Catholics 1620s–1670s', 178.

52 Ohlmeyer, *Civil War and Restoration*, 83; Gillespie, in *Natives and Newcomers*, 198–9.

53 *Cal. S.P. Ire., 1633–1647*, 274; Gilbert, *Contemporary History*, vol. i, pt. i, 'Aphorismical Discovery', 12.

54 O'Riordain and Gillespie, in Mac Cuarta, ed., *Ulster 1641*, 83 and 110; Dunlop, ed., *Ireland under the Commonwealth: Being a Selection of Documents Relating to the Government of Ireland, 1651–9*, ii, 363, 423.

55 Gillespie, 'Destabilising Ulster, 1641–42', in Mac Cuarta, ed., *Ulster 1641*, 112.

56 [John Lodge] ed., *Desiderata Curiosa Hibernica, or, a Select Collection of State Papers*, ii, 78, 86–8; Perceval-Maxwell, 'Ulster 1641 in the Context of Political Developments in the Three Kingdoms', in Mac Cuarta, ed., *Ulster 1641*, 100–103; Lecky, *Ireland in the Eighteenth Century*, i, 94; Canny, 'What Really Happened in 1641?', in Ohlmeyer, *Ireland from Independence to Occupation 1641–1660*, 29–30.

57 *Desiderata Curiosa*, ii: 'The Humble Remonstrance of the Northern Catholicks of Ireland, Now in Arms', 99. But see Moody, *et al.*, eds., *New History of Ireland*, ix, 605, which does not support their accusation about the prorogation of parliament.

58 But see Stevenson, *Scottish Covenanters and Irish Confederates*, 83–102, for the confusion of attitudes towards the Scots.

59 Hamilton, *The Irish Rebellion of 1641*, 106.

60 Hickson, *Ireland in the Seventeenth Century or the Irish Massacres of 1641–2*, ii, 216–17.

61 Hamilton, *Irish Rebellion*, 150.

62 IFC, MS vol. 1215/214; Hickson, *Irish Massacres*, i, 176–82.

63 Hill, ed., *The Montgomery Manuscripts (1603–1706)*, 131–2; Hamilton, *Irish rebellion*, 256.

64 Murray, 'The History of the Parish of Creggan in the 17th and 18th Centuries', *Louth Arch. Soc. Jn.*, viii, no. 2, 124.

65 John Lynch, *Cambrensis Eversus*, 1, 12. Clarke, *The Old English in Ireland, 1625–42*, 224–6.

66 Gillespie, 'Destabilising Ulster', 112–13.

67 Simms, 'Violence in County Armagh, 1641', in Mac Cuarta, ed., *Ulster 1641*, 130–31.

68 McCall, 'The Gaelic Background to the Settlement of Antrim and Down 1580–1641', 130; McSkimin, *Carrickfergus*, 41–57, detailed account of the controversy over the numbers of Catholics killed.

69 Simms, 'Violence in County Armagh', 127; Hamilton, *Irish Rebellion*, 217–18, 149–52; Russell and Prendergast, eds., *The Carte Manuscripts*, 147–51.

70 Ohlmeyer, *Civil War and Restoration*, 110–13; Stevenson, 'The Desertion of the Irish by Coll Keitach's Sons, 1642', *I.H.S.*, xxi, 75–84.

71 Kennedy, 'Eagla an Ghallsmacht.', 178–83.

72 Jones, *A Remonstrance of Divers Remarkable Passages Concerning the Church and Kingdome of Ireland*, 1.

73 Most historians would not now go so far as Lecky in totally denying the stories of massacre (*Ireland in the Eighteenth Century*, i, 45–100), but would accept the Depositions as a valuable source, if used with utmost caution; see e.g. Canny, 'What Really Happened in Ireland in 1641', in Ohlmeyer, ed., *Ireland . . . 1641–1660*, 24–42.

74 Barnard, 'The Uses of 23 October 1641 and Irish Protestant celebrations', *E.H.R.*, cvi, 892.

75 Stewart, *The Narrow Ground. Aspects of Ulster*, 49.

76 Elliott, *Partners in Revolution*, 8–9; Stewart, *Narrow Ground*, 108; *Northern Star*, 22 August 1792; Harris, *The Ancient and Present State of the County of Down*, 106, also 35, 81, 84–6, 92–3, 97; David Hayton, 'The Propaganda War', in Maguire, ed., *Kings in Conflict*, 118–19.

77 Dunlop, ed., *Ireland under the Commonwealth*, i, 179. In August 1652 Jones was instructed by the commissioners to discover the perpetrators of such outrages with a view to their punishment (*ibid.*, 242).

78 The words are Walter Love's, quoted in Bottigheimer, *English Money and Irish Land*, 127–8.

79 Young, *Historical Notices of Old Belfast and Its Vicinity*, 75; Dunlop, ed., *Ireland under the Commonwealth*, ii, 370.

80 Corish, in Moody *et al.*, eds., *New History of Ireland*, iii, 359–60; Dunlop, ed., *Ireland under the Commonwealth*, ii, 322.

81 Dunlop, ed., *Ireland under the Commonwealth*, ii, 323–4.

82 *Ibid.*, ii, 486, 499, 515, 516, 542, and i, 299; 29 November 1652, Sir Charles Coote being reprimanded for moving Donegal creaghts, their families and stocks to his lands in Connacht. Simington, *The Transplantation to Connacht, 1654–58*, xii–xiii.

83 Dunlop, ed., *Ireland under the Commonwealth*, ii, 614, also i, 78–96, and ii, 339, 346–50, 351–4, 360–61 for the Scots to be transplanted, 254 from Antrim and Down alone, including a John Tennent from Lecale.

84 See *Montgomery Manuscripts*, Viscount Montgomery, like most other outlawed Protestants, 'composing' for their property, 218–19; Dunlop, ed., *Ireland under the Commonwealth*, ii, 363, 580, 711, and Burke, *The Irish Priests in Penal Times*, 42–3, on Cromwellian soldiers marrying Catholic

Irishwomen; Ohlmeyer, *Civil War and Restoration*, 245, on Cromwellian soldiers selling up; IFC, MS vol. 815/361–2: traditions in Cavan about purchase of the soldiers' portions.

85 Duffy, 'The Evolution of Estate Properties in South Ulster, 1600–1900', in Smyth and Whelan, eds., *Common Ground*, 100–104; Bottigheimer, 'The Restoration Land Settlement in Ireland', *I.H.S.*, xviii, 17; Barnard, 'Planters and Policies in Cromwellian Ireland', *Past and Present*, no. 61, 31–69.

86 The most recent general survey ignores it entirely: Fitzpatrick, *Seventeenth-century Ireland*. The most comprehensive (Bottigheimer) concentrates largely on the Adventurers, Barnard, 'Planters and policies', on the 'Old Protestants'. Given its place in popular demonology, it is at least odd that the best overall account of the consequences for the Catholic populace remains Butler, *Confiscation in Irish History*, whilst Ohlmeyer's *Civil War and Restoration* provides some valuable material on Antrim. A welcome exception for west Ulster (Tyrone, Londonderry, Donegal) is McKenney, 'The Seventeenth-century Land Settlement in Ireland', in Ohlmeyer, ed., *Ireland . . . 1641–1660*, 181–200.

87 Kerry and Tipperary saw most transplantation, which probably explains the strength of anti-Cromwellian sentiment there, reflected in the bitterness of the Munster poetry and in living popular tradition. It was a tradition very much alive in my Kerry mother's family and Tipperary grandmother's.

88 Gillespie, 'Continuity and Change', in Brady *et al.*, *Illustrated History of Ulster*, 117.

89 McKenny, 'The Seventeenth-century Land Settlement in Ireland: Towards a Statistical Interpretation', 196–8; Butler, *Confiscation*, 150–53; also map in Bottigheimer, *English Money and Irish Land*, 214–15; see also Dunlop, ed., *Ireland under the Commonwealth*, ii, 702–3.

90 These were the Articles of Cloughoughter signed with O'Reilly, Lord Enniskillen, Miles O'Reilly, Col. MacMahon, Hugh Maguire, Con O'Neill, Dan O'Cahan, and various others of 'the Ulster party', Dunlop, ed., *Ireland under the Commonwealth*, ii, 336–7n, 362, 429.

91 Ohlmeyer, *Civil War and Restoration*, 234–48; Dunlop, ed., *Ireland under the Commonwealth*, ii, 369.

92 Ó Fiaich, 'The O'Neills of the Fews,' ii, *Seanchas Ard Mhacha*, 2, 287–92; Murray, 'The History of the Parish of Creggan', 121–3; Russell and Prendergast, eds., *The Carte Manuscripts*, 147–51. But Bottigheimer, 'The Restoration Land Settlement', 17, suggests he was eventually declared innocent. Archbishop Plunkett refers to him in 1671 as one of only three Catholic landowners left in Ulster (Hanly, ed., *The Letters of Saint Oliver Plunkett*, 247).

93 Schlegel, 'The MacDonnells of Tyrone and Armagh: A Genealogical Study', *Seanchas Ard Mhacha*, x, 193–219; Ó Doibhlin, *Domhnach Mór*, 140–54.

94 Cullen, *Emergence of Modern Ireland*, 42; Livingstone, *Monaghan*, 124; Maguire, 'The Estate of Cú Chonnacht Maguire of Tempo', *I.H.S*, xxvii, 141, shows throughout the century hardly any British settlement on his estate.

95 Lin. Lib., Joy MSS, Commonplace Book, fos. 33–7, 'An Account of the

Ancient Family of Magennis of Iveagh'. The outcome of this case, however, was to show that the original trust was not necessarily guaranteed if the offspring of the Protestant friend were ill-disposed. Edmond Oge Magennis was still trying to recover the lands from the son of the family friend when he joined James II's cause in 1688 and was later killed at the battle of Aughrim (1691). By the second half of the eighteenth century some of the Magennises of Waringstown had converted to the established church, see Atkinson, *An Ulster Parish*, 62, 86, also Coote, *Statistical Survey of County Armagh*, 126. Ó Doibhlin, *Domhnach Mór*, 159–63, the 1666 hearth-money rolls show the O'Loughrans still on former erenach land.

96 Lecky, *Ireland in the Eighteenth Century*, i, 106.

97 Bagwell, *Ireland under the Stuarts*, iii, 22–3.

98 Connolly, *Religion, Law and Power*, 13; also Ohlmeyer, *Civil War and Restoration*, 263–4.

99 Bottigheimer, 'Restoration Land Settlement', 19.

100 Russell and Prendergast, eds., *The Carte Manuscripts*, 87; Butler, *Confiscation*, 188.

101 Bagwell, *Ireland under the Stuarts*, iii, 49; Connolly, *Religion, Law and Power*, 13–17; *Cal. S.P. Ire., 1663–1665*, 687–9, 699.

102 Russell and Prendergast, eds., *The Carte Manuscripts*, 91–2.

103 Giblin, ed., 'Catalogue of Material of Irish Interest in the . . . Vatican Archives', Part I, 102–5.

104 Bagwell, *Ireland under the Stuarts*, iii, 39–43; *Cal. S.P. Ire., 1663–1665*, 29, 44, 90, 115, 208–21, 338, 687; Hill, *MacDonnells of Antrim*, 290–344.

105 Butler, *Confiscation*, 172, 191; and see Moody *et al.*, eds., *New History of Ireland*, iii, 572–3.

106 Butler, *Confiscation*, 192, 196, 203; Laverty, *Down and Connor*, ii, 243, lx–lxxii.

107 *Cal. S.P. Ire., 1663–5*, 361–2, 714, and *1669–70*, 433, 460, 523–4, 534–5; Butler, *Confiscation*, 203.

108 *Savages of the Ards*, 195, 250; O'Laverty, *Down and Connor*, ii, 145–6.

109 Livingstone, *Monaghan Story*, 123.

110 Moody *et al.*, eds., *New History of Ireland*, iii, 428; *Cal. S.P. Ire., 1666–1669*, 543–9, long, forceful memorandum showing utter amazement and a sense of deep injustice at the way the interest of former Cromwellians had been placed above those who had been loyal royalists.

111 Cited Ó Buachalla, 'Jacobitism and Nationalism: the Irish Literary Evidence', in O'Dea and Whelan, eds., *Nations and Nationalism*, 104.

112 Ó Buachalla, 'Lillibulero agus eile', *Comhar* (April, 1987), 29.

113 Bagwell, *Ireland under the Stuarts*, iii, 231; Connolly, *Religion, Law and Power*, 35.

114 Barnard, 'The Uses of 23 October 1641', 894.

115 Hugh Reily, *The Impartial History of Ireland*, iv.

116 Elliott, *Wolfe Tone*, 137; Simms, *The Jacobite Parliament of 1689*, 21–6.

117 Lin. Lib., Joy MSS, Commonplace Book, fo. 35.

118 Atkinson, *An Ulster Parish*, 37–8.

119 Simms, ed., 'Irish Jacobites', *Anal. Hib.*, xxii, 22–187, lists of outlawries and pardons; idem, 'Land Owned by Catholics in Ireland in 1688', *I.H.S.*, vii, 180–90, in which he also explains why more land survived in Catholic hands in the west of Ireland.

120 Atkinson, *An Ulster Parish*, 34–48.

121 Maguire, 'The Estate of Cú Chonnacht Maguire', 133–5; Simms, 'Land Owned by Catholics', 185. He died at sea en route to France after being outlawed. His brother Charles, who had become a Protestant, was granted the estate by William on payment of a fine. But this was voided by the Act of Resumption (Russell and Prendergast, eds., *The Carte Manuscripts*, 101).

122 See case of Antrim O'Haras in Connolly, *Religion, Law and Power*, 309; also Quinn, 'Religion and Landownership in County Louth 1641–c.1750', chap. 2.

123 Lin. Lib., Joy MSS, Commonplace Book, op. cit.; Ó Fiaich, 'O'Neills of the Fews', ii, 294–5, 300, 302, also shows O'Neills of the Fews intermarrying with Magennises, Clandeboye O'Neills and O'Donnells into the eighteenth century.

124 Maguire, ed., *Kings in Conflict*, 64.

125 Ó Fiaich, 'O'Neills of the Fews', iii, 386.

126 See Roebuck, in Mitchison and Roebuck, eds., *Economy and Society*, 85–6, showing considerable bargaining power of tenants in Ulster, even under the penal laws.

127 Silke, 'The Irish Abroad, 1533–1691', in Moody *et al.*, eds., *New History of Ireland*, iii, 593; Hill, *Plantation*, 205.

128 Henry, 'Ulster Exiles in Europe, 1605–1641', in Mac Cuarta, ed., *Ulster 1641*, 37–60. This is the best short survey of this topic. See Dunlop, ed., *Ireland under the Commonwealth*, i, cxxxvi, for a reported 27,000 leaving in 1656.

129 Ó Fiaich, 'O'Neills of the Fews', ii, 283; Silke, 'The Irish Abroad', in Moody *et al.*, eds., *New History of Ireland*, iii, 606.

130 Hanly, ed., *Letters of Saint Oliver Plunkett*, 160; Connolly, *Religion, Law and Power*, 206, which sheds new light on the tory phenomenon.

131 Russell and Prendergast, eds., *The Carte Manuscripts*, 98; Ó Fiaich, 'The Registration of the Clergy in 1704', *Seanchas Ard Mhacha*, 6, 52. Brian McHugh, priest in Longford, imprisoned 1708 for marrying a Catholic and Protestant, escaped and became a tory.

132 Gillespie, 'Transformation of the Borderlands', 84–6; Dunlop, ed., *Ireland under the Commonwealth*, i, 49–50.

133 Smyth, 'Society and Settlement . . . "1659 Census"', 75.

134 See for e.g. Ó Doibhlin, *Domhnach Mór*, 167ff. Glassie, *Ballymenone*, 110: in this region of Fermanagh popular tradition has the rapparees robbing the rich to give to the poor, rather than submit to 'English law and religion'.

135 For examples of English and Scots tories see McSkimin, *History of Carrickfergus*, 459–61; *Cal. S.P. Ire.*, *1666–1669*, 608; and 'Protestant Rapparees', Story, *Impartial History*, 161.

136 Casey, 'Carleton and the Count', *Seanchas Ard Mhacha*, viii, 7–22;

Adams, *The Printed Word and the Common Man*, 15, 90; Bardon, *History of Ulster*, 143–5; Moody, 'Redmond O'Hanlon, *c.*1640–1681', *Proceedings and Reports of the Belfast Natural History and Philosophical Society*, 2nd ser., i, pt 1, 17–33.

137 IFC, MS 1113/50 and 975/31; Story, *Impartial History*, 15; Murphy, *Ulster Folk of Field and Fireside*, 10. See also Murray, 'A Previously Unnoticed Letter of Oliver Plunkett's', *Seanchas Ard Mhacha*, viii, 23–33; Dunlop, ed., *Ireland under the Commonwealth*, i, 17.

138 Story, *Impartial History*, 15, 59; Macafee, 'Population of Ulster', 56; *Cal. S.P. Ire., 1666–1669*, 256–7.

139 Reily, *Impartial History of Ireland*, 39.

140 Livingstone, *Monaghan Story*, 123, makes this point; Simms, *The Williamite Confiscation in Ireland*, 16, shows that the successive land upheavals of the seventeenth century affected the Gaelic proprietors far more adversely than the Old English.

141 Duffy, 'The Territorial Organisation of Gaelic Landownership and Its Transformation in County Monaghan, 1591–1640', *Irish Geography*, xiv, 19.

142 Hill, *MacDonnells of Antrim*, 362.

143 See e.g. on Brownlow estate in Armagh, Cunningham and Gillespie, 'An Ulster Settler and his Irish Manuscripts', *Éigse*, xxi, 30; Macafee, 'Population of Ulster', 75, 92.

144 Hanly, ed., *Letters of Saint Oliver Plunkett*, 247, also 74–5, 410, 455; MacCurtain, 'Rural Society in post-Cromwellian Ireland', in Cosgrove and McCartney, eds., *Studies in Irish History*, 133.

5 THE MERGER OF 'IRISHNESS' AND CATHOLICISM IN EARLY MODERN ULSTER

1 O Connor, *In Search of a State*, 11.

2 The hymnn was used by the GAA until the 1960s as a kind of anthem for major fixtures, see Hayes, *Minority Verdict*, 56.

3 Ohlmeyer, *Civil War and Restoration*, 35–6, 287. 'Travels of Sir William Brereton in Ireland, 1635', in Falkiner, *Illustrations of Irish History and Topography*, 372–3; see e.g. Russell and Prendergast, eds., *The Carte Manuscripts*, 124; *Cal. S.P. Ire., 1663–5*, 138, 566, for sense of persecution.

4 Hanly, ed., *Letters of Saint Oliver Plunkett*, 144, 452; O'Laverty, *Down and Connor*, i, 313; Harkin, *Inishowen*, 142–3.

5 Cullen, *The Emergence of Modern Ireland, 1600–1900*, 131–2.

6 McCone and Simms, eds., *Progress in Medieval Irish Studies*, 212.

7 See e.g. Ó Muirgheasa, *Céad de Cheoltaibh Uladh*, 9–12, by Patrick Plunkett, early nineteenth century, contains all the standard themes first used in the seventeenth century, Catholicism the true religion of the Gael, the Protestants insincere, the Catholic who converts doomed, the Irish language exclusively theirs; idem, *Dánta Diadha Uladh*, 257, an 1824 poem of Thomas O'Connor.

8 Hanly, ed., *Plunkett Letters*, 546, shows Phelim O'Neill and his son Gordon adopting Catholicism and Protestantism at different points in their life.

9 Harkin, *Inishowen*, 74–5; Gillespie, *Devoted People*, 121–2, 140–41.

10 Perceval-Maxwell, *Scottish Migration to Ulster*, 272–3; *Cal. S.P. Ire., 1625–32*, 512–13; Hanly, ed., *Plunkett Letters*, 226, Captain John Hamilton 'a Scottish gentlemen', a Catholic 'and a great support of our religion in those parts', 1671.

11 Hill, 'The Origins of the Scottish Plantations in Ulster to 1625', *Jn. Brit. Studs.*, 32, 40; O'Laverty, *Down and Connor*, 430; Ohlmeyer, *Civil War and Restoration*, 75.

12 Gillespie, 'Continuity and Change', 124–9; Robinson, *Plantation of Ulster*, 187–8.

13 Even before the plantation a number of the Ulster Irish had studied in Scotland and were credited with speaking 'Scots' (as well as Irish, English and Latin), this 'The O'Kane Papers', *Anal. Hib.*, xii, 100–104. See also Adams, 'The Emergence of Ulster as a Distinct Dialect Area', *Ulster Folklife*, iv, 68–9. Montgomery and Robinson, 'The Linguistic Landscape of Seventeenth-century Ulster', unpublished paper delivered to the annual ACIS conference, Belfast, June 1995.

14 See e.g. Morgan, 'The End of Gaelic Ulster', 30; Ó Fiaich and Ó Caithnia, *Art Mac Bionaid*, 66–8, Art Bennett's 1852 poem 'A ghleann na suailce' ('O valley of virtue'), the belief that you only became Protestant if bribed or deceived; also IFC, MS 815/289, Cavan story of a woman in Cromwell's time 'turning to keep her land', struck down by supernatural forces as a result.

15 Reily, *Impartial History of Ireland*, iv–v.

16 Dunlop, *Commonwealth*, ii, 515, 517, also 355–7, 370, 413; Hill, *Plantation*, 414–15.

17 Phil Kilroy, 'Sermon and Pamphlet Literature in the Irish Reformed Church, 1613–34', *Archiv. Hib.*, xxxiii, 113–14.

18 Barnard, *Cromwellian Ireland*, 179n, and 90–91, 171–82 for this section; the press seems to have been taken to London in the 1650s and then lost – see McGuinne, *Irish Type Design*, 22.

19 Gilbert, *Contemporary History*, vol. I, pt. i, xviii; Burnett, *The Life of Bishop Bedell*, 140–41; Moody *et al.*, eds., *New History of Ireland*, iii, 574.

20 Burke, *Irish Priests in Penal Times (1660–1750)*, 43; Canny, 'Why the Reformation Failed', 443.

21 'Miscellanea Vaticano-Hibernica', *Archiv. Hib.*, v, 105; Gillespie, 'The End of an Era', in *Natives and Newcomers*, 197; Gillespie, 'Destabilizing Ulster, 1641–2', 110.

22 Ohlmeyer, *Civil War and Restoration*, 55, 249–50; O'Laverty, *Down and Connor*, i, 399–401, 423–4, ii, 316–27; Maguire, 'Estate of Cú Chonnacht Maguire', 140; Hill, ed., *Montgomery Manuscripts*, i, 89–91.

23 Dunlop, *Ireland under the Commonwealth*, ii, 363, 423; PRONI, T3022/4/2A–C, shows Gaelic names among the Cromwellian commissioners in Antrim, 1657; IFC, MS 976/92, folk traditions of Cromwellians turning

Catholic; MacCurtain, 'Rural Society in Post-Cromwellian Ireland', 131; Burke, *Irish Priests in Penal Times*, 43; Tynan, *Catholic Instruction in Ireland, 1720–1950*, 19–20: *c.*1720s, O'Reilly, Bishop of Derry, published an English language catechism for 'the newly converted colonists'.

24 Gillespie, 'The Presbyterian Revolution in Ulster, 1660–1690', in Sheils and Wood, eds., *The Churches, Ireland and the Irish*, 159–70.

25 Macafee and Morgan, 'Population in Ulster, 1660–1760', 47–59.

26 See Elliott, 'Origins and Transformation of Early Irish Republicanism', *Internat. Rev. Soc. Hist.*, xxiii, 415.

27 Crawford, 'The Ulster Irish in the Eighteenth Century', *Ulster Folklife*, vol. 28, 26; Gillespie, 'The Transformation of the Borderlands', 80–81.

28 Hanly, ed., *Plunkett Letters*, 530.

29 I am grateful to Dr Art Hughes, Institute of Irish Studies, Queen's University, Belfast, for advice here. Ó Baoill, *An Teanga Bheo: Gaeilge Uladh*, 123; see also Day and McWilliams, eds., *Ordnance Survey Memoirs of Ireland*, vol. 15, 15.

30 Flynne, 'Hugh MacMahon, Bishop of Clogher 1707–15 and Archbishop of Armagh 1715–37', *Seanchas Ard Mhacha*, 7 (1973), 110; Gilbert, *Contemporary History*, vol. I, pt i, xx; PRONI, T.3022/4, op. cit.; Gillespie, 'Destabilizing Ulster, 1641–2', 109.

31 See e.g. Ó Muirgheasa, *Dánta Diadha Uladh*, 227–32, Lament for Daniel Mackey, Bishop of Down, 1673, clearly a patron of the poets; translator Eugene O'Curry, in *Louth Arch. Soc. Jn.*, 267–72. Ó Fiaich, 'The Political and Social Background of the Ulster Poets', *Léachtaí Cholm Cille*, i, 30–32. Carrigan, 'Catholic Episcopal Wills in the PRO, Dublin, 1683–1812', *Archiv. Hib.*, i, 173–4, dynasty of MacCartan priests at Loughinisland. Heusaff, *Filí agus Cléir san Ochtú hAois Déag*, 5–6: Fr Phelim O'Neill, so beloved of the poets, direct descendant of Turlogh MacHenry.

32 Hughes, 'Landholdings of Gaelic poets', unpublished paper, kindly made available to me by the author.

33 Kennedy, *'Eagla an Ghallsmacht'*, 49–59.

34 O'Rahilly, ed., *Five Seventeenth-century Political Poems*, 140–41; Leerssen, *Mere Irish and Fíor Ghael*, 239–41.

35 Ó Fiaich, 'Filíocht Uladh', 92–3.

36 *Maol* – bald, bare, naked – possibly a reference to clean-shaven, shorn, cropped hair, singling them out from the bearded and long-haired Irish.

37 Walsh, ed., 'The Memorial Presented to the King of Spain on Behalf of the Irish Catholics, A.D. 1619', *Archiv. Hib.*, vi, 54.

38 Bennett acknowledges as much in his praise of Ó Doirnín, Mac Cuarta, Mac Cooey, in 'Don Sagart Pádraig Ó Luain' ('For the priest Patrick Lamb', parish priest of Cullyhanna), in Ó Muirgheasa, *Céad de Cheoltaibh Uladh*, 165; Heusaff, *Filí agus Cléir*, 56, Fr Phelim O'Neill (much respected by the poets), transcribing Keating, 'An Síogaí' and 'Tuireamh na hÉireann', in the eighteenth century.

39 Welch, *The Oxford Companion to Irish Literature*, 237. Hardiman, *Irish Minstrelsy*, ii, 306–39. O'Rahilly, *Five . . . Political Poems*, 12–16.

40 Mag Uidhir, *Pádraig Mac a Liondain: Dánta*: the works of these poets were never published.

41 See e.g. Hagan, ed., 'Miscellanea Vaticano-Hibernica', *Archiv. Hib.*, iii, 302–5, the Irish Earls (O'Neill, O'Donnell etc.) to Pope Paul V. *c.*1613; Corish, ed., 'Two Reports on the Catholic Church in Ireland in the Early Seventeenth Century', *Archiv. Hib.*, xxii, 141–2.

42 Mag Uidhir, *Pádraig Mac a Liondain*, 6–8.

43 *Ibid.*, 19–22. There is a similar fatalism in church documents (Moran, *Spicil. Ossor.*, i, ccxv, 1654); also Maguire, 'Pádraig Mhac a Lionnduinn of the Fews', 20, 106–7.

44 *"Sé mo Ghéardheachair Chlíse mar d'Éag Treibh no dTíortha* (Painfully troubled is my heart for the way the tribe of the countries died), in Ó Gallachóir, 'Filíocht Shéamais Dhaill Mhic Cuarta', 263; Mag Uidhir, *Pádraig Mac a Liondain*, 7, Keating's influence.

45 Ó Gallachóir, 'Filíocht', 259, and *'Ní maith is léir damh'* ('It's not well that I see), 239.

46 *'Ceist agam ort a Chúirt na Féile'* (I've a question for you, O Court of Hospitality), O'Gallachóir, 'Filíocht', 121–7.

47 *'A Phlanda'* (O Scion), *ibid.*, 58.

48 His treatise had gone through six editions by 1733, see O'Laverty, *Down and Connor: The Bishops*, 514–15.

49 Either Calvin or Seán Buí ('swarthy John'), the Irish reference for the English.

50 Niall of the Nine Hostages, a favourite figure in Ulster nationalist rhetoric and iconography; this poem taken from Ó Gallachóir, ed., *Séamas Dall Mac Cuarta: Dánta*, 52.

51 QUB, Belfast, Gaelic Manuscripts 17: Mic A/428 (xviii), 'An essay on Séamus Mac Cuarta'.

52 *'Ní maith is léir damh'*, in praise of Brian, son of Art O'Neill of the Fews, Ó Gallachóir, 'Filíocht Shéamais Dhaill Mhic Cuarta', 239.

53 Ó Gallachóir, *Séamus Dall Mac Cuarta: Dánta*, 63–9, 90. However, Ó Fiaich, 'Filíocht Uladh mar Fhoinse don Stair Shóisialta san 18ú hAois', *Stud. Hib.*, no. 11, 82, sees the poem as a lament rather than a call to action, a proclamation that Jacobitism is no more. See also Ó Buachalla, ed., *Nua Dhuanaire*, ii, 2–3, 'Eachroim,' *c.*1730, another Ulster poem of stark imagery at the scale of the defeat at Aughrim.

54 *'Sé is léir liom uaim'* ('What's evident to me'), Ó Gallachóir, 'Filíocht . . . Mhic Cuarta', 191–4.

55 Ó Buachalla, 'Lillibulero agus Eile', *Comhar*, 27.

56 Murray, *History of the Parish of Creggan*, 61–7.

57 Ó Fiaich, 'Art Mac Cooey and His Times', *Seanchas Ard Mhacha*, vi, 235; idem, *'Filíocht Uladh'*, 82–4, says Jacobitism was much weaker in Ulster.

58 Ó Muirgheasa, *Dánta Diadha Uladh*, 376.

59 Ó Fiaich, 'Art Mac Cooey and His Times', *Seanchas Ard Mhacha*, vi, 242–3; the poems are in Ó Fiaich, *Art Mac Cumhaigh: Dánta*, 102–4.

60 Heussaff, *Filí agus Cléir san Ochtú hAois Déag*, 74–5, 161–2; Murray,

'Three Documents Concerning the Deanery of Dundalk during the Eighteenth Century', *Archiv. Hib.*, v, 68–73.

61 Ó Buachalla, *Cathal Buí: Amhráin*, 21ff.

62 The key scribes are also from this area, Maguire, 'Pádraig Mhac a Lionnduinn of the Fews', 18–19. Even after Cromwellian persecution this area, next to Meath, had the largest numbers of priests in the country. See Ó Fiaich, 'Edmund O'Reilly', 192–3; also Dunlop, *Commonwealth*, ii, 491, for the numbers of schoolmasters operating there; Hanly, ed., *Plunkett Letters*, 73–5, on the Old English families.

63 Maguire, 'Pádraig Mhac a Lionnduinn of the Fews', 9–10; Pádraig Ó Pronntaigh (Patrick O'Pronty), a minor County Down poet, but considered one of the finest scribes of the eighteenth century, was an assistant to MacAlindon; on the scribes see also Cullen, 'Patrons, Teachers and Literacy in Irish: 1700–1850', in Daly and Dickson, eds., *The Origins of Popular Literacy in Ireland*, 15–44.

64 Ó Mórdha, 'Simon Macken; Fermanagh Scribe and Schoolmaster', *Clogher Rec.*, ii, 432–44. For other examples of the most dramatic of the Irish-language material being passed on see Duffy, *Nicholas O'Kearney: The Last of the Bards of Louth*, 11–12; Art Murphy, the poet-teacher of Nicholas as a youth (he was born 1807), used Mac Cuarta's works (notably his *Tuireamh*), also Keating; Ó Muirgheasa, *Céad de Cheoltaibh Uladh*, 191, shows frequent later copies of this elegy for Owen Roe, written 1649 by a County Down priest.

65 Burke, ed., 'The Diocese of Derry in 1631', *Archiv. Hib.*, v, 2–3; Hunter, 'English Undertakers in the Plantation of Ulster', 486; Rogan, *Synods and Catechesis in Ireland, c.445–1962*, i, 4–5; Hill, *Plantation*, 494–5, 130 n.

66 Moran, *Spicil. Ossor.*, i, 407–12, 'An Account of the Irish Church in 1654', also pp. 415–16, 'The State of Ireland in 1656'; MacCaffrey, ed., 'Commonwealth Records', *Archiv. Hib.*, vi, 175–202, details Cromwellian policies, directed exclusively against clergy, though those willing to abjure papal supremacy allowed to stay.

67 Corish, *The Catholic Community*, 49; see also Barnard, *Cromwellian Ireland*, 172–5, and Edwards, 'Irish Catholics and the Puritan Revolution', in Franciscan Fathers, eds., *Father Luke Wadding*, 93–118. Barnard, 'Irish Images of Cromwell', in Richardson, ed., *Images of Cromwell*, 180–206.

68 See e.g. the influential little volume Millett OFM, 'Survival and Reorganisation 1650–1695', in Corish, ed., *A History of Irish Catholicism*, iii, ch. 7, 1–12. In his more recent bibliographical survey, 'The Seventeenth Century', in Ó Muirí, ed., *Irish Church History Today*, 42, he likens Cromwellian policy to that of the Nazis towards the Jews.

69 Rogan, *Synods and Catechesis*, i, 38–9.

70 According to Archbishop Plunkett, see Hanly, ed., *Plunkett Letters*, 145.

71 Russell and Prendergast, eds., *The Carte Manuscripts*, 124.

72 Giblin, ed., 'Catalogue of material of Irish interest . . . Part 1', *Coll. Hib.*, i, 60 (1624).

73 The word 'Palesman' appears frequently in Ó Doibhlin, *Domhnach Mór*, for Plunkett's activities contradict the association in this book between Catholicism and a Gaelic race, and his foreign roots can be the only explanation (see e.g. pp. 171–3). The appointment of Patrick Tyrrell to Clogher a few years later was similarly resisted. See Ó Fiaich, 'The Appointment of Bishop Tyrrell and Its Consequences', *Clogher Rec.*, i, no. 3, 1–14.

74 O'Connell, *The Diocese of Kilmore: Its History and Antiquities*, 448.

75 Russell and Prendergast, eds., *The Carte Manuscripts*, 125.

76 Quoted Burke, *Irish Priests in Penal Times*, 47.

77 Stuart, *Historical Memoirs of the City of Armagh*, by Revd Ambrose Coleman, OP, 237–9, deals at length with the Franciscan accusers. They are denounced as 'nefarious wretches' for betraying their own. Plunkett was canonised October 1975.

78 Burke, *Irish Priests in Penal Times*, 77, also, 61–5, 74–7, 282–3; Hanly, ed., *Plunkett Letters*, 442, 463; Lecky, *Ireland in the Eighteenth Century*, i, 255.

79 Hanly, ed., *Plunkett Letters*, 78, 86–7, 166, 306, 481; Moran, *Spicil. Ossor.*, i, 193 and 212–13; Burke, *Irish Priests in Penal Times*, 61.

80 Hayton, 'The Propaganda War', in Maguire, ed., *Kings in Conflict*, 113–18.

81 Flynne, 'Hugh MacMahon', 125; James MacCaffrey, ed., 'Commonwealth Records', *Archiv. Hib.*, vi, 191.

82 O'Laverty, *Down and Connor: Bishops*, 496; Burke, *Irish Priests in Penal Times*, 74–6.

83 Ryan, 'Religion and State in Seventeenth-century Ireland', *Archiv. Hib.*, xxxiii, 110–21.

84 Kennedy, '*Eagla an Ghallsmacht*', 177–86; Henry, 'Ulster Exiles in Europe', in Mac Cuarta, ed., *Ulster 1641*, 56, thinks fears of the Ulster clergy inciting rebellion were justified; *Cal. S.P. Ire.*, *1663–5*, 359–61.

85 See *Cal. S.P. Ire.*, *1669–70*, 560–63, for the full text and list of subscribers.

86 Giblin, ed., 'Catalogue of Material . . . in the Vatican Archives', Part I, 102–5; Stuart, *Historical Memoirs of the City of Armagh*, 242.

87 Flynne, 'Hugh MacMahon Bishop of Clogher', 125 – only three of these were from Ulster.

88 Giblin, ed., 'Catalogue of Material . . . in the Vatican Archives', Part II, 24ff, also Part I, 123.

89 Flynne, 'Hugh MacMahon', 136–40.

90 Ó Fiaich, 'Edmund O'Reilly, Archbishop of Armagh, 1657–1669', in Franciscan Fathers, eds., *Father Luke Wadding*, 214; Burke, *Irish Priests in Penal Times*, 11–14; O'Connell, *Diocese of Kilmore*, 433–4.

91 Ó Fiaich, 'The Registration of the Clergy in 1704', *Seanchas Ard Mhacha*, vi, 59.

92 Burke, *Irish Priests in Penal Times*, 65.

93 Moran, *Spicil. Ossor*, i, 192; Giblin, ed., 'Catalogue of Material . . . in the Vatican Archives', Part I, 115–16.

94 Cited Corish, *Catholic Community*, 42.

95 Hanly, ed., *Plunkett Letters*, 407; Smyth, 'Blessed Oliver Plunkett in Down and Connor', *Down and Connor Hist. Soc. Jn.*, viii, 76–80.

96 Ó Fiaich, 'Edmund O'Reilly', 197; R. Gillespie, *The Sacred in the Secular*, 13–14; Gillespie, *Devoted People*, 152.

97 Flynne, 'Hugh MacMahon', 115; Crawford, 'Ulster Irish', 27; Ó Gallachair, 'Clogherhici. A Dictionary of the Catholic Clergy of the Diocese of Clogher (1535–1835)', *Clogher Rec.*, i, no. 3, 169; Hanly, ed., *Plunkett Letters*, 361–2, 380–81.

98 *Comhairle Mhic Clámha ó Achadh na Muilleann: The Advice of MacClave from Aughnamullen*, translated by Ó Dufaigh and Rainey.

99 See e.g. of Father McQuaid of Knockaraven, in Ó Gallachair, 'Clogherici', *Clogher Rec.*, xii, no. 2, 237.

100 See e.g. Ó Fiaich, 'The appointment of Bishop Tyrrell', 7; Ó Gallachair, 'Clogherhici', *Clogher Rec.*, i, no. 3, 68–9; Gallagher, 'Sources for the History of a Diocese', *Procs. Ir. Cath. Hist. Committee*, 29–30.

101 Hanly, ed., *Plunkett Letters*, 517–19, 522; also O'Laverty, *Down and Connor: Bishops*, 483; Bartlett, *Fall and Rise*, 5.

102 Hanly, ed., *Plunkett Letters*, 277.

103 *Ibid.*, 238; and Burke, *Irish Priests in Penal Times*, 75, for meetings of clergy in ale-houses.

104 Hanly, ed., *Plunkett Letters*, 340–41.

105 *MacClave from Aughnamullen*, 68–71.

106 Hanly, ed., *Plunkett Letters*, 75, 152–3, 277–8.

107 Gillespie, *The Sacred in the Secular*, 40.

108 The words are those of George Andrews, dean of Limerick, in 1625, cited in Kilroy, 'Sermon and Pamphlet Literature', 115.

109 Ó Muirgheasa, ed., *Dánta Diadha Uladh*, 139, also 97, 123, 125; Murray, 'A Previously Unnoticed Letter', 24, one of the papers found on the tory, Patrick Fleming, had prayers to the devotion of 'the print of Our Lady's Foot, with instructions for saying the Pater Noster and Ave Maria'.

110 Ó Muirgheasa, ed., *Dánta Diadha Uladh*, particularly useful here as it records poetry which survived in the popular oral tradition down to this century, e.g. poems by Ó Prontaigh, pp. 163–4, Cathal Buí, p. 139, Owen O'Donnelly, pp. 214–16.

111 Croker, ed., *The Tour of the French Traveller M. de la Boullaye le Gouz in Ireland in A.D. 1644*, 39 and 45.

112 Troyer, ed., *Five Travel Scripts Commonly Attributed to Edward Ward [1698]*, 10.

113 Litton-Falkiner, *Illustrations of Irish History*, 418 – the date is 1667–8, the location two miles from Drogheda.

114 Tynan, *Catholic Instruction in Ireland, 1720–1950*, 14; also Rogan, *Synods and Catechesis*, xiv–xv, showing very intermittent reference to such instruction in the synods of the seventeenth century.

115 Hanly, ed., *Plunkett Letters*, 141, 145; Briggs, *Early Modern France 1560–1715*, 172.

116 Ó Muirgheasa, ed., *Dánta Diadha Uladh*, 147–8.

117 Gillespie, *The Sacred in the Secular*, 2.

118 This is an Ulster poem of the 1640s. Its authorship is in contention,

sometimes attributed to a Protestant clergyman from Co. Down; if so, he is clearly of native Irish stock and/or the text must have been doctored by a scribe, given its content. Ó Muirgheasa, *Dhá Chéad*, poem 1, also in Ó Buachalla, *Nua-Dhuanaire*, i, 38.

119 Hickson, *Ireland in the Seventeenth Century*, i, 189–40; *An Account of the Bloody Massacre in Ireland*, 3.

120 *Cal. S.P. Ire., 1633–1647*, 355; Gilbert, *Contemporary History*, i (1), 360.

121 Hickson, *Ireland in the Seventeenth Century*, i, 173.

122 Ó Fiaich, 'Filíocht Uladh', 124; Ó Muirgheasa, *Céad de Cheoltaibh Uladh*, 13; Hanly, ed., *Plunkett Letters*, 220; *Montgomery Manuscripts*, 139, also says reading the scriptures has become the dividing line.

123 O'Dwyer, *Mary*, 232; the same image is reproduced in the nineteenth century, Ó Muirgheasa, ed., *Dánta Diadha Uladh*, 257.

124 Ó Muirgheasa, ed., *Dánta Diadha Uladh*, poems 50–51, 53, 54, 56.

125 Millett, 'Survival and Reorganization', 36; Moran, *Spicil. Ossor*, i, 120–21.

126 Ó Muirgheasa, ed., *Dánta Diadha Uladh*, 276–7; Robinson, *Plantation of Ulster*, 189: report of the woodkerne hanging an Irishman because he had conformed, 1615.

127 O'Donovan, *The Topographical Poems of John Ó Dubhagain*, 29–30; also Ó Muirgheasa, *Céad de Cheoltaibh Uladh*, 186–90, songs attacking priests who conformed still being sung in the twentieth century, particularly in Donegal and Tyrone.

128 Ó Muirgheasa, ed., *Dánta Diadha Uladh*, 348 (this about the two MacLochlain brothers of Inishowen; idem, *Céad de Cheoltaibh Uladh*, 186–90).

129 IFC, MS 1922/58.

130 IFC, MS 975/106.

131 IFC, MS 1275/212 and 214; see Murphy, *Tyrone Folk Quest*, 23. The original Catholicism of the Hamiltons is lost to local Tyrone traditions; see also Ó Fiaich, 'O'Neills of the Fews', 55, on local Armagh traditions of Turlough MacHenry changing his religion to keep his land.

132 IFC, MS 976/168, this from south Armagh; also MS 1923/97.

133 Cunningham, in *Natives and Newcomers*, 169–70.

134 See Edwards, 'The Priest, the Layman and the Historian', *European History Quarterly*, xvii, 87–93.

6 LIFE UNDER THE PENAL LAWS

1 UFTM, School Textbook Collection, E2/61/10: *The Programme of History Irish and English*, Book II, 34e; Ó Danachair, 'The Penal Laws and Irish Folk tradition', *Procs. Ir. Cath. Hist. Comm.*, 10–16.

2 Young, *Tour in Ireland* (1776–1779), i, 114; Cullen, 'Catholics under the Penal Laws', *Eighteenth-Century Ireland*, i, 71.

3 Ó Fiaich, 'The Registration of the Clergy in 1704', *Seanchas Ard Mhacha*, vi, 49.

4 Bishop MacMahon claimed this the situation as early as 1714: Flanagan, 'The Diocese of Clogher in 1714', *Clogher Rec.*, i, no. 3, 126. Many clergy would not have been averse to taking the oath, but disapproval from their flocks deterred them, see Fagan, *Divided Loyalties*, 45–6.

5 Corish, 'Catholic Marriage under the Penal Code', in Cosgrove, ed., *Marriage in Ireland*, 70–71.

6 Synge, *The Case of Toleration Considered with Respect Both to Religion and Civil Government*; Richardson, *A Short History of Attempts That Have Been Made . . . to Convert the Popish Inhabitants of Ireland*, 44; see also Connolly, *Religion, Law and Power*, 285–88; Fagan, *An Irish Bishopric in Penal Times*, 48–9, 74–5; and Lecky, *Ireland in the Eighteenth Century*, i, 271, 304, 306–7. These works by Synge and Richardson became bestsellers in their day, showing the level of debate on the issue.

7 Young, *Tour*, ii, 66.

8 Fagan, *Divided Loyalties*, 166–7, 189–92.

9 Shaw, *Cullybackey*, 132; Quinn, 'Religion and Landownership in Louth', 7.

10 Though not, it seems, by the Catholic clergy. The draft of a satirical pamphlet by Michael MacDonagh, Bishop of Kilmore, arrested near Lough Neagh in 1739, speaks scathingly of such converts: see Fenning, ed., *The Fottrell Papers, 1721–39*, 133–6; also Bishop MacMahon's criticism in Flanagan, ed., 'The Diocese of Clogher in 1714', *Clogher Rec.*, i, 128.

11 O'Laverty, *Down and Connor*, iii, 425, and i, 382, also iii, 407, for the continued pro-Catholic leanings of the McManuses. See Fagan, *An Irish Bishop in Penal Times*, 67–8, 94 and O'Brien, *The Great Melody*, 56–7, for similar examples from elsewhere in Ireland.

12 Bigger, *The Ulster Land War of 1770*, 51–2; see case also of Rowland Kane, a Protestant discoverer, PRONI, D.627/13; Lecky, *Ireland in the Eighteenth Century*, i, 47 on the sense of insecurity caused by this among propertied Catholics; Macaulay, *William Crolly: Archbishop of Armagh, 1835–49*, ix. Crolly's family lost land when one of the family conformed in 1774 and claimed all under the penal laws.

13 Simms, 'Irish Catholics and the Parliamentary Franchise, 1692–1728', in Hayton and O'Brien, eds., *War and Politics in Ireland, 1649–1730*, 224–34.

14 Cited in Elliott, *Partners in Revolution*, 37–8; Fagan, *Divided Loyalties*, 112, on the extreme prejudices of the Irish parliament.

15 Doyle, *Ireland, Irishmen and Revolutionary America, 1760–1820*, 70.

16 *BNL*, 23 January 1756; Ian McBride, 'Presbyterians in the Penal Era', *Bullán: An Irish Studies Journal*, i–ii, 82–3. Gebbie, ed., *An Introduction to the Abercorn Letters*, 144; Crawford and Trainor, eds., *Aspects of Irish Social History, 1750–1800*, 164.

17 *The Parliamentary Register Or, History of the Proceedings and Debates of the House of Commons of Ireland, 1781–97*, i, 258–9, xiii, 165, 169, xiii, 296; Moody, McDowell and Woods, eds., *The Writings of Theobald Wolfe Tone*, i, 121–2.

18 Brady, *Catholics and Catholicism in the Eighteenth-century Press*, 69. *A Test of Roman Catholic Liberality, Submitted to the Consideration of Both*

Roman Catholicks and Protestants. By a Citizen of London-Derry. Even this liberal Protestant feared that were Catholics to be given power they might close Protestants' churches and schools and persecute their religion.

19 Wall, 'Catholic Loyalty to King and Pope in Eighteenth-century Ireland', in O'Brien, ed., *Catholic Ireland in the Eighteenth Century*, 107–14. Fagan, *An Irish Bishop in Penal Times*, 97–8, 112.

20 PRONI, D.1514/9/71, Frederick Hervey to unnamed Catholic, 31 October 1767.

21 De Valera, 'Antiquarianism and Historical Investigations in Ireland in the Eighteenth Century', 39–43; Gamble, *View of Society and Manners in the North of Ireland in the Summer and Autumn of 1812*, 264–5.

22 Brady, *Catholics and Catholicism*, 111–25; Ó Gallachair, 'Clogherici. A Dictionary of the Catholic Clergy of the Diocese of Clogher (1535–1835)', *Clogher Rec.*, vol. 8, no. 2, 211; Leerssen, *Mere Irish and Fíor Ghael*, 361.

23 'Act for the Security of Protestant Purchasers' (I Geo. III, *c*.12) and 'Act for Quieting the Possessions of Protestants Deriving under Converts from the Popish Religion' (I Geo III, *c*.13).

24 Elliott, 'The Origins and Transformation of Early Irish Republicanism', *Internat. Rev. of Soc. Hist.*, xxiii, 415; Connolly, *Religion, Law and Power*, 144–9; Brady, *Catholics and Catholicism*, 96–7, 226; Crawford, 'The Political Economy of Linen: Ulster in the Eighteenth Century', in Brady *et al.*, eds., *Ulster: An Illustrated History*, 152–5.

25 Adams, *Printed Word*, 96–7.

26 O'Byrne, ed., *The Convert Rolls*, viii–ix; Brady, *Catholics and Catholicism*, 13–14, 58–9, 129–37, 146–50, 197; Bigger, *The Ulster Land War of 1770*, 51–2.

27 Quoted P. McNally, *Parties, Patriots and Undertakers*, 28.

28 Richardson, *A Proposal for the Conversion of the Popish Natives of Ireland to the Established Religion*; Hill, 'Popular Protestantism in Ulster in the Post-Rebellion Period, *c*.1790–1810', in Shields and Wood, eds., *The Churches, Ireland and the Irish*, 25, 191–202; Blaney, *Presbyterians and the Irish Language*, 20–27; Corkery, 'Gaelic Catechisms in Ireland', 56–63.

29 Harris, *The Ancient and Present State of the County of Down*, 17–18, 77, 109. Connolly, *Religion, Law and Power*, 304–7; Laverty, *Down and Connor*, i, 156–7.

30 Milne, *The Irish Charter Schools, 1730–1830*, 328.

31 Cited Milne, *Charter Schools*, 300; Stevenson, trans., *A Frenchman's Walk through Ireland, 1796–7*, 75, popular fear of such institutions in 1790s Munster.

32 Quinn, 'Religion and Landownership', 25.

33 Flanagan, ed., 'Clogher in 1714', 125–6; Fenning, ed., *Fottrell Papers*, 123.

34 The fullest accounts are in Connolly, *Religion, Law and Power*, 263–94, and his 'The Penal Laws', in Maguire, ed., *Kings in Conflict*, 157–72; also the articles by Simms, in Hayton and O'Brien, eds., *War and Politics in Ireland 1649–1730*, particularly 225–76.

35 Larkin, ' "Popish Riot" in south County Derry', *Seanchas Ard Mhacha*, 8, no. 1, 94–111.

36 Ó Gallachair, 'Clogher's Altars of the Penal Days', *Clogher Rec.*, 2, 103; idem, 'Clogherici', *Clogher Rec.*, i, no. 3, 68; IFC, MS 1359/153; Farry, 'Penal Day Traditions in Mourne', *Down and Connor Hist. Soc. Jn.*, ix, 42–9; Creighton, 'The Penal Laws in Ireland and the Documents in the Archives of Propaganda (1690–1731)', *Procs. Irish Cath. Hist. Committee*, 9, shows the penal laws against the clergy rarely fully enforced; McKeown, 'Friars Bush', *Down and Connor Hist. Soc. Jn.*, vi, 72–5; [Harkin], *Inishowen*, 68; Wall, 'Penal Laws', in O'Brien, ed., *Catholic Ireland*, 23.

37 Brady, *Catholics and Catholicism*, 16, 19; Lecky, *Ireland in the Eighteenth Century*, i, 258, 312; Flannagan, 'MacMahon', 127.

38 Shaw, *Cullybackey*, 127–9, Ó Danachair, 'The Penal Laws and Irish Folk Tradition', 15; Duffy, *Landscapes*, 36 (Caldwells of Fermanagh); [Harkin] *Inishowen*, 98–9, (Campbell family); Laverty, *Down and Connor*, i, 246–7, 313n., 317–8, 325, and ii, 353; Renehan, *Collections on Irish Church History*, 2 vols., ii, 93; UFTM, R.85.249, taped interview with Jim O'Neill of Warrenpoint, concerning the Presbyterian Glenny family holding land in trust for the Marmions and handing it back 'honourably'; Cogan, *Meath*, ii, 243, 266–7, 282.

39 Examples are the Hamiltons of mid-Ulster (Abercorn) and Louth (Clanbrassill); the O'Neills, McManuses and MacDonnells of Antrim; the Savages and Magennises of Down; the McCanns of Armagh.

40 Brady, *Catholics and Catholicism*, 146; also *BNL*, 9 July 1756, 12 July and 11 November 1757, advertisements for Protestant tenants exclusively; Laverty, *Down and Connor*, i, 317. In 1750 the recently rebuilt chapel at Struell, outside Downpatrick, was torn down by a mob headed by the Protestant curate and with the sanction of the landlord, the Southwell family.

41 W. H. Crawford, 'Economy and Society in Eighteenth-Century Ulster', 33–5; also his 'The Ulster Irish in the Eighteenth Century', *Ulster Folklife*, 28, 26; Roebuck, 'The Economic Situation and Functions of Substantial Landowners, 1660–1815', in Mitchison and Roebuck, eds., *Economy and Society in Scotland and Ireland, 1500–1939*, 84–9.

42 PRONI, D.207/5/46, report of the English Attorney and Solicitor-General to the English Privy Council, 16 July 1778.

43 Rushe, *Monaghan in the Eighteenth Century*, 131–7; Lecky, *Ireland in the Eighteenth Century*, i, 282, also 312; Brady, *Catholics and Catholicism*, 89, 272; Flynn, 'Hugh MacMahon', 129–30; Crawford, 'Economy and Society', 34; Osborough, 'Catholics, Land and the Popery Acts of Anne', in Power and Whelan, eds., *Endurance and Emergence*, 21–56.

44 Fenning, *Fottrell Papers*, xiii; Brady, *Catholics and Catholicism*, 90.

45 PRONI Mic.147/9/93–5, Clanbrassill to 'My Lord' [Roden?], November 1757; Lord Chesterfield (Lord Lieutenant 1745–6) had also tried to introduce such a bill.

46 PRONI, T.808/14895/7–10; also T.808/14895–6, Abstracts of County Antrim Assizes and quarter sessions, 1711–31 and ANT 4/1/1, Antrim Grand Jury Presentment Books for 1711–21.

47 The complaint 1788 'we had popish G[rand] Juries and Protestant Petit Juries', cited Miller, *Peep O'Day Boys and Defenders*, 65–7.

48 Mac Giolla Easpaig, *Tomás Ruiséil*, 56; *The Parliamentary Register: or, History of the Proceedings and Debates of the House of Commons of Ireland, 1781–97*, 7 vols., xiii, iii–2, speech by Dr Duigenan, 4 February 1793, in opposition to the Catholic relief bill, where he lists the incidences when Catholics can be debarred from juries.

49 O'Laverty, *Down and Connor*, iv, 129, 247.

50 Miller, *Peep O'Day Boys*, 73.

51 O'Laverty, *Down and Connor*, iii, 382, also ii, 49–50.

52 Gebbie, *Abercorn Letters*, 65–7; Brady, *Catholics and Catholicism*, 202.

53 Flanagan, ed., 'Diocese of Clogher', 40–41.

54 O'Laverty, *Down and Connor*, ii, 206.

55 James Stuart, *Historical Memoirs of the City of Armagh*, 349–50.

56 PRONI, T.1392: Memorial of the Proprietors of the Fews, 2 December 1743; Donaldson, *A Historical and Statistical Account of the Barony of the Upper Fews in the County of Armagh* (Dundalk, 1923), 10–16, 86–7.

57 Macafee, 'Colonisation of the Maghera Region', 88–9; McBride, 'Presbyterians in the Penal Era', 77.

58 Crawford, 'Ulster Irish', 26.

59 Crawford and Trainor, eds., *Aspects of Irish Social History*, 112–13; also Roebuck, ed., *Macartney of Lissanoure*, 146; and see Laverty, *Down and Connor*, iii, 294, 323, for other examples of liberal Protestant gentry in Antrim.

60 Gebbie, *Abercorn Letters*, 36; Corish, 'Catholic Marriage under the Penal Code', 72–5; Brady, *Catholics and Catholicism*, 50; Cogan, *Meath*, ii, 282, iii, 59.

61 Carleton, *Autobiography*, 235–6.

62 Adams, *Printed Word*, 12–14, 144–5; see also Ó Mórdha, 'Simon Macken; Fermanagh Scribe and Schoolmaster'; and Corish, *Catholic Community*, 109–10, on their dislike of the printing press and how they even transcribed things printed in English; Szövérffy, '*Rí Naomh Seoirse*: Chapbooks and Hedge-Schools', *Éigse*, 9, 114–17.

63 Ashton, *The Battle of Aughrim, or the Fall of Monsieur St. Ruth. A Tragedy*; Adams, *Printed Word*, 70–72; Ó Cíosáin, *Print and Popular Culture*, 107–11.

64 'Report on the State of Popery in Ireland, 1731', *Archiv. Hib.*, i, 10–27; Fenning, *Undoing of the Friars*, 196–7.

65 Brady, 'Catholics and Catholicism', 253.

66 Macaulay, *William Crolly. Archbishop of Armagh, 1835–49*, 2; see also O'Connell, *The Diocese of Kilmore: Its History and Antiquities*, xxxv.

67 Carleton, *Autobiography*, 72–3; idem, *Traits and Stories*, i, 41; Cullen, 'Patrons, Teachers and Literacy in Irish', in Daly and Dickson, eds., *Origins of Popular Literacy*, 30–31.

68 McPolin, 'An Old Irish Catechism from Oriel', *Ir. Eccles. Rec.*, 509–15;

Ó Cíosáin, 'Printed Popular Literature in Irish', in Daly and Dickson, eds., *Origins of Popular Literacy*, 50, discussed also in his *Print and Popular Culture*, ch. 9; Ó Casaide, *Irish Language in Belfast and County Down*, 45–6; Wall, *The Sign of Dr Hay's head*, 109–11.

69 Buttimer, 'An Irish Text on the "War of Jenkins' Ear"', *Celtica*, xxi, 80–82.

70 Young, *Historical Notices of Old Belfast*, 182–3; Brady, *Catholics and Catholicism*, 131.

71 Parker, *The History of Londonderry, Comprising the Towns of Derry and Londonderry, New Hampshire*, 74 – my thanks to Dr Ian McBride for drawing this to my attention. See also Sampson, *Statistical Survey of the County of Londonderry*, 457, for a description of such a wedding. Ó Danachair, in Cosgove, ed., *Marriage in Ireland*, 113, also notes this custom as being peculiar to the north, though he thinks it came from Scotland.

72 Ó Fiaich, *Art Mac Cumhaigh: Dánta*, 88, 186–7.

73 Ó Muirgheasa, *Abhráin . . . Mhic Chubhthaigh*, 56, 64; Ó Fiaich, *Art Mac Cumhaigh: Dánta*, 85.

74 Ó Muirgheasa, *Abhráin . . . Mhic Chubhthaigh*, 281.

75 PRONI, Mic.147/9/111–14, the earl of Roden to his sister Charlotte, 3 April 1811; for Count Nugent's family, see O'Callaghan, *Irish Brigades in France*, 154–5.

76 Ó Muirgheasa, *Dhá Chéad de Cheoltaibh Uladh*, 18; Rushe, *Monaghan*, 66–7, and McEvoy, 'The United Irishmen in Co. Tyrone', *Seanchas Ard Mhacha*, iii, no. 2, 288, for Irish interpreters at the courts.

77 McGarvey, 'The Heather Edge', *Seanchas Ard Mhacha*, ii, no. 1, 184; Ó Mórdha, 'Maurice O'Gorman in Monaghan', *Clogher Rec.*, ii, 20–24; Ó Gallachair, 'Clogherici', *Clogher Rec.*, ii, no. 1, 51; Carleton, *Traits and Stories*, i, 44n; see McMahon and Ó Fiaich, 'Inscriptions in Creggan Graveyard', *Seanchas Ard Mhacha*, vi, no. 2, 330.

78 Francis Hutchinson, *A Defence of the Ancient Historians*, 128–9; Hutchinson, *The Reformed Presbyterian Church in Scotland*, 221.

79 Madden, *The United Irishmen, Their Lives and Times*, 3rd ser., i, 312–13.

80 See PRONI, D.668/3, lengthy description by Revd Philip Skelton, rector of Templecarn, Co. Donegal, 10 February 1776, to the Protestant bishop of Clogher. For continued gatherings at other holy wells see Harris, *The Ancient and Present State of the County of Down*, 25, 35; PRONI, D.605/1/12, detailed 1720 description of a pattern at Saint Ternan's well in Fermanagh.

81 Flanagan, 'Diocese of Clogher', 129–30; Donnelly Jr., 'Lough Derg' in Ronan *et al.*, eds., *Donegal: History and Society*, 491–507; Carleton, *Autobiography*, pp. 88–95.

82 Sir Charles Coote, *Statistical Survey of the County of Monaghan*, 39; Gebbie, *Ardstraw*, 52–61.

83 *The Distress'd State of Ireland Considered* ([Dublin], 1740); Macafee, 'Population of Ulster', 111–21.

84 Gebbie, ed., *Abercorn Letters*, 12–13; Day, *Letters from Georgian Ireland*, 215; Ó Gallachóir, *Séamas Dall Mac Cuarta. Dánta*, 70. 'Irish Catholics

Licensed to Keep Arms (1704)', *Archiv. Hib.*, iv, 59–65. Of 115 granted, only three went to Ulster, two Magennises, one Major Stafford, Co. Donegal.

85 Kirkham, 'Economic Diversification in a Marginal Economy', 80.

86 Young, *Tour*, i, 161, 166, 174–5, 184, 196–8, 205.

87 Cullen, 'Catholics under the Penal Laws', 23–36; Whelan, 'Regional Impact', 258–60; Dickson, 'Derry's Backyard: The Barony of Inishowen, 1650–1800', in Dunlevy, Nolan and Ronayne, eds., *Donegal. History and Society*, 417–18.

88 Ó Fiaich, 'O'Neills of the Fews', *Seanchas Ard Mhacha*, viii, 386; see Bigger, *Ulster Land War*, 125–6, MacCartans and their undertenants being turned out from lands of Clanvarraghan; Lin. Lib., Joy MSS, Commonplace Book, f. 32: similarly with the Magennises in Annachlone; Ó Fiaich, '*Filíocht Uladh mar Fhoinse don Stair Shóisialta san 18ú hAois*', *Stud. Hib.*, no. 11, 95–6; Ó Muirgheasa, *Dánta Diadha Uladh*, 276–7, Farney (Monaghan). Ó Mearáin, 'The Bath Estate, 1700–1777', *Clogher Rec.*, vol. 6, no. 2, 333–60, shows a great variety of leases, improving later in the century with Catholics letting directly from the landlord after 1777. The Irish generally maintained their presence on the old O'Neill lands around Dungannon (Crawford, 'Political Economy', 155), also Armagh (Glancy, *Primate Lands*, 387).

89 Crawford, 'Economy and Society in South Ulster', 246; Gebbie, *Abercorn Letters*, 49.

90 Plowden, *An Historical Review of the State of Ireland*, iv, 53; Tone, *Writings*, i, 365–71.

91 Ó Casaide, *Irish Language in Down*, 27.

92 Ó Fiaich, 'O'Neills of the Fews', *Seanchas Ard Mhacha*, viii, 389–90; idem, *Mac Cumhaigh. Dánta*, 148–9; idem, 'MacCooey and His Times', 242, the O'Callaghans; Crawford, 'Economy and Society in Eighteenth-Century Ulster', 25; Rushe, *Monaghan*, 38–9, for the MacMahons of Ballybay; Duffy, *Landscapes of South Ulster*, 66, 70, 74, for the McKennas and Murphys; Gebbie, *Abercorn Letters*, 76.

93 Simms, ed., *Rev James O'Coigley, United Irishman*, 11–12.

94 PRONI, Whyte Papers, D.298/1/11–26, D.2918/5/3/1–12, D.2918/8/63, various leases and legal papers. I am grateful to Dr Alan Blackstock for alerting me to the contents of these papers. *Burke's Irish Family Records* (1976), 1214–16.

95 Tone, *Writings*, i, 243; Ó Casaide, *The Irish Language in Belfast and County Down*, 12.

96 Carrigan, 'Catholic Episcopal Wills in the Public Record Office, Dublin, 1683–1812', *Archiv. Hib.*, i, 151–90; [Harkin], *Inishowen*, 186–7: this the account of a journey to the Collège des Lombards by Charles O'Donnell, future Bishop of Derry (1798–1823), his baggage every bit that of a gentleman; Crawford, 'Economy and Society in Eighteenth-century Ulster', 23; Duffy, *Landscapes of South Ulster*, 66.

97 McVeigh, ed., *Richard Pococke's Irish Tours*, 71.

98 *Burke's . . . Landed Gentry of Ireland*, 4th edn, 683–4.

99 However, since they were destroyed in the Four Courts fire of 1922, we

are dependent on highly deficient secondary lists. See excellent discussion of this in Fagan, *Divided Loyalties*, 176–88.

100 NLI, T.1,898 (Catholic Qualification Rolls, 1778–90); only twelve out of a national total of 1,526 took the 1774 oath, and those, it seems, in areas where the bishops endorsed the oath, or where there was a significant landed interest (Fagan, *Divided Loyalties*, 176–9).

101 Quoted Lecky, *Ireland in the Eighteenth Century*, iii, 339–40. A similar argument was made in *A Candid and Impartial Account of the Disturbances in the County of Meath, in the Years 1792, 1793, and 1794. By a County Meath Freeholder*.

102 Leighton, *Catholicism in a Protestant Kingdom: a Study of the Irish Ancien Régime*, 153–4.

103 PRONI, D.1325/3/35 and 37, for documents referred to above – also very useful 'Introduction' to the collection by Dr. A. P. W. Malcomson. I am grateful to Dr Alan Blackstock for drawing my attention to this collection.

104 I am grateful to Dr C. J. Woods for showing me this article on Coile for the *Dictionary of Irish Biography*.

105 Livingstone, *Monaghan Story*, 139–40.

106 This is the theme of MacCooey's 'Churls of the Barley', see Ó Fiaich, 'Art MacCooey and his times', *Seanchas Ard Mhacha*, vol. 6, no. 2, 242–3; idem, *Art Mac Cumhaigh. Dánta*, 102–4; Watson, '*Coimhlint an Dá Chultúr – Gaeil agus Gaill i bhFilíocht Chúige Uladh san Ochtú hAois Déag*', Eighteenth-Century Ireland, 3, 97; Crawford, 'The Ulster Irish in the Eighteenth Century', 29.

107 Ó Fiaich, 'MacCooey and his Times', 223.

108 Garret Fitzgerald, 'The Decline of the Irish Language', in Daly and Dickson, eds., *Origins of Popular Literacy*, 59–72.

109 Ó Fiaich, 'The Political and Social Background of the Ulster Poets', *Léachtaí Cholm Cille*, i, 29; de Brún, 'Some Irish MSS with Breifne Associations', *Breifne*, iii, no. 12, 560–61.

110 Crawford, 'Economy and Society in Eighteenth-century Ulster', 32, also 11, 28–32, 54–6.

111 In elections of 1773 only Enniskillen nominated representatives; in 1791 Carrickfergus, Monaghan, Armagh, Donegal, Derry, Newry, Belfast and Coleraine had joined, see Edwards, ed., 'The Minute Book of the Catholic Committee, 1773–92', *Archiv. Hib.*, 9, 12, 56–7, 92–3, 118–20; Whelan, 'Regional Impact', 262. For Orangemen attacking propertied Catholics see Brady, 'Catholics and Catholicism', 301–3; Hogan, 'The Migration of Ulster Catholics to Connaught, 1795–6', *Seanchas Ard Mhacha*, 9, no. 2, 286–301.

112 Young, *Tour*, ii, 57.

113 Cited Dickson, *Ulster Emigration*, 35.

114 Brockliss and Ferté, 'Irish Clerics in France in the Seventeenth and Eighteenth Centuries', 540.

115 De Valera, 'Antiquarianism and Historical Investigations', 195–8; McCarthy, 'Ulster Office', 208–12. Proof of noble rank would have been necessary to attain officer rank in the armies of the Continental powers.

116 [McKenna], *Devenish (Lough Erne) Its History, Antiquities and Traditions*, 125–34; also Simms in Moody and Vaughan, eds., *New History of Ireland*, iv, 642–3; Ó Gallachair, 'Clogherici', *Clogher Rec.*, i, no. 4, 137–56; Murray, *History of the Parish of Creggan*, 54; Ó Coinne and Ó Fiaich, 'Tombstone Inscriptions in Drumglass Cemetery', *Seanchas Ard Mhacha*, vii, no. 2, 316–19.

117 Livingstone, *Monaghan Story*, 591–2.

118 Ó Ceallaigh, *Gleanings from Ulster History*, 94–5.

119 Chart, ed., *The Drennan Letters*, 79.

120 Flanagan, 'The Diocese of Clogher in 1714', *Clogher Rec.*, i, no. 2, 40; Crawford, 'Economy and Society in South Ulster in the Eighteenth Century', 18.

121 *A Candid and Impartial Account of the Disturbances in the County of Meath, in the Years 1792, 1793, and 1794* (Dublin, 1794), 2; Crawford, 'Political economy', 153–6; Duffy, *Landscapes of South Ulster*, 42–4, 52, 64; Ó Fiaich, 'The 1766 Religious Census', *Seanchas Ard Mhacha*, iv, 147–70; Macafee, 'The Colonisation of the Maghera Region of South Derry during the Seventeenth and Eighteenth Centuries', 76–86, analyses this process of segregation; idem, 'Population of Ulster', Harris, *The Ancient and Present State of the County of Down*, 78, 97.

122 Crawford, 'Economy and Society in Eighteenth-century Ulster', 27, 61–80. Duffy, *Landscape of South Ulster*, 21; Houston, 'Literacy and Society in the West, 1500–1850', *Social History*, viii, no. 3, 285–7, shows how areas which do not speak the 'official' language are more traditional and economically less developed; in Scotland Highland Gaelic-speakers were viewed by the Presbyterian Lowlanders as popish and barbarous. But see Young, *Tour*, i, 161–2, showing Rundale in largely Presbyterian areas also; Anderson, 'Rundale, Rural Economy and Agrarian Revolution: Tirhugh, 1715–1855', in Nolan, Ronayne and Dunlevy, eds., *Donegal. History and Society*, 447–69. Macafee, 'The Population of Ulster', 56: in 1712 Catholics were still 60 per cent of the Ulster population and were largely concentrated in the remoter parts of the country.

123 Molyneux's Tour, 1708, in Young, *Historical Notices of Old Belfast*, 153. Crawford, 'Economy and Society in Eighteenth-century Ulster', 21; Duffy, *Landscapes of South Ulster*, 23; Sir Charles Coote, *Statistical Survey of County Armagh*, particularly 22–3, 35, 300; Gebbie, ed., *Abercorn Letters*, 205.

124 Patterson, 'The Territory of Ballymacone and Its Associations with the McCones', *Seanchas Ard Mhacha*, i, no. 1, 139; Donaldson, *A Historical and Statistical Account of the Upper Fews*, 139; Harris, *The Ancient and Present State of the County of Down*, 125, 'Booleying in the Mournes'.

125 Crawford and Trainor, eds., *Aspects of Irish Social History*, 90.

126 McParlan, *Statistical Survey of the County of Donegal*, 91–2, 100–101; Duffy, *Landscapes of South Ulster*, 79: in the hills of west Monaghan a 1760 commentator noted whiskey for sale in almost every house, though no inns in the area. Also Kirkham, 'Economic Diversification in a Marginal Economy:

a case study', in Roebuck, ed., *Plantation to Partition*, 65–81; Ó Muirgheasa, *Dhá Chéad de Cheoltaibh Uladh*, iii, 394–5: *c*.1780, poem about smuggling from Gortahork, Co. Donegal; *Sources for the Study of Local History in Northern Ireland. Northern Ireland Public Record Office*, 70; Gebbie, ed., *Abercorn Letters*, 126, 140, attempts to discourage whiskey production. Ó Fiaich, 'Filíocht Uladh', 117–19, on attitudes to new modes of travel in the poetry, limited popular use of new roads. Ó Muirgheasa, *Dhá Chéad de Cheoltaibh Uladh*, iii, poem 195.

127 Gebbie, *Abercorn Letters*, 205; Duffy, *Landscapes of South Ulster*, 26–7; Miller, *Peep O'Day Boys and Defenders*, 105, for Protestant fears of Catholics in the mountains in the 1790s, their distinctive great coats distinguishing them at the Battle of the Diamond, 1795.

128 Carleton, *Traits and Stories of the Irish Peasantry*, ii, 258; Madden, *United Irishmen*, 2nd ser., ii, 507, 125–6 n.

129 Carleton, *Traits and Stories*, i, 'The Party Fight and Funeral', 216.

130 Crawford, 'Economy and Society in Eighteenth-century Ulster', 26, 28.

131 O'Laverty, *Down and Connor*, iv, xxv–xxx.

132 John Dubourdieu, *Statistical Survey of the County of Antrim*, 429–48; Latocnaye, *A Frenchman's Walk through Ireland*, 217; Conolly, 'Spoken English in Ulster in the Eighteenth and Nineteenth Centuries', *Ulster Folklife*, xxviii, 33–9; Donaldson, *Upper Fews*, 165.

133 Gamble, *Sketches of History, Politics, and Manners in Dublin and the North of Ireland in 1810*, 246; Day, *Letters from Georgian Ireland*, 221.

134 O'Connell, *Diocese of Kilmore*, 461.

135 Tynan, *Catholic Instruction in Ireland*, 14.

136 Flanagan, 'Clogher in 1714', 127; Corish, *Catholic Community*, 129; Kelly, 'The Formation of the Modern Catholic Church in the Diocese of Kilmore, 1580–1880', in Gillespie, ed., *Cavan. Essays on the History of an Irish County*, 125.

137 McVeigh, ed., *Richard Pococke's Irish Tours*, 63.

138 O'Laverty, *Down and Connor*, iii, 107–9.

139 There is even a tradition of Catholics and Protestants sharing church accommodation at Loughinisland, County Down, till a dispute in 1720, see O'Laverty, *Down and Connor. Bishops*, 549.

140 'Report on the State of Popery, Ireland, 1731', *Archiv. Hib.*, i (1912), 10–27 (for Ulster), and for the rest of the country, ii (1913), 108–56, iii (1914), 124–59, and iv (1915), 131–77; Duffy, *Landscapes of South Ulster*, 29, 36, 40–44, 54, 58, 62–6, 92, PRONI, T.808/15261, 1744 religious return for Fermanagh; Donaldson, *Upper Fews*, 86, description of Presbyterian meeting house.

141 Crawford, 'Society and Economy in Eighteenth-century Ulster', 39.

142 [Harkin], *Inishowen*, 55–8; Carrigan, 'Wills', 262–4; Maguire, *Diocese of Raphoe*, i, 163; PRONI, T.808/15261, '1744 Committee on religion'.

143 Carleton, *Autobiography*, 43–4.

144 Tynan, *Catholic Instruction in Ireland*, 34; McPolin, 'An Old Irish Catechism from Oriel', *Irish Eccles. Rec.*, lxix, 510; Cogan, *Meath*, ii, 210, iii, 136, 139, 222–5: expansion in number of schools, churches, etc., reflecting a determined return to public worship.

145 Flanagan, 'Clogher in 1714', 128; Madgett, 'Constitutio Ecclesiastica', 81–2.

146 McGrath, 'The Tridentine Evolution of Modern Irish Catholicism, 1563–1962', in Ó Muirí, *Irish Church History Today*, 84–99.

147 [Richard Phillips] *Journal of a Tour in Ireland . . . 1804*, 16–17.

148 O'Connell, *Kilmore*, 505; Corish, *Catholic Community*, 108.

149 Delumeau, *Catholicism between Luther and Voltaire*, 9; Hennig, 'The First Liturgical Catechism in Ireland', *Ir. Eccles, Rec.*, 310.

150 Ó Maonaigh O.F.M., ed., *Seanmónta Chúige Uladh*, 42; Ó Muirgheasa, *Dhá Chéad*, ii, 159–63, 192–3; Heussaff, *Filí agus Cléir san Ochtú hAois Déag*, 61–2.

151 Fenning, *Fottrell Papers*, 10.

152 Tynan, *Catholic Instruction in Ireland*, 34, 49.

153 IFC, MS 102/231; also Taylor, *Occasions of Faith*, 99, 115, on their enduring popularity.

154 McGlinchey, *The Last of the Name*, 12.

155 Bourke, ed., *Sermons in Irish-Gaelic by the Most Rev. James O'Gallagher.*

156 Though see Ó Buachalla, *I mBéal Feirste Cois Cuain*, 58n, Irish still spoken between Ballynahinch and Newry until 1820.

157 Pulleine D.D., *An Teagasg Críosaidhe Angoidhleig* (c.1782); McPolin, 'An Old Irish Catechism', 509–17.

158 Harris, *The Ancient and Present State of the County of Down*, 17–18, 76–7, 105–6, 109.

159 Hyde, trans., 'An Irish Funeral Oration over Owen O'Neill, of the House of Clanaboy', *U.J.A.*, vol. 3, 258–70 and vol. 4, 50–55.

160 Fenning, ed., *Fottrell Papers*, 13.

161 Fenning, *Undoing of the Friars*, vi–ix, 156, 178–9, 195.

162 McGlinchy, *Last of the Name*, 69–70.

163 Brady, 'Catholics and Catholicism', 85–9, 97–103; Millett, *Survival and Reorganization*, 47; Fenning, ed., *Fottrell Papers*, 37.

164 Carleton, *Traits and Stories*, i, 336; Ó Dufaigh, 'James Murphy, Bishop of Clogher, 1801–24', *Clogher Rec.*, vi, no. 3, 491–93.

165 Fenning, *Undoing of the Friars*, 282–3: my own account is heavily dependent on this excellent book.

166 Whelan, 'Anthony Blake, Archbishop of Armagh 1758–1787', *Seanchas Ard Mhacha*, v, no. 2, 289–323; Murray, 'Three Documents Concerning the Deanery of Dundalk during the Eighteenth Century', *Archiv. Hib.*, v, 70–71.

167 Brady, ed., 'A Pastoral of Arch. O'Reilly, 1788', *Seanchas Ard Mhacha*, 4, no. 1, 176.

168 'A List of Regulars Registered in Ireland Pursuant to the Catholic Relief Act of 1829', *Archiv. Hib.*, iii, 34–86.

169 Fenning, *Undoing of the Friars*, 294; see O'Laverty, *Down and Connor*, i, 40–41: the Dominicans had a small community at Kilcoo, near Castlewellan. In 1817 its last friar died.

170 Duffy, *Landscapes of South Ulster*, 74, 92; Murray, *History of Creggan*, 16; Ó Muirgheasa, *Céad de Cheoltaibh Uladh*, 187.
171 Lecky, *History of Ireland*, i, 147; Tynan, *Catholic Instruction in Ireland*, 24; IFC, MS 1215/215.

7 REFORM TO REBELLION: THE EMERGENCE OF REPUBLICAN POLITICS

1 The words of Theobald Wolfe Tone, cited Elliott, *Tone*, 411.
2 Rushe, *Monaghan in the Eighteenth Century*, 35; Adams, 'Ulster Folklife, 1738–40 from the pages of the Belfast Newsletter', *Ulster Folklife*, 31, 43, 46; Larkin, ' "Popish Riot" in Co. Derry 1725', *Seanchas Ard Mhacha*, viii, no. 1, 97–110; *BNL*, 1 and 26 June 1739.
3 Fagan, *An Irish Bishop in Penal Times*, 84.
4 Ó Fiaich, 'Filíocht Uladh', 82; Heusaff, *Filí agus Cléir*, 51, 170; Maureen Wall, 'Catholic Loyalty to King and Pope in Eighteenth-century Ireland', in O'Brien, ed., *Catholic Ireland*, 109.
5 Ó Buachalla, *Nua-Dhuanaire*, II, 2–3; Ó Muirgheasa, *Céad de Cheoltaibh Uladh*, ii, 151: '*Oró 'sé do bheatha abhaile*' – Jacobite song collected in both Tyrone and Donegal, in support of victory by 'Young Charles', but a feeling that the author will never see it.
6 Woods, *Journals and Memoirs of Thomas Russell*, 66–7 – Russell describing how one of the Tyrone Grand Jury had thrown a glass at the head of a blind fiddler in Omagh for playing 'The White Cockade'.
7 Leerssen, *Mere Irish and Fíor-Ghael*, 275–6.
8 De Rís, ed., *Peadar Ó Doirnín: a Bheatha Agus a Shaothar* (Dublin, 1969), 7–8.
9 Howell, *State Trials*, xxv, 754.
10 Good example of this in Fagan, *Irish Bishop in Penal Times*, 58–9.
11 Brady, *Catholics and Catholicism*, 209: case of clergy Diocese of Derry subscribing to Volunteers when Catholic leaders generally stand aside from them, seeing London and Dublin governments as better allies than the Protestants.
12 Giblin, ed., 'Catalogue of Material of Irish Interest in the . . . Vatican Archives', *Coll. Hib.*, v, 80–82; Flynn, 'Hugh MacMahon', 144–5.
13 Chart, ed., *The Drennan Letters*, 72, 79, 115, 219, 232, 323.
14 This was the Bishop of Clogher, the Franciscan Denis Maguire, clearly residing in Fermanagh among his relatives.
15 The records are so deficient (only the index surviving the 1922 fire) that it is impossible to arrive at a totally accurate analysis. See Fagan, *Divided Loyalties*, 142–88 on this. Even so I have tried to reach some conclusions based on NLI, Pos. 1898, Index to the Catholic Qualification Rolls; Ó Gallachair, 'Catholic Qualification Rolls Index: Fermanagh and Monaghan', *Clogher Rec.*, ii, no. 3, 544–51; Ó Domhnaill, 'County Donegal in the Catholic Qualification Rolls, 1778–1790', *Co. Donegal Hist. Soc. Jn.*, i, no. 3, 204–5;

Wall in O'Brien, ed., *Catholic Ireland*, 110–14; Gebbie, ed., *Abercorn Letters*, 180.

16 Young, *Historical Notices of Old Belfast*, 183.

17 NLI, Pos. 1899: Index to Catholic Qualification Rolls, Ulster, 1793–6.

18 Miller, ed., *Peep O'Day Boys and Defenders*, 131.

19 Marshall, *History of the Parish of Tynan*, 50–51.

20 Crawford and Trainor, eds., *Aspects of Irish Social History*, 38–9; Rushe, *Monaghan in the Eighteenth Century*, 42–3.

21 Bigger, *Ulster Land War*, 12, 25–6, 50, 133–50.

22 McVeigh, ed., *Pococke's Irish Tour*, 60.

23 Dickson, 'Taxation and Disaffection in Late Eighteenth-century Ireland', in Clarke and Donnelly, Jr., eds., *Irish Peasants. Violence and Political Unrest*, 37–63; Crawford, 'Economy and Society in Eighteenth-century Ulster', 56–8; Miller, *Peep O'Day Boys and Defenders*, 14.

24 Bigger, *Ulster Land War*, 36, 101–3.

25 Beresford, 'Ireland in French Strategy, 1691–1789', 334.

26 Macafee, 'Population of Ulster', ch. 5.

27 *FDJ*, 10 June 1790; Young, *Tour*, i, 115, 164.

28 D. W. Miller, 'Politicisation in Revolutionary Ireland: the Case of the Armagh Troubles', *Ir. Econ. & Soc. Hist.*, 23, n. 46; Dickson, *A Narrative of the Confinement and Exile of William Steel Dickson, D.D.*, 10–11, says that Catholic offers were rejected and the Volunteers were anti-papist; Burns agrees: 'The Belfast Letters, the Irish Volunteers 1778–9 and the Catholics', *Review of Politics*, xxi, 678–91; Ó Snodaigh, 'Class and the Volunteers', 165–84. O'Laverty, *Down and Connor*, i, 472, thinks the Volunteers 'a very overpraised body', they generally excluded Catholics and, with a few exceptions, the Catholics 'remained unfriendly towards them'. PRONI, T.2541/IB1/4/12: G. Knox to Abercorn, 14 February 1793, shows even new corps of Volunteers divided; Gebbie, ed., *Abercorn Letters*, 15.

29 *Charlemont Mss*, ii, 76.

30 The religious topography of Armagh is an important topic in every work on the Armagh troubles. But there is a good overview in Wright, *Two Lands in One Soil*, 31–2; Cullen, *Modern Ireland*, 206–8.

31 Miller, 'Armagh Troubles', 158.

32 Ibid., 123; see also Stuart, *Historical Memoirs of the City of Armagh*, 417n. In 1784 people who had actually fought at the Boyne were still alive.

33 Miller, ed., *Peep O'Day Boys and Defenders*, 105. See Duffy, *Landscapes*, 42, 44, 52, 64, for other examples of population increase leading to movement by Protestants into hilly, Catholic areas, with inevitable sectarian clashes in the 1790s.

34 The most comprehensive account of the Armagh situation is Miller, ed., *Peep O'Day Boys*. See also his 'The Armagh Troubles, 1784–95', in Clark and Donnelly, eds., *Irish Peasants*, 155–91. Latocnaye, *Walk Through Ireland*, 258–60. *BNL*, 28 Aug. 1989: Armagh Assizes. *A View of the Present State of Ireland . . . by an Observer*, (n.p., 1797), 5–11.

35 Miller, *Peep O'Day Boys*, 123.

36 Cited Hogan, 'The Migration of Ulster Catholics to Connaught, 1795–96', *Seanchas Ard Mhacha*, ix, 286.

37 'Ulster Folk in Tipperary', *Béaloideas*, x, 300–301; Seamas Mac Manus, *Rocky Road to Dublin*, 90; IFC, MS 976/193: May 1945, recollections of Thomas Mulholland, aged sixty-five, of Newtown, Rostrevor; also account of attacks on the O'Coigleys in 1796, in Simms, ed., *Rev James O'Coigley, United Irishman*, 11–12.

38 Camden's correspondence with London: PRO, London, HO 100/62–64; NAI, SOC 1015/6–11, 21, also in Down, Tyrone, Cavan, Monaghan.

39 Elliott, 'Origins and Transformation', 414, 424–5; Lecky, *Ireland in the Eighteenth Century*, iii, 421–50 (also shows fugitive Catholics being sheltered by Presbyterians in Antrim and Down); MacNeven, *Pieces of Irish History*, 186–7; Kent, CKS, U840/015 1/4, returns of Catholics who had fled to Mayo, December 1796.

40 Elliott, *Tone*, 180–81; Tone, *Life*, i, 172–5; Hillsborough had succeeded to the Downshire title in 1793; *FJ*, 8 September 1792 on Annesley.

41 *An Argument on Behalf of the Catholics of Ireland* (Dublin, 1791).

42 Tone, *Life*, i, 149–50.

43 McEvoy, 'The United Irishmen in Co. Tyrone', *Seanchas Ard Mhacha*, iii, 303–4, and v, 37; Mac Suibhne, 'Up Not Out: Why did North-west Ulster not Rise in 1798?', in Portéir, ed., *The Great Irish Rebellion*, 83–100.

44 David Hempton, paper delivered to Conference of Irish Historians in Britain, Oxford 1992.

45 Crawford and Trainor, eds., *Aspects of Irish Social History*, 42; Hill, 'Popular Protestantism in Ulster in the Post-Rebellion period, *c.*1790–1810', in Sheils and Wood, eds., *The Churches, Ireland and the Irish*, 196.

46 See Miller's Intriguing 'Presbyterianism and "Modernization" in Ulster', *Past and Present*, 80, 66–90.

47 McEvoy, 'United Irishmen in Co. Tyrone', v, 60–61.

48 Keogh, *'The French Disease'*, 70.

49 *NS*, 11 July 1792.

50 *NS*, 30 May 1796; Keogh, *'The French Disease'*, 50–51, for the hierarchy's fears of a Catholic-Presbyterian alliance.

51 Teeling, *Observations on the '. . . Battle of the Diamond'*, 13.

52 Tone, *Life*, i, 367–8.

53 Adams, *Printed Word*, 86. The best analyses of the content of United Irish songs are Thuente, *The Harp Re-strung: The United Irishmen and the Rise of Irish Literary Nationalism*, and Zimmermann, *Songs of Irish Rebellion*. The best overview of United Irish propaganda is Curtin, *The United Irishmen*, chs. 8 and 9. PRO, HO 100/38/373: the gatherings at the churches to elect delegates to the Convention, also to sign a declaration against 'certain unpopular doctrines'.

54 Crawford and Trainor, eds., *Aspects of Irish Social History*, 76–7; Latocnaye, *A Frenchman's Walk through Ireland*, 204–5; McEvoy, 'United Irishmen in Tyrone', 307; Keogh, *'The French Disease'*, ch. 6; *NS*, 5 December 1792.

55 BL, Add. Mss. 38, 759/37v, unsigned narrative, June 1797.

56 Miller, *Peep O'Day Boys*, 137.

57 NAI, 620/18/88a, A new song addressed to Irishmen, written by Wolfe Tone for the 1792 Belfast Harpers' Festival; also *NS*, 26 August 1796, 'Ireland: an Ode'.

58 *NS*, 30 May 1796; Curtin, *United Irishmen*, 185.

59 Woods, ed., *Journals and Memoirs of Thomas Russell*, 69.

60 Tone, *Life*, i, 377–8.

61 Madden, *United Irishmen*, 2nd ser., ii, 402–3, McCracken and Cuthbert employing counsel for those in Armagh; *FJ*, 20 April 1793; Elliott, *Tone*, chs. 12–14.

62 Tone, *Life*, i, 87–8.

63 Teeling, *History of the Irish Rebellion of 1798*, 12–14; Madden, *United Irishmen*, 3rd ser., i, 186–8; Tone, *Life*, i, 221–2; Elliott, 'The Defenders in Ulster', in Dickson, Keogh and Whelan, eds., *The United Irishmen*, 222–31.

64 Rogers, *The Irish Volunteers and Catholic Emancipation*, 144–66.

65 PRO, HO 100/42/248–51, Hobart to Nepean, 5 February 1792, summarising his speech; *Parl. Reg.*, xiii, 94, seq; Elliott, *Tone*, 202–5.

66 O'Laverty, *Down and Connor*, ii, 150.

67 PRO, HO 100/44/115–8: 'A Roman Catholic to Mr Braughall of the Catholic Committee', 29 May 1793.

68 Bartlett, *Fall and Rise*, 181–2.

69 PRONI, D.607/C/56: McNally to Downshire, 8 December 1794.

70 Ó Muirgheasa, *Céad de Cheoltaibh Uladh*, ii, 152.

71 Teeling, *Observations on the '. . . Battle of the Diamond'*, 7–13.

72 Carleton, *Autobiography*, 76–80.

73 Details of the very general arming of the Defenders in south Ulster are in PRO, HO 100/42/195–8, 270–72, 100/43/47–50, 145–51, 100/44/115–V8. More detailed accounts of the Defenders can be found in my articles, 'Origins and transformation', 'The Defenders in Ulster', and *Partners in Revolution*, 39–44. A sample of their oaths is conveniently located in Bartlett, 'Defenders and Defenderism in 1795', *I.H.S.*, xxiv (1985), 373–94. For Defenders' trials see Howell, *State Trials*, xxv, 750–84 and xxvi, 226–462.

74 *NS*, 23 March 1793; see PRO, HO 100/42/13–14, 27–8, 194–8 and 100/43/71–3, for the disturbances and trials; also Elliott, *Partners in Revolution*, 43–4.

75 PRO, HO 100/44/115–18, 'Extracts of various letters of information relative to the late insurrections', 8 June 1793; HO 100/38/243, [John Keogh] to the Revd. Hussey, 29 March 1792.

76 Bartlett, 'An End to the Moral Economy', *Past and Present*, xcix, 57–8.

77 PRO, HO 100/46/59, Gen. Whyte to Nepean, 8 April 1793; *NS*, 6 April 1793.

78 Teeling, *Observations on the '. . . Battle of the Diamond'*, 16–17; Coigley too praised the support the Catholics received from the Presbyterians and the Quakers (Madden, *United Irishmen*, 3rd ser., ii, 10).

79 *NS*, 30 March 1795.

80 Cullen, 'The Political Structures of the Defenders', in Dickson and Gough,

eds., *The French Revolution and Ireland*, 129–30; *Report from the Committee of Secrecy of the House of Commons of Ireland, 1798*, 58; PRONI, D.272/149, Cooke to Nugent [January 1796].

81 PRONI, D.607/G/200: T. Lane to Downshire, 12 October 1799; Elliott, 'The Defenders in Ulster', 225.

82 Gebbie, ed., *Abercorn Letters*, 175–6, 180.

83 Miller, *Peep O'Day Boys*, 138–9.

84 Zimmerman, *Songs of Irish Rebellion*, 297; Blackstock, *Ascendancy Army*, 92–7.

85 Madden, *Antrim and Down*, 25–6. The United Irishmen seem to have made particular headway among the Kerry Militia, *Report from the Committee of Secrecy*, 1797 (Append. II of 1798 report), 82.

86 Blackstock, 'The raising of the Yeomanry in Ulster', in Dickson, Keogh and Whelan, eds., *The United Irishmen*, 234–43.

87 Chart, ed., *Drennan Letters*, 259; Dr Haliday too protests, *Charlemont MSS*, ii, 294, 303.

88 Lecky, *Ireland in the Eighteenth Century*, iv, 62–4; Ó Muirí, 'The Killing of Thomas Birch', *Seanchas Ard Mhacha*, x, no. 2, 298–300.

89 Latocnaye, *A Frenchman's walk through Ireland*, 221–2, 252–3.

90 Chart, ed., *Drennan Letters*, 252; Gebbie, ed., *Abercorn Letters*, 196–9.

91 NAI, 620/34/54: the notebooks of John Maxwell (member of the United Irish Ulster provincial committee, appointed colonel of Co. Down); PRONI, D.272/1: 1798 'Black Book'; also Ó Muirí, 'The Killing of Thomas Birch', 279, 284. McEvoy, 'United Irishmen in Co. Tyrone', v, 8–15.

92 Elliott, *Partners in Revolution*, 127. Later the regiment was part of the force which quelled the Ulster rebellion in 1798 (see PRONI, D.607/F/236 and 255).

93 Curtin, *United Irishmen*, 82–3; Newell, *The Apostasy of Newell*, partly reprinted in Madden, *United Irishmen*, 2nd ser., i, 345–425; Latocnaye, *A Frenchman's Walk through Ireland*, 255, 268–9. For folk memory of the military suppression, see IFC, MS 976/137, the Ancient Britons, MS 976/522, 'terrible time of the Light Horsemen' in Kilkeel, MS 1113/515, and Richill (Armagh); also the yeomanry, MS 976/522 and 555.

94 *Charlemont MSS*, ii, 321; *Report from the Committee of Secrecy, 1798*, Append. vi, information of Charles McFillin, a Derry Catholic United Irishman, on how they were specifically targeting Catholics at this time.

95 See also *Castlereagh Corr.*, i, 206; Dickson, *Revolt in North*, 240. However, Keogh, 'The French Disease', 169, thinks that most priests – under tremendous pressure from all sides – simply 'laid low'.

96 Adams, *Printed Word*, 88–9, the huge numbers of these prophecies were rolling off the presses in Ulster in these years; Curtin, *United Irishmen*, 188–9; Connolly, *Priests and People*, 109–10; Lecky, *Ireland in the Eighteenth Century*, iv, 125–6. See *Report from the Committee of Secrecy of the House of Commons of Ireland, 1798*, append. no. xxvi, and *Beauties of the Press*, 152–3 for reports of Orange oath to massacre all Catholics; Donnelly Jr., 'Propagating the Cause of the United Irishmen', *Studies*, lxix, 15–21, northern

United Irishmen adept at exploiting popular millenarianism. Dix, *Books and Pamphlets Printed in Strabane in the Eighteenth Century*, 14, lists a 1795 pamphlet, *Prophetical extracts . . . the Revolution in France and the Decline of Papal Power in the World*. Young, *Ulster in '98*, 28–35, suggests that Catholic United Irishmen in the south and northern Presbyterians may have been swearing different oaths.

97 NLI, MS G.200 (b), 'Ollamh Éigin. An Revolution. The French Revolution. By an Uncertain Author'. It seems to be from the Dundalk area, for the scribe was Ó Gallóglaigh of Dundalk. See also Ó Mórdha, 'Dán Faoi Mhuirthéacht na Frainnce', *Éigse*, 7, 202–4, on this poem.

98 Howell, *State Trials*, xxv, 754 – also McEvoy, 'United Irishmen in Co. Tyrone', *Seanchas Ard Mhacha*, iv, 11.

99 McSkimin, *Annals of Ulster*, 65.

100 Latocnaye, *A Frenchman's Walk through Ireland*, 263–4.

101 Keogh, 'The French Disease', 163; NAI, SOC 1016/30: similar case from the Polls area of Meath/Cavan/Monaghan borders.

102 Miller, *Peep O'Day Boys*, 62; Ó Muirí, 'The Killing of Thomas Birch, United Irishman, March 1797 and the Meeting of the Armagh Freeholders, 19 April 1797', *Seanchas Ard Mhacha*, x, 289–90. See Dickson, *Revolt in the North*, 103, for more examples of sympathetic Protestants being harassed, and Steel Dickson, *Narrative*, 30–31, for new fears about neighbours.

103 Gebbie, ed., *Abercorn Letters*, 204–5. There is some dispute whether news from Wexford would have arrived in time to materially affect attitudes in Ulster on the eve of its rebellion. The following sources show that it did, likewise with reports from other counties: McBride, *Scripture Politics*, 202; PRONI Downshire Papers D607/F/185, 190, 192, 195, 196, 199, 218 (25 May–9 June); Lecky, *Ireland in the Eighteenth Century*, iv, 394–5; Stewart, *The Summer Soldiers*, 257; Gahan, *The People's Rising*, 132–3; Curtin, *United Irishmen*, 260–62; Hill, ed., *Rebellion in County Down*, 55.

104 Madden, *Antrim and Down*, 42–3.

105 Curtin, *United Irishmen*, 267.

106 Madden, *Antrim and Down*, 98, also 113 and 116, where, initially at least, the 'old' Defenders are being sworn as United Irishmen; *Charlemont MSS*, ii, 321.

107 Elliott, *Partners in Revolution*, 246; idem, 'The Defenders in Ulster', in Dickson, Keogh and Whelan, *The United Irishmen*, 222–33.

108 NAI, 620/31/128: [J. Lee] to George Anderson. 20 June 1797.

109 *Report from the Committee of Secrecy of the House of Commons of Ireland*, 1798, 162–4.

110 Stewart, *Summer Soldiers*, 206; Dickson, *Revolt in the North*, 227–31; Madden, *Antrim and Down*, 129 seq.

111 Cited Dickson, *Revolt in the North*, 227–31; also Teeling, *History of the Irish Rebellion*, 136.

112 Musgrave, *Memoirs of the Different Rebellions in Ireland* – the second edition published within two months of the first – 557: Musgrave claimed that as many as 2,000 Catholics defected and watched from the Seaforde road with satisfaction as the Protestants were destroying each other.

113 On this see Cullen, 'The Internal Politics of the United Irishmen', in Dickson, Keogh and Whelan, *United Irishmen*, 194, 344. Cullen – in a revision of his earlier conclusions in 'The Political Structures of the Defenders', in Gough and Dickson, eds., *Ireland and the French Revolution* – argues that Magennis and Lowry returned prior to June 1798. If this were proved, it would significantly alter our understanding. There was a rumour reported by Leonard McNally on 2 June (NAI, 620/10/121/108) that Lowry was in the North. However since he signed a petition in Paris on 16 June (Elliott, *Tone*, 379 and 469) it seems unlikely that he was in Down at the time stated.

114 Madden, *Antrim and Down in '98*, 240.

115 NAI, 620/40/140: information contained in MacCary to Edward Cooke, under-secretary at Dublin Castle, 8 October 1798.

116 Rushe, *Monaghan in the Eighteenth Century*, 37; Teeling, *History of the Irish Rebellion . . . Sequel*, 202–3.

117 Keogh, 'The French Disease', 197–8; Hill, ed., *Rebellion in County Down*, 131.

118 NAI, 620/4/41: 'Narrative of the Rebel Army within C. Down'; Stewart, *Summer Soldiers*, 271.

119 Wright, *Two Lands in One Soil*, 42–3.

120 Madden, *Antrim and Down*, 131; see Elliott, *Partners in Revolution*, 237–8, for the many examples of this feeling throughout the country.

121 *BNL*, 24 July 1798. Priests involved in Ulster were: Magennis, and Coigley; two involved in the purely sectarian politics in Killevy, south Armagh; MacCary; Patrick Gribben – newly appointed parish priest of Glenravel – also imprisoned in Carrickfergus till 1803. The people of Rathlin seem to have been very generally involved and Father McMullen was arrested and brought to Ballyclare. However, to seek evidence of priests actually turning out may be inappropriate. Wexford was quite unusual in this. There is some circumstantial evidence that in the south Down, south Armagh, and the north Louth axis of successful United Irish-Defender co-operation, a number of priests at least subscribed to the political views of the United Irishmen. Keogh, 'The French Disease', 186–99; *Charlemont MSS*, ii, 340–41; O'Laverty, *Down and Connor*, iii, 111–13.

122 *BNL*, 24 July 1798; Musgrave, *Memoirs of the Different Rebellions*, 558.

123 D. H. Akenson and W. H. Crawford, *James Orr*, 10–11, 39–40.

124 Young, *Ulster in '98*, 14–17; Elliott, *Partners*, 205–6; Stewart, *Summer Soldiers*, 247, 264.

125 O'Laverty, *Down and Connor*, ii, 292, 329, 332, 352–3; NAI, SOC 1019/6: March 1800: anon to Col Littlehales, on how the yeomanry in 1798 did not distinguish between guilty and innocent, nor respect protections issued by the officers; that there were ten times more killed who had remained peaceably at home than took up arms or fled to the mountains.

126 Akenson and Crawford, *James Orr*, 16.

127 NAI, SOC 1567/10, Sir George Hill to Chief Secretary Peel, 9 March 1814.

128 *Charlemont MSS*, II, 327–55; for the spread of Defenderism see NAI, 620/46/38; Elliott, *Partners in Revolution*, 245–7; SOC 1091/4–7, 1020/3–7, 1383. *A Concise Account of the Material Events and Atrocities, Which Occurred in the Present Rebellion*, by 'Verdicus' (Dublin, 1799), claims that all the Defenders who migrated to Mayo from Ulster 'were virulent republicans, and drenched with superstitious credulity, being all of the scapular order'. He also cites Dickey's declaration to show it was a popish rebellion after 23 May.

129 McCoy, *Ulster's Joan of Arc* (Bangor, 1987), 30–33; Lyttle, *Betsy Gray or the Hearts of Down*, Append., 162–3; Stewart, *Summer Soldiers*, 227–9. IFC, MS 976/388, how Betsy Gray has been incorporated into the nationalist canon.

130 PRO, HO 100/87/5–7: Castlereagh to the Duke of Portland, 3 June 1799.

131 NAI, SOC 1019/6, anon to Col. Littlehales, March 1800; Elliott, *Partners*, 237–9.

132 O'Laverty, *Down and Connor*, i, 99–101, also iii, 356, for another loyalty address by Revd Hugh Devlin and 600 parishioners of Duncane, Grange, Cranfield and Ballyscullenbeg (Co. Antrim); Elliott, *Partners*, 311–12.

133 Donnelly Jr., 'Pastorini and Captain Rock', in Clark and Donnelly, eds., *Irish Peasants*, 127.

134 *Charlemont MSS*, ii, 180.

135 Teeling, *History of the Irish Rebellion ... Sequel*, 325, 328, 331–2; Madden, *United Irishmen*, 3rd ser., i, 192–4. Unlike his sons Luke Teeling had not become a United Irishman, even shunning his friend Thomas Russell in 1803.

8 THE REVIVAL OF 'POLITICAL' CATHOLICISM

1 See my 'Religion and Identity in Northern Ireland', in W. Van Horne, ed., *Global Convulsions: Race, Ethnicity and Nationalism at the End of the Twentieth Century* (New York, 1997), 152.

2 Emmet Larkin, 'The Devotional Revolution in Ireland, 1850–1875', *Amer. Hist. Rev.*, lxxvii, no. 3 (1972), 625–52; Rogan, *Synods and Catechesis in Ireland*, 73–9, uses evidence in the Vatican Archives to argue that the 'devotional revolution' was already in progress before Cullen. This my own research largely bears out.

3 Hugh McLeod, *Religion and the People of Western Europe 1789–1989* (Oxford, 1997), 47ff.

4 [Harkin], *Inishowen*, 172.

5 Mr and Mrs S. C. Hall, *Ireland: Its Scenery, Character etc.*, 3 vols. (London, 1841–3), iii, 57; Corish, *Irish Catholic Experience*, 169; David Miller, 'Irish

Catholicism and the Great Famine', *Jn. of Soc. Hist.*, ix, no. 1 (1975), 87; Ambrose Macaulay, *Patrick Dorrian, Bishop of Down and Connor 1865–85* (Dublin, 1987), 22, in 1834 there were only three priests for all Belfast; Revd Donal Kerr, 'James Browne Bishop of Kilmore, 1829–65', *Breifne*, vol. 6, no. 22 (1983–4), 128–9, poor state of church in Cavan 1820s–30s, though also shows reform already under way before Cullen.

6 MacAulay, *Crolly*, 63–5.

7 Bartlett, *Fall and Rise*, particularly 329–31.

8 See K. Whelan, 'Regional Impact', 265, shows the O'Connell 'rent' in Ulster the lowest in the country, except for Belfast and Newry, and a band stretching through south Ulster.

9 Desmond Murphy, *Derry, Donegal and Modern Ulster 1790–1921* (Londonderry, 1981), 41–6; Thomas D'Arcy M'Gee, *A Life of the Rt. Rev. Edward Maginn* (New York, 1857), 54.

10 Bardon, *History of Ulster*, 245–7; Macaulay, *Crolly*, 81; Livingstone, *Monaghan*, 190–91; HC 1835 (476) XVI: *Third Report from the Select Committee on Orange Lodges . . . in Ireland*, 36, 145.

11 Kerr, 'James Browne Bishop of Kilmore', 122–3; also S. Ó Dufaigh, 'James Murphy, Bishop of Clogher, 1801–24', *Clogher Rec.*, vi, no. 3 (1968), 422, 447–8, and Philip O'Connell, 'A Dublin Convert Roll: The Diary of the Rev. P. E. O'Farrelly', *Irish Eccles. Rec.*, lxxi (January–June 1949), 533–44 and lxxii (July–December 1949), 27–35, for the bitter contest going on between the proselytising societies and the Catholic Church for the souls of the young in particular.

12 MacManus, *Rocky Road to Dublin*, 159; IFC, MS 1,074/55 and 1,069/98.

13 Tomás Ó Fiaich and Liam Ó Caithnia, *Art Mac Bionaid: Dánta*, 66–8; Ó Muirgheasa, *Dánta Diadha Uladh*, 361.

14 See e.g. Ó Muirgheasa, *Dánta Diadha Uladh*, poem 58, pp. 363–4.

15 Colm Beckett, *Aodh MacDomhnaill: Dánta* (Dublin, 1987), poems no. 9 and 34, also the excellent introduction; Fr Luke Walsh, *The Home Mission Unmasked* (Belfast, 1844).

16 HC 1835 (476) XVI: *Third Report from the Select Committee on Orange Lodges . . . in Ireland*, 163.

17 Beckett, *Aodh Mac Domhnaill: Dánta*, 29–31, poem 2, and on O'Connell, poems 3, 4, 6, 7, 8, 12, 13 (on John O'Connell). There is also considerable admiration for Young Irelanders William Smith O'Brien, Thomas Davis and Charles Gavan Duffy. See also Seosamh Ó Duibhginn, *Séamas Mac Giolla Choille* (Dublin, 1972), 61–2, and Séan Ó Dufaigh and Diarmaid Ó Doibhlin, *Nioclás Ó Cearnaigh: Beatha Agus Saothar* (Dublin, 1989), 100–101, for other O'Connellite poetry from south Ulster, north Leinster. For the prevalence of the prophecies see Connolly, *Priest and People*, 109–10, and Donnelly, 'Pastorini and Captain Rock', 102–37.

18 The French priest, Adolphe Perraud, *Ireland under English Rule* (Dublin, 1864), describes Catholic 'fury' at such proselytising, 394–401; Ó Dufaigh, 'James Murphy, Bishop of Clogher', 422, 447–8.

19 Macaulay, *Crolly*, 155–7. Miller, *Church, State, and Nation*, 29–30, shows the Catholic clergy broadly happy with the National school system, despite a number of irritants.

20 Emmet Larkin, *The Consolidation of the Roman Catholic Church in Ireland, 1860–1870* (Dublin, 1987), 179; Rogan, *Synods in Catechesis in Ireland*, 107–8, 180–97.

21 Macaulay, *Dorrian*, 45–50.

22 Larkin, *Making of the Roman Catholic Church 1850–60*, 35–6.

23 Rafferty, *Catholicism in Ulster*, 139. See also Desmond Bowen, *The Protestant Crusade in Ireland 1800–70* (Dublin, 1978), 262–72 on Cullen's intense anti-Protestantism. Crolly he considered a 'Castle bishop' and he (Crolly) was severely criticised by the ultramontanes for his tolerance of Protestantism.

24 Patrick J. Corish, 'Cardinal Cullen and the National Association of Ireland', in Alan O'Day, ed., *Reactions to Irish Nationalism, 1865–1914* (London, 1987), 117–65; Larkin, *Making of the Roman Catholic Church 1850–60*, 387.

25 Connolly, 'Catholicism in Ulster', 165.

26 Mr and Mrs S. C. Hall, *Ireland: Its Scenery, Character etc.*, 3 vols. (London, 1841–3), iii, 271, found even Lough Derg much 'fallen' and 'superstition' generally in decline.

27 Marie O'Connell, 'The Genesis of Convent Foundations and Their Institutions in Ulster, 1840–1920', in Janice Holmes and Diane Urquhart, eds., *Coming into the Light: The Work, Politics and Religion of Women in Ulster 1840–1940* (Belfast, 1994), 179–206.

28 Macaulay, *Dorrian*, 263–5.

29 Carleton, 'The Station', in *Traits and Stories*, i, 145–80.

30 Corish, *Irish Catholic Experience*, 172; Macaulay, *Crolly*, 102; Rev. Patrick Rogers, 'The Minute Book of the Belfast Rosarian Society', *Down and Connor Historical Soc. Jn.*, viii (1937), 17–23 – this would explain why there was such a surfeit of New Testaments in its circulating library (estbld. 1819).

31 UFTM, field-recording transcripts vols. 17/101 and 23/1.

32 W. M. Thackeray, *Irish Sketchbook*, 35–6, 80, 100, 180, 241.

33 Keenan, *The Catholic Church in Nineteenth-century Ireland*, 114–25; Kerr, 'Browne, Bishop of Kilmore', 133.

34 Macaulay, *Dorrian*, particularly 106, 130, 140–57; A. C. Hepburn, *A Past Apart*, 131, 146–7.

35 Macaulay, *Dorrian*, 118–19; Fitzpatrick, *Oceans of Consolation*, 305; Vaughan, ed., *New History of Ireland*, v, 737–8, on their pleasure at Cullen's official welcome at the Castle; Taylor, *Occasions of Faith*, 169–70; Mary Louise Peckham, 'Catholic Female Congregations and Religious Change in Ireland, 1770–1870' (Univ. Wisconsin, Madison, Phd. thesis, 1993), 271–2. In the more prosperous counties in the east, there seems to have been no problem financing religious institutions – see Marie O'Connell, 'The Genesis of Convent Foundations and Their Institutions in Ulster', in Holmes and Urquhart, eds., *Coming into the Light*, 124–5.

36 Margaret Purdy, 'Some aspects of the Religious and Cultural Identity of Pre-Famine Rural Ulster as Portrayed in William Carleton's Traits and Stories of the Irish Peasantry' (Univ. of London, MA dissertation, 1992), 23; Connolly, *Priests and People*, 265–6, on the absence of popular irreligion among the Irish peasantry; McGlinchy, *Last of the Name*, 74–5.

37 Carleton, *Autobiography*, 61–2.

38 UFTM, V-19/22: recollections of Mrs Francilla Stevenson of her teenage days in Portrush at the close of the 19th century. For an excellent overview of priest-people relations see Connolly, *Priest and People*, 135–74.

39 Breandán Mac Suibhne, 'Canon James McFadden (1842–1917)', in Gerard Moran, ed., *Ten Radical Priests*, 149–84; Corish, *Irish Catholic Experience*, 235–6.

40 Murphy, *Ulster Folk of Field and Fireside*, 149–50. However Frank McKenna (b. Tyrone, near Omagh 1916) remembered the bishops' pastorals condemning poteen in his own time, so their success was not total – see UFTM, Tape R85.33.

41 Cited Brozyna, *Labour, Love and Power*, 176.

42 Enrí Ó Muirgheasa, 'The Holy Wells of Donegal', *Béaloideas*, 6 (1936), 141–62.

43 Taylor, *Occasions of Faith*, 66–7, also 18, 35, 43–4; Ronald H. Buchanan, 'Calendar Customs', *Ulster Folklife*, viii (1962), 15–34.

44 MacGowan, *Hard Road to Klondike*, 29; MacManus, *Rocky Road*, 291, also found in Donegal extraordinary 'praying powers' in the excessively long rosaries and other 'pedantic prayers'.

45 See IFC, MS 974/72–3, 146–8, MS 1057/7–8, 154–61, MS 2081/35–6; Murphy, *Tyrone Folk Quest*, 17, 77; Taylor, *Occasions of Faith*, 3, 26, 93; Linda-May Ballard, 'Three Local Storytellers: A Perspective on the Question of Cultural Heritage', in Gillian Bennett and Paul Smith (eds.), *Monsters with Iron Teeth*, 166–70; Gamble, *View of Society and Manners in the North of Ireland*, 324.

46 Ballard, 'Three Local Storytellers', 162; also UFTM Collectors' Books, V12/16/8: interview with Miss Campbell of Newcastle, 1956.

47 Opsahl Commission, 1993, submission no. 325.

48 O'Laverty, *Down and Connor*, iii, 395–7; Fionnuala Williams, 'A Fire of Stones Curse', *Folk Life*, xxxv (1996–7), 63–73; also UFTM, Collectors' Books V12/19/27 and V12/3/21–25; Glassie, *Ballymenone*, 66.

49 UFTM, Field Recording Transcripts, vol. 23/1–8; McLeod, *Religion and the People of Western Europe*, 54–74, for an excellent overview of popular attitudes to magic and the supernatural.

50 See e.g. Curley, 'Northern Irish Poets and the Land since 1800', 43, 56, 88–91, 113–20; Taylor, *Occasions of Faith*, 80, 98–100.

51 Seymour, *Irish Witchcraft and Demonology* (New York, 1992), notably 1–24 and 194seq.; O'Laverty, *Down and Connor*, iii, 395–7; [Harkin], *Inishowen*, 177; Connolly, *Priest and People*, 100–108.

52 Murphy, *Tyrone Folk Quest*, 27; Bourke, *The Burning of Bridget Cleary*, a study of an infamous case of fairy possession in Tipperary, 1895, in particular

pp. 24–38; Thuente, *W. B. Yeats and Irish Folklore*, 99; Andrews, *Ulster Folklore*, vi, 10–11.

53 Carleton, *Autobiography*, 18–19; Harris, 'The Schools' Collection', *Ulster Folklife*, iii, 12–13.

54 MacManus, *Rocky Road to Dublin*, 98–9.

55 Gamble, *View of Society and Manners in the North of Ireland*, 344–5; Glassie, *Ballymenone*, 64–8; Murphy, *Ulster Folk of Field and Fireside*, 82–4; Andrews, *Ulster Folklore*, 37–9.

56 Lucas, 'The Sacred Trees of Ireland', *Cork Hist. Soc. Jn.*, lxviii, 16–54, particularly 24–9, 46–8; Low, *Celtic Christianity and Nature*, 79–104; also Murphy, *Ulster Folk of Field and Fireside*, 82, 121–9; idem, *Tyrone Folk Quest*, 51.

57 Macaulay, *Dorrian*, 213.

58 Bardon, *History of Ulster*, 356; Comerford, *The Fenians in Context*, 147; Walker, *Ulster Politics*, 49.

59 Miller, *Church, State and Nation*, 31–6, 61; this is the central theme of this seminal study.

60 Macaulay, *Dorrian*, 240–41.

61 Hoppen, *Elections, Politics and Society*, 243.

62 Walker, *Ulster Politics*, 113–15; Corish, 'Cardinal Cullen and the National Association of Ireland'.

63 Walker, *Ulster Politics*, 219–21.

64 Bardon, *History of Ulster*, 408; Gray, *City in Revolt*, 52–5; Phoenix, ed., *A Century of Northern Life*, 15–17; Woods, 'The General Election of 1892', in Lyons and Hawkins, eds., *Ireland under the Union*, 310, 318–19; Walker, *Party Election Results, 1801–1922*, 144–9.

65 Macaulay, *Dorrian*, 149.

66 Hepburn, *A Past Apart*, 148–56; Miller, *Church, State and Nation*, 96–7; Harris, 'Catholicism, Nationalism and the Labour Question', 20.

67 Hepburn, *A Past Apart*, 157ff; Fitzpatrick, 'The Geography of Irish Nationalism', 420–27.

68 Murphy, *Derry, Donegal and Modern Ulster*, 180–81.

69 John B. Dooher, 'Tyrone Nationalism and the Question of Partition, 1910–25' (Univ. of Ulster M. Phil. thesis, 1986), 184 – Bishop McHugh's letter in the nationalist *Ulster Herald*, 24 June 1916. The bishops' utter insistence on denominational education further alienated moderate Unionists, see Miller, *Church and State*, ch. xviii.

70 Phoenix, *Northern Nationalism*, 32.

71 *Ibid.*, 49–53; Miller, *Church, State and Nation*, 422; idem, 'The Roman Catholic Church in Ireland: 1898–1918', in O'Day, ed., *Reactions to Irish Nationalism*, 197–203, charting the uncharacteristic confusion in church leadership about which horse to back in the 1916–22 period.

72 Hopkinson, *Green against Green: The Irish Civil War* (Dublin, 1988), 21–2.

73 Laffan, *The Partition of Ireland, 1911–1925*, 104; Darby, *Northern Ireland: Background*, 20.

9 THE FAMINE AND AFTER: CATHOLIC SOCIAL CLASSES IN NINETEENTH-CENTURY ULSTER

1 Connolly, 'Catholicism in Ulster', 158.

2 See e.g. Fitzpatrick, *Oceans of Consolation*, 366–9, for the terrible insecurity of a semi-literate Protestant peasant family in south Armagh, 1843–64.

3 Young, *Tour*, i, 150–51, 166.

4 O'Kelly, *Early Ireland*, 232–3.

5 Mokyr, *Why Ireland Starved*, 177, 244, 281; Atkinson, *Ireland in the Nineteenth Century* (London, 1833), 349, reports able-bodied poor 'with long trains of children' soliciting relief in the towns of Tyrone and Donegal.

6 Daly, 'Revisionism and the Great Famine', in Boyce and O'Day, eds., *The Making of Modern Irish History*, 71–89; Kennedy, 'The Rural Economy, 1820–1914', in Kennedy and Ollerenshaw, eds., *An Economic History of Ulster, 1820–1939*, 25–30; Wright, *Two Lands in One Soil*, ch. 4; Fitzpatrick, 'The Disappearance of the Agricultural Labourer, 1841–1912', *Ir. Econ. Soc. Hist.*, vii, 66–92; O'Neill, *Family and Farm in Pre-Famine Ireland*, 120–21; Mokyr, *Why Ireland Starved*, 268–75; Vaughan, ed., *New History of Ireland*, v. 351–4; Cormac Ó Gráda, *Black '47 and Beyond*, 77–83, 122–5.

7 Ó Gráda, *Economic History*, 122–4 – e.g. the London Companies, major absentees, considered caring landlords, also his *Black '47*, 126 seq.; Mokyr, *Why Ireland Starved*, 197–212; MacLaughlin, 'The Politics of Nation-Building in Post-Famine Donegal', in Dunlevy, Nolan and Ronayne, eds., *Donegal. History and Society*, 608.

8 Gamble, *Sketches of History, Politics, and Manners in Dublin and the North of Ireland in 1810*, 246–7; Grant, 'Some Aspects of the Great Famine in County Armagh', *Seanchas Ard Mhacha*, 8, no. 2, 353–4; Wright, *Two Lands in One Soil*, 76.

9 Akenson, *Small Differences*, 144–5, on how the Famine became the centre-piece of Catholic nationalist tradition.

10 Clarkson, 'Population Change and Urbanisation, 1821–1912', in Kennedy and Ollerenshaw, eds., *Economic History of Ulster*, 137–43; Fitzpatrick, *Oceans of Consolation*, 15–16, sees Fermanagh, Tyrone and Armagh as among those counties sending most emigrants to Australia in the decades after the Famine; Grant, 'The Great Famine and the Poor Law in Ulster: the Rate-in-Aid Issue of 1849', *I.H.S.*, xxvii, 30–47; Crawford, 'Poverty and Famine in County Cavan', in Gillespie, ed., *Cavan*, 140–41, 156; Mokyr, *Why Ireland Starved*, 267, shows excess deaths during the Famine at 43–57%, higher than any county in Munster, though not Connacht – the worst affected province.

11 McCavery, 'The Famine in County Down', in Kinealy and Parkhill, eds., *The Famine in Ulster*, 107.

12 Bardon, *History of Ulster*, 286.

13 See IFC, MSS 975/81–2, 976/163 and 168, and 1112/373; Quinlan, 'A Punishment from God: the Famine in the Centenary Folklore Questionnaire', *The Irish Review*, xix, 78–9. Begley and Lally, 'The Famine in County

Donegal', in Kinealy and Parkhill, eds., *Famine in Ulster*, 80; Kinealy, *The Great Calamity. The Irish Famine, 1845–52*, 349.

14 Parkhill, 'The Famine in County Londonderry', in Kinealy and Parkhill, eds., *Famine in Ulster*, 164.

15 McCavery, 'Famine in County Down', 120–21, 126–7.

16 Cunningham, 'The Famine in County Fermanagh', in Kinealy and Parkhill, eds., *Famine in Ulster*, 141; MacAtasney, *'This Dreadful Visitation'*, 84–6; Grant, 'The Great Famine and the Poor Law in Ulster', 30–47.

17 Cunningham, 'The Famine in County Fermanagh', in Kinealy and Parkhill, eds., *Famine in Ulster*, 141; Wright, *Two Lands in One Soil*, ch. 5.

18 Wright, *Two Lands in One Soil*, 118, 124, see Ó Gráda, *Black '47 and Beyond*, 56–8; Gallogly, 'The Famine in County Cavan', in Kinealy and Parkhill, eds., *Famine in Ulster*, 69.

19 Bardon, *History of Ulster*, 296; MacAtasney, *'This Dreadful Visitation'*, 32. 102.

20 Dallat, 'The Famine in County Antrim', in Kinealy and Parkhill, eds., *Famine in Ulster*, 21–3. McEvoy, 'The Parish of Errigal Kieran in the Nineteenth Century', *Seanchas Ard Mhacha*, i, 128, tells of the soup-kitchens in Armagh, but no tradition of souperism in this part.

21 IFC, MS 1361/103, unnamed interviewee, April 1953, also an excellent example of the elision of different periods and experiences into one historical narrative of oppression – in this case the penal laws, notably the £5 clause, spoken of as if they still operated at the time of the Famine.

22 Cited Póirtéir, ed., *Famine Echoes*, 167; also IFC MS 1359/129, 143.

23 IFC, MS 1360/143; Póirtéir, *Famine Echoes*, 169.

24 Gallogly, 'Famine in County Cavan', 72–3, citing *Freemans Journal*, 27 January 1849.

25 IFC, MS 1113/1G; also Póirtéir, *Famine Echoes*, 139, 140–41, 178–9.

26 IFC, MS 1072/315, 335 and 338, for the taunting of descendants of families who turned; MS 1072/359, it was always given out in the 'big Protestants' houses'; MS 1072/315, 335, 338 ('Benson's Gravy', Benson doling out the soup at Chambree's place); IFC, MS 976/163, and Póirtéir, *Famine Echoes*. 173, 178–9, on Ribbon retaliation; Ó Muirgheasa, *Dhá Chéad*, 31–2, Bennett's scathing poem on the O'Callaghans.

27 David Hempton and Myrtle Hill, *Evangelical Protestantism in Ulster Society 1740–1890* (London, 1992), 138–40 on the philanthropy.

28 See also Donnelly, in Vaughan, ed., *New History of Ireland*, v, 311–12, and Ó Gráda, *Ireland. A New Economic History*, 174, on widespread popular sense of the soup-kitchens as demeaning.

29 Cited Begley and Lally, 'Famine in County Donegal', 79; Ó Gráda, *Black '47*, 50–51.

30 McCavery, 'Famine in County Down', 107; Patrick Duffy, 'The Famine in County Monaghan', in Kinealy and Parkhill, eds., *Famine in Ulster*, 191.

31 Póirtéir, *Famine Echoes*, 139.

32 Beckett, *Aodh Mac Domhnaill: Dánta*, 41 – Brady is taunted as a spy because of his pro-English outlook.

33 UFTM, R85.249, taped interview with Owen O'Rourke, b.1889, Catholic farmer of Omeath, also favourable local tradition of the Protestant McGarrys running the soup-kitchen at Drumla 'there was no souperism, just charity'; Kinealy, *Great Calamity*, 164.

34 See Foster, *The Story of Ireland*, 8–13 on Sullivan's *Story*.

35 Duffy, 'The Famine in Monaghan', 195; Fitzpatrick, *Oceans of Consolation*, 536, also finds little mention of it.

36 Quinlan, 'A punishment from God', 72–3, 82; Ó Gráda, *Ireland: A New Economic History*, 174.

37 Beckett, *Aodh Mac Domhnaill: Dánta*, poems 15 and 16, 'Agallamh idir Aindrias Ó hÉigeartaigh agus an Bard um Mheath na bPrátaí' ('A dialogue ... about the rotting of the potatoes'); *Report of Royal Commission on the Belfast Riots*, HC 1857–8 (2309), xxvi, 241.

38 Clarkson, 'Population Change and Urbanisation', 155.

39 Anne O'Dowd, *Spalpeens and Tattie Hokers. History and Folklore of the Irish Migratory Agricultural Worker in Ireland and Britain* (Dublin, 1991), 30–31, 42–3, 103–17, 233, 287–8. See Fitzpatrick, *Oceans' of Consolation*, 337 seq.; also his 'A Peculiar Tramping People', in Vaughan, ed., *New History of Ireland*, v, 623–4, 646–50; Foster, *Modern Ireland*, 345–9.

40 O'Dowd, *Spalpeens and Tattie Hokers*, 287–8.

41 Ó Muirgheasa, *Dhá Chéad de Cheoltaibh Uladh*, iii, 345–6.

42 Patrick MacGill, *Children of the Dead End* (London, 1985, reprint of 1914 original), 30.

43 Colm Tóibín, *Bad Blood*, 13–21; UFTM, Collectors' Books, V-19 (Tyrone), 46–7, hiring fairs in Tyrone after 1920; also Murphy, *Tyrone Folk Quest*, 13 and *Ulster Folk of Field and Fireside*, 151, on the sense of degradation of the hiring fair.

44 Michael MacGowan, *The Hard Road to Klondike* (London, 1962), 40.

45 O'Dowd, *Spalpeens and Tattie Hokers*, 130–31. 217–19.

46 MacGowan, *Hard Road to Klondike*, 142–3; Paddy [the Cope] Gallagher, *My Story*, 204 (*c.*1914) also highlights the real improvement in the life of the rural poor. His aged parents had feared eviction because he had spoken harshly to the Protestant minister. He assured them that eviction was no longer possible except for non-payment of rent.

47 Fitzpatrick, *Oceans of Consolation*, 446–7; UFTM, Collectors' Books V.19/7/18–20 also shows landlords having a bad name in Protestant traditions.

48 Walker, *Ulster Politics*, 18–21.

49 R. W. Kirkpatrick, 'Origins and Development of the Land War in Mid-Ulster, 1879–85', in Lyons and Hawkins, eds., *Ireland Under the Union*, 208, shows sudden increase in evictions in 1880, Ulster experiencing the highest of any province.

50 See e.g. Walker, *Ulster Politics*, 22, on Protestant fears that the aim of the Land League was to dispossess Protestants.

51 O'Laverty, *Down and Connor*, i, 389.

52 Paul Bew and Frank Wright, 'The Agrarian Opposition in Ulster Politics,

1848–87', in Clarke and Donnelly, *Irish Peasants*, 192–229; Wright, *Two Lands in One Soil*, ch. 7; Walker, *Ulster Politics*, 19–21; Samuel Clarke, *Social Origins of the Irish Land War* (New Jersey, 1979), 211–12.

53 *Report on the Derryveagh Evictions*, HC 1861 (316) lii, 539–79; Mac-Gowan, *Hard Road to Klondike*, 18–19; also Bardon, *History of Ulster*, 321–2; W. E. Vaughan, *Sin, Sheep and Scotsmen: John George Adair and the Derryveagh Evictions, 1861* (Belfast, 1983).

54 Fitzpatrick, *Oceans of Consolation*, 421; MacPhilib, 'Profile of a Landlord in Folk Tradition and in Contemporary Accounts – the Third Earl of Leitrim', *Ulster Folklife*, xxxiv, 26–40.

55 Walker, 'The Land Question and Elections in Ulster, 1868–86', in Clarke and Donnelly, eds., *Irish Peasants*, 238–9.

56 Kirkpatrick, 'Origins and Development of the Land War in mid-Ulster, 1879–85', 227–9.

57 Bew and Wright, 'Agrarian Opposition', 215, particularly in south Ulster where it sparks a major Orange revival; also Kirkpatrick, 'Origins . . . of the Land War', 228–35. Walker, *Ulster Politics*, 24–5: in the growing towns Catholics tend to be over-represented among the poorest and in consequence under-represented among the new town councils. The local government enquiry of 1877 shows only two Catholics out of forty on Belfast town council (though a third of its populace) and in Derry only two out of twenty-four. There were more elsewhere, but still less than their proportions warranted – and it was a source of grievance.

58 Kennedy, 'The Rural Economy', 60 n.127; Clarkson, 'Population Change and Urbanisation', 153–5.

59 Budge and O'Leary, *Belfast: Approach to Crisis*, 28–33.

60 Hall, *Ireland: Its Scenery, Character*, iii, 52–3; Ó Gráda, *New Economic History*, 285–6.

61 Thackeray, *Irish Sketchbook*, 310.

62 Macaulay, *Dorrian*, 122–8 – by 1884 over 20,000 Catholics were located on the Falls Road (almost a third of the city's Catholic populace), with a building programme of churches, schools and parochial facilities to match.

63 Thackeray, *Irish Sketchbook*, 308.

64 Baker, 'Orange and Green: Belfast 1832–1912', in Dyos and Wolff, eds., *The Victorian City*, ii, 806.

65 O'Hanlon, *Walks among the Poor of Belfast*, notably 4–19, 27, 38; also Hepburn, *A Past Apart*, 75, and Walker, *Ulster Politics*, 23–6, for the significant numbers of Church of Ireland (though not Presbyterian) members among the under-privileged.

66 Hepburn, *A Past Apart*, 38–40, 63; Baker, 'Orange and Green', 801. Morris, 'Inequality, Social Structure and the Market', 200–203, argues that one of the reasons for this is that skilled wages were tied to the Scottish urban model (from which many of the skilled tradesmen were imported), while unskilled labour wages were decided by the rural rates from which most of the unskilled came, producing a 'dual economy'.

67 Baker, 'Orange and Green', 802.

68 *Ibid.*, 799; Hepburn, *The Conflict of Nationality in Modern Ireland* (London, 1980), 24–31, reproduces a number of documents to illustrate the rising sectarian temperature in Belfast.

69 Hepburn, *A Past Apart*, 118–19, Budge and O'Leary, *Approach to Crisis*, ch. 3; John Gray, *City in Revolt: James Larkin and the Belfast Dock Strike of 1907* (Belfast, 1985), 15–17.

70 Hepburn, *A Past Apart*, 34–5, 39–44; Clarkson, 'Population Change', 138–41.

71 James H. Murnane, 'Dr James Donnelly, Bishop of Clogher (1865–1893) and the Ascendancy in Monaghan', *Clogher Rec.*, xiii, no. 1 (1988), 1–25.

72 Mac Suibhne, 'Canon James McFadden', 153–4; Ó Gráda, *New Economic History*, 268–70; Paddy [the Cope] Gallagher, *My Story*, 189, 267–8: how the gombeenmen try to stop the co-op by denouncing them as Orange and Unionist stooges; they were much worse than the landlords, indeed they reaped most benefit from the dismantling of landlordism. See Walker, *Ulster Politics*, 17–26, for the occupational statistics.

73 Hepburn, *A Past Apart*, 129; Jim MacLaughlin, 'The Politics of Nation-building in Post-Famine Donegal', 609–10; see also Hoppen, *Elections*, 171–2 for national ratios.

74 Jim MacLaughlin, 'The Politics of Nation-Building in Post-Famine Donegal', 615; James O'Shea, *Priest, Politics and Society in Post-Famine Ireland* (Dublin, 1983), 241–6.

75 Murphy, *Derry*, 173, church providing networks of support for incoming rural Catholics, permits employers to resist unionisation.

76 Macaulay, *Dorrian*, 36–7, 51, 105, 121–2, 128. Hughes was the first ever Catholic to be elected to municipal office in Belfast (1855): see Budge and O'Leary, *Approach to Crisis*, 61, and *Reports of the Commissioners of Inquiry into the Origin and Character of the Riots in Belfast, July and September, 1857*, HC 1857–8 [2309] xxvi, 1, 147, 242–4; Hughes thought some 100 to 150 Catholics in Belfast capable of being made Peace Commissioners, three – William Ross, McCue of Rosemary Street and Joseph Magill – being worth £100,000. The report into the 1886 riots found three-quarters of all the public houses in Belfast (even in Protestant areas) owned by Catholics, *Belfast Riots Commission*, HC 1887 [C.4925], xviii, 525, 533.

77 Macaulay, *Dorrian*, 124–5.

78 Fitzpatrick, *Oceans of Consolation*, 393, 408, 555, 560.

79 Mac Suibhne, 'Canon James McFadden', 150–51; MacGill, *Children of the Dead End*, 3–5, 11, 21–2.

80 MacManus, *Rocky Road to Dublin*, 228.

81 Gray, *City in Revolt*, 44, 152.

82 *Ibid.*, 33–8.

10 ACROSS THE DIVIDE:
COMMUNITY RELATIONS AND SECTARIAN
CONFLICT BEFORE PARTITION

1 Gamble, *View of Society and Manners in the North of Ireland in the Summer and Autumn of 1812*, 63, 83–4, 104.

2 Gamble, *Sketches of History, Politics, and Manners in Dublin and the North of Ireland in 1810*, 217–20, 233. In 1870 the Governor of the Apprentice Boys made a similar objection to granting equal marching rights to nationalists, *Royal Commission of Inquiry into Riots and Disturbances in the City of Londonderry*, HC 1870 [C.5*] xxxii, 575.

3 Duffy, *My Life in Two Hemispheres*, i, 6–8.

4 MacManus, *Rocky Road to Dublin*, 204, 214.

5 Doyle, *An Ulster Childhood*, 36–9.

6 Gamble, *View of Society . . . in the North of Ireland*, 116–7.

7 Doyle, *Ulster Childhood*, 39–40.

8 IFC, MS 975/87–88.

9 IFC, MS 1215/127.

10 Wright, *Two Lands*, 186–7; *Return of the Number of Murders and Waylayings in the Baronies of Upper and Lower Fews, in County Armagh, 1844–50*, HC 1850 [566] li, 577; *Return of . . . Murders, Waylayings . . . of Agrarian Character . . . Louth, Armagh and Monaghan, 1849–52*, HC 1852 (448) xlvii, 465–75.

11 Doyle, *Ballygullion*, 135; also his *Rosabelle and other Stories*, 200 (from *The Leprechaun*).

12 MacManus, *Rocky Road to Dublin*, 112; Fitzpatrick, *Oceans of Consolation*, 412–15.

13 UFTM, Collectors' Books V-19/7/64–5.

14 Bullock, *Dan the Dollar*. In Irish-language sources, this shunning of materialism is usually associated also with reminders that this world is not for long: see Ó Muirgheasa, *Dánta*, 164, 172–3, 271–4, 363, 365–6; idem, *Céad*, poem 4.

15 Ó Coinne and Ó Fiaich, 'Tombstone Inscriptions in Drumglass Cemetery'; however Corish, *Irish Catholic Experience*, 157, notes the beginning of its decline elsewhere in Ireland from 1820. This partly reflects the new ability of the Catholic Church to purchase land for its own cemeteries, whereas previously all cemeteries were in the hands of the established Church.

16 Wright, *Two Lands*, 392–3.

17 Akenson, *Small Differences*, 109–15.

18 Fitzpatrick, *Oceans of Consolation*, 391–5; Donaldson, *Historical Account of the Upper Fews*, 71, very few inter-faith marriages.

19 Fitzpatrick, *Oceans of Consolation*, 391n.

20 O'Dowd, *Spalpeens*, 281, 283.

21 Ó Muirgheasa, *Dánta Diadha Uladh*, no. 60; idem, *Dhá Chéad*, poem 14; frequent recitations of England's cruelty against Catholicism (very notable in

Bennett, see Ó Fiaich and Ó Caithnia, eds., *Art Mac Bionaid, Dánta*, notably poem 29.

22 RIA, MS 23B.19, p. 100.

23 Ó Muirgheasa, *Dánta Diadha Uladh*, no. 44.

24 Beckett, *Aodh Mac Domhnaill*, 40–43, 'A Conversation between Brady the Spy and an Irish Poet'.

25 Ó Muirgheasa, *Dhá Chéad*, 42–3, poem 14.

26 Indeed it looks as if the phrase may have been regularly used by Orangemen, Wright, *Two Lands*, 56.

27 *Belfast Riots Commission*, HC 1887 [C.4925] xviii, 535.

28 Gamble, *Sketches*, 287.

29 *Royal Commission of Inquiry into Riots and Disturbances in the City of Londonderry*, HC 1870 [C.5*] xxxiii, 428, 478, 497, 586.

30 Macaulay, *Crolly*, 92.

31 Gamble, *Sketches*, 269.

32 Duffy, *My Life in Two Hemispheres*, i, 13.

33 *Third Report from the Select Committee . . . [on] Orange Lodges*, HC 1835 [476], xvi, 110–21, 171–212; Hereward Senior, *Orangeism in Britain and Ireland, 1795–1836* (London, 1966), 247–8.

34 Senior, *Orangeism*, 267–8.

35 *Third Report from the Select Committee . . . [on] Orange Lodges*, 12–21, 32, 41, 69–70, 216–45. Milne, *Charter Schools*, 295, in 1822 it was revealed that the Blacker family had sent thirty-five boys and girls from the Portadown area to Charter schools at Strangford and Dundalk.

36 *Third Report from the Select Committee . . . [on] Orange Lodges*, 23.

37 Carleton, *Autobiography*, 34–40.

38 Doyle, *Ballygullion*, 131.

39 *Third Report from the Select Committee . . . [on] Orange Lodges*, 16.

40 Carleton, *Autobiography*, 188–9, 122–3.

41 Duffy, *Landscapes of South Ulster*, 62.

42 Ó Mórdha, 'The Rising of Burke', *Clogher Rec.*, iv, nos. 1–2. 50–53.

43 Livingstone, *Fermanagh Story*, 161–6; *Third Report from the Select Committee . . . [on] Orange Lodges*, 83 seq.; IFC, MS 1923/17–20; Ó Mórdha, 'Notes and Comments. Party Quarrels in Nineteenth-century Monaghan', *Clogher Rec.*, II, 2, 355–7, extracts from contemporary papers on sectarian clashes and killings in the Clones area, 1823–28; Murphy, *Derry*, 48–9.

44 Glassie, *Ballymenone*, 237, also 223–40; *Memorial of Prisoners Charged with Murder at Macken*, HC 1830 (150) xxvi, 301; also *Third Report from the Select Committee . . . [on] Orange Lodges*, 83 seq.; IFC, MS 1923/17–20, for folk memory of Mackan incident.

45 *Third Report from the Select Committee . . . [on] Orange Lodges*, Append. 129.

46 *Papers Relating to the Investigation held at Castlewellan into the Occurrences at Dolly's Brae, on the 12th July, 1849*, HC 1850 [1143] li, 331ff. IFC MS 975/267, 294–8, 584–5, 589: for memories of sectarian clashes in this area in the nineteenth century. Apparently five Catholics were executed and

two transported for killing an Orangeman in the 1840s; there was a commemoration of them a century later.

47 Zimmermann, *Songs of Irish Rebellion*, 311–13.

48 Hempton and Hill, *Evangelical Protestantism in Ulster Society*, ch. 9, 161–87.

49 Doyle, *An Ulster Childhood*, 54–5.

50 Hepburn, 'The Catholic Community in Belfast, 1850–1940', [though reproduced in his *Past Apart*, not the opening pages], in Engman *et al.*, eds., *Ethnic Identity in Urban Europe*, 41.

51 Doyle, 'A Flag and a Flapper', in his *Rosabelle and Other Stories*, 82–100.

52 'Letters written by John O'Donovan, relating to the History and Antiquities of the County of Down ... in 1834' (unpubd. typescript in the RIA). The same outsider shock at the levels of sectarian bitterness is reflected in successive parliamentary reports into Belfast's riots, e.g. *Belfast Riots Commission*, HC 1887 [C.4925] xviii, 417. Boyd, *Holy War in Belfast*, 9, cites the occurrence of serious riots in 1835, 1843, 1857, 1864, 1872, 1880, 1884, 1886, 1898.

53 Boyd, *Holy War in Belfast*, 70–71; Baker, 'Orange and Green', 807. Duffy, *Life in Two Hemispheres*, i, 42, Catholics coming from predominantly Catholic counties regard Belfast as hostile territory.

54 *Report of the Commission of Inquiry into the Origin and Character of the Riots in Belfast in July and September 1857* HC 1857–8 [2309] xxvi, 248–51, also 3, 27. The September 1857 riots were likewise sparked by Revd Hugh Hanna's open-air preaching in the docks area (ibid., 11–14, 111); Hempton and Hill, *Evangelical Protestantism in Ulster Society*, 124–5; Boyd, *Holy War in Belfast*. 22–3, 26–7.

55 *Report of the Commission of Inquiry into ... the Riots in Belfast in July and September 1857*, 8, 2, 124.

56 Ibid., 142, also 87, 123, 130.

57 Ibid., 138–9.

58 Ibid., 11.

59 Ibid., 87, 101, 124, 138–9.

60 Ibid., 125.

61 Brozyna, *Labour, Love and Power*, 22, 47–8.

62 Boyd, *Holy War*, 89–91.

63 Hepburn, *Past Apart*, 161; Budge and O'Leary, *Belfast. Approach to Crisis*, 92–4.

64 Baker, 'Orange and Green', 808.

65 Walker, *Ulster Politics*, 77–221.

66 *Belfast Riots Commission*, 1887, 638; Budge and O'Leary, *Belfast: Approach to Crisis*, 87–90.

67 *Belfast Riots Commission*, 1887, 538.

68 Ibid., 11, 533.

69 *Royal Commission of Inquiry into Riots and Disturbances in the City of Londonderry*, HC 1870 [C.5*] xxxiii, 581–5; The Apprentice Boys' annual celebrations were banned on the recommendation of the Commission.

70 Lacy, *Siege City*, 93, 173; McBride, *The Siege of Derry in Ulster Protestant Mythology*, 50–51.

71 Doak, 'Rioting and Civil Strife in the City of Londonderry during the Nineteenth and Early Twentieth Centuries', 147–58.

72 *Correspondence between Ld. Chancellor of Ireland and R. McClintock, in Reference to His Conduct as a Magistrate ... March 1884*, HC 1884 [C.5057] lxiii, 513.

73 *Report of the Royal Commission to Inquire into Disturbances in the City of Londonderry, 1 November 1883*, HC 1884 [C.3954] xxxviii, 611. For similar Orange counter-demonstrations elsewhere, and official rebuke of magistrates involved, see the various reports in HC 1884 [C.4065] lxiii, 517 (Newry), HC 1884 (95) lxiii, 461 (Dromore, Tyrone); HC 1884 [C.3891] lxiii, 547 (Rosslea, Fermanagh – also on magistrates in Monaghan and Cavan).

74 McBride, *Siege of Derry*, 54–57; Murphy, *Derry*, 133; Doak, 'Rioting and Civil Strife in ... Londonderry', 145–6, 249.

75 See Darby, *Intimidation and the Control of Conflict in Northern Ireland* (Dublin, 1986), 14–18.

76 *Belfast Riots Commission*, HC 1887 [C.4925] xviii, 448.

77 [W. Shankill], *The Belfast Riots, 1886. The Islandmen and Shankill Road Defended* (Belfast, 1886).

78 Budge and O'Leary, *Belfast: Approach to Crisis*, 83.

79 Cited, Macaulay, *Dorrian*, 79, 47n, see also Cogan, *Diocese of Meath*, iii, 86: 'We are told, a Catholic might be known by his stooped carriage and subdued manner.'

80 Rushe, *Monaghan in the Eighteenth Century*, 93.

81 Stuart, *Historical Memoirs of the City of Armagh*, new edn. by Revd Ambrose Coleman, OP (Dublin, 1900), vii, xxi–xxiii.

82 Connolly, *A Sermon Preached in the Church of St Mary Belfast, on the Occasion of the Centenary on Sunday, November 11th (1883)*, 16–17.

83 Gamble, *View of Society*, 267.

84 Hill, 'The Disputed Lessons of Irish History', *Past and Present*, 118, 96–129. For similarity of Catholic 'in the time of persecution' approach in O'Laverty, *Down and Connor* (e.g. iii, 468), also *Derry Journal*, 14 July 1957, and Presbyterian in 'time of tyranny' in Latimer, *A History of the Irish Presbyterians*, ch. xxix.

85 Quinlan, 'A Punishment from God', 73–4; Foster, *The Story of Ireland*; Adams, 'The Validity of Language Census Figures in Ulster, 1851–1911', *Ulster Folklife*, 25, 113–122, shows the impact being made on Ulster – particularly Belfast and particularly in the under-30s generation – of the Gaelic League's Irish language revival.

86 Donaldson, *A Historical and Statistical Account of the Barony of the Upper Fews*, 71.

87 See e.g. *The Irish Magazine*, i (1807–8), 36–37, ii (1809), 2, 162–5; Clifford, ed., *The Origin of Irish Catholic Nationalism*.

88 Duffy, *Life in Two Hemispheres*, i, 17–18.

89 *Correspondence and Reports Relating to the Removal of Lord Rossmore*, HC 1884 [C.3891] lxiii, 547.

90 Duffy, *My Life in Two Hemispheres*, i, 17–18.

91 Ó Fiaich and Ó Caithnia, eds., *Art Mac Bionaid: Dánta*, 71–5, poem 29.

92 Elliott, 'Religion and Identity in Northern Ireland', 150–53.

93 Taylor, *Occasions of Faith*. 118–44.

94 Connolly, *Sermon Preached in the Church of St Mary*, 26–7.

95 Conor Cruise O'Brien, *Ancestral Voices*, 43.

96 Miller, *Church, State, and Nation*, 61–2; Foster, *Modern Ireland*, 446–56.

97 Duffy, *My Life in Two Hemispheres*, i, 44; Ó Muirgheasa, *Dánta*, 270; Ó Muirí, ed., *Lámhscríbhinn Staire an Bhionadaigh*, 193.

98 Malachi O'Doherty, *The Trouble with Guns*, 18.

99 Glassie, *Ballymenone*, 223, also 199 and 234; MacManus, *Rocky Road to Dublin*, 304–5; Paddy [the Cope] Gallagher, *My Story*, 41.

100 *Irish History Reader* by The Christian Brothers [Br J. M. O'Brien from Co. Clare]. Coldrey, *Faith and Fatherland: The Christian Brothers and the Development of Irish Nationalism 1838–1921*, particularly ch. 6, also 68–76.

101 O'Brien, *Ancestral Voices*, 22–9.

102 Miller, 'The Roman Catholic Church in Ireland', 124–7.

103 Ó Cuív, 'Irish language and literature, 1845–1921', in Vaughan, ed., *New History of Ireland*, vi, 408.

104 IFC, MS 1360/279, 285–6, traditions from Antrim, MS 1215/262–3, from Tyrone; UFTM, R85.242, taped interview with Mrs Bridget Gilhooley, Mullaghbawn, Co. Armagh.

105 Murphy, *Tyrone Folk Quest*, 67.

106 Ó Snodaigh, *Hidden Ulster*, 80–81; also Blaney, *Presbyterians and the Irish Language*, particularly 143–51 and 175–82.

107 UFTM, M3 12: McPeake Transcripts, 109, 114–5; Blaney, *Presbyterians and the Irish Language*, 175–6.

108 C. Milligan Fox, *Annals of the Irish Harpers*, 198–9.

109 MacLaughlin, 'The Politics of Nation-Building in Post-Famine Donegal', 583–604.

110 Ó Danachair, 'The Progress of Irish Ethnology, 1783–1982', *Ulster Folklife*, 29, 7–10.

111 MacLaughlin, 'The Politics of Nation-Building in Post-Famine Donegal', 583–604, on the historical writings of the priests; also Miller, *Church, State, and Nation*, 308 on the anti-Englishness of the hierarchy. Fitzpatrick, 'The Geography of Irish Nationalism', 420–22.

112 Murphy, *Tyrone Folk Quest*, 64.

113 Foster, *Modern Ireland*, 453.

II CATHOLICS IN NORTHERN IRELAND
1920-2000

1 Laffan, *Partition of Ireland*, 93; O'Halloran, *Partition and the Limits of Irish Nationalism*, 18; Farrell, *Northern Ireland. The Orange State*, 24-5.

2 Bardon, *History of Ulster*, 468.

3 Phoenix, 'Political Violence, Diplomacy and the Catholic Minority in Northern Ireland, 1922', in Darby, Dodge and Hepburn, eds., *Political Violence: Ireland in a Comparative Perspective*, 34.

4 The fullest contemporary account of the Belfast troubles is McKenna [Fr John Hassan, curate of St Mary's], *Facts and Figures of the Belfast Pogrom 1920-1922* – a private printing, only eighteen copies run off; Boyd, 'Father Hassan and the Pogrom', *The Irish Press*, 9 September 1970; *Irish News*, 5 January 1939, article on the death of Father Hassan.

5 'McKenna', *Belfast Pogrom*, 81; Phoenix, *Northern Nationalism*, 195-7; Farrell, *Orange State*, 51, 58, 96, 346; Hezlet, *The 'B' Specials: A History of the Ulster Special Constabulary*, 69, whilst condemning this, absolves the Specials of any involvement.

6 There are similar scenes in Frank Burton's account of another Catholic ghetto in Belfast in the Troubles of the 1970s, *The Politics of Legitimacy: Struggles in a Belfast Community*, 18-19. They could have been transposed to the 1920s and not seemed out of time.

7 *Irish News*, 22 May 1922.

8 UFTM, Collectors' Books, Tyrone, V-19-7, recollections of May Brunt, 1960; Bowman, *De Valera and the Ulster Question 1917-1973*, 72; Dooher, 'Tyrone Nationalism and the Question of Partition, 1910-25', 431; Hopkinson, *Green against Green: the Irish Civil War*, 83-6.

9 Phoenix, 'Political Violence', 29-47; Hopkinson, *Green against Green*, 248-52.

10 'McKenna', *Belfast Pogrom*, op. cit.

11 Shea, *Voices and the Sound of Drums*, 112.

12 Harkness, *Northern Ireland since 1920*, 89. Whyte, 'How Much Discrimination Was There under the Unionist Regime, 1921-68?', in Gallagher and O'Connell, eds., *Contemporary Irish Studies*, 3-7.

13 Shea, *Voices and the Sound of Drums*, 96.

14 Laffan, *Partition of Ireland*, 103-5.

15 Phoenix, *Northern Nationalism*, 197, 226, 237-9.

16 Farrell, *Arming the Protestants: The Formation of the Ulster Special Constabulary, 1920-27*, 267-9; Brewer with Higgins, *Anti-Catholicism in Northern Ireland, 1600-1998*, 93; Arthur, *Government and Politics of Northern Ireland*, 26-7.

17 It is extremely difficult to find a dispassionate account of the USC. The fullest accounts are the favourably disposed Hezlet, *The 'B' Specials: A History of the Ulster Special Constabulary*, and the hostile Farrell, *Arming the Protestants* – although both try to be fair and the latter is particularly well

researched. More recently Follis, *A State under Siege: The Establishment of Northern Ireland, 1920–1925*, 82, 88–9, vividly conveys Unionists' sense of siege in this period. But his case, largely absolving the USC from sectarianism, is marred by excessive pleading, particularly in his efforts to explain away the McMahon murders, 94–5, 111–12.

18 Bew, Gibbon and Patterson, *Northern Ireland 1921–1994*, 35–41.

19 Farrell, *Arming the Protestants*, 153.

20 Buckland, *James Craig*, 86–7.

21 Idem, *A History of Northern Ireland*, 46–7; idem, *Craig*, 87; Phoenix, *Northern Nationalism*, 223ff. There were only a handful of occasions when the Special Powers Act was used against Protestants and usually this was belatedly and reluctantly. It was not until 1966 that the power to ban an organisation under the Act was used against a non-republican body (in this case the UVF). See Whyte, 'Discrimination', 27–8; Farrell, *Orange State*, 63–4; and the traditional nationalist account of Gallagher, *The Indivisible Island*, 194–5.

22 Ultach, 'Orange Terror: the Partition of Ireland', reprinted from *The Capuchin Annual*, 25. Ultach speaks of young men being constantly stopped and harassed in Catholic areas (pp. 4–5). In my recollection actual incidents of this happening were central to nationalist consciousness in Northern Ireland.

23 Maurice Hayes, *Minority Verdict*, 74.

24 Whyte, 'How Much Discrimination Was There under the Unionist Regime?', 29; *Disturbances in Northern Ireland: Report of the Commission Appointed by the Governor of Northern Ireland [The Cameron Report]* (Belfast, 1969), para. 181, also 168.

25 See for e.g. PRO, DO 35/893/123/4, 40–43, 'Treatment of the Catholic minority in Northern Ireland', informal British enquiries, 1924 and 1938; Craigavon's dismissal of Nationalist complaints in 1934, *Northern Ireland House of Commons Debates (NIHC)*, vol. 16, 1933–34, cols. 1092–1094.

26 Barritt and Carter, *The Northern Ireland Problem*, 62; NIHC, 16, col. 1091, on a Nationalist motion about discrimination Craigavon declared himself 'an Orangeman first' ahead of his political status.

27 Opsahl Commission, private hearing, 18 February 1993.

28 Whyte, 'Discrimination under the Unionist Regime', 7; Barritt and Carter, *The Northern Ireland Problem*, 98; Gallagher, *The Indivisible Island* (London, 1957), 225–65; as a publicist employed by the Dublin government, Gallagher was able to use the gerrymandering issue to demonise Ulster Unionists in Irish nationalist thinking generally.

29 *Cameron Report*, para. 141.

30 See Hewitt, 'Catholic Grievances, Catholic Nationalism and Violence in Northern Ireland during the Civil Rights Period: a Reconsideration', *British Jn. of Sociology*, 32, 362–80; the subsequent debate between himself and O'Hearn, ibid., 34 (1983), 438–45, 446–51, 36 (1985), 94–101, 102–5; 38 (1987), 88–100; and the critique of both by Kovalcheck, 'Catholic Grievances in Northern Ireland: Appraisal and Judgement', ibid., 38 (1987), 77–87.

31 PRO, DO 35/893/251/6–9, 'Allegations made by Éire Govt. as to the

Maltreatment of the Minority in Northern Ireland, Arising out of the Partition Question', November 1938.

32 Bardon, *History of Ulster*, 591–3; Harkness, *Northern Ireland*, 71.

33 *Cameron Report*, paras. 139–40.

34 Heskin, *Northern Ireland*, 50.

35 Whyte, 'Discrimination under the Unionist Regime', 18; idem, *Interpreting Northern Ireland*, 54–64; Simpson, 'Economic Development: Cause or Effect in the Northern Irish Conflict', in Darby, ed., *Northern Ireland*, 100–107.

36 *Cameron Report*, para. 138; also Gallagher, *Indivisible Island*, 208–9; Barritt and Carter, *Northern Ireland Problem*, 97–8; Whyte, 'Discrimination under the Unionist Regime', 8–9.

37 Shea, *Voices and the Sound of Drums*, 112–13.

38 *Cameron Report*, para. 141.

39 Buckland, *The Factory of Grievances*, 278–9, 280.

40 Arthur, *Government and Politics*, 62–3.

41 Phoenix, ed., *A Century of Northern Life*, 41; Buckland, *Factory of Grievances*, 22.

42 Shea, *Voices and the Sound of Drums*, 113.

43 Ibid., 98, 142 and 197.

44 Ibid., 159; Barritt and Carter, *Northern Ireland Problem*, 96; Buckland, *Factory of Grievances*, 20; Whyte, 'Discrimination under the Unionist Regime', 13; Bew *et al.*, *Northern Ireland*, 57–94.

45 Ultach, 'Orange Terror', 10–15; this pamphlet went through four reprints, August–September 1943. The author was thought to be J. J. Campbell, then a teacher in St Malachy's, Belfast, later head of the Education Department at Queen's University and a BBC Governor.

46 *Fermanagh Times*, 13 July 1933.

47 *NIHC*, 16, cols. 612–19, 20 March 1934.

48 PRO, DO 35/893/123/44: note prepared by Mr Markbreiter for Sir Samuel Hoare, 3 March 1938.

49 PRO, DO 35/893/123/6, 'Treatment of the Catholic Minority in N. Ireland'; also Bowman, *De Valera and Ulster*, 182.

50 *The Autobiography of Terence O'Neill*, 27–9, 40, 47.

51 *Belfast Telegraph*, 17–18 February 1969.

52 *NIHC*, 16, cols. 1086–7.

53 UFTM, Tape R83.25, interview 9 November 1983.

54 Ultach, 'Orange Terror', 24–6; Hepburn, *A Past Apart*, 174–202; Munck and Rolston, *Belfast in the Thirties*, 46–56; Farrell, *Orange State*, 137–42; Jones, 'The Distribution and Segregation of Roman Catholics in Belfast', *Sociological Review*, 4, 174–5, on the increased residential segregation in this period.

55 Mageean's word (Ultach, 'Orange Terror', 24).

56 Harold Jackson, *The Two Irelands*, 10.

57 Richard Rose, *Governing without Consensus: An Irish Perspective*, 272–3.

58 Ultach, 'Orange Terror', 14. Despite the shock-horror title, Ultach is a

moderate nationalist, whose preferred solution is to publicise the plight of Catholics.

59 Dooher, 'Tyrone Nationalism and the Question of Partition, 1910–25', 321–3, 391–2, 420–25, 539.

60 *NICH*, 14, cols. 44–5; Phoenix, *Northern Nationalism*, 369; Kennedy, 'Catholics in Northern Ireland, 1926–1939', in MacManus, ed., *The Years of the Great Test, 1926–39*, 142.

61 See e.g. Dervla Murphy, *A Place Apart*, 76, 125, 126, interviewees' criticism of the Nationalist party for not accepting the state and getting what was rightfully 'theirs' in the early days of partition.

62 *The Irish Weekly*, 5 April 1958.

63 Farrell, *Orange State*, 194–6.

64 Robert Harbinson, *No Surrender*, 16.

65 O Connor, *In Search of a State*, 231.

66 McCluskey, *Up off Their Knees*, 16; O Connor, *In Search of a State*, 149–50; O'Halloran, *Partition and the Limits of Irish Nationalism*, particularly chs. 3 and 5.

67 *Irish News*, 17 November 1932.

68 *NIHC*, 16, col. 1095: 'We are a Protestant Parliament and a Protestant State'. See *BNL*, 13 July 1932 for the earlier speech, also Farrell, *Orange State*, 136.

69 *Irish News*, 19 and 23 November (editorial) 1932.

70 *Ibid.*, 2 July 1953, Alderman McKearney.

71 McCluskey, *Up off Their Knees*, 7.

72 Hayes, *Minority Verdict*, 15.

73 Barritt and Carter, *The Northern Ireland Problem*, 51.

74 Rose, *Governing without Consensus*, 229; McAllister, *The Northern Ireland Social Democratic and Labour Party*, 21.

75 *NIHC*, 16, cols. 1115–1117, Sir Basil Brooke, saying as much in a debate on the 'Rights of the Minority', 24 April 1934.

76 McCracken, 'The Political Scene in Northern Ireland, 1926–1937', in MacManus, ed., *The Years of the Great Test*, 154; Jackson, *The Two Irelands – a Dual Study of Inter-Group Tensions*, Minority Rights Group, Report no. 2, 10.

77 Bell, *The Secret Army: A Story of the IRA 1916–1970*, 156–69; Barritt and Carter, *The Northern Ireland Problem*, 129.

78 Hepburn, *A Past Apart*, 194.

79 Interview in the 1980s with O'Donnell, in Munck and Rolston, *Belfast in the Thirties*, 183–4. See *Irish News*, 28 March 1932: the march was to Milltown cemetery and had been banned by the Minister of Home Affairs. A priest led the marchers as they recited the rosary in Irish. The protest passed off peacefully.

80 Barritt and Carter, *The Northern Ireland Problem*, 133.

81 Bardon's moving description of the blitz, *History of Ulster*, 564–74.

82 Paddy Devlin, *Straight Left: An Autobiography*, 22–9; this dislike for the IRA in the 1940s finds confirmation in Ultach, 'Orange Terror', 45, 53.

83 Bardon, *History of Ulster*, 587–8.

84 My italics – Bell, *Secret Army*, 334; *Irish News*, 27–28 February 1962; *Ulster Herald*, 3 March 1962.

85 *Fermanagh Herald*, 9 March 1957 – Lenten Pastoral.

86 Shea, *Voices and the Sound of Drums*, 160–64.

87 Harkness, *Northern Ireland*, 126–7; Rose, *Governing without Consensus*, 98–9; Arthur, *Government and Politics of Northern Ireland*, 76–7.

88 Interview with McCrystal on BBC Radio Ulster, 4 June 1998.

89 Shea, *Voices and the Sound of Drums*, 183.

90 Arthur, *Government and Politics of Northern Ireland*, 93; Whyte, *Interpreting Northern Ireland*, 75–9; Brian Faulkner, *Memoirs of a Statesman*, 52.

91 Budge and O'Leary, *Approach to Crisis*, 220, 356 and 369.

92 Rose, *Governing Without Consensus*, 522, notes 55 and 61.

93 The final choice of name – Queen Elizabeth Bridge – was better, but only marginally so.

94 O'Neill, *Autobiography*, 114–17.

95 Arthur, *Government and Politics*, 69; Whyte, *Interpreting Northern Ireland*, 151–4, reaches the conclusion that Protestants in the south of Ireland did not suffer active discrimination. However, the rulings of the Catholic Church on the children of 'mixed marriages' did cause long-term decline in numbers; see also Livingstone, *Monaghan Story*, 447, shows discrimination against Protestants in the border areas and very high outward migration.

96 Murphy, *A Place Apart*, 157, 259–62.

97 O'Neill, *Autobiography*, 78–82. There is a sad little picture in the *Autobiography* of O'Neill opening a minor road in the Belfast suburb of Glengormley. Yet even here he had been sought out by placard-waving Paisleyites – the caption 'The Paisleyites in the background are an example of what I had to contend with'.

98 Barritt and Carter, *The Northern Ireland Problem*, 158–9.

99 Arthur, *Government and Politics of Northern Ireland*, 100.

100 McCluskey, *Up off Their Knees*, 19.

101 *Cameron Report*, para. 12.

102 McCluskey, *Up off Their Knees*, 122.

103 Devlin, *Straight Left*, 90–91.

104 The fullest account of the PD is Arthur, *The People's Democracy 1968–1973*; also Purdie, *Politics in the Streets*, 198–243; personal accounts in Bernadette Devlin, *The Price of My Soul*, 99ff. Devlin, *Straight Left*, 93–5; Farrell, *Orange State*, 247ff.

105 Boal and Buchanan, 'The 1969 Northern Ireland Election', *Irish Geography*, vi, 80–83.

106 Bardon, *History of Ulster*, 674.

107 O'Neill, *Autobiography*, 113.

108 *Cameron Report*, para. 127, also 128–47.

109 Gordon, *The O'Neill Years, Unionist Politics 1963–1969*; Bew et al., *Northern Ireland*, 114, 138–9; Devlin, *Straight Left*, 96–101, says much the same; he also found that O'Neill was being bullied by his own party.

110 Murphy, *A Place Apart*, 126 (but also generous tributes from moderate Catholics, pp. 126–67). Bernadette Devlin, *Price of My Soul*, 114, says much the same of O'Neill. Heskin, *Northern Ireland*, 114, substantiates the kind of perverse pride which Paisley evoked even among his opponents, signs of this also in IFC MS 1923/92–3. The above account of the O'Neill era is based on: his *Autobiography*, Faulkner, *Memoirs of a Statesman*, 38–56, Rose, *Governing Without Consensus*, 97–109, Harkness, *Northern Ireland*, 139–57, *Sunday Times* Insight Team, *Ulster*, chs. 3–5; Arthur, *The People's Democracy*, 1968–73, idem, *Government and Politics*, the most balanced analysis of the O'Neill years; personal memories and those of friends and colleagues.

111 The *Sunday Times* Insight Team, *Ulster*, 126ff.

112 Precise figures for such enforced relocation have remained elusive and controversial. Figures for 1969 were prepared for the Scarman Report: *Violence and Civil Disturbances in Northern Ireland in 1969: Report of the Tribunal of Enquiry (Scarman Report)*, 2 vols. (Belfast, 1972), i, 248–9. The Community Relations Commission updated the figures to 1972: Darby and Morris, *Intimidation in Housing*. See Darby, *Intimidation and the Control of Conflict*, 58–98, for an overview; and O Connor, *In Search of a State*, 108, 116, also Morrison, *West Belfast*, 107–14, and Adams, *The Politics of Irish Freedom*, 54, for their place in republican traditions.

113 *Cameron Report*, paras. 213–15.

114 Devlin, *Straight Left*, 127.

115 Maurice Hayes, *Minority Verdict*, 104.

116 'Where Death Stalks the Streets', *Irish News*, 25–29 January 1993; McKeown, *Two Seven Six Three*, 49–54; Burton, *Politics of Legitimacy*, 18–19.

117 Opsahl Commission, 18 February 1993 oral hearings, Argyle Business Centre, Shankill Road, Belfast.

118 McAllister, *Social Democratic and Labour Party*, 56–9, 130–31.

119 Hayes, *Minority Verdict*, 158.

120 Flackes, *Northern Ireland*, 167–8.

121 Devlin, *Straight Left*, 210.

122 Faulkner, *Memoirs of a Statesman*, 262, 271.

123 An opinion poll of March 1974 – just before the collapse of the power-sharing executive – revealed 65 per cent Protestant and 94 per cent Catholic support for the concept of power-sharing (McAllister, *Social Democratic and Labour Party*, 137).

124 Whyte, *Interpreting Northern Ireland*, 74; Arthur, *Government and Politics of Northern Ireland*, 138; Bardon, *History of Ulster*, 746. See Moloney, 'Where are the Provos Going?', in Bell, Johnstone and Wilson, eds., *Troubled Times*, 1983 commentary on the Provos' political threat to the SDLP; also O'Malley, *The Uncivil Wars*, 122–32.

125 Interview with O Connor, *In Search of a State*, 90–91.

126 Faulkner, *Memoirs*, 205, also 104, 110–11, 166–7, 187, 253. He found the Belfast SDLP less 'Dublin-orientated' than its rural (and Derry) supporters

– it was the latter who pushed the Council of Ireland. John Hume he described as 'a formidable political thinker with great personal integrity but a sometimes exasperating dogmatism'.

127 Though see Darby, *Northern Ireland*, 24–5, who suggests that this might be part of moderate mythology about 'the tolerant sixties' and that basic attitudes had not altered.

12 A RESENTFUL BELONGING: CATHOLIC IDENTITY IN THE TWENTIETH CENTURY

1 Breen, Devine, Dowds, eds., *Social Attitudes in Northern Ireland*, 149, also 90–91, 144; Rose, *Governing without Consensus*, 248, 496; *Belfast Telegraph*, 11 December 1992, Barry White's analysis of the 1991 census: 'Experience shows that when someone refuses to declare their religious denomination in a survey, a follow-up question such as "Do you consider yourself Protestant or Catholic?" usually gets a positive response, revealing true allegiance.'

2 Murphy, *A Place Apart*, 163.

3 My thanks to Vivienne Anderson, Director of the North Belfast Community Centre, for this information.

4 Longley, *The Living Stream*, 95.

5 McKittrick, *Independent on Sunday*, 21 March 1993, and follow-up in the *Independent*, 22 March 1993.

6 Opsahl Commission, oral hearings, Belfast 19–20 January and 16–17 February 1993 (particularly communications of Sally McErlean, Kathleen Feenan, Mary Leonard, May Blood, Kathleen Kelly and Geraldine Reagan on conditions in west Belfast); *Social Attitudes in Northern Ireland*, 184; also reports on the changing religious demography of north Belfast in 'Where Death Stalks the Streets', *Irish News*, 25–29 January 1993.

7 The extent to which this is practised was revealed in BBC Radio Ulster's 'Talkback' programme throughout the week beginning 11 January 1999. New regulations against the practice were brought in by government on 1 March 1999, but the views of many interviewed on 'Talkback' that day were that they would be unworkable.

8 Beckett, *A Belfast Woman*, 84–5; Devlin, *Straight Left*, 4, 16; Darby, *Intimidation and the Control of Conflict in Northern Ireland*, ch. 5. Breen *et al.*, eds., *Social Attitudes in Northern Ireland*, 190–91, found such stereotyping of the 'other' also determining job applications, where there was an expectation of discrimination, even though it was never directly experienced. McLaverty, *Call My Brother Back*, 122, reflects on how different Belfast is to Rathlin, where Protestants and Catholics mixed amicably. Boal, 'Territoriality on the Shankill–Falls Divide, Belfast', *Irish Geography*, vi, 30–50. An earlier study, Jones, 'The Distribution and Segregation of Roman Catholics in Belfast', *Sociological Review*, 4, 167–89, traced the segregation through the nineteenth and twentieth centuries.

9 UFTM, R.83/151: interview with Linda Ballard, 30 November 1983.

10 Beckett, *Give Them Stones*, 131. See discussion of this work in Smyth, *The Novel and the Nation*, 135–8.

11 O'Shea, *Voices and the Sound of Drums*, 196.

12 Brewer with Higgins, *Anti-Catholicism in Northern Ireland, 1600–1998*, 156; Clayton, *Enemies and Passing Friends*, 50–83.

13 Parker, *May the Lord in His Mercy be Kind to Belfast*, 331.

14 Linenhall Lib., NI Poll. Coll., P.637, Continuous Household Survey, June 1985.

15 Heskin, *Northern Ireland: A Psychological Analysis*, 28; for other examples of such stereotyping see my 'Religion and Identity in Northern Ireland', in *Global Convulsions*, edited by Van Horne, 149–67, Brewer, *Anti-Catholicism*, 100, and Parker, *May the Lord in His Mercy*, 129–30, 139–40.

16 Initiative '92-Opsahl Commission focus groups in Derry City, Castledawson, Keady, Auchnacloy and Belfast (Shankill Road). These are now in the Linenhall Library, Belfast.

17 Articles 2 and 3 of the Irish constitution were removed in December 1999 under the terms of the 1998 Good Friday Agreement.

18 'In these rural areas, a disproportionate number of the IRA's victims were the only sons of Protestant farmers', Fintan O'Toole, 'The End of the Troubles', *New York Review of Books*, 19 February 1998, 10.

19 White, 'Predicting the Balance', *Belfast Telegraph*, 11 December 1992. See Brewer, *Anti-Catholicism*, 92, for scares and prejudices concerning this issue since the foundation of the state.

20 Brewer, *Anti-Catholicism*, 87–8, 162–3, 234 n.1; Arthur, *Government and Politics of Northern Ireland*, 69.

21 Harris, *Prejudice and Tolerance*, 143–4; Boal, 'Shankill–Falls Divide', 43–7. This seems to have been a very long-running source of dispute, Ó Mórdha, 'The Rising of Burke', 52, details such an incident early in the nineteenth century.

22 Linenhall Lib., NI Pol. Coll. P.666, cheaply printed song-sheet 'Orange Loyalist Songs' (Belfast, 1970). Harris, *Prejudice and Tolerance*, 8, 88–9, 143–4, 171, provides an excellent account of how this ultimate taboo operates, even in communities with otherwise good communal relations.

23 Breen *et al.*, eds., *Social Attitudes in Northern Ireland*, 18–19; Whyte, *Interpreting Northern Ireland*, 40–42.

24 Ultach, 'Orange Terror', 10.

25 *Ibid.*, 23.

26 UFTM, R85.44, taped 1985 interview with Bridget and Brian Murphy of Forkhill, County Armagh, but this was also commonplace in everyday humour prior to the ceasefires.

27 Leo Howe, 'Doing the Double', in Curtin and Wilson, eds., *Ireland from Below*, 144–64; Heskin, *Northern Ireland*, 50, as in so many other areas, Heskin found attitudes to work remarkably similar in both communities.

28 BBC Radio Ulster, 'Talkback', Tuesday 8 January 1991.

29 Frank Burton, *The Politics of Legitimacy*, 187–8 n.43.

30 *The Guardian Weekend*, 3 April 1993; see also Burton's analysis of the importance of reading the sectarian signs correctly, *The Politics of Legitimacy*, 37–67.

31 Harris, *Prejudice and Tolerance*, 143–4; Stringer and Robinson, eds., *Social Attitudes in Northern Ireland: The Second Report*, 146.

32 McCann, *War and an Irish Town*, 81; also McCrystal, *Reflections on a Quiet Rebel*, 80–81; Harris noted such polarisation even in mixed rural schools, *Prejudice and Tolerance*, 137–8.

33 Cited Dunlop, *A Precarious Belonging*, 98–9.

34 I have learnt much of the situation in these Ulster counties which are part of the Irish Republic from conversations with Dr C. J. Woods.

35 McCann, *War in an Irish Town*, 73; Dervla Murphy, *A Place Apart*, 103–11; the best recent account of Protestant sensitivities about Catholic culture is by former Presbyterian moderator John Dunlop, *A Precarious Belonging*, particularly ch. 3.

36 Heskin, *Northern Ireland*, 44–7; Brewer, *Anti-Catholicism*, 124, 130–31.

37 Opsahl Commission, public hearing, Council Offices, Dungannon, 5 February 1993.

38 Tony Parker, *May the Lord in His Mercy*, 136.

39 The words of the psychiatrist John E. Mack, cited in Arthur, '"Reading" Violence: Ireland', in Apter, ed., *The Legitimization of Violence*, 284.

40 O Connor, *In Search of a State*, 123–4; Cardinal Cahal Daly has always been vociferous in his condemnation of the IRA, yet even he saw earlier rebels as more noble, Daly, *The Price of Peace*, 69, though generally denouncing violence, 51–71, 191–3.

41 Murphy, *A Place Apart*, 203–4.

42 Devlin, *Price of My Soul*, 30, 39, 59–69.

43 McCourt, *Angela's Ashes*, e.g. 122, 162; *Irish News*, 2 January 1939 on the enthusiasm with which a rendering of Pearse's Oration over the grave of O'Donovan Rossa was received at the Christian Brothers past pupil association's annual *céilí* in Belfast; personal recollection of its recitation by Belfast nationalists.

44 See e.g. Breen *et al.*, eds., *Social Attitudes in Northern Ireland: the fifth report* (1996), 17.

45 Personal recollections and notes of the Schools Assembly, QUB, 25 February 1993; for a summary see *Citizens' Inquiry: the Opsahl Report on Northern Ireland*, 384–6.

46 O Connor, *In Search of a State*, 246.

47 *Irish News*, 11 November 1932.

48 Jeffrey, 'The Great War in Modern Irish Memory', in Fraser and Jeffery, eds., *Men, Women and War*, 148–51; Clayton, *Enemies and Passing Friends*, 117, 126–7. UFTM, Field Recording Transcripts, vol. 10, p. 71: Mary Sheehy's family were staunch republicans in Derry during World War I, yet she remembered the great sadness at the losses of the Somme.

49 *Irish News*, 9, 19, 20, 27 January, 19 March and 12 April 1932.

50 O Connor, *In Search of a State*, 293; Burton, *Politics of Legitimacy*, 73–4.

51 Dr Paddy McNally, paper read at Conference of Irish Historians in Britain, April 1998.

52 *Irish News*, 14 September 1953, Revd J. Maguire of St Malachy's College, at an open-air mass at Drumnaquoile, Co. Down; also *Irish News*, 20 and 23 February 1932 and *Fermanagh Herald*, 9 March 1957.

53 *Irish Weekly*, 15 March 1958, similar speech opening Strabane parochial carnival, by Revd Hugh Gallagher, *Derry Journal*, 14 July 1959.

54 *Irish News*, 21 June 1932.

55 *Ulster Herald*, 10 March 1962.

56 Moore, *The Emperor of Ice-Cream*, 29. Boal, 'Shankill–Falls Divide', 36, shows a massive 83 per cent readership of the *Irish News* in the Catholic Clonard area of west Belfast, although in Northern Ireland generally by then, British papers and the more neutral *Belfast Telegraph* were overtaking the *Irish News* and *Belfast Newsletter* in popularity, see Darby, *Conflict in Northern Ireland*, 142–3.

57 The words are those of the then Sinn Féin's publicity Director – Danny Morrison – reported in Padraig O'Malley's brilliant and disturbing account of the hunger strikes and their aftermath (on which much of the above account is based), *Biting at the Grave*, 60; see also Paul Arthur's revealing analysis of how the hunger strikes adapted the key concepts of Catholicism to their cause: ' "Reading" Violence', 234–91; Beresford, *Ten Men Dead*, notably 338–44, the Church's role.

58 Murphy, *A Place Apart*, 132.

59 McAllister, in Darby, ed., *Northern Ireland*, 77; Murphy, *A Place Apart*, 93–4, 132; Darby, *Intimidation and the Control of Conflict*, 136–7; Moxon-Browne, *Nation, Class and Creed in Northern Ireland*, 58, attitude survey of 1978 shows Catholics softer on IRA than on loyalist paramilitaries, but see 21–2, for an example of confused thinking; also O Connor, *In Search of a State*, 304, and McElroy, *The Catholic Church and the Northern Ireland Crisis*, 138–40 on the inadequacies of Church thinking on the 'just war' theory. An excellent analysis of violence in nationalist and republican traditions is Arthur, 'Republican Violence in Northern Ireland: the Rationale', in Darby *et. al.*, eds., *Political Violence*, 48–63; Clayton, *Enemies and Passing Friends*, 152–3, on similar ambivalence in Protestant thinking.

60 O Connor, *In Search of a State*, 88–9, interview with Peter O'Hagan, SDLP councillor.

61 Both Arthur, *Government and Politics of Northern Ireland*, 42, and Donnelly, 'Political Identity in Northern Ireland: An Issue for Catholic Theology', *Studies*, vol. 86, no. 343, 242–3, discuss this issue.

62 *Irish News*, 17 and 30 March 1932; Harvey, 'At the Edge of the Union': Derry Newspapers and the Rhetoric of Nationalism, 1937–39', 26.

63 Arthur, 'Republican Violence', 49 and 59; *Irish News*, 28 March 1932, 10 April 1939.

64 *Fermanagh Herald*, 12 January 1957.

65 *Irish News*, 19 April 1958; Harris, 'Catholicism, Nationalism and the Labour Question in Belfast, 1925–38', *Bullán: an Irish Studies Journal*, iii, no. 1, 25.

66 Ó Snodaigh, *Hidden Ulster*, 81.

67 Murphy, *Tyrone Folk Quest*, 67; idem, *Rathlin*, 96; UFTM, R85.249, interview with Mrs Bridget Gilhooley, Mullaghbawn, Co. Armagh, b. 1917, stories from her mother's time about the local priest discouraging Irish; IFC, MS 1360/285 and MS 1215/262–3, similar accounts from North Antrim and Tyrone.

68 UFTM, Collectors Books V-12-3/51, a Ballycarry Protestant's recollections of being taught Irish culture and history in her National school before partition.

69 Hayes, *Black Puddings with Slim*, 244; O Connor, *In Search of a State*, 318–19; also personal experiences in the 1950s and 1960s. Liam Andrews, '"The very dogs in Belfast will bark in Irish." The Unionist Government and the Irish language 1921–43', in Mac Póilin, ed., *The Irish Language in Northern Ireland*, 69.

70 UFTM, Field Recording Transcripts, vol. 16, pp. 4–20: interview 12 May 1976; this claim about the polarising effect of the Troubles also finds endorsement in ibid., vol. 15, p. 171; see also Harvey, 'At the Edge of the Union', 31, for this notion of the '98-type Presbyterians.

71 Opsahl Commission, submission no. 325, summarised in *Citizens' Inquiry*, 341–2.

72 PRONI, CAB 9D/44/1, 1928 correspondence between 'The Loyalty League' and Government – this shows a decline in the numbers of children studying Irish from 5,531 in 1923 to 1,290 in 1927; Andrews, 'Unionist Government and the Irish language 1921–43', 74–6; Harvey, 'At the Edge of the Union', 76, citing Education Minister John Robb's 1943 rebuttal of the Orange Order's attempt to have the Irish language outlawed in the schools, on the grounds that it was 'part of that freedom of the individual for which we profess to be fighting this war'.

73 Mac Póilin, 'Aspects of the Irish Language Movement in Northern Ireland', in Nic Craith, *Watching One's Tongue: Aspects of Romance and Celtic Languages*, 156–9; also O'Reilly, 'Nationalists and the Irish Language in Northern Ireland: Competing Perspectives', in Mac Póilin, ed., *Irish Language in Northern Ireland*, 98–113.

74 *Newry Reporter*, 7 February 1957; UFTM, M3/12, McPeake Transcripts, the renowned traditional musician, Francis McPeake, recalls (1983) family traditions of early Gaelic League activities in Belfast. The language side seems to have been politicised at an early stage, even though he suggests that ordinary people on the Falls Rd (126) would have preferred it otherwise. The music side seems to have attracted much Presbyterian support (this finds endorsement in UFTM, Field Recording Transcripts, vol. 16, pp. 1–20, 1976 interview with the piper Jack O'Rourke).

75 O'Reilly, 'Nationalists and the Irish language in Northern Ireland', 100.

76 The poet Michael Longley recalls as an Arts Council officer being instructed to discontinue the funding to the Conway Education Project in west Belfast. This, together with the more notorious case of the removal of funding from the *Glór na nGael* language group in 1990, he thought short-sighted and

counter-productive (*A Citizen's Inquiry: The Opsahl Report*, 331–2); O'Reilly, 'Nationalists and the Irish Language', 118–27, examines the controversy in some detail, and comes to much the same conclusion.

77 Submission to the Opsahl Commission – *Citizen's Inquiry: The Opsahl Report*, 335. Although there is indeed a strong move elsewhere in the country to remove the GAA ban mentioned here.

78 See *The Agreement*, 19–20, for clauses on the language issue.

79 McCrystal, *Reflections on a Quiet Rebel*, 109–16, 142–6.

80 Devlin, *Price of My Soul*, 60; Loftus, *Mirrors, Orange and Green*, 88.

81 O Connor, *In Search of a State*, 178–9; McCrystal, *Reflections*, also his interview, BBC Radio Ulster, 4 June 1998.

82 May McCann, 'Belfast Ceilidhes', *Ulster Folklife*, 29, 55–105; Bardon, *History of Ulster*, 422–3; UFTM, Field Recording Transcripts, vol. 17, pp. 65–6; IFC, MS 976/203, Mrs Anne Mulholland of Rostrevor, recalling (in 1945) 'house *ceilidhes*': 'They'd only be wee dances of course, for the priest wouldn't allow a big dance. And you wouldn't stay late, for in them times you had to be home to say the Rosary.'

83 Hayes, *Minority Verdict*, 50.

84 Linenhall Lib., NI Political Coll., 'A New Song for Nationalist Heroes', in 'Micí bocht', *Dance to Democracy: A Collection of Broadsides with Insights into Our Present Troubles* (Belfast, n.d.); McCann, 'Belfast Ceilidhes', 64, for the GAA vigilantes.

85 As an articulate team of Tyrone sixth-formers did in their public presentation to the Opsahl Commission, Dungannon, 5 February 1993.

86 Harris, *Prejudice and Tolerance*, 176 (though it should be pointed out that her informant was a hostile source).

87 O Connor, *In Search of a State*, 293.

88 Keogh, *The Vatican, the Bishops and Irish Politics, 1919–39*, 212–15; *Irish News*, 9–20, 27–28 January, 8 February, 17 March 1932. Needless to say, MacRory's comments became part of the Unionists' association of Catholicism and 'disloyalty', see e.g. NIHC, 16, cols. 618 and 1115.

89 Hayes, *Minority Verdict*, 29–30.

90 The words are those of Monsignor Denis Faul (one of the very few senior clergy courageous enough to speak on the issue) to the public hearing of the Opsahl Commission at Dungannon, 5 February 1993; Rogan, *Irish Catechesis*, i, 22–3, shows that by the twentieth century the Irish hierarchy had established a control over education unique in the world, though somewhat similar situations obtained in Scotland, the Netherlands and Quebec.

91 'Submission from the Northern Catholic Bishops on the Consultative Document "Education in Northern Ireland – Proposals for Reform"', news release by the Catholic Press and Information Office, 23 June 1988, p. 3.

92 *Irish News*, 2 May 1953.

93 Murray, *Worlds Apart*, 23; Cardinal Daly's *Irish Times* interview (7 November 1990), in which he did not deny such when asked by the reporter; also McAllister, *Social Democratic and Labour Party*, 136, on reactions to integration proposals of 1974.

94 Breen *et al.*, eds., *Social Attitudes in Northern Ireland: The Fifth Report*, 19–20.

95 Gallagher and Worrall, *Christians in Ulster 1968–1980*, 169, 153–72.

96 Whyte, *Interpreting Northern Ireland*, 47, also 42–8; see also Education section of *A Citizen's Inquiry: the Opsahl Report*, 105–10.

97 Murray, 'Schools and Conflict', in Darby, ed., *Northern Ireland: The Background to the Conflict* (Belfast, 1983), 136–50.

98 Devlin, *Price of My Soul*, 62–70.

99 Barritt and Carter, *Northern Ireland Problem*, 89.

100 See Farren, *The Politics of Irish Education 1920–65*, 24–34.

101 Akenson, *Education and Enmity*, 95, 188 – much of this education section is based on Akenson's findings.

102 Shea, *Voices and the Sound of Drums*, 159–72. Indeed, in 1988 the Northern Ireland bishops paid tribute to 'the harmonious relationship' which had existed between them and the Northern Ireland Ministry of Education (see 'Submission from the Northern Catholic Bishops', op. cit., p. 9).

103 Farren, *Politics of Irish Education*, 49–58.

104 O Connor, *In Search of a State*, 311–14.

105 Murray, *Worlds Apart*, 21; Akenson, *Education and Enmity*, 117, 168.

106 Barritt and Carter, *The Northern Ireland Problem*, 87–8.

107 Murray, *Worlds Apart*, 26–30.

108 Akenson, *Education and Enmity*, 119–24.

109 Titley, *Church, State and the Control of Schooling in Ireland 1900–1944*, 106, 119, 132.

110 Harris, 'Catholicism, Nationalism and the Labour Question in Belfast, 1925–38', *Bullán: An Irish Studies journal*, iii, 17; Rafferty, *Catholicism in Ulster*, 248.

111 Akenson, *Education and Enmity*, 169; Farren, *Politics of Irish Education*, 167. Not all higher clergy were utterly opposed to state social welfare, notably Monsignor Arthur Ryan of Belfast (a professor at Queen's University) and the future bishop of Down and Connor, William Philbin (Whyte, *Church and State*, 272, also Hayes, *Minority Verdict*, 315 on Ryan); see Lee, *Ireland 1912–1985*, 318–19 for a reassessment of the hierarchy's role in the 'Mother and Child' episode.

112 UFTM, R83.135, Fred Heatley's memories of working-class Belfast in the 1940s: areas where the women did not work seemed to mark them out as 'decent working-class' areas; Harvey, 'At the Edge of the Union', 19–20.

113 Munck and Rolston, *Belfast in the Thirties*, 82–3.

114 Barritt and Carter, *Northern Ireland Problem*, 109–19; *Irish News*, 24 April 1953; Whyte, *Church and State in Modern Ireland 1923–1970*, 149–50.

115 Devlin, *Price of My Soul*, 63; also Farren, *Politics of Irish Education*, 89.

116 McCann, *War and an Irish Town*, 74.

117 Harris, *Prejudice and Tolerance*; 130, Hayes, *Sweet Killough*, 197; idem, *Black Puddings*, 154; idem, *Minority Verdict*, 117, 93–4.

118 Hayes, *Minority Verdict*, 117.

119 Rogan, *Synods and Catechesis in Ireland*, 436, 442, also 326–32, 431.

120 O Connor, *In Search of a State*, 314–17.

121 See also very good discussions of Moore's work in Norman Vance, 'Catholic and Protestant Literary Visions of "Ulster": Now You See It, Now You Don't', in *Religion and Literature*, 28, 134–6 and Sullivan, *A Matter of Faith: The Fiction of Brian Moore*.

122 Hayes, *Black Puddings*, 49, 102–4.

123 McCann, *War and an Irish Town*, 69–70.

124 Hayes, *Black Puddings with Slim*, 153–4; idem, *Sweet Killough*, 14–15, 186; Devlin, *Straight Left*, 3–4; O Connor, *In Search of a State*, 278.

125 Harvey, 'At the Edge of the Union', 35.

126 *Irish News*, 9 January 1939 and 23 January 1962, Bishop O'Kane's funeral in January 1939, and Dr Mageean's in 1962; also *Irish News*, 28 June and 5 July 1958, and Rafferty, *Catholicism in Ulster*, 236, 245–6, for the 1958, 1947 and 1934 references.

127 *Irish News*, 21 June 1932; every issue in June carries reports and there had been a build-up of preparation since the beginning of the year.

128 McElroy, *The Catholic Church and the Northern Ireland Crisis*, 144–5. The subsequent account relies heavily on this very interesting book.

129 O'Malley, *Biting at the Grave*, 173–8.

130 See e.g. Faul and Murray, *The Alienation of Northern Catholics*.

131 O Connor, *In Search of a State*, 172–4; Rafferty, *Catholicism in Ulster*, 275–81; David Beresford, *Ten Men Dead*, 178–91, 218–19, for Ó Fiaich's role in the hunger strikes and the dilemma of the Church.

132 Barritt and Carter, *Northern Ireland Problem*, 117–19.

133 Darby, *Intimidation and the Control of Conflict in Northern Ireland*, 111, also pp. 109–11, 121–2, 155–6; Burton, *Politics of Legitimacy*, 93–104, for a similar heart and minds battle in Ardoyne. However, for concern also within the Church that it was assuming a role better left to lay people see Lennon, *After the Ceasefires*, 97.

134 Except by the ever-impressive O Connor, *In Search of a State*, 282; also Dara O'Hagan, 'Sinn Féin and the Catholic Church', 17, 134–8, 142–59, also 194–5, on a general softening of relationships between republicans and the church since the 1994 ceasefire.

135 *A Citizen's Inquiry. The Opsahl Report*, 340.

136 There is an excellent overview of recent research into Catholic religious sisters in Ireland in Margaret MacCurtain, 'Late in the Field: Catholic Sisters in Twentieth-Century Ireland and the new Religious History', *Journal of Women's History*, 6–7, 49–63. This also highlights the struggle of female religious within the Catholic Church.

137 *A Citizen's Inquiry. The Opsahl Report*, 96.

138 See Moxon-Browne, *Nation, Class and Creed*, 49–51, useful survey of reforms since 1970; BBC Radio Ulster, 'Talkback', 12 January 1999, reporting the large increase in Catholic applications to the RUC since the Good Friday Agreement.

139 Longley, *The Living Stream*, 88–9.

140 Deane, *Reading in the Dark*, 231–2.

141 Beckett, *Give Them Stones*, 119, 130–31.

142 There is a good survey of Troubles writing in Michael Parker, *The Hurt World*, 1–8.

143 Arthur, ' "Reading" Violence', 282; for this concentration of violence in Catholic areas, both rural and urban. Michael Poole, 'The Geographical Location of Political Violence in Northern Ireland', in Darby *et al.*, *Political Violence*, 64–82, also shows Armagh top of the league.

144 *Citizen's Inquiry: The Opsahl Report*, 421.

145 See the interesting collection of papers to the 1995 conference: 'Beyond 2000 for Northern Ireland', published by the Jigsa Group in 1998 – notably those by Paddy Doherty and Michael Smyth. The extraordinary bitterness of much of Catholic historiography is exemplified in the otherwise excellent local history of Tyrone, *Domhnach Mór*, written in 1963, in which there are only two overarching themes, 'dispossession' and 'the Church'. It also characterises the work of the otherwise respected folklorist Michael J. Murphy, the most important collector and compiler for the Ulster section of the Irish Folklore Commission in Dublin.

146 Glassie, *Ballymenone*, 639.

147 There is an excellent overview of recent opinion in Joseph Ruane and Jennifer Todd, eds., *After the Good Friday Agreement: Analysing Political Change in Northern Ireland* (Dublin, 1999), notably the essay by Bernadette C. Hayes and Ian McAllister, 'Ethnonationalism, Public Opinion and the Good Friday Agreement', 30–48.

Select Bibliography

PRIMARY

Northern Ireland

Linenhall Library

Joy MSS
Broadside Collection
N.I. Political Collection
Opsahl Commission papers (originals in possession of the author)

Queen's University, Belfast

Gaelic Manuscripts 17: Mic A/428 (xviii), 'An essay on Séamus Mac Cuarta'

Public Record Office of Northern Ireland

Ant 4/1/1: Antrim Grand Jury presentment books, 1711–21
CAB 9D: N.I. Ministry of Education
D.272: McCance Collection
D.605: Survey of Col. Mervyne Archdal's estate, Co. Fermanagh, 1720
D.607: Downshire MSS
D.627: Family and estate papers of the Montgomery family, Blessingbourne,
    Co. Tyrone, 1880–94
D.1375: McGildowny Papers
D.1514: Hervey-Bruce Papers
D.2714/5H1: General notes on Viscount Magennis of Iveagh
D.2918: Whyte Papers
DIO (RC)/1: Clogher Diocesan Papers.
Mic.147/9: Papers and correspondence of the Roden family, Newcastle, Co.
    Down
T.808/14895–6:Tennison Groves Abstracts of the County Antrim assizes and
    quarter sessions
T.808/15261: 1744 Committee on Religion

T.1392: Memorial of the proprietors of the Fews, 2 Dec. 1743
T.2541: Abercorn MSS
T.3022/4/2A-C: Cromwellian Inquisition taken in the town and county of
    Antrim, 1657.

Ulster Folk and Transport Museum

Collectors' Books
Field Recordings, transcripts
Schools Text-Book Collection
Sound recordings (taped interviews), R83–90
M3 12: McPeake Transcripts

Republic of Ireland

Irish Folklore Commission, University College, Dublin

Collectors' books, vols. 57, 89, 102, 105, 270, 975–6, 1033, 1057, 1112–13,
    1215–17, 1359–60, 1364–5, 1386–7, 1483, 1844, 1922–6, 2034–5,
    2037–8, 2080–82, 2094, 2099, 2104, 2176

National Archives of Ireland

State of the Country Papers
Rebellion Papers, 620/1–67

National Library of Ireland

T.1898: Catholic Qualification Rolls, 1778–90
Pos. 1899: Index to the Catholic Qualification Rolls, Ulster, 1793–6
MS G.200(b): *Ollamh éigin. An Revolution. The French Revolution. By an
    uncertain author*

Royal Irish Academy

Ordinance Survey Letters

England

Public Record Office

HO 100/38, 42–4, 87, 62–4: Home Office Papers
DO 35/893/123: 'Treatment of the Catholic minority in Northern Ireland',
    1924, 1938

Centre for Kentish Studies

U840 Pratt Mss

PRINTED PRIMARY

Newspapers and periodicals

An Phoblacht. Republican News
Belfast News Letter
Belfast Telegraph
Derry Journal
Fermanagh Herald
Fermanagh Times
Fortnight Magazine
Guardian
Irish News
Irish Weekly
Newry Reporter
Northern Star
Ulster Herald

Official reports and papers (by date)

Cal.S.P.Ireland, 1598–1670
[David Bindon], *An Abstract of the Number of Protestant and Popish Families in the Several Counties and Provinces of Ireland taken from the Returns Made by the Hearth-money Collectors . . . in the Years 1732 and 1733* (Dublin, 1736)
The Parliamentary Register, or, History of the Proceedings and Debates of the House of Commons of Ireland, 1781–97, 17 vols. (Dublin, 1782–1801)
Report from the Committee of Secrecy of the House of Commons of Ireland (Dublin, 1798) – also reproducing 1793 and 1797 secret committee reports
Memorial of Prisoners Charged with Murder at Macken, H.C.1830 (150) xxvi, 301
Third Report from the Select Committee . . . [on] Orange Lodges, H.C.1835 (476) xvi,1
Papers Relating to the Investigation Held at Castlewellan into the Occurrences at Dolly's Brae, on the 12th July, 1849, H.C.1850 [1143] li, 331
Return of Number of Murders and Waylayings in the Baronies of Upper and Lower Fews, in County Armagh, 1844–50, H.C.1850 [566] li, 517

Report from the Lord Lieutenant . . . Proclaiming of a District in the County of Down, H.C.1851 (250) l, 435

Return of Numbers of Murders, Waylayings . . . or Other Crimes of Agrarian Character . . . Louth, Armagh and Monaghan, 1849–52, H.C.1852 (448) xlvii, 465–75

Report . . . into Conduct of Constabulary during Disturbances at Belfast, July and Sept. 1857, H.C.1857–8 (333) xlvii, 781

Royal Commission of Inquiry into . . . Riots in Belfast, July and Sept. 1857, H.C.1857–8[2309], xxvi, 1

Report on the Derryveagh Evictions, H.C.1861 (316), lii, 539–79

Notes of Trials at Armagh, Arising out of Riots at Derrymacash, H.C.1861 (315), lii,1

Papers relating to Donaghmore Riot, with Report of Commission . . . into Conduct of Justices of the Peace . . . at Dungannon, Oct. 1866, H.C.1867 [3906], lix,191

Royal Commission of Inquiry into Riots and Disturbances in the City of Londonderry, H.C. 1870 [C.5*] xxxii, 411

Royal Commission of Inquiry into Disturbances in the City of Londonderry, Nov. 1883, H.C.1884 [C.3954] xxxviii, 515

Correspondence Relating to the Action of Certain Magistrates . . . at Londonderry, Nov.1883, H.C.1884[C.4010] lxiii, 491

Correspondence between the Lord Chancellor of Ireland and R. McClintock, in Reference to His Conduct as a Magistrate . . . Mar. 1884, H.C. 1884 [C.5057] lxiii

Reports into other Orange meetings: H.C. 1884 [C.4065] lxiii, 517 and 527 (Newry); H.C. 1884 (95) lxiii, 461 (Dromore, Tyrone); H.C. 1884 [C.3891] lxiii, 547 (Rosslea, Fermanagh – also on magistrates in Monaghan and Cavan)

Correspondence and Reports Relating to the Removal of Lord Rossmore, H.C. 1884 [C.3891] lxiii, 547

Belfast Riots Commission, H.C.1887 [C.4925] [C.4925-I], xviii, 1, 25; [C.5029], xviii, 631

Northern Ireland House of Commons Debates, 1932–4

Disturbances in Northern Ireland: Report of the Commission Appointed by the Governor of Northern Ireland (Cameron Report), (Belfast, 1969)

Violence and Civil Disturbances in Northern Ireland in 1969: Report of the Tribunal of Enquiry (Scarman Report), 2 vols. (Belfast, 1972)

The Agreement: Agreement Reached in the Multi-party Negotiations [so-called Good Friday Agreement] (1998)

We Will Remember Them. Report of the Northern Ireland Victims Commissioner Sir Kenneth Bloomfield, KCB (April 1998)

Contemporary printed works

A. F. O'D. Alexander, ed., 'The O'Kane Papers. Bishop Montgomery's Survey of the Bishoprics of Derry, Raphoe and Clogher', *Anal. Hib.*, xii (1943), 67–127

'A List of Regulars Registered in Ireland Pursuant to the Catholic Relief Act of 1829', *Archiv. Hib.*, iii (1914), 34–86

An Account of the Bloody Massacre in Ireland . . . (London, 1678)

Annála Uladh: Annals of Ulster, edited by W.M. Hennessy, 4 vols. (Dublin, 1887–1901)

Annals of the Kingdom of Ireland by the Four Masters, from the Earliest Period to the Year 1616, edited and translated by John O'Donovan, 7 vols. (Dublin, 1851)

Robert Ashton, *The Battle of Aughrim, or the Fall of Monsieur St. Ruth. A Tragedy* (Dublin, 1756)

Thomas Bartlett, 'Select Documents: Defenders and Defenderism in 1795', *I.H.S.,* xxiv (1985), 373–94

Beauties of the Press (Dublin, 1800)

'Bodley's Visit to Lecale, County of Down, A.D. 1602–3', *U.J.A.,* ii (1854), 73–99

Revd Canon Ulick J. Bourke, ed., *Sermons in Irish-Gaelic by the Most Rev. James O'Gallagher* (Dublin, 1877)

John Brady, *Catholics and Catholicism in the Eighteenth-Century Press* (Maynooth, 1965)

J. S. Brewer and W. Bullen, eds., *Calendar of the Carew Manuscripts Preserved in the Archiepiscopal Library at Lambeth,* 6 vols. (London, 1867–73)

Cornelius G. Buttimer, 'An Irish Text on the "War of Jenkins' Ear"', *Celtica,* xxi (1990), 75–98

Michael J. Byrne, ed., *The Irish War of Defence, 1598–1600: Extracts from De Hibernia Insula Commentarius of Peter Lombard, Archbishop of Armagh* (Cork, 1930)

— *Ireland under Elizabeth* . . . *Being a Portion of the History of Catholic Ireland by Don Philip O'Sullivan Bear* (Dublin, 1903)

Edward Campion, *A Historie of Ireland Written in the Yeare 1571,* in James Ware, ed., *Ancient Irish Histories: The Works of Spencer, Campion, Hanmer, and Marleburrough,* 2 vols. (Dublin, 1809)

A Candid and Impartial Account of the Disturbances in the County of Meath, in the Years 1792, 1793, and 1794. By a County Meath Freeholder (Dublin, 1794)

Nicholas Canny, ed., 'Rowland White's "The Dysorders of the Irishery, 1571"', *Stud. Hib.,* xix (1979), 147–60

Charlemont MSS. The Manuscripts and Correspondence of James, First Earl of Charlemont, HMC, 12th report, append pt. 10 and 13th report, append pt. 8, 2 vols., (London, 1891–4)

D. A. Chart, ed., *The Drennan Letters* (Belfast, 1931)

The Christian Brothers, *Irish History Reader* (Dublin, 1905)

A Collection of Certain Horrid Murthers in Several Counties of Ireland Committed since 23 October 1641 (London, 1641)

A Concise Account of the Material Events and Atrocities, Which Occurred in the Present Rebellion, by 'Verdicus' (Dublin, 1799)

Revd James Connolly, *What Mean These Stones: A Sermon Preached in the Church of St Mary Belfast, on the Occasion of the Centenary on Sunday, November 11th (1883)* (London, 1883)

Charles Coote, *Statistical Survey of County Armagh* (Dublin, 1804)

— *Statistical Survey of the County of Monaghan* (Dublin, 1801)

Patrick J. Corish, ed., 'Two Reports on the Catholic Church in Ireland in the Early Seventeenth Century', *Archiv. Hib.*, xxii (1959), 140–62

M. A. Costello, *De Annatis Hiberniae: A Calendar of the First Fruits Fees Levied on Papal Appointments to Benefices in Ireland, 1400–1535* (Dublin, 1912)

W. H. Crawford and B. Trainor, eds., *Aspects of Irish Social History, 1750–1800* (Belfast, 1969)

Revd Séamus Creighton, 'The Penal Laws in Ireland and the Documents in the Archives of Propaganda (1690–1731)', *Procs. Irish Cath. Hist. Committee* (1961), 5–9

Sir John Davies, 'A Discovery of the True Causes Why Ireland was Never Entirely Subdued', in H. Morley, ed., *Ireland under Elizabeth and James I* (London, 1890)

Angélique Day, ed, *Letters from Georgian Ireland: the Correspondence of Mary Delaney 1731–68* (Belfast, 1991)

Angélique Day and Patrick McWilliams, eds., *Ordnance Survey Memoirs of Ireland*, 40 vols. (Belfast 1990–98)

Seamus Deane, ed., *The Field Day Anthology of Irish Writing*, 3 vols. (Derry, 1991)

John Derricke, *The Image of Irelande* (Edinburgh, 1883)

William Steel Dickson, *A Narrative of the Confinement and Exile of William Steel Dickson, D.D.* (Dublin, 1812)

The Distress'd State of Ireland Considered; More Particularly with Respect to the North. In a Letter to a Friend ([Dublin], 1740)

John Dubourdieu, *Statistical Survey of the County of Antrim* (Dublin, 1812)

Robert Dunlop, ed., *Ireland under the Commonwealth: Being a Selecion of Documents Relating to the Government of Ireland, 1651–9*, 2 vols. (Manchester, 1913)

R. D. Edwards, ed., 'The Minute Book of the Catholic Committee, 1773–92', *Archiv. Hib.*, ix (1942), 1–172

Patrick Fagan, ed., *Ireland in the Stuart Papers: Correspondence and Documents of Irish Interest from the Stuart Papers in the Royal Archives, Windsor Castle*, 2 vols., (Dublin, 1995)

C. Litton Falkiner, *Illustrations of Irish History and Topography* (London, 1904)

Hugh Fenning, ed., *The Fottrell Papers, 1721–39* (Belfast, 1980)

Revd P. J. Flanagan, 'The Diocese of Clogher in 1714', *Clogher Record*, i (1954), 39–42, 125–30

John H. Gebbie, ed., *An Introduction to the Abercorn Letters* (Omagh, 1972)

Gerald of Wales (Giraldus Cambrensis), *The History and Topography of Ireland*, translated by John O'Meara (Harmondsworth, 1988)

Cathaldus Giblin, ed., 'Catalogue of Material of Irish Interest in the Collection *Nunziatura di Fiandra*', Vatican Archives: Part I, vols. 1–50, *Coll. Hib.*, i (1958), 7–136; Part 4, vols. 102–122, *Coll. Hib.*, v (1962), 7–125

J. T. Gilbert, ed., *A Contemporary History of Affairs in Ireland from A.D. 1641 to 1652 Containing the . . . Narrative Entitled an 'Aphorismical Discovery of Treasonable Faction'*, 3 vols. (Dublin 1879–80)

William Gillies, 'A Poem on the Downfall of the Gaodhil', *Éigse*, 13 (1969–70), 203–10

Mrs Stephen Gwynn, *Stories from Irish History* (Dublin and Belfast, 1920)

John Hagan, ed., 'Miscellanea Vaticano-Hibernica', *Archiv. Hib.*, iii (1914), 227–365; iv (1915), 215–318; v (1916), 74–185; vi (1917), 94–155; vii (1918–21), 67–356

Revd W. Hamilton, *Letters Concerning the Northern Coast of the County of Antrim* (Belfast, 1822)

John Hanly, ed.,*The Letters of Saint Oliver Plunkett* (Dublin, 1979)

William Harris, *The Ancient and Present State of the County of Down* (Dublin, 1744)

— *Translation of the Works of Sir James Ware* (Dublin, 1739)

George Hill, ed., *The Montgomery Manuscripts (1603–1706): Compiled from the Family Papers by William Montgomery of Rosemount Esquire* (Belfast,1869)

Herbert F. Hore, ed., 'Marshal Bagenal's Description of Ulster, Anno 1596', *U. J. A.*, 1st ser., ii (1854), 153–4

T. B. and T. J. Howell, eds., *A Complete Collection of State Trials*, 33 vols. (London, 1809–28)

Francis Hutchinson, *A Defence of the Antient Historians: with a Particular Application of It to the History of Ireland* (Dublin, 1734)

Irish Catholic Directory, 1932–79

'Irish Catholics Licensed to Keep Arms (1704)', *Archiv. Hib.*, iv (1915), 59–65

H. Jones, *A Remonstrance of Divers Remarkable Passages Concerning the Church and Kingdome of Ireland* (London, 1641)

Geoffrey Keating, *Foras Feasa ar Éirinn, the History of Ireland*, edited by D. Comyn and P.S. Dineen (Dublin, 1987)

John Lawless, *The Belfast Politics, Enlarged; Being a Compendium of the Political History of Ireland for the Last Forty Years* (Belfast, 1818)

Les Martyrs de la Province Dominicaine d'Irlande (Paris, 1890)

A. G. Little, ed., *Liber Exemplorum* (n.p., 1908)

[John Lodge], ed., *Desiderata Curiosa Hibernica, or, a Select Collection of State Papers*, 2 vols. (Dublin, 1772)

Marquess of Londonderry, ed., *Memoirs and Correspondence of Viscount Castlereagh*, 12 vols. (London, 1848–54)

John Lynch, *Cambrensis Eversus*, edited by Matthew Kelly, 3 vols. (Dublin, 1848–52)

James MacCaffrey, ed., 'Commonwealth Records', *Archiv. Hib.*, vi (1917), 175–202; vii (1918–21), 20–66

G. B. McKenna [Fr John Hassan – curate of St. Mary's], *Facts and Figures of the Belfast Pogrom 1920–1922* (Dublin, 1922)

W. J. MacNeven, *Pieces of Irish History* (New York, 1807)

James McParlan, *Statistical Survey of the County of Donegal* (Dublin, 1802)

Francis McPolin, 'An Old Irish Catechism from Oriel', *Ir. Eccles. Rec.* (1947), 509–17

Samuel McSkimin, *Annals of Ulster from 1790–1798*, new edn. by E. J. McCrum (Belfast, 1906)

Dr Nicholas Madgett, 'Constitutio ecclesiastica', edited by Michael Manning, *Kerry Arch. Soc. Jn.*, ix (1976), 68–91

Cuthbert Mhág Craith, *Dán na mBráthar Mionúr* (Dublin, 1980)

Henry Joseph Monck Mason, *The Testimony of St Patrick against the False Pretensions of Rome to Primitive Antiquity in Ireland* (Dublin, 1846)

W. Shaw Mason, *A Statistical Account, or Parochial Survey of Ireland*, 3 vols. (Dublin, 1814)

C. Maxwell, *Irish History from Contemporary Sources, 1509–1610* (London, 1923)

Benignus Millet, O.F.M., 'Archbishop Edmund O'Reilly's Report on the State of the Church in Ireland, 1662', *Coll. Hib.*, ii (1959), 105–14

T. W. Moody, ed., 'Ulster Plantation Papers, 1608–13', *Anal. Hib.*, no. 8 (1938), 179–298

P. F. Moran, *Spicilegium Ossoriense, Being a Collection of Original Letters and Papers Illustrative of the History of the Irish Church from the Reformation to the Year 1800*, 3 vols. (Dublin, 1874)

— ed., *The Analecta of David Rothe, Bishop of Ossory* (Dublin, 1884)

Henry Morley, ed., *Ireland under Elizabeth and James I* (London, 1809)

Fynes Moryson, *An Itinerary*, new edition, 4 vols. (Glasgow, 1907–8)

Revd L.P. Murray, 'Three Documents Concerning the Deanery of Dundalk during the Eighteenth Century', *Archiv. Hib.*, v (1916), 39–73

— 'Archbishop Cromer's Register', *Louth Arch. Soc. Jn.*, vii (1929–32), 516–24; viii (1933–6), 38–49, 169–88, 322–51; ix (1937–40), 36–41, 124–30

— 'The History of the Parish of Creggan, *Louth Arch. Soc. Jn.*, viii (1933–6), 117–63; ix (1937–40), 135–61

— 'The Last Abbot of Mellifont', *Louth Arch. Soc. Jn.*, viii (1933–6), 223–33

Richard Musgrave, *Memoirs of the Different Rebellions in Ireland*, second edition (Dublin, 1801)

John Edward Newell, *The Apostasy of Newell* (London, 1798)

Eileen O'Byrne, ed., *The Convert Rolls* (Dublin, 1981)

Sean Ó Domhnaill, 'County Donegal in the Catholic Qualification Rolls, 1778–1790', Co. Donegal Hist. Soc. Jn., i (1949), 204–5

Comhairle Mhic Clamha ó Achadh na Muilleann: The Advice of MacClave from Aughnamullen, translated by S. Ó Dufaigh and Brian Rainey (Lille, 1981)

Tomás Ó Fiaich, 'The 1766 Religious Census', Seanchas Ard Mhacha, iv (1960–62), 147–70

P. Ó Gallachair, '1622 Survey of Cavan', Breifne, i (1958), 60–75

— 'Catholic Qualification Rolls Index: Fermanagh and Monaghan', Clogher Record, ii (1959), 544–51

W. M. O'Hanlon, Walks among the Poor of Belfast (Belfast, 1853)

'The O'Kane Papers' presented by A.F. O'D. Alexander, Anal. Hib., xii (1943), 79–111

Cainneach Ó Maonaigh O.F.M., ed., Seanmónta Chúige Uladh (Dublin, 1965)

— ed., Smaointe Beatha Chríost (Dublin, 1944)

Réamonn Ó Muirí, ed., Lámhscríbhinn Staire an Bhionadaigh: Comhrac nGael agus na nGall le Chéile [Bennett's historical manuscript: the conflict of the Gaeil and Gaill with each other], (Monaghan, 1994)

Thomas F. O'Rahilly, ed., Desiderius, Otherwise Called Sgáthán an Chrábaidh, by Flaithrí Ó Maolchonaire, 1616 (Dublin, 1941)

J. P. O'Reilly, 'Remarks on Certain Passages in Capt. Cuellar's Narrative of His Adventures in Ireland ... 1588–89', Proc. R.I.A., iii (1893–6), 175–217

Adolphe Perraud, Ireland under English Rule (Dublin, 1864)

F. Plowden, An Historical Review of the State of Ireland, 5 vols. (Philadelphia, 1806)

Revd James Pulleine D.D., An Teagasg Críosaidhe Angoidhleig (1748 and 1782)

L. F. Renehan, Collections on Irish Church History, 2 vols. (Dublin,1861–74)

Revd William Reeves, ed., Acts of Archbishop Colton in his Metropolitan Visitation of the Diocese of Derry (Dublin, 1850)

— ed., 'The Irish Itinerary of Father Edmund MacCana',U.J.A., ser.1., vol. ii (1854), 44–59

Hugh Reily, The Impartial History of Ireland (London, 1754; first printed Louvain, 1695)

Report of the Lough Foyle Fishery Case of Allen v. Donnelly and Others Tried at the Tyrone Spring Assizes at Omagh, 1856 ... Reported by W. McLaughlin, Londonderry Standard Office (London, 1857)

'Report on the State of Popery in Ireland, 1731', Archiv. Hib., i (1912), 10–27 (for Ulster); for the rest of the country: ii (1913), 108–56, iii (1914), 124–59, and iv (1915), 131–77

John Richardson, A Proposal for the Conversion of the Popish Natives of Ireland to the Established Religion (London, 1711)

— A Short History of Attempts That Have Been Made ... To Convert the Popish Inhabitants of Ireland (London, 1712)

E. Rogan, *Synods and Catechesis in Ireland, c. 445–1962*, 2 vols. (Rome, 1987)

C. W. Russell and J.P. Prendergast, eds., *The Carte Manuscripts in the Bodleian Library, Oxford* (London, 1871)

Revd G. Vaughan Sampson, *Statistical Survey of the County of Londonderry* (1802)

[W. Shankill], *The Belfast Riots, 1886: The Islandmen and Shankill Road Defended* (Belfast, 1886)

E. P. Shirley, ed., *Original Letters and Papers in Illustration of the History of the Church in Ireland* (London, 1851)

Sources for the Study of Local History in Northern Ireland. Northern Ireland Public Record Office: a catalogue for an exhibition (January–July 1968)

Edmund Spenser, *A View of the State of Ireland* [1596], in James Ware, ed., *Ancient Irish Histories: The Works of Spencer, Campion, Hanmer, and Marleburrough*, 2 vols. (Dublin, 1809)

[George Story], *A True and Impartial History of the Most Material Occurrences in the Kingdom of Ireland during the Two Last Years* (London, 1691)

'Submission from the Northern Catholic Bishops on the Consultative Document "Education in Northern Ireland – Proposals for Reform" ', news release by the Catholic Press and Information Office, 23 June 1988

Edward Synge, *The Case of Toleration Considered with Respect Both to Religion and Civil Government* (Dublin, 1726)

Charles Hamilton Teeling, *Observations on the 'History and Consequences' of the 'Battle of the Diamond'* (Belfast, 1838)

— *History of the Irish Rebellion of 1798* and *Sequel to the History of the Irish Rebellion of 1798* (Shannon, 1972, reprint of 1876 edition)

A Test of Roman Catholic Liberality, Submitted to the Consideration of Both Roman Catholicks and Protestants. By a Citizen of London-Derry (Londonderry, 1792)

Ultach, 'Orange Terror: The Partition of Ireland', reprinted from *The Capuchin Annual* (1943)

James Ussher, *An Epistle Written by the Rev. James Ussher, Bishop of Meath, Concerning the Religion Anciently Professed by the Irish and Scottish* (Dublin, 1631)

A View of the Present State of Ireland . . . by an Observer (n.p., 1797)

Reginald Walsh, O.P., 'The Memorial Presented to the King of Spain on Behalf of the Irish Catholics, A.D. 1619', *Archiv. Hib.*, vi (1917), 27–54

Fr Luke Walsh, *The Home Mission Unmasked* (Belfast, 1844)

N. J. A. Williams, ed., *Pairlement Chloinne Tomáis* (Dublin, 1981)

C. J. Woods, *Journals and Memoirs of Thomas Russell* (Dublin, 1991)

Georges-Denis Zimmermann, *Songs of Irish Rebellion: Political Street Ballads and Rebel Songs, 1780–1900* (Dublin, 1967)

Memoirs and Autobiography

Gerry Adams, *The Politics of Irish Freedom* (Dingle, 1986)

William Carleton, *Autobiography* (London, 1968)

Bernadette Devlin, *The Price of My Soul* (London, 1969)

Paddy Devlin, *Straight Left: An Autobiography* (Belfast, 1993)

Lynn Doyle, *An Ulster Childhood*, (Belfast, 1985, facsimile of 1926 edition)

Charles Gavan Duffy, *My Life in Two Hemispheres*, 2 vols. (London, 1898)

Brian Faulkner, *Memoirs of a Statesman* (London, 1978)

Paddy [the Cope] Gallagher, *My Story* (London, 1939)

Robert Harbinson, *No Surrender: An Ulster Childhood* (Belfast, 1987, reprint of 1960 first edition)

Maurice Hayes, *Sweet Killough: Let Go Your Anchor* (Belfast, 1994)

— *Minority Verdict: Experiences of a Catholic Public Servant* (Belfast, 1995)

— *Black Puddings with Slim: A Downpatrick Boyhood* (Belfast, 1996)

Eamonn McCann, *War and an Irish Town* (London, 1993)

Conn McCluskey, *Up off Their Knees: A Commentary on the Civil Rights Movement in Northern Ireland* (Galway, 1989)

Cal McCrystal, *Reflections on a Quiet Rebel* (Harmondsworth, 1998)

Patrick MacGill, *Children of the Dead End: The Autobiography of a Navvy* (London, 1985, reprint of 1914 original)

Charles McGlinchy, *The Last of the Name* (Belfast, 1989, reprint of 1986 edition)

Michael MacGowan, *The Hard Road to Klondike* (London, 1962)

Seamas MacManus, *The Rocky Road to Dublin* (New York, 1947)

Terence O'Neill, *The Autobiography of Terence O'Neill* (London, 1972)

Patrick Shea, *Voices and the Sound of Drums: An Irish Autobiography* (Belfast, 1981)

Samuel Simms, ed., *Rev. James O'Coigley, United Irishman* (Belfast, 1937)

William T. W. Tone, ed., *The Life of Theobald Wolfe Tone*, 2 vols. (Washington, 1826). (However, the most authoritative edition of Tone's writings is now T.W. Moody, R.B. McDowell and C.J. Woods, eds., *The Writings of Theobald Wolfe Tone, 1763–98,* 3 vols. (Oxford, 1998–) – only vol. i published to date.)

Fiction and poetry

Colm Beckett, ed., *Aodh Mac Domhnaill: Dánta* (Dublin, 1987)

Mary Beckett, *A Belfast Woman* (Dublin, 1987)

— *Give Them Stones* (London, 1991, reprint of 1987 edition)

Osbert Bergin, *Irish Bardic Poetry* (Dublin, 1970)

Shan Bullock, *Dan the Dollar* (Dublin, 1906)

William Carleton, *Traits and Stories of the Irish Peasantry*, 2 vols. (Gerrards Cross, 1990, reprint of 1844–5 edition)

— *Valentine McClutchy: The Irish Agent* (London, 1845)
— *The Black Prophet: A Tale of Irish Famine* (London, 1847)
(Both novels were used in the edition: *The Works of William Carleton,* 2 vols. (New York, 1970))
Seamus Deane, *Reading in the Dark* (London, 1996)
Seán de Rís, *Peadar Ó Doirnín: a Bheatha agus a Shaothar* (Dublin, 1969)
Lynn Doyle, *Ballygullion* (London, 1924)
— *Rosabelle and Other Stories* (London, 1933)
James Hardiman, *Irish Minstrelsy, or, Bardic Remains of Ireland,* 2 vols. (Dublin, 1831)
Douglas Hyde, translator, 'An Irish Funeral Oration over Owen O'Neill, of the House of Clanaboy', *U.J.A.,* ser. 2, vol. 3 (1897), 258–70 and vol. 4 (1898), 50–55
E. Knott, ed.,*The Bardic Poems of Tadhg Dall Ó Huiginn,* Irish Texts Soc., 2 vols. (London, 1920–21)
Frank McCourt, *Angela's Ashes* (London, 1996)
Michael McLaverty, *Call My Brother Back* (Swords, 1976)
Seosamh Mag Uidhir, *Pádraig Mac a Liondain: Dánta* (Dublin, 1977)
Brian Moore, *The Emperor of Ice-Cream* (London, 1970)
— *The Lonely Passion of Judith Hearne* (London, 1956)
— *The Feast of Lupercal* (London, 1957)
Danny Morrison, *West Belfast* (Cork, 1989)
Breandán Ó Buachalla, *Cathal Buí: Amhráin* (Dublin, 1975)
— ed., *Nua-Dhuanaire II* (Dublin, 1976)
John O'Donovan, *The Topographical Poems of John Ó Dubhagain* (Dublin, 1862)
Séan Ó Dufaigh and Diarmaid Ó Doibhlin, *Nioclás Ó Cearnaigh: Beatha agus Saothar* (Dublin, 1989)
Seosamh Ó Duibhginn, *Séamas Mac Giolla Choille* (Dublin, 1972)
Tomás Ó Fiaich, *Art Mac Cumhaigh: Dánta* (Dublin, 1973 and 1981)
Tomás Ó Fiaich and Liam Ó Caithnia, *Art Mac Bionaid: Dánta* (Dublin, 1979)
Seán S. Ó Gallachóir, ed., *Séamas Dall Mac Cuarta: Dánta* (Dublin, 1971)
Séamus P. Ó Mórdha, 'Maurice O'Gorman in Monaghan: A Second Poem on Fr. Francis MacMahon', *Clogher Record,* ii (1957), 20–24
Énri Ó Muirgheasa, 'Domhnall Mac Craigh; easpag Dúin', *Louth Arch. Soc. Jn.* (1914), 267–72
— *Céad de Cheoltaibh Uladh* (Dublin, 1915)
— *Dhá Chéad de Cheoltaibh Uladh* (Dublin, 1934)
— *Dánta Diadha Uladh* (Dublin, 1936)
— ed., *Abhráin Airt Mhic Chubhthaigh* (Dublin, 1916)
Cecille O'Rahilly, ed., *Five Seventeenth-century Political Poems* (Dublin, 1952)
Michael Parker, ed., *The Hurt World. Short Stories of the Troubles* (Belfast, 1995)
Robert McLiam Wilson, *Ripley Bogle* (London, 1997 edn.)

Tours

A. Atkinson, *Ireland in the Nineteenth Century* (London, 1833)

Charles Topham Bowden, *Tour through Ireland* (Dublin, 1791)

William Brereton, *Travels in Holland the United Provinces England Scotland and Ireland, 1634–1635*, edited by Edward Hawkins (Manchester, 1844)

James Buckley, ed., 'A Tour in Ireland in 1672–4', *Cork Hist. and Arch. Soc. Jn.*, x (1904), 85–100.

T. Crofton Croker, ed., *The Tour of the French Traveller M. de la Boullaye le Gouz in Ireland in A.D. 1644* (London, 1837)

John Gamble, *View of Society and Manners in the North of Ireland in the Summer and Autumn of 1812* (London, 1813)

— *Sketches of History, Politics, and Manners in Dublin and the North of Ireland in 1810* (London, 1826)

Mr and Mrs S. C. Hall, *Ireland: Its Scenery, Character etc.*, 3 vols. (London, 1841–3)

Revd W. Hamilton, *Letters Concerning the Northern Coast of the County of Antrim* (Belfast, 1822 edition)

Chevalier de Latocnaye, *A Frenchman's Walk through Ireland*, translated by John Stevenson (Belfast, 1917 – 1984 facsimile)

Phillip Luckombe, *A Tour through Ireland* (London, 1780)

John McVeigh, ed., *Richard Pococke's Irish Tours* (Dublin, 1995)

J. P. Mahaffy, ed., 'Two Early Tours in Ireland', *Hermathena*, xl (1914), 13

Howard William Troyer, ed., *Five Travel Scripts Commonly Attributed to Edward Ward* [1698] (New York, 1933)

Molyneux's Tour, 1708, in Robert M. Young, *Historical Notices of Old Belfast and Its Vicinity* (Belfast, 1896)

Dervla Murphy, *A Place Apart* (London, 1978)

[Richard Phillips] *Journal of a Tour in Ireland . . . August, 1804 . . .* (1804) (London, 1806)

W. M. Thackeray, *The Irish Sketchbook* (Glos. 1990, 1st edition 1843)

Colm Tóibín, *Bad Blood: A Walk along the Irish Border* (London, 1994)

A Trip to Ireland, Being a Description of the Country . . . As Also Some . . . Observations on Dublin ([London] 1699)

Arthur Young, *Tour in Ireland* (1776–1779), 2 vols. (London, 1892 edition)

SECONDARY

The Ancient and Noble Family of the Savages of the Ards, compiled by G.F.A. (London, 1888)

F. H. A. Aalen, *Man and Landscape in Ireland* (London, 1978)

G. B. Adams, 'The Emergence of Ulster as a Distinct Dialect Area', *Ulster Folklife*, iv (1958), 61–73

— 'The Validity of Language Census Figures in Ulster, 1851–1911', *Ulster Folklife,* xxv (1979), 113–22

J. R. R. Adams, *The Printed Word and the Common Man: Popular Culture in Ulster 1700–1900* (Belfast, 1987)

— 'Ulster Folklife, 1738–40 from the Pages of the Belfast Newsletter', *Ulster Folklife,* xxxi (1985), 41–52

Ian Adamson, *The Identity of Ulster,* 2nd edition (Belfast, 1987)

N. B. Aitchison, 'The Ulster Cycle: Heroic Image and Historical Reality', *Jn. Med. Hist.,* 13 (1987) 87–116

D. H. Akenson, *Small differences: Irish Catholics and Irish Protestants, 1815– 1922, An International Perspective* (Dublin, 1991)

— *Education and Enmity: The Control of Schooling in Northern Ireland, 1920–50* (Newton Abbot, 1973)

— and W.H. Crawford, *James Orr: Bard of Ballycarry* (Belfast, 1977)

Elizabeth Andrews, *Ulster Folklore* (London, 1913)

J. H. Andrews, 'Geography and Government in Elizabethan Ireland', in Nicholas Stephens and Robin E. Glasscock, eds., *Irish Geographical Studies* (Belfast, 1970), 178–91

Liam Andrews, ' "The Very Dogs in Belfast Will Bark in Irish." The Unionist Government and the Irish language 1921–43', in Aodán Mac Póilin, ed., *The Irish Language in Northern Ireland* (Belfast, 1997)

Paul Arthur, *The People's Democracy 1968–1973* (Belfast, 1974)

— *Government and Politics of Northern Ireland,* 2nd edition (London, 1987)

— 'Republican Violence in Northern Ireland: the Rationale', in John Darby *et al.,* eds., *Political Violence: Ireland in a Comparative Perspective* (Belfast, 1990) 48–63

— ' "Reading" Violence: Ireland', in David E. Apter, ed., *The Legitimization of Violence* (New York, 1997), 284

E. D. Atkinson, *An Ulster Parish: Being a History of Donaghcloney* (Dublin, 1818)

Richard Bagwell, *Ireland under the Stuarts,* 3 vols. (London, 1909–16)

S. E. Baker, 'Orange and Green: Belfast 1832–1912', in H.J. Dyos and M. Wolff, eds., *The Victorian City: Image and Reality,* 2 vols.(London, 1973), ii, 789–814

Linda-May Ballard, 'Three Local Storytellers: A Perspective on the Question of Cultural Heritage', in Gillian Bennett and Paul Smith, eds., *Monsters with Iron Teeth: Perspectives in Contemporary Legend,* iii (Sheffield, 1988), 161–82

Jonathan Bardon, *A History of Ulster* (Belfast, 1992)

T. C. Barnard, 'Planters and Policies in Cromwellian Ireland', *Past and Present,* no. 61 (1973), 31–69

— *Cromwellian Ireland: English Government and Reform in Ireland, 1649– 1660* (Oxford, 1975)

— 'The Uses of 23 October 1641 and Irish Protestant Celebrations', *Eng. Hist. Rev.,* cvi (1991), 889–920

— 'Irish Images of Cromwell', in R.C. Richardson, ed., *Images of Cromwell* (1993), 180–206

Denis P. Barritt and Charles F. Carter, *The Northern Ireland Problem: A Study in Group Relations* (Oxford, 1972)

Thomas Bartlett, 'An End to the Moral Economy: The Irish Militia Disturbances of 1793', *Past and Present*, xcix (1983), 41–64

— 'Defenders and Defenderism in 1785', *I.H.S.*, xiv (1985), 373–94

— *The Fall and Rise of the Irish Nation: The Catholic Question 1690–1830* (Dublin, 1992)

— and Keith Jeffrey, eds, *A Military History of Ireland* (Cambridge, 1996)

Brian Barton, *Brookeborough. The Making of a Prime Minister* (Belfast, 1988)

J. Bowyer Bell, *The Secret Army: The Story of the IRA 1916–1970* (London, 1970)

Robert Bell, *The Book of Ulster Surnames* (Belfast, 1988)

David Beresford, *Ten Men Dead* (London, 1987)

Paul Bew, Peter Gibbon and Henry Patterson, *Northern Ireland 1921–1994: Political Forces and Social Classes* (London, 1995)

F. J. Bigger, *The Ulster Land War of 1770* (Dublin, 1910)

D. A. Binchy, 'A pre-Christian Survival in Medieval Irish Hagiography', in Dorothy Whitelock, Rosamund McKitterick and David Dumville, eds., *Ireland in Early Medieval Europe: Studies in Memory of Kathleen Hughes* (Cambridge, 1982), 165–78

— 'Patrick and his Biographers, Ancient and Modern', *Stud. Hib.*, ii (1962), 7–173

B. Bjersby, *The Interpretation of the Cuchulainn Legend in the Works of W. B. Yeats* (Uppsala, 1950)

Allan Blackstock, *An Ascendancy Army: The Irish Yeomanry 1796–1834* (Dublin, 1998)

Roger Blaney, *Presbyterians and the Irish Language* (Belfast, 1996)

F. W. Boal, 'Territoriality on the Shankill–Falls Divide, Belfast', *Irish Geography*, vi (1969), 30–50

— and R.H. Buchanan, 'The 1969 Northern Ireland Election', *Irish Geography*, vi (1969), 80–83

John Bossy, 'The Counter-Reformation and the People of Catholic Europe', *Past and Present*, no. 47 (May, 1970), 51–70

— 'The Counter-Reformation and the People of Catholic Ireland, 1596–1641', in T.D. Williams, ed., *Historical Studies,* viii (Dublin, 1971), 155–69

— *The English Catholic Community, 1570–1850* (London, 1975)

— 'Catholicity and Nationality in the Northern Counter-Reformation', in Stewart Mews, ed., *Religion and National Identity: Studies in Church History,* xviii (Oxford, 1982), 285–96

Karl S. Bottigheimer, *English Money and Irish Land* (Oxford, 1971)

— 'The Restoration Land Settlement in Ireland: A Structural View', *I.H.S.*, xviii (1972), 1–21

— 'The Failure of the Reformation in Ireland: *une question bien posée*', *Jn. Eccles. Hist.* xxxvi (1985), 196–207

Angela Bourke, *The Burning of Bridget Cleary: A True Story* (London, 1999)

Andrew Boyd, *Holy War in Belfast* (Tralee, 1969)

Desmond Bowen, *The Protestant Crusade in Ireland 1800–70* (Dublin, 1978)

John Bowman, *De Valera and the Ulster Question 1917–1973* (Oxford, 1982)

Brendan Bradshaw, *The Dissolution of the Religious Orders in Ireland under Henry VIII* (Cambridge, 1974)

Ciaran Brady, Mary O'Dowd and Brian Walker, eds., *Ulster: An Illustrated History* (London, 1989)

Ciaran Brady and Raymond Gillespie, eds., *Natives and Newcomers: Essays on the Making of Irish Colonial Society 1534–1641* (Dublin, 1986)

John Brady, *Catholics and Catholicism in the Eighteenth-Century Press* (Maynooth, 1965)

W. J. Brady, 'The Story of Donaghmore', *Down and Connor Hist. Soc. Jn.*, x (1939), 36–43

P. A. Breatnach, 'Metamorphosis 1603: Dán le hEochaidh Ó hEódhasa', *Éigse*, xvii (1977–9), 169–80

Caoimhín Breatnach, *Patronage, Politics and Prose* (Maynooth, 1996)

Richard Breen, Paula Devine, Lizanne Dowds, eds., *Social Attitudes in Northern Ireland: The Fifth Report* (Belfast, 1996)

John D. Brewer with Gareth I. Higgins, *Anti-Catholicism in Northern Ireland, 1600–1998: The Mote and the Beam* (Basingstoke, 1998)

L. W. B. Brockliss and P. Ferté, 'Irish Clerics in France in the Seventeenth and Eighteenth Centuries', *Proc. R.I.A.*, C.87/9 (1987), 527–72

Andrea Ebel Brozyna, *Labour, Love and Prayer: Female Piety in Ulster Religious Literature, 1850–1914* (Ithaca and Belfast, 1999)

Alan Bruford, *Gaelic Folktales and Medieval Romances* (Dublin, 1969)

Ronald H. Buchanan, 'Calendar Customs', *Ulster Folklife*, viii (1962), 15–34

Patrick Buckland, *James Craig* (Dublin, 1980)

— *A History of Northern Ireland* (Dublin, 1981)

— *The Factory of Grievances: Devolved Government in Northern Ireland 1921–39* (Dublin, 1979)

Anthony Buckley, 'Neighbourliness – Myth and History', *Oral History Jn.*, xi (1983), 44–51

— 'Collecting Ulster's Culture: Are There Really Two Traditions?', in *The Use of Tradition*, edited by Alan Gailey (UFTM, Cultra, 1988), 49–60

— '"We're Trying to Find Our Identity": Uses of History among Ulster Protestants', in Elizabeth Tonkin, Maryon McDonald and Malcolm Chapman, eds., *History and Ethnicity* (London and New York, 1988), 183–97

— 'Collecting Ulster's Culture: Are There Really Two Traditions?', in Alan Gailey, ed., *The Use of Tradition: Essays Presented to G.B.Thompson* (UFTM, Cultra, 1988), 49–60

Anthony D. Buckley and Kenneth Anderson, *Brotherhoods in Ireland* (UFTM, Cultra, 1988)

Ian Budge and Cornelius O'Leary, *Belfast: Approach to Crisis: A Study of Belfast Politics 1613–1970* (London, 1973)

Burke's Genealogical and Heraldic History of the Landed Gentry of Ireland, 4th edition, edited by L.G. Pine (London, 1958)

Burke's Irish Family Records (London, 1976)

William P. Burke, *Irish Priests in Penal Tmes 1660–1750* (Shannon 1969, reprint of 1914 edition)

— ed., 'The Diocese of Derry in 1631', *Archiv. Hib.,* v (1916)

G. Burnett, *The Life of Bishop Bedell* (Dublin, 1736)

R. E. Burns, 'The Belfast Letters, the Irish Volunteers 1778–9 and the Catholics', *Review of Politics,* xxi (1959), 678–91

Frank Burton, *The Politics of Legitimacy: Struggles in a Belfast Community* (London, 1978)

W.F. Butler, 'Irish Land Tenures: Celtic and Foreign', *Studies,* xiii (1924), 530

William T. Butler, *Confiscation in Irish History* (London,1917), 291–305, 524–40

Francis John Byrne, 'Tribes and Tribalism in Early Ireland', *Ériu,* xxii (1971), 128–66, 160–66

— 'Seventh-Century Documents', *Irish Eccles. Rec.,* cviii (1967), 164–82

Marc Caball, *Poets and Politics: Reaction and Continuity in Irish Poetry, 1558–1625* (Cork, 1998)

Euan Cameron, *The European Reformation* (Oxford, 1991)

Nicholas Canny, 'The Treaty of Mellifont and the Re-organisation of Ulster, 1603', *Irish Sword,* ix (1969–70), 249–62

— 'Hugh O'Neill, Earl of Tyrone, and the Changing Face of Gaelic Ulster', *Stud. Hib.,* x (1970), 7–35

— 'Why the Reformation Failed in Ireland: *une question mal posée*', *Jn. Eccles. Hist.,* xxx (1979), 423–50

— *From Reformation to Restoration: Ireland, 1534–1660* (Dublin, 1987)

Andrew Carpenter, ed., *Place, Personality and the Irish Writer* (Gerrards Cross, 1977)

Revd W. Carrigan, 'Catholic Episcopal Wills in the PRO, Dublin, 1683–1812', *Archiv. Hib.,* i (1912), 151–90

Daniel J. Casey, 'Carleton and the Count', *Seanchas Ard Mhaca,* viii (1975–6), 7–22

Lucian Ceyssens, 'Florence Conry, Hugh de Burgo, Luke Wadding and Jansenism', in the Franciscan Fathers, eds., *Father Luke Wadding,* 295–331

D. A. Chart, 'The Break-up of the Estate of Con O'Neill', *Proc. R.I.A.,* xlviii (1942–3), sect. C, 119–51

Aidan Clarke, *The Old English in Ireland, 1625–42* (London, 1966)

Samuel Clarke, *Social Origins of the Irish Land War* (New Jersey, 1979)

— and J. R. Donnelly, Jr., eds., *Irish Peasants: Violence and Political Unrest, 1780–1914* (Dublin, 1983)

Pamela Clayton, *Enemies and Passing Friends: Settler Ideologies in Twentieth-Century Ulster* (London, 1996)

Brendan Clifford, ed., *The Origin of Irish Catholic Nationalism: Selections from Walter Cox's 'Irish Magazine'* (Belfast, 1992)

A. Cogan, *The Ecclesiastical History of the Diocese of Meath*, 3 vols. (Dublin, 1867–74)

Barry M. Coldrey, *Faith and Fatherland: The Christian Brothers and the Development of Irish Nationalism 1838–1921* (Dublin, 1988)

D. Comyn and P.S. Dineen, eds., *The History of Ireland by Geoffrey Keating*, Irish Texts Soc., 4 vols (London, 1902–14)

S. J. Connolly, 'Catholicism in Ulster, 1800–1850', in Roebuck, ed., *Plantation to Partition*, 157–71

— *Priests and People in pre-Famine Ireland 1780–1845* (Dublin, 1982)

— *Religion and Society in Nineteenth-Century Ireland* (Dundalk, 1985)

— *Religion, Law and Power: The Making of Protestant Ireland 1660–1760* (Oxford, 1992)

—ed., *The Oxford Companion to Irish History* (Oxford, 1998)

Linde Conolly, 'Spoken English in Ulster in the Eighteenth and Nineteenth Centuries', *Ulster Folklife*, xxviii (1982), 33–9

Patrick J. Corish, 'The Re-Organisation of the Irish Church, 1603–41', *Ir. Cath. Hist. Comm. Proc.* (1957), 9–14

— *The Origins of Irish Catholic Nationalism* (Dublin, 1968)

— *The Christian Mission* (Dublin, 1981)

— *The Catholic Community in the Seventeenth and Eighteenth Centuries* (Dublin, 1981)

— 'Catholic Marriage under the Penal Code', in Art Cosgrove, ed., *Marriage in Ireland* (Dublin, 1985), 67–77

— *The Irish Catholic Experience: A Historical Survey* (Dublin, 1986)

— 'Cardinal Cullen and the National Association of Ireland', in Alan O'Day, ed., *Reactions to Irish Nationalism, 1865–1914* (London, 1987), 117–65

Art Cosgrove, 'The Writing of Irish Medieval History', *I.H.S.*, xxvii (1990), 97–111

— 'The Early Irish Church and the Western Patriarchate', in Proinséas Ní Chatháin and Michael Richter, eds., *Irland und Europa, die Kirche in Frühmittelalter. Ireland and Europe, the Early Church* (Stuttgart, 1984), 9–15

— ed., *Marriage in Ireland* (Dublin, 1985)

— ed., *A New History of Ireland, ii: Medieval Ireland, 1169–1534* (Oxford, 1987)

W. H. Crawford, 'Economy and Society in South Ulster in the Eighteenth Century', *Clogher Record*, viii (1975), 241–58

— 'The Ulster Irish in the Eighteenth Century', *Ulster Folklife*, xxviii (1982), 24–32

— 'The Political Economy of Linen: Ulster in the Eighteenth Century', in Ciaran Brady *et al.*, eds., *Ulster: An Illustrated History* (London, 1989), 134–57

Donal F. Cregan, 'The Social and Cultural Background of a Counter-Reformation Episcopate, 1618–60', in Art Cosgrove and Donal McCartney, eds., *Studies in Irish History Presented to R. Dudley Edwards* (Dublin, 1979), 85–117

L. M. Cullen, *Life in Ireland* (London, 1979)

— *The Emergence of Modern Ireland, 1600–1900* (Dublin, 1981)

— 'Catholics under the Penal Laws', *Eighteenth-Century Ireland*, i (1986), 23–36

— 'Patrons, Teachers and Literacy in Irish: 1700–1850', in Mary Daly and David Dickson, eds., *The Origins of Popular Literacy in Ireland: Language Change and Educational Development 1700–1920* (Dublin, 1990), 15–44

Bernadette Cunningham, 'The Culture and Ideology of Irish Franciscan Historians at Louvain 1607–1650', in Ciaran Brady, ed., *Ideology and the Historians* (Dublin, 1991), 11–30

— and Raymond Gillespie, 'The East Ulster Bardic Family of Ó Gnímh', *Éigse*, xx (1984), 106–14

— and Raymond Gillespie, 'An Ulster Settler and His Irish Manuscripts', *Éigse*, xxi (1986), 25–36

E. A. Currie, 'Field Patterns in County Derry', *Ulster Folklife*, xxix (1983), 70–80

E. Curtis, 'Janice Dartas', *Roy. Soc. Antiq. Jn.* lxiii (1933), 182–205

Cahal B. Daly, *The Price of Peace* (Belfast, 1991)

Mary Daly, 'Revisionism and the Great Famine', in George Boyce and Alan O'Day, eds., *The Making of Modern Irish History. Revisionism and the Revisionist Controversy* (London, 1996), 71–89

— and David Dickson, eds., *Origins of Popular Literacy in Ireland: Language Change and Educational Development 1700–1920* (Dublin, 1990)

P. de Brún, 'Some Irish Manuscripts with Breifne Associations', *Breifne*, iii (1969), 552–61

John Darby, ed., *Northern Ireland: The Background to the Conflict* (Belfast, 1983)

— *Intimidation and the Control of Conflict in Northern Ireland* (Dublin, 1986)

— and Nicholas Dodge and A.C. Hepburn, eds., *Political Violence: Ireland in a Comparative Perspective* (Belfast, 1990)

— and Geoffrey Morris, *Intimidation in Housing* (Belfast, 1974)

— and Geoffrey Morris, *Conflict in Northern Ireland: The Development of a Polarised Community* (Dublin, 1976)

Jean Delumeau, *Catholicism between Luther and Voltaire* (London, 1977)

Liam de Paor, *The Peoples of Ireland. From Pre-History to Modern Times* (London, 1986)

Liam and Máire de Paor, *Early Christian Ireland* (London, 1958)

Hugh Deery, 'Ancient Christian Burial places of Drumholm', *Donegal Annual*, iii (1956), 110–13

Charles Dickson, *Revolt in the North: Antrim and Down in 1798* (Dublin, 1960)

David Dickson and Hugh Gough, eds., *The French Revolution and Ireland* (Dublin, 1990).

— and Daire Keogh and Kevin Whelan, eds., *The United Irishmen* (Dublin, 1993)

E. R. M. C. Dix, *Books and Pamphlets Printed in Strabane in the Eighteenth Century* (Dublin, 1901)

John Donaldson, *A Historical and Statistical Account of the Barony of the Upper Fews in the County of Armagh, 1838* (Dundalk, 1923)

Colm J. Donnelly, *Living Places. Archaeology, Continuity and Change at Historic Monuments in Northern Ireland* (Belfast, 1997)

J. S. Donnelly, Jr., 'Propagating the Cause of the United Irishmen', *Studies*, lxix (1980), 5–23

— and Kerby A. Miller, eds., *Irish Popular Culture* (Dublin, 1999)

Peter Donnelly, 'Political Identity in Northern Ireland: An Issue for Catholic Theology', *Studies*, vol. 86, no. 343 (1997), 238–47

Martin W. Dowling, *Tenant Right and Agrarian Society in Ulster, 1600–1870* (Dublin, 1999)

David Noel Doyle, *Ireland, Irishmen and Revolutionary America, 1760–1820* (Dublin, 1981)

Patrick J. Duffy, 'The Territorial Organisation of Gaelic Landownership and Its Transformation in County Monaghan, 1591–1640', *Irish Geography*, xiv (1981), 1–26

— 'Patterns of Landownership in Gaelic Monaghan in the Late Sixteenth Century', *Clogher Record*, x (1979–81), 304–22

— 'The Evolution of Estate Properties in South Ulster, 1600–1900', in Smyth and Whelan, eds., *Common Ground*, 84–109

— *Landscapes of South Ulster: A Parish Atlas of the Diocese of Clogher* (Belfast, 1993)

Seán Duffy, *Nicholas O'Kearney: The Last of the Bards of Louth* (Tyrone, 1989)

— 'The First Ulster Plantation: John de Courcy and the Men of Cumbria', in T.B. Barry, Robin Frame and Katharine Simms, eds., *Colony and Frontier in Medieval Ireland. Essays presented to J.F. Lydon* (London, 1995), 1–27

— *Ireland in the Middle Ages* (Dublin, 1997)

David Dumville, ed., *Kathleen Hughes: Church and Society in Ireland A.D. 400–1200* (London, 1987)

John Dunlop, *A Precarious Belonging. Presbyterians and the Conflict in Northern Ireland* (Belfast, 1995)

Tom Dunne, 'Haunted by History: Irish Romantic Writing, 1800–50', in Roy Porter and Mikulás Teich, eds., *Romanticism in National Context* (Cambridge, 1988), 68–91

John Edwards, 'The Priest, the Layman and the Historian: Religion in Early Modern Europe', *European History Quarterly*, xvii (1987), 87–93

Marianne Elliott, 'Origins and Transformation of Early Irish Republicanism', *Internat. Rev. Soc. Hist.*, xxiii (1978), 405–28

— *Partners in Revolution: The United Irishmen and France* (London and New Haven, 1982)

— *Wolfe Tone: Prophet of Irish Independence* (London and New Haven, 1989)

— 'The Defenders in Ulster', in Dickson, *et al.*, eds.,*The United Irishmen*, 222–33

— 'Religion and Identity in Northern Ireland', in Winston A. Van Horne, ed., *Global Convulsions: Race, Ethnicity and Nationalism at the End of the Twentieth Century* (New York, 1997), 149–68

Steven G. Ellis, *Ireland in the Age of the Tudors 1447–1603. English Expansion and the End of Gaelic Rule* (London and New York, 1998)

Colmán Etchingham, 'The Implications of Paruchia', *Ériu*, xliv (1993), 139–62

E. Estyn Evans, 'The Ulster Farmhouse: A Comparative Study', *Ulster Folklife*, iii (1957), 14–18

Patrick Fagan, *Divided Loyalties: The Question of an Oath for Irish Catholics in the Eighteenth Century* (Dublin, 1997)

— *An Irish Bishop in Penal Times: The Chequered Career of Sylvester Lloyd OFM, 1680–1747* (Dublin, 1993)

Cyril Falls, *The Birth of Ulster* (London, 1936)

Michael Farrell, *Northern Ireland: The Orange State*, 2nd edition (London, 1980)

— *Arming the Protestants: The Formation of the Ulster Special Constabulary 1920–27* (London, 1983)

Sean Farren, *The Politics of Irish Education 1920–65* (Belfast, 1995)

Revd P.P. Farry, 'Penal Day Traditions in Mourne', *Down and Connor Hist. Soc. Jn.*, ix (1938), 42–9

D. Faul and R. Murray, *The Alienation of Northern Catholics* (Dungannon, 1984)

Anselm Faulkner, 'The Right of Patronage of the Maguires of Tempo', *Clogher Record*, ix (1977), 167–86

Brendan Fitzpatrick, *Seventeenth-Century Ireland: the War of Religions* (Dublin, 1988)

David Fitzpatrick, 'The Disappearance of the Agricultural Labourer, 1841–1912', *Ir. Econ. Soc. Hist.*, vii (1980), 66–92

— *Oceans of Consolation: Personal Accounts of Irish Migration to Australia* (Ithaca, 1994)

W. D. Flackes, *Northern Ireland: A Political Directory 1968–79* (Dublin, 1980)

Robin Flower, *The Irish Tradition* (Oxford, 1979 imprint of 1947 work)

Laurence J. Flynn, 'Hugh MacMahon, Bishop of Clogher 1707–15 and Archbishop of Armagh 1715–37', *Seanchas Ard Macha*, vii (1973–4), 108–75

Bryan A. Follis, *A State under Siege: The Establishment of Northern Ireland, 1920–1925* (Oxford, 1995)

Alan Ford, *The Protestant Reformation in Ireland, 1590–1641* (Frankfurt am Main, 1987).

R. F. Foster, *Modern Ireland, 1600–1972* (London, 1988)

— *The Story of Ireland: An Inaugural Lecture Delivered before the University of Oxford on 1 December 1994* (Oxford, 1995)

— ed., *The Oxford Illustrated History of Ireland* (Oxford, 1989)

Robin Frame, *Colonial Ireland, 1169–1369* (Dublin, 1981)

— *English Lordship in Ireland 1318–1361* (Oxford, 1982)

Franciscan Fathers, eds., *Father Luke Wadding: Commemorative Volume* (Dublin, 1957)

Eric Gallagher and Stanley Worrall, *Christians in Ulster 1968–1980* (Oxford, 1982)

Frank Gallagher, *The Indivisible Island: The History of Partition in Ireland* (London, 1957)

Revd Patrick Gallagher, 'Sources for the History of a Diocese: Seventeenth-Century Clogher', *Procs. Ir. Cath. Hist. Committee* (1957), 25–37

Jeffrey Gantz, *Early Irish Myths and Sagas* (Harmondsworth, 1988)

Cathaldus Giblin, 'The Processus Datariae and the Appointment of Irish Bishops in the Seventeenth Century', in Franciscan Fathers, eds., *Father Luke Wadding*, 508–616

Raymond Gillespie, *Colonial Ulster: The Settlement of East Ulster 1600–1641* (Cork, 1985)

— 'The Presbyterian Revolution in Ulster, 1660–1690', in W.J. Sheils and Diana Wood, eds., *The Churches, Ireland and the Irish* (Oxford, 1989), 159–70

— *The Sacred in the Secular: Religious Change in Catholic Ireland, 1500–1700* (Colchester, Vermont, 1993)

— ed., *Cavan: Essays on the History of an Irish County* (Blackrock, 1995)

— ed., *Devoted People: Belief and Religion in Early Modern Ireland* (Manchester, 1997)

— and Harold O'Sullivan, eds., *The Borderlands: Essays on the History of the Ulster–Leinster Border* (Belfast, 1989)

Michael Glancy, 'The Primates and the Church Lands of Armagh', *Seanchas Ard Mhacha*, v (1969–70), 370–96

Henry Glassie, *Irish Folk History: Folktales from the North* (Dublin, 1982)

— *Passing the Time in Ballymenone* (Bloomington, 1995, reprint of 1982 edition)

David Gordon, *The O'Neill Years: Unionist Politics 1963–1969* (Belfast, 1989)

B. J. Graham and L. J. Proudfoot, eds., *An Historical Geography of Ireland* (London, 1993)

Jean M. Graham, 'Rural Society in Connacht 1600–1640', in Glasscock and Stephens, eds., *Irish Geographical Studies*, 192–208

James Grant, 'Some Aspects of the Great Famine in County Armagh', *Seanchas Ard Mhacha*, viii (1977), 344–59

— 'The Great Famine and the Poor Law in Ulster: the Rate-in-Aid Issue of 1849', *I.H.S.*, xxvii (1990), 30–47

John Gray, *City in Revolt: James Larkin and the Belfast Dock Strike of 1907* (Belfast, 1985)

Alice Stopford Green, *History of the Irish State to 1014* (London, 1925)

Aubry Gwynn and R. Neville Hadcock, eds., *Medieval Religious Houses. Ireland* (London, 1970)

Lord Ernest Hamilton, *The Irish Rebellion of 1641* (London, 1920)

— *Elizabethan Ulster* (London, 1919)

R.P.C. Hanson, *Saint Patrick: His Origins and Career* (Oxford, 1968)

Philip Dixon Hardy, *The Holy Wells of Ireland* (Dublin, 1836)

Michael Harkin [Maghtochair], *Inishowen: Its History, Traditions and Antiquities* (Londonderry, 1867)

David Harkness, *Northern Ireland since 1920* (Dublin, 1983)

K. M. Harris, 'The Schools' Collection', *Ulster Folklife,* iii (1957), 8–13

Mary Harris, 'Catholicism, Nationalism and the Labour Question in Belfast, 1925–38', *Bullán: an Irish Studies Journal*, iii (1997), 15–32

Rosemary Harris, *Prejudice and Tolerance in Ulster: A Study of Neighbours and 'Strangers' in a Border Community* (Manchester, 1972)

G. A. Hayes-McCoy, *Scots Mercenary Forces in Ireland* (Dublin, 1937)

— 'The Making of an O'Neill: A View of the Ceremony at Tullahoge, Co. Tyrone', *U.J.A.*, xxxiii (1970), 89–94

David Hempton and Myrtle Hill, *Evangelical Protestantism in Ulster Society 1740–1890* (London, 1992)

A. C. Hepburn, *A Past Apart: Studies in the History of Catholic Belfast 1850–1950* (Belfast, 1996)

Ken Heskin, *Northern Ireland: A Psychological Analysis* (Dublin, 1980)

Anna Heussaff, *Filí agus Cléir san Ochtú hAois Déag* (Dublin, 1992)

Christopher Hewitt, 'Catholic Grievances, Catholic Nationalism and Violence in Northern Ireland during the Civil Rights Period: A Reconsideration', *British Jn. of Sociology*, 32 (1981), 362–80; the subsequent debate between himself and Denis O'Hearn, ibid., 34(1983), 438–45, 446–51, 36 (1985), 94–101, 102–5; 38 (1987), 88–100

Sir Arthur Hezlet, *The 'B' Specials: A History of the Ulster Special Constabulary* (London, 1972)

Mary Hickson, *Ireland in the Seventeenth Century or the Irish Massacres of 1641–2*, 2 vols. (London, 1884)

George Hill, *An Historical Account of the Plantation of Ulster* (Belfast, 1877)

— *An Historical Account of the MacDonnells of Antrim* (Belfast, 1978, reprint of 1873 edition)

Jacqueline R. Hill, 'Popery and Protestantism, Civil and Religious Liberty: The Disputed Lessons of Irish History 1690–1812', *Past and Present*, 118 (1988), 96–129

J. Michael Hill, 'The Origins of the Scottish Plantations in Ulster to 1625: A Reinterpretation', *Jn. Brit. Studs.*, xxxii (January 1993), 24–43

Myrtle Hill *et al.*, eds., *1798 Rebellion in County Down* (Newtownards, 1998)

Patrick Hogan, 'The Migration of Ulster Catholics to Connaught, 1795–6', *Seanchas Ard Mhacha*, ix (1978–9), 286–301

Michael Hopkinson, *Green Against Green: The Irish Civil War* (Dublin, 1988)

K. Theodore Hoppen, *Elections, Politics and Society in Ireland 1832–1885* (Oxford, 1984)

Rab Houston, 'Literacy and Society in the West, 1500–1850', *Social History*, viii (1983), 269–93

Leo Howe, 'Doing the Double', in Chris Curtin and Thomas M. Wilson, eds., *Ireland from Below: Social Change and Local Communities* (Galway, 1989), 144–64

Kathleen Hughes, *The Church in Early Irish Society* (London, 1966)

R. J. Hunter, 'The Settler Population of an Ulster Plantation County', *Donegal Annual*, x (1971–3), 124–54

— 'English Undertakers in the Plantation of Ulster, 1610–41', *Breifne*, iv (1973–75), 471–99

Revd Matthew Hutchinson, *The Reformed Presbyterian Church in Scotland: Its Origin and History 1680–1876* (Paisley, 1893)

Douglas Hyde, *A Literary History of Ireland* (new edition, London and New York, 1967)

Alvin Jackson, *Ireland: 1798–1998* (Oxford, 1999)

Harold Jackson, *The Two Irelands: A Dual Study of Inter-Group Tensions* (Minority Rights Group, London, 1971)

K. H. Jackson, *The Oldest Irish Tradition: A Window on the Iron Age* (Cambridge, 1964)

Neil Jarman, *Displaying Faith: Orange, Green and Trade Union Banners in Northern Ireland* (Belfast, 1999)

Henry A. Jefferies and Ciarán Devlin, eds., *History of the Diocese of Derry from the Earliest Times* (Dublin, 1999)

Keith Jeffrey, 'The Great War in Modern Irish Memory', in T.G. Fraser and Keith Jeffrey, eds., *Men, Women and War* (Dublin, 1993), 148–51

Revd Brendan Jennings, *Michael Ó Cléirigh: Chief of the Four Masters and His Associates* (Dublin, 1936)

Emrys Jones, 'The Distribution and Segregation of Roman Catholics in Belfast', *Sociological Review*, 4 (1956), 167–89

F. M. Jones, *The Counter-Reformation* (Dublin, 1967)

Desmond Keenan, *The Catholic Church in Ireland in the Nineteenth Century* (Dublin, 1983)

Fergus Kelly, *A Guide to Early Irish Law* (Dublin, 1988)

James Kelly, 'The Formation of the Modern Catholic Church in the Diocese of Kilmore, 1580–1880', in Gillespie, ed., *Cavan.*, 115–38

David Kennedy, 'Catholics in Northern Ireland, 1926–1939', in Francis Mac-Manus, ed., *The Years of the Great Test, 1926–39* (Cork, 1967), 138–60

Liam Kennedy, *Colonialism, Religion and Nationalism in Ireland* (Belfast, 1996)

— and Philip Ollerenshaw, eds., *An Economic History of Ulster, 1820–1939* (Manchester, 1985)

Daire Keogh, *'The French Disease': The Catholic Church and Radicalism in Ireland 1790–1800* (Dublin, 1993)

Dermot Keogh, *The Vatican, the Bishops and Irish Politics 1919–39* (Cambridge, 1986)

Revd Donal Kerr, 'James Browne Bishop of Kilmore, 1829–65', *Breifne*, vi (1983–4), 109–54

Phil Kilroy, 'Sermon and Pamphlet Literature in the Irish Reformed Church, 1613–34', *Archiv. Hib.*, xxxiii (1975), 110–21

Christine Kinealy, *The Great Calamity: The Irish Famine, 1845–52* (Dublin, 1994)

— and Trevor Parkhill, eds., *The Famine in Ulster* (Belfast, 1997)

Thomas Kinsella, trans., *The Tain* (Oxford, 1989)

G. Kirkham, 'Economic Diversification in a Marginal Economy: A Case Study', in Roebuck, ed., *Plantation to Partition*, 65–81

R. W. Kirkpatrick, 'Origins and Development of the Land War in mid-Ulster, 1879–85', in F.S.L. Lyons and R.A.J. Hawkins, *Ireland Under the Union: Essays in Honour of T.W. Moody* (Oxford, 1980), 201–35

Kassian A. Kovalcheck, 'Catholic Grievances in Northern Ireland: Appraisal and Judgement', *British Jn. of Sociology*, xxxviii (1987), 77–87

Brian Lacy, *Siege City: The Story of Derry and Londonderry* (Belfast, 1990)

— *Colum Cille and the Columban Tradition* (Dublin, 1997)

Michael Laffan, *The Partition of Ireland, 1911–1925* (Dublin, 1983)

Emmet Larkin, 'The Devotional Revolution in Ireland, 1850–75', *Amer. Hist. Rev.*, lxxii (1967), 852–4

— *The Making of the Roman Catholic Church in Ireland, 1850–60* (Chapel Hill, 1980)

— *The Consolidation of the Roman Catholic Church in Ireland, 1860–1870* (Dublin, 1987)

J. Larkin, '"Popish Riot" in South County Derry', *Seanchas Ard Mhacha*, viii (1975–6), 94–111

W. T. Latimer, *A History of the Irish Presbyterians* (Belfast, 1893)

W. E. H. Lecky, *A History of Ireland in the Eighteenth Century*, 5 vols. (London, 1892)

J. J. Lee, *Ireland 1912–1985* (Cambridge, 1989)

J. Leerssen, *Mere Irish and Fíor-Ghael: Studies in the Idea of Irish Nationality, Its Development and Literary Expression prior to the Nineteenth Century* (Amsterdam and Philadelphia, 1986)

Brian Lennon, *After the Ceasefires* (Dublin, 1995)

Peadar Livingstone, *Fermanagh Story* (Enniskillen, 1969)

— *Monaghan Story* (Enniskillen, 1980)

Belinda Loftus, *Mirrors, Orange and Green* (Dundrum, 1994)

Edna Longley, *The Living Stream. Literature and Revisionism in Ireland* (Newcastle Upon Tyne, 1994)

Mary Low, *Celtic Christianity and Nature: Early Irish and Hebridean Traditions* (Edinburgh, 1996)

A. T. Lucas, 'The Sacred Trees of Ireland', *Cork Hist. and Arch. Soc. Jn.*, lxviii (1963), 16–54

A. Lynch, 'Religion in Late Medieval Ireland', *Archiv. Hib.*, xxxvi (1981), 3–15

Revd John Lynch, *The Life of St. Patrick from Walter Harris's Translation of Sir James Ware's Works* (London and Dublin, 1870)

Brendan Lynn, *Holding the Ground: The Nationalist Party in Northern Ireland, 1945–72* (Aldershot, 1997)

Ian McAllister, *The Northern Ireland Social Democratic and Labour Party: Political Opposition in a Divided Society* (London, 1977)

Gerard MacAtasney, *'This Dreadful Visitation': The Famine in Lurgan/Portadown* (Belfast, 1997)

Ambrose Macaulay, *Patrick Dorrian, Bishop of Down and Connor 1865–85* (Dublin, 1987)

— *William Crolly: Archbishop of Armagh, 1835–49* (Dublin, 1994)

I. R. McBride, 'Presbyterians in the Penal Era', *Bullán: an Irish Studies Journal,* i–ii (1994), 73–86

— *Scripture Politics: Ulster Presbyterians and Irish Radicalism in the Late Eighteenth Century* (Oxford, 1998)

— *The Siege of Derry in Ulster Protestant Mythology* (Dublin, 1997)

May McCann, 'Belfast Ceilidhes', *Ulster Folklife,* 29 (1983), 55–105

Donal MacCartney, 'The Writing of History in Ireland, 1800–30', *I.H.S.,* x (1957), 347–62

Kim McCone, *Pagan Past and Christian Present in Early Irish Literature* (Maynooth, 1990)

— and Katharine Simms, eds., *Progress in Medieval Irish Studies* (Maynooth, 1996)

Desmond McCourt, 'The Rundale System in Donegal. Its Distribution and Decline', *Donegal Annual,* iii (1954–5), 47–60

— 'Surviving Openfield in County Londonderry', *Ulster Folklife,* iv (1958), 17–28

Jack McCoy, *Ulster's Joan of Arc. An Examination of the Betsy Gray Story* (Bangor, 1987)

J. L. McCracken, 'The Political Scene in Northern Ireland, 1926–1937', in Francis MacManus, ed., *The Years of the Great Test, 1926–39* (Cork, 1967), 26–39

Brian Mac Cuarta, ed., *Ulster 1641: Aspects of the Rising* (Belfast, 1993)

Margaret MacCurtain, 'Rural Society in post-Cromwellian Ireland', in Art Cosgrove and Donal McCartney, eds., *Studies in Irish History Presented to R.Dudley Edwards* (Dublin, 1979), 118–36

— 'Late in the Field: Catholic Sisters in Twentieth-Century Ireland and the New Religious History', *Journal of Women's History,* vi–vii (1995), 49–63

— and Mary O'Dowd, eds., *Women in Early Modern Ireland* (Edinburgh, 1991)

R. B. McDowell, *Ireland in the Age of Imperialism and Revolution* (Oxford, 1979)

G. McElroy, *The Catholic Church and the Northern Ireland Crisis* (Dublin, 1991)

Thomas McErlean, 'The Irish Townland System of Landscape Organisation', in Terence Reeves-Smyth and Fred Hammond, eds., *Landscape and Archaeology in Ireland* (Oxford, 1983), 315–39

Revd Brendan McEvoy, 'The Parish of Errigal Kieran in the Nineteenth Century', *Seanchas Ard Mhacha*, i (1954–5), 118–31

— 'The United Irishmen in Co.Tyrone', *Seanchas Ard Mhacha*, iii (1958–9), 283–314, and v (1969), 37–65

John McGarry and Brendan O'Leary, *Explaining Northern Ireland: Broken Images* (Oxford, 1995)

Revd Charles McGarvey, 'The Heather Edge', *Seanchas Ard Mhacha*, ii (1956–7), 178–88

Séamus N. Mac Giolla Easpaig, *Tomás Ruiséil* (Dublin, 1957)

Charles McGlinchy, *The Last of the Name* (Belfast, 1986)

Dermot McGuinne, *Irish Type Design* (Dublin, 1992)

[Revd G.E. McKenna], *Devenish (Lough Erne): Its History, Antiquities and Traditions* (Enniskillen, 1897)

Revd L. McKeown, 'Friars Bush', *Down and Connor Hist. Soc. Jn.*, vi (1934), 72–5

Michael McKeown, *Two Seven Six Three: An Analysis of Fatalities Attributable to Civil Disturbances in Northern Ireland in the Twenty Years between July 13 1969 and July 12 1989* (Lucan, 1989)

Jim MacLaughlin, 'The Politics of Nation-Building in Post-Famine Donegal', in Dunlevy, Nolan and Ronayne, eds., *Donegal History and Society*, 583–624

Hugh McLeod, *Religion and the People of Western Europe 1789–1989* (Oxford, 1997)

K. McMahon and T. Ó Fiaich, 'Inscriptions in Creggan Graveyard', *Seanchas Ard Mhacha*, vi (1971–2), 309–32

Paddy McNally, *Parties, Patriots and Undertakers* (Dublin, 1997)

Eoin MacNeill, *Celtic Ireland* (Dublin, 1921)

T. E. McNeill, *Anglo-Norman Ulster: The History and Archaeology of an Irish Barony 1177–1400* (Edinburgh, 1980)

Gearóid Mac Niocaill, *Ireland before the Vikings* (Dublin, 1972)

— 'The Contact of Irish and Common Law', *N. Ireland Legal Quarterly*, 23 (1972), 16–23

Séamas MacPhilib, 'Profile of a Landlord in Folk Tradition and in Contemporary Accounts – the Third Earl of Leitrim', *Ulster Folklife*, xxxiv (1988), 26–40

Aodán Mac Póilin, 'Aspects of the Irish Language Movement in Northern Ireland', in Máiréad Nic Craith, ed., *Watching One's Tongue: Aspects of Romance and Celtic Languages* (Liverpool, 1996), 156–9

Samuel McSkimin, *The History and Antiquities of the County of the Town of Carrickfergus, from the Earliest Records till 1839*, edited by E.J. McCrum (Belfast, 1909)

Breandán Mac Suibhne, 'Canon James McFadden (1842–1917)', in Gerard Moran, ed., *Ten Radical Priests* (Dublin, 1997), 149–84

R. R. Madden, *The United Irishmen, Their Lives and Times*, 3 ser., 7 vols. (London,1842–5), and revised edition, 4 vols. (London, 1857–60)
— *Antrim and Down in '98* (Glasgow, n.d)
W. A. Maguire, ed., *Kings in Conflict: The Revolutionary War in Ireland and Its Aftermath, 1689–1750* (Belfast, 1990)
— 'The Estate of Cú Chonnacht Maguire of Tempo: A Case History from the Williamite Land Settlement', *I.H.S.*, xxvii (1990), 130–44
J. P. Mahaffy, 'Two Early Tours in Ireland', *Hermathena*, xl (1914), 1–16
J. P. Mallory, ed., *Aspects of the Táin* (Belfast, 1992)
— and T.E. McNeill, *The Archaeology of Ulster from Colonization to Plantation* (Belfast, 1991)
John J. Marshall, *History of the Parish of Tynan in the County of Armagh* (Dungannon, 1932)
F. X. Martin, 'Derry in 1590: A Catholic Demonstration', *Clogher Record*, vi (1968), 597–602
Thomas D'Arcy M'Gee, *A Life of the Rt. Rev. Edward Maginn* (New York, 1857)
David Miller, *Church, State and Nation in Ireland 1898–1921* (Dublin, 1973)
— 'Irish Catholicism and the Great Famine', *Jn. Soc. Hist.*, ix (1975), 81–8
— 'Presbyterianism and "Modernization" in Ulster', *Past and Present*, 80 (1978) 66–90
— *Peep O'Day Boys and Defenders: Selected Documents on the County Armagh Disturbances 1784–96* (Belfast, 1990)
— 'Politicisation in Revolutionary Ireland: The Case of the Armagh Troubles', *Ir. Econ. Soc. Hist.*, 23 (1996), 1–17
Benignus Millett, *The Irish Franciscans 1651–1665* (Rome, 1964)
— *Survival and Reorganization 1650–1695* (Dublin, 1968)
Kenneth Milne, *The Irish Charter Schools, 1730–1830* (Dublin, 1997)
Frank Mitchell and Michael Ryan, *Reading the Irish Landscape* (Dublin, 1997)
Joel Mokyr, *Why Ireland Starved: A Quantitative and Analytical History of the Irish Economy, 1800–1850* (London, 1985)
William Monter, *Ritual, Myth and Magic in Early Modern Europe* (Sussex, 1983)
T. W. Moody, 'The Treatment of the Native Population under the Scheme for the Plantation of Ulster', *I.H.S.*, i (1938), 59–63
— *The Londonderry Plantation, 1609–4: The City of London and the Plantation in Ulster* (Belfast, 1939)
— 'Redmond O'Hanlon, c.1640–1681', *Proceedings and Reports of the Belfast Natural History and Philosophical Society*, 2nd ser., i, pt 1 (1937), 17–33
— and F. X. Martin and F. J. Byrne, eds., *A New History of Ireland*, iii: *Early Modern Ireland, 1534–1691* (Oxford, 1978)
— *A New History of Ireland*, viii: *A Chronology of Irish History to 1976* (Oxford, 1982)
— *A New History of Ireland*, ix: *Maps, Genealogies, Lists* (Oxford, 1984)

— and W. E. Vaughan, eds., *A New History of Ireland, iv: Eighteenth-century Ireland 1690–1800* (Oxford, 1986)

Canice Mooney, 'The Irish Church in the Sixteenth Century', *Ir.Eccles. Rec.*, xcix (1963), 102–13

— *The First Impact of the Reformation* (Dublin, 1967)

— *The Church in Gaelic Ireland, Thirteenth to Fifteenth Centuries* (Dublin, 1969)

— 'The Friars and Friary of Donegal, 1474–1840', in Terence O'Donnell, ed., *Franciscan Donegal* (Donegal, 1952), 3–49

Hiram Morgan, 'The End of Gaelic Ulster: A Thematic Interpretation of Events between 1534 and 1610', *I.H.S.*, xxvi (1988), 8–32

— *Tyrone's Rebellion: The Outbreak of the Nine Years War in Tudor Ireland* (Suffolk, 1993)

— 'The Colonial Venture of Sir Thomas Smith in Ulster, 1571–1575', *Hist. Jn.*, xxviii (1985), 261–78

R. J. Morris, 'Inequality, Social Structure and the Market in Belfast and Glasgow, 1830–1914', in S.J. Connolly, Rab Houston and R.J. Morris, eds., *Conflict, Identity and Economic Development* (Preston, 1995), 189–203

E. Moxon-Browne, *Nation, Class and Creed in Northern Ireland* (Aldershot, 1983)

Ronnie Munck and Bill Rolston, *Belfast in the Thirties. An Oral History* (Belfast, 1987)

James H. Murnane, 'Dr James Donnelly, Bishop of Clogher (1865–1893) and the Ascendancy in Monaghan', *Clogher Rec.*, xiii, no 1 (1988), 1–25

Desmond Murphy, *Derry, Donegal and Modern Ulster 1790–1921* (Londonderry, 1981)

Gerard Murphy, *Saga and Myth in Ancient Ireland* (Dublin, 1955)

Michael J. Murphy, *Tyrone Folk Quest* (Belfast, 1973)

— *At Slieve Gullion's Foot* (Dundalk, 1975)

— *Ulster Folk of Field and Fireside* (Dundalk, 1983)

— *Rathlin: Island of Blood and Enchantment. The Folklore of Rathlin* (Dundalk, 1987)

Dominic Murray, 'Schools and Conflict', in John Darby, ed., *Northern Ireland: The Background to the Conflict* (Belfast, 1983), 136–50

— *Worlds Apart: Segregated Schools in Northern Ireland* (Belfast, 1985)

James Murray, 'The Church of Ireland: A Critical Bibliography', Part I: 1536–1603, and Part II: 1603–41, by Alan Ford, *I.H.S.*, xxviii (Nov. 1993), 345–8

Revd L. P. Murray, 'The History of the Parish of Creggan in the 17th and 18th Centuries', *Louth Arch. Soc. Jn.*, viii (1934), 117–63, later reissued as *History of the Parish of Creggan* (Dundalk, 1940)

— 'Franciscan Monasteries after the Dissolution', *Louth Arch. Soc. Jn.*, viii (1934), 275–82

P. G. Murray, 'A Previously Unnoticed Letter of Oliver Plunkett's', *Seanchas Ard Mhacha*, viii (1975–6), 23–33

Kenneth Nicholls, *Gaelic and Gaelicised Ireland in the Middle Ages* (Dublin 1972)

Próinséas Ní Chatháin and Michael Richter, eds., *Irland und Europa, die Kirche in Frühmittelalter: Ireland and Europe, the Early Church* (Stuttgart, 1984)

William Nolan, Liam Ronayne and Mairead Donlevy, eds., *Donegal. History and Society* (Dublin, 1995)

E. R. Norman and J.K.S. St. Joseph, *The Early Development of Irish Society. The Evidence of Aerial Photography* (Cambridge, 1969)

Dónall P. Ó Baoill, *An Teanga Bheo: Gaeilge Uladh* (Dublin, 1996)

Conor Cruise O'Brien, *The Great Melody: A Thematic Biography of Edmund Burke* (London, 1992)

— *Ancestral Voices: Religion and Nationalism in Ireland* (Dublin, 1994)

Breandán Ó Buachalla, *I mBéal Feirste Cois Cuain* (Dublin, 1968)

— 'Na Stíobhartaigh agus an tAos Léinn: Cing Séamas', *Proc. R.I.A.*, 83, sect. C (1983), 81–134

— 'Lillibulero agus Eile', *Comhar* (April 1987), 27–9

— 'Poetry and Politics in Early Modern Ireland', *Eighteenth-Century Ireland*, vii (1992), 149–75

— 'Foreword' to Geoffrey Keating, *Foras Feasa ar Éirinn*, edited by D. Comyn and P.S. Dineen (1987 reprint of London, 1902)

— 'Poetry and Politics in Early Modern Ireland', *Eighteenth-Century Ireland*, vii (1992), 149–75

— 'Jacobitism and Nationalism: The Irish Literary Evidence', in Michael O'Dea and Kevin Whelan, eds., *Nations and Nationalism: France, Britain, Ireland and the Eighteenth-Century Context* (Oxford, 1995), 103–16

Cathal O'Byrne, *As I Roved Out* (Belfast, 1982, reprint of 1946 edition)

John Cornellius O'Callaghan, *Irish Brigades in the Service of France* (Shannon, 1968, reprint of 1870 edition)

Séamus Ó Casaide, *Irish Language in Belfast and County Down, 1601–1850* (Dublin,1930)

S. Ó Ceallaigh, *Gleanings from Ulster History* (Cork, 1951)

N. Ó Cíosáin, *Print and Popular Culture in Ireland 1750–1850* (Basingstoke, 1997)

Séan Ó Coinne and T. Ó Fiaich, 'Tombstone Inscriptions in Drumglass Cemetery', *Seanchas Ard Mhacha*, vii (1974), 316–19

Marie O'Connell, 'The Genesis of Convent Foundations and Their Institutions in Ulster, 1840–1920', in Janice Holmes and Diane Urquhart, eds. *Coming into the Light: The Work, Politics and Religion of Women in Ulster 1840–1940* (Belfast, 1994), 179–206

Philip O'Connell, *The Diocese of Kilmore: Its History and Antiquities* (Dublin, 1937)

— 'A Dublin Convert Roll: The Diary of the Rev. P.E. O'Farrelly', *Ir. Eccles. Rec.*, lxxi, (January–June,1949), 533–44 and lxxii (July–December, 1949), 27–35

Fionnuala O Connor, *In Search of a State* (Belfast, 1993)

Donnchadh Ó Corráin, *Ireland before the Normans* (Dublin, 1972)

— 'Nationality and Kingship in pre-Norman Ireland', in T.W. Moody, ed., *Nationality and the Pursuit of National Independence* (Belfast, 1978), 1–35

P. S. Ó Dalaigh, 'Sketches of Farney', *Clogher Record*, I, no. 2 (1954), 56–62

Caoimhín Ó Danachair, 'The Penal Laws and Irish Folk tradition', *Proc. Ir. Cath. Hist. Comm.* (1961), 10–16

— 'The Progress of Irish Ethnology, 1783–1982', *Ulster Folklife*, 29 (1983), 7–10

— 'Representations of Houses in Some Irish Maps of 1600', in Geraint Jenkins, ed., *Studies in Folk Life. Essays in Honour of Iorwerth C. Peate* (London, 1969), 91–104

Alan O'Day, ed., *Reactions to Irish Nationalism, 1865–1914* (London, 1987)

Éamon Ó Doibhlin, 'Conn O'Neill of Kilskeery', *Clogher Record*, vi (1967), 388–93

— 'The Deanery of Tulach Óg', *Seanchas Ard Mhacha*, vi, no 1 (1971), 141–82

— *Domhnach Mór (Donaghmore): An Outline of Parish History* (2nd edition, Dungannon, 1988)

Terence O'Donnell, ed., *Franciscan Donegal* (Donegal, 1952)

Anne O'Dowd, *Spalpeens and Tattie Hokers: History and Folklore of the Irish Migratory Agricultural Worker in Ireland and Britain* (Dublin, 1991)

Mary O'Dowd, *Power, Politics and Land: Early Modern Sligo 1568–1688* (Belfast, 1991)

Revd Seosamh Ó Dufaigh, 'The Mac Cathmhaoils of Clogher', *Clogher Record*, ii (1957), 25–48

— 'James Murphy, Bishop of Clogher, 1801–24', *Clogher Record*, vi (1968), 419–93

Revd Eoghan O'Duffy, *The Apostasy of Myler Magrath, Archbishop of Cashel* (No place of pub., 1864)

B. W. O'Dwyer, 'Gaelic Monasticism and the Irish Cistercians, c.1228', *Ir. Eccles, Rec.*, 108 (1967), 19–28

Peter O'Dwyer, *Mary: A History of Devotion in Ireland* (Dublin,1988)

Tomás Ó Fiaich, 'The Appointment of Bishop Tyrrell and Its Consequences', *Clogher Record*, i (1953–6), 1–14

— 'Diocese of Armagh: Sources and Problems', *Proc. Ir. Cath. Hist. Committee* (1955), 6–9

– ed., 'The 1766 Religious Census for Some County Tyrone Parishes', *Seanchas Ard Mhacha*, iv, no 1 (1960–61), 147–70

— 'The Political and Social Background of the Ulster Poets', *Léachtaí Cholm Cille*, i (1970), 23–56

— 'Filíocht Uladh mar Fhoinse don Stair Shóisialta san 18ú hAois', *Stud. Hib.*, xi (1971), 80–129

— 'The Registration of the Clergy in 1704', *Seanchas Ard Mhacha*, vi, no 1(1971), 46–69

— 'Art Mac Cooey and his Times', *Seanchas Ard Mhacha*, vi (1971), 217–46

— 'The O'Neills of the Fews', *Seanchas Ard Mhacha*, vii (1973–4), 1–63, 263–315, and viii (1977), 386–413

Revd P. Ó Gallachair, 'Clogher's Altars of the Penal Days', *Clogher Record*, ii (1957–9), 97–130

— 'Clogherhici. A Dictionary of the Catholic Clergy of the Diocese of Clogher (1535–1835)', *Clogher Record*, i, no. 3 (1955), 66–87, no. 4 (1956), 137–60; ii (1957–9), 170–91, 272–9, 504–11; iv (1960–62), 54–94; vi (1966–8), 126–36, 379–87, 578–96; vii (1969–72), 89–104, 514–28; viii (1973–4), 93–103, 207–20; ix (1976), 67–75; xi (1982–4), 374–86; xii (1986), 233–46

Cormac Ó Gráda, *The Great Irish Famine* (London, 1989)

— *Ireland: A New Economic History 1780–1939* (Oxford, 1994)

— *Black '47 and Beyond. The Great Irish Famine in History, Economy, and Memory* (Princeton, 1999)

— *An Drochshaol: Béaloideas agus Amhráin* (Dublin, 1994)

Standish O'Grady, *History of Ireland: The Heroic Period* (London, 1878)

Clare O'Halloran, *Partition and the Limits of Irish Nationalism* (Dublin, 1987)

— 'Irish Re-creations of the Gaelic Past: The Challenge of MacPherson's Ossian', *Past and Present*, 124 (1989), 69–95

Jane H. Ohlmeyer, *Civil War and Restoration in Three Stuart Kingdoms: The Career of Randal MacDonnell, Marquis of Antrim 1609–1683* (Cambridge, 1993)

— ed., *Ireland from Independence to Occupation 1641–1660* (Cambridge, 1995)

Michael J. O'Kelly, *Early Ireland. An Introduction to Irish Pre-History* (Cambridge, 1989)

Revd J. O'Laverty, *An Historical Account of the Diocese of Down and Connor, Ancient and Modern*, 5 vols. (Dublin, 1878–95)

Padraig O'Malley, *The Uncivil Wars* (Belfast, 1983)

— *Biting at the Grave: The Irish Hunger Strikes and the Politics of Despair* (Belfast, 1990)

Revd Lorcán Ó Mearáin, 'The Bath Estate, 1700–1777', *Clogher Record*, vol. 6, no. 2 (1967), 333–60

Séamas P. Ó Mórdha, 'Dán Faoi Mhuirthéacht na Frainnce', *Éigse*, vii (1953–4), 202–4

— 'Simon Macken: Fermanagh Scribe and Schoolmaster', *Clogher Record*, ii (1986), 432–44

— 'Maurice O'Gorman in Monaghan', *Clogher Record*, ii (1957), 20–24

— 'Notes and Comments. Party Quarrels in Nineteenth-Century Monaghan', *Clogher Record*, ii (1958), 355–7

— 'The Rising of Burke', *Clogher Record*, iv (1960–61), 50–53

Énrí Ó Muirgheasa, 'The Holy Wells of Donegal', *Béaloideas*, vi (1936), 141–62

Réamonn Ó Muirí, 'The Killing of Thomas Birch', *Seanchas Ard Mhacha*, x, (1980–82), 267–319

— ed., *Irish Church History Today* (Armagh, n.d.)

Kevin O'Neill, *Family and Farm in Pre-Famine Ireland* (Wisconsin, 1984)

T. F. O'Rahilly, *Early Irish History and Mythology* (Dublin, 1946)

Michelle O'Riordan, *The Gaelic Mind and the Collapse of the Gaelic World* (Cork, 1990)

Camille O'Reilly, 'Nationalists and the Irish Language in Northern Ireland: Competing Perspectives', in Mac Póilin, ed, *Irish Language in Northern Ireland*, 98–113

W.N. Osborough, 'Catholics, Land and the Popery Acts of Anne', in T.P. Power and Kevin Whelan, eds., *Endurance and Emergence: Catholics in Ireland in the Eighteenth Century* (Dublin, 1990), 21–56

James O'Shea, *Priest, Politics and Society in Post-Famine Ireland* (Dublin, 1983)

P. Ó Snodaigh, 'Class and the Volunteers', *Irish Sword*, xvi (1984–6), 165–84

— *Hidden Ulster* (Belfast, 1995)

Edward L. Parker, *The History of Londonderry, Comprising the Towns of Derry and Londonderry, New Hampshire* (Boston, 1851)

Tony Parker, *May the Lord in His Mercy be Kind to Belfast* (London, 1993)

T. G. F. Patterson, 'The Territory of Ballymacone and Its Associations with the McCones', *Seanchas Ard Mhacha*, i (1954–5), 132–50

— 'Housing and House Types in County Armagh', *Ulster Folklife*, vi (1960), 8–17

M. Perceval-Maxwell, *The Scottish Migration to Ulster in the Reign of James I* (1990 reprint of London, 1973 edition)

J. R. S. Phillips, 'The Irish Remonstrance of 1317: An International Perspective', *I.H.S.*, xxvii (1990), 112–29

E. Phoenix, ed., 'Political Violence, Diplomacy and the Catholic Minority in Northern Ireland, 1922', in John Darby, Nicholas Dodge and A.C. Hepburn, eds., *Political Violence: Ireland in a Comparative Perspective* (Belfast, 1990), 29–47

— *Northern Nationalism: Nationalist Politics, Partition and the Catholic Minority in Northern Ireland 1890–1940* (Belfast, 1994)

— ed., *A Century of Northern Life: The Irish News and 100 Years of Ulster History 1890s–1990s* (Belfast, 1995)

Stuart Piggott, *The Druids* (London, 1968)

Cathal Póirtéir, *Famine Echoes* (Dublin, 1995)

Andy Pollak et al., *A Citizens' Inquiry: The Opsahl Report on Northern Ireland* (Dublin, 1993)

Michael Poole, 'The Geographical Location of Political Violence in Northern Ireland', in Darby et al., *Political Violence*, 64–82

T. P. Power and Kevin Whelan, eds., *Endurance and Emergence. Catholics in Ireland in the Eighteenth Century* (Dublin, 1990)

Lindsay Proudfoot, ed., *Down. History and Society. Interdisciplinary Essays on the History of an Irish County* (Dublin, 1997)

H. Pryce, ed., *Literacy in Medieval Celtic Societies* (Cambridge, 1998)

Bob Purdie, *Politics in the Streets. The Origins of the Civil Rights Movement in Northern Ireland* (Belfast, 1990)

C. Quinlan, 'A Punishment from God: The Famine in the Centenary Folklore Questionnaire', *Irish Review*, xix (1996), 68–86

David Quinn, *The Elizabethans and the Irish* (Ithaca, 1966)

Oliver P. Rafferty, *Catholicism in Ulster 1603–1983: An Interpretive History* (Dublin, 1994)

Patrick Rafroidi, 'Imagination and Revolution: The Cuchulain Myth', in Oliver MacDonagh, W.F. Mandle and Pauric Travers, eds., *Irish Culture and Nationalism, 1750–1950* (Canberra, reprint 1985), 137–48

Michael Richter, *Medieval Ireland. The Enduring Tradition* (London, 1988)

Philip Robinson, 'Vernacular Housing in Ulster in the Seventeenth Century', *Ulster Folklife*, xxv (1979), 1–28

— *The Plantation of Ulster* (Dublin, 1984)

Peter Roebuck, 'The Economic Situation and Functions of Substantial Landowners, 1660–1815: Ulster and Lowland Scotland Compared', in Rosalind Mitchison and Peter Roebuck, eds., *Economy and Society in Scotland and Ireland, 1500–1939* (Edinburgh, 1988), 84–9

— ed., *Plantation to Partition: Essays in Ulster History in Honour of J.L. McCracken* (Belfast, 1981)

— ed., *Macartney of Lissanoure* (Belfast, 1983)

R. S. Rogers, 'The Folklore of the Black Pig's Dyke', *Ulster Folklife*, iii (1957), 29–36, and the response by T.G. Barron, ibid., iv (1958), 75–6

Revd Patrick Rogers, *The Irish Volunteers and Catholic Emancipation* (Belfast, 1934)

— 'The Minute Book of the Belfast Rosarian Society', *Down and Connor Hist. Soc. Jn.*, viii (1937), 17–23

Richard Rose, *Governing without Consensus: An Irish Perspective* (London, 1971)

Joseph Ruane and Jennifer Todd, eds., *After the Good Friday Agreement: Analysing Political Change in Northern Ireland* (Dublin, 1999)

D. C. Rushe, *Monaghan in the Eighteenth Century* (Dundalk, 1916)

Conor Ryan, 'Religion and State in Seventeenth-Century Ireland', *Archiv. Hib.*, xxxiii (1975), 110–21

John Ryan, *The Monastic Institute* (Dublin, 1971), 49–50

Donald M. Schlegel, 'The MacDonnells of Tyrone and Armagh: A Genealogical Study', *Seanchas Ard Mhacha*, x (1980–82), 193–219

R. W. Scribner, 'Interpreting Religion in Early Modern Europe', *European Studies Review*, xiii (1983), 89–105

Hereward Senior, *Orangeism in Britain and Ireland, 1795–1836* (London, 1966)

St John D. Seymour, *Irish Witchcraft and Demonology* (New York, 1992)

Richard Sharpe, 'St Patrick and the See of Armagh', *Cambridge Medieval Celtic Studies*, 4 (Winter, 1982), 33–59

William Shaw, *Cullybackey: The Story of an Ulster Village* (Edinburgh, 1913)

W. J. Sheils and Diana Wood, eds., *The Churches, Ireland and the Irish,* Studies in Church History, no. 25 (Oxford, 1989)

Robert C. Simington, *The Transplantation to Connacht, 1654–58* (Dublin, 1970)

J. G. Simms, *The Williamite Confiscation in Ireland* (London, 1956)

— ed., 'Irish Jacobites', *Anal. Hib.*, xxii (1960), 22–187

— 'Land Owned by Catholics in Ireland in 1688', *I.H.S.* vii (1950), 180–90

— *The Jacobite Parliament of 1689* (Dundalk,1966)

— 'Irish Catholics and the Parliamentary Franchise, 1692–1728', in D.W. Hayton and Gerard O'Brien, eds., *War and Politics in Ireland, 1649–1730* (London, 1986), 224–34.

Katherine Simms, 'The Archbishops of Armagh and the O'Neills, 1347–1471', *I.H.S.*, xix (1974), 38–55

— 'Warfare in the Medieval Gaelic Lordships', *Irish Sword*, xii (1975–6), 102–8

— 'The Medieval Kingdom of Loch Erne', *Clogher Record*, ix (1977), 126–41

— 'Guesting and Feasting in Gaelic Ireland', *Roy. Soc. Archives Jn.*, 108 (1978)

— 'The O'Hanlons, the O'Neills and the Anglo-Normans in Thirteenth-Century Armagh', in *Seanchas Ard Mhacha*, ix (1978), 70–94

— 'The O'Reillys and the Kingdom of East Breifne', *Breifne*, vi (1979), 305–19

— ' "The King's Friend": O'Neill, the Crown and the Earldom of Ulster', in J. Lydon, ed., *England and Ireland in the Later Middle Ages* (Dublin, 1981), 214–36

— 'Propaganda Use of the Táin in the Later Middle Ages', *Celtica*, xv (1983), 142–9

— 'Nomadry in Medieval Ireland: the Origins of the Creaght or Caoraigheacht', *Peritia*, v (1986), 379–91

— 'Bardic Poetry as a Historical Source', in Tom Dunne, ed., *The Writer as Witness: Literature as Historical Evidence* (Cork, 1987), 58–75

— *From Kings to Warlords: The Changing Political Structure of Gaelic Ireland in the Later Middle Ages* (Suffolk, 1987)

— 'Bards and Barons: The Anglo-Irish Aristocracy and Native Culture', in R. Bartlett and A. Mackay, eds., *Medieval Frontier Societies* (Oxford, 1989), 188–94

— 'Gaelic Warfare', in T. Bartlett and K. Jeffery, eds., *A Military History of Ireland* (Cambridge, 1996), 99–115

— 'The Contents of Later Commentaries on the Brehon Law Tracts', in *Ériu*, xlix (1998), 23–40

Peter Smith, *Oidhreacht Oirghiall. A Bibliography of Irish Literature and Philology Relating to the South-East Ulster–North Leinster Region: Printed Sources* (Belfast, 1995)

Gerry Smyth, *The Novel and the Nation: Studies in the New Irish Fiction* (London, 1997)

Revd J. Smyth, 'Blessed Oliver Plunkett in Down and Connor', *Down and Connor Hist. Soc. Jn.*, viii (1937), 76–80

William J. Smyth, 'Society and Settlement in Seventeenth-Century Ireland: The Evidence of the "1659 Census"', in Smyth and Whelan, eds., *Common Ground*, 55–83

— and Kevin Whelan, eds., *Common Ground: Essays on the Historical Geography of Ireland* (Cork, 1988)

Roger Stalley, 'The Long Middle Ages. From the Twelfth Century to the Reformation', in Brian de Breffny, ed., *The Irish World. The History and Cultural Achievements of the Irish People* (London, 1977), 72–98

David Stevenson, *Scottish Covenanters and Irish Confederates* (Belfast, 1981)

— 'The Desertion of the Irish by Coll Keitach's Sons, 1642', *I.H.S.*, xxi (1978), 75–84

A. T. Q. Stewart, *The Narrow Ground. Aspects of Ulster* (London,1977)

— *The Summer Soldiers: The 1798 Rebellion in Antrim and Down* (Belfast, 1995)

Peter Stringer and Gillian Robinson, eds., *Social Attitudes in Northern Ireland: The Second Report* (Belfast, 1992)

James Stuart, *Historical Memoirs of the City of Armagh* (Newry, 1819), also new edition (Catholic version) by Revd Ambrose Coleman, OP, (Dublin, 1900)

Robert Sullivan, *A Matter of Faith: The Fiction of Brian Moore* (Westport, CT, 1996)

Sunday Times Insight Team, *Ulster* (London, 1972)

Joseph Szövérffy, '*Rí Naomh Seoirse*: Chapbooks and Hedge-Schools', *Éigse*, ix (1958–61), 114–28

Lawrence Taylor, *Occasions of Faith. An Anthropology of Irish Catholics* (Dublin, 1995)

Mary Helen Thuente, *The Harp Re-strung: The United Irishmen and the Rise of Literary Nationalism* (New York, 1994)

— *W.B.Yeats and Irish Folklore* (Dublin, 1980)

E. Brian Titley, *Church, State and the Control of Schooling in Ireland 1900–1944* (Canada and Dublin, 1983)

Michael Tynan, *Catholic Instruction in Ireland, 1720–1950* (Dublin, 1985)

Norman Vance, 'Celts, Carthaginians and Constitutions: Anglo-Irish Literary Relations, 1780–1820', *I.H.S.*, xxii (1980–81), 216–38

— 'Catholic and Protestant Literary Visions of "Ulster": Now You See It, Now You Don't', in *Religion and Literature*, 28 (1996), 127–40

W. E. Vaughan, *Sin, Sheep and Scotsmen: John George Adair and the Derryveagh Evictions, 1861* (Belfast, 1983)

— ed., *A New History of Ireland. v: Ireland Under the Union. i. 1801–70* (Oxford, 1989), 515–20

— ed., *A New History of Ireland. vi: Ireland Under the Union. ii. 1870–1921*(Oxford, 1996)

John Waddell, 'The Question of the Celticization of Ireland', *Emania*, ix (1991), 5–16

Thomas Wall, *The Sign of Dr Hay's Head* (Dublin, 1958)

B. M. Walker, *Party Election Results, 1801–1922* (Dublin, 1978)

— 'The Land Question and Elections in Ulster, 1868–86', in Clarke and Donnelly, eds., *Irish Peasants*, 230–68

— *Ulster Politics: The Formative Years, 1868–86* (Belfast, 1989)

Paul Walsh, *Leabhar Chlainne Suibhne. An account of the MacSweeney families in Ireland* (Dublin, 1920)

— *The Four Masters and Their Work* (London, 1944)

— *Irish Men of Learning* (Dublin, 1947)

— *Irish Chiefs and Leaders* (Dublin, 1960)

Seosamh Watson, 'Coimhlint an Dá Chultúr – Gaeil agus Gaill i bhFilíocht Chúige Uladh san Ochtú hAois Déag', *Eighteenth-Century Ireland*, iii (1988), 85–104

John Watt, *The Church in Medieval Ireland* (Dublin, 1972)

J. A. Watt, 'The Papacy and Ireland in the Fifteenth Century', in Barrie Dobson, ed., *The Church, Politics and Patronage* (Glos., 1984), 133–43

Robert Welch, *The Oxford Companion to Irish Literature* (Oxford, 1996)

Kevin Whelan, 'The Regional Impact of Irish Catholicism, 1700–1850', in Smyth and Whelan, eds., *Common Ground*, 253–77

— 'The Catholic Parish, the Catholic Chapel and Village Development in Ireland', *Irish Geography*, xvi (1983), 1–15

Patrick Whelan, 'Anthony Blake, Archbishop of Armagh 1758–1787', *Seanchas Ard Mhacha*, v (1970), 289–323

Newport B. White, ed., *Extents of Irish Monastic Possessions, 1540–1541* (Dublin, 1943)

John Whyte, *Church and State in Modern Ireland 1923–1970* (Dublin, 1971)

— 'How Much Discrimination was There under the Unionist Regime, 1921–68', in Tom Gallagher and James O'Connell, eds., *Contemporary Irish Studies* (Manchester, 1983), 3–7

— 'How is the Boundary Maintained between the Two Communities in Northern Ireland?', *Ethnic and Racial Studies*, ix (1986), 219–34

— *Interpreting Northern Ireland* (Oxford, 1990)

Fionnuala Williams, 'A Fire of Stones Curse', *Folk Life*, xxxv (1996–7), 63–73

C. J. Woods, 'The General Election of 1892: The Catholic Clergy and the Defeat of the Parnellites', in F. S. L. Lyons and R. A. J. Hawkins, eds., *Ireland under the Union: Essays in Honour of T. W. Moody* (Oxford, 1980), 289–319

Frank Wright, *Two Lands in One Soil: Ulster Politics before Home Rule* (Dublin, 1996)

R. M. Young, *The Town Book of the Corporation of Belfast 1613–1816* (Belfast, 1892)

— *Ulster in '98: Episodes and Anecdotes* (Belfast, 1893)

— *Historical Notices of Old Belfast and Its Vicinity* (Belfast, 1896)

UNPUBLISHED THESES

Marcus de la Poer Beresford, 'Ireland in French strategy, 1691–1789' (Univ. of Dublin M.Litt. thesis, 1975)

John Corkery, 'Gaelic Catechisms in Ireland' (NUI, MA thesis, St Patrick's College, Maynooth, 1944)

W. H. Crawford, 'Economy and Society in Eighteenth-Century Ulster' (QUB, PhD. thesis, 1982)

James Connor Doak, 'Rioting and Civil Strife in the City of Londonderry during the Nineteenth and Early Twentieth Centuries' (QUB, MA thesis, 1978),

John B. Dooher, 'Tyrone Nationalism and the Question of Partition, 1910–25' (Univ. of Ulster, M.Phil. thesis, 1986)

Patrick Harvey, 'At the Edge of the Union': Derry Newspapers and the Rhetoric of Nationalism, 1937–39' (Univ. Ulster, M.A. thesis, 1988)

R. J. Hunter, 'The Ulster Plantation in the counties of Armagh and Cavan, 1608–41' (Univ. Dublin, M.Litt. thesis, 1969)

Mary Catherine Kennedy, '*Eagla an Ghallsmacht*. The Religion and Politics of Irish Catholics 1620s-1870s' (NUI, Galway, MA thesis, 1987)

William McAfee, 'The Population of Ulster, 1630–1841: Evidence from mid-Ulster' (Univ. of Ulster, D.Phil. thesis, 1987)

T. P. J. McCall, 'The Gaelic Background to the Settlement of Antrim and Down, 1580–1641' (QUB, M.A. thesis, 1983)

Terence Francis McCarthy, 'Ulster Office, 1552–1800' (QUB, M.A. thesis, 1983)

Patrick J. Curley, 'Northern Irish Poets and the Land since 1800' (QUB, MA thesis, 1977)

Anne De Valera, 'Antiquarianism and Historical Investigations in Ireland in the Eighteenth Century' (NUI, UCD, MA thesis, 1978)

Hugh Joseph Maguire, 'Pádraig Mhac a Lionnduinn of the Fews' (QUB, PhD thesis, 1965)

V. Morley, 'The American Revolution and Opinion in Ireland, 1760–83' (Univ. of Liverpool, PhD. thesis, 1999)

Seán Seosamh Ó Gallachóir, 'Filíocht Shéamais Dhaill Mhic Cuarta' (MA thesis, St Patrick's College, Maynooth, 1967)

Mary Louise Peckham, 'Catholic Female Congregations and Religious Change in Ireland, 1770–1870' (Univ. Wisconsin, Madison, PhD. thesis, 1993)

Margaret Purdy, 'Some Aspects of the Religious and Cultural Identity of Pre-Famine Rural Ulster as Portrayed in William Carleton's Traits and Stories of the Irish Peasantry' (Univ. of London, Birkbeck Coll., MA dissertation, 1992)

Michael G. Quinn, 'Religion and Landownership in County Louth 1641 – c.1750' (Univ. Ulster, MA thesis, 1984)

Katharine Simms, 'Gaelic Lordships in Ulster in the Later Middle Ages' (Univ. of Dublin, PhD. thesis, 1976)

Index

abbots 14
Abercorn, Claud Hamilton, 4th Earl
  116
Abercorn, Lord (John James
  Hamilton, 1st marquis) 217
Abercorn estate, Tyrone 179
abjuration, oath (1708) 148
abstention, Nationalist 383, 396,
  397
Act(s)
  Arms (1793) 242
  Banishment (1697) 166
  Black (1639) 146
  Catholic Emancipation (1829)
    209
  Catholic Relief (1793) 217, 233,
    235, 242
  Charitable Bequests (1844)
    278
  Coercion (1885) 361
  Convention (1793) 242
  Disestablishment (1869) 167
  Ecclesiastical Titles (1851) 319
  Education (1930) 462; (1944)
    462; (1947) 407
  Flags and Emblems (1954) 406,
    454
  Franchise (1884) 294
  Government of Ireland (1920)
    300, 373
  Health Services (Northern
    Ireland) (1948) 407
  Home Rule Bills 297, 300, 325,
    357
  Irish Poor Law (1838) 311,
    (1847) 310
  Land 320, 321
  MacPherson Bill (1919) 460
  Militia (1793) 242
  Offences Against the State (1939)
    402
  Party Emblems (1860) 350
  Party Processions (1832) 345,
    349, 356
  Party Processions (1850) 350
  Popery (1704) 166
  Public Order 406
  Quebec (1774) 168
  Registration (1704) 176
  Settlement (1662) 111–12, 115
  Special Powers (1922) 382, 386,
    411
  of Union (1800) 261, 271, 342
  Wyndham (1903) 321
Adair, John 319
Adair family 312
Adams, Gerry 445, 446
Adeir Clann Liútair (MacCooey)
  182
Áed mac Loingsich 17
*Agallamh idir Brádaigh an spiadhóir
  agus Bard Gaeilge* (McDonnell)
  312
Agnew family 29
agriculture 305–6, 320
Ahoghill, Co. Antrim 167
Airgialla 10, 18, 19
Airthir 19, 49

Aisling Airt Mhic Cumhaigh
140–41
aisling poems 134
Akenson, D. H. 341, 460, 462
Albanach, use of word 132
alliances, medieval 48–9
America, emigration to 168, 192,
338
Ancient Britons regiment 247, 248
Ancient Order of Hibernians (AOH)
296, 326, 353, 356, 469
Andrews, John 307, 308, 389
Anglo-Irish 34, 48–9
Anglo-Irish Agreement (1985)
427–8, 450
Anglo-Irish Treaty (1921) 377, 378
Anglo-Irish war (1919–21) 373,
374
Anglo-Normans 13, 25, 26–8, 29,
30, 34, 48–9, 75
Annals of the Four Masters 64, 76
Annesley, Lord (Francis Charles, 1st
earl) 226, 227, 235
Annesley family 109
antiquarianism, patriotic 75, 232
Antrim, earls of 190
    land confiscation 109–10
    recruiting 98
    status 95, 113, 120
Antrim, Randal MacDonnell, earl of
95
Antrim county xxxix–xli
    Anglo-Norman 26, 27
    bog xli–xlii
    Catholics in 87, 195, 243, 252
    coast 3
    Coast Road xl
    community relations (1790s) 238
    Convention (Catholic) members
    237
    Cromwellian confiscations 109
    excluded from Plantation 89, 91
    Famine 307, 308, 309, 313
    Gaelic-speaking Scots 178
    National schools 277
    and oath of allegiance 217

1641 Rebellion 103–4
1798 Rebellion 252–4, 255
    religious demography xlii
    settlers 86–8
    'souperism' 309–10
    toryism 176
    United Irishmen 251, 252
    Volunteers 221–3
    Williamite settlement 120
Antrim plateau xl
Antrim town 253, 260
AOH
see Ancient Order of Hibernians
Apprentice Boys of Derry 359, 360,
413, 417
Arboe, Co. Tyrone 251
Ardoyne, Belfast 125, 160, 326,
394, 418
Ards peninsula 27, 86–7, 255–6
Ardstraw, Co. Tyrone 341
*Argument on Behalf of the Catholics
of Ireland* (Tone) 228, 231
A Rí lér fuasclaíodh (McAlindon)
136
Armagh, *see* of 60, 61, 65, 136, 151,
180, 208, 209, 280, 328
Armagh city 7, 12, 13–14, 62–3,
221
Armagh county
    Boundary Commission and 379
    Cromwellian confiscations 110
    Famine 186, 305, 307, 313
    IRA activity 406
    local councils 373
    Oakboys 217
    Orangeism 345–6
    parliamentary elections 385
    Plantation 91
    poor land 93
    population 219
    population movement 93
    raths 6
    religious demography xli,
    222
    sectarian clashes (1780s and
    1790s) 176, 221–7

tories 118
Ulster Irish in 93
arms, Catholics and 182, 186, 242, 347
Arnon St, Belfast 377
Ar Thargair Cholmcille mhic Féilim (MacDonnell) 276
Ascendancy, Protestant 227, 233, 236, 239, 343, 440
asceticism, medieval 62, 101
Ash Wednesday 451
Athlone, battle (1691) 116
atrocities
    1641 101–7
    1790s 224, 247
Audley family 86–7
Augher, Co. Tyrone 102–3
Aughrim, battle (1691) 116, 137, 138, 139, 140, 344
Augustinian friars 60
Austria, military service 193

Bagenal, Sir Henry 27, 28
Baker, Sybil 325, 356–7
Ballard, Linda May 287
Ballintoy, Co. Antrim 310
Ballybay, Co. Monaghan 272, 319
ballybetaghs 42
ballybo 42
Ballycastle, Co. Antrim 176, 237
Ballydonellan, Co. Antrim 174
Ballygullion (Doyle) 339, 347, 352–3
Ballymacarrett, Belfast 357–8, 375
Ballymena, Co. Antrim 253, 261, 275, 326
Ballymenone, Co. Fermanagh 306, 479
Ballymoney, Co. Antrim 320, 329
Ballynahinch, Co. Down 256–7, 258, 260, 263
Banbridge, Co. Down 374
Bancroft, Edward 219
Bangor, Co. Down 239
Bannaugh, Co. Donegal 120

Banner of Ulster (McKnight) 319
Bann River xli, 26, 28, 103
Bann valley 3, 8
Bardon, Jonathan 405, 407
bards 45–8, 126–7
Barkeley, Alexander 224
barricades, Catholic 471
Barritt, Denis 411, 460, 465
Barthelet, cartographer 52
Bates, Richard Dawson 381, 389, 390
Battle of Aughrim (play) 180
BBC Northern Ireland 408
Beckett, Mary 432, 433, 477, 480
Bede, Venerable 15
Bedell, Bishop William 129, 130
Belfast 321–7
    attacked (1793) 242
    borough police 343
    Catholics in 283, 321, 322, 323–5, 374–8, 388, 398, 409, 417
    Catholic convention (1792) delegates and 236–7
    Catholic view of 398
    churches, shortage 270
    City Council 323, 324, 437
    death, average age 323
    dock strike (1907) 330
    east 437
    expansion xxvi, 321
    Famine 308
    in fiction 477
    first Catholic school 277
    as fount of sedition (1790s) 243
    household franchise 324
    intimidation 324, 325, 326
    Labour politics 330–31
    middle-class Catholics 322, 323
    murals 431, 447
    murder, sectarian 422
    IRA 403–4, 419
    'pogrom' (1920s) 374–6, 377–8
    population 321
    poverty 323

Belfast – *cont.*
  as Protestant 321, 322, 324
  Protestant demonstrations 181
  religious segregation 325, 326,
    432
  rural influx 321, 326
  sectarian geography 322
  sectarian riots 324, 325, 343,
    353–6, 357–8, 392, 393–4
  shipyard 323–4, 330, 356, 375,
    394
  soup kitchens 309
  state schools 439
  textile mills 321–3
  Town Council 357, 358
  Troubles (1969-) 418–21
  west 437, 478
  World War II xxii, 386, 403–4
Belfast Agreement (1998)
  see Good Friday Agreement
Belfast Morning News 295
Belfast News Letter 168, 259, 356,
  362, 368, 445
Belfast Relief Fund 309
Belfast Telegraph 408, 465
Belfast Woman, A (Beckett) 432,
  480
bells, saints' 21, 64
Benburb, Co. Tyrone 223
benefices, outsiders appointed to
  72–3, 280
Bennett, Art 135, 141, 273–4, 364,
  366–7
Benson family 86–7
Beresford family 109
Betsy Gray and the Hearts of Down
  (Lyttle) 262–3
Bible
  as anti-popish symbol 156, 157
  Catholics' ignorance of 129
  Douay version 282
  foreign 137
  Irish-language 129, 273, 274,
    275, 277
  Protestant 282
  in vernacular 202

Bigger, F. G. 368
bigotry
  Catholic 468
  Catholics and 366, 439
  Protestant 468
  qualitative difference 468
'Big Wind' (1839) 282
'Billy Bluff and Squire Firebrand'
  (satire) 232–3
Bíobla Gallda 273
bishops 71, 72
  authority 66, 71
  and Catholic loyalty 214
  church-building 199, 200, 201
  and landed families 190
  and mixed marriage 179
  penal laws and 167, 175, 176,
    177, 198–9
  political quietism 279
  status 59
  Stuart nomination 207
  support for friars 208, 209
  titles 319
  titles, use 167
  and welfare state 464
  see also hierarchy
Black, Samuel 361–2
black economy 437
Blacker, Col. William 345–6
Black Pig's Dyke 9
Blake, Anthony, archbishop of
  Armagh 208–9
Blaney, Neil 419
Bloody Sunday (Derry 1972) 421,
  422, 473, 476
Bloomfield, Ken 424
Boer War (1899–1902) 283
bog xxx, 27, 31, 195
Bogside, Derry 358, 417
Bonamargy friary, Ballycastle 128
Book of Invasions
  see Lebor Gabála
Book of Martyrs (Foxe) 336
Book of the Taking of Ireland
  see Lebor Gabála
booleying 35, 36

Boullaye le Gouz 154
boundaries, provincial 8–9, 378
Boundary Commission (1925) 300,
    301, 373, 378, 379, 396
boycotts 223, 383, 393
Boylaugh, Co. Donegal 120
Boyne, battle (1690) 116, 344
Boyne valley, Co. Meath 5
Brantry, Co. Tyrone 62
Brehon Laws 43, 45
brehons 45–6
Breifne (Cavan) 26, 50
Brennan, Francis 275
Brennan, Mary 341
Brennan family, Drumcullen 339
Brewer, John 440
Brian Boru, High King 17, 18
Brigid, St 76, 286
British Army
    Bloody Sunday (1972) 421, 422
    Catholics in 446
    mistakes leading to IRA
        recruitment 419, 420–21
    post-1798 264
    Troubles (1969-) 419–20
    welcomed by Catholics 419
British Government
    and discrimination 394, 395
    post-partition 423
    and prisoners 448, 449
    Troubles, view of 423
'Brockan-men' 310
Brooke, Sir Basil, Lord
    Brookeborough 391–2, 393,
    407
Brooke, Charlotte 232
Broughshane, Co. Antrim 275
Browne, Noel 464
Brown Square, Belfast 325, 353
Bruce Wars (1315–18) 27, 29
Bruford, Alan 60
Brunt, May 339–40
'B' Specials
    Catholics to join 376
    deployment (1969) 418
    disbanded (1970) 419, 422

    petty harassment 381, 382–3
    sectarianism 380–82
    see also Ulster Special
        Constabulary
Buckland, Patrick 388
Bullock, Shan 340
burial customs 63, 154, 178
Burke, David 348
Burke, Raymond 379
Burntollet ambush (1969) 415,
    416–17
Burton, Frank 438
business vote 385
Byrne, John 221, 222, 255
Byrne, Patrick 255

Cait Bhreaca 273
Caldwell, Sir James 188
Caledon, Co. Tyrone 103, 412–13
Call My Brother Back (McLaverty)
    375–6
Calvinism 70, 71
Camden, Lord (John Jeffreys Pratt,
    2nd earl) 245
Cameron Commission (1969) 385,
    387, 388, 412, 419
    and police 383, 415–16
Campaign for Social Justice (CSJ)
    412
Campbell, T. J. 397
Campbells, MacDonnells' enmity
    for 104
Campion, Edmund 48, 62, 65, 66,
    67
Carleton, William 179, 180, 181,
    185, 201, 207–8, 241, 284,
    289, 346
Carlingford, Co. Down 244
Carlisle Circus, Belfast 358
Carrickfergus, Co. Antrim 69, 181
Carrick Hill, Belfast 358
Carrive, Co. Armagh 224
Carson, Sir Edward 409
Carter, Charles 411, 460, 465
Carter, Revd Dean 346
Casement, Roger 368

Cashel, Synod of (1101) 44
cashels 14
Castleblaney, Co. Monaghan 311
Castle of Glasdrummond
    (MacCooey) 140
Castlereagh, Lord (Robert Stewart,
    Viscount) 237, 263
Castlewellan, Co. Down 349–51
Catherine of Braganza, Queen
    Consort 113
Catholic Book Society 282
Catholic Church
    authoritarianism xxxvii, 466,
        468, 475
    catechesis, popular 155, 202–5,
        206, 207
    as community 283–4, 469, 474
    conservatism 230
    criticism, internal 466, 468, 475,
        476, 479
    denounces IRA 402
    'devotional revolution' 280–86
    and education 180, 277
    18th-century recovery 198–210
    episcopal structure 71–2
    and Gaelic Revival 455–6
    and integrated education 459
    internal debate 472, 475
    Irish, separate development 149,
        154
    liberalisation 475
    and MacPherson Bill (1919) 460,
        461
    and mixed marriage 341
    modern characteristics 269
    modernism, campaign against 365
    in nationalist press 450–51
    national *vs* universal 59
    19th-century revival 269–70,
        278, 280–86, 291
    penal laws and 163–4, 165–77,
        180, 198–9
    power, growing 351
    Protestant perception of xxiv, 273
    and 1798 rebellion 259
    secularism, campaign against 365

secular leadership 265, 293
    and separate education 277–8,
        458–9
    and Sinn Féin 472, 474
    social status within 132–3
    and Troubles (1969–) 470–81
    and United Irishmen 230
    voluntary work 474
    see also Catholicism; clergy
Catholic Committee 190, 227, 244,
    330
    Convention (1792–3) 236–9
    and Defenders 235
    elections 231, 236, 239
    middle class and 192, 213
    and oath of allegiance 216
    perceived threat 235
    Ulster and 187
    and ultra-Protestantism 241–2
    and United Irishmen 190
Catholic Convention (1792–3)
    236–9
Catholic Emancipation 168,
    220–21, 228–9, 236–7,
    238–9, 271–2, 292, 342, 347,
    348
Catholic Enlightenment 173
Catholic Institute, Belfast 295,
    329–30
Catholicism
    anti-English nationalism 76,
        294
    anti-Protestantism 294
    Calvinist hostility towards 70
    church-based devotions 282
    as cultural and political identity
        450–57
    as dangerous political system
        105–6
    Gaelic heritage 75–80
    middle-class morality in 284–5
    militant continental 146
    nationalism and 457
    and oath of supremacy 143
    oral tradition 130
    persecution 126, 149

'pick-and-mix' 475
political 143–9, 168, 291
politics, clerical domination of
  294–6
private practice 144
public practice as defiance 451
as religion 457–70
and sacred landscape 288
southern 475
superiority, perceived 183
survival 126–7
see also Catholics, popery
Catholic Qualification Oath (1774)
  216
Catholic Qualification Rolls 189
Catholics, Ulster 127–32
  alienation from state xxiv–xxv,
    264, 266, 271, 422, 458
  arms, keeping 182, 186, 221, 242,
    347
  and arts 323
  assertiveness 335, 336, 351
  attendance at mass 431
  and Belfast xxvi
  bitterness 442–3
  British 456–7
  and British connection 481
  community organisation 323,
    466, 470
  conservatism 396, 398
  discrimination against 384–94
  disinheriting 175
  disloyalty, perceived 100, 106,
    146, 147–8, 170, 181, 221,
    226, 238, 248, 391–2, 393,
    395–6, 401, 406, 435
  distinctive qualities 121
  divided by Troubles 428
  and early church 13
  Elizabethan stereotypes 361
  emigration 192–3
  employment 194, 323–4, 327,
    330, 341, 384, 387, 460
  family size 192, 407
  and fundraising 328–9
  as Gaels xxv, 128, 363, 369

inferiority, perceived 182, 335,
  343, 432–3
and integrated education 459
jury service 176
land ownership 116
and the law 225, 343–4
as minority 131
mobility, resistance to 192, 198
moral dignity 441, 442
nationalism 215, 396
occupations 327–8
oppression, theme 365
as people 440
and polite society 163
political awareness, 18th-century
  213–19
political identity 335
and political Protestantism 479
population, percentage of xx,
  325, 435
powerlessness, perceived 422
Presbyterians, perceptions of 233
prosperity 186–91
in Protestant areas 432
Protestant perceptions of 146,
  170–71, 181–2, 210, 216, 221,
  230–31, 343, 417–18, 434–5,
  436–7, 440
Protestants, perceptions of 156,
  215, 337, 446
as 'real' Irish xxv, 4, 363, 369
rebelliousness, perceived 383–4,
  441, 481
'Roman' prefix 168, 362
romantic nationalism 367–8
rural 318
self-image 456
self-protective mechanism 446
sensitivity to scorn 362
social class 327–31
social life 326
and southerners 338
status 121–2, 185–94, 217,
  305
stereotypes 163, 228, 231, 238,
  432–40

Catholics, Ulster – *cont.*
structural disadvantage 323–5,
327
touchiness 432–3
as underclass 194
unemployment 358
victimhood xxxviii, 362–3
voting pattern 291, 294, 299
wealth 328–9
winners, perceived as 422
Catholic Truth Society of Ireland
369, 451, 470
cattle 32, 35, 36
Cattle Raid of Cooley
see Táin Bó Cuailnge
Cavan county xli–xlii
Cromwellian confiscations 109
English in 90
Famine 305, 307, 309
Home Rule 297
land grants 90
land tenure 41
and Partition xlii
Plantation 91
proselytism in 273, 275
succession disputes 51
ceasefires, IRA 473
Céili Dé movement 20
céilís 452, 455
Celtic Ulster 4–6, 7–10
cemeteries, sharing 166, 340
Cenél Conaill 10
Cenél nEógain 10, 18, 19, 26
censuses, religious 170, 195, 198
'chapel-gate' election (1949) 399
Charlemont, Lord (James Caulfield,
1st earl) 153, 222, 265
Charles I, King 108, 144, 337
Charles II, King 107, 111–14
Charter schools 171–3, 178, 180,
205, 277
Chichester, Arthur, Lord Deputy 85,
88–9, 90, 94
chiefs, Gaelic
inauguration ceremonies 36–8, 40
loss of 84, 85, 92

and Plantation 96
and settlers 86
see also lordships
Chiericati, Bishop 61, 66
children, in textile industry 323
Children of the Dead End (MacGill)
315
Chonaire, Flaithrí Ó Maoil 75, 76
Christian Brothers 278, 281, 283,
328, 389
history teaching 366, 367
Christianity 9, 10, 12–17, 20–21
Church Education Society 277
churches
building 270, 282, 283, 309, 328,
329
early Protestant 200
medieval 64
shortage 199–201, 202, 282
Churchill, Lord Randolph 358
Churchill, W. S. 379
church lands 38
attacked 69
confiscated 52
landholding 43–5
Plantation and 45, 96
repossession 99
Church of Ireland
Calvinism 70
conformity with England 99
disestablishment (1869) 167
exclusivity 70
land 91, 327
and National schools 277
and poor Irish 129
churls 43, 84
Cistercian friars 60, 62
civil liberties, suspension 382
civil rights campaign 385, 422
aims 476
bishops and 471
and Catholic confidence 476
emergence (1960s) 408
Protestant perceptions of 395,
415, 417
protests 411–15, 433–4

reforms, achieving 442
see also Northern Ireland Civil
    Rights Association
civil service, Catholics and 378, 383,
    388, 389–91, 393, 409
Clanbrassil, Lord (James Hamilton,
    1st earl) 176
Clandeboye estates 88, 89
Clare county 107
Clark (Lisburn innkeeper) 257–8
Claudy seminary, 201
Cleland, Revd John 233
clergy
    absentee 61, 72, 73
    alms, questing for 152, 153
    assertiveness 340
    authority 207–8
    civic culture, lack 458
    and civil-rights movement 471
    constitutional nationalism 299,
        300
    continental training 70–71, 74,
        150, 169
    dress 282
    economic dependence 147,
        149–50
    education 150–51, 282
    and education 459, 462, 476
    18th-century 202
    executions 69, 72
    failings of 151, 152–3, 155
    and Famine relief 309
    hereditary succession 65
    history, teaching 364–5, 366
    increase 327–8
    independence 202
    and IRA 457, 471–2
    and Irish language 67, 71,
        451–2
    and the law 184
    lay nomination 149
    lower 149, 152
    loyalty 264
    marriage 44, 65, 72
    in medieval tales 60–61
    and modern politics 446

and nationalism 292, 293, 295–6,
    474, 476
oath of abjuration (1709) 165
and oath of allegiance 217
and O'Connell campaign 271
penal laws and 164, 165–6
persecution 149–50
and Plunkett 144
as political leaders 457
politics, non-involvement 229–30
poverty 149–50
pro-Spanish 72, 73
Protestant 461, 462
Protestant perceptions of 292
and republicans 446
respect for 151, 203, 239, 242–3,
    264
role xxiv
'Rome-running' 61, 65
and 'Second Reformation' 272–3
secular 209
sheltering 174
shortage 208, 209
as social leaders 117
and state schools 461, 462
status 132–3, 151, 159
training 66, 202, 466–7
Troubles and 475–6
and United Irish Society 230
violence, opposition to 457
Clifton St, Belfast 358
Cloghaneely, Co. Donegal 316
Clogher, Co. Tyrone 6, 65
Clogher diocese 60, 177, 199, 406
Clonard Monastery, Belfast 404,
    470
Clondehorky parish, Co. Donegal
    65
Cloughcur, Co. Antrim 310
coarb land 44
Coigley, Revd James 244, 248, 255
Coigley family 188
Coile, Bernard 190–91
Coleman, Revd Ambrose 362
Coleraine, Co. Derry 29, 30, 92,
    409

Collins, Michael 376, 377, 379, 396

Colton, John, archbishop of Armagh 44

Columba
see Colum Cille

Colum Cille 16, 37, 64, 76, 249, 250–51, 276

Combe, Barbour and Combe foundry, Belfast 324

comfort, Gaelic disregard 32–3, 101, 186, 340

Common Law, English 85, 86

Commonwealth, Ulster Catholic support 126, 147

communism, Catholic Church and 469

community relations
landlords and 307
marching season 346–7, 349–51, 352–3
O'Connell campaign and 272
post-1798 263–4
rural 317, 318, 319, 320
1920s 374–9
17th century 153
18th century 178–85, 219
19th century 272, 276, 338–42

Community Relations Commission 420, 424, 467

Conall Cernach 5

Conchobar mac Nessa, king of Ulaid 5, 49

concubinage 65

Confederate War (1641–53) 147, 148

confession, sacrament 66

Confessions (St Patrick) 13

confirmation, sacrament 66, 201, 202

Congested Districts Board 316

Connacht 98, 107, 108, 110, 118

Connachta 5, 9

Connolly, Revd Francis 447

Connolly, Revd James 362, 365

Conroy, Felix 257

Conry, Florence 75, 76

Conry family 118

conscience, freedom of 147, 166

Conservative party 320, 321, 357, 420, 422

Constitution, Irish (1937) 458

conversational topics, avoidance 437–8, 445

conversion, religious 251
Charter schools and 171–3
death-bed 287
food-relief and 310, 311
material reward for 273
as treason 157–8

Conway, Cardinal William 409, 471, 472, 474

Cooke, Revd Henry 180, 231, 271, 275, 279, 305

Cooper, Ivan 423

Coote family 109

Corish, Monsignor Patrick 143, 270

Cork county 118

Cornwallis, Lord (Charles, 1st marquis) 260

Corrigan Park, Belfast 470

Cosgrave, John 119

Cosgrave, Liam, Taoiseach 379

Costello, John, Taoiseach 406

cottiers 284

council housing, discrimination in 378, 386–7, 408, 411

Council of Ireland (1920) 300, 425

Council of Trent (1545–63) 70, 75, 276, 282

Counter-Reformation 65, 66, 68, 70–72, 73–4, 75, 78, 129, 146, 150

'country', overlordship 38

'couple-beggars' 179

Court of Claims, Restoration 112, 115

Covenanters, Scottish 99, 229

Cox, Watty 363

'coyne and livery' 30, 50

Craig, James (Lord Craigavon) 375,

376, 377, 379, 382, 392, 394,
397, 399–400, 452
Craig, William 413, 414–15, 425
Craigavon, Co. Armagh 409
crannogs 6, 14
Crawford, W. H. 131
creaghting 35, 36
Crebilly, Co. Antrim 95
Creevy Rocks rebel camp 255
Creggan, Co. Armagh 63, 222, 223
Creichton, George 101
Cress-stoney, Co. Cavan 180–81
criminal law 55
Crolly, William, archbishop of
Armagh 181, 272, 277, 278,
279, 291
Cromwell, Henry 107
Cromwell, Oliver 100, 106–7,
107–11, 143
Crossmaglen, Co. Armagh 310–11
Cruithin 4, 10, 17, 19
CS gas 420
Cú Chulainn 4–5, 7, 139, 404, 443
Culdees 20, 62
Cullen, Cardinal Paul 270, 279–81,
284, 291, 293, 368
Cullen, Louis 244
Cullyhana, Co. Armagh 473
Cultural Traditions Group 453
culture, Irish 195, 369
Education Ministry and 452
medieval pride in 46
rebelliousness and 452–3
religion as 478–9
18th-century revival 214
written works in 78
Cummins, Anne 355
'cures' 287–8
curfew (1970) 420
Curran, Bob 287–8, 452
Currie, Austin 412, 423
Curtin, Nancy 247
Cuthbert, Joseph 243

Dáil Éireann 373, 396, 399
Daley, Charles 409

Dál Fiatach 9, 49
Dál nAraide 10, 16, 17, 18
Dál Riata 9, 17
Daly, Cardinal Cahal 474
Daly, Edward, bishop of Derry 473
Dane's Cast, Co. Armagh 9
Dan the Dollar (Bullock) 340
Davies, Sir John 31, 39, 41, 45, 51,
52, 85–6, 90
Day, Judge 358
Deane, Seamus 477
De Cobain, Wesley 361
decommissioning, arms 481
de Courcy, John 26, 31
Defenderism 239–43, 249
Defenders 215, 225, 235, 249, 296
excommunication 248
revived 254, 262
and United Irishmen 230, 237,
244–9, 253, 254, 265
deference, traditional 198, 227
Deirdriu (Deirdre) of the Sorrows 5
demesne lands 38, 41
Democratic Unionist Party 425, 437
demography
change, Protestants and 435
religious xxxix–xlii, 194–8, 229
17th-century changes 131
Dempsey, Larry 253
Denvir, Cornelius, bishop of Down
and Connor 278, 283
derbfine 5
Derricke, John 63
Derry city
Bloody Sunday (1972) 421, 422,
473
borough police 343
Catholic Church in 359
Catholics in 335
community relations 358–60
Council 373, 415
in fiction 477
first Catholic mayor 373
PD march (1968) 414–15
Plantation 91
religious demography xlii, 326

Derry city – *cont.*
  RUC behaviour 416
  sectarian riots (1920s) 374
  Troubles (1969-) 417
  unemployment (1960s) 411
  as university site 409
  use of name xx–xxi
Derry county 10
  bog xli
  Catholics in minority 195
  improving landlords 307
  land tenure 41
  United Irish Society 257
  Volunteers 221
Derry diocese 60, 201
detention
  powers (1920s) 382
  see also internment
De Valera, Eamon 299, 386, 394,
    402, 405, 406, 458
Devenish cemetery, Fermanagh 193
Devlin, Bernadette xxiv, 414, 443,
    455, 466
Devlin, Joe 296, 297, 299, 330, 379,
    396–7, 398, 399, 404
Devlin, Paddy 404, 420, 422–3,
    425, 428
devolved government, and
    discrimination 388
Devon Commission 307
devotional literature 64, 66
devotions, Catholic 469
Dickey, James 259, 262
Dickey family 174
Dickson, George 262
Dickson, Revd William Steel 252
difference, badges of 335
Digest of Popery Laws (Butler) 231
diocesan organisation 17
direct rule 422, 426
discrimination 384–94
  Catholic institutions and 465
  Protestant perceptions of 395
  use in explanation 441
dispensations 65
dispossession 52, 54, 83

Dissenters, emigration 192
distilling, forbidden 218
Divis Flats, Belfast 418
Divis St, Belfast 418
divorce, attitudes to 475
Dockside, Belfast 326, 393, 394
Doherty, Paddy 83, 479
Dolan, Myles 158–9
Dolly's Brae, Co. Down 349–51
domestic service 341
dominion status 300
Domhnach Mór (Ó Doibhlin) 158
Donaghmore, Co. Tyrone 65, 96
Donaldson, John 363
Donegal county 10
  Catholic life (1870s) 287
  Cromwellian confiscations 109
  as escape 477
  fairies, belief in 289–90
  hiring fairs 313, 314
  holy wells 286
  Home Rule 297
  inauguration ceremonies 36
  landlords 307, 319–20
  mountain ranges 31
  19th-century life 313–14, 316–17
  and oath of allegiance 217
  and Partition xlii
  Plantation 91
  and Protestant tenants 195
  1798 Rebellion 252
  tories 118
  Ulster Irish in 93
  United Irishmen 246
  Volunteers 221
Donegall Rd, Belfast 394
Donegan family 310
Donegore Hill, Co. Antrim 259–60
Donnelly, Alex 393
Donnelly, Patrick 299
Donoghue, Betty 354–5
Doon Well, near Kilmacrenan 286,
    287
Dorrian, Patrick, bishop of Down
    and Connor 281, 283, 284,
    292–3, 295–6, 328, 329–30

Dorsey, Co. Armagh 9
Douay Bibles 282
Dougall, Hugh 379
Down and Connor diocese 60, 451,
    466–7
Down county xl
    Anglo-Norman 26, 27
    Boundary Commission and 379
    Catholic Convention members
        237
    Catholics in minority 195, 243
    community relations (1790s) 238
    constituency size 217
    excluded from Plantation 89, 91
    Famine 308, 313
    Irish language in 205
    local councils 373
    National schools 277
    Patrick cult 26
    Protestant fears 352
    1641 rebellion 106
    1798 rebellion 255–8
    settlers 86–8
    Troubles (1780s/1790s) 223, 224,
        226–7
    Ulster Irish in 93
    United Irishmen 233, 238, 251,
        252
Downpatrick, Co. Down 6, 12, 14,
    45, 61, 86–7, 181, 319, 326,
    383, 458, 468
Downshire, Lord (Arthur Hill, 2nd
    marquis) 227, 235, 244
Doyle, Lynn 337, 338, 339, 344,
    347, 352–3
Drennan, William 194, 216
dress, Irish 34, 92
Drew, Revd Thomas 354, 355–6,
    362
Drogheda, synod (1614) 74
Dromintee, Co. Armagh 316
Dromore, Co. Down 181
Dromore diocese 60
druids 36, 61
Druim Cett, Convention of (AD
    575) 16

Drumbanagher pattern 223
Drumbee 223
drumlins xxix, 3
Drumswords churchyard,
    Monaghan 348
drunkenness, Catholic Church and
    285
Dublin, 1798 rebellion 252
Dublin University 239
Duffy, Charles Gavan 336, 338,
    344, 364, 367
Duigenan, Patrick 238
Dundalk, Co. Louth 181, 316
Dunfanaghy, Co. Donegal 200
Dungannon, Co. Tyrone 387, 412,
    413
Dunleavy family 49

earldoms 50
Easter Rising (1916) 299, 443–4,
    451, 453
Echlin family 86–7
ecumenism (1960s) 410
education xxxvii
    capital grants 462
    Catholic 277, 278, 407, 440, 447,
        452, 461, 462, 467–8
    history teaching 364–5, 366
    integrated 179–80, 336–7, 439,
        459, 476
    legislation, fairness 386
    means test 462–3
    monastic 15
    proselytising 273, 277
    segregated 276–8, 281, 294, 340,
        439, 458–64, 459, 462
    state 439, 463
Education and Enmity (Akenson)
    460
Education Bill (1923) 461, 462
Education Ministry xxxvii, 452,
    460, 463
elections
    Catholic Committee 231, 236,
        239
    Catholics and 181, 217

elections – *cont*
  'chapel-gate' election (1949) 399
  local government 373, 378, 385
  nationalists and 449
  parliamentary 299, 385, 397
  Westminster 401
elementary schools 461
  see also primary schools
eleven-plus examination 463
elite, Gaelic 126, 127
  decline 127
  disunity 111, 113
  and England 89
  and land settlements 84
  status 159
elite, Protestant 117
Elizabeth I, Queen 134
Elizabeth II, Queen 400
Emain Macha (Navan Fort), Armagh
  4, 6–7, 9, 11–12, 47, 49
Émer 5
emigration 192, 306–7, 317, 338
Emmet, Robert 443, 450
Emperor of Ice-Cream, The
  (Moore) 448, 468
employment
  Catholics 194, 323–4, 327, 330,
    384, 387, 460
  discrimination in 386, 387–92
  growth (1950s) 408
  religion and 378
endurance, Catholic tradition 239,
  468–9
engineering industry 408, 417–18,
  437
England
  Catholics and 481
  and Gaelic lords 49–52
  IRA campaign (1939) 402
  land-hunger 86
  Revolutionary wars (1793) 238
  rule over Ireland 25, 61
  war with Spain (1625–30) 94
  war with Spain (1739) 181
  see also British...
English language, status and 181

Enlightenment 172, 207
Enniskillen Co Fermanagh 451
  IRA bomb (1987) 441, 473
  Protestant demonstrations 181
Eóganacht 17
equality in government 481
Érainn 4
erenach land 96
erenachs 44–5, 152
Essex, Arthur Capel, earl of 112,
  144–5
Eucharistic Congress (1932) 443,
  447–8, 470
European Court of Human Rights
  421
evangelism, Protestant 129, 307,
  309–11
eviction, Famine and 309, 310–11
exorcism, priestly 287
extreme unction, sacrament 287

Factory of Grievances (Buckland)
  388
fáinne 454
Fair Employment Agency 387
fairies 8, 282–3, 288
'Faith of Our Fathers' (hymn) 125,
  455
Falls Rd, Belfast 358
  as Catholic area 325, 326
  mills 322
  Troubles (1969–) 394, 404, 420
family allowance 407
famine
  1741 186
  see also Great Famine
Farney, Monaghan 119
Farnham, Lord (John Maxwell, 5th
  baron) 273, 275, 310
Farrell, Michael 398
Farren, Neil, bishop of Derry 458,
  462, 469
Faughart, Co. Louth 141
Faul, Monsignor Denis 441, 472
Faulkner, Brian 410, 416, 425, 426,
  428

Feargal, king 77
feasting, Celtic 7
Feast of Lupercal (Moore) 467
Fenian, use of term 358
Fenians 291–2, 335, 368
Fergus mac Róich 5
Fermanagh county xli
  bog xli
  Boundary Commission and 379
  'B' Specials 380
  confiscated lands conspiracy
    (1625) 94
  Cromwellian confiscations 110
  elections 385, 386
  gavelkind 39
  genealogies 39
  IRA activity 406
  land tenure 41
  local councils 373
  Maguire lands 40
  Nine Years War 54
  and oath of allegiance 217
  Plantation xlii, 91
  succession disputes 51
Fews barony, Co. Armagh 119, 120,
  136, 140, 196, 363
Fews mountain 9
Fianna Fáil government 419
Fianna (Finn MacCumhail) 10–11
Fianna (republican youth) 404
fiction, Northern Irish 477–8, 480
Fife, William 320
Fife family 339
Finnian, St 15, 16
Finn MacCumhail 10–11
Fitt, Gerry 412, 413, 422–3, 425,
  428
Fitzpatrick, David 317, 341
Fitzsimmons family 87
Fitzwilliam, Sir William, Lord
  Deputy 52
Fitzwilliam, William Wentworth,
  2nd earl 243, 245
Flanders 118
flashpoints, traditional 195, 243,
  327

Flight of the Earls (1607) 53, 54, 55,
  85, 89, 92
floggings (1922) 382
Flood family 339–40
Flower, Robin 10
folklore, Protestant view 287–8
Foras Feasa ar Éirinn 79
forenames, as labels 455
forests 27, 30, 35–6
Forkhill, Co. Armagh 141, 222,
  223, 224, 273–4, 406
Fortnight magazine xliii
Foster, Anthony 165
Foster, Roy 369
France, and United Irishmen 246,
  249–50, 262
franchise
  business vote 385
  Catholics 291, 294, 324
Franciscan friars 60, 61, 62
  and Gaelic heritage 75–80
  missions 73–4
  and Plunkett 144
  Plunkett and 150, 151, 152, 153
  Third Order Secular 62
Franciscan Observant friars 63–4
Franco, General Francisco 469
Freeduff, Co. Armagh 178, 222
freeholders 40, 41, 42, 50–52, 53,
  88–9, 92
Freeman's Journal 310
Free State, Irish
  civil war (1922–3) 373, 377, 378
  and compulsory Irish 452
  and discrimination in NI 394
  emergency powers (1920s) 382
  and northern Catholics 376–7,
    379
  and northern sectarianism 376–7
  pact with Craig 376–7, 379, 381
  Protestants in 363, 373
  provisional government 376
  retaliatory sectarianism 394
  schools 461
  Ulster counties in 379
French Revolution 213, 215

friaries, foundation 63
friars 62–4
  abuses 207
  affection for 203, 207, 209–10
  Counter-Reformation 73–4, 78
  decline 207, 208, 209, 210
  devotional literature 67
  education abroad 207
  episcopal authority 71, 72
  as Gaelic elite 75
  itinerant 200, 207
  power 203
  pro-Spanish 73
  recruitment 75
  suppressing 173
  traditional training 72
  and weddings 179
friendship, across divide 126, 174,
  339
fundamentalist preachers 353–4,
  355–6, 410
fund-raising, Catholic 465–6

Gael, use of word 132
Gaelic Athletic Association (GAA)
  xxxiv, 369, 454, 455
Gaelic culture 195, 369
Gaelic League 368–9, 452–3, 454
Gaelic Revival 46, 285–8, 367–8,
  369, 455
Gaelic Ulster xxxviii, xxxix, 4, 25
  Counter-Reformation and 70–72
  disunity 111, 113
  familial structure 61–2
  frontier 29
  gallowglass families 29–30
  life in 30–34
  lords 30, 87, 94, 97
  power in 113
  pragmatism 26
  Protestantism and 69
  provincialism 73
  Reformation in 61, 68–70
  religious practice 60, 64–5, 66–8
  society in 84, 95
  status in 117

Gaeltacht, Donegal 454
Gall, use of word 46, 132
Gallagher, Revd Eric 459
Gallagher, James, bishop of Raphoe
  204, 205, 282
gallowglasses 29–30, 86, 110
Galway county 109
Gamble, John 198, 287, 290,
  335–7, 341, 362
gavelkind 39–40, 41
genealogy
  falsification 19, 77
  importance 5, 95, 118, 193
  religion and 72
  and status 39–40
  tracing 19
'general confession of Fiachra Mac
  Brádaigh, The' 155–6
General Remonstrance of the
  Catholics of Ireland (1641)
  156–7
gentry, Catholic 189, 190
geography, religious
  see demography, religious
George I, King 200
George III, King 243, 261
George VI, King 400
Germany, IRA negotiations with
  403
gerrymandering 378, 385, 388, 392
ghettos, religious 295, 326, 328,
  356, 378, 381
Giffard, John 247
Giraldus Cambrensis 8, 11, 13, 20,
  106
Give Them Stones (Beckett) 433,
  477
Gladstone, W. E. 167, 294, 320,
  357
Glassie, Henry 306, 348, 479
Glenard estate, Belfast 394
Glenarm, Co. Antrim 309
Glencolumbkille, Co. Donegal 365
Glens of Antrim 190
  Catholicism xl
  Gaelic-speaking 171

landscape xl, xlii
linen industry and 195
Protestant tenants 195
Scots settlers 29
toryism 118, 176
Ulster Irish in 93
Glenties, Co. Donegal 311, 329
Glenveagh evictions (1861) 319
gods, Celtic 8
Golden Age, Irish 15
gombeenmen 327, 329
Good Friday Agreement (1998) 426,
476–7, 481
Gortin, Co. Tyrone 95
Gosford Castle, Co. Armagh 225,
245
grammar schools, means test 462–3
grand juries 236
Grattan, Henry 168
Gray, Elizabeth (Betsy) 263
Gray, John 330
Great Famine (1845–9) xl, 305–13
Catholics affected by 305
collective amnesia and 308
cottiers decimated 284
in folk memory 306, 469
Protestants in 306, 308
relief schemes 307–8, 309–11,
312
souperism 273
Green, Alice Stopford 368
Greencastle, Belfast 326
Gregory, Augusta, Lady 11
Grianán of Ailech, Co. Donegal 6
grievance, culture of 362–3, 440–50
Grimshaw's Mill 354, 355
guns
see arms
Gwynn family 312

Haliday, Dr Alexander 265
Hall, S. C., Mr and Mrs 322
Hall-Thompson, Colonel 407,
461
Hamill, John 328
Hamilton, Sir Claud 95

Hamilton, Sir George 114, 128
Hamilton, Sir James 87, 88
Hamilton family 339–40
Hancock, John 345
Hanna, Revd Hugh 276, 356, 361
Harbison, Thomas 299
Harkness, David 378
Harland & Wolff shipyard, Belfast
323–4, 325, 330
Catholics in 323–4, 375, 394
intimidation in 324
Orangeism 356
Harris, Rosemary 466
Harris, Walter 45, 172, 178, 205,
206
Hassan, Revd John 377–8
Haughey, Charles 419
Hayes, Maurice 383, 420, 423–4,
466–7, 468, 469
healing 287–8
Healy, Cahir 396
hearth-money 218
Hearts of Steel 218–19
Heath, Sir Edward (later Lord) 424,
425
Heatley, Fred 394
hedge-schools 164, 179–81, 277,
447
Henry, Henry, bishop of Down and
Connor 296, 330
Henry II, King 13, 25, 36, 60, 61,
136
Henry VIII, King 50, 134
Hepburn, Tony 326
Hercules St (later Royal Ave),
Belfast 253, 325
hereditary land title 50, 51
heretic, use of word 136
Hervey, Frederick, Bishop of Derry
169–70
Heskin, Ken 434, 440
Hezlet, Sir Arthur 381
hierarchy, Catholic
authoritarianism 295
gradualist approach 227, 270
as outsiders 151

hierarchy, Catholic – *cont.*
  and partition 297–8, 300–301
  see also Catholic Church; bishops
higher education xxxvii, 433–4
High Kingship 12, 17
Hill, Sir George 307
Hill, Jacqueline 363
Hill, Sir Moses 87, 113
Hill family 113, 227
hill-forts 6–7
hills 27, 35–6, 131
Hillsborough, Wills Hill, 2nd
  viscount (later Downshire) 175,
  218
hiring fairs 313–15
Historical Memoirs of Armagh
  (Stuart) 362
history, Irish
  Protestants and 452, 479
  teaching 364–5, 366, 452, 460
Hobson, Bulmer 368
Hole in the Wall Gang 431
holy days 201–2
holy places, importance 45
holy wells 286
Holywood, Co. Down 178
Home Affairs Ministry 382, 389,
  390, 413
Home Rule
  campaign 293–4, 344, 360, 364
  opposition to 357
  Protestants and 295, 297
  and Protestant unemployment
  357, 361
  as 'Rome Rule' 320, 363
  Ulster excluded 297–9
Hood family 193
Hope, Bob 404
Hope, James 254, 256, 258, 259
horsemanship 33
hospitality, Gaelic 94–5, 198
housing
  allocation xxii, 378, 386–7, 408,
  411
  exchanges 378, 379
  Gaelic 30–31, 32–3

plantation 91
points system 411
provision xxxv
shortage 386–7, 408
two-storey 32
Housing Trust xxii, 386, 408
Howe, Leo 437
Hudson, Revd Edward 223, 262
Hughes, Bernard 329, 330
Hughes, Terence 189
Hume, Cardinal 472
Hume, John 366, 401, 423, 425,
  427, 428
humour, Ulster xxxv–xxxvi, 431,
  477
hunger strikes (1981) 426–7,
  448–50, 472, 473, 476
Hussey, Thomas, Bishop of
  Waterford and Lismore 248
huts, monastic 14, 60, 62

identity
  anti-popery in 440
  axioms of 83
  Catholicism as 450–57
  dual, conflict between 427, 437–8
  formation in opposition 156–7
  and past 445
  political 335
  republican 446–7
  sectarian awareness and 269
  secular 160
  social class and 328
  stereotypical cues 198
  in transition 476, 478
  Ulster Catholic xxxiii–xxxiv, 152,
  156, 361–9, 440, 442, 445,
  476–8
  Ulster Protestant 70, 352, 353, 440
Ignorantia sacerdotum 66
illegitimacy 65
illuminated manuscripts 15
image-worship 64
Impartial History of Ireland, The
  (Reily) 128–9, 170
inauguration ceremonies 36–8, 40

independence
  Northern Irish 423
  Protestants and 295, 297
indulgences 282
industry
  decline 408, 417–18
  location 437
informers
  IRA and 404
  and penal laws 175
Inishowen, Co. Donegal 3, 86,
    91–2, 128, 149, 178
Inquisition of Dungannon (1609) 44
In Search of a State (O Connor) 125
insecurity, Ulster xxxiii
insult, use 354–5
internment
  clergy and 472
  powers (1920s) 382
  torture in 421
  use (1957) 406
  use (1970) 421
  wartime 403, 423
intimidation 355
  anticipation of 432
  IRA campaign 435
  1790s 226
  Troubles (1969-) 418–19, 432
Iona abbey 37
Irish Catholic Confederacy 91, 134
Irish Church
  and England 61
  English influence 36
  Gaelic chiefs and 60, 70, 73, 74,
    79, 80
  in Gaelic Ulster 36
  indiscipline, monasteries 66–7
  as localised family fiefdom 149–50
  medieval reform 59–60, 61,
    64–5, 68–70
  popular culture 66–7
Irish Folklore Commission 93, 369
Irish Labour Party 398
Irish language
  as Catholic code 369, 453
  communication and 314–15

compulsory 452
decline 126, 181, 191, 205, 451
  18th-century revival 214
  evangelisation and 171
  Gaelic League and 368
  IRA and 453–4
  mountain areas 197
  19th-century decline 368
  post-partition revival 451–4
  Protestant interest in 452
  and rebellion 369
  religion and 67, 71, 129–30
  sectarian vocabulary 132
  Unionist condemnation 452–3
  use in politics 182
Irish Magazine 363–4
Irish Minstrelsy (Hardiman) 135
Irish Monthly 285
Irish News xxxvi, 295, 377, 389,
    391, 399, 400, 409, 445–6,
    447, 448, 451, 454, 470
Irish Parliament
  abolition 261
  anti-Papist 167–8
  Catholic Relief Bill (1793) 238
  Catholics barred 167, 239
  Catholics in 294
  Old Irish in 97
  prorogation 100
  and Settlement Act 112
  and Temple 115
  and Treaty of Limerick 165
  Williamite 116
Irish Parliamentary Party 294, 295,
    296, 297, 298, 299
Irish Rebellion (Temple) 105–6, 170
Irish Republican Army (IRA) 396,
    442
  Catholics and 419
  and Catholics in police 381
  defence role 403, 419
  growth (1930s) 394
  internment (1970) 421
  1920s 373, 374, 377, 380
  Operation Harvest 406
  post-partition 402–6, 408

Irish Republican Army – *cont.*
  and Troubles (1969-) 419
  see also Official IRA; Provisional
    IRA
Irish Society 277
Irish Volunteers 298
Irish Weekly 445, 447
Irvine, John 337
Islandmagee, Co. Antrim 102, 104
Iveagh, Co Down 26, 49

Jacobitism 164, 168, 169, 213–14
James I, King 50, 69–70, 77, 78, 85,
  86, 89
James II, King 114–16, 131, 199,
  359
James III (Old Pretender) 148, 165,
  169, 207
Jesuits 71, 146
Jesus Christ 64, 67, 139, 154
John, King 29
Johnston, William 320, 363
John XXIII, Pope 408, 409
Jones, Henry, bishop of Clogher
  105, 107, 109, 129, 156
Jonesborough, Co. Armagh 222
Jordan family 86–7
juries
  kin ties 55
  Orange 347, 348

Keating, Geoffrey 79, 137
Kelly, Edward 193
Kelly, James 389
Kelly, Liam 406
Kelly, Revd Terence 145–6
Kennedy, John F. 408
Kernan, Michael 358
Kernan family 193
kerne 30, 92
Kerr, Anne 413
Kerr, Russell 413
Kerry county 118
Kerry militia 246
Killala friary 67
Killeavy, Co. Armagh 93

Killough, Co. Down 114, 172
Killsherdany, Co. Cavan 310
Kilmacrenan, Co. Donegal 36, 37,
  101
Kilmore diocese 60, 202
Kinawley, Co. Fermanagh 329, 367
Kinelarty, Co. Down 26
King, William, archbishop of Dublin
  171, 192
kin-group
  importance 65, 439–40
  as unit of social control 5–6
kingship, concept of 18
Kinnaird, Co. Tyrone 103
Klondike 287
Knox, George 190

Labour party
  and Ulster Workers Strike 426
labour politics 330–31
Lafferty, H. A. 341
laity, religious instruction 282
Lake, General Gerard 246, 259
Lamb, Revd Patrick 274, 364
'Lament for Sorley MacDonnell'
  (Mac Cuarta) 139, 142–3, 214
land
  as commodity 53
  competition for 221
  confiscation 84, 107–11
  Cromwellian settlement 93,
    107–11
  at Crown disposal 85
  discoverers 112
  dispossession 52, 54
  familial 14, 18, 37, 38–9, 41–2,
    318–19
  fertile, natives leave 93
  and Gaelic tradition 35–8, 40
  loss to Protestants 158
  marriage with chief 37
  mortgaged 94
  peasant proprietorship 317
  poor, assignation xl–xlii, 18, 93,
    195–7
  Protestant fears for 167–8, 170

redistribution by lord 40, 42–3
rents 55
Restoration settlement 111–14,
    120, 147
17th-century settlement 120–22
shortage 219, 221
subdivision 40, 41, 42, 305–6
tenure 38–45
tenure, Gaelic 86, 91
title 42, 86–7, 92, 96
units of measurement 42
Williamite settlement 115–17
see also freeholders; land-
    ownership
land-conformism 167
land law, early 14
Land League 293, 319, 320, 321
landlords
    Anglican 318
    Catholic 311
    18th-century 186
    electoral interests 217
    evangelical 273
    in Famine 307–8
    in folk memory 306, 307, 310–11
    improving 307
    Protestant 117
    removal 317–18
    as trustees 319
land-owners
    Catholic, transplantation 108
    Church of Ireland 327
    Protestant 108–9, 110–11, 115
    as tenants 187
land-ownership
    Catholic 114, 121–2
    Gaelic 38, 40–42
    increase 91
    as Protestant 270
    status and 55, 84
'land Protestants' 158–9, 167
landscape
    Catholic 195–7
    Protestant 196, 197
    sacred 288
    see also topography

Land War (1879–82) 318
Larkin, Emmet 270
Larkin, James 330
Larne, Co. Antrim 326
last rites 287
La Tène Celtic culture 4
Latocnaye, Chevalier de 246, 247,
    251
Laudabiliter papal bull 25, 61, 136
law
    Catholics and 225
    Catholics in 327
    Common Law 43, 85, 86
    criminal code 55
    and English language 126, 343–4
    evasion, and penal laws 176
    extension 31
    Irish language and 184
    and landholding 43
    outwitting, culture of 184
Lawless, John 272, 345
Leader, The 366
learning, respect for 231
leases 86
    annual 92
    long 159, 185
Lebor Gabála 9, 15, 48, 76
Lecale, Co. Down 27, 36
Lecky, W. E. H. 111, 247
Lee, Simon xliii
Leech Committee 383
Leinster 248, 252
Leitrim, William Sydney Clements,
    3rd earl 320
Leitrim county 108, 118
Leix county 85
Lemass, Seán 409, 410
Leslie, Henry 129
Leslie family of Monaghan 312
Leth Cuinn 17
Leth Moga 17
Letterkenny, Co. Donegal 313, 314
Letter to Coroticus (Patrick) 13
Liberal party 291, 294, 300,
    320–21, 357
liberty, as Protestant 169

'Lillibullero' 114–15
Limerick, Treaty of (1697) 116
linen industry
    agriculture and 305–6
    Catholics in 186, 187, 188, 189,
        191, 192
    collapse 306
    exports 192
    importance 191–2
    mechanisation 321–3
    Orangeism 345–6
    prosperity and 186
    Protestant 191
    United Irishmen and 244
Lisburn, Co. Antrim 218, 326, 374
Lisnaskea, Co. Fermanagh 290, 308
Lissane parish 65
Lissanoure, Co. Antrim 178–9
Lisselby Roodan, Co. Londonderry
    73
literacy
    English 181
    Ulster Irish 130
Lloyd George, David 300, 378
local government
    elections 373, 378, 385
    employment practices 324, 386,
        387–92
    gerrymandered 462
    Orange influence 324
    and 1641 Rebellion 97
localism, Gaelic 42
Lóegaire, King of Tara 14
Loghenesolyn, Londonderry 73
Logue, Cardinal 300
Loinsigh (Lynch) family 187
Lombard, Peter, archbishop of
    Armagh 72, 73
London companies 143
Londonderry
    County Borough 91–2
    boundaries redrawn 385
    creation 32
    housing, discrimination 387
    Grand Jury 236
    Plantation 91

tories 118
    see also Derry
Londonderry, Charles Stewart
    Henry, 7th marquis 461–2
Londonderry, Charles William
    Stewart, 3rd marquis 307, 309
Londonderry, Robert Stewart, 1st
    marquis 233, 246–7
Londonderry Standard 319–20
London Hibernian Society 170, 277
Lonely Passion of Judith Hearne
    (Moore) 468
Longley, Edna 475, 477
Long Parliament (1640) 99
Lord Lieutenants, weakness 235
lordship, Gaelic 48–56
    and English lordship 49–52
    hospitality 94–5
    and landholding 38
    leadership 94
    and power 38
    succession 51–2
    and toryism 119
    transformed to estates 40
Lough Derg, Co. Donegal 184–5
Lough Foyle fisheries 89
Loughgall, Co. Armagh 49, 91, 103,
    225
Loughgall Volunteers 221
Loughinisland, Co. Down 187
Loughlinstown, Co. Derry 120
Lough Neagh xli, 3, 8, 260
Loughrea, Co. Galway 107
Lough Swilly 218
Louis XIV, King of France 115
Louth county 151, 165, 216–17,
    221, 224–5
Louvain seminary 72, 73, 75–6,
    78–9, 148, 202
Lowry, Alexander 255
loyalty, use of term 395–6
Loyalty League 453
Lurgan, Co. Armagh 326, 327,
    346
Lynch, John 98
Lynch family 187

Lynn, Brendan 398
Lynn Committee (1921) 383, 461–2
Lyons, Maura 410
Lyttle, W. G. 263

MacAingil, Hugh 75
McAlester, Robert 310
McAlindon, Patrick 136–7
Macan, Arthur 251
Macan, Thomas 251
Mac an Bhaird, Aodh 75, 76
Mac an Bhaird, Fearghal Óg 78
Mac Artáin 19
Macartney, Lord 178–9
McAteer, Eddie 399, 401, 413
McAughtry, Sam 453
MacBrádaigh, Fiachra 155–6
McCabe, William Putnam 184
MacCabe family 29
Mac Caghwell, Hugh 75
McCahy, Hugh Roe 241
McCall sept 40
MacCana, Edmund 88
McCann, Anthony 255
McCann, Eamonn 466, 468–9
McCann, Toole 103
McCann family 49
MacCartan, John 116
MacCartan, Revd Patrick 248
MacCartan, Theophilus, bishop of
    Down and Connor 188, 208
MacCartan family 19, 26, 87, 188
MacCary, Revd James 257
McCasey family 96
Mac Cathmhaoil family 75
Mac Cathmhaoil sept 40
MacCawell family 44, 65
McCawll sept 40
MacClave of Aughnamullen
    (O'Donnelly) 150–51, 153
McClay, Bab 290
McClelland, Revd 275
McCluskey, Conn 399, 400,
    411–12, 413
McCluskey, Patricia 411–12, 413
McComiskey, William 338

MacConnell family 29
MacCooey, Art 139–42, 143, 182,
    183, 186, 204, 213, 217, 223
McCourt, Frank 444
McCourt, Malachy 444
McCracken, Henry Joy 217, 252–3,
    254, 255, 264
McCracken, Mary Anne 182, 217
McCrudden, Turlough 73, 74, 78
McCrystal, Cal 408, 454
Mac Cuarta, Séamus Dall 136,
    137–9, 142–3, 157, 214
McCullough, Rose 315
McDaid (tory leader) 139
McDevitt, Philip 201, 208
Mac Domhnaill, Aodh 274–5, 276,
    366
MacDonald, Alistair 103–4
MacDonald, Ramsay 331
MacDonnell, Alexander 103–4
McDonnell, Hugh 274–5, 276, 312,
    313, 342–3, 366
McDonnell, Patrick 255
MacDonnell, Sorley Boy 139, 142–3
MacDonnells of Antrim 72, 138
    friaries 63
    and James I 87
    lands 87–8
    and 1641 Rebellion 98
    religion 117
    restored 113, 116–17
    Scots Catholic tenants 128
    and settlers 88
    status 87–8, 95
McDonnells of Antrim
    see also Antrim, earls
MacDonnells of Ballygawley 29
MacDonnells of the Isles 27, 29,
    30
MacDowall family 29
Mac Duinn Slébhe 49
McElroy, Gerald 475, 476
MacEnaney, Patrick 193
MacEnaney family 193
McEnhill, Hugh 338
MacFadden, Canon James 329

McFadden, Mrs 433
McFall, Michael 189
MacGerrity, Hugh 139
McGildowney, Edmund 237
McGildowney, Eugene 190
MacGill, Patrick 285, 315, 329
MacGill family 29
McGlinchey, Patrick 204, 207
McGlone, John 298, 299, 343
McGlone, Teag 73
MacGowan, Michael 287, 313–14, 315–17, 319, 326
McGuinness, Martin 459
McGurk, Revd Bernard 145
Macha, horse-goddess 7
MacHale, John, archbishop of Tuam 278, 279
McHugh, Charles, bishop of Derry 298
Mack, John 441
Mackan, Co. Fermanagh 348–9
McKee, Joseph 341
Macken, Simon 142–3
McKenna, Nugent 175
McKenna family 188
McKittrick, David 432
McKnight, James 319–20, 359, 368
McLaughlin family 237
MacLaverty, Bernard 438
McLaverty, Michael 375–6
McLaverty, Revd B. 448
McLeod, Hugh 270
Mac Liammóir, Mícheál 443
Mac Lochlainn family 19, 28
McLorinan, Paul 167
MacLoughlin family 49
MacMahon, Colla MacBrian 114
MacMahon, Hugh, archbishop of Armagh 97, 132, 136, 177, 194, 199, 215–16
MacMahon, Hugh, bishop of Clogher 173
MacMahon, Hugh Roe 52
McMahon, Owen 375
McMahon murders 375, 443

MacMahons of Monaghan 19, 29, 31, 34, 40, 188
   mortgaged lands 94
   and surrender and regrant 50
McManus, Honoria 167
MacManus, Seamas 226, 273, 289–90, 329, 337, 339, 367
Mac Mathgamna 19
McNally, Leonard 239
McNeill, Daniel 189
McParlan, James 197
McPeake, Francis 368
McQuaid, Revd Matt 310
MacQuillans of the Route 29, 63, 87
MacRory, Cardinal Joseph 374, 457–8
MacRory family 29
MacShane, Andrew 187
McShanes 237
MacSheehy family 29
McSkimin, Samuel 253–4
McSparran, J. D. 397
MacSweeney, Maire 68
MacSweeney, Maolmhuire 89, 94–5
MacSweeney, Miles 114
MacSweeney family 29, 36–7, 45, 63, 89, 92, 138
McVeagh, Fergus 176
MacVeagh, Jeremiah 299
Madden, R. R. 254, 256
Mag Aonghusa 19
Mageean, Daniel, bishop of Down and Connor 382–3, 394, 458, 470
Magee College, Derry 409
Magennis, Revd Bernard 255, 258
Magennis, Bonaventure, bishop of Down and Connor 72–3
Magennis, Brian Oge McRory 113
Magennis, Edmund Oge 115, 116
Magennis, Ever 113
Magennis, John 237, 238, 248, 255, 256–7, 257–8
Magennis, Phelimy 113

Magennis family 19, 26, 36, 40, 49, 60, 87, 94, 116, 187, 188
Magennis family of Clanconnel 116
Magennis family of Iveagh 34, 50, 98, 110, 113, 117, 138
Magennis family of Kilwarlin 113
Magennis family of Tollymore 130–31
Maghera, Co. Derry 251
Magherally, Co. Down 218–19
magic, Catholicism and 286–90
Magill, Revd Robert 261
Magin, Nicholas 253
Maginn, Edward, bishop of Derry 272, 359
Maginn, Revd Patrick 113
magistrates
    Orangeism 345–6, 350
    Protestant 327
    stipendiary 343, 345
Magroarty, Revd John 365
Mag Uidir 19
Maguire, Brian 90, 95, 116
Maguire, Bryan 193
Maguire, Conor Rua 89
Maguire, Constantine 237
Maguire, Cú Chonnacht 116
Maguire, Denis, bishop of Dromore 193, 208
Maguire, Hugh 52
Maguire, Hugh O'Dugan 156
Maguire, Philip 237
Maguire, Terence 237
Maguire family 19, 29, 40, 64, 65, 110, 188, 193, 208
    and Anglo-Normans 26
    decline 97
    Flight (1607) 54
    genealogy 45–6
    land 40, 90
    and 1641 Rebellion 98
    as turncoats 158–9
Malan, Rian 438
Mallon, Seamus 477
Mandeville family 86–7, 346
manuscripts, Gaelic 76, 79

maps, making 52
marches, anti-internment 421
    see also parades
marching season
    community relations and 346–7, 349–51
    see also parades
Markethill, Co. Armagh 225
Markets, Belfast 326
Marlborough Street College, Dublin 463
marriage
    to close relatives 65, 173
    delayed 317
    religion and 436
    see also mixed marriage
martial law (1797–8) 247, 251, 253
martyrs 13
Mary, Virgin 154
    devotion to 70, 286
    as ideal 204
    politicisation 157
    portrayal 64, 67
mass
    attendance at 201, 474
    in vernacular 469
Massarene, Sir John Clotworthy, Lord 99, 114
Massarene family 109
mass-houses 166, 199, 200
mass-rocks 164, 174, 199, 200, 201, 447, 469
Mater Infirmorum hospital, Belfast 283
    Craigavon and 397
    funding 464–5
    Prince of Wales visits 400
    state funding 407
Maynooth, St Patrick's seminary 209, 248, 284, 433
meat, eaten on Fridays 310, 316
Meath diocese 60
Medb, Queen of Connachta 5
media 41, 440
    Catholic, repressive culture 467
    nationalist 445–6, 447

and peace process 445
meeting-houses, early 200
Mellifont, Treaty of (1603) 53
mendicant friars 62–4
mensal lands 38
mercenaries 25, 28, 30
  Scottish 28–30
  see also gallowglasses
Mesolithic Ulster 3
Methodists 171, 229, 339
Middle Ages 18
middle class
  culture of 284
  Presbyterian 232
middle class, Catholic 192–4, 243
  in Belfast xxvi, 322, 323
  in civil-rights movement 465
  18th-century 187, 228
  leadership 265
  19th-century 327
  prejudice encountered 479
  and prophecies 250
  and republicans 442
middlemen 95, 187
Mide, province 8
Midgley, Harry 407, 461
Midnight Mass, The (Carleton) 208
migration, seasonal 315–17
Milesian origin-myth 16, 137
militarisation, medieval 25, 29
militia 242, 246, 247, 260–61, 264
millenarianism 249
Miller, Glenn 404
Millfield, Belfast 353, 355
Milltown cemetery, Belfast 283
Mindzenty, Cardinal 469
Minority Rights Group 395
Mise Éire (film) 443
missions, Catholic 280, 286
Mitchel, John 311, 312
mixed marriage 340–41, 435–6, 439, 475
  Catholic Church and 341, 435, 475
  Catholics and 440
  18th-century 179

intimidation and 355
Protestants and 341, 435
sectarian violence and 394
  17th-century 130–31
mobility, Gaelic 30–31, 32, 33, 34, 35, 86
Modest Proposal (Swift) 186
Moira, Francis Rawdon, 2nd earl 226, 247
Molyneux, Thomas 196
Monaghan county xli, 19
  Cromwellian descendants 185
  excluded from Plantation 89, 91
  Famine 305, 307
  freeholders 88–9
  Gaelic land-holding system 120
  Home Rule 297
  militia 247
  and Partition xlii–xliii
  1798 rebellion 257
  sectarian incidents 347–8
  succession disputes 51, 52
  troubles (1790s) 225
Monaghan town 181, 336, 364
monarchy, Catholic support 400
monasteries
  buildings 31, 60, 62
  decline 59–60, 61
  dissolution 61, 62, 69
  land gifted 43–4
  and learning 75
  new orders 59–60, 61
  priorities 20
  as social centres 14
  succession within 14
  Viking raids 16–17
money economy 53
Montgomery, George, bishop 73
Montgomery, Revd Henry 233
Montgomery, Sir Hugh 87, 88
Montgomery, Sir James 102
Montgomery of Ards, Viscount 107
Mooney, Canice 64
Mooney, Donatus 71–2
Moore, Brian 448, 467–8
Moore, Thomas 46, 47, 285

Moran, D. P. 366
Morgan, Lady 197
Morris, Henry 240
Moryson, Fynes 33
'Mother and Child Scheme' 464
mountain people, and government
   234–5
Mountjoy, Charles Blount, 8th
   baron 54, 145
Mount Stewart, Co. Down 309
Mourne Mountains, Co. Down 102
Movilla, Co. Donegal 15, 16
Mulholland, Thomas 226
Mulholland's mill, Belfast 322–3
Mullins, Mrs 353
Munro, Henry 252, 255–6, 257,
   258
Munster 85, 133, 135
murders, sectarian 422, 435, 438
Murney, George 329
Murphy, Dervla 416, 431
Murphy, Michael J. 38, 158, 159,
   310, 368, 369
Murphys of Monaghan 188
Murray, Daniel, archbishop of
   Dublin 278
Murray, Revd Raymond 472
Musgrave, Sir Richard 253
music, sectarian 223, 358

names
   anglicisation 157–8
   Gaelic forms 455
Naoise 5
Nation, The 364
national anthem, Catholics and 400
National Association of Ireland 293
National Health Service 464–5
nationalism
   ascetic, pious 454, 455
   battle hymn 125–6
   Catholicism and 83, 450–51, 457,
     478
   clergy and 292, 293, 295–6
   constitutional 292–3, 299, 300,
     444

   development 83, 351–2, 363
   early 291, 294
   politics (1970–99) 422–8
   post-1921 373, 377, 383
   as rebellious 344
   romantic 367–8, 399, 443–4,
     445, 449
   secular 295–6
   and Stormont 396–402
nationalists
   abstentionism 396, 397
   Catholic disillusionment with 401
   division in elections 449
   in government 424–5
   and Irish Republic 399
   meeting (1916) 297–8
   middle-class takeover 397–8
   need to belong 399
   and oath of allegiance 400–401
   secular identity 160
   self-confidence 481
   self-examination 480
   southern 299, 300
   in Stormont 396–7
   and unity 481
   Westminster election (1955) 401
National schools 277–8, 281, 337,
   340, 368
Navan Fort
   see Emain Macha
Ned McKeown (Carleton) 183
neighbourliness 126, 339
Neilson, James 181
Nendrum, Co. Down 14
Neolithic Ulster 3
Ne Temere papal decree (1907) 341,
   435
Newell, Edward 247
New English 28, 46, 69
New Ireland Forum (1983–4) 427,
   450, 478
New Irish Army 99, 101
'New Light' Presbyterians 229
New Lodge, Belfast 326
Newry, Co. Down 181, 244, 326,
   379, 388

Newry Register 363
newspapers
  separate 448
  see also media
New Testament 67
Newtownards, Co. Down 307
Newtownards Independent 312
Newtownbutler, Co. Fermanagh
  391
Niall of the Nine Hostages 10
NICRA
  see Northern Ireland Civil Rights
  Association
Nine Years War (1593–1603) 32,
  37, 43, 53, 54, 59, 86, 87
Nixon, D.-I. J. W. 375
no-go areas, Catholic 471
nomadism, Gaelic
  see mobility
Normans 14
Northern Ireland, use of term xxxiii
Northern Ireland Assembly (1973)
  424–6
Northern Ireland Assembly (1999)
  454
Northern Ireland Civil Rights
  Association (NICRA) 412–14,
  419, 423
Northern Ireland Conservative Party
  433
Northern Ireland Labour Party 398,
  420
Northern Ireland Office 424
Northern Ireland state
  boundaries 373, 379
  Catholic Church and 470–71,
  472, 473
  Catholic minority 300, 373, 379
  Catholic ownership 384, 476,
  481
  Catholics and 384, 395, 396, 398,
  399, 402, 409, 458
  discrimination in 384–94
  foundation (1921) 300, 373,
  374
  'in danger' 379

nationalist recognition 373, 376,
  383, 423
sectarian pronouncements 389
Unionist domination 386
Northern Irish parliament
  see Stormont
Northern Star newspaper 230,
  231–2, 242, 250
novitiates, reopening 209
Nugent, Major-General George 253,
  256, 261
nuns 155
  and Church 476
  introduction 281, 283, 356
  modern role 474, 476
nursery schemes, Catholic Church
  and 464

Oakboys 217–18
oath of allegiance
  Catholics and 169, 189, 216–17,
  248
  Nationalist Party and 400–401
oaths of abjuration 169
O'Boyle, Turlough 89
O'Boyle family 44, 65, 138
O'Brien, Conor Cruise 366, 367
Ó Bruadair (poet) 11
Ó Buachalla, Breandán 77
O'Cahan, Donal
  case against O'Neill 54, 55
  in Nine Years War 53
O'Cahan family 19, 26, 30, 32,
  37–8, 92, 94
O'Callaghan, Owen 237
O'Callaghan family 141, 188, 189,
  311
O'Carroll family 19
Ó Catháin family 19
Occasions of Faith (Taylor) 286
Ó Cerbaill family 19
O'Clery, Michael 75–6
O'Connell, Daniel 325, 328
  campaign 271–2, 279, 347
  clergy as agents 271, 292
  Protestants and 353

support 271–2, 276, 342, 344
O'Connellism 262
O Connor, Fionnuala 125, 399, 442, 446, 462, 467, 473
O'Corry family 65
O'Devany, Bishop of Down and Connor 69, 72
Ó Dochartaigh 19
O'Doherty, Sir Cahir 85
O'Doherty, Malachi 366, 367
O'Doherty, Rose 204
O'Doherty family 19
Ó Doibhlin, Revd Éamon 158
Ó Doirnín, Peadar 139, 203, 213, 214–15, 223
Ó Domhnaill, Aodh 314
Ó Domhnaill family 19
O'Donnell, Dominick 183
O'Donnell, General 188–9
O'Donnell, Manus 34
O'Donnell, Peadar 403
O'Donnell family 19, 33, 72, 193
  and friaries 63
  hereditary poets 75–6
  inauguration ceremonies 36, 37
  lands 94, 132–3
  marriages 28–9
  as priests 65, 132–3
  territorial dispute with O'Neill 41–2, 47
  see also Tyrconnell
O'Donnelly, Owen 150–51, 153
O'Donnelly, Shane McPhelimy 73
O'Donovan, John 353
O'Donovan Rossa, Jeremiah 443, 444
O'Dufferne, Patrick Groome 95
Offaly, plantation 85
Official IRA 402, 419, 421
  targeted by military 419
Ó Fiaich, Cardinal Tomás 140, 149, 473–4
O'Flynn family 26
Ó Gallachair, Revd P. 174
O'Gallagher, Owen 180
O'Gallagher, Tuathal Balbh 66

O'Gallagher family 65
'O Gentle Cleric' (Bennett) 364
Ogle, John 244–5
Ó Gnímh, Fear Flatha 96–7
Ó Gnímhs 29, 78
O'Grady, Standish 11
O'Hagan, Peter 427–8
O'Hagan family 32, 37–8, 41
O'Hanlon, Fergal 406, 444, 451
O'Hanlon, Hugh 255
O'Hanlon, Paddy 423
O'Hanlon, Redmond 119–20
O'Hanlon, Revd W. 323
O'Hanlon family 19, 26, 40, 49, 89, 227
O'Hara, Charles 189
O'Hara, Oliver 167
O'Hara family 95, 189
Ó hEódhasa, Eochaidh 48, 77–8
Ó Huiginn, Tadhg Dall 47
O'Kane, bishop of Derry 470
O'Laverty, Revd James 88, 130, 288, 319, 366
Old English 28, 46
  and compromise 147
  and freedom of conscience 147
  and land 100, 109, 120
  and loyalty 120
  O'Neill and 59
  outlawed 116
  and 1641 Rebellion 100, 102, 104
  status 113
  Tridentine Catholicism 71
  and Ulster Irish 100, 104
Old Irish 28
  and compromise 147
  and land 109, 120
  outlawed 116
  in Parliament 97
  as royal officials 97
Old Lodge, Belfast 358, 394
ollamhs 76, 77, 193
O'Loughran family 44, 65, 96
Omagh, Co. Tyrone 120, 315, 387
Ombudsman 411

Ó Muirgheasa, Énri 240, 286, 314, 342, 343
O'Neill, Aedh Reamhar 33
O'Neill, Art 369
O'Neill, Captain Art 118
O'Neill, Art McBaron 91
O'Neill, Brian Crossagh 95
O'Neill, Daniel of Clandeboye 113–14
O'Neill, Daniel of the Fews 188
O'Neill, Henry of Killeleagh 113
O'Neill, Sir Henry of the Fews 110
O'Neill, John 188, 237
O'Neill, Sir Neill of Killeleagh 116
O'Neill, Nelan 64
O'Neill, Niall Óg 47
O'Neill, Owen of Clandeboye 206
O'Neill, Owen Roe 91, 100, 134, 135, 136, 146
O'Neill, Sir Phelim 90, 100, 101, 103, 107, 108
O'Neill, Phelim (Felix Neel) 158
O'Neill, Shane 37, 43, 90
O'Neill, Sir Terence xxxvi, 392–3, 423
    Catholics and 384, 390, 411, 414, 416
    modernisation programme 409
    Paisley and 410–11, 415, 416
    reconciliation policy 407, 409, 410, 414
    resignation (1969) 401, 407–12, 414–16, 415, 425
    Unionist party and 409–11, 414, 415
O'Neill, Terence (Convention representative) 237
O'Neill, Turlough Luineach 34
O'Neill, Turlough MacHenry 89
O'Neill family 187, 193
    alliances against 49
    and Anglo-Normans 26, 27, 28
    and church lands 44
    declining branches 97
    earldom 50, 51
    and friaries 63
    inauguration 41
    land grants 89
    land loss 132–3
    and lineal succession 51
    lordship 31–2
    marriages 28–9
    as priests 132–3
    territorial dispute with O'Donnell 41–2, 47
    'the', use of 37
    and Ulaid dynasty 47, 49
    see also Tyrone, earls
O'Neill family of Antrim 189, 392
O'Neill family of Armagh 63, 188
O'Neill family of Banvale 188, 227
O'Neill family of Clandeboye 26, 27, 40, 49, 87, 130–31, 188
O'Neill family of Killeleagh 98
O'Neill family of the Fews 36, 40, 49, 89, 98, 138, 140, 188
O'Neill family of Tyrone 36, 37, 72
Ó Néills, emergence 19
On the prophecy of Colum Cille son of Phelim (MacDonnell) 276
Opsahl, Torkel xliii
Opsahl Commission xliii, 83, 384, 432, 434–5, 476, 478
O'Rahilly, Cecile 133
O'Rahilly, T. F. 4
Óráid (Pulleine) 206
Orangeism
    aggression 240, 244–5, 262, 325, 346–7
    Catholics and 264, 351
    gentry and 224
    growth 344
    as necessary evil 246
    Presbyterians and 351
    and 1798 rebellion 253–4
    revival (1880s) 352
    and state apparatus 264, 266
    United Irishmen and 251
    working class and 264
'Orangeman, The' (verse) 343
Orange Order
    and Catholic employment 391–2

Glaswegians in 393
Grand Lodge of Ireland 345
influence of 389
lower-class Presbyterians in 229
and mixed marriage 341
parliamentary enquiry (1835) 275
temporary dissolution (1836–40)
265
and tenant right 320
United Irishmen join 262
Ordnance Survey Memoirs 281, 284
O'Reilly, archbishop of Armagh 248
O'Reilly, Daniel 208
O'Reilly, Edmund, archbishop of
Armagh 148, 150
O'Reilly, Revd Michael 181
O'Reilly, Michael, archbishop of
Armagh 203–4, 206, 208, 209
O'Reilly, Miles 101
O'Reilly, Philip 101, 109, 208
O'Reilly, Revd Tom 329
O'Reilly family 26, 50, 65, 90, 119,
188
Oriel
see Airgialla
Orior, Co. Armagh 91
Ormond, James Butler, 1st duke
111, 114, 147, 148, 149
O'Rorke family 189
O'Rourke, Jack 452
Orr, James 259–60, 262
O'Shea, Kitty 295
O'Sheil, James, bishop of Down and
Connor 137–8
'Oultachs' 192, 226
Our Boys magazine 367
outdoor relief strike (1932) 393
overlords
curtailing power 117
England and 86, 88
and power 40

Paddy's Resource song collection
232
paganism, Celtic 7, 8, 14–15, 20, 60
Paine, Thomas 239

Pairlement Chloinne Tomáis 97
Paisley, Revd Ian 410–11, 425, 440
and O'Neill 410–11, 415, 416
Paisleyism 406, 413–15, 434
Pale 25, 29, 31, 34, 43, 85, 119
Papacy
authority 209
Catholic loyalty to 164
dogmatism 351
and politics 293
popular devotion to 61
temporal powers 146, 148, 209,
270
papist, use of term 136, 141, 182,
199
parades 223
and sectarian riots 344–61
parades, Catholic 356, 360
parades, Orange 344–51
banned (1832) 265, 325, 345,
349, 352, 354, 356
in Catholic areas 440–41
challenged by Catholic youths
348
Conservative Government and
420
continuing effects 480
18th-century 225
as legitimate loyal display 344
rights 356
riots and 393–4
Parades Commission 476
paramilitaries, Loyalist 417–18
Parker, Edward 182
Parker, Tony 436
parliamentary elections 385, 397
Parnell, Charles Stewart 292,
293–4, 295
Parnellism 367–8
parochial development 14
partible inheritance 39–40
partition
Catholic hierarchy and 297–8,
300–301
IRA and 402
south and 406

partnership leases 195, 197
Passionist order 281
pastoralism, Gaelic 30, 33, 35, 43, 86
Patrick, St 7, 12–14, 16, 21, 26, 64, 76, 457
patriotism, death and 443–4, 449
Patten Commission (1999) 431–2, 476
patterns 153, 286
peace, desire for 434
peace-lines 432
peace process, and meaning of Ulster 481
Pearse, Patrick 11, 299, 443–4, 449, 450
peasants 43, 285–8, 369
Peden, Alexander 249
Peep O'Day Boys 222, 223, 224, 225, 226, 240, 244, 245
penal laws 140, 165–77, 210
    added value 479
    enforcement 177
    evasion 174
    intention behind 173–4
    leases, length 174–5
    Mass legal under 447
    modern reading 164
    and property 167
    repeal 220
    severity 165
    traditional view 163–4, 174, 447, 469
penance, sacrament 201, 202
People's Democracy (PD) 414–15, 416–17
Perrot, Sir John 48
persecution 126, 143, 146–9, 149
    elite and 159
    republicanism and 447–8
personality, Ulster xxxiii
Peter's Hill, Belfast 355
Philbin, William, bishop of Down and Connor 470–71, 474
Phoenix, Eamon 398
Phoenix Park, Dublin 447, 470

physiognomy, and religious affiliation 361–2
Pioneer Total Abstinence Society 285
Pius IX, Pope 282
place, pride of 46, 480–81
Plantation xxxviii, xli, 43, 53, 84–97
    added value 479
    beneficiaries of 89–90, 91
    categories 91
    church lands in 96
    co-operation with 89, 91
    counties 91
    and Cromwellian confiscations 110
    and 'deserving Irish' 48, 73, 90–91
    initial welcome 86
    Irish majority in 92, 97
    land allotment 48, 73
    landlords as trustees 319
    land tenure 38, 41
    as mixed settlement 102
    as religious campaign 83
    and resentment 93–4
    and status 95–7
Plunkett family 188, 193
Plunkett, Oliver, archbishop of Armagh 118, 121, 132, 149, 151–5, 155
    execution 144–5
    and Franciscans 74, 144, 150, 151, 152, 153
    in hiding 150
    and Protestant authorities 151–2
    snobbishness 151
Pococke, Richard, Bishop of Ossory 188, 199–200, 218
poetry
    anti-clerical 203
    anti-English, anti-Scottish 133–5
    Irish 77, 126–7, 195, 274, 342–3
    Jacobitism 213–14
    and James I 77, 78
    proselytisers in 274–5
    religions, attributes in 183

religious 154
settlers insulted 135
Ulster 133, 135
poets
druids as 61
Gaelic 45–8
and preservation of tradition 46,
47–8, 49
role 36
and settlers 96–7
17th-century 133–43
status 96–7, 133
polite society, emergence 163
politics
denominational 294
electoral 294
religious polarisation 291
'poll' 42
Pooler, Revd L. A. 263
Poor Law Unions 308–9
Poor Scholar (Carleton) 197
popery
fear of 269, 271, 434, 435
loyalist view 449–50
penal laws and 168
as political system 168
as threat 352
population decline 30, 86, 306–7,
313
population growth 219, 341
Portadown, Co. Armagh 103, 104,
223, 326, 327, 346
Porter, Revd James 233
Portnaw 103–4
Portnorris 221, 222
potato, reliance on 305
Pound, Belfast 353, 355
poverty
Protestant 318, 323
rural 317, 318
power
clerical 365
overlordship and 40
as Protestant 159, 343, 363, 365
power-sharing 423, 424–6, 427,
428

Powis Commission (1868–70) 281
Poyntz Pass, Co. Armagh 399
PR
see proportional representation
Prehistoric Ulster 3–12
Presbyterianism xxxviii, xxxix
anti-Catholicism 132
evangelism 171
Home Mission 275
introduction in Ireland 256
persecution 126
radicalism 262
suspicion of government 230
varieties of 229
Presbyterians
and Black Oath 99
Catholic perceptions of 156, 228,
233, 263–4
and Catholic rights 238
Catholics, perception of 230–31
increase 131
and Irish language 368
loyalty 226–7
mobility 198
and Orangeism 351
in Orange Order 229
penal laws and 166
stereotype 314
teachers, training 463
and United Irishmen 229, 244
and unjust rule 146
voting pattern 291, 294
Price, Elizabeth 102
pride of place 46, 480–81
priests
see clergy
primary education 461–2
prisoners, republican
and Irish language 453
political status 448–9
prisoners, treatment 66
privilege, Protestant 324
professions
traditional 193–4
property
modern definition 159

prophecies 276
prophecy, ancient 249, 250–51
proportional representation (PR)
    373
  abolition 378, 385, 397
  Northern Ireland Assembly and
    424
proselytism, Protestant 272–7, 278,
    307, 309–11, 458, 460
Protestantism
  anti-popery 479
  Cardinal MacRory and 457–8
  civility and 59
  and clerical marriage 65
  European adoption 69
  and evil 210
  and Gaelic society 69
  as heretical 76
  and land-owning 108–9, 110–11,
    115
  and pagan survivals 21
  perceived materialism 183, 340
  'Second Reformation' 270, 272,
    275–6, 276–7, 282
  as test of loyalty 59
  textual tradition 130
  tithes 69
Protestants
  and Catholic neighbours 126
  Catholic perceptions of 156, 337,
    440, 446
  Catholics, perception of 83, 84,
    146, 170–71, 181–2, 210, 216,
    221, 230–31, 343, 417–18,
    434–5, 436–7
  collusion over penal laws 174
  and demographic change 435
  and early church 13
  evangelism 171–3, 272–7, 278
  in Famine 306, 308
  fear of Catholics 228, 352, 410
  fears for property 167–8, 170
  as foreign usurpers 363–4
  and friars 153
  and fundamentalist preachers
    353–6

Gaelic traditions 130
  insecurity 481
  and Irish history 479
  and Irish language 368
  land acquisition xxxviii, xli, 110
  majority 131
  and mixed marriage 341
  nationality 128
  and National schools 277
  patronising attitude 433–4, 442
  persecution 169
  political identity 335
  population decline 410
  and 1641 Rebellion 99, 100–107
  self-perception 434, 436–7
  sincerity 128
  Solemn League and Covenant 297
  Special Powers Act invoked
    against 411
  status 122
  support for Catholics 174–5
  unemployment 357, 361, 434
  vulnerability 373, 379, 380
Protestant Telegraph 434
provinces 8–9, 17
Provisional IRA 410, 419
  border campaign 435
  British Army mistakes and 419,
    420–21
  Catholic Church and 471–2
  ceasefires 473
  constitutional nationalists and
    442
  damage in nationalist areas 478
  hunger-strikes (1981) 448–50,
    472, 473
  Official IRA, feud with 419
  recruitment 420–21
  and Ulster Workers' Strike 425–6
  war, claim of 448
public service, Catholics and 388
public services, Catholic
    employment in 378, 383, 388,
    389–91, 393, 460
public works, Famine and xl,
    308

Pulleine, James, dean of Dromore 204–5, 206
Pym, John 100

Quakers 312
Queen's Colleges 278–9
Queen's University, Belfast xxxvii
  student protests (1968–9) 413–15
Quigley family 188
Quin family 193
Quinn, Mary 142

radio stations, southern 438–9
Rafroidi, Patrick 11
Randalstown, Co. Antrim 253
Raphoe, Co. Donegal 180
Raphoe diocese 60
rapparees 118–20, 195, 196
rate-in-aid scheme 308–9
Rathcoole estate, Belfast 449
Rathfriland, Co. Down 244, 349–51
Rathlin Island 30, 104, 375, 376
raths 6–7, 14
  as fairy forts 290
Reading in the Dark (Deane) 477
Rebellion
  1541 (Shane O'Neill's) 43, 51
  1595 (Tyrone's) 51
  1641 89, 90, 94, 97–107, 132, 156, 164
    in popular tradition 83, 101, 103, 106
  1798
    aftermath 261–7
    Catholic clergy in 248, 261
    executions 260–61
    leadership, middle-class 265
    religious dissension within 253–4
    rumoured Catholic desertions 256–7, 258, 263
    southern rising 262, 263
    timing 255
    in Ulster 249–61

  1803 (Emmet's) 264
recusancy fines 69, 99
Redemptorist order 281
Redmond, John 295, 297, 298
Rees, Merlyn 426
Reformation 13, 52, 61, 68–70, 130
regionalism, intense 135
Reid, Revd Alex 472–3
Reilly, Daniel 187
Reily, Hugh 128–9, 170
religion
  admitting to 431
  ascertaining 437–8
  elite 160
  external features 361–2, 437–8
  fluidity of affiliation 130–31
  physical characterics 361–2, 431
  popular 160
  transformed into culture 478–9
religious affiliation, ascertaining 361–2, 437–8
religious education 458
religious orders, introduction 281, 283
Reliques of Irish Poetry (Brooke) 232
'Remonstrance' (1661) 147, 148, 149
Remonstrance (Jones) 105
rents 94, 218
Report on the State of Popery (1731) 180
Republic, Irish
  Catholic revisionism 475
  declaration (1948) 398
  nationalism 479–80
  need for involvement 424, 425, 427
  and Northern Catholics 399
  Protestant population 435
  school funding 462
republicanism
  clergy and 300
  militant 299, 300
  rural, Plantation and 84

Restoration (1660) 143
  land settlement 111–14, 147
Ribbonmen 241, 296, 311, 325,
  335, 347, 348, 349–50, 353
Richardson, John 171
Rich Hill, Co. Armagh 226
rights, natural 227
Rights of Man (Paine) 231
ring-forts 6–7
Rinuccini, Giovanni Battista,
  Archbishop 100, 134, 146, 147,
  148, 150
riot, sectarian 218, 324, 325,
  344–51, 353–6, 357–8, 374,
  375, 392, 393–4, 420
Ripley Bogle (Wilson) 478
'Robbery Cut' 177
Rochefort, Jouvin de 155
Roden, Earls of 183, 350
Rodgers, W. R. 439
'Roman' Catholic, use of term 168,
  362
romantic nationalism 367–8, 399,
  443–4, 445, 449
Rome, early Church and 13–14
rosary, devotion to 284, 287, 403,
  451
Rose, Richard 395, 409, 441, 474
Ross, William 329
Rossmore, Henry Robert Westenra,
  3rd baron 364
Route, The, Co. Antrim 29, 87
Royal Belfast Academical Institution
  279
Royal Irish Constabulary (RIC)
  343, 345, 357, 360–61, 374,
  375, 380
Royal Ulster Constabulary (RUC)
  Catholic perception of 380
  Catholics in 376, 380, 381
  demoralisation 418
  disarmed (1970) 419
  Patten Report and 431–2
  proposed reorganisation (1922)
    376–7, 379–80
  reforms 476

sectarianism 375, 377, 415–16
  and student marches (1968–9)
    414, 415
rundale system 317
rural conditions, improvement 317
rural values, as ideal 455
Rushe, D. C. 362
Russell, Revd Matthew 285
Russell, Patrick 114, 187
Russell, Thomas 176, 234, 252, 264
Russell family 27, 86–7, 116
Ryan, John 413

Saintfield, Co. Down 235, 255
St Leger, Anthony, Lord Deputy
  41–2
St Malachy's College, Belfast 328,
  343, 408, 467
St Mary's Christian Brothers School,
  Belfast 460
St Mary's Strawberry Hill,
  Twickenham 463, 464
St Mary's Training College, Belfast
  463
St Matthew's church, Ballymacarrett
  375
St Patrick's Well, Inishowen 286
St Peter's pro-Cathedral, Belfast 284
saints 14–15
  as familial figures 21, 64, 66, 78
  local importance 64, 66, 76, 286
  relics 64, 283, 286
St Vincent de Paul Society 328, 464,
  469
Sands, Bobby 448–9
Sandy Row, Belfast 325, 353, 354,
  355, 357, 452
Saoirse (film) 443
Savage, Hugh 237
Savage, Thomas 237
Savage family 27, 34, 63, 86–7,
  114, 116, 130–31, 187, 188,
  189
Scarman Tribunal (1972) 383
scholars 89, 90–91, 96, 231
schools

see elementary; grammar;
 National; primary; secondary
see also education
Scotland 86, 315–16
Scots settlers xxxix, 28–30, 88, 121,
 128, 129, 131
Scullabogue massacre (1798) 252,
 261
Scullion, Phelix 200
Seceders 229
secondary schools 462–3
'Second Reformation' 270, 272,
 275–6, 276–7, 282
sectarian conflict
 pre-Famine 275–6
 19th-century 338
 1920s 374
 1935 392, 393–4
 1969- 415, 418–19, 420, 421
sectarian polarisation 251
security forces
 in anti-Catholic riots 375
 and Catholics 444, 450
 Protestants and 450
 see also British Army; Royal
  Ulster Constabulary
segregation 432
 in education 459–64
Senchas Már 15
septs 39, 42, 49
settlers 121
 Anglo-Norman xli
 and cultural seepage 131
 English 27
 influx after Plantation 43
 New English 55
 and 1641 Rebellion 101–7
 and resentment 93–4
 and toryism 119
 Tudor 28
 see also Plantation; Scots settlers
Shake Hands with the Devil (film)
 443
Shanaghan, Daniel 244
Shane Fadh's Wedding (Carleton)
 208

Shane's Castle, Randalstown 392
Shankill Rd, Belfast 353, 355, 357,
 358, 404, 418, 420, 452
Shannon valley 8
Shea, Patrick 378, 379, 382, 388,
 389–91, 409, 433
Shewie, Co. Armagh 103
shiring, Ulster (1585) 50
Simms, Katharine 65, 126–7
Simms, Robert 254
Sinn Féin 296, 476
 abstentionism 299–300
 Catholic Church and 466, 474
 Catholic support 427, 450, 457
 elections (1918) 299
 emergence 426
 hunger strikes (1981) 426–7
 and integrated education 459
 and Irish language 453
 and landscape 11–12
 strategy 427
 success 426
 Westminster election (1955) 401
Síogaí Rómhánach, An 133–5, 140,
 215
Sisters of Mercy 281, 464
Six Counties, use of term
 xxxiii–xxxiv
Slieve Gullion, Sinn Féin and 11–12
Small Differences (Akenson) 341
Smaointe beatha Chríost 67
Smith family 86–7
Smithfield, Belfast 324, 325, 326
social class 327–31
Social Democratic and Labour Party
 (SDLP) 422–8, 476
 and consensual unity 423
 as dominant Nationalist party
  424, 427, 428
 in government 424–5
 and Irish Republic 427
 Sinn Féin and 426, 427, 450
 Unionist party and 426
socialism
 Catholicism and 328, 454, 464
 and sectarianism 331

soldiers
  Continental enlistment 92,
    117–18, 192–3
  land settlement 108, 109–10
  recruitment, geography 118
  see also British Army; mercenaries
Solemn League and Covenant 297
'souperism' 273, 309–10, 311, 312
soup kitchens 309–10, 311, 312
South, Sean 405, 444, 451
Spain 59, 193
Spender, Sir Wilfred 390
Spenser, Edmund 34, 39, 43, 46
Sperrin mountains 32, 118, 195,
    305
sport, nationalism in 455
Springfield Rd, Belfast 418
Stanhope St, Belfast 377
state schools 439
station masses 202, 282
status
  declining 37–8, 38–9, 40, 50
  Irish language and 191
  land and 55, 84, 95
  lineage and 39–40, 95
  Plantation and 95–7
  traditional Irish concept 117
stereotypes xxxv–xxxvii, 432–40
  Catholic 228, 231, 238
  Elizabethan 361
  influence on behaviour 432–3
  Irish 456
  1641 Rebellion and 127
  reinforcing 439
  1790s 261
Stewart, Joe 397
Stewartstown, Co. Tyrone 246
Story, George 120
Stormont parliament 399–400
  Catholic chaplain 471
  Catholics employed at 389
  Irish premiers' visits 409, 410
  Nationalist politics and 383,
    396–400
  nationalist politics and 457
  suspended (1972) 422

as Unionist symbol 400
Story of Ireland (Sullivan) 313
Strabane, Claud Hamilton, Lord
    114
Strabane, Co. Tyrone 86, 181, 315,
    326
Strafford, Thomas Wentworth, earl
    88, 92, 98–9, 101
Strangford Lough 3, 27, 28
Stranmillis College, Belfast 463–4
street-rhymes, sectarian 439
Stuart, James 362
Stuart monarchs 33, 77, 111–14,
    134, 199, 214
subsistence farming 195–7, 317
succession
  disputes 39, 51, 52
  Gaelic 40, 50
  lineal 51
suffering, Catholic tradition of
    468–9
Sullivan, A. M. 313
Sunday school, mixed 181, 277
Sunday Times 417
Sunningdale Agreement (1973) 377,
    424, 426
supernatural, Catholicism and
    286–90
superstition
  Catholicism and 207, 208,
    286–90
  Protestantism and 288
surnames 19
surrender and regrant 40, 50, 51,
    52, 53, 92
Sussex, Lord Deputy (Thomas
    Radcliffe, earl) 66, 69
Swanlinbar, Co. Cavan 329
Sweden 118
Swift, Jonathan 186
Syllabus of Errors (1864) 330
Synge, Edward 166
Synod of Thurles (1850) 279, 282

Taaffe, Revd Lawrence 142
Taaffe family 189

Tagra an dá Theampall (MacCooey) 141, 143
Táin Bó Cuailnge 5, 7, 9–10, 139
Tametsi papal decree 179
Tanderagee, Co. Armagh 223, 346, 347
Tara, Kings of 8
'tate' 42
taxes, collecting 218
Taylor, Lawrence 286, 365
teachers
    Catholic 327, 396
    paid from Dublin 461
    and state 396
    trade unionism among 328
    training 460, 463–4
Teeling, Bartholomew 237, 238, 244, 248, 255
Teeling, Charles 230, 237, 241, 243, 244, 248, 254, 257
Teeling, Luke 189, 236, 237, 265–6
Teeling family 187, 189, 244, 248
Temple, Sir John 105–6, 115, 170
Templepatrick, Co. Antrim 102, 104
tenant-right campaign (1850s) 318–21, 339
tenants
    Catholic 175, 185
    Cromwellian 130–31
    independence 217
    Irish 93–4
    Presbyterian 178, 318
    Protestant 159, 175, 194
    religion 128
    rights 318–21, 339
    security 27, 185
    shortage 121
    status 40
    sub-tenancies 131
tenants-at-will 38–9
Teresa, Mother 466
Termonagurk, Co. Tyrone 44
termon families 152
termon lands 43–5, 96

territory, religion and 195
textile industry 321–3, 394
Thackeray, W. M. 322–3
Thatcher, Margaret 448, 449
Thomas the Rhymer 249
Thompson, James 256
thorn trees 290
Three Tasks, The (Carleton) 181
Tipperary county 109
tithe war (1830–33) 345
Tohill, Revd John 343
Tóibín, Colm 315
tolerance, religious 99, 126
tombstones, survey of 193
Tone, Theobald Wolfe 168, 188, 228–9, 235, 237, 366, 367, 450
Toole, John 189
topography xxxix–xlii
    and Celtic myth 11–12
    and mobility 30, 31
    shaping history 28, 34–5
tories 92, 118–20, 139, 176, 195, 196
tower houses 32
townlands 41, 42
transhumance 35, 36, 86
transitional poets 136
Treaty of Limerick (1691) 165, 169, 175
trees, magical 290
Trew, Revd 326
tricolour, usage 454–5
Tridentine Catholicism 70–71, 75, 149, 151, 199, 202, 203
Trinity College Dublin 91, 105, 129
triumphalism, Catholic 114, 283, 325, 363, 481
Troubles (1969–) 416–22
    Catholic Church and 470–81
    deaths 418, 421–2
    Plantation and 84
Troy, Thomas, archbishop of Dublin 209, 230
tuatha 5–6, 8, 15, 17, 18, 19, 38

Tudor monarchy
  civilising mission 33
  and Gaelic revival 75
  land laws 25
  and overlords 88–9
Tullahoge inauguration site 36, 37,
  41, 51
turncoats 157–9, 273, 309–10, 311
Turner, Samuel 238, 259, 262
Twinbrook estate, Belfast 449
Tynan, Co. Armagh 96
Tyrconnell, Richard Talbot, earl of
  114, 115
Tyrconnell, Ruari O'Donnell, earl of
  54
Tyrconnell earls 51, 53, 74
Tyrone, Conn O'Neill, earl of
  hereditary title 51
  lands, loss 87, 88, 94
  overlordship of Ulster 47
  secrecy 35
Tyrone, Hugh O'Neill, 2nd earl 3
  appeals for return from Pale 43
  and churls 84
  and England 51, 52
  flight abroad (1607) 54, 94
  freehold granted 53
  inauguration 51
  James I and 77
  Jesuits and 71
  lands 40
  lineage expansion 53–4
  O'Cahan's case 54, 55
  in popular tradition 134, 135
  and religion 59, 77
  Tudor support 50
Tyrone county 10
  bog xli
  Boundary Commission and 379
  Church of Ireland 277
  Cromwellian confiscations 109
  dynastic instability 51
  elections 386
  fairies, belief in 289
  Famine 305, 307
  IRA activity 406

local councils 373
lordship 51, 53
O'Neill lands 40
Plantation 91
religious demography xlii
Scots Catholic tenants 128
tories 118
troubles (1790s) 225
United Irishmen 246
Volunteers 221

Uí Echach Cobo 10, 49
Uí Néill 9, 10, 13–14, 16, 17, 18,
  19
Uisliu 5
Uí Thuirtri 18, 26
Ulaid 4–6, 7–10, 14, 15, 16, 18, 47,
  49
Ulidian Tales
  see Ulster Cycle
Ullans 128, 454
Ulster
  boundary 8–9
  east xxxix–xl, 28
  and Leinster, animosity 248
  north-west xli
  pride in 366–7
  as Protestant 121
  south xl, 117
  south-west 118
  topography xxxix–xliii
  use of term xx, 445–6, 481
Ulster Custom 318
Ulster Cycle 4–5, 7–8, 9, 10, 11, 12,
  290
Ulster Examiner 291
Ulster Herald 448
Ulster Irish
  alliances 100
  literacy 130
  Old English and 100, 104
  and settlers 101
  17th-century 117–22
  social leadership 94
Ulster Office 95, 193, 235, 236,
  238

Ulster Protestant Action 410
Ulster Protestant Association 380
Ulster Protestant League 393
Ulster-Scots dialect 128, 454
Ulster Special Constabulary (USC) 373, 380–81, 381–2, 415–16
Ulster Volunteer Force (UVF) 297, 380
Ulster Workers' Strike (1974) 425–6
'Ultach' (J. J. Campbell) 391, 392, 394, 395, 436
Ultach Trust 453
ultramontanism 148, 215, 279
undertakers, Plantation 88, 91
under-tenants 43
unemployment
   industry and 408
   1960s 411
   Protestant 417–18
   religion and 387, 434
Unigenitus (papal bull) 215–16
Union flag 400, 457, 460, 481
Unionist party
   and Boundary Commission 379
   Catholic mistrust 416
   Catholics, perception of 383–4
   Catholic support 409, 416
   and Conservative party 300
   and Council of Ireland 425
   and Home Rule 297, 298
   militant support 381, 384
   Orangeism 352, 384, 389, 391, 393
   patronising attitude 433–4, 442
   and SDLP 426
   splinter groups 425
United Irishmen 106, 184, 225, 342
   aims 231
   and Armagh outrages 226
   assassination committee 247
   Catholic Committee and 190
   Catholics in 229, 246, 248, 254–5, 259, 261
   defections 256–7, 258, 259, 263

and Defenders 230, 237, 244–9, 253, 254, 265
and education of public opinion 227, 235
foundation 213
leadership 255
and oath of allegiance 249
Pearse and 443
Presbyterians in 254, 256, 258–9, 262–3
propertied supporters 258, 259
publications 231–3, 250
1798 rebellion 249–61
satire 231, 232–3
songs 231, 232, 233–4
tactics, early success 234
United States 425
unity, as aspiration 481
urbanisation
   increasing 284, 321
   18th-century 187
Ussher, James, archbishop of Armagh 76

values, inherited 444–5
Vatican II, Council 467, 469, 471, 476
victimhood
   Catholic 384–5, 480–81
   egoism of 441–2
   IRA and 441–2
   Protestant 363
   traditions of xxxvi–xxxix, 206, 362–3
Vikings 16–17, 75
violence
   ambivalence about 449–50
   Catholic Church and 449, 451, 471, 472–3, 475
   Catholics and 441
   demography of 478
   medieval 40, 55
   republican 481
Volunteers 220–23, 230
vulnerability, Protestant 373, 379, 380

Wales, Edward, Prince of 400
Walker, Brian 318
Walker, Revd George 359
Walker, William 330
'Walking the Dog' (MacLaverty)
    438
Walsh, Peter 148, 149
Ward, Hugh 75, 76
Warden, David Bailie 254, 255,
    256, 258
Waring, William 115, 116
War of the Revolution (1688) 225
Watson, William 328–9
wealth
    modern definition 159
    sectarian division xli
weapons decommissioning 481
wedding customs 182
welfare societies, Catholic 464
welfare state 405, 407, 433, 464,
    465
West, Harry 425
Western Isles 28, 29, 30, 88
Westminster election (1955) 401
Westmorland, Lord (John Fane,
    10th earl) 168
Whigs, and Catholic emancipation
    228–9
whiskey, illicit 218
White, Rowland 115
Whiteboys 174
White City, Belfast xxxv
White/Whyte family 27, 29, 86–7,
    116, 188
Whyte, General 243
Whyte, John 385, 386, 387, 460

Willes, Chief Baron 196
William III, King 137, 138, 144,
    222
Williamite land settlement 115–17
Wilson, Harold 408, 426
Wilson, Paddy 423
Wilson, Robert McLiam 478
Wilson, Robin xliii
Wilson, Sammy 437
witchcraft 289
women
    employment 464
    evangelism 311
    in textile industry 322
woodkerne
    see kerne
work ethic 128, 387
workhouses 308, 309, 311–12
working class
    Catholic 457, 474
    Orangeism 356–7
    Protestant 342, 347, 384, 408,
        422, 433–4
World War I (1914–18) 189, 297
World War II (1939–45) 402,
    403–4
Worrall, Stanley 459
Wright, Frank 258, 308
Wyse, A. N. Bonaparte 391

Yeats, W. B. 11
yeomanry 245, 262, 263, 264, 345
York St, Belfast 358, 394
Young, Arthur 165, 166, 192, 305
Young, Revd Henry 273–4
YP pools 465